the ENCYCLOPEDIA of PUNK

BY BRIAN COGAN

FOREWORD BY PENELOPE SPHEERIS

the ENCYCLOPEDIA of PUNK

BY BRIAN COGAN

FOREWORD BY PENELOPE SPHEERIS

STERLING
New York / London

DEDICATION

To the memory of my late, great mentor, Neil Postman,
of New York University, who despised any punk music he heard,
but whose ability as a teacher, mentor, and friend
taught me how to write for an audience and
how to think critically.

Originally published as *The Encyclopedia of Punk Music and Culture*

Published by Sterling Publishing Co., Inc.
387 Park Avenue South, New York, NY 10016

© 2006, 2008 by Brian Cogan
Foreword © by Penelope Spheeris

Originally published in 2008 by arrangement with Greenwood Press.
This 2010 edition published by Sterling Publishing Co., Inc.

Book design by Phil Yarnall - SMAY DESIGN

Distributed in Canada by Sterling Publishing
c/o Canadian Manda Group, 165 Dufferin Street,
Toronto, Ontario, Canada M6K 3H6

Distributed in the United Kingdom by GMC Distribution Services,
Castle Place, 166 High Street, Lewes, East Sussex, England BN7 1XU

Distributed in Australia by Capricorn Link (Australia) Pty. Ltd.
P.O. Box 704, Windsor, NSW 2756, Australia

ISBN 978-1-4027-7937-4

For information about custom editions, special sales, premium and
corporate purchases, please contact Sterling Special Sales
Department at 800-805-5489 or specialsales@sterlingpub.com.

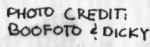

-core
CH
AFTER THE LIGHTS GO
CHANNEL THREE'S
The
PROLET
$ Idle
VERIE
ASSA

PHOTO CREDIT:
BOOFOTO & DICKY

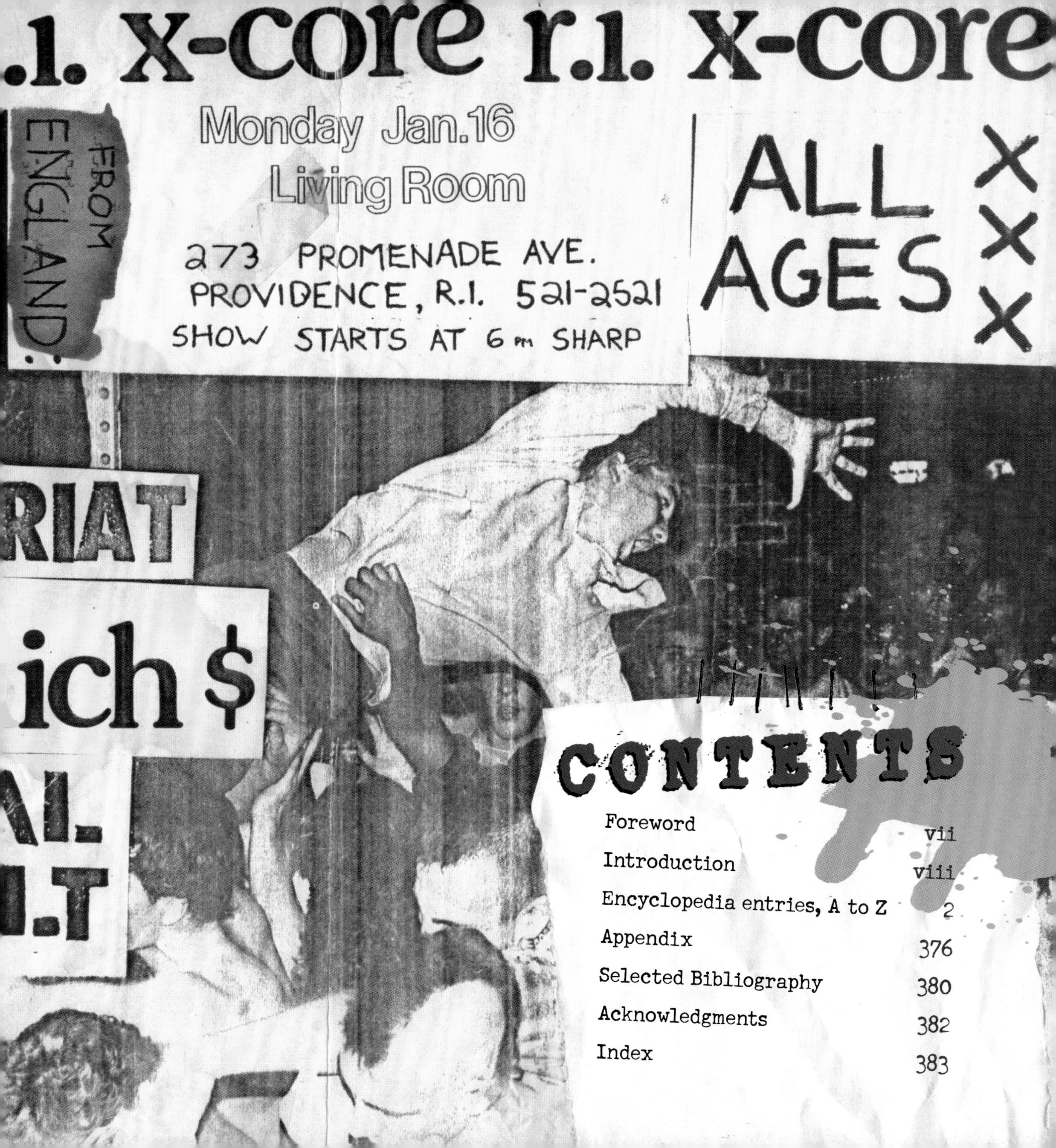

r.1. x-core r.1. x-core

FROM ENGLAND.

Monday Jan.16
Living Room

273 PROMENADE AVE.
PROVIDENCE, R.I. 521-2521
SHOW STARTS AT 6 PM SHARP

ALL
AGES
XXX

RIAT

ich $

I.
I.T

CONTENTS

HE DEC
western civi

Filmed December 1979

Spheeris Films Inc.
presents

**ALICE BAG BAND   BLACK FLAG   CATHOLIC DISCIPLE
CIRCLE JERKS   FEAR   GERMS
and X**

Directed by Penelope Spheeris   Executive Producers Gordon Brown

LP ON SLASH

FOREWORD

Punk rock came into the world like a cataclysmic force of nature, hell-bent on transforming not only music, but also our very social fiber.

In doing so, it coincidentally performed the much-needed task of annihilating disco. While some unsuspecting souls were thrust into a state of terrified confusion, others of us found a new reason to believe. Most people fear change. Back in the day, the fragile and the scared desperately needed a survival guide to make sense of it all. Over 30 years later we now have Brian Cogan's comprehensive work, which expertly presents the genre of punk rock, indisputably one of the most revolutionary movements in music history.

Like so many, I came from a chaotic, abusive childhood and in my teenage years always found sanctuary and solace in hard-edged rock 'n' roll. However, by the mid-1970s the airwaves were permeated with bubblegum pop, boring progressive rock, and the vapid drones of disco fueled by cocaine, or as we called it, disco dust. Long hair prevailed, flared jeans boogied on the dance floors, and everybody was in zone-out heaven. Personally I had sworn off music at that point, but when I caught glimpse of the angst-ridden, obnoxious reverberations of punk rock, my life would be forever affected.

Throughout history, change has been implemented by those who walk a thin line between genius and insanity. To this day John Lydon, aka "Johnny Rotten," continues to gracefully skate that line. Fueled by Rotten's brilliance and insanity, the Sex Pistols gave new meaning to "break all the rules." They ferociously tore down tradition, not only with music and fashion, but with attitude and philosophy. Rhythms were hyper-speedy, guitars discordant, and the lyrics were plain old pissed off. There were no more love songs. Anger and rebellion were the order of the day. They were anti-everything superficial. The most shocking thing about punk was the mayhem of the pit where a bloody nose or a broken bone was a badge of honor. It spread like a disease across continents, across the world. New bands sprouted up like weeds after a thunderstorm. The music and the lifestyle would become the manifesto for a new tribe: the punks.

When the scene was coming into its own, an uncontrollable urge fell upon me to document it. I sensed the historical importance of the movement and felt possessed, if not obligated, to document it. Filmed on a whistle and a prayer, *The Decline of Western Civilization* was said to be the most written-about movie of 1979. The general population, critics, musicians, believers and naysayers were all desperately trying to integrate the new landscape into their stilted logic systems and it just wasn't working. These punks I had put up on the screen had created an all-out assault on the senses. At the first screening a woman stood up and screamed, "Damn you for glorifying these heathens!" This sort of response rattled me at first, but then I realized I was part of a revolution. Each generation instinctively tries to make their mark in the world. The punks, for their part, came up with one of the few lasting efforts.

Punk saturated the very fabric of our existence and gave rise to a new way of thinking. Even though it is in your face and defiant, at its core it is really about honesty and integrity. The music spawned a new lifestyle, an evolved philosophy, a way of being. Corporate greed, ego-driven commerciality, and a society that did not care about its needy had all helped give birth to this generation of morality warriors.

Most true punks are highly intelligent and honorable; they live their lives by pure intentions. They are generally very compassionate; they don't care how old you are or how beautiful you are, or what color you are, only if you are a decent and ethical person. Many are outcasts; social misfits who just never fit in. Now that their look has been integrated into the mainstream it is more difficult to sort out the posers, but punks have good instincts. (Things like self-made clothes, holes repaired with green dental floss and a generous sprinkling of studs will generally mark the real deal.) Many of the gutterpunks are nomadic, traveling from city to city, forming new families as they go. As witnessed in *The Decline of Western Civilization Part III*, many are homeless because they will not buy into the vapid American Dream; they will not abide by the general immoral behavior of our society.

Over the decades, pure punk rock has kept a steady course, and its far-reaching effects and cultural legacy are undeniable, even as its look and sound have been shamelessly usurped by most other genres of popular music. However, in countries around the world there are thriving punk communities, a subculture perfectly content with being kept off the media radar. You don't hear a lot about them because they despise self-promotion, commerciality, and selling out. However, their music still rings out loud and rebellious. There are those who want to believe that punk is dead, but as you will witness in this book, it is more alive than ever.

—PENELOPE SPHEERIS
Los Angeles, California
February 2008

Introduction

In writing about punk rock, certain contradictions must be considered, because no two people seem to agree on an exact definition of the term, how and when punk began, and if punk still exists or if its modern-day expression is merely a nostalgic imitation of a dead art form. These are legitimate questions, ones that punk theorists and zines have been debating for years, reaching little or no consensus. Although I do not wish to add fuel to the fire or incite the ire of the many who believe that writing about punk for public consumption in the mass media is an act of selling out, I nonetheless believe that this book will prove a useful resource for historians, students, and others who share a fascination with punk.

In defining punk, basic consensus among academics is that it is a cultural and musical movement that began roughly in the early-1970s and then concluded during the early-'80s, when other popular musical movements, such as post-punk, hardcore, and new wave, became the dominant musical forms of the day, and when many of the early members of the punk scene left punk behind. This book does not regard punk as such a static phenomenon, however, and instead examines punk in all its complexity, contradictions, and inconsistencies. Punk is herein shown not as a historical epoch with a clearly defined timeline, but instead as a social and political subculture that is constantly changing, sometimes far beyond the scope of the original punks' intent. Punk rock is not so much about "What happened and when?" as it is about "What's been going on, and where is it happening now?"

Ultimately, *The Encyclopedia of Punk* is an attempt, no more or less, to examine the huge scope of punk rock with as much objectivity as possible. This book is not so much an effort to be definitive—an impossible task—but instead to provide a general reference for, and guide to, the vast expanse of work that has been labeled *punk rock* over the past few decades and to capture some of the DIY power of punk on the printed page.

How Did Punk Happen and What Is It, Exactly?

Many people (particularly in the United States) think of punk rock as an outgrowth of the many experimental and hard-to-categorize bands playing at the CBGB club on New York's Lower East Side, starting around 1974. These bands included the Ramones, Patti Smith, Television, the Heartbreakers, Suicide, Richard Hell and the Voidoids, and many others discussed in this book. Punk then exploded out of this scene, whereupon it was given a name and focus by *Punk* magazine (debut issue 1976), a fashion sense and literary vision courtesy of gutterpoet Richard Hell, and increased visibility by London punks who never quite gave proper credit to the Americans who inspired them. The music was loud and raw, and those who created it or loved it looked (to the general public) like dangerous, drug-addicted freaks, with chopped and colored hair, studded dog collars, piercings, and shredded second-hand clothing. It was a musical genre and a lifestyle choice that practically guaranteed incoming abuse for anyone identified with it. Punk upset mainstream society with its unfocused fury and rebellious stance, taking a vocal stand against the musical conformity foisted upon American consumers by corporate record labels obsessed with middle-of-the-road soft rock and self-indulgent bloated soloing, both on recordings and in huge arenas filled with cattle-like masses. Punk laid bare the idiocy of the rock dinosaurs and the consumerist culture they supported and reflected, and in doing so pointed the way toward a more egalitarian future.

To those who subscribe to the above scenario, punk (after its initial blaze of glory in the late-1970s) was then quickly co-opted by record labels, which marketed the more accessible bands (such as Blondie) as new wave and ignored the rest. This corporate interference led to punk's eventual demise and mutation into the much more underground hardcore scene. In later years, punk would resurface again from time to time, but it was never the same.

Other observers—including practically every English academic who has ever written on the subject—believe in a different, and much more Brit-centric, variation on punk's creation myth. The subscribers of this doctrine believe punk started out as a British working-class movement fired up by the class discontent erupting throughout the country in reaction to both 1970s economic malaise and the repressive ideals of the Conservative party and its exemplar, Margaret Thatcher. The leaders of the punk movement—inspired by the political and subversive movements of the 1960s in general and radicals like the Situationists specifically—tended to be wily, older anarchists (for instance, Malcolm McLaren and Bernie Rhodes). In the key years of 1976 and 1977, the likes of McLaren and Rhodes acted as pied pipers to young, disaffected British kids, such as Joe Strummer and John Lydon, who then formed bands to articulate the revolutionary politics and brash, new musical styles favored by their mentors. In the wake of these forerunners followed an impressive parade of bands who might have had a vast stylistic range—the lean and angular goth-rock of Joy Division or the in-your-face yelpings of X-Ray Spex, for example—but who were nevertheless given punk's approving brand by dint of sheer individuality and nonconformity. Punk then spread across the world (including the U.S., whose New York bands were all well and good, but nothing compared to the real thing) and nothing was ever the same again.

For believers in *that* scenario, punk rock was uniquely British and inspired American punk rock. According to this point of view, American punk simply did not understand the unique nature of the original British movement, which in any case burned out around 1980 due to creative stagnation and then mutated into the much more musically adventurous post-punk.

The Cramps' Lux Interior explains punk, 1984.

The obvious difficulty with both scenarios (and most of their variations) is that they set limits on the life span and geographic reach of punk, whereas anyone with eyes and ears can tell you that punk still thrives today all over the world. Certainly in almost every small American town groups of young kids are starting bands, photocopying zines and flyers, and creating websites and blogs devoted to punk. These kids are not merely devoted to a hopelessly moribund movement, like the backward-looking British Teddy Boy faction of the 1970s; instead, they are still finding something relevant and empowering in the original message of punk. Most of all, these two scenarios don't adequately explain why punk was so dynamic and attractive to society's marginalized population in the first place.

Punk is a subculture, and although subcultures have founders and are characterized by codes, established fashions, and (very often) rules, this does not mean that these communities remain static or come to an end after the founders have left the scene. In his book *The Rastafarians: Sounds of Cultural Dissonance*, Leonard E. Barrett points out that though its founders are long gone, Rastafarian ideology is an evolving culture whose flexible dogma takes into account the passage of time. In my view, the same thing is true of punk rock, which continues, adapting to changes in the cultural milieu. New punks constantly reinvigorate the scene, creating new rules, new fashions, and new symbols that many of the originators would not recognize but that are still demonstrably punk. This book does not put dates on punk or even consider punk one unified subculture. Punk is inclusive enough to hold a motley assemblage of queercore activists, Riot Grrrls, Christian skateboarders, straight-edge kids, performance-art freaks, hardcore jocks, goths, retro ska fanatics, and skinheads, some of whom may be hostile to each other but all of whom certainly fit under the countercultural umbrella of punk.

Though many critics were saying punk was dead as early as 1979 (depending on who's telling the story, punk "died" with Sid Vicious, or on the day that Green Day signed to a major label, or when the Clash started playing stadiums, or after CBGB closed, or....), to a teen living in the modern age in a soulless American suburb, a grim British council estate, or a Brazilian *favela*, punk is just as much a way of forging an identity today as it was in 1976, 1984, or 1991. Punk may be dead for some who no longer identify with it, but for those still following its loose overall precepts (the DIY aesthetic, general disregard for authority, overall resistance to the mainstream co-option of subculture, and so on), punk is best seen as a virus, one that mutates constantly and resists codification—or vaccination.

Punk Enough?

The debate over what can be labeled *punk rock* is pretty much never-ending, which made determining the criteria for inclusion in *The Encyclopedia of Punk* problematic. Many punks who were either in the scene during punk's early days, or who listened only to music from that time period, would argue that punk simply didn't exist after, say, 1980. Of course, some in the hardcore scene—a punk variant that spread in America during the 1980s after the decline of punk's first wave—make a similar argument about non-hardcore punk, decrying its lack of authenticity. And so it goes. But restricting punk, or even one of its subgenres, to a specific period of time (1977–1982, for instance) or place (New York, say, or London) misses the point—to those who need what punk has to offer, it doesn't ever go away and can exist anywhere the disaffected happen to be.

I consider punk a set of overlapping subcultures with a shared canon of music, but nowhere in this book are specific bands and movements canonized as the true face of or standard-bearers for punk music, fashion, style, or politics. Although Craig O'Hara's *The Philosophy of Punk: More Than Noise* (1999) makes a compelling argument about a common set of shared punk ideals, it can also be argued that punk is an open and constantly morphing movement. This quickly becomes clear when trying to carbon-date, or create a family tree, for punk. For instance, John Holmstrom, creator of *Punk* magazine (and a man better qualified than most to offer a definition), told me he thought the idea of punk predated even his magazine naming the movement in 1976, pointing not just to earlier genres such as rockabilly,

garage, and proto-punk, but to such works as Alfred Jarry's *Ubu Roi* (1896), perhaps the most scandalous play of its day. Although stretching the definition of punk back to nineteenth-century theater could potentially open the debate so wide that it would be impossible to *ever* define punk (a friend asked, "Why isn't Mozart punk?"), this idea led me to be as inclusive as possible in this work.

Although I have tried to include every major band that has been labeled *punk* over the years, this book confines itself mostly to bands from the United States and England, not only because these countries were ground zero locations for the movement, but because even a cursory examination of worldwide punk rock over the last several decades would require several additional volumes. Punk bands from other countries such as Japan, Australia, France, Ireland, Belgium, the Netherlands, and Canada are covered, usually because those bands are acknowledged as being influential on the overall movement or because they have influenced the scene in the United States. And while this book is mainly historical, I have attempted to keep its contents as up-to-date as possible, including some current bands (the Ergs, Smokewagon, and others) that are regarded by critics and punk zines as keeping the spirit of punk alive.

Because the punk scenes in large cities were best known and best documented, this book omits many bands who might have been influential locally but never achieved recognition outside their respective regions. And anyway, many punk bands provided little documentation (aside from records and other musical archives) about their existence at all, featured members who often worked under stage names or used only first names, or changed members so rapidly that an accurate history is nearly impossible.

Also included are entries on other music genres that have influenced punk, such as reggae, ska, and rockabilly. Likewise, musicians as diverse as the Velvet Underground and Napalm Death are included for their influence on punk rock, and some bands that are not musically very punk are included for their creative proximity to certain punk scenes (such as the decidedly non-punk Talking Heads, who were nevertheless an important component of the CBGB punk scene in its heyday). While I generally err on the side of discussing bands and even subgenres that some would not associate with punk, I have taken great pains *not* to include bands that merely pay lip service to punk through fashion accessories. For that reason, many modern emo bands are not included, nor are those that use punk as a marketing tool, such as Avril Lavigne, Blink 182, and Sum 41.

Simply recording for a major label is not a disqualifier for inclusion in this book (after all, the Ramones recorded for Sire, and the Clash for CBS Records). Similarly, this book does not disqualify bands as insufficiently punk (as some might prefer) due to their association with the mainstream media, despite my great respect for those bands and record labels that eschew such marketing (for example, Fugazi and Dischord Records). And finally, bands are not excluded simply for possessing hit songs. Even though some bands in this book had Top 10 singles (Blondie and Green Day, to name two), it only means they operated differently from more underground performers. Early punk bands—the Clash, the Sex Pistols, and the Ramones, for instance—could not draw upon the enormous underground networks created in later years by the relentless international touring of bands such as Black Flag and the Minutemen, and so they had to rely in some sense on preexisting structures to sell, produce, and perform music.

If you disagree with the inclusion of a particular band in this book, scribble over the offending entry or put a sticker from a band you prefer over the entry (but only if the book is not a library copy). And if you think I unjustly left a band out, mail me a flyer with your thoughts.

Ultimately, the mission of *The Encyclopedia of Punk* is to provide the reader with a sense of the urgency and importance of punk rock, to convey how brazenly raw and revolutionary it was in the beginning, and to provide an illustration of the movement's vitality in the present day, when mainstream music seems just as bland and corporate as it was in the 1970s before punk smashed the doors in. Despite what the graffiti might say, punk is not dead. As long as bored teenagers get together and work on zines, start their own bands, and try to live by their own artistic and aesthetic code, punk is very much alive.

"ALL SUCCESSFUL REVOLUTIONS ARE THE KICKING IN OF A ROTTEN DOOR."

— JOHN KENNETH GALBRAITH

ABC NO RIO
LOCATION: NEW YORK

Founded in 1980, ABC No Rio is an independent club and social center located at 156 Rivington Street on New York's Lower East Side, owned and operated by a punk collective. Bands that play at ABC No Rio range from national acts to local punk bands to those touring on the grassroots level. All prospective performers have to submit song lyrics or recordings beforehand so that they can be screened for potentially racist, sexist, or homophobic content. The club faced numerous financial difficulties over the years due to rising rents and the gentrification of the Lower East Side that started in the 1990s. The social center was largely the result of the Real Estate Show of 1979, during which a radical artists' collective occupied 123 Delancey Street and turned it into a gallery that was shut down by New York's Housing Preservation and Development Agency before they granted the collective use of the Rivington Street building. The city eventually agreed to sell the building to the collective, as long as they raised enough money for necessary renovations. In addition to hosting the weekly punk/hardcore matinees on Saturday afternoons, the building also holds an extensive zine library, a computer lab, a darkroom, a silk-screen printing facility, and numerous other community-oriented groups and projects. ABC No Rio is a classic example of the **DIY** ethos at work and an indication that collectives, despite their reputation for rancor and squabbling, can work together and create artistic spaces for punks of all ages to collaborate.

THE ACCUSED
1982–early 1990s, 2003–present

LINEUP: John Dahlin (vocals, replaced by Blaine Cook, Brad Mowen); Tom Niemeyer (guitar); Chibon Batterman (bass, replaced by Alex "Maggot Brain" Sibbald, James Davis); Dana Collins (drums, replaced by Steve Nelson, Mike Peterson)

The Accused, from Seattle, Washington, were one of the more popular and influential of the early grindcore bands (bands who mixed extreme heavy metal with science fiction/horror film lyrics and punk, all played at the speed of light). The early period with Dahlin marked the band's most straightforward **hardcore** punk era, and when Dahlin left in 1984 the band moved in a more metallic direction. The band broke up in the early 1990s, but re-formed in 2003 with a lineup whose only original member is Tom Niemeyer on guitar. The Accused are well known for their mascot "Martha Splatterhead," a ghoulish woman usually pictured either killing someone or holding some sort of weapon, a sort of female variation on Iron Maiden's "Eddie." Along with the **Misfits**, the Accused were a strong influence on punk's horror-rock subgenre, and evidence of their look and style can be found in the worlds of White Zombie, Lamb of God, and others.

Discography:

Return of Martha Splatterhead (Subcore, 1986); *More Fun Than an Open Casket Funeral* (Combat, 1987; Relativity, 1991); *Hymns for the Deranged* (Musical Tragedies/Empty, 1988); *Martha Splatterhead's Maddest Stories Ever Told* (Combat, 1988); *Grinning Like an Undertaker* (Nastymix, 1990); *Straight Razor* EP (Nastymix, 1991); *Splatter Rock* (Nastymix, 1992)

ACME ATTRACTIONS
LOCATION: LONDON

The second most influential fashion shop in London during the early days of British punk, Acme Attractions first opened in 1975. The store was located at 135 King's Road in Chelsea and employed **Don Letts** as a DJ and also his then-girlfriend Jeanette Lee, who later went on to join **Public Image Ltd.** and manage the British band Pulp. The store sold punk clothing but also mod 1960s suits and retro and soul clothing. It had numerous punk customers, such as Johnny Rotten (born **John Lydon**), Billy Idol, Tony James, and **Sid Vicious**, as well as Bob Marley. Along with **Malcolm McLaren** and **Vivienne Westwood**'s Let It Rock and **Sex** stores, Acme Attractions was the key store involved in punk fashion during the mid-1970s.

THE ADICTS
1977–present

LINEUP: Keith Warren, aka "Monkey" (vocals); Pete Davidson (guitar); Mel Ellis (bass); Michael Davidson, aka "Kid Dee" (drums)

Seemingly unstoppable and quite catchy British group founded in Ipswich, Suffolk, England, in the mid-1970s, the Adicts were known for their colorful clown makeup and bowler hats, eerily reminiscent of *A Clockwork Orange*'s gang of Alex and his Droogs. The band is notable for being the longest-running punk band with all original members, a fact that's even more impressive, given the sheer lunacy of their performances, not to mention the wearing of those hats and suspenders for all these years. The Adicts briefly experimented with mainstream music and added synths in the mid-1980s, even changing their name temporarily to ADX in an effort to get more mainstream airplay. Eventually, though, the Adicts returned to form, sounding much like they did during their prime in the early-1980s.

Discography:

Songs of Praise (Dwed, 1981); *Sound of Music* (Cleopatra, 1982); *Bar Room Bop* (Fall Out, 1985); *Smart Alex* (Cleopatra, 1985); *This is Your Life* (Fall Out, 1985); *Fifth Overture* (Fall Out, 1987); *Live and Loud* (Cleopatra, 1993); *Twenty-Seven* (Cleopatra, 1993); *Rockers into Orbit* (Fallout/Jungle, 1998); *Joker in the Pack* (Harry May, 2000); *Rise and Shine* (Captain Oi!, 2002); *Made in England* (SOS, 2005); *Rollercoaster* (SOS, 2005)

Viddy this horrorshow band of Adicts, my droogs.

THE ADOLESCENTS

1980-1982, 1986-1989, 2003-present

CURRENT LINEUP: Tony (Brandenburg) Cadena (vocals); Steve Soto (bass); Rikk Agnew (guitar); Frank Agnew Jr. (guitar); Derek O'Brien (drums)

The Adolescents were a poppy and melodic Southern California band whose original lineup consisted of Tony (Brandenburg) Cadena on vocals, Rikk Agnew on guitar, Frank Agnew, Jr. on guitar, Steve Soto on bass, and Casey Royer on drums. After an early rough start, scenester **Rodney Bingenheimer** played their first single, "Amoeba," on his influential *Rodney on the Rock* radio program in 1980 and generally championed them thereafter. The band released their self-titled debut in 1981 to critical acclaim and healthy sales. Rikk Agnew soon departed, however, to record a solo record and play with goth band Christian Death. Though he was replaced by Steve Roberts, the band broke up in 1982. Royer went on to front **DI**. The Adolescents reunited in 1986 for a series of shows, but Frank Agnew left soon after, as did Royer, and the two were replaced by Alfie Agnew and Sandy Hansen, the lineup that recorded the *Brats in Battalions* album. After that album, Alfie Agnew, Rikk Agnew and Cadena quit and Soto took over lead vocals for the *Balboa Fun Zone* record before the band splintered again in 1989. Cadena toured with Adz for a while and Rikk Agnew returned to Christian Death. The band sporadically reunites for tours and in 2005 released a new album with the lineup of Tony Cadena on lead vocals, Frank Agnew on guitar, his son Frank Agnew Jr. on guitar, Steve Soto on bass, and Derek O'Brien (formerly of **Social Distortion**) on drums. Lead singer Tony Cadena teaches third grade in California. The Adolescents remain an important part of punk history, despite the almost *Spinal Tap*-like nature of their ever-changing lineup.

Discography:

Adolescents (Frontier, 1981; Epitaph, 1997); *Brats in Battalions* (Triple X, 1987, 1994); *Balboa Fun Zone* (Triple X, 1988, 1994); *Live 1981* and *Live 1986* (Triple X, 1989, 1994); *Return to the Black Hole* (live; Triple X, 1997); *Live at the House of Blues* (Kung Fu, 2004); *The Complete Demos 1980–1986* (Frontier, 2005); *O.C. Confidential* (Finger Records, 2005).
Rikk Agnew: *All by Myself* (Frontier, 1982, 2003); *Emotional Vomit* (Triple X, 1990, 1994); *Turtle* (Triple X, 1994)

The Adverts' TV Smith (right) and Gaye Advert.

THE ADVERTS

1977-1980

LINEUP: TV Smith (vocals); Howard Pickup (guitar, replaced by Paul Martinez); Gaye Advert (bass); Laurie Driver (drums, replaced by Rod Latter, Rick Martinez); Tim Cross (keyboards)

An early English band from punk's first wave, the Adverts were led by front man TV Smith and bassist Gaye Advert. Originally to be called One Chord Wonders (the title of their first single), the Adverts were best known for their second single, "Gary Gilmore's Eyes," which actually cracked the Top 20 in the UK. In February 1978, the Adverts released their first album, *Crossing the Red Sea with the Adverts*, which featured their latter-day keyboard player, Tim Cross. The Adverts endured unfair criticism about having a woman in the band, revealing the scene's inherent sexism (sadly still quite prevalent), and Gaye Advert was used as a reluctant sex symbol in advertising and in music magazines. One of the first bands to criticize the growing conformity within the British punk scene, the Adverts had already made considerable musical strides by the time of their demise in 1980. TV Smith went on to a sporadic but lengthy solo career.

Discography:

Crossing the Red Sea with the Adverts (Bright, 1978; Butt, 1982; Link Classics, 1990; Phantom, 1997; Fire Records, 2002); *Cast of Thousands* (Anagram Punk, 1980, 1999; Fire Records, 2005); *The Peel Sessions* EP (Strange Fruit, 1987); *Live at the Roxy* (Receiver, 1990, 1999); *Radio 1 Sessions* (Pilot, 1997); *The Best of the Adverts* (Anagram Punk, 1999); *The Wonders Don't Care* (Pilot, 2001); *Live and Loud* (Step 1, 2002; Harry May, 2005); *Anthology* (Fire Records, 2003); *The Punk Singles Collection* (Anagram Punk, 2004)

AFI

1991-present

LINEUP: Davey Havok (vocals); Mark Stopholese (guitar, replaced by Jade Puget); Vic Chalker (bass, replaced by Jeff Kregse, Hunter Burgan); Adam Carson (drums)

AFI (A Fire Inside) is a California goth/punk hybrid band that started out as your standard **Misfits**-influenced **hardcore** band, but later experimented with synths and programmed sounds, mixed with high-speed mid-1990s melodic punk. The band's politics don't extend much beyond vocalist Davey Havok's proclaimed allegiance to being not only drug- and alcohol-free but vegan. The early AFI records are akin to a spooky, cleaned-up **emo** version of the Misfits (particularly *Black Sails in the Sunset*), and Havok gained some attention for his range and intensity. Their later records, however, are pure fluff as the band shed more and more of their hardcore trappings and increasingly moved toward becoming the house band of mall punk store Hot Topic. Though having clearly alienated the punker-than-thou crowd with their pop mainstreaming, since AFI's *Sing the Sorrow* went gold, it's clear they can afford to do just that.

Discography:
Answer That and Stay Fashionable (Wingnut, 1995); *Very Proud of Ya* (Nitro,1996); *Shut Your Mouth and Open Your Eyes* (Nitro, 1997); *Black Sails in the Sunset* (Nitro, 1999); *The Art of Drowning* (Nitro, 2000); *Sing the Sorrow* (Dreamworks, 2003); *Decemberunderground* (Interscope, 2006)

AGAINST ME

2000-present

LINEUP: Tom Gabel (vocals); James Bowman (guitar); Andrew Seward (bass); Warren Oakes (drums)

Founded in Gainesville, Florida, Against Me is one of the key punk bands of the present day, being one of the most honest, lyrically and musically diverse bands on the scene. Their debut album *Reinventing Axl Rose* was a folk/punk hybrid with lyrics that embraced the absurd as well as the anarchist stance of front man Tom Gabel. Although Against Me has long championed the **DIY** aesthetic, they upset many fans when they signed to major label subsidiary Sire (ironically, also the longtime label of the **Ramones**) for their 2007 album *New Wave*. The resulting uproar led to much fan unrest and the vandalizing of their tour van. Although it should be noted that some of their purist fans called them sellouts when the band signed to **Fat Wreck Chords** in 2003 (hardly a major label), this anger also reflects the high expectations of Against Me's listeners, as well as the close relationship between them and the band itself. Even though Against Me has written a masterpiece of a protest song about the futility of protest songs—"White People for Peace"—it remains to be seen if the band is just griping for its own sake or actually making a difference. At any rate, their lyrical intelligence and the sheer sonic power of Against Me's music, a cross between folk/classic punk and **Nirvana**'s crunch (Butch Vig, producer on *Nevermind*, also produced *New Wave*), make them one of the most promising young punk bands in America.

Discography:
Reinventing Axl Rose (No Idea, 2002); *As the Eternal Cowboy* (Fat Wreck Chords, 2003); *Searching for a Former Clarity* (Fat Wreck Chords, 2005); *New Wave* (Sire, 2007)

ABOVE: Against Me's Tom Gabel looks nothing like Axl Rose.

Davey Havok of AFI takes a wee nap at the Berkeley Square.

AGENT ORANGE

1979–present, with lengthy hiatuses

LINEUP: Mike Palm (vocals/guitar); Steve Soto (bass, replaced by James Levesque); Scott Miller (drums)

A surf-guitar punk band from Placentia, California, Agent Orange formed in 1979

and are led by longtime scene stalwart Mike Palm. They were best known for their electrifying first album, *Living in Darkness*, and the surf-punk classic "Bloodstains" (years later, the **Offspring** paid tribute to the song's distinctive riff in their hit single "Keep 'em Separated"). Agent Orange were one of the earliest punk bands to add a surf-rock direction to their music and influenced numerous bands in addition to the Offspring, including many of the garage-rock revivalists of the 1990s. Original bassist Steve Soto went on to form the **Adolescents**. Although influential in Californian **hardcore**, Agent Orange never capitalized on their success. The band has reunited in recent years and toured in 2005. Although Agent Orange recorded sparsely, they are remembered as one of the most important early Southern California bands of the early-1980s.

Essential Discography:
This is the Voice (Restless, 1986, 1997); *Living in Darkness* (Restless, 1992); *Virtually Indestructible* (Fearless, 1996); *Real Live Sound* (Restless, 1997); *When You Least Expect It* (Restless, 1997); *Sonic Snake Session* (Restless, 2003)

AGNOSTIC FRONT

1980–1992, 1997–present

LINEUP: "Jimmy the Russian" (vocals, replaced by Roger Miret); Vinnie Stigma (guitar); Joe James (guitar); Adam Moochie (bass, replaced by Diego, Rob Kabula, Alan Peters, Craig Setari, and others, now Mike Gallo); Ray Barberi, aka "Raybeez" (drums, replaced by Lou Beatto, Jim Coletti, Dave Jones, and many others, now Steve Gallo)

New York City's seminal activist, **skinhead**, **hardcore** band, Agnostic Front performed regularly at the **CBGB** hardcore matinees during the mid- to late-1980s. In the mid-1980s, with the addition of a second guitar player, Stigma stopped playing guitar, and the band became more metallic, writing songs with guitarist Pete Steele of Carnivore. In 1988, several members formed a still-extant side project, Madball. The band had a resurgence on the **Epitaph** label in the late-1990s and has continued with various shifts in personnel. Their classic first album, *Victim in Pain*, contained numerous skinhead anthems. By the second LP, *Cause for Alarm*, the band's increasingly metallic sound reflected their internal turmoil at the time. The next album, *Liberty & Justice For...*, was a return to form, but Miret went to jail for two years for drug possession following its completion, derailing Agnostic Front's momentum at a crucial point. The lineup of the band, as of late 2007, was Miret, Stigma, Steve Gallo on drums, and Mike Gallo on bass. The band performs sporadically, and lead singer Roger Miret performs with his new band, Roger Miret and the Disasters. Agnostic Front was one of the many bands who tried to save CBGB, and a live DVD of the band performing there was released in 2007.

Discography:
Live in New York (Combat, 1983); *Victim in Pain* (Rat Cage, 1984; Combat Core, 1986); *Cause for Alarm* (Relativity, 1986); *Liberty & Justice For...* (Combat, 1987; Relativity, 1991); *Live at CBGB* (Combat, 1989; Relativity, 1990); *Cause for Alarm/Victim in Pain* (Relativity, 1991); *One Voice* (Relativity, 1992, 1999); *To Be Continued: The Best of Agnostic Front* (Relativity, 1992); *Last Warning* (Relativity, 1993); *Raw Unleashed* (Grand Theft Auto, 1995); *Raw* (Grand Theft Auto, 1996); *Something's Gotta Give* (Epitaph, 1998); *Riot, Riot, Upstart* (Epitaph, 1999); *Dead Yuppies* (Epitaph, 2001); *Working Class Heroes* (Knockout, 2003); *Another Voice* (Nuclear Blast, 2004); *Warriors* (Nuclear Blast, 2007). **Madball:** *Ball of Destruction* EP (In Effect/Relativity, 1989). **Roger Miret and the Disasters:** *Roger Miret and the Disasters* (Hellcat Records, 2002)

Agent Orange rocks a skate ramp opening in San Diego, circa 2007.

October 8, 2006: Agnostic Front plays the final hardcore matinee at CBGB.

ALKALINE TRIO

1996–present

LINEUP: Matt Skiba (vocals/guitar); Nolan McGuire (guitar, live performances only); Rob Doran (bass, replaced by Dan Andriano); Glenn Porter (drums, replaced by Mike Felumlee, Derek Grant)

One of the best bands of the mid-1990s, Alkaline Trio developed their own distinct style and musical direction, with Matt Skiba's vocal dexterity and increasingly intricate guitar parts showing that **hardcore** does not have to be one-dimensional and surly. The band was briefly on a major label, but fans of Alkaline Trio are not as punk orthodox as those of other bands, and didn't take them to task for it. The band is also unusual for their use of Satanic or anti-Christian imagery from time to time, something the band's parents hope is simply a phase they will soon outgrow.

Discography:

Goddamnit! (Asian Man, 1998); *Maybe I'll Catch Fire* (Asian Man, 2000); *Alkaline Trio* (Asian Man, 2000); *From Here to Infirmary* (Vagrant, 2001); *Good Mourning* (Vagrant, 2003); *Crimson* (Vagrant, 2005); *Remains* (Vagrant, 2007)

ALL

1987–present

LINEUP: Dave Smalley (vocals, replaced by Scott Reynolds, Chad Price); Stephen Egerton (guitar); Karl Alvarez (bass); Bill Stevenson (drums)

The experimental, musically bewildering, and jazz-inflected group All was formed by the remaining members of the **Descendents** when Milo Aukerman left to return to graduate school. Perhaps the tightest and most musically adept punk group outside of **Bad Brains**, despite a rotating cast of lead singers, All was also inspired by the philosophy of life supposedly developed by Bill Stevenson and friend Pat McCuistion after a revelation from the "Basemaster General." While these obsessions with caffeine, girls, food, farting, and other silly pursuits are meant to be taken tongue-in-cheek, the band often played it straight (though still writing more songs about the joys of caffeine than the **Pogues** had about whiskey). Led by master drummer Stevenson and including guitarist Stephen Egerton and bassist Karl Alvarez, All took its name from the title of the last Descendents record and Bill Stevenson's philosophy of always going for "All." The original singer was Dave Smalley of **DYS**

STEVE ALBINI

Controversial producer, musician, and punk and indie theorist, Steve Albini is just as famous for his production techniques (lo-fi and low involvement) as for his client list (everyone from **Nirvana** to Robert Plant) and his feuds (almost anyone he has come in contact with over the last two decades). Albini has been associated with the Chicago scene since the 1980s, when he wrote about music for publications like *Forced Exposure* and **Maximum RocknRoll**; an oft-reproduced article he wrote called "The Problem with Music" for Issue No.5 of the Chicago journal *The Baffler* broke down, dollar-for-dollar, all of the horrible things that happen to an indie band when they sign with a major label. During the same decade, Albini fronted the seminal proto-industrial noise band **Big Black** and began producing records, later opening his own recording studio, Electrical Audio. A polarizing and often purposely obnoxious foil who is equally noted for his intemperate mouth as for his undisputed musical and recording abilities, Albini is also an iconic figure on the punk and indie scenes, and would be regarded as such even if his career had simply ended after disbanding Big Black in 1987. Albini continued as a musician, however, and after forming the short-lived (and controversial) band Rapeman, he returned to form in the 1990s with the more adventurous Shellac. His lengthy list of engineering credits (Albini refuses to be credited as a "producer") include Nirvana's *In Utero* and the **Pixies**' *Surfer Rosa*.

and the first incarnation of **Dag Nasty**, who had left Dag Nasty to take a graduate fellowship in Israel. Smalley left All after the *Allroy for President* EP to form his own band, **Down by Law**. The band also recorded an album as Tony All with ex-Descendent Tony Lombardo, Reynolds, and bassist/songwriter Karl Alvarez singing songs Lombardo had recorded about girls and breakups.

Stevenson, Alvarez, and Egerton moonlight in numerous other bands (including the Lemonheads) and continue to be in high demand as producers of other bands from their base in Fort Collins, Colorado. The three core members also periodically reunite with Milo Aukerman for Descendents projects and tours. Although the All family grew to an extended one with the addition of key roadies Bug and Gooch, they went on a lengthy hiatus in 2002 while the members pursued other projects. Stevenson and Alvarez played on the Lemonheads reunion record and were touring with Lemonheads front man Evan Dando in 2007. Stevenson operates the recording studio The Blasting Room in Colorado, and also tours with Only Crime.

Discography:
Allroy Sez . . . (Cruz, 1988); *Allroy for Prez . . .* (Cruz, 1988); *Allroy's Revenge* (Cruz, 1989); *Trailblazer* (Cruz, 1989); *Allroy Saves* (Cruz, 1990); *Percolater* (Cruz, 1992); *Breaking Things* (Cruz, 1993); *Pummel* (Interscope/Atlantic, 1995); *Mass Nerder* (Epitaph, 1998); *All: The Best of* (Owned & Operated, 1999); *Problematic* (Epitaph, 2000); *Live Plus One* (Epitaph, 2001). **Tony All:** *New Girl, Old Story* (Cruz, 1991)

GG ALLIN

Notorious for his drug- and alcohol-fueled escapades, not to mention so-called performances in which few songs were played, the legendary GG Allin—whose real name has been reported to be Kevin Allin, or less believably, Jesus Christ Allin (it appears that his father was a religious maniac, but as with most GG stories, there is rarely a definitive truth)—made a name for himself by, for instance, pursuing audience members with human feces. He put out numerous recordings with his band the Murder Junkies, but is far better known for his scatological life and early death. GG started off as a fairly pedestrian version of **Iggy Pop**, confronting the audience and breaking glasses, but soon his antics increased to the point of rarely completing an entire set. Usually after two or three songs, GG would defecate on stage and chase audience members around with clumps of his own feces in each hand, and maybe (if the crowd was lucky), also eat or throw women's used sanitary napkins. GG promised to kill himself onstage on October 31, 1987, but after a

woman in the crowd alleged that he had assaulted and burned her, he was arrested and eventually served three years in prison, where the date of his promised suicide came and went without incident. After his release, GG resumed touring in 1991 with the Murder Junkies (featuring his brother Merle) and played in any club foolish or naive enough to book him. After returning to New York City at the commencement of their tour, GG Allin played a show at the Gas Station Club in Alphabet City and subsequently overdosed on a combination of drugs on June 28, 1993. The 1994 film *Hated: GG Allin and the Murder Junkies* documented his life and scandals.

After GG Allin's demise, his former roadie Evan Cohen wrote a book, *I Was a Murder Junkie*, detailing his work on GG's last U.S. tour. Merle Allin continues to tour with the Murder Junkies and keeps GG's flame burning by selling assorted GG merchandise and memorabilia to fans who can't quite get enough. Despite the notorious antics, some of GG's records are actually quite enjoyable, and the early material with the Jabbers and Scumfucs include some great punk songs, not that audiences ever

got to hear them. Among the followers of GG's legacy is the forgettable Bloody Mess of Bloody Mess and the Scabs.

Discography:
GG Allin: *Live Fast, Die Fast* EP (Black & Blue, 1984, 1998); *Hated in the Nation* (ROIR, 1987, 1992, 1994, 1998); *Freaks, Faggots, Drunks & Junkies* (Homestead, 1988; Aware One, 1994); *Suicide Sessions* (Awareness, 1989; Aware One, 1998); *Doctrine of Mayhem* (Black & Blue, 1990); *Anti-Social Personality Disorder: Live* (Evergreen, 1993); *Brutality and Bloodshed for All* (Alive, 1993); *Dirty Love Songs* (New Rose Blues, 1994); *War in My Head* (Aware One, 1995); *Aloha from Dallas* (ROIR, 1995; Last Call, 2002); *Hated* (soundtrack; Aware One, 1995); *Carnival of Excess* (Rockside Media, 1996); *Terror in America* (live; Alive, 1996); *Boozin' & Pranks* (live; Black & Blue, 1998); *Res-Erected* (live; ROIR, 1999); *Singles Collection, Vol. 1* (Temperance, 1999); *Troubled Troubadour* (Aware One, 2000); *Rock 'n' Roll Terrorist* (Last Call, 2003); *Expose Yourself: The Singles Collection 1977–1991* (Aware One, 2004). **GG Allin and the Holy Men:** *You Give Love a Bad Name* (Homestead, 1987; Aware One, 1995). **GG Allin and the Jabbers:** *Always Was, Is and Always Shall Be* (Orange, 1980; Black & Blue, 1988; Halycon, 1998); *Public Animal #1* EP (Orange, 1982; Black & Blue, 1998); *No Rules* EP (Orange, 1983); *Banned in Boston, Vols. 1 & 2* (Black & Blue, 1989, 1998). **GG Allin and the Scumfucs:** *Eat My Fuc* (Blood, 1984; Black & Blue, 1988, 1998); *Hard Candy Cock* EP (Blood, 1984); *I Wanna Fuck Your Brains Out* EP (Blood, 1985). **GG Allin and the Scumfucs/Artless:** *GG Allin and the Scumfucs/Artless* (Ger. Starving Missle/Holy War, 1985). **GG Allin & Antiseen:** *Murder Junkies* (New Rose Blues, 1994; Last Call, 2002; TKO Round 2004)

ALTERNATIVE TENTACLES

LOCATION: SAN FRANCISCO

An independent record label founded in June 1979, and operated by **Jello Biafra**, lead singer of the **Dead Kennedys**, Alternative Tentacles released not only the Dead Kennedys' catalog but also records by **NOmeansno**, **Butthole Surfers**, **Neurosis**, Leftover Crack, and the long-lost Los Angeles-based space alien band Zolar X. The label also releases more political work such as spoken-word recordings of Biafra and radical historian Howard Zinn. Biafra remains the owner, even though he lost the rights to the name Dead Kennedys in a bitter lawsuit with his ex-bandmates and no longer has the rights to reissue the band's albums (although he still sells the "Nazi Punks Fuck Off" single). Alternative Tentacles relocated to Emeryville, California, in 2002 and continues to fill a much-needed niche by putting out new music, as well as books and T-shirts, and lately also reissuing long-forgotten records by bands like **JFA** and the Eat (no Dead Kennedys, of course, but such is punk life).

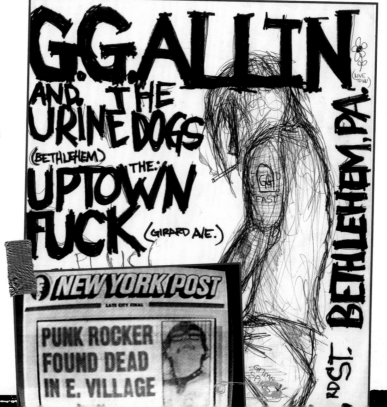

G.G. ALLIN AND THE URINE DOGS (BETHLEHEM) THE: UPTOWN FUCK (GIRARD AVE.)

NEW YORK POST

PUNK ROCKER FOUND DEAD IN E. VILLAGE

ALTERNATIVE TV

1977-1979, 1985-present

LINEUP: Mark Perry (vocals/guitar); Alex Fergussen (guitar); Tyrone Thomas (bass); Chris Bennett (drums)

An experimental and Frank Zappa-esque **post-punk** band led by Mark Perry (former editor of the influential zine *Sniffin' Glue*), Alternative TV tried to make punk live up to its promise of actually breaking rules as opposed to making them. Their poppiest and best-known song was the classic "Action Time Vision." The band went through various personnel changes and eventually called it quits in March 1979. Perry revived the band in 1985 and recorded sporadically with a variety of lineups, eventually even recording a version of the **Ramones**' song "Now I Wanna Sniff Some Glue," which inspired the zine's name in the first place.

Discography:

The Image Has Cracked (Deptford Fun City, 1978); *Vibing up the Senile Man (Part One)* (Deptford Fun City, 1979); *Live at the Rat Club '77* (Crystal/Red, 1979); *Action Time Vision* (Deptford Fun City, 1980); *Strange Kicks* (IRS, 1981); *Peep Show* (Anagram, 1987); *Splitting in 2* (Anagram, 1989); *Sol* EP (Chapter 22, 1990); *Dragon Love* (Chapter 22, 1990). **Here & Now/Alternative TV:** *What You See...Is What You Are* (Deptford Fun City, 1978). **Good Missionaries:** *Fire from Heaven* (Deptford Fun City, 1989). **Mark Perry:** *Snappy Turns* (Deptford Fun City, 1981)

ANGELIC UPSTARTS

1977-present

LINEUP: Thomas Mensforth, aka "Mensi" (vocals, replaced by Chris Wright); Ray Cowie, aka "Mond" (guitar); Steve Forsten (bass); Decca Wade (drums)

Mentored by Jimmy Pursey of **Sham 69** and influenced by the political punk of the **Sex Pistols** and the **Clash**, the Angelic Upstarts' music put an emphasis on working-class issues. Initially proponents of the **DIY** aesthetic, the band released their first independent single, "The Murder of Liddle Towers" (about a police murder) in 1978. Like many punk bands of the time, the Angelic Upstarts were quickly signed to Warner Bros., and key supporter Pursey produced their debut album, *Teenage Warning*, which came out in July 1979. They were prone to invasions from **skinhead** members of the British fascist movement the **National Front**, who disrupted sets and shouted Nazi slogans. The Angelic Upstarts, like Sham 69, tried to be inclusive in their approach, reasoning that allowing fascist skins to attend gigs was a good way to educate them. But in practice (as with Sham 69), the clashes between working-class fascists and art school punks often caused the band to walk

LEFT: Alternative TV's Mark Perry (center) provides non-televisual entertainment.

ABOVE: The Angelic Upstarts' Mensi gets possessed at a Northumberland prison show in 1979.

off stage. The band toured relentlessly and played numerous gigs in support of causes such as Rock Against Racism (**RAR**), trying to get their positive message across to their working-class audience until finally breaking up in 1983. The Angelic Upstarts have reformed many times and have gone through countless bass players and drummers. The band records and tours to this day with a variety of new lineups—as of 2006, the only remaining original member was drummer Decca Wade. Although successful in England, the Angelic Upstarts never achieved the level of fame they deserved in America, where they enjoy only a cult following.

Discography:

Teenage Warning (Warner Bros., 1979; Captain Oi!, 2003); *We Gotta Get Out of This Place* (WEA, 1980; Phantom, 2003); *2,000,000 Voices* (EMI, 1981; Captain Oi!, 2002); *Live* (EMI, 1981); *Still from the Heart* (EMI, 1982; Castle Music, 1994; Import, 2003); *Reason Why* (Anagram, 1983; Import, 2001); *Angel Dust (The Collected Highs 1978–1983)* (Anagram, 1983, 1999); *Last Tango in Moscow* (Picasso, 1984; Razor, 1988; Captain Oi!, 2000); *Live in Yugoslavia* (Picasso, 1985; Griffin, 1995); *Power of the Press* (Gas, 1986; Link Classics, 1990; Step 1, 2001); *Bootlegs and Rarities* (Dojo, 1986); *Blood on the Terraces* (Link, 1987; Captain Oi!, 2000); *Brighton Bomb* (Chameleon, 1987); *Live and Loud!!* (Link, 1988; Harry May, 2005); *England's Alive* EP (Skunx, 1988); *Bombed Out* (Dojo, 1992); *Kids on the Streets: Best Of* (Cleopatra, 1993); *Who Killed Liddle?* (Recall, 1999); *Independent Punk Singles Collection* (Anagram, 1999); *BBC Punk Sessions* (Captain Oi!, 2000); *Lost and Found* (Harry May, 2000, 2002); *Rarities* (Captain Oi!, 2000); *EMI Punk Years* (Captain Oi!, 2000); *Live from the Justice League* (TKO, 2001); *Greatest Hits Live* (Harry May, 2002); *Collection* (EMI, 2002); *Sons of Spartacus* (Captain Oi!, 2002); *Anthems Against Scum* (Import, 2002)

ANGRY SAMOANS

1978-present
LINEUP: "Metal" Mike Saunders (vocals);
Gregg Turner (guitar); Kevin Saunders
(guitar); Todd Homer (bass);
Billy Vockeroth (drums)

A Los Angeles joke-punk band led by "Metal" Mike Saunders (who claims to have coined the term *heavy metal*) and guitarist Gregg Turner, Angry Samoans are best known for short, jokey, **hardcore** songs such as "My Old Man's a Fatso," "They Saved Hitler's Cock" (possibly an answer song to **Unnatural Axe**'s "They Saved Hitler's Brain"), and the ode to compulsory blindness "Lights Out" (later covered by Boston **ska** band the Mighty Mighty Bosstones). Angry Samoans were unapologetic fans of obscure 1960s tunes (such as the ones you

might find on the *Nuggets* compilation) and often tried to "out-obscure" the audience in their choice of cover versions. While their output was limited, the Angry Samoans were among more important early punk bands in Southern California, and added a much-needed sense of humor to a scene that was then becoming increasingly serious and violent. The band sporadically gets back together and tours with a lineup of Saunders, Billy Vockeroth, and whoever else is on hand at the moment.

Discography:

Inside My Brain EP (Bad Trip, 1980; PVC, 1987; Triple X, 1994); *Back from Samoa* (Bad Trip, 1982; PVC, 1987; Triple X, 1992); *Yesterday Started Tomorrow* EP (PVC, 1987; Triple X, 1992); *Gimme Samoa: 31 Garbage-Pit Hits* (PVC, 1987); *STP Not LSD* (PVC, 1988; Triple X, 1992); *Live at Rhino Records* (Triple X, 1992); *Return to Samoa* (Shakin' Street, 1990); *The Unboxed Set* (Triple X, 1995); *The '90s Suck & So Do You* (Triple X, 1999). **Metal Mike:** *Plays the Hits of the 90's* EP (Triple X, 1991); *Fuck the War* EP (Triple X, 2006)

THE ANTHRAX
LOCATION: STAMFORD, CT

The popular Connecticut hole-in-the-wall The Anthrax was famous for allowing **hardcore** and **straight-edge** shows when many clubs would not. Run by brothers Brian and Sean Sheridan, The Anthrax was located first in Stamford but eventually moved to Norwalk, where it hosted numerous shows featuring local bands like **76% Uncertain**, **Bold**, **Vatican Commandos** (featuring a pre-techno Moby on guitar), and **Youth of Today**, before it moved to New York City. Other notable visitors included the **Cro-Mags**, **Judge**, NY Citizens, **Token Entry**, Toxic Reasons, **Bad Religion**, and many others. The Anthrax was a popular place for many in the local scene who did not

have the money or the time to go see their favorite bands play in New York, and was also one of a string of clubs across the country that helped support the touring band network in the pre-Internet age. The club shut down after the New York and Connecticut scenes lost momentum in the mid- to late-1980s.

THE ANTI-CLUB
LOCATION: LOS ANGELES

In Los Angeles, the Anti-Club had a short but memorable life as one of the spots where many bands played during the city's 1970s punk heyday, including early luminaries such as the **Circle Jerks** and the **Leaving Trains**. The club's eclectic programming also included rockabilly nights and roots rock, as well as experimental bands and noise-rock acts. The Anti-Club's booker, Russell Jessum, was known for his open-minded attitude when the punk scene was at its start and far more widespread in its taste for and embracement of all kinds of music. For a time, the Anti-Club was one of the more welcoming scenes for L.A.'s earlier punk pioneers, before the influx of the more violent Orange County **hardcore** crew.

TOO SMART TO FIGHT, TOO SMART TO KILL

JOIN NOW

A NEW KIND OF ARMY

ANTI-FLAG

1988–1989, 1993–present

LINEUP: Justin Sane (vocals/guitar); Andy Flag (vocals/bass, replaced by "Chris #2," among others); Pat Thetic (drums)

Antiauthority, antireligion, and anticorporate culture, Anti-Flag is a band from Pittsburgh whose near-constant desecration of the U.S. flag as a logo marks their out-of-the-mainstream stance pretty clearly. The band coalesced in the early 1990s after an original version in the previous decade fell apart. Despite their frantic sound, the band is far more melodic than even they would like to admit, with touches of early **Bad Religion** mixed with the Southern California **pop-punk** sound. Anti-Flag remains resolutely anticapitalist and is one of the most politically active and consistent bands in the modern punk scene. This can be read as ironic by some, as the band was putting out anticorporate and anticapitalist music even after they signed in 2005 to major label RCA, a subsidiary of megagiant Sony/BMG, which didn't seem to mind Anti-Flag biting the corporate hand that fed them. Critics who thought that the band's sound and attitude would change upon signing with the major label were in for a shock, because their first RCA release, *For Blood and Empire*, is a particularly vicious attack on the George W. Bush administration (albeit, the kind of very well-produced and well-recorded bromide that corporate backing provides). Still, Anti-Flag remains a killer live band and an eloquent voice for radical causes. They even continue to run their own independent label, A-F, which has released music by Modey Lemon and others.

Discography:

Die for the Government (New Red Archives, 1996); *Their System Doesn't Work for You* (A-F, 1998); *A New Kind of Army* (Go-Kart, 1999); *Underground Network* (Fat Wreck Chords, 2001); *The Terror State* (Fat Wreck Chords, 2003); *Live at Fireside Bowl* EP (Liberation, 2003); *For Blood and Empire* (RCA, 2006)

ANTI-FLAG
A NEW KIND OF ARMY

Anti-Flag does not mean Anti-American. Anti-Flag means anti-war. Anti-Flag means unity.

Anti-Flag brings the revolution to Vancouver, 2006.

ANTI-NOWHERE LEAGUE

1980–1987, 1992–present

LINEUP: Nick Culmer, aka "Animal" (vocals); Chris Exall, aka "Magoo" (guitar); Clive "Winston" Blake (bass); Djahanshah Aghssa, aka "PJ/Persian John" (drums)

This notorious British punk band from the early-1980s was formed by Animal and Magoo, two former motorcycle gang members, with Winston Blake on bass and PJ on drums joining early on. The band toured with the **Exploited** and other bands early on, but is perhaps best known for a shocking incident that occurred on tour with the **Damned** in 1981 in which Winston allegedly put a mayonnaise-covered carrot up his rectum and then proceeded to eat the carrot. Since the band's early records were banned from radio programs, including *Top of the Pops*, for their lyrical content, Anti-Nowhere League survived by touring constantly. After enduring various personnel changes due to internal and substance-abuse problems, the band went more **new wave**/new romantic in look and sound for subsequent albums (a radical switch that must have puzzled longtime fans and certainly did not win them any new converts). After returning to form—and more personnel changes—Anti-Nowhere League disbanded in 1987, but after Metallica invited "Animal" onstage at Wembley Stadium in 1992 to sing their song "So What," it reinvigorated him enough that he spearheaded a reunion in the early-1990s. Although in some respects an important early punk band, Anti-Nowhere League will be less remembered for their music than for their drug- and booze-fueled demolitions of hotel rooms and tour buses.

Discography:

We Are... The League (WXYZ, 1982); *Live in Yugoslavia* (ID, 1983); *Long Live the League* (ABC, 1985); *RIP* (Dojo, 1985); *The Perfect Crime* (GWR, 1987); *Live and Loud!* (Link, 1990); *The Horse is Dead* (Receiver, 1996); *Scum* (Pavement, 1997); *Return to Yugoslavia* (Knock Out, 1998); *Out of Control* (Receiver, 2000); *So What* (Harry May, 2000); *Live Animals* (Step 1, 2002); *I Hate People... Long Live the League* (Harry May, 2002); *Kings & Queens* (Captain Oi!, 2005); *Pig Iron* (Nowhere, 2006); *The Road to Rampton* (Nowhere, 2007)

ANTI-PASTI
1979-1983

LINEUP: Martin Roper (vocals); Dugi Bell (guitar); Stu Winfield (bass, replaced by Will Hoon); Stan Smith (drums, replaced by Kevin Nixon)

A British outfit from the early-1980s, Anti-Pasti released only a few punk protest albums before breaking up. Anti-Pasti's debut *The Last Call* is considered their best record; it actually charted on the mainstream album charts in Britain and propelled the fairly handsome lads to British semi-stardom. Although closely identified with bands like Chron Gen and the **Exploited**, Anti-Pasti had more range than either band and could play mid-tempo numbers as well as the usual generic thrash so popular in the second wave of British punk. They briefly regained prominence in 2005 when a member of the British boy band Busted was seen wearing an Anti-Pasti T-shirt in a video. Despite the obvious provocation, it is unclear if the band will reunite.

Discography:
Four Sore Points EP (Rondelet, 1980); *The Last Call...* (Shatter, 1981); *Caution in the Wind* (Rondelet, 1982); *Anti-Pasti* (Rondelet, 1983)

AOD
1981-1990, 2005

LINEUP: Paul Richards (vocals); Jim Foster (guitar, replaced by Bruce Wingate); Jack Steeples (bass); Dave Scott/Schwartzman (drums)

A New Jersey **hardcore** band largely active in the mid-to-late 1980s, AOD was known for their humor, hyper-fast music, and garish outfits. They gradually evolved into a more melodic band as they progressed and experimented with metal, pop, and psychedelic music. AOD wrote what is considered the best punk song ever about race relations and hamburgers (a tall order) in "White Hassle," a song about inadvertently getting into a fight at 4:00 A.M. at a White Castle burger joint. The band has reunited sporadically for benefits and performed at the series of concerts to save **CBGB**.

Discography:
The Wacky Hijinks of... (Buy Our Records, 1984); *Humungousfungousamongus* (Buy Our Records, 1986); *Cruising with Elvis in Bigfoot's UFO* (Wasteland, 1983; Buy Our Records, 1988); *Ishtar* (Restless, 1989); *Sittin' Pretty* (Grand Theft Audio, 1995)

ARTICLES OF FAITH
1981-1985

LINEUP: Vic Bondi (vocals/guitar); Joe Scuderi (guitar); Dave Shield (bass); Virus X (drums)

A raw and aggressive **hardcore** band from Chicago, Articles of Faith were led by the eloquent but controversial Vic Bondi, who had definite ideas as to what qualified as hardcore and what did not. Articles of Faith started out in 1981 as a melodic **Clash**-inspired band, but shifted gears when Bondi saw **Bad Brains** and was inspired to move the band in a faster and harder direction. This went against the then-prevailing trend in Chicago for **oi**-style bands such as the **Effigies** to play slower songs. Bondi actually got into a prolonged feud with the Effigies and became another example of a punk pleading for unity while engaging in silly and pointless rivalries. None of that takes away, however, from Articles of Faith's aggressive but melodic hardcore and dynamic stage shows, which were legendary in Chicago and eventually across the country. Articles of Faith imploded in 1985, while Bondi went on to join several other hardcore and post-hardcore bands, currently playing in the band Report Suspicious Activity.

Discography:
What We Want is Free (Wasteland, 1982); *Wait* (Wasteland, 1983); *Give Thanks* (Bitzcore 1984, 1996); *In This Life* (Lone Wolf, 1987); *AoF Complete Volume 1* (Alternative Tentacles, 2002); *AoF Complete Volume 2* (Alternative Tentacles, 2003)

A7
LOCATION: NEW YORK

During the early days of **hardcore** in New York City, the A7 club played host to numerous bands (**Bad Brains** played many of their earliest shows in the city here) and was a frequent gathering place for many of the often-underage punks who populated New York's East Village and Lower East Side during the early 1980s. The club was also occasionally known for drug use and violence due to the large population of homeless punks who lived in nearby Tompkins Square Park. The club closed for good during the mid-1980s, and the neighborhood has changed so drastically since then that the punk community has almost completely left the area (except for the holdouts in Tompkins Square Park).

AVAIL
1990-present

LINEUP: Tim Barry (vocals); Joe Banks (guitar); Gwomper (bass); Ed Trask (drums); Beau Beau (cheerleader)

The ferocious Virginia band Avail is known for having one of the most energetic and relentless live shows in the U.S. post-**hardcore** scene (augmented by "cheerleader" Beau Beau's manic dancing). The band was originally formed during the late-1980s in Washington, D.C., with Joe Banks on guitar, Tim Barry on drums, and several other members who quickly quit. After a band reconfiguration and a move to a new headquarters in Richmond, Virginia

Articles of Faith in an undated scene from the film *American Hardcore*.

The Wacky Hi-Jinks of....

ADRENALIN O.D.

Avail's super-roadie Beau Beau goes airborne in Utah, 1996.

the avengers died for your sins

(which figures prominently in the band's lyrics), Barry took over lead vocal duties, Ed Trask was added on drums, and the enigmatic Gwomper took over on bass. Known for their intensely personal lyrics, Avail straddled the line between the experimental and straight-out hardcore groups that characterized the D.C. scene during the late-1980s, and played gigs with almost every luminary of the scene. The band was one of many who had to take their original masters back from **Lookout! Records** when the label ran into trouble early in 2005.

Discography:

Satiate (Lookout!, 1992); *Dixie* (Lookout!, 1994); *4 AM Friday* (Lookout!, 1996); *The Fall of Richmond* EP (Lookout!, 1997); *Over the James* (Lookout!, 1998); *V.M. Live* (Liberation, 1999); *One Wrench* (Fat Wreck Chords, 2000); *Front Porch Stories* (Fat Wreck Chords, 2002); *Live at the Kings Head Inn* (Old Glory, 1999)

THE AVENGERS

1977–1979, 2004–present

LINEUP: Penelope Houston (vocals); Greg Ingraham (guitar, replaced by Brad Kunt); Jimmy Wilsey (bass); Danny Furious (drums)

An early U.S. punk band led by singer Penelope Houston, the Avengers (along with another female-led punk band, the **Nuns**) opened for the **Sex Pistols** during their 1978 U.S. tour stop at San Francisco's Winterland. The band's androgynous look and particularly American brand of punk weren't well received during their lifespan due to a scene that was not only sexist but also resistant to anything other than UK-style punk. While punk may have been tolerant of many things, in the early years a female-fronted band such as the Avengers was in certain ways a threat to the estab-

lished punk orthodoxy. The band released little legitimate material during its lifetime, and various releases of their album, usually poor-quality bootlegs, had been floating around for years until **Lookout! Records'** official release years later. After the band's dissolution, Penelope Houston became a prolific solo artist but still toured sporadically with various incarnations of the Avengers and with her own band. The Avengers' current lineup consists of Houston and Ingraham with Joel Reader on bass and Luis Illades on drums.

Discography:

Avengers EP (White Noise, 1978, 1981); *Avengers* (CD Presents, 1983); *The Avengers Died for Your Sins* (Lookout!, 1999). **Penelope Houston:** *Birdboys* (Subterranean, 1988)

Penelope Houston, backstage at the Whisky in 1978.

BACK DOOR MAN

This influential early Los Angeles zine started by Phast Phreddie (Fred Patterson) covered the Hollywood scene but also wrote about influential early punk and garage music and bands such as **Iggy Pop**, **Pere Ubu**, Roxy Music, and Brian Eno. From 1974 to 1978, *Back Door Man* provided valuable information to the first generation of L.A. punks who could rely on no real radio or mainstream coverage of the new and fast-growing scene. Phast Phreddie was also a popular DJ and emcee and was a key player in the early L.A. punk scene. Phreddie now frequently deejays in New York and is known for his encyclopedic knowledge of obscure albums and singles.

⑪   75¢

BACK DOOR MAN

KINKS, IGGY POP

INTERVIEWS WITH
BLONDIE
TELEVISION
RAMONES
CHEAP TRICK
MINK DE VILLE

PHIL SPECTOR
ELLIOTT MURPHY
HOLLYWOOD STARS
NITE CITY

ABOVE: Blondie graces *Back Door Man*'s May 1977 cover.
LEFT: Bad Brains' H.R. considers Babylon.

BAD BRAINS
1979–present
LINEUP: Paul "H.R." Hudson (vocals);
Gary "Dr. Know" Miller (guitar);
Darryl Jenifer (bass); Earl Hudson (drums)

An incendiary but internally troubled Rastafarian-**hardcore** band, Bad Brains fused hardcore's acceleration with metallic crunch and spacey **reggae**. Extremely influential on both the New York and Washington, D.C., scenes (inspiring everyone from Living Color to **Agnostic Front** to the Beastie Boys), they released an equal number of groundbreaking works and complete duds. Bad Brains have long been famous for both the members' unmatched virtuosity and the electrifyingly spiritual performances of lead singer H.R.

First formed in Maryland by a group of jazz-fusion-loving African Americans, Bad Brains originally called themselves Mind Power. In 1978, friend Sid McCray introduced them to punk rock via the **Dead Boys**, among others, after which they took their new name from the **Ramones** song, and left jazz fusion behind forever. A series of furious and now-legendary shows around the D.C. area in 1979 and 1980 cemented Bad Brains' reputation among young and impressionable types like **Ian MacKaye** and **Henry Rollins**. Although they started out as typical American middle-class suburbanites, the band members became Rastafarians after seeing the movie *Rockers* and a double bill of Stanley Clarke and Bob Marley. They grew their hair out into dreadlocks, introduced reggae into their set list, began speaking in Jamaican patois, and ate according to Rastafarian dietary restrictions.

In 1980, Bad Brains decamped for New York City (a move inspired, oddly enough, by the book *Think and Grow Rich* by Napoleon Hill) where they gigged at a frantic pace, eventually becoming the tightest band in hardcore. They were invited by the **Damned** to tour England but were not allowed into that country. Back in the U.S., they recorded the blisteringly fast "Pay to Cum" single and opened for the **Clash** at the legendary Bond's Casino. The band went on a national tour in 1982 to promote their first album, the self-titled, cassette-only ROIR Records release.

In April 1982 in Texas, Bad Brains ran into trouble when H.R. got into an altercation with the **Big Boys** singer Biscuit over the latter's open homosexuality, and the band later allegedly stiffed the Big Boys in a marijuana deal. **MDC**, friends of the Big Boys, spread the word via flyers and newsletters warning of Bad Brains' intolerance, and the band became persona non grata to many punks. It was just one of the many episodes of erratic and intolerant behavior that would hamper the band throughout its lifetime. That same year, however, the band met the Cars front man

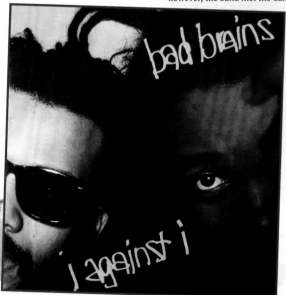

bad brains

i against i

Bad Brains' Dr. Know (left) and H.R.

and fan Ric Ocasek, who produced their album *Rock for Light* for the Gem label, which quickly folded. Following a brief breakup over whether to sign to Elektra Records, Bad Brains regrouped in 1986 for the powerful **SST** release *I Against I*. Although H.R. had been arrested for selling pot (he recorded the vocals for "Sacred Love" over the phone from jail), the record was a huge success in underground circles and firmly established Bad Brains as musically light-years ahead of their peers and many imitators.

After *I Against I*, whose metal-tinged anthems represent for many of their fans the band's high-water mark, H.R. quit again. Bad Brains continued without him, but he returned in time to record vocals for 1989's *Quickness* album (Mackie from the **Cro-Mags** played drums, although Earl is featured on the cover). H.R. then quit again, and the band recorded *Rise* with Israel Joseph I (Dexter Pinto) on lead vocals. H.R. returned once again to record the disappointing 1995 *God of Love* album for Madonna's Maverick label. The band subsequently broke up, toured, and re-formed, this time as Soul Brains because they no longer had the right to use their original name. In 2007, they released the impressively raw *Build a Nation* album, produced by Beastie Boy Adam Yauch.

Although Bad Brains are musically, and perhaps ideologically, one of the most important U.S. punk bands, their legacy of

internal turmoil doomed the band to years of struggle. They went through several line-up changes involving the Hudson brothers at various points, with H.R. struggling for years with questions of whether his Rastafarian beliefs fit in with the commercial nature of rock 'n' roll or whether his beliefs even allowed the rhythms used in rock 'n' roll. (Many Rastafarians believe that only a pure form of reggae music is spiritually acceptable, with some feeling even some of Bob Marley's songs constituted secular, non-reggae music). According to other sources, H.R. also struggled with over-use of drugs, emotional or psychological problems, trouble with the law, and arguments and physical altercations with everyone from fellow bandmates, members of other groups, and even record executives. Although Bad Brains never achieved their true potential, they remain a seminal band in punk, hardcore, heavy metal, and hard rock history.

Essential Discography:
Bad Brains (tape; ROIR, 1982; Dutch East India Trading, 1991; ROIR, 1996); *Bad Brains* EP (Alternative Tentacles, 1982); *I and I Survived* EP (Important, 1982); *Rock for Light* (PVC, 1983; Caroline, 1991); *I Against I* (SST, 1986); *Live* (SST, 1988); *Attitude: The ROIR Sessions* (In-Effect/Relativity, 1989); *Quickness* (Caroline, 1989); *The Youth Are Getting Restless* (Caroline, 1990); *Spirit Electricity* (SST, 1991); *Rise* (Epic, 1993); *God of Love* (Maverick/Warner Bros., 1995); *Black Dots* (Caroline, 1996); *The Omega Sessions* (Victory, 1997); *Banned in D.C.: Bad Brains Greatest Riffs* (Caroline, 2003); *Build a Nation* (Megaforce, 2007). **H.R.:** *Its About Luv* (Olive Tree, 1985; SST, 1988); *Human Rights* (SST, 1987); *H.R. Tapes '84–'86* (SST, 1988); *Singin' in the Heart* (SST, 1989); *Charge* (SST, 1990)

BAD RELIGION
1980–present
LINEUP: Greg Graffin (vocals); "Mr." Brett Gurewitz (guitar, replaced by Brian Baker); Greg Hetson (guitar); Jay Bentley (bass); Pete Finestone (drums, replaced by Bobby Schayer and Brooks Wackerman)

Bad Religion has long been one of the most prolific, politically active, lyrically dense, and melodically driven bands in punk rock and **hardcore** music. Well known for the multisyllabic lyrics of guitarist Mr. Brett and lead singer (and Ph.D. candidate and eventual professor) Greg Graffin, Bad

Religion put out a number of classic albums like *No Control*, *Suffer*, and *Stranger than Fiction* that gave a melodic but still musically ferocious edge to punk rock. The band had several radio and **MTV** hits like "21st Century (Digital Boy)," "Infected," and "Stranger than Fiction." For a time during the 1990s, while signed to a major label, Bad Religion was one of the best-known breakthrough punk bands in America.

Bad Religion was originally formed in 1980 in California's San Fernando Valley by students Greg Graffin and "Mr." Brett Gurewitz (who also founded and runs **Epitaph**, possibly the most successful and profitable independent record label in punk history), along with Jay Bentley on bass and Pete Finestone on drums. The band started to get noticed when a 15-year-old Graffin gave the **Circle Jerks'** Greg Hetson a demo tape that indicated their raw talent. Their first EP, the eponymous *Bad Religion*, came out in 1981, followed later that year by the somewhat more melodic *How Could Hell Be Any Worse?*. After touring Southern California and becoming one of the more popular live acts of the early-1980s, the band evidently became disillusioned with the limitations inherent in the punk scene. With Graffin away studying at the University

Bad Religion's Jay Bentley shows some skin, 2004.

of Wisconsin in 1983, Bad Religion went though a radical change of musical direction, releasing the keyboard-driven and confusing (at least to punk fans of the time) *Into the Unknown*. For Bad Religion's fans, the release of the **new wave**-sounding album—which closely follows the **Devo** template—was tantamount to heresy. The band went on hiatus following the critical pans given to *Into the Unknown* (eventually deleted by Epitaph, the album is still not available legally).

In 1984, the band was re-formed at the suggestion of Hetson (who had previously provided a guitar solo for the song "Part III" on the first album), with Hetson on second guitar, and released the far more orthodox punk *Back to the Known* EP, which was partially made to reassure their fans that the band had gone back to basics. After another hiatus, during which Graffin acquired a master's degree and started work on a Ph.D. at Cornell, the full quintet lineup of Graffin, Gurewitz, Hetson, Bentley, and Finestone was finally reestablished in 1988 for *Suffer*, the first release in a string of remarkable albums.

In the 1980s and early-1990s, when most punk and hardcore acts had broken up, Bad Religion continued to tour and release records that were some of the most interesting and vital of the time. After punk rock was back on the mass media radar in the early-1990s, Bad Religion was signed to Atlantic, which re-issued the *Recipe for Hate* album in 1993 and then their major-label debut

Stranger than Fiction in 1994, which led to MTV videos for "Infected" and the remake of the earlier "21st Century (Digital Boy)."

After *Stranger than Fiction*, however, founder Mr. Brett left to work on running Epitaph full time and was believed to be dealing with a drug problem. Mr. Brett was replaced by Brian Baker (of **Minor Threat**, **Dag Nasty**, and the embarrassing metal band Junkyard). With Baker in the mix, the band recorded several more albums and toured extensively, including several times on the **Vans Warped** tour.

Bad Religion left Atlantic Records in 2001 and re-signed with their old friends at Epitaph. Drummer Bobby Schayer, who had replaced Finestone, also retired from the band that year and was replaced by Brooks Wackerman, formerly of **Suicidal Tendencies**. Major contributors to keeping the punk aesthetic alive during the lean years of the mid- to late-1980s, Bad Religion continues to perform and record.

Discography:

Bad Religion EP (Epitaph, 1981); *How Could Hell Be Any Worse?* (Epitaph, 1982; remastered, Epitaph, 2004); *Into the Unknown* (Epitaph, 1983); *Back to the Known* EP (Epitaph, 1984); *Suffer* (Epitaph, 1988; remastered, Epitaph, 2004); *No Control* (Epitaph, 1989; remastered, Epitaph, 2004); *Against the Grain* (Epitaph, 1990; remastered, Epitaph, 2004); *80–85* (Epitaph, 1991); *Generator* (Epitaph, 1992; extra tracks and remastered, Epitaph, 2004); *Recipe for Hate* (Epitaph, 1993; Atlantic, 1993); *Stranger than Fiction* (Atlantic, 1994); *All Ages* (Epitaph, 1995); *The Gray Race* (Atlantic, 1996); *Tested* (live; Epic, 1997); *No Substance* (Atlantic, 1998); *The New America* (Atlantic, 2000); *The Process of Belief* (Epitaph, 2002); *The Empire Strikes First* (Epitaph, 2004); *New Maps of Hell* (Epitaph, 2007)

BELOW: At a USC frat party, 1980. (L to R) Brett Gurewitz, Greg Graffin, Jay Ziskrout, Jay Bentley.

THE BAGS

1977-1980

LINEUP: Alice Bag/Armandariz (vocals);
Craig Lee (guitar); Rob Ritter (guitar);
Patricia Bag/Morrison (bass);
Terry Graham (drums)

This early Los Angeles punk group was formed in 1977 and led by Alice Bag on lead vocals, Craig Bag (Craig Lee, later of Catholic Discipline) and Rob Ritter (later of **45 Grave**) on guitars, Terry "Dad" Bag (Terry Graham) on drums, and Pat Bag (Patricia Morrison, who later joined the **Gun Club**, the Sisters of Mercy, and the **Damned**) on bass. Later members included D.J. Bonebrake of **X** on drums, Geza X on guitar, and Jane Koontz on guitar. The band formed when Alice and Patricia met at an audition for **Kim Fowley**'s first post-**Runaways** project, and decided they were better off forming a band on their own. The Bags were originally supposed to perform with bags over their heads in a bid for anonymity, but the plan was foiled when **Darby Crash** took the bag off Alice Bag's head during a show. The band was one of the better of the raw L.A. bands and were more musically adept than the **Germs,** but also raucous and sloppy in an endearing way. The Bags appeared in Penelope Spheeris's *Decline of Western Civilization* before breaking up in 1980. Ritter (who had changed his name to Rob Graves) died in 1991 and Lee died in the 1980s, while Alice Bag continues to perform in various bands today.

Discography:
Survive 7" (Dangerhouse, 1978);
Disco's Dead (Artifix, 2003)

LESTER BANGS

An iconic critic who wrote for *Creem Magazine* and many other publications, Lester Bangs had a love-hate relationship with punk rock and especially with Ur-punk **Lou Reed**, about whom Bangs often wrote. He was especially appreciated for his early interest in the **Clash** and the disdain he had for the elements of racism and white supremacy that he saw in the nascent scene. Bangs was one of the first American writers to truly "get" early punk and to try to contextualize it in terms of the music industry and fan culture. He was famous for the visionary, often surrealistic rants in his rock criticism, and for his espousal of the rock 'n' roll lifestyle, including the prerequisite substance abuse and fast living. His writing style is often imitated but rarely equaled, as was his lifestyle.

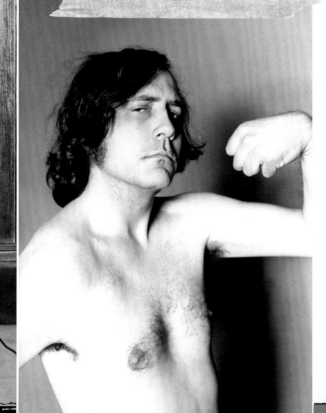

LEFT: Alice Bag at a benefit show for the Masque, February 1978.
BELOW: Lester Bangs: critical muscle, 1980.

Bangs was also a musician and wrote and played in Birdland with Mickey Leigh, **Joey Ramone**'s younger brother. While the band's garage rock redux was hardly groundbreaking, it was proof that Bangs had a musical and artistic vision in addition to being a critic.

Bangs died of a prescription-drug overdose in 1981. His work has been anthologized in two volumes, *Psychotic Reactions and Carburetor Dung* and *Mainlines, Bloodfeasts, and Bad Taste.*

BATTALION OF SAINTS

1978-1984, 1994-1998, 2004-present

CLASSIC LINEUP: George Anthony (vocals); Chris Smith (guitar); James Cooper (bass, replaced by Dennis Frame, Captain Scarlet, Greg Kramer, Ken Ortman, others); Ted Olsen (drums)

A **hardcore** band from San Diego, formed in the early-1980s, Battalion of Saints emulated heavily political, metal-influenced British bands such as **Discharge**. Originally founded by George Anthony and Chris Smith as the Nutrons in 1978, the band switched names after a few lineup changes in the early-1980s. They first broke up in 1984 when Smith left to join **Kraut**; he subsequently died of an overdose. Battalion later re-formed in the late-1990s with only Anthony left from the original lineup. The band was briefly known as Battalion of Saints A.D. and featured a mostly British lineup of Anthony, Terry "Tezz" Bones (of Discharge and **Broken Bones**) on guitar, plus **U.K. Subs** members Greg Kramer and Matt McCoy, but this lineup fell apart in 1998. They re-formed again in 2004 with new members, including ex-**Adolescents** guitarist Rikk Agnew. Although Battalion of Saints didn't break any new musical ground, their fast, aggressive West Coast style and politically adept lyrics put them in the top tier of early hardcore bands.

Discography:

Fighting Boys EP (Nutrons, 1982); *Second Coming* (Nutrons/Enigma, 1984, 1995); *Rock in Peace: The Best of the Battalion of Saints* (Mystic, 1988, 1995); *Death-R-Us* (Taang!, 1995); *Best Of* (Mystic, 2003). **Battalion of Saints A.D.**: *Cuts* (Taang!, 1996)

Battalion of Saints' Chris Smith does his rooster impression in L.A., 1983.

BEAT HAPPENING

1982–present

LINEUP: Calvin Johnson (vocals/guitar); Heather Lewis (drums/guitar); Brett Lunsford (drums/guitar)

The minimalist and intentionally amateurish Beat Happening are led by indie rock giant and K Records mastermind Calvin Johnson. Considered punk less for their music than the **DIY** aesthetic of Johnson and collaborators Heather Lewis and Brett Lunsford, whose bassless trio echoes a more childlike version of the **Cramps** on their early records. Several of the earliest releases are on cassette and difficult to find, but the band's essential material has been repackaged for CD in a variety of formats. Although Beat Happening had impeccable punk cred, their repetitious style was an acquired taste, and could wear thin through the course of an album or concert. (Sometimes Beat Happening would play longer opening slots than the headliner.)

Select Discography:
Beat Happening EP (tape; K, 1984); *1983–1985* (K/Feel Good All Over, 1990); *You Turn Me On* (K, 1992), *Beat Happening* (K, 1996). *Music to Climb the Apple Tree by* (K, 2003)

BEEFEATER

1984–1986

LINEUP: Tomas Squib (vocals); Fred Smith (guitar); Douglas Birdwell (bass); Bruce Taylor (drums)

A Washington, D.C., political punk band who recorded for **Dischord Records** during the 1980s and were active in various D.C. political movements such as **Revolution Summer** in 1985, Beefeater was started by singer Tomas Squib as an outlet for his radical politics and provocative lyrics. Beefeater, despite their name, were dedicated to vegetarianism and radical politics, and played in a punk-funk style quite rare in the scene at the time. Squib was known for his energetic but pacifist shows, including one notorious episode during which he stripped off all his clothes in an effort to quell an extraordinarily violent **pit**. The band was also committed to examining spirituality and living an honest punk life as opposed to simply talking and dressing

Are we not Beat Happening?

like punks. After the band broke up Squib went on to form Fidelity Jones, a less punk-influenced, but still indie, Dischord band.

Discography:
Plays for Lovers (Dischord, 1985, 1995); *Need a Job* (Olive Tree, 1986); *House Burning Down* (Dischord, 1987, 1995)

BETTER YOUTH ORGANIZATION

LOCATION: LOS ANGELES

The Better Youth Organization movement and record label was started by the Stern brothers (Shawn, Mark, and Adam) of the Los Angeles band **Youth Brigade** in 1979. The Stern brothers tried to create a positive space where members of the punk rock community could release albums and play (the band also occasionally ran a club)

outside of the corporate structure of the traditional recording industry. The label released its first album, the compilation *Someone Got Their Head Kicked In*, in 1982. That same year Youth Brigade organized the Someone Got Their Head Kicked In tour with **Social Distortion**, which was later made into the notorious punk documentary *Another State of Mind*. BYO put out records by **7 Seconds**, the Briefs, Four Letter Word, and others. The label still exists, although the political aspects of the BYO seem to have been put on the back burner.

JELLO BIAFRA

Jello Biafra (real name Eric Boucher) is lead singer for the **Dead Kennedys**, author, activist, a former mayoral candidate in San Francisco, and frequent collaborator with other musicians. When his career with the Dead Kennedys came to an end in the late-1980s, Biafra reinvented himself as a political provocateur, punk rock story-teller, political comedian, and musician, touring clubs and college campuses, spreading mischief and agitation against conformist and establishment politics. Biafra was also busy creating music with disparate collaborators, such as Al Jourgensen from Ministry (under the moniker Lard) and **Ian MacKaye** from **Fugazi**, as well as more straight-ahead punk material with **D.O.A.**, NOmeansno, and Mojo Nixon on his **Alternative Tentacles** label. In a strange turn of events, Biafra was the target of a savage beating at the **Gilman Street** club in 1994 by young street punks who doubted his underground authenticity.

In the late 1990s, Biafra was the subject of a contentious lawsuit filed against him by the other former members of the Dead Kennedys (East Bay Ray, D.H. Peligro, and Klaus Flouride) alleging he withheld royalty payments from them. He ultimately lost the case and the rights to the name Dead Kennedys, leading the rest of the band to re-form and tour with a different singer. The polarizing Biafra remains a punk icon not only for his groundbreaking work with the Dead Kennedys (who changed the very nature of **hardcore**, making it more politically aware and open to satire), but also for his relentless activism and refusal to compromise his principles.

Select Solo Discography:
No More Cocoons (Alternative Tentacles, 1987); *High Priest of Harmful Matter—Tales from the Trial* (Alternative Tentacles, 1989); *I Blow Minds for a Living* (Alternative Tentacles, 1991); *Beyond the Valley of the Gift Police* (Alternative Tentacles, 1994); *If Evolution is Outlawed, Only Outlaws Will Evolve* (Alternative Tentacles, 1998); *Become the Media* (Alternative Tentacles, 2001); *Machine Gun in the Clown's Hand* (Alternative Tentacles, 2002); *The Big Ka-Boom Part One* (Alternative Tentacles, 2002). **Witch Trials:** *The Witch Trials EP* (Subterranean/Alternative Tentacles, 1981). **Lard:** *The Power of Lard EP* (Alternative Tentacles, 1988); *The Last Temptation of Reid* (Alternative Tentacles, 1990); *Pure Chewing Satisfaction* (Alternative Tentacles, 1997). **Jello Biafra with D.O.A.:** *Last Scream of the Missing Neighbors* (Alternative Tentacles, 1990). **Jello Biafra with NOmeansno:** *The Sky Is Falling and I Want My Mommy* (Alternative Tentacles, 1991). **Tumor Circus:** *Tumor Circus* (Alternative Tentacles, 1991). **Jello Biafra with Plainfield:** *Jello Biafra with Plainfield EP* (Alternative Tentacles, 1993). **Jello Biafra with Mojo Nixon:** *Will the Fetus Be Aborted?* EP (Alternative Tentacles, 1993)

"It's a safe little punk womb to have *Maximum RocknRoll* as your bible and to think the world's most important issue is whether Jawbreaker sold out, while ignoring the homeless people outside. That's not community. Bickering endlessly over stuff that doesn't matter is not community, it's junior high."

—Jello Biafra,
Punk Planet 18, May/June 1997

BIG BLACK

1982-1987

LINEUP: Steve Albini (vocals/guitar); Santiago Durango (guitar); Jeff Pezzati (bass, replaced by Dave Riley)

Chicago's confrontational and aggressively noisy Big Black, led by the mercurial **Steve Albini**, were one of the key bands that established the indie rock touring and musical blueprints of the 1980s. Big Black was started in 1982 with Albini and a drum machine, but after the *Lungs* EP, Jeff Pezzati came aboard on bass and Santiago Durango on guitar (both had played in **Naked Raygun**). After recording two EPs, Pezzati was replaced by Dave Riley. Big Black is known not only for its combative and harsh music (a style of stripped-down, industrial punk with some comparison to fellow Chicagoans Ministry; only you weren't supposed to necessarily enjoy it), but also for the controversial lyrics of Albini, who turned a penchant for black humor into a career, leading to accusations of racism and sexism against the band. In 1987, Durango left to go to law school, and the band decided to retire after releasing the *Songs About Fucking* album. Albini later formed the short-lived Rapeman and the longer-lasting Shellac. Today, Albini is one of the most sought-after engineers in music, working on albums by **Nirvana**, Jesus Lizard, the **Pixies**, and even Robert Plant.

Discography:
Lungs EP (Ruthless, 1982); *Bulldozer* EP (Ruthless, 1983); *Racer-X* EP (Homestead, 1984); *Atomizer* (Homestead, 1986; Touch and Go, 1986); *The Hammer Party* (Homestead, 1986); *Headache* EP (Touch and Go, 1987); *Songs About Fucking* (Touch and Go, 1987); *Pigpile* (Touch and Go, 1992)

"There are some people that (thought of Big Black) as some sort of dark and scary charging industrial rock machine, and I think of it as three goofballs playing a slightly bent version of rock music."

—**Steve Albini,** *Maximum RocknRoll* **issue #112**

(L to R) Big Black's Steve Albini, Santiago Durango, and Dave Riley lurk in the shadows.

THE BIG BOYS

1978-1984

LINEUP: Randy Turner, aka "Biscuit" (vocals); Tim Kerr (guitar); Chris Gates (bass); Steve Collier (drums, replaced by Greg Murray, Fred Shultz, and Rey Washam)

One of the first groups to merge funk rhythms with **hardcore** punk, the Big Boys were a clear influence on many more successful bands such as the Red Hot Chili Peppers. Notable for having openly gay members at a time when many in the punk community did not tolerate homosexuality, the Big Boys redefined punk as more inclusive in terms of musicality and sexuality. The Big Boys first formed in Austin, Texas, in 1978 with vocalist "Biscuit" (Randy Turner), guitarist Tim Kerr, bassist Chris Gates, and drummer Steve Collier, which proved to be the quintessential lineup. The band gigged mostly in Texas, and although they released albums only on minor labels, their influence was felt around the country. In 1983, they were the opening band at the Washington, D.C., Punk Funk Spectacular, which featured local go-go band Trouble Funk and **Minor Threat** in their last performance.

The Big Boys were among the few hardcore bands who tried to musically expand punk's limited palette. Also, along with other more tolerant Austin punks such as the **Dicks**, the band challenged the limited worldviews of many supposedly "tolerant" punks, who were in some ways as straight-laced as the people they mocked. The band broke up in the mid-1980s. Guitarist Tim Kerr went on to form Poison 13 and remains a part of the Austin scene, mentoring younger bands. Bassist Gates put together the Los Angeles glam-metal band Junkyard with Brian Baker of Minor Threat, **Dag Nasty** and Bad Religion. "Biscuit" remained a popular artist in Austin until his untimely death on August 17, 2005.

Discography:
Live at Raul's Club (split LP with the Dicks; Rat Race, 1980); *Where's My Towel* (Wasted Talent, 1981); *Fun, Fun, Fun...* EP (Moment, 1982); *Lullabies Help the Brain Grow* (Moment/Enigma, 1983); *No Matter How Long the Line at the Cafeteria, There's Always a Seat* (Enigma, 1984); *Wreck Collection* (Unseen Hand, 1989; Gern Blandsten, 2002); *The Skinny Elvis* (Touch and Go, 1993); *The Fat Elvis* (Touch and Go, 1993)

BIG DRILL CAR

1987-1995

LINEUP: Frank Daly (vocals); Mark Arnold (guitar); Bob Thomson (bass, replaced by Darrin Morris); Danny Marcroft (drums, replaced by Keith Fallis)

A loud and poppy punk band from Orange County, California, who recorded during the late-1980s to mid-1990s (mostly on Bill Stevenson's Cruz label), Big Drill Car featured vocalist Frank Daly and guitarist Mark Arnold (previously in the punk band MIA) with a revolving rhythm section. The band played a particularly adept version of Orange County punk, better than most, but not enough to make a living. Big Drill Car broke up in the mid-1990s, after which several members joined with John Kastner of the **Doughboys** to form the punk supergroup All Systems Go.

Discography:
Small Block EP (Variant, 1988); *Album Type Thing* (also known as *Tape* or *CD Type Thing*; Cruz, 1989); *Batch* (Cruz, 1991); *Toured (A Live Album)* (Headhunter/Cargo, 1993); *No Worse for the Wear* (Headhunter/Cargo, 1994)

RONNIE BIGGS

Ronald Arthur Biggs (born August 8, 1929), usually called Ronnie Biggs, is best known as a participant in the Great Train Robbery of 1963 and, briefly, as a member of the disintegrating **Sex Pistols**. After escaping from a British prison he fled first to France, where he underwent plastic surgery, then to Australia. He was forced into exile in Brazil in 1965, from which England could not extradite him because his girlfriend was pregnant. After Johnny Rotten (born **John Lydon**) quit the Sex Pistols in 1978, remaining members Paul Cook and Steve Jones (minus a dope-sick **Sid Vicious**) flew down to Rio de Janeiro at the request of manager **Malcolm McLaren** to record two songs and make a video with Biggs. The two resulting songs, "A Punk Prayer" and "No One is Innocent," were released as an EP and were also included on the soundtrack of the Sex Pistols' posthumous film, *The Great Rock 'n' Roll Swindle*, in which the video with Biggs appears. The recordings where Biggs sang are problematic at best.

The collaboration with Biggs can be seen as either another cheap publicity stunt by McLaren or a true punk statement of

LEFT: The Big Boys' Randy "Biscuit" Turner, in happy times.
BELOW: Mr. Biggs' mugshot photo, early-1960s.

rebellion against authority, depending on one's viewpoint. Biggs spent his years after recording with the Sex Pistols as a celebrity fugitive, charging curious tourists money to meet him or have their pictures taken with him. He later recorded a song, "Carnival in Rio (Punk Was)," with Germany's **Die Toten Hosen** on their 1991 album *Learning English, Lesson One*. Biggs eventually tired of life in exile and returned to England in 2001 to face charges. Upon arrival, he was arrested and returned to prison. He is mostly remembered as a footnote to the Sex Pistols' career and an illustrative example of McLaren's attempts to milk the dying cow for all it was worth.

BIKINI KILL

1990-1998

LINEUP: Kathleen Hanna (vocals); Billy Karren, aka "Billy Boredom" (guitar); Kathi Wilcox (guitar/bass); Tobi Vail (drums/vocals)

Definitely the best known and probably the most dynamic band of the so-called **Riot Grrrl** movement of the early to mid-1990s, Bikini Kill featured the sometimes screaming, sometimes cooing vocals of lead singer **Kathleen Hanna** and some extremely emotional and sometimes outright confrontational songs about gender, identity, and violence. Formed in the late-1980s in Olympia, Washington, the band recorded and released their first cassette, *Revolution Girl Style*, by themselves but soon signed to the progressive **Kill Rock Stars** label, an ideal place for Bikini Kill's furiously independent, stripped-down style of punk rock. Many of the band's songs were influenced by the degradation Hanna experienced as a stripper, as well as her later work as a founder (along with Molly Neumann, Erin Smith, Allison Wolfe, later of **Bratmobile**, and Jen Smith) of *Riot Grrrl* zine; the band relocated from Olympia to Washington, D.C., in 1991 to take advantage of that city's far more hospitable scene (D.C. mainstay **Ian MacKaye** produced their eponymous EP). After they started getting noticed in 1993, the band was befriended by proto-Riot Grrrl **Joan Jett**, who produced the electrifying and raw "New Radio/Rebel Girl" single.

During their prime, Bikini Kill was not only one of the most politically engaged bands in punk, but by doing things like banning **stage diving** at shows and forcing men out of the **pit**, worked to create a safe environment for women to actually participate in shows without being attacked or groped. After the band's demise in 1998, Hanna went on to form the equally confrontational and gender-questioning (but much more danceable) **Le Tigre**.

Discography:
Revolution Girl Style Now (cassette; no label, 1991); *Bikini Kill* EP (Kill Rock Stars, 1991); *New Radio* EP (Kill Rock Stars, 1993); *Pussy Whipped* (Kill Rock Stars, 1994); *The C.D. Version of the First Two Records* (Kill Rock Stars, 1994); *Reject All American* (Kill Rock Stars, 1996)

THE C.D. VERSION OF THE FIRST TWO RECORDS.

RODNEY BINGENHEIMER

A Los Angeles scenemaker and DJ on L.A.'s influential KROQ radio station, Rodney Bingenheimer was an early proponent of both glam and punk rock and played numerous punk bands on his radio show before punk was popular or had any mainstream exposure. Although extremely unprepossessing physically, Bingenheimer was a key figure in the L.A. music scene and like **John Peel**, was an influential tastemaker. Early in the 1970s, he ran the English Disco club (where the **New York Dolls** and the **Stooges** played), and he started playing punk music on KROQ in August 1976, introducing Southern California listeners to the likes of the **Ramones**, the **Donnas**, and **Agent Orange**. His status as champion of underground music gained him cameos in *Repo Man* and the Roger Corman-produced Ramones film *Rock 'n' Roll High School*. Bingenheimer's life was analyzed in the 2004 documentary, *Mayor of the Sunset Strip*.

(L to R) Blondie's Frankie Infante, Joey Ramone, Iggy Pop, and Rodney Bingenheimer, 1988.

Bikini Kill's Kathleen Hanna (right) elicits rock backup from Joan Jett (left), 1994.

BLACK FLAG

1977-1986

LINEUP: Henry Rollins (vocals); Greg Ginn
(guitar); Dez Cadena (guitar); Keith Morris
(bass, replaced by Ron Reyes, Dez Cadena,
Chuck Dukowski, Kira Roessler); Robo
(drums, replaced by Bill Stevenson,
Anthony Martinez)

A tremendously influential Los Angeles
band who best articulated the early **hardcore** sound, Black Flag was founded by
guitarist **Greg Ginn** before he became an
indie recording impressario. Subject to constant lineup changes, Black Flag are known
for slowing down hardcore and combining
it with the sludgy riffs of Black Sabbath,
and for the lyrics and unmatchable stage
presence of latter-day lead singer **Henry
Rollins**. The band is also largely responsible
for establishing the ethos of touring regularly across the United States and keeping
the hardcore scene alive during the 1980s.
Black Flag contributed almost more than
any other band to establishing a network
of regionally connected scenes and **squats**,
touring without major label promotion or
support, and blazing the way for subsequent bands to follow the cross-country
trail they helped to create.

Black Flag was founded in 1977 as
Panic by Ginn in Hermosa Beach, California,
after Ginn had become excited by the first
Ramones album. Panic included **Keith
Morris** (later to found the **Circle Jerks**)
on vocals, Greg's brother, the artist
Raymond Pettibon on bass, and drummer
Brian Migdol. Pettibon soon left the band
and was replaced by Gary McDaniel, who
changed his name to Chuck Dukowski in
a thinly veiled tribute to the drunken
writer Charles Bukowski. Soon after,
Migdol was replaced by Robo, an illegal
alien from Colombia, marking the band's
first serious lineup. After learning of a
British band of the same name, Panic
changed their name to Black Flag at
Pettibon's suggestion, named after the
symbol of anarchy. (Pettibon designed
the band's logo, the waving black flag
often referred to as "the bars," as well as
numerous band flyers and album covers.)

In 1978 Ginn formed **SST** to release the
Nervous Breakdown EP. At the first the band
had a hard time finding places to play, as
the L.A. scenesters looked down on the guys

from Hermosa Beach who didn't live in the cooler parts of town and eschewed the punk uniform for T-shirts and jeans. Black Flag made their official public debut at an outdoor Parks Department concert at Hollywood Park, where the band was met by an unappreciative, food-throwing crowd (to the crowd's credit, Ginn had booked the gig by claiming that they were a Fleetwood Mac cover band). The group soon started playing with like-minded bands and helped release the **Minutemen**'s *Paranoid Time* EP, cementing a long partnership between the two bands (there was even a short-lived collaborative outfit named Minuteflag). Black Flag suffered a setback when Morris departed in August 1979, but the members recruited Ron Reyes (aka Chavo Pederast), the drummer from teen punk band **Red Kross**, to record the *Jealous Again* EP. During a show at the Fleetwood in L.A., Reyes quit mid-set, and the band went into an epic version of "Louie Louie" to pacify the crowd. Yet another former member of Red Kross, guitarist Dez Cadena, took over on vocals, and Black Flag began to play much more frequently in the early-1980s.

Black Flag gained a (mostly unearned) reputation for violence when police

and punks clashed outside a show at the **Whisky** on Sunset Boulevard in L.A., which led to even more police surveillance and harassment and eventually to Black Flag's name becoming synonymous with "punk violence" at L.A. shows. After recording several singles with Dez before he decided to move to guitar in July 1981, the band recruited superfan Henry Garfield as their new vocalist after an audition in New York (Garfield, who later adopted the name Rollins, had often driven from Washington, D.C., to New York with friend **Ian MacKaye** to catch Black Flag whenever they were in the area). Black Flag toured constantly, and Rollins soon gained a reputation for confronting the crowds, including grabbing back at fans, male or female, who grabbed him onstage or who heaped abuse on him. Rollins got into numerous fights with "fans" during his tenure as Black Flag vocalist, partially because he had replaced earlier singers and in the eyes of many punks "ruined the band," and partially for his long hair. The band at first lived on starvation wages, eating paste and stealing food, along with most of the SST staff and their faithful

roadie Mugger (Steve Corbin), who also played in the frequent Black Flag opening band Nig Heist (with Ginn, Dukowski, and Stevenson).

In 1981, Black Flag recorded the classic album *Damaged*, which featured the famous cover image of Rollins smashing his fist into a mirror, blood apparently dripping from his hand. Greg Ginn had made a deal with a small label, Unicorn, to distribute the album, but the parent label, MCA, objected and declared the album "antifamily," which the band promptly made into a sticker and placed it on the album. After a disastrous tour of England that found the band almost starving, the now-departed Robo was replaced briefly by Bill Stevenson, then by Emil, who lasted for one or two recording sessions, and then Chuck Biscuits of **D.O.A.**, who stayed in the band for six months before being fired by the workaholic Ginn. Because the **Descendents** singer Milo Aukerman was in college and the Descendents were on hiatus, Bill Stevenson rejoined the group, just in time for legal wrangling with Unicorn that put the band in recording limbo. Aside from the nonlabeled *Everything Went Black* compilation of

early material (which led to brief incarceration for Ginn and Dukowski), the band was unable to record until 1984.

In the meantime, Black Flag went through stylistic and musical changes, with Rollins and Ginn growing their hair and the band moving in a slower, more metallic direction, as evidenced by the next release, *My War*, which demonstrated the band at its most experimental, especially on side two, with three grindingly slow songs that may have been too much for fans to process. Kira Roessler stood in for Dukowski (who had been replaced briefly by "Dale Nixon," a pseudonym for guitarist Greg Ginn, who also played bass on the *My War* album) and added some adventurous bass lines that complemented and grounded Ginn's radical experimentation. Rollins continued with his bodybuilding, while his lyrics became both increasingly convoluted and personal as time went on, and his stage presence became more assertive and confrontational. The prolific band released two more metallic records, *Loose Nut* and *In My Head* in 1985 alone, but things were coming to a close. That summer, drummer Bill Stevenson left and rejoined the Descendents, and later in the year Kira was dismissed from the band

FAR LEFT: Black Flag in Tuscon, 1983: (L to R) Greg Ginn, Chuck Dukowski, Henry Rollins.
LEFT: At the Starwood, 1980: (L to R) Greg Ginn, Dez Cadena, Robo, Chuck Dukowski.

after the live recording *Who's Got the 10 1/2?* (she went on to play in the dual bass band Dos with her then-husband **Mike Watt** of the Minutemen). After a final tour that included several instrumental Black Flag shows, Rollins was sacked and Ginn finally broke up the band in early 1986. In 2004, Ginn organized a rather sad Black Flag "reunion" show in L.A. without any of the key members of the band and with a bass machine labeled "Dale Nixon."

Although synonymous with hardcore during the 1980s, Black Flag was a band that couldn't be pigeonholed. At a time when hardcore meant playing fast and sloppy, Black Flag's technically proficient members (particularly Ginn), were keen on improvisation and jamming, even releasing an entirely instrumental album, *The Process of Weeding Out.* And during a period when punks often looked for "hippies" to beat up, Rollins and Ginn's lengthy tresses made it clear they wouldn't bow to hardcore fashion. Even though Black Flag ended ignobly, they remain one of the most popular and influential hardcore punk bands of all time, with both Ginn's guitar playing and Rollins's vocals having inspired an entire generation of punks and the grunge scene that followed them.

Discography:
Nervous Breakdown EP (SST, 1978, 1992); *Jealous Again* EP (SST, 1980, 1991); *Damaged* (SST, 1981, 1990); *Everything Went Black* (SST, 1983, 1990); *The First Four Years* (SST, 1984, 1990); *My War* (SST, 1984, 1990); *Family Man* (SST, 1984, 1990); *Slip It In* (SST, 1984, 1990); *Live '84* (SST, 1984, 1998); *Loose Nut* (SST, 1985, 1990); *The Process of Weeding Out* EP (SST, 1985, 1990); *In My Head* (SST, 1985, 1990); *Who's Got the 10 1/2?* (SST, 1986, 1990); *Wasted...Again* (SST, 1987, 1990); *I Can See You* EP (SST, 1989); *Six Pack* EP (SST, 1992); *TV Party* EP (SST, 1992)

BLACK RANDY AND THE METROSQUAD

1977–1980

LINEUP: Jon "Black Randy" Morris (vocals); Bob Dead (guitar); K.K. Garrett (guitar); Pat Garrett (bass); Dan Brown (piano)

A chaotic band led by the incredibly charismatic Black Randy (John Morris), a diabetic, alcoholic street hustler, the Metrosquad usually consisted of members of other bands in the late-1970s Los Angeles scene, such as K.K. Garrett from the **Screamers** on guitar, Pat Garrett from the **Dils** on bass, Bob Dead on guitar, and Dan Brown on piano. A number of other L.A. scenesters like Exene Cervenka of **X**, Belinda Carlisle and Jane Wiedlin of the Go-Gos, and Alice Bag of the **Bags** performed as backup vocalists, the Blackettes. The Metrosquad were one of the first American bands to utilize purposefully shocking imagery for their often tongue-in-cheek songs about horrendous subjects. In a deliberate attempt to horrify his audience, Black Randy would often use blaxploitation humor and a sort of early rap delivery for songs about things like African dictator Idi Amin and cannibalism (as well as less serious material like James Brown and Isaac Hayes covers). Black Randy was a true punk and a good example of punk's ability to piss people off (although it may just have been for the sake of pissing people off). Black Randy died of AIDS in 1988 after years of drug abuse.

Discography:
Pass the Dust, I Think I'm Bowie (Dangerhouse, 1980)

Black Randy in his Angel costume, 1978.

BLACK TRAIN JACK

1992–1995

LINEUP: Ernie Parada (vocals/guitar); Rob Vitale (vocals); Brian Goldstein (bass); Nick (drums)

A New York **hardcore** band formed by former **Token Entry** drummer Ernie Parada, Black Train Jack featured Parada

overshadowed by Black Flag, due to their soundalike quality. Still, Bl'ast! was one of the bands who represented the peak of SST's roster as a major indie label, however by the time they broke up the label was on a slow downhill slide.

Discography:
The Power of Expression (Wishing Well, 1984; SST, 1987, 1990); *It's in My Blood* (SST, 1987, 1990); *Take the Manic Ride* (SST, 1989, 1991)

THE BLISTERS

1990-1995
LINEUP: Steve Bahr (vocals/bass); Steve Schifferman (guitar); Dennis Marmon (guitar); Bill Kleenmeyer (drums)

The Blisters were a New Jersey pop-punk band of the early 1990s who played an earnest variety of high-speed odes to the problems inherent in leaving adolescence behind and joining the race of adulthood. The band went through numerous personnel changes, at one point adding second guitarist Steve Schifferman and a variety of new drummers. The second album, *Pissed to Meet Me*, playfully acknowledged the band's appreciation for the **Replacements** as well as the **Ramones**. The Blisters later put out a cassette-only album that went in a more metallic direction, and fans are probably better off buying the two albums when the band was at their young and innocent peak.

Discography:
Off My Back (Albertine, 1991); *Pissed to Meet Me* (Incognito, 1992), *Meow: The Claude Coleman Sessions EP* (tape; no label, 1995)

Black Train Jack play in the Save CBGB's series, 2005.

on guitar, and the lyrics mostly concerned **straight-edge** topics and remaining true to one's core values. Although they played numerous gigs with heavy hitters, Black Train Jack never achieved anything more than a cult following. The band reunited for a show with **Gorilla Biscuits** and **Bold** at the 2005 benefit concerts to save **CBGB**.

Discography:
No Reward (Roadrunner, 1993); *You're Not Alone* (Roadrunner, 1994)

BL'AST!

1982-1990
LINEUP: Clifford Dinsmore (vocals); Steve Stevenson (guitar, replaced by Mike Neider); Dave Cooper (bass); Bill Torgerson (drums)

A California **hardcore** band signed to the **SST** label and (not surprisingly) very similar in sound to early **Black Flag**, Bl'ast! started as M.A.D. in 1982 but changed their name to Bl'ast! in 1984. Most of their songs were about surfing, most memorably their

anthem "Surf and Destroy." Dinsmore left in the early-1990s, and the band broke up shortly thereafter but reunited in 2001 for several reunion shows. Guitarist Mike Neider later put together the similarly named Ghetto-Blast while Dinsmore went on to form Space Boy. While Bl'ast! was a great band, they were

BL'AST!

IT'S IN MY + BLOOD!

BLONDIE

1974-1982, 1997-present

LINEUP: Debbie Harry (vocals); Chris Stein (guitar); Gary Valentine (bass, replaced by Frank Infante; Frank Infante (bass, then guitar); Clem Burke (drums); Jimmy Destri (keyboards)

Although hardly a punk band as most would define the term, Blondie was one of the most successful groups to evolve from the fertile **CBGB** scene of the mid-1970s, and one of the few to break out to popular success almost immediately. While Blondie did not play the hyper fast rhythms of the **Ramones**, they were nonetheless a punk band by virtue of their attitude, and the fact that when the band started in New York, punk had not yet calcified into a rigid set of rules. Blondie was as influenced by pop and girl-group sounds as the Ramones, and their frenetic, fast-paced take on pop, and later reggae and rap, made them punk pioneers.

Led by the arresting stage presence and beauty of Debbie Harry—controversy over her being the public face of Blondie led to a campaign by the record company to promote the slogan "Blondie is a Group" on T-shirts and stickers—Blondie scored numerous chart hits such as "Heart of Glass" and "Call Me" in a few short years. Later singles such as "The Tide is High" and "Rapture" saw them dabbling in, and helping to popularize, **reggae** and rap, respectively. Blondie disbanded in 1982 (due as much to lack of inspiration after the lackluster album *The Hunter* as to Stein's lengthy illness), but regrouped in the late 1990s with several core members, released a number of well-received records, and continued to tour sporadically. Many punks were annoyed by Blondie's popularity and saw them as selling out the promise of early punk by adopting disco rhythms and rap in their quest for commercial success. Hardly the punk sellout that many thought, Blondie's experimentation and use of different rhythms and musical styles actually grounds them more firmly in punk's **DIY** aesthetic than many bands that stuck to the traditional beat and guitar sound.

Discography:

Blondie (Private Stock, 1976; Chrysalis, 1977); *Plastic Letters* (Chrysalis, 1977); *Parallel Lines* (Chrysalis, 1978); *Eat to the Beat* (Chrysalis, 1979); *Autoamerican* (Chrysalis, 1980); *The Best of Blondie* (Chrysalis, 1981); *The Hunter* (Chrysalis, 1982); *Blonde and Beyond* (Chrysalis/ERG, 1993); *The Platinum Collection* (Chrysalis/EMI, 1994); *Remixed Remade Remodeled: The Remix Project* (Chrysalis/EMI, 1995); *Picture This Live* (Chrysalis/EMI-Capitol, 1997); *No Exit* (Beyond/BMG, 1999); *Blondie Live* (Beyond/BMG, 1999); *Greatest Hits* (Chrysalis/Capitol, 2002); *The Curse of Blondie* (Epic, 2003; Sanctuary, 2004); *Live by Request* (Sanctuary, 2004). **Debbie Harry/Blondie:** *Once More into the Bleach* (Chrysalis, 1988); *The Complete Picture: The Very Best of Deborah Harry and Blondie* (Chrysalis, 1991). **Debbie Harry:** *KooKoo* (Chrysalis, 1981); *Rockbird* (Geffen, 1986; Geffen Goldmine, 1997); *Def, Dumb & Blonde* (Sire/Reprise, 1989); *Debravation* (Sire/Reprise, 1993). **Jimmy Destri:** *Heart on a Wall* (Chrysalis, 1982)

LEFT: Blondie's Debbie Harry at CBGB, 1976.

ABOVE: (L to R) Jimmy Destri, Frank Infante, Debbie Harry, Nigel Harrison, Chris Stein.

THE BLUE HEARTS

1985–1995

LINEUP: Hiroto Kohmoto (vocals); Masatoshi Mashima (guitars); Junnosuke Kawaguchi (bass); Tetsuya Kajiwara (drums)

Japan's answer to the **Clash** and the **Ramones** (with the **Undertones** involved in the formula as well), the Blue Hearts were one of the key Japanese punk bands of the 1980s and early-'90s. Popular enough to inspire both a major musical as well as a movie based on their best-known song "Linda Linda"—*Linda Linda Linda* (2005) followed a high school band as they struggled to learn the song in time for a talent show—the Blue Hearts started out as a typical, **pop-punk** band, singing songs about girls, alienation, and loneliness with poppy choruses shouted by the band over lead singer Hiroto Kohmoto's deep and resonant voice. As they advanced in their career, the Blue Hearts grew increasingly adventurous. If their American records are pop masterpieces, akin to the Ramones' *Rocket to Russia* or *The Clash*, the Blue Hearts' later Japanese albums are the equivalent of the Clash's *London Calling* or even *Sandinista!* in ambition. In their later material, the Blue Hearts incorporated a weird variety of instrumentation including steel drums, harpsichord, and even marching band drum syncopations (one song is just marching band drums).

A major influence on almost every Japanese and Asian punk band that came after, and one of the great lost bands of punk history, the Blue Hearts are worth a listen whether you understand Japanese or not—their emotional music will make you remember why you got into punk in the first place. (And be honest, how many **Exploited** lyrics can you understand?)

Discography:

The Blue Hearts (Meldac, 1987, 2007); *Young and Pretty* (Meldac, 1987, 2007); *Train Train* (Meldac, 1988, 2007); *Super Best* (Meldac, 1995); *Singles 1990–1993* (East West Japan, 1999)

BOLD

1983–1989, 1994

LINEUP: Matt Warnke (vocals); Tim Brooks (bass); John Zuluago (guitar); Drew Thomas (drums)

An East Coast **straight-edge** band who originally performed as Crippled Youth when the members were in the seventh grade and were mentored by **Youth of Today** (drummer Drew Thomas played in both bands), Bold renamed themselves in 1986. Influenced by **Bad Brains**, Youth of Today, **Cro-Mags**, and **D.R.I.**, they played primarily in the Connecticut and New York scenes. The band was known for an ability to mix its straight-edge militancy with a sense of humor. Bold was also one of the youngest bands on the New York hardcore scene and in 1986 when the band played out most, the average age of the Bold members was 15. After the band broke up, Drew Thomas went on to play with Into Another.

Discography:

Speak Out (Revelation, 1988)

THE BOOMTOWN RATS

1975–1986

LINEUP: Bob Geldof (vocals); Gerry Cott (guitar); Garrick "Garry" Roberts (guitar); Pete Briquette (bass); Simon Crowe (drums); Johnnie Fingers (keyboards)

Irish pop-punkers among the most clever and soulful of the first wave of punk bands, the Boomtown Rats were led by the irascible "Saint Bob" (as he would later be sarcastically called by the British tabloids). The band's unusual name was taken from a line in the Woody Guthrie autobiography *Bound for Glory* and their sense of slightly smirking detachment along with their well-written pop hooks made them perennial hit-makers in the UK and Ireland. To many, the Rats were a perfect melding of punk, pop, and soul, just tuneful enough, but noted for their revved-up punk sound when heard live. Although best known for their crossover hit "I Don't like Mondays"—based on a news story and written from the perspective of a girl who went on a shooting spree in her school and later explained that she had done it because she didn't like Mondays—the Rats also had many other killer tracks such as "Joey's on the Streets Again" and "Rat Trap." The band had petered out by the mid-1980s, after which Geldof started a solo career to middling success. The high point of Geldof's post-Rats career was organizing the Band-Aid project in 1984, which featured the cream of British rock and **new wave** musicians on the charity single "Do They Know It's Christmas?"

Discography:

The Boomtown Rats (Mercury, 1977); *A Tonic for the Troops* (Columbia, 1978); *The Fine Art of Surfacing* (Columbia, 1979); *Mondo Bongo* (Columbia, 1980); *Rat Tracks* EP (Vertigo, 1981); *The Boomtown Rats* EP (Columbia, 1982); *V Deep* (Columbia, 1982); *Ratrospective EP* (Columbia, 1983); *In the Long Grass* (Columbia, 1984); *Greatest Hits* (Columbia, 1987)

The Boomtown Rats' Bob Geldof shows off his gymnastics training, 1977.

TATTOOS AND BODY ART

Although most of the original punks did not have tattoos or piercings, tattoos later became almost *de rigueur* for band members, and the practice of body modification eventually became quite prevalent among street punks. In retrospect, it seems natural that punks would adopt the practices of tattoos and body art—as practiced in cultures like Japan and Polynesia—because these symbols have often marked the bearer as an outsider from mainstream culture, and as an initiate to a secret society or cult; in the same way that the typical punk "uniform" of leather and spikes marked one as an outsider from mainstream American or British culture. There was, in short, almost no simpler form of societal rebellion.

Early New York hardcore punks such as Harley Flanagan and John Joseph McGeown of the Cro-Mags were largely responsible for introducing tattoos to the New York scene in the early-1980s, as was Henry Rollins of Black Flag, who tattooed images from his favorite bands on his body along with quotes and other designs. Many punks used tattoos as a way of demonstrating their loyalty to a variety of bands or movements within punk rock. Facial tattoos, in particular, are graphic markers—even today, when tattoos have become more prevalent in society—that the recipient did not want to work in a corporate job. Today, many punks in hardcore and emo bands sport tattoos, and the practice is quite wide-spread, although the symbolic meaning can vary from punk to punk. Tattoos can often be signs of tribal allegiance, markers of rites of passage, or simply body decorations that make sense only to the wearer.

Earrings and body piercing also have a long history of marking tribal allegiance. Although earrings were fairly common in the early U.S. and British scenes, more radical types of piercings did not become prevalent until the early-1980s. Piercings were also relatively uncommon during the early days of punk, except for earrings on men and the occasional safety pin though the nose. Pioneers such as Genesis P-Orridge of Throbbing Gristle, however, started ritual scarification, outlandish and ritualistic tattoos, and elaborate piercings and weights, including his notoriously pierced genitals. Although most did not take piercing or body art to the extreme that P-Orridge did, he nevertheless inspired many punks to get piercings in places that society, even underground society, had previously considered taboo.

For many punks, there was no better way to indicate allegiance to one's favorite band then by wearing the band's logo, permanently inscribed on an arm, leg, or the torso. Many bands highlighted the body art of their fans and displayed it in album inserts, perhaps to demonstrate (and reward) the extreme loyalty of their fans.

The Boredoms, July 2002.

THE BOREDOMS

1982-present

LINEUP: Yamatsuka Eye (vocals); Yoshikama Toyohito (drums/percussion/vocals); Tabata Mara (guitar, replaced by Yamamote Seiichi); Hosoi (bass, replaced by Hira); Hasegawa Chu (percussion, replaced by ATR); Taketani (drums, replaced by Yoshimi Yokoto)

An insanely diverse Japanese noise-punk band, the Boredoms can at times be noise-oriented to the point of being completely unlistenable. The prolific band's voluminous output and sheer level of sonic force makes **Big Black** look like a bubblegum pop act, and their excursions into stratospheric levels of sound experimentation would prompt even Ornette Coleman to scratch his head looking for a melody.

The Boredoms first started in 1982 but only began to record in earnest in 1985, when they still had a fairly stable lineup.

Along the way they lost and gained members with stunning regularity, eventually ending up with a drummer and two percussionists who double on other instruments alongside band leader and mainstay Yamatsuka Eye, who has also collaborated with other noise adherents such as Thurston Moore and John Zorn's Naked City. Krautrock and psychedelia also figure in to the Boredoms' sonic approach, occasionally sounding as though they are either cleverly planning emotional dynamics in their music, like Sigur Rós, or are just adhering to a set of rules only they understand, like Zorn at his most dissonant. Either way, the Boredoms are among the most exciting bands around, even when they verge on the dissonant. On July 7, 2007, the band played in a special concert at New York's Brooklyn Bridge Park in honor of the date's convergence of three sevens, reflected by the number of drummers the

Boredoms recruited for the concert (77 drummers total!). Although the Boredoms are not everyone's cup of sake, the band has changed styles and members enough that at least one or two records will be of interest to fans of **Can**, Einstürzende Neubaten, **Sonic Youth**, and others. Those of the straight-edge inclination should definitely check them out, as the experience will be the closest one will ever get to doing hard drugs, only without the buzzkill after the junk wears off.

Discography:

Anal by Anal (Trans, 1986); *Osorezan to Stooges Kyo* (Selfish, 1988); *Onanie Bomb Meets the Sex Pistols* (WEA, 1989); *1994 Soul Discharge* (Shimmy-Disc, 1991); *Pop Tatari* (WEA, 1992, Reprise, 1993); *Super Roots* EP (WEA, 1993; Reprise, 1994; Vice, 2007); *Wow-2* (Avant, 1993); *Super Roots 2* EP (WEA, 1994); *Chocolate Synthesizer* (WEA, 1994; Reprise, 1995); *Super Roots 3* (WEA, 1994; Vice, 2007); *Super Roots 5* (WEA, 1995; Vice, 2007); *Super Roots 6* (Reprise, 1996; Vice, 2007); *Super 8* (Birdman, 1998); *Super Roots 7* EP (Warner Bros., 1998; Vice, 2007); *Vision Creation Newsun* (WEA, 1999); *Super Roots 8* EP (Aka, 2004; Vice, 2007)

BORIS THE SPRINKLER

1992-2000

LINEUP: Rev. Norb (vocals/guitar); Paul Schroder (guitar); Erik Lee (bass, replaced by Eric James, then Ric 6); Ronny Johnny Kispert (drums, replaced by Paul 2)

A Green Bay, Wisconsin, band led by brilliant and deranged zine writer and lead singer Rev. Norb, Boris the Sprinkler released numerous singles and several albums in a whimsical **Ramones**-influenced style highlighted by Rev. Norb's lyrics, which were honed by his years of writing for zines such as *Maximum RocknRoll*, *Razorcake*, and *Go Metric*. Rev. Norb started out with the zine *Sick Teen* and formed Boris the Sprinkler around 1992 to provide an outlet for his love of pop culture and topics such as *Star Trek*, *The Simpsons*, and comic books. Rev. Norb is also known for writing the world's longest song ("R' rilly Gonna Mess U Up," which clocks in at 13,000 words and 74 minutes) and for his collection of Bob Dylan covers released by **Alternative Tentacles**. Norb continues to be one of the most creative and funniest voices in punk rock today.

Discography:

Drugs and Masturbation (Mutant Pop, 1995); *End of the Century* (Clear View, 1998); *Suck* (Go Kart, 1999); *Gay* (Go Kart, 2000); *Mega Anal* (Bulge Records, 2000). **Nob Dylan and the Nobsolettes:** *Positively 12 Stiff Dylans* (Alternative Tentacles, 2007)

BOUNCING SOULS

1987–present

LINEUP: Greg Attonito (vocals); Pete Steinkopf (guitar); Bryan Papillion (bass); Michael Shal Khichi (drums, replaced by Michael McDermott)

One of New Jersey's oldest and most popular punk bands, Bouncing Souls play a melodic form of **hardcore**, toying with the formula from time to time, but still staying true to their roots. Formed in 1987 when the members were still in high school and looking for a way to escape their suburban Jersey life, Bouncing Souls released their early material on its own Chunksaah label. The band recorded several albums for **Epitaph** and toured extensively, remaining a very popular act, particularly in the New York, New Jersey, and Connecticut tri-state area. While Bouncing Souls may never be the biggest band name on the scene, they have established themselves as elder statesmen, consistently putting out great albums every few years.

Discography:
Argyle EP (Chunksaah, 1993); *Neurotic* EP (Chunksaah, 1993); *The Greenball Crew* (Chunksaah, 1993); *The Good, the Bad, and the Argyle* (Chunksaah, 1994; BYO, 1995); *Maniacal Laughter* (BYO, 1995); *The Bouncing Souls* (Epitaph, 1997); *Tie One On* EP (live; Epitaph, 1998); *Hopeless Romantic* (Epitaph, 1999); *The Bad, the Worse and the Out of Print* (Chunksaah, 2000); *How I Spent My Summer Vacation* (Epitaph, 2001); *Anchors Aweigh* (Epitaph, 2003); *Do You Remember?* (Chunksaah, 2003); *The Gold Record* (Epitaph, 2006)

DAVID BOWIE

Though primarily noted for his seminal status as alien, glam-rock superstar, David Bowie was a huge influence on punk, particularly in his Ziggy Stardust and Berlin periods, also helping to promote the careers of proto-punks **Lou Reed** and **Iggy Pop**. Bowie was perhaps most influential to the earlier, more frenetic, "louder and faster" version of punk that had some of its roots in his particular brand of glam rock. Bowie's Berlin-based collaborations with musical soundscaper Brian Eno during his three-record experiment in mood and dynamics became a key influence on **post-punk** bands such as **Joy Division** (who may have taken their original name, Warsaw, from the song "Warszawa" on Bowie's *Low* record). Bowie also produced Lou Reed's *Transformer* album, and his company MainMan provided the finances for the recording of Iggy and the **Stooges**' *Raw Power*. Although many punks were disappointed by Bowie's later stylistic changes, many of the younger generation were inspired by his music and fluidity in changing identity. Johnny Rotten (born **John Lydon**) of the **Sex Pistols** was clearly a fan, bringing in a Bowie album (alongside numerous **reggae** records) to play on the air during his famous radio interview on the Tommy Vance show on London's Capital Radio in July 1977.

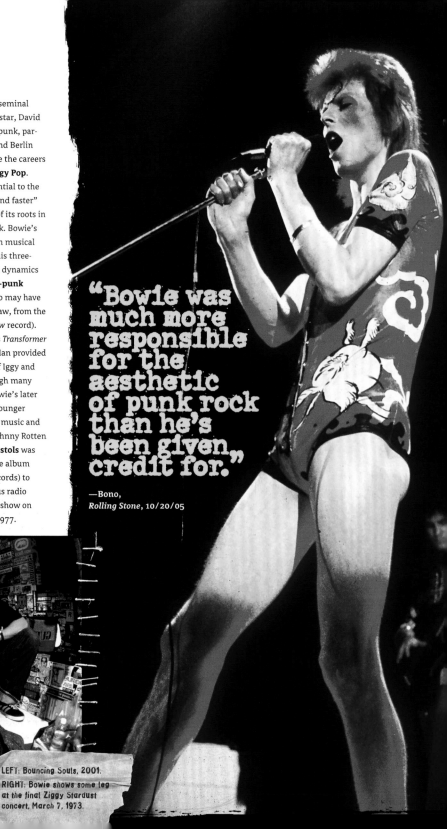

> "Bowie was much more responsible for the aesthetic of punk rock than he's been given credit for."
>
> —Bono, *Rolling Stone*, 10/20/05

LEFT: Bouncing Souls, 2001.
RIGHT: Bowie shows some leg at the final Ziggy Stardust concert, March 7, 1973.

Although never a punk except in looks and imagination, Bowie is one of the most formative figures in the genre's creation, and it would be particularly impossible to think of British punk without Bowie's contribution.

Essential Discography:
The Rise and Fall of Ziggy Stardust and the Spiders from Mars (RCA, 1972); *Aladdin Sane* (RCA, 1973); *Pin-Ups* (RCA, 1973); *Diamond Dogs* (RCA, 1974); *Low* (RCA, 1977); *Heroes* (RCA, 1977); *Lodger* (RCA, 1979); *Scary Monsters* (RCA, 1980)

THE BOYS

1976–1981
LINEUP: Duncan "Kid" Reid (vocals/bass); John Plain (guitar); Jack Black (drums); Casino Steel (keyboards)

A minor band from London best known for the single "Brickfield Nights"—an engaging slice of pop-punk later covered by **Die Toten Hosen** on their album *Learning English, Lesson One*—the Boys featured the youthful Duncan "Kid" Reid on vocals and bass, Casino Steel on keyboards, "Honest" John Plain on guitar, and Jack Black (not the actor) on drums. The band broke up in 1981 but still get together for periodic reunions. The Boys also released a Christmas album as the Yobs. Never one of the big 1977-era punk bands, the Boys were still great for a laugh.

Discography:
The Boys (NEMS, 1977; Link Classics, 1990; Captain Oi!, 2000); *Alternative Chartbusters* (NEMS, 1978; Link Classics, 1990; Captain Oi!, 2001); *To Hell with the Boys* (Safari, 1979; Captain Oi!, 2002); *Boys Only* (Safari, 1980; Captain Oi!, 2003); *Power Cut* (Anagram, 1999); *Live at the Roxy Club* (Receiver, 1999); *BBC Sessions* (live; Vinyl Japan, 1999, 2003); *Sick on You* (Harry May, 2000); *Complete Punk Singles Collection* (Anagram, 2000); *Punk Rock Rarities* (Captain Oi!, 2000); *Svengerland* (Captain Oi!, 2002); *Very Best of the Boys* (Anagram, 2002). **Yobs:** *The Yobs Christmas Album* (Safari, 1980; Great Expectations, 1989)

BRACKET

1992–present
LINEUP: Marty Gregori (vocals/guitar); Larry Tinney (guitar); Zack Charlos (bass); Ray Castro (drums)

A **pop-punk** band from Forestville, California, who initially followed the same musical template popularized in the early to mid-1990s, Bracket signed to a major label at the time when record companies were eager to capitalize on **Green Day**'s million-records-selling popularity. Bracket

The Boys, 1977.

maintains a relentlessly charming pop-punk sound with some metallic edges. *Requiem*, the band's first self-produced record, peels away some of the lavish production of *4-Wheel Vibe* and showcases the members at their peak.

Discography:
924 Forestville St. (Caroline, 1994); *4-Wheel Vibe* (Caroline, 1995); *"E" is for Everything* on Fat Wreck Chords, 1996); *Novelty Forever* (Fat Wreck Chords, 1997); *When All Else Fails* (Fat Wreck Chords, 2000); *Live in a Dive* (Fat Wreck Chords, 2002); *Requiem* (Takeover, 2006)

BRATMOBILE

1991–1994, 1999–2003
LINEUP: Allison Wolfe (vocals/guitar/drums); Molly Neuman (vocals/guitar/drums); Erin Smith (guitar)

Bratmobile may not have been the tightest group but they were certainly poppier and more accessible than the similar-sounding **Bikini Kill**, the other most influential and respected band of the **Riot Grrrl** movement of the late-1980s and early-1990s. Consisting of the geographically far-flung singer Allison Wolfe, guitarist Erin Smith, and drummer Molly Neuman (although the band frequently switched instruments), Bratmobile originally formed on a dare in 1991 to play at the K Record's International Pop Underground convention in Olympia, Washington. The band released several singles, followed by the brilliant, blink-and-you'll-miss-it *Pottymouth* in 1993. Bratmobile broke up in 1994 but re-formed in 1999 to tour and release new records. Wolfe and Neuman worked on the zine *Girl Germs* as well as the *Riot Grrrl* zine and

movement. Drummer Molly Neuman played in the band Peechees in the mid-1990s and managed the **Donnas**.

Discography:
Pottymouth (Kill Rock Stars, 1993); *The Real Janelle EP* (Kill Rock Stars, 1994); *The Peel Session EP* (Strange Fruit, 1994); *Ladies, Women and Girls* (Lookout!, 2000); *Girls Get Busy* (Lookout!, 2002). **Peechees:** *Scented Gum EP* (Lookout!, 1995); *Do the Math* (Kill Rock Stars, 1996); *Games People Play* (Kill Rock Stars, 1997); *Life* (Kill Rock Stars, 1999)

Bratmobile c.1997: (L to R) Erin Smith, Allison Wolfe, Molly Neuman.

BROKEN BONES

1983-1992, 1998-present

LINEUP: Nick "Nobby" Dobson (vocals, replaced by Craig Allen); Tony "Bones" Roberts (guitar); Paul "Oddy" Hoddy (bass, briefly replaced by Tezz Roberts, Darren Harris); Darren "Baz" Burgess (drums, replaced by Cliff Moran, Dave Bridgewood)

An English **hardcore** band along the lines of **Discharge**, Broken Bones were formed by ex-Discharge guitarist Bones. Their first album *Dem Bones* was a punk-metal hybrid, while subsequent recordings were more standard metal. Broken Bones were among the earliest bands to mix horror and splatter rock with punk and metal, somewhat reminiscent of a more metallic version of the **Misfits**. The band would have been more influential if not for all-too-frequent lineup changes that kept them from achieving the popularity of **Discharge**. While the band's official correspondence allegedly went to a scarily named "The Meatman," it was actually opened and answered by Bones' mum. Broken Bones were notoriously kicked out of Disneyland in 1985 during an American tour, as they were proving to be a more compelling photo op than Mickey or Goofy.

Discography:
Dem Bones (Fall Out, 1984); *Seeing thru My Eyes* EP (Fall Out, 1985); *Live at the 100 Club* (Subversive Sounds, 1985); *Bonecrusher* (Combat Core, 1986); *F.O.A.D.* (Combat Core, 1987); *Decapitated* (Fall Out, 1987); *Losing Control* (Heavy Metal, 1989); *Stitched Up* (Rough Justice, 1991); *Brain Dead* (Rough Justice, 1992); *Without Conscience* (Rhythm Vicar, 2001)

BROMLEY CONTINGENT

This loose-knit group of early punks, who took their name from a south London neighborhood where some lived, followed the **Sex Pistols** around from gig to gig and spread the word about the band early on. Some of the original members were William Broad (better known as Billy Idol), Steve Bailey (later Steve Severin of **Siouxsie and the Banshees**), Sue Catwoman (Sue Lucas), and future goth icon and punk front woman, Siouxsie Sioux, who went on to greater fame in Siouxsie and the Banshees. The Bromley

Contingent first saw the Sex Pistols at Ravensbourne Art College outside London and pursued the band, at one point even renting a van to drive to Paris for a gig. A number of Bromley members accompanied the Pistols to the band's foul-mouthed TV interview with Bill Grundy in 1976. Eventually, many members went on to form bands of their own, to varying degrees of success.

THE BUTCHIES

1998-2005

LINEUP: Kaia Wilson (vocals/guitar); Alison Martlew (bass); Melissa York (drums)

A queer female band from Durham, North Carolina, started by former members of **Team Dresch** after that band's demise, the Butchies recorded for indie label Mr. Lady Records (founded by singer/guitarist Kaia Wilson and Tammy Rae Carlson) before moving to the slightly larger indie label Yep Roc in 2004. The Butchies worked to increase awareness of queer social issues and the permeability of gender while rocking with a gleeful sense of humor. (Their first album, *Are We Not Femme?*, with a front cover picture of the Butchies in skirts and wigs, plays not only on the title of the first **Devo** album but also on the idea that butch lesbians can toy around with traditional notions of gender and femininity.) Wilson's label, meanwhile, released albums from **Le Tigre** among others.

Discography:
Are We Not Femme? (Mr. Lady, 1998); *Population 1975* (Mr. Lady, 1999); *Three* (Mr. Lady, 2001); *Make Yr Life* (Yep Roc, 2003)

make yr life / butchies

The Butchies model the 2004 spring line: (L to R) Melissa York, Alison Martlew, Kaia Wilson.

BUTTHOLE SURFERS

1981–present

LINEUP: Gibson "Gibby" Haynes (vocals); Paul Lear (guitar); Jeff Pinkus (bass, replaced by Quinn Matthews, Nathan Calhoun); Scott Mathews (drums, replaced by Paul Coffey, aka "King Koffee"); Teresa Taylor, aka "Teresa Nervosa" (drums)

An almost uncategorizable noise-punk circus led by the dynamic Gibson "Gibby" Haynes, who often "sang" through a megaphone, the Butthole Surfers were formed in San Antonio, Texas, in 1981 by Haynes (the son of local children's TV show host,

"Mr. Peppermint"). They achieved notoreity for their bizarre permutations of existing song structures and nonsensical lyrics about subjects such as the Shah of Iran sleeping in Lee Harvey Oswald's grave. One early song was composed almost entirely of snorting and spitting. The Butthole Surfers also stood apart with their original dual drummers, "King Koffee" and "Teresa Nervosa" (who gained a degree of indie immortality with her role as the woman trying to sell Madonna's Pap smear in the 1991 film *Slacker*).

The Butthole Surfers made increasingly indefinable music that challenged and often offended audiences, touring relentlessly more as a circus sideshow than as a

band, blinding the audience with strobe lights, showing films of medical experiments in the background, or throwing thousands of photocopies of roaches into the audience during gigs. They eventually signed to a major label, and although garnering a surprise hit in the early 1990s with the relatively tame song "Pepper," they were eventually dropped by a record label that had difficulty promoting a band whose name alone discouraged radio stations from playing their music. A particularly interesting harmonic convergence occurred in 1992 when former Led Zeppelin bass player John Paul Jones produced *Independent Worm Saloon* (the Surfers had recorded the Zeppelin-esque

gag "Hairway to Steven" in 1988). The band went on hiatus in the late-1990s, after which Gibby toured with his own band, Gibby Haynes and His Problem.

Discography:

Butthole Surfers (Alternative Tentacles, 1983); *Live PCPPEP* (Alternative Tentacles, 1984); *Psychic… Powerless…Another Man's Sac* (Touch and Go, 1985); *Cream Corn from the Socket of Davis* EP (Touch and Go, 1985); *Rembrandt Pussyhorse* (Touch and Go, 1986); *Locust Abortion Technician* (Touch and Go, 1987); *Hairway to Steven* (Touch and Go, 1988); *Double Live* (Buggerveil, 1989); *Widowermaker* EP (Touch and Go, 1989); *Pioughd* (Rough Trade, 1990); *Independent Worm Saloon* (Capitol, 1993); *The Hole Truth…and Nothing Butt* (Trance Syndicate, 1995); *Electric Larryland* (Capitol, 1996); *Weird Revolution* (Hollywood, 2001); *Humpty Dumpty LSD* (Latino Beggerveil, 2002); *Butthole Surfers/Live PCPPEP* (Latino Beggerveil, 2003)

The Butthole Surfers explore the boundaries of artistic license, April 1987.

BUZZCOCKS

1976-1981, 1989-present

LINEUP: Howard Devoto (vocals/guitar);
Pete Shelley (vocals/guitar); Steve Diggle
(bass/guitar); Steve Garvey (bass, replaced
by Tony Barber); John Maher (drums,
replaced by Phil Barker, Danny Farrant)

This seminal punk band's poppy harmonies and insightful love songs by Pete Shelley helped to bridge the gap between punk rock and power pop. The Buzzcocks first formed in Manchester, England, in 1976 and debuted on July 20 of that year, opening for the **Sex Pistols** at the Manchester Lesser Free Trade Hall, the same spot at which they had originally seen the Pistols and were inspired to start a band. In January 1977, the Buzzcocks became one of the first bands in Britain to put out an independent 7" record, the seminal *Spiral Scratch* EP. The next month, Devoto quit the band to pursue other projects, including **Magazine** (best known for their song "Shot by Both Sides") and Luxuria. Even without him, after *Spiral Scratch*, the Buzzcocks became a major draw, launching a long and productive career in meteoric fashion. New bassist Garth Davies, who had taken over when Diggle moved to guitar, proved to be unreliable, and he was quickly replaced by Steve Garvey, who remained with the band until the early-1980s.

Initially known as a singles band, the Buzzcocks put out a number of seminal early punk songs such as "Ever Fallen in Love (With Someone You Shouldn't Have)" and "What Do I Get?" in a short amount of time. After pivotal singles like "Orgasm Addict" and "What Do I Get?", the Buzzcocks released their first full-length

album, *Another Music in a Different Kitchen*, to critical acclaim and reasonable sales. Soon after, the band settled into a rigorous touring and recording schedule that would eventually tear them apart. Their second album, *Love Bites*, was rushed out seven months later to capitalize on the first album's success. The Buzzcocks experimented musically with their third album, *A Different Kind of Tension*, which featured the epic philosophical essay "I Believe," in which Shelley gloomily lists a contradictory set of beliefs before proclaiming "There is no love in this world anymore" over and over to end the song. The band toured the United States in 1979 and courted controversy at a gig at Club 57 in New York, where drummer John Maher tore down a banner for the sponsoring station WPIX-FM, and the band was forced to flee the venue. Attempting to regroup when they returned to England, the Buzzcocks recorded the EPs *Parts One, Two, and Three* with drug-crazed producer Martin Hannet (who had previously produced **Joy Division** as well as the *Spiral Scratch* EP), but the sessions turned into chaos. After some halfhearted attempts

to record a fourth album, Shelley and regular producer Martin Rushent recorded the song "Homosapien," which became Shelley's debut solo single.

In 1981, Shelley dissolved the band by writing letters to the other members, and then embarked on a solo tour. Maher and Diggle briefly formed Flag of Convenience, and Garvey played on Shelley's first tour before moving to New York and retiring. The original Buzzcocks (although without Garvey and Maher, who retired and were replaced by bassist Tony Barber and drummer Phil Barker) reunited in the late-1980s for a reunion tour; after which they continued to record and tour. Having cemented their place as punk's romantic conscience, the Buzzcocks consistently released new material that evoked their old songs, not only musically, but also in their examination of the same themes of alienation and loneliness they dealt with on their first three albums. Shelley also recorded some electronic material with former lead singer Howard Devoto in 2002 as the Buzzkunts. The full version of the sessions recorded for the *Spiral Scratch* EP were eventually

released on the Mute label in 2000 after years of bad bootleg copies had circulated. The Buzzcocks remain today the only original punks from the class of 1977 who to continue to make compelling music. A British comedic quiz show entitled "Never Mind the Buzzcocks" has been a success since the 1990s, much to the chagrin of the band.

Discography:

Spiral Scratch EP (New Hormones, 1977, 1981); *Another Music in a Different Kitchen* (UA, 1978); *Love Bites* (UA, 1978); *A Different Kind of Tension* (UA, 1979; IRS, 1989); *Singles Going Steady* (IRS, 1979); *Parts One, Two, Three* EPs (IRS, 1980); *Total Pop 1977–1980* (Weird Systems, 1987); *The Peel Sessions* EP (Strange Fruit, 1988); *Lest We Forget* (ROIR, 1988); *Live at the Roxy Club April '77* (Absolutely Free, 1989; Receiver, 1990); *Product* (Restless Retro, 1989); *The Peel Sessions Album* (Strange Fruit, 1989; Strange Fruit/Dutch East India Trading, 1991); *Time's Up* (Receiver, 1991); *Operators Manual: Buzzcocks Best* (IRS, 1991); *Alive Tonight* EP (Planet Pacific, 1991); *Entertaining Friends: Live at the Hammersmith Odeon March 1979* (IRS, 1992); *Trade Test Transmissions* (Caroline, 1993); *French* (IRS, 1996); *All Set* (IRS, 1996); *Modern* (Go-Kart, 1999); *Buzzcocks S/T* (Merge, 2003); *Flat-Pack Philosophy* (Cooking Vinyl, 2006) **Steve Diggle:** *Heated and Rising* EP (Three Thirty, 1993). **Various Artists:** *Something's Gone Wrong Again: The Buzzcocks' Covers Compilation* (C/Z, 1992)

Buzzcocks charm the natives: (L to R) Pete Shelley, Steve Diggle, old lady, old lady, Steve Garvey, John Maher.

CAN
1969–1979

LINEUP: Malcolm Mooney (vocals, replaced by Damo Suzuki); Michael Karoli (guitar/vocals); Holger Czukay (bass/vocals); Jaki Liebezeit (drums/vocals); Rebop Kwaku Baah (percussion); Irmin Schmidt (keyboards/vocals)

An experimental German band who were extremely influential to **post-punk** in general, and to **John Lydon** and **Public Image Ltd.** in particular, Can was years ahead of their time, particularly in their early adoption of electronic music and Eno-esque soundscapes, which often got them lumped under the term *Krautrock*. In 1969, Can released their first album, *Monster Movie*, which included the epic funk/drone "You Doo Right," which demonstrated the potential of Can's approach. The following year, now featuring Japanese singer Damo Suzuki, Can went even more out there, combining bassist Holger Czukay's tape experiments with tight and focused songwriting. Suzuki left in 1973, but the band continued until 1978, even reuniting with original singer Malcolm Mooney for a short-lived reunion in 1989. The various members continued with solo careers, Czukay's being the most prolific. Guitarist Michael Karoli died in 2001.

Discography:
Monster Movie (UA, 1969; Spoon/Mute/Restless Retro, 1990; Mute, 1998; remastered, Mute, 2004); *Soundtracks* (UA, 1970; Spoon/Mute/Restless Retro, 1990; Mute, 1998; remastered, Mute, 2004); *Tago Mago* (UA, 1971; Spoon/Mute/Restless Retro, 1990; remastered, Mute, 2004); *Ege Bamyasi* (UA, 1972; Spoon/Mute/Restless Retro, 1990; remastered, Mute, 2004); *Future Days* (UA, 1973; Spoon/Mute/Restless Retro, 1990; Mute, 2005); *Limited Edition* (UA, 1974); *Soon over Babaluma* (UA, 1974; Spoon/Mute/Restless Retro, 1990; Mute, 2005); *Landed* (Virgin, 1975; Spoon/Mute/Restless Retro, 1990; remastered, Mute, 2005); *Unlimited Edition* (Caroline, 1976; Spoon/Mute/Restless Retro, 1990; remastered, Mute, 2005); *Opener 1971–1974* (Sunset, 1976); *Flow Motion* (Virgin, 1976; Spoon/Mute/Restless Retro, 1990; Mute, 1993); *Saw Delight* (Virgin, 1976; Spoon/Mute/Restless Retro, 1990; Mute, 1993); *Out of Reach* (Peters International, 1978; Tko Magnum Midline, 1999); *Cannibalism* (UA, 1978); *Can* (Laser, 1979; Spoon/Mute/Restless Retro, 1990; Mute, 1993); *Cannibalism 1* (Spoon, 1980; Spoon/Mute/Restless Retro, 1990; Mute, 1998); *Delay 1968* (Spoon, 1980; Spoon/Mute/Restless Retro, 1990; Mute, 1998); *Incandescence 1969–1977* (Virgin, 1981); *Onlyou* (tape; Pure Freude, 1982); *Prehistoric Future—June, 1968* (tape; Tago Mago, 1984); *Rite Time* (Mercury, 1989; Mute, 1997); *Cannibalism 2* (Spoon/Mute/Restless Retro, 1990; Mute, 1998); *Cannibalism 3* (Spoon/Mute/Restless Retro, 1990; Mute, 1998); *Radio Waves* (Sonic Platten, 1997); *Sacrilege: The Remixes* (Mute, 1997); *Inner Space* (Tko Magnum Midline, 1998); *Anthology 1968–1993* (Mute, 1998); *Can Box Music (Live 1971–1977)* (Mute, 1999); *Box* (boxed set; Mute, 1999); *Can & Out of Reach* (Audelic, 2003).

Can: (L to R) Irmin Schmidt, Michael Karoli, Rebop Kwaku Baah, Jaki Liebezeit, Holger Czukay, Malcolm Mooney, c.1970s.

CANDY ASS RECORDS
LOCATION: PORTLAND, OR

Run by influential **queercore** rocker Jody Bleyle (formerly of **Team Dresch** and later of Family Outing), Candy Ass Records (1992–1999) released albums by bands such as Team Dresch, **Heavens to Betsy**, and **Sleater-Kinney** (in partnership with Chainsaw Records). Their 1995 double album *Free to Fight* featured songs about women's safety from all-female bands like Fifth Column, Excuse 17, Cheesecake, and Lois; it also included a 75-page illustrated booklet about self-defense against harassment and rape, as well as practical advice, stories, and poems. Other artists on the Candy Ass roster were Containe, Cypher in the Snow, Hazel, the Third Sex, New Bad Things, and Vegas Beat. By sticking to their indie principles, Candy Ass Records was another example of how a politicized **DIY** company made a difference in giving voice to artists who might otherwise have been marginalized.

JIM CARROLL

Author of numerous books of punk poetry and short stories, and occasional rock star, Jim Carroll was a junkie for many years before cleaning up his act and performing on a more regular basis. Between 1980 and 1984 he produced three albums with his descriptively named Jim Carroll Band, the highlight of whose output was by far the epic song "People Who Died" from the album *Catholic Boy*. From the mid-1980s on, Carroll concentrated primarily on his writing, and recorded more spoken-word pieces than music. The 1995 film *The Basketball Diaries*, starring Leonardo DiCaprio, was based on one of Carroll's autobiographical books published in 1978. Along with **Richard Hell** and Tom Verlaine, Carroll brought a literary sensibility to punk and was able to use his druggy past to evocative effect in chronicling a life almost wasted, but in which a true poetic talent was somehow nurtured through an opiate haze.

Discography:
Music: *Catholic Boy* (Atco, 1980, 1989); *Dry Dreams* (Atco, 1982); *I Write Your Name* (Atlantic, 1983, 1991); *A World Without Gravity: The Best of the Jim Carroll Band* (Rhino, 1993); *Pools of Mercury* (Polygram, 1998); *Runaway EP* (Kill Rock Stars, 2000). **Spoken Word:** *Rimbaud Lectures* (The American Poetry Archive, 1978); *Naropa Institute* (Naropa Institute Archives Project, 1986); *Praying Mantis* (Giant, 1991); *The Basketball Diaries* (Audio Literature, 1994); *Curtis's Charm* (Rabid Dog Productions, 1996); *Pools of Mercury* (Mercury, 1998).

CATHAY DE GRANDE

LOCATION: HOLLYWOOD

A Chinese club turned punk venue that operated in Hollywood from 1981 to 1985, Cathay de Grande (along with **Madame Wong's** and Hong Kong Garden) served as a welcome venue for bands like the **Minutemen**, **Social Distortion**, **Battalion of Saints**, and **Suicidal Tendencies** who often had a hard time finding places to perform. A then up-and-coming Los Lobos—who shared bills with many star performers in the early-1980s Los Angeles punk scene such as **X**, the **Circle Jerks**, and particularly the Blasters—frequently took the stage there as well. Cathay de Grande was one example of how early artistic punks could adapt pretty much any location for performances.

CAUSE FOR ALARM

1982-present

LINEUP: Keith Burkhardt (vocals); Eric Britto (guitar); Stephen Fuller (bass); Carl Dynamo (drums)

One of the more positive bands in the New York **hardcore** scene of the mid-1980s, Cause for Alarm eventually became adherents of the **Hare Krishna** mantra, along with other like-minded bands such as **Youth of Today** and **Shelter**. While many groups talked a lot about the scene and the need for unity, Cause for Alarm seemed to actually care about it. Although the band never had as much success as similar bands, such as **Bold**, they still remain popular in New York and continue to play out live, albeit infrequently. Singer Keith Burkhardt remains one of the most arresting hardcore punk front men on the New York scene.

Discography:

Beyond Birth and Death (Victory, 1995); *Cheaters and the Cheated* (Victory, 1997); *Birth After Birth* (Victory, 1997); *Beneath the Wheel* (Victory, 1998); *Nothing Ever Dies* (Victory, 2000)

CBGB

LOCATION: NEW YORK

The seminal club run by **Hilly Kristal**, CBGB was where the early punk scene in New York was born. Located at the corner of Bowery and Bleecker streets for over three decades, CBGB served as a launching pad for new bands with its Monday night Audition Showcase, and provided a platform for aging punk bands, and the cream of lame Jersey metal bands on weeknights. The club was founded by Kristal in 1973 at 315 Bowery (in the heart of the then-decrepit Bowery area), and named it CBGB & OMFUG (which stands for "Country, Bluegrass, Blues and Other Music for Uplifting Gormandizers"). Kristal was unable to make ends meet until **Television** and other like-minded underground groups started playing there in March 1974. Soon, bands such as **Talking Heads**, **Blondie**, the **Ramones**, and the **Dead Boys** dominated the burgeoning punk scene coalescing around CBGB.

As the 1970s ended, more of the first wave of bands had either broken up or moved on to the national stage, and a new group took its place at CBGB: the New York **hardcore** scene. In the early-to-mid-1980s, bands like **Youth of Today**, **Bold**, **Judge**, **Warzone**, **Agnostic Front**, **Cause for Alarm**, **Cro-Mags**, and **Murphy's Law** played the fabled Sunday afternoon hardcore matinees, which the club eventually stopped due to violence. After that, the CBGB scene quieted down when fewer national bands played the club. Unknowns could be found at the club most nights, although national acts such as **Green Day** would stop by for surprise visits. The club became part of the punk legend, and Kristal's decision to market the club's brand saw CBGB T-shirts popping up all over the world.

In August 2005, after being threatened with eviction due to unpaid

rent, Kristal—who maintained that most of the estimated $2 million the club received each year from merchandising simply went back into the business—organized a number of star-studded benefit concerts to save the club. Their efforts were ultimately for naught, though, and CBGB officially closed its doors in October 2006 after a farewell performance by **Patti Smith**. Less than a year after the club's closing, Hilly Kristal died of lung cancer on August 28, 2007.

The legacy that CBGB left behind is enormous. Discounting for a moment the thousands of bands who played there over a three-decade span, there were also the squalid and terminally broken toilets (where **Johnny Thunders** and **Dee Dee Ramone** shot up), the back rooms where **Legs McNeil** and **Richard Hell** would bring willing punk groupies, the surly bartenders, and the ubiquitous presence of Hilly lounging somewhere near the door, seemed more than the punk haven it was, feeling more like a friendly squat open to anyone, albeit one with overpriced beers and rickety furniture. Always a firetrap, and aging badly toward the end, CBGB became more of a brand and punk legend than it did a working club. The last year saw a fitting tribute with the farewell concerts, and as long as the T-shirts adorn everyone from Japanese tourists to heavy-metal wannabes, the name of CBGB will not be forgotten. (One could say the same for the smell of the toilets.)

After Joey Ramone's death in April 2001, this shrine to the lanky legend sprouted in front of CBGB.

CELIBATE RIFLES

1978–present

LINEUP: Damien Lovelock (vocals); Kent Steedman (guitar); Dave Morris (guitar); Michael "Mickey" Couvret (bass); Paul Larsen (drums)

An Australian punk band formed in 1978 by high school friends influenced by **Radio Birdman**, **Iggy** and the **Stooges**, the **Ramones**, and to an extent, the **Sex Pistols** (which accounts for their in-joke name). The Celibate Rifles toured extensively in the late-1980s and early-'90s. They garnered some minor college radio success with the release of *Platters Du Jour* and *Turgid Miasma of Existence*, and even some **MTV** airplay for the anti-television evangelist song "Jesus on TV" in 1987. The Celibate Rifles briefly disbanded in the early-2000s, but resumed touring with key members Lovelock, Steedman, and Morris still going strong over the last three decades. Lovelock released a solo record, Steedman released a record as Crent, and former member James Darroch recorded as Eastern Dark. Although the Celibate Rifles were never as well known as their Australian compatriots the **Saints** (possibly to do with their rare touring outside of Australia), the band's combination of high-speed Ramones-style punk and intelligent lyrics have kept them consistently engaging.

Discography:

But Jacques, the Fish? EP (no label, 1982); *Sideroxylon* (Hot, 1983); *The Celibate Rifles* (Hot, 1984); *Quintessentially Yours* (What Goes On, 1985); *The Turgid Miasma of Existence* (Hot/Rough Trade, 1986); *Mina Mina Mina* (What Goes On, 1986); *Kiss Kiss Bang Bang* (What Goes On, 1986); *Roman Beach Party* (What Goes On, 1987); *Dancing Barefoot* EP (What Goes On, 1988); *Blind Ear* (True Tone/EMI, 1989); *Platters du Jour* (Hot/Rattlesnake/Normal, 1990); *Heaven on a Stick* (Hot, 1992); *Yizgarnnoff* (Hot, 1993);

Sofa (Hot, 1993); *Spaceman in a Satin Suit* (Hot, 1994); *On the Quiet* (Hot, 1996); *Wonderful Life* (Tronador, 1997); *Mid-Stream of Consciousness* (Real-O-Mind, 2002). *Beyond Respect* (MGM Distribution, 2007). **Eastern Dark:** *Long Live the New Flesh!* EP (What Goes On, 1986); *Girls on the Beach (With Cars)* (Waterfront, 1990). **Damien Lovelock:** *It's A Wig, Wig, Wig, Wig World* (Hot/Survival, 1988). **Crent:** *Crent* (Waterfront, 1990)

CHALK CIRCLE

1981–1983

LINEUP: Sharon Cheslow (vocals/guitar); Mary Green (vocals/guitar); Jan Pumphrey (bass, replaced by Sally Berg, Tamera Edminster, Chris Niblack); Anne Bonafede (drums)

The first all-female band from the Washington, D.C., **hardcore** scene—definitely not to be confused with the melodic Canadian group of the same name—Chalk Circle (named for Bertolt Brecht's *Caucasian Chalk Circle*) were relatively popular around D.C., but still had to face the usual sexism and allegations that female bands could not rock as hard as male bands could surely rock. Sharon Cheslow and Mary Green had been friends with scenesters **Ian MacKaye** and Jeff Nelson, and after seeing a **Clash** show in Philadelphia, were inspired to form a band of their own like so many of the other bands forming in D.C. during that fertile time. **Henry Rollins**, still named Garfield, declined the drummer's seat as he preferred to sing (and the rest, as they say, is history), but Anne Bonafede soon filled in as drummer, with a variety of people taking over on bass. Although Chalk Circle only recorded a few demos and compilation tracks, they are fondly remembered as being one of the more adventurous and emotionally real bands in the D.C. scene of the early-1980s.

CHELSEA

1976–present

LINEUP: Gene October (vocals); Billy Idol (guitar, replaced by James Stevenson, numerous others, Stevenson again); Dave Martin (guitar/vocals); Tony James (bass, replaced by Geoff Myles, others, now Phil Barber); John Towe (drums, replaced by many others, now Chris Bashford)

A British band best remembered for the classic punk single "Right to Work" and for birthing the original lineup of **Generation**

Leee Black Childers (right) with David Bowie's wife Angie, 1985.

X, Chelsea started out supporting noise terrorists **Throbbing Gristle** at an art gallery opening in October 1976, even though the bands' disparate styles did not mesh well. When the instrumentalists in Chelsea left to form Generation X in November 1976, singer Gene October regrouped the band with Dave Martin on guitar and vocals, James Stevenson on guitar, Geoff Myles on bass, and Chris Bashford on drums; they released their debut album, *Chelsea*, in 1979. October continued to record and tour with new lineups of Chelsea when not working as a garbage man in London. October is also the uncredited force behind convincing the management of former gay nightclub Shageramas to convert the venue to the **Roxy** and cater to punk bands and clientele.

Discography:

Chelsea (Step Forward, 1979; Captain Oi!, 2000); *No Damage* (IRS, 1980); *Alternative Hits* (Step Forward, 1980; Weser, 1996; Captain Oi!, 2000); *No Escape* (IRS, 1980); *Evacuate* (IRS, 1982; Captain Oi!, 2005); *Live and Well* (Punx, 1984; Rhythm Vicar, 2003); *Just for the Record* (Step Forward, 1985); *Original Sinners* (Communique, 1985); *Rocks Off* (Jungle, 1986); *Backtrax* (Illegal, 1988); *Ultra Prophets* (IRS, 1989); *Underwraps* (IRS, 1989); *Unreleased Stuff* (Clay, 1989); *Traitors Gate* (Weser, 1996); *Fools and Soldiers* (Receiver, 1997); *Punk Singles* (Captain Oi!, 2000); *Punk Rock Rarities* (Captain Oi!, 2000); *BBC Punk Sessions* (live; Captain Oi!, 2001); *Metallic F.O.: Live at CBGB* (Captain Oi!, 2002); *Urban Kids: A Punk Anthology* (Castle Us/Ryko, 2005); *Live & Loud* (Harry May, 2005); *Faster, Cheaper & Better Looking* (Captain Oi!, 2005)

LEEE BLACK CHILDERS

Manager, scenester, and photographer Leee Black Childers worked with **David Bowie** at MainMan management and at times had the unenviable task of keeping **Iggy Pop** from overindulging. Childers, a one-time assistant of Andy Warhol's at The Factory, was present from the early days of punk and later managed the **Heartbreakers** on their drug-fueled tour of Europe in 1976. It is unclear why Childers has yet to publish his story, but then again the libel lawsuits may be cost prohibitive. Childers is also regarded as one of the best photographers of the early punk era, having definitely benefited from his ready access to members of the scene.

CH3

1980–mid-1990s, 2005–present

LINEUP: Mike Magrann (vocals/guitar); Kimm Gardener (vocals/guitar); Larry Kelley (bass, now Andy Thompson); Mike Burton (drums, now Fredo Silva)

A Cerritos, California, band, also known as Channel 3, CH3 went though numerous rhythm sections and stylistic changes in the mid-1980s and alienated many fans with experimental albums such as *Airborne*. Although CH3 had started out as a fast melodic punk band, Mike Magrann's desire to add instruments such as saxophone and harmonica to newer and slower songs led to a higher profile in the indie rock scene, and opening spots for such bands as the Red Hot Chili Peppers. Fans who remembered the louder and faster CH3, however, were not satisfied until the band returned to its roots for a 2005 tour. A little-known fact about the band is that Magrann's mother was imprisoned in an internment camp for Japanese-Americans during World War II, leading to the band's classic track "Manzanar" from *I've Got a Gun* EP.

Discography:

CH3 EP (Posh Boy, 1981); *Fear of Life* (Posh Boy, 1982); *I've Got a Gun* (No Future, 1983); *After the Lights Go Out* (Posh Boy, 1984); *Airborne* EP (Enigma, 1984); *Last Time I Drank* (Enigma, 1985); *Rejected* (Lone Wolf, 1989); *How Do You Open the Damn Thing* (Lost and Found, 1996); *Channel Three* (Dr. Strange, 2002)

CHUMBAWAMBA

1984–present

LINEUP: Alice Nutter (vocals);
Danbert Nobacon (vocals/guitar);
Boff (guitar); Paul Grecco (bass);
Jude Abbot (trumpet/vocals);
Harry Hamer (drums/programming);
Dunstan Bruce (percussion/vocals);
Lou Watts (vocals/keyboards)

This British punk anarchist collective formed in Leeds 13 years before their catchy single "Tubthumping" became an unlikely radio and **MTV** hit in 1997. Before then, Chumbawamba (the name is purposefully meaningless) had a long and politically active career, and were notorious throughout the 1980s for playing at anti-Margaret Thatcher protests and leftist benefits that were often the target of raids by British police. However, the band's catchy brand of satire didn't limit itself to easy targets on the right: Their first album, 1986's *Pictures of Starving Children Sell Records*, took a stab at the era's ultimate symbol of mainstream lefty do-goodism—Live Aid.

Being a stalwart, independent, anarchist collective unwilling to avoid sacred cows of any ideological stripe, Chumbawamba caused a bit of controversy among anarchist punks when they signed to EMI (the members made a preemptive strike by sending letters to zines, which claimed that they could have more success bringing about social change by working within the system). Their 1997 EMI debut *Tubthumper* contained the bouncy "Tubthumping" which turned into a surprise hit, while the success of the follow-up single "Amnesia" cemented their international fame. The troublemaking band immediately caused controversy with subversive actions, such as playing the song in a country-and-western style when promoting the record or advocating on American television that punks had a right to shoplift from major record stores (which led some chains to stop carrying their records).

Subsequent albums were just as politically abrasive, and EMI dropped the band in 2000, much later than anyone really expected, considering the lyrical content of most of their songs. Afterwards, Chumbawamba returned to independent recording, and their message remained as staunchly anticapitalist as it was when the band started. Although their danceable,

Chumbawamba's Alice Nutter fails at her Maria von Trapp impersonation during a show in Cannes, 1998.

idiosyncratic sound has little to do with the bombast that most people associate with punk (they often tour with an accordionist), the band's strident consistency and ideological stance defines them as more squarely within the punk camp than many bands with louder guitars and better fashion accessories. As of 2005, the band essentially splintered in half, with Dunstan, Danbert, Nutter, and Harry all pursuing solo careers (Nutter is now a successful playwright and Danbert now tours as a solo artist and has put out a record with Jon Langford) and the rest of the band toured as the acoustic, often a cappella Chumbawamba to support the re-recorded version of *English Rebel Songs*.

Discography:

Pictures of Starving Children Sell Records (Agit Prop, 1986); *Slap!* (Agit Prop, 1990); *Homophobia* (Import, 1994); *Showbusiness (Live)* (One Little Indian, 1995); *Swinging with Raymond* (One Little Indian, 1996); *Tubthumper* (Republic/Universal, 1997); *Shhh* (Agit Prop, 1997); *Anarchy* (EMI, 1998); *English Rebel Songs 1381–1984* (Import, 1998); *What You See is What You Get* (Republic/Universal, 2000); *Readymates* (Republic/Universal, 2002); *Shhlap!* (Mutt, 2003); *UN* (Koch, 2004); *Singsong and a Scrap* (No Masters, 2006); *Get On With It: Live* (No Masters, 2007)

CIRCLE JERKS

1979–1990, 1995–present

LINEUP: Keith Morris (vocals); Greg Hetson (guitar); Roger Rogerson (bass, replaced by Ron Reyes, Earl Liberty, Zander Schloss); Lucky Lehrer (drums, replaced by Keith Clark, Chuck Biscuits, Kevin Fitzgerald)

One of the most popular of the many Southern California **hardcore** bands of the early-1980s, the Circle Jerks were equally adept at party anthems, biting social commentary, and high-speed covers of 1970s kitsch material. The original lineup was typical of the incestuous Southern California scene, featuring former **Black Flag** singer **Keith Morris** on vocals (he appeared only on the Jerks' first 7" single) and Greg Hetson, who also played in the early lineup of **Red Kross**, **Bad Religion**, and Black Flag. The best-remembered lineup of the band appeared on the *Golden Shower of Hits* album and subsequent tour,

which featured Earl Liberty (formerly of Saccharine Trust) on bass and Chuck Biscuits (previously of Black Flag and **D.O.A.**) on drums. The band also famously (though briefly) appeared in *Repo Man*, parodying themselves as cheesy lounge singers laconically covering their classic "When the Shit Hits the Fan."

Over their lifetime, the Circle Jerks released several key albums, including *Group Sex*, *Wild in the Streets*, and *Golden Shower of Hits*, and although bass players (such as Ron Reyes) and drummers (such as powerhouse Chuck Biscuits) came and went, the core songwriting group remained. The band gained a more stable lineup and veered into more metallic territory with the release of *Wonderful* in 1985, going almost full-out, slowed-down metal with *VI* in 1987. While the first three albums are punk rock must-haves, the later stuff, well, it's...mediocre...(Keith Morris, as a rule, should not sing slow songs.)

The Circle Jerks became less visible in the late-1980s and early-'90s as Hetson began to concentrate more on Bad Religion and Morris took an increasing interest in artist representation for record companies and production. Between the 1980s and '90s, the band occasionally re-formed with key members Morris and Hetson, plus the addition of Zander Schloss from the **Weirdos** (who also appeared in *Repo Man* and numerous other bands and projects) on bass.

The band reunited for the 1995 record *Oddities, Abnormalities and Curiosities*, which featured a puzzling guest appearance by Debbie Gibson on a cover of "I Wanna Destroy You" by the Soft Boys (Robyn Hitchcock's original band), and though they are still nominally together, the band hasn't released another new album since. Today, Hetson mostly tours with Bad Religion, and Schloss tours with the reunited Weirdos, although

the Circle Jerks occasionally re-form with at least Morris and Hetson for sporadic tours. The band achieved a form of skate immortality in 2007 when Vans released a line of Circle Jerks-themed shoes. Morris has one of the truly original voices in hardcore and will be equally remembered for his work with Black Flag as with the Circle Jerks. For a while, the Circle Jerks were as powerful and compelling as any hardcore band around, but then they changed with the times and for the worse; perhaps a sign that punk bands are not meant to adapt to commercial imperatives? Either way, Morris is still one of the best singers/screamers in punk rock, and with his long dreads flying in the air, remains a vital force at shows.

Discography:

Group Sex (Frontier, 1980); *Wild in the Streets* (Faulty Products, 1982); *Golden Shower of Hits* (LAX, 1983); *Wonderful* (Combat Core, 1985); *VI* (Relativity, 1987); *Gig* (Relativity, 1992); *Oddities, Abnormalities and Curiosities* (Mercury, 1995)

The Circle Jerks, 1984: (L to R) Earl Liberty, Keith Morris, Chuck Biscuits, Greg Hetson.

CIV

1994-1998

LINEUP: Anthony Civarelli (vocals); Charlie Garriga (guitar); Arthur Smilios (bass); Sammy Siegler (drums)

The short-lived, melodic New York band Civ were led by charismatic, bald-headed singer Civ (Anthony Civarelli) and featured former members of **Gorilla Biscuits** (Civarelli, bassist Arthur Smilios, and drummer Sammy Siegler). Civ scored a minor radio hit and video success with the catchy song "Can't Wait One Minute More" off their smash 1995 record *Set Your Goals*, produced by former Gorilla Biscuits and **Quicksand** guitarist Walter Schreifels, and which capitalized on the temporary mainstream vogue for punk music being given a high-polished commercial gloss. A follow-up album was less successful, and the band called it quits in 1998. "Can't Wait One Minute More" was eventually used in a car commercial, and is a frequent karaoke favorite for aging punks or indie kids. Civarelli went on to reunite Gorilla Biscuits for several successful tours, and is also renowned as a tattoo artist. While never as beloved as Gorilla Biscuits, Civ was one of the few punk bands signed to a major label who truly lived up to the hype.

Discography:
Set Your Goals (Revelation/Lava/Atlantic, 1995);
Thirteen Day Getaway (Atlantic, 1998)

THE CLASH

1976-1986

LINEUP: Joe Strummer (vocals/guitar); Mick Jones (vocals/guitar); Paul Simonon (vocals/bass); Keith Levene (guitar, not on records); Terry Chimes, aka Tory Crimes (drums, replaced by Nicky Headon, aka Topper Headon)

One of the most famous, critically acclaimed, politically committed, artistically experimental, and commercially successful punk bands of all time—among the few that non-punks can name—the Clash were ultimately, after the demise of the **Sex Pistols**, the public face of punk rock as far as mass media was concerned. The Clash are to many the single most important English punk band, and although boneheaded career moves, intra-band fighting, naïve allegiance to managers, and trendy political causes have dated their trendsetting appeal, the music still stands as powerful today as it was during the band's late-1970s heyday.

Very much like the Pistols, the Clash were more or less the idea of a Svengali, in this case Bernie Rhodes, a **Situationist** and friend of **Malcolm McLaren**, who wanted to form a band to rival McLaren's media sensations. The band was formed in London in June 1976 out of the ashes of the **London SS** (featuring Mick Jones, future **Generation X** bassist Tony James, and future **Public Image Ltd.** member Keith Levene) and the 101'ers, **Joe Strummer's** pub rock band. Strummer had been convinced to quit the 101'ers by Rhodes, who simply introduced him to the others and announced that Strummer would be working with them. (Some have disputed this story, saying that the members got together independent of Rhodes, but Rhodes was ultimately a major influence on the band's

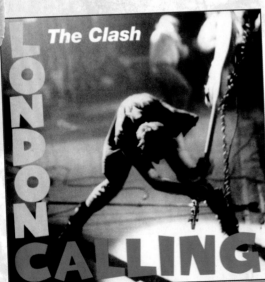

The Clash, 1979: (L to R) Joe Strummer, Topper Headon, Paul Simonon, Mick Jones.

politics, if not their songwriting). A search for a drummer eventually found Terry Chimes (sometimes known as Tory Crimes), who supported the band until their first record. After fighting over musical direction, Levene was forced out, and the lineup solidified with Strummer on lead vocals and guitar, Mick Jones on guitar and vocals, and Paul Simonon on bass (which he did not play as such, but learned his parts). Aided by Rhodes, Simonon (a painter of no small talent) provided much of the artistic direction and look, which included paint-splattered clothes, ripped jeans, patches sewn on suit jackets, and some of the best hair this side of Vidal Sassoon. Strummer and Jones soon formed a musical partnership that would rival John Lennon and Paul McCartney for sheer output and musical breadth, from short, catchy punk tunes to longer experimental pieces that proclaimed their love of **reggae**. Before almost anyone else, the Clash realized that pub rock, punk, roots rock, and reggae were all genres of music that had more in common, at least socially and politically, than the idiotic and sectarian fights between the Teds, Punks and Mods and Rockers had led most people to believe.

A major turning point for the Clash musically and politically was the Notting Hill riot of August 1976 in which the police clashed violently with young black men during the annual Carnival street festival.

The Clash on the first night of their 1979 American tour.

The subsequent violence inspired two of the Clash's best early songs, "White Riot" and "White Man in Hammersmith Palais," which demonstrated their commitment to social change as opposed to the mere nihilism then ascendant in the British scene. These songs also showed that the Clash could approach the same topic from two different musical perspectives, part **hardcore** punk, part slow, **dub**-like reggae. The Clash then joined the notorious Anarchy tour of December 1976, with the Sex Pistols, the **Damned**, the **Heartbreakers**, and (later) the **Buzzcocks**, but the initial 19 dates were marked by chaos, confrontation, cancellations, and the removal of the **Damned** from the tour. The Clash then stunned the nascent punk community by signing to CBS Records in January 1977; not surprisingly, many, including the zine *Sniffin' Glue*, saw this as a sellout of the first degree. The band began recording in early 1977 with former Blue Oyster Cult member, producer Sandy Pearlman. Their eponymous album was released in England that November but was not released at that time in the United States due to CBS' concerns about the supposedly poor production quality. They needn't have been concerned, as the album's brutal and direct, but also strangely melodic and harmonious, blend of Jones' guitar, and Simonon's reggae-esque bass playing meld perfectly with Strummer's anguished vocals, and the album also proved one thing that both Led Zeppelin and Eric Clapton had been used to argue against: that white men could indeed, play reggae.

After the first album, the apolitical Chimes left the band and was replaced by the more musically adventurous Topper Headon, who would stay with the band until their last record. In October 1978, the Clash released *Give 'Em Enough Rope*, technically their second album but, due to contractual disputes, their first release in the United States. Since the first album, *The Clash*, hadn't been considered commercial enough, by the time it finally hit stores in America during the summer of 1979, several of the "less commercial" tracks on the UK album, including "Cheat," "Protex

The Clash in more innocent times, 1976.

Blue," "Deny," and "48 Hours" had been substituted with songs that were arguably better, such as the sensational "Clash City Rockers," "Complete Control," "White Man in Hammersmith Palais," "I Fought the Law," and "Jail Guitar Doors." One could quibble, but it seems clear that the American version is stronger and more consistent in terms of tracking and dramatic shifts between songs. Although *Give 'Em Enough Rope* was a worthy follow-up, with its huge, wall-of-guitars sound—as though Phil Spector had been let loose on the punk world—the band felt constrained by the growing consistency of British punk, and Strummer and Simonon were in particular fascinated by the reggae sounds of Britain's Caribbean subculture.

In 1979, the Clash followed with the masterful 19-song double LP *London Calling*, which contained a number of instant classics like the title track, "Hateful," and "Rudie Can't Fail." The unlisted final track on side four, the R&B-flavored "Train in Vain" (often mistakenly called "Stand by Me"), which had been left off the original

track listing because it was intended to be included as a flexi-disc, became a hit for the band when it was released as a single. The cover of *London Calling* was a parody/homage to the first Elvis Presley album, and some ads promoting the album featured a young Elvis holding the album aloft while sneering. At this time, with a critical and commercial success of an album—it mixed funk, reggae, punk, **rockabilly**, and jazz over ambitious riffs and critiques of capitalism and consumer culture—the Clash found themselves tasting success through experimentation. They were also well on their way to becoming one of the most formidable live bands in rock history, a fact that can be seen in two excellent documentaries, *Rude Boy* (1980) and *Westway to the World* (2000). Critic **Lester Bangs** memorably described the Clash in concert as being like "a desperation uncontrived, unstaged, a fury unleashed on the stage and writhing upon itself in real pain that connects with the nerves of the audience." While Bangs was given to hyperbole (partic-

ularly when on the "cough syrup diet") in the case of the Clash, he was dead on, the band was a live force to be reckoned with, as passionate as they were experimental.

In June 1981, the Clash played a now-famous extended stay at New York's Bond's Casino in Times Square, where they allowed a diverse melange of bands ranging from **Kraut** to **Bad Brains** to early rap stars like Grandmaster Flash to support them. The more parochial punks were already upset by the disturbingly non-punk flavor of their opening acts, and generally disappointed by the Clash's suspicious embrace of world music, and the musically all-over-the-map triple LP *Sandinista!*, released in December of 1980. The label initially balked at its unwieldy size but later relented when the Clash agreed to lose money by selling it at a single-album price (as they had done with *London Calling*). *Sandinista!* was much more musically diverse and politically ambitious, but the quality suffered underneath all the sprawl. After the Clash lost money on both

"As a mix of personalities, the Clash was a perfect engine."

—writer Lenny Kaye

the record and touring, they regrouped to record the much more accessible (at least on side one) *Combat Rock*, which was released in 1982 and spawned the hit singles "Should I Stay or Should I Go?" and "Rock the Casbah." The Clash then embarked on their highest profile tour, with drummer Terry Chimes returning to replace the drug-addicted Topper Headon, and then opened for the Who on their 1982 farewell tour.

Personnel problems within the band seemed to escalate at the same rate as their commercial success. Tensions between Strummer and Jones were reaching a peak during 1983, and Jones was summarily axed that September. Drummer Chimes left quickly thereafter, and Strummer and Simonon recruited guitarists Nick Sheppard (from the English punk band the Cortinas)

and Vince White, and a new drummer Pete Howard to tour under the Clash name (including some interesting and unusual acoustic busking tours) and to eventually record the much-maligned *Cut the Crap* album, largely produced and overdubbed by a returned Bernie Rhodes. The Clash finally called it quits following the tours for *Cut the Crap*. (Although roundly despised, *Cut the Crap* is not that bad a record, even if the lineup suffers without Mick Jones, and certainly songs like "This is England" and "Dirty Punk" should at least be included on Clash compilations with more regularity.)

Several ex-Clash members kept up a stream of creativity afterward, particularly Strummer, who briefly joined the **Pogues** in 1991, did some interesting soundtrack work, and released a number of solo

albums, including three with his band the Mescaleros, before his sudden death from a heart attack in December 2002. Mick Jones had a few hits with his adventurous dance-funk group Big Audio Dynamite (although Joe Strummer is strongly missed from all but the one BAD record on which he co-wrote songs) before forming Carbon/Silicon with ex-Generation X bassist Tony James. Paul Simonon was briefly in Havana 3 A.M. before concentrating on his painting, though later he played in the Good, the Bad and the Queen, with Blur's Damon Albarn, the Verve's Simon Tong, and Tony Allen from Fela Kuti's band.

The Clash were rightfully inducted into the Rock and Roll Hall of Fame in 2003. Their legacy is impossible to overestimate, and the members' commitment to their ideals, no matter how tenuous some of those

The Anarchy tour bus, December 1976. (L to R) Mick Jones, John Lydon, Billy Rath (The Heartbreakers), Paul Simonon, Joe Strummer.

CONFLICT

1981-present

LINEUP: Colin Jerwood (vocals, replaced by Steve Ignorant, Pauline Beck); Steve (guitar, then others); John Clifford (bass, replaced by Paul Hoddy); Paco Correna (drums); Paul Friday, aka "Nihilistic Nobody" (visuals)

The British **hardcore** band Conflict was started by vocalist Colin Jerwood, who loudly espoused causes like vegetarianism and animal rights and smashing the violent and corrupt British empire by any means necessary. Conflict, like **Crass** before them, was extremely vocal in their opposition to Great Britain's political structure (particularly Margaret Thatcher, of course) and demanded that their followers be similarly dedicated to fighting injustice, in essence advocating real political action as opposed to simply singing about anarchy. They also pushed a **DIY** philosophy that led to them starting their own label, Mortarhate. The band's agitprop political positions caused continual controversy in the British press as well as clashes with the increasingly nervous British police force (one 1987 show actually turned into a full-fledged riot). Steve Ignorant from Crass joined the band in the late-1980s as a co-lead vocalist and contributed songs from the Crass repertoire to the band's live shows. After Ignorant departed in 1989, the band released *The Final Conflict*, supposedly announcing their demise, but Conflict re-formed in the early-1990s and continued to record and tour sporadically. Conflict still tours with original vocalist Jerwood and drummer Paco Correna—when his health permits it. One of the most extreme and long lasting bands on the English anarcho-punk scene, Conflict has resolutely refused to compromise, simply cranking out great records that challenge the dominant ideology whenever they get a chance to record.

Discography:

It's Time to See Who's Who (Corpus Christi, 1983); *Increase the Pressure* (Mortarhate, 1984); *Only Stupid Bastards Help EMI* (Model Army, 1986); *The Ungovernable Force* (Mortarhate, 1987); *Turning Rebellion into Money* live; Mortarhate, 1987); *From Protest to Resistance* (Mortarhate, 1988); *Against All Odds* (Mortarhate, 1989); *The Final Conflict* (Mortarhate, 1989); *Conclusion* (Cleopatra, 1994); *We Won't Take No More* (Conflict, 1995); *Deploying All Means Necessary* (Cleopatra, 1997); *In the Venue* (Mortarhate, 2000); *In America* (Go Kart, 2001); *Carlo Giuliani* (Jungle, 2003); *There's No Power Without Control* (Mortarhate, 2003); *Rebellion Sucks* (Mortarhate, 2004)

ideals may have been, has been extremely inspirational to legions of punks who continue to idolize the Clash. Strummer in particular was looked up to for his consistency and dedication to his own vision, acting as a sort of spiritual godfather to the British and American scenes. (In fact, one of the bands who took the most musically from the Clash was **Rancid**, whose lead singer Tim Armstrong later returned the favor by signing the Mescaleros to his **Epitaph**-backed boutique label, Hellcat Records.) The Clash are also famous for expanding punk's sonic palette to include rap, reggae, funk, dub, and world music and for educating numerous young punks to the fact that their music could be more than just three chords and a fast beat. The level of admiration they have garnered led some to call them the "only band that matters"; a statement that may in fact not be hyperbole.

Discography:

The Clash (CBS, 1977, 1999); *Give 'Em Enough Rope* (Epic, 1978, 1999); *The Cost of Living* EP (CBS, 1979); *The Clash* (Epic, 1979, 1999); *London Calling* (Epic, 1979, 1999, 2004); *Black Market Clash* (Epic, 1980); *Sandinista!* (Epic, 1980, 1999); *Combat Rock* (Epic, 1982, 1999); *Cut the Crap* (Epic, 1985); *I Fought the Law* EP (CBS, 1988); *The Story of the Clash Volume 1* (Epic, 1988); *Crucial Music: The Clash Collection* (CBS Special Products/Relativity, 1989); *Crucial Music: 1977 Revisited* (CBS Special Products/Relativity, 1990); *Return to Brixton* EP (Epic, 1990); *Clash on Broadway* (Epic/Legacy, 1991); *The Singles* (Epic, 1999); *Super Black Market Clash* (Epic, 1999); *From Here to Eternity* (Epic, 1999). **Joe Strummer**: *Walker* (Virgin Movie Music, 1987); *Earthquake Weather* (Epic, 1989); *Gangsterville* EP (Epic, 1989); *Island Hopping* EP (Epic, 1989). **Joe Strummer and the Mescaleros**: *Rock Art and the X-Ray Style* (Mercury, 1999); *Global a Go-Go* (Hellcat, 2001); *Streetcore* (Hellcat, 2003). **Havana 3 a.m.**: *Havana 3 a.m.* (IRS, 1991)

THE COCKNEY REJECTS

1979-1990, 1999-present

LINEUP: Jeff "Stinky" Turner (vocals); Mickey Geggus (guitar); Chris Murrel (bass, replaced by Vince Riordan, others); Paul Harvey (drums, replaced by Andy Scott, others)

English punks the Cockney Rejects were associated with the **oi** movement both because of their working-class lyrics and for the 1980 song "Oi! Oi! Oi!" The band was one of the earliest to pioneer the British football-terrace sing-alongs that didn't need elaborate vocals and harmonies, just a huge chorus of yobbos chanting along. (Sadly, the football terrace crowd was also a violent lot and the band had to dodge the occasional beer.) After gaining some success, the Cockney Rejects developed an unfortunate following of **National Front** members, who simply did not get the band's working-class message of solidarity, racial and otherwise. The truth of the matter was that the Rejects were into West Ham United, not Hitler, a fact often lost on the crowd. The Cockney Rejects soon became the premiere oi band, while putting out three quality records in a row, including the "live" *Greatest Hits Vol. 3*, one of the highlights of their career. *The Power and the Glory* was a step back toward hard rock territory, a direction they continued in for the next decade until breaking up in 1990. They reunited in 1999 and went on to join the punk package tour circuit.

Discography:

Greatest Hits Vol. 1 (EMI, 1980); *Greatest Hits Vol. 2* (EMI, 1980); *Greatest Hits Vol. 3* (EMI, 1981); *The Power and the Glory* (Zonophone, 1981); *The Wild Ones* (AKA, 1982); *Quiet Storm* (Heavy Metal, 1984); *Unheard Rejects* (Wonderful World, 1985); *Lethal* (Neat, 1990); *The Punk Singles Collection* (Dojo, 1997); *Greatest Hits Vol. 4* (Rhythm Vicar, 1997); *Out of the Gutter* (Captain Oi!, 2003)

BOOKS

Given that so much of what happened in punk's various heydays took place under the cultural radar, much of it went undocumented at the time. In recent years, however, numerous books have been written about punk history and philosophy, with subjects ranging from particular **scenes** or movements to personal memoirs to academic discourses on what it all meant (and still means). Although punk will forever be known more for its music than its literature, here's a quick guide to some of the more notable and worthwhile books on the subject.

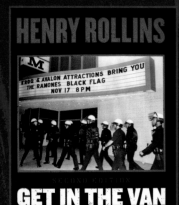

GET IN THE VAN: ON THE ROAD WITH BLACK FLAG (1994)

Years after leaving **Black Flag**, **Henry Rollins** published this collection of tour diaries from his days leading the band on their blitzkrieg cross-country tours. *Get in the Van* documented the squalid lifestyle and police harassment that the band endured on their frequent journeys across the United States in a van during the early- to mid-1980s. Rollins' writing provides a characteristically realistic and gritty look at the extremely unglamorous life of early **DIY** bands on the road, the abuse from audiences, and the lack of food that bands of that period often had to withstand on a regular basis. The diary

serves as an entertaining but also excellent analysis of how difficult it was for early punks such as Black Flag to establish themselves in a frequently hostile environment. It also demonstrates Rollins's evolution as a writer.

DANCE OF DAYS: TWO DECADES OF PUNK IN THE NATION'S CAPITAL (2001)

This key work is a fascinating and well-informed look at the Washington, D.C., **hardcore** scene and political movements during the 1980s to the '90s. *Dance of Days* contains numerous interviews with key players from **Minor Threat**, **Bad Brains**, **Fugazi**, **Rites of Spring**, and **Bikini Kill** as well as more obscure bands such as Urban Verbs. It is also packed with invaluable information on the origins of **straight edge**, the rise of

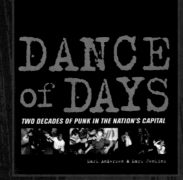

Dischord Records, and the politicization of punk. Authors Mark Jenkins (a journalist who covered many of the bands in the book) and Mark Andersen (who provides an insider's account of the role of **Positive Force** D.C. on the politicization of the punk scene) cover all the bases regarding the important figures in one of the country's most electrifying scenes.

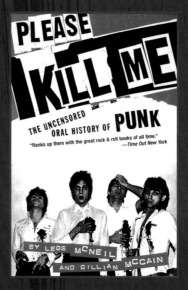

PLEASE KILL ME: THE UNCENSORED ORAL HISTORY OF PUNK (1996)

An oral history of New York punk, *Please Kill Me* was written and compiled by original punks, **Legs McNeil** and Gillian McCain. McNeil's strength is his close involvement with those among the early New York scene and his tight relationships with many of the musicians interviewed for the book. *Please Kill Me* gives an account of the genre's origins in the proto-punk of the 1960s, with context from many of that decade's major players, such as **Iggy Pop**, John Sinclair, the

MC5, and **Lou Reed**. When the book reaches the 1970s, McNeil himself becomes a participant because he and **John Holmstrom** of *Punk* magazine had a major influence not only in naming the new scene centered at **CBGB** but also in interviewing and promoting the bands and artists they most enjoyed, such as the **Dictators** and the **Ramones**. A noble attempt to document the often contradictory history of punk rock.

DHARMA PUNX (2004)

This memoir by former addict and petty criminal Noah Levine tells of how he reformed into a **straight-edge** punk and eventually became a Buddhist teacher in training, now leading meditation retreats and groups in juvenile detention halls and prisons. Levine's rejection of violence and nihilism goes strongly against the media image of many punks as inherently antisocial, providing a positive counterpoint to the mainstream image that often equates punk with criminality. *Dharma Punx* fits squarely within the tradition of punks seeking spirituality—as epitomized by **Bad Brains**' conversion to Rastafarianism and the embrace of Krishna Consciousness by members of **Youth of Today**, **Shelter**, and the **Cro-Mags**—and as such is primarily of interest to punks in recovery (**Social Distortion**'s Mike Ness, an ex-junkie, provides a cover testimonial) or to students of spirituality.

PRETTY IN PUNK: GIRLS' GENDER RESISTANCE IN A BOYS' SUBCULTURE (2002)

Lauraine Leblanc's academic take on women in punk examines how they are often marginalized—even abused—in this primarily male-dominated subculture, despite the supposedly liberal climate fostered by punk's anarchist ideology. Drawing on interviews with street punks, *Pretty in Punk* looks at how, despite this, many young women see the scene as a place of protest, where they can express themselves in less "feminine" ways than in mainstream culture.

FROM THE VELVETS TO THE VOIDOIDS: A PRE-PUNK HISTORY FOR A POST-PUNK WORLD (1993)

Clinton Heylin's book relates in exhaustive and meticulous detail how the punk scene coalesced in various cities across the United States from the mid-1960s to the mid-'70s. *From the Velvets to the Voidoids* was recently reissued in 2005 and in the new introduction Heylin takes issue with other punk history books such as **Legs McNeil**'s *Please Kill Me* as being inadequate for the task at hand and insufficiently rigorous.

LIPSTICK TRACES: A SECRET HISTORY OF THE TWENTIETH CENTURY (1989)

This dense work is rock historian Greil Marcus' brave and (occasionally) successful attempt to contextualize punk and the **Sex Pistols** in terms of historical, political,

LIPSTICK TRACES
A SECRET HISTORY OF THE TWENTIETH CENTURY
GREIL MARCUS

and artistic trends, particularly highlighting connections between punk and movements such as the **Situationists**. Although the links found by Marcus were denied by many (including the Sex Pistols' **John Lydon**), *Lipstick Traces* makes a compelling point that punk did not simply spring out of nothing but instead came from a long and complex tradition of artistic and social rebellion against dominant power structures, a tradition from which punk rock was then able to draw for philosophical and social insight. *Lipstick Traces* is also a moving account of the potential power of creative subcultures. Overall, one of the most intellectual examinations of punk and the power of protest.

PHILOSOPHY OF PUNK: MORE THAN NOISE (1999)

Here, Craig O'Hara tries to codify the disparate elements of punk, arguing that punk is by its nature antiestablishment, antiracist, antisexist, antihomophobic, profeminist, in support of animal rights, and inherently inclusive of diversity and difference. Although the book is an extremely worthy effort to give coherence to a massively incoherent and amorphous movement, it is unclear that the majority of those who identify themselves as punks would agree with the rather monolithic portrait of the movement

that is portrayed in *Philosophy of Punk*. It is also unclear if a philosophy of punk can be, or should be, articulated, given the wide disparity of movements, cultures, and subcultures that exist within punk.

WE GOT THE NEUTRON BOMB: THE UNTOLD STORY OF L.A. PUNK (2001)

Brendan Mullen and Marc Spitz's oral history of the Los Angeles punk scene during the late-1970s and early-'80s details its development before the predominance of **hardcore**. Assembled from interviews with most of the surviving key players and assorted hangers-on, *We Got the Neutron Bomb* describes how the L.A. scene began as an artistic movement fueled by revolutionaries and those dissatisfied with the vagaries of life, including bands as diverse as the **Weirdos** (whose classic song gave the book its title), the **Screamers**, **X**, the **Dils**, and the **Bags**. Also included is the rise and spectacular fall of the legendary **Germs** and the charismatic and twisted **Darby Crash**, as well as the increased marginalization of the original scenesters by the violence and machismo that permeated L.A. in the 1980s. Cowriter Mullen (whose account of the L.A. scene has been vociferously disputed by some) ran the legendary club the **Masque** and also wrote *Lexicon Devil: The Fast Times and Short Life of Darby Crash and the Germs*.

JOHN COOPER CLARKE

An English poet from Manchester who opened for many prominent punk acts (**Sex Pistols**, the **Fall**, **Joy Division**) and released several records of spoken-word social commentary, John Cooper Clarke battled a heroin addiction for several years, but eventually returned to touring and live performance. Cooper Clarke can be seen as more analogous to punk poets like **Jim Carroll**, as opposed to spoken-word artists like **Henry Rollins** and **Jello Biafra**. Also, Cooper Clarke's cadences, set to minimalist music, prove that he was several years ahead of his time and anticipated not only the modern spoken-word movement, but

BELOW LEFT: John Cooper Clarke in Nottingham, 1979.
RIGHT: Corrosion of Conformity, 1995.

also explored the dynamics of the human voice (similar to the manner in which performers like Björk have done) better than almost any other writer working during that time. Cooper Clarke appeared as a commentator in **Don Letts**'s 2005 documentary *Punk Attitude* and more recently made a cameo as himself in the 2007 Joy Division biopic *Control*.

Discography:
Disguise in Love (CBS, 1978); *Où est la Maison de Fromage s'il Vous Plait?* (Epic, 1978); *Walking Back to Happiness* (Epic, 1979); *Snap, Crackle & Bop* (Epic, 1980); *Me and My Big Mouth* (Epic, 1981); *Zip Style Method* (Epic, 1982)

CORROSION OF CONFORMITY

1982–present

LINEUP: Mike Dean (vocals/bass, replaced for several years by Phil Swisher, returned 1993); Woody Weatherman (guitar/vocals); Reed Mullin (drums, replaced by others, now Jason Patterson)

North Carolina's Corrosion of Conformity (often known as simply COC) helped pioneer the crossover between punk rock and heavy metal during the mid-1980s. Corrosion of Conformity's 1983 debut album, *Eye for an Eye*, was standard thrash,

but *Animosity* in 1985 helped pave the way for punk-metal hybrid, as done by punk bands such as **Suicidal Tendencies**, **D.R.I.**, and **T.S.O.L**. Corrosion of Conformity is noted for adding metal influences to punk's energy and speed, spearheading both the cross-genre sound and the introduction of many metal fans to punk rock and vice versa. They continued to make music well into the 1990s, even with numerous personnel changes. In the early 2000s, Corrosion of Conformity did not generate much output, but reemerged in 2005 and continue thrashing to this day.

Discography:
Eye for an Eye (Caroline, 1983, 1990); *Animosity* (Combat, 1985; Metal Blade, 1994); *Technocracy* (Combat, 1987; remastered, Sony, 1995); *Blind* (Combat, 1991; extra tracks and remastered, Sony 1995); *Vote with a Bullet* (Relativity, 1992); *Deliverance* (Sony, 1994); *Wiseblood* (Sony, 1996); *America's Volume Dealer* (Sanctuary, 2000); *Live Volume* (Sanctuary, 2001); *In the Arms of God* (Sanctuary, 2005)

WAYNE/JAYNE COUNTY

The campy, preoperative, budding transsexual Wayne/Jayne County was a major influence on the early days of punk and a key scenemaker at **Max's Kansas City** during its heyday. First as a DJ and later as the leader of Wayne County and the Electric Chairs, Wayne County—who was born Wayne Rogers in Dallas, Georgia, and grew up feeling like an outcast—pioneered a raunchy, glam-influenced version of punk that dealt with gender issues in songs such as "Man Enough to be a Woman" and "Wonder Woman." He gained notoriety performing at drag shows in Atlanta before moving to New York and joining the downtown theater and gay club scene, taking part in the Stonewall riots. After they met at Stonewall, County became roommates with **Leee Black Childers**, and with Andy Warhol associates Holly Woodlawn and Jackie Curtis, and soon was performing in the Warhol play *Pork* in England. There, County became a local celebrity and encountered **David Bowie**, who signed her to his MainMan management company. But Bowie never got around to producing a record for County's first band, Queen Elizabeth, which also featured Jerry Nolan, later of the **New York Dolls**.

After the breakup of Queen Elizabeth, Wayne continued deejaying at Max's (allegedly the first U.S. DJ to play the **Sex Pistols'** "Anarchy in the UK") and formed a second band, Wayne County and the Back Street Boys. Excited by the musical possibilities there, County relocated to England and solidified the band (now called the Electric Chairs) with guitarist Greg Van Cook, bassist Val Haller, and eventually J.J. Johnson on drums. While in England, the Back Street Boys appeared in the Derek Jarman film *Jubilee* and put out a single on Miles Copeland's Illegal Records label (which also released the first record by the Police; Miles being the brother of Police drummer Stewart Copeland) but did not find much success until 1978 when Safari Records put out the landmark punk single "Fuck Off" (featuring piano by Jools Holland from Squeeze). That song solidified County's reputation for provocation, which was furthered by the release of the band's first album, *The Electric Chairs*, which featured Henry Padovoni (formerly of the Police). After the record's release, Van Cook left and was replaced by former Back Street Boy Elliot Michaels for the second record, *Storm the Gates of Heaven*. By the time *Things Your Mother Never Told You* came out in 1979, Wayne had begun having surgeries in his quest to change his identity to Jayne County. At that point, the Electric Chairs and Jayne split amicably, and Jayne moved to Berlin.

County was also the focus of a famous incident at **CBGB** in March 1976. After being heckled by Handsome Dick Manitoba of the **Dictators**, County attacked him with a microphone stand, sending Manitoba to the hospital with a broken collarbone. The local scene divided over whom to support, with some punks siding with Manitoba and some playing a benefit show for County. County continued to record and tour, sometimes sharing a stage with Manitoba, old wounds seemingly forgotten. The legacy of Wayne/Jayne County can be seen in the gender-bending experiments of David Bowie and others of the glam movement, who, if not directly influenced by County, were certainly aware of her work before they began their own experimentations. County eventually became revered in the **queercore** movement, which later adopted him as a sort of elder statesman/woman who reveled in the role of gender provocateur.

Discography:
The Electric Chairs (Safari, 1978); *Storm the Gates of Heaven* (Safari, 1978); *Blatantly Offensive* (Safari, 1978); *Man Enough to be a Woman* (Safari, 1978); *Things Your Mother Never Told You* (Safari, 1979); *Rock 'n' Roll Resurrection* (live; Safari, 1980); *The Best of Jayne/Wayne County and the Electric Chairs* (Safari, 1981); *Private Oyster* (Revolver, 1986); *Amerikan Cleopatra* (Konnexion, 1987); *Betty Grable's Legs* EP (Jungle, 1989); *Goddess of Wet Dreams* (ESP, 1993); *Rock 'n' Roll Cleopatra* (RPM, 1993); *Let Your Backbone Slip* (RPM, 1995, 2000); *Deviation* (Royalty, 1996); *Wash Me in the Blood of Rock and Roll* (Fang, 2002); *So New York* (Ratcage, 2003); *At the Tracks!* (Munster, 2006)

Wayne County performing with the Electric Chairs in London, 1977.

The Cramps plot dark and unspeakable deeds, time and place unknown.

THE CRAMPS

1976–present

LINEUP: Erick Purkhiser, aka "Lux Interior" (vocals); Kristy Wallace, aka "Poison Ivy Rorschach" (guitar); Sean Yseult (bass); Nick Knox (drums, replaced by others, then Harry Drumdini)

Crossing punk with U.S. roots music, **rockabilly**, blues, and country, the Cramps formed a unique hybrid later adapted by numerous underground bands around the world, particularly in Europe and Japan. The nucleus of the **Cramps** came together in California in 1972 when Lux Interior picked up a hitchhiker who turned out to be Poison Ivy Rorschach. They briefly relocated to Akron, Ohio, before moving to New York and debuting at an audition night at **Max's Kansas City** in 1976. The Cramps released their first record in March 1978, a cover of "Surfing Bird" done in a manner best described as a campy cross between frenetic, raved-out rockabilly and 1960s psychedelic rock. This style, the Cramps' B-movie signature, would later serve as the impetus for the psychobilly subgenre (a term the band apparently coined). For many of their early albums (the first of which, 1980's *Songs the Lord Taught Us*, was recorded in Memphis with producer Alex Chilton), the band had no bass player. Throughout the band's thirty-odd-year lifespan, various second guitarists have come and gone, and after the 1983 departure of Kid Congo Powers (aka Brian Tristan, also of **Gun Club** and Nick Cave and the Bad Seeds), the Cramps largely stuck to bass players backing up Ivy on guitar. The nucleus has remained solid, though, with a continuous stream of new musicians supporting the ever-agile Interior and the ever-vamping Ivy. Although having received almost no mainstream recognition, the Cramps have nevertheless made their mark, their pulpy stamp able to be found in acts as diverse as the Reverend Horton Heat and White Zombie.

Discography:

Lucky 13 (Drug Fiend, 1978); *Gravest Hits* EP (Illegal/I.R.S., 1979); *Songs the Lord Taught Us* (Illegal/I.R.S., 1980; A&M, 1990); *Psychedelic Jungle* (I.R.S., 1981); *Voodoo Rhythm* (OK, 1983); *Off the Bone* (Illegal, 1983); *Smell of Female* (Ace Records, 1983, 1990; Restless, 1994; Vengeance, 2001); *Bad Music for Bad People* (I.R.S., 1984; A&M, 1990); *A Date with Elvis* (Big Beat, 1986; Enigma, 1990; Restless, 1994; Vengeance, 2001); *Rockin n Reelin in Auckland New Zealand* (live; Vengeance, 1987; Vengeance/Restless, 1994, 2001); *What's Inside a Ghoul* (Pow Wow, 1988); *Gravest Hits/Psychedelic Jungle* (IRS, 1989); *Stay Sick!* (Enigma, 1990; Dutch East Wax, 1991; Vengeance, 2001); *All Women are Bad* EP (Enigma, 1990); *Eyeball in my Martini* (Big Beat, 1991); *Look Mom, No Head!* (Restless, 1991, 1993); *Flame Job* (Medicine, 1994; Epitaph, 1994); *Big Beat from Badsville* (Epitaph, 1997); *Off the Bone* (Phantom, 1998); *Fiends of Dope Island* (Vengeance, 2003); *Off the Bone/Songs the Lord Taught Us* (Empire, 2003); *How to Make a Monster* (Vengeance, 2004)

DARBY CRASH

The infamous lead singer of Los Angeles trailblazers the **Germs**, Darby Crash (actual name Jan Paul Beahm) made his mark in early punk history due to his manipulative powers of persuasion, introspective lyrics, and oft-romanticized early death. Even before changing his name—first to Bobby Pyn and then to Darby—Crash had been a powerful and influential student at the experimental IPS program for gifted students at L.A.'s University High School in the 1970s. There, Crash learned techniques of brainwashing and manipulation from both the program's pseudo-Scientologist methods, and his own intensive reading of Nietzsche, Spengler, and Aleister Crowley. Crash and friend Georg Ruthenberg (aka Pat Smear) formed a quasi-cult of their own, and talked very early of his eventual suicide.

Crash later put his powers of manipulation to unholy use as the ringleader of the smashcircus better known as the Germs, which he and Smear formed in 1977. Known these days as one of the cornerstones of late-1970s L.A. punk, the Germs were also a great front for Crash's cult mania, which he called "Circle One," complete with neo-fascist insignias and armbands. The group had a simple initiation process: Crash or one of his female acolytes would grind a lit cigarette into a recruit's wrist, creating the circular "Germ Burn"—and a new Germs fan. Although it's difficult to tell from the band's often muffled recordings, the Germs were by all accounts a phenomenon on stage (at least early on), particularly due to Crash's hypnotic presence (best preserved in all its chaotic splendor in the film *The Decline of Western Civilization*).

Though severely hobbled by Crash's erratic, junkie lifestyle (by some accounts he had been doing speed as early as the

A purposefully bloodied Darby Crash showcases his dentition at L.A.'s The Masque, November 1977.

"I'm not going to save up for my old age because I'm not going to have an old age. If we run out of money, I can always kill myself."

—Darby Crash, *No Magazine*, 1979

seventh grade), the band burned bright and hot before Crash started casting about for something else to do. A brief sojourn in England was followed by a successful reunion show in December 1980, which should have augured a better time in Crash's life. However, by then Crash's mood had become even darker and his friendship with Casey Cola, local scene-maker and Crash's heroin enabler, was turning increasingly self-destructive. Four days after the reunion show, Darby Crash

and Casey Cola overdosed. Cola survived, but Crash died, though the news would be buried amid coverage of the murder of John Lennon. Of the several books on Crash's life and times, the biography *Lexicon Devil* by **Brendan Mullen**, Don Bolles, and Adam Parfrey stands apart. The legacy of Darby Crash's life is a tragically wasted talent cut short by drugs and mental illness, allowing him to live on in a sense as an American version of Sid Vicious, *sans* Nancy.

CRASS

1977–1984

LINEUP: Steve Ignorant (vocals);
Eve Libertine (vocals); Joy de Vivre
(vocals); Phil Free (guitar); Andy Palmer
(guitar); Pete Wright (bass); Penny Rimbaud
(drums); Gee (art/design); Mick (films)

The best-known and most politically active British punk band to espouse anarchy and the communal life along with the **DIY** aesthetic, Crass rejected the empty slogans of their late-1970s scenemates for an atonally discordant sound and a dedication to a

radically anticapitalist lifestyle. Led by drummer and songwriter Penny Rimbaud (born Jeremy John Ratter) and singer Steve Ignorant (born Oscar Thompson), the group began as a radical art collective in 1977, living together in a farmhouse that Rimbaud had established as a commune. The original band lasted for only a few performances before calling it quits.

The second version of Crass—named after the line from "Ziggy Stardust" where

Crass leads a polite discussion about capitalism, time and place unknown.

WELCOME HOME

David Bowie sang that "the kids was just Crass"—featured Rimbaud on drums, Pete Wright on bass, Andy Palmer (who apparently never learned a single chord but played by open-tuning and sliding his hand on the guitar neck) and Phil Free on guitars, and Steve Ignorant, Eve Libertine, and Joy de Vivre on vocals. In the spirit of the commune and the band's artistic philosophy, Crass also included Gee, responsible for their stark and oft-imitated album covers and posters, and Mick, who did the disturbing experimental films projected during the band's live performances. The band worked as a true collective, and each member had veto power over band decisions, guaranteeing that any band product, lyrics, or statements represented the entire band, not just a particular member. Accordingly, flyers were produced and handed out at every show to explain the band's philosophical approach and vegetarian beliefs. True to form, Crass's first gig was a benefit concert for a group of squatters held in a children's playground in London.

After gigging for a while, the band released its first record, *The Feeding of the 5000* (named for the 5,000 copies originally pressed), which was reissued when the initial pressing on the Small Wonder label sold out. (The first pressing was notable for the Irish pressing plant's refusal to duplicate the record unless the original opening track, "Asylum," an antireligious rant, was deleted. The original versions were released without the song, which was replaced by two minutes of silence called "Free Speech.") The second pressing, and all future Crass releases, were put out on their own **Crass Records** label, which eventually released numerous other records by like-minded bands such as the **Poison Girls**. Crass's next album, 1979's *Stations of the Crass*, celebrated the anticapitalism graffiti campaign on the London Underground pioneered by Rimbaud and Libertine. The third Crass record was a remarkable feminist statement called *Penis Envy*, on which all vocals were sung by the band's two female vocalists, Eve Libertine and Joy de Vivre. The album made waves particularly because of a prank the band played in conjunction with its release: Under the pseudonym Creative Recordings and Sound Services, Crass offered the schmaltzy track "Our Wedding" as a free flexi-disc to a British teen magazine called *Loving*, which, unaware of the band's views or reputation, accepted the flexi-disc and made it a part of their special bridal issue. Controversy erupted when it was discovered that the song was a parody.

Subsequent recordings such as *Christ—The Album* reiterated the band's philosophy, but when Great Britain declared war against Argentina over the Falkland Islands, Crass was reenergized and released an extremely polarizing attack on Prime Minister Margaret Thatcher; "How Does it Feel to be the Mother of 1,000 Dead?" led to much hand-wringing in the British media and in Parliament. In 1982, in response to government pressure and facing possible obscenity charges, Crass engaged in a program of civil disobedience, culminating in several "Stop the City" protests designed to grind London's business district to a halt. Thousands of protesters participated, which led to greater inspiration for worldwide days of civil disobedience.

Since Crass was more dedicated to getting out the members' anarchistic, antireligion, anticapitalist views than to making money as a band, they felt that groups like the **Clash** and the **Sex Pistols** had betrayed punk's original promise by signing to major labels. Putting Crass's beliefs front and center, former communard (of the commune, not the **new wave** band) Dave King designed the band's ambiguous logo, which combined elements of the swastika, the Christian cross, and two serpents' heads. That logo was later used by many anarchist punks as a symbol of rebellion against the dominant power structure, along with the anarchy *A* symbol, which the band also quickly adopted for their stage shows. Most of Crass's shows were benefits for various causes, including the Campaign for Nuclear Disarmament (CND) and squatters' rights. The band was also notorious for the so-called Thatchergate tapes, which were doctored by band member Pete Wright to mimic a phone call between Thatcher and U.S. President **Ronald Reagan** in which the Prime Minister indicated her responsibility for the sinking of a British warship. The prank led to a statement from the U.S. State Department denouncing the tape as a KGB forgery. A considerable media outcry ensued until the hoax was discovered by the British newspaper, *The Observer*.

Crass eventually succumbed to internal strife and an early promise to have a built-in expiration date of 1984, thanks to its Orwellian connotations (although constant police harassment certainly hastened their decision). The band broke up in 1984 after playing a final benefit performance for striking miners in southern Wales.

Crass is still regarded as one of the most important political punk bands and certainly one of the few that have kept rigorously close to their anarchistic DIY ideals. Various members went on to other projects, most notably Steve Ignorant, who worked with **Conflict**, and Penny Rimbaud, who wrote several books on his life and philosophy. Out of the entire, and generally endless, dispute over what constitutes punk rock, Crass made the most compelling argument that its benchmark does not have to be a simple loud-and-fast sound but rather a particular antiauthoritarian attitude, authenticity, and system of ethics. A really cool name does not hurt, either. Although the band's legacy lives on, some just do not seem to "get" the band; witness multimillionaire soccer superstar David Beckham photographed in 2005 talking to Elton John while wearing a Crass T-shirt. All in all, considering their nonstop political agitation and their raging antiestablishment music, Crass made bands like the Sex Pistols look and sound like the Bay City Rollers.

Discography:

Reality Asylum 7" (Crass, 1978); *The Feeding of the 5000* (Small Wonder, 1978; second pressing, Crass, 1980, 1995); *Stations of the Crass* (Crass, 1979, 1995); *Penis Envy* (Crass, 1981, 1995); *Christ—The Album* (Crass, 1982, 1995); *Yes Sir, I Will* (Crass, 1983, 1995); *10 Notes on a Summer's Day* (Crass, 1986, 1998); *Best Before 1984* (Crass, 1995); *Christ: The Bootleg* (live; Allied, 1996; No Idea, 1999); *You'll Ruin it for Everyone* (Import, 2001). **Penny Rimbaud & Eve Libertine:** *Acts of Love* (Crass, 1985)

finest, particularly when they played at San Quentin Penitentiary in full cop gear. Crime's best-known song was their first, the classic rocker "Hotwire My Heart," later covered by **Sonic Youth**. The best compilation of Crime's recordings was released in 2004 as *San Francisco's Still Doomed*.

Discography:

All the Stuff, Vols. I–III (unknown label, 1990s); *San Francisco's Doomed* (Solar Lodge, 1992); *Terminal Boredom* (Out of Darkness, 1992); *Hate Us or Love Us, We Don't Give a Fuck* (live; Planet Pimp/Repent, 1994); *San Francisco's First and Only Rock 'n' Roll Band* (Criminal, 1999); *Piss on Your Turntable* (Lady Butcher, 2001); *Cadillac Faggot* (live; Red Legacy, 2003); *San Francisco's Still Doomed* (Swami, 2004)

CRO-MAGS

1982–1993, 2000

LINEUP: John Joseph McGeown (vocals); Kelvin "Parris" Mitchell Mayhew (guitar); Doug Holland (guitar); Harley Flanagan (bass/vocals); Mackie Jayson (drums)

One of the hardest and heaviest bands in New York **hardcore**, the Cro-Mags were led by Harley Flanagan (of the **Stimulators**) and influenced heavily by **Bad Brains** (with whom drummer Mackie Jayson would later play). Among the most impressive live bands of the mid-1980s hardcore matinee scene at **CBGB**, the Cro-Mags were renowned for shows that often turned into violent contests where audience members fought gladiator-style with each other and sometimes with the band members themselves. Also politically outspoken, the band sang about Krishna Consciousness (courtesy of lead singer John Joseph) alongside brutal

CRASS RECORDS

LOCATION: LONDON

Independent label Crass Records was formed by anarchist collective and band **Crass** to promote their own music and that of similar bands who also wished to work outside of the capitalist music industry. Bands on Crass Records at one point or another included **Poison Girls**, Donna and the Kebobs, **Zounds**, Snipers, Dirt, **Rudimentary Peni**, **Conflict**, **Flux of Pink Indians**, and like-minded U.S. band **MDC**. The motivating theory behind Crass Records was not to make money, but to change the nature of the music industry and to support other bands through the lucrative (by punk standards) sales of Crass albums. After the band Crass broke up, the label was mostly dormant, although a cassette recording by Crass drummer Penny Rimbaud came out in the 1990s.

CRIME

1976–1980, 1986, 2004

LINEUP: Johnny Strike (guitar/vocals); Frankie Fix (guitar and vocals); Ron "the Ripper" Greco (bass); Chris Cat (drums, replaced by Ricky Tractor, Brittely Black, Hank Rank)

San Francisco's Crime had a surprisingly traditional rock background and regarded itself as "San Francisco's first and only rock 'n' roll band." One of the few strictly **DIY** American bands, they released mostly singles on their own label, Crime Music. Notorious for performing in police uniforms, they incurred the enmity of the Bay Area's

The Cro-Mags' Harley Flanagan lets the spit fly, 1989.

riffs that attracted both hardcore punks and metalheads to the scene. John Joseph left the band after the first record, and Harley took over on lead vocals for the next two albums. Although the Cro-Mags disbanded acrimoniously, and John Joseph later served time in a naval brig for desertion, the band continued to reunite sporadically. Conflicts between Harley and other members of the band make a full reunion unlikely, particularly with Harley and John Joseph trading off vocals on some records.

There may have been many other violent New York hardcore bands, but the Cro-Mags, justifiably or not, took the blame for much of the mayhem that dogged the scene; in any case, John Joseph's turn to spirituality in the 1980s located the band in the same Krishna-core axis as **Youth of Today** and **Shelter**.

Discography:
The Age of Quarrel (Rock Hotel/Profile, 1986, 1994); *Best Wishes* (Profile, 1989); *Alpha-Omega* (Century Media, 1992); *Near Death Experience* (Century Media, 1993); *Age of Quarrel/Best Wishes* (Another Planet, 1994); *Hard Times in an Age of Quarrel* (live; Century Media, 1994; Import, 2000); *Before the Quarrel* (Cro Mag, 2000); *Revenge* (Cro Mag, 2000). **Harley Flanagan:** *Harley's War-Cro-Mag* (Loudfast, 2003)

CRUCIAL YOUTH

1986-1990
LINEUP: Joe Crucial (vocals); Ollie Grind (guitar); Maynard Krebs (guitar); Melvin Berkley (bass); Gentleman Jim (drums)

Goofy punk band Crucial Youth satirized the **straight-edge** movement by taking it to its extreme and ridiculing the healthy pretensions of many of the most orthodox in the **hardcore** scene. The band was formed primarily as a response to bands like **Youth of Today**, **Bold**, and the New York vegan/straight-edge alliance, where extremist younger kids would knock bottles of beer (or even iced tea, as caffeine was considered a drug) out of concertgoers' hands. A great band, but who knows if they were satirizing themselves as well as the scene, and ultimately, who cares? Needless to say the same bands who preached unity on stage *hated* Crucial Youth.

Discography:
Straight and Loud (Faith, 1987); *A Gig Too Far* (live; B-core, 1991); *Posi Machine* (New Red Archives, 1995); *Singles Going Straight* (New Red Archives, 2001)

CRUCIFUCKS

1982-1995, 1998
LINEUP: Doc Corbin Dart (vocals); Gus Varner (guitar); Marc Hauser (bass); Steve Shelley (drums)

The cheerfully provocative Crucifucks of Lansing, Michigan, made a habit of being offensive whenever possible through the use of blasphemous images and lyrics which, although getting a bit trite in punk circles, were nonetheless always effective in provoking the attention of some local minister or politician. An example of this was the album cover for the record *Our Will Be Done*, which featured a dead police officer and resulted in a lawsuit from the Philadelphia Fraternal Order of Police in 1992. The Crucifucks broke up in the mid-1990s but re-formed—with Dart, Dave Breher on bass, Nat Warren on guitar, and Steve Merchant on drums (original drummer Steve Shelley having long been in **Sonic Youth** by that point)—to play the **Alternative Tentacles** 20th anniversary party in 1998. Dart has since played around with various other bands and numerous solo shows.

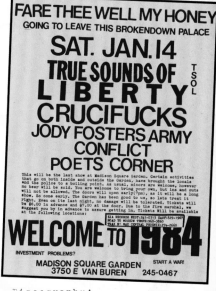

Discography:
The Crucifucks (Alternative Tentacles, 1985); *Wisconsin* (Alternative Tentacles, 1987); *Our Will Be Done* (Alternative Tentacles, 1992); *L.D. Eye* (Alternative Tentacles, 1996). **Doc Corbin Dart:** *Patricia* (Alternative Tentacles, 1990)

CRUST PUNK

A term used to denote a particularly abrasive offshoot of anarcho-punk, crust punk adherents are generally known as *crusties* or *gutter punks*. Their beliefs center around such core topics as animal rights, veganism, and the complete abolition of capitalism. Key principles and elements of their politics and lifestyle—living communally, often in squats if not on the streets, listening to and producing ear-bleedingly loud, metallic, and furiously antiestablishment music—can be traced back to key British bands like **Crass** and **Conflict**. The look trends toward a mix of classic 1977-style brightly-colored mohawks or dreadlocks with a plethora of metal-spiked leather (except for the vegans) and a determined absence of personal hygiene. Some key crust bands include Amebix, Deviated Instinct, and **Nausea**, with one of the more important labels/collectives being Minneapolis' **Profane Existence**. Penelope Spheeris' 1998 documentary, *The Decline of Western Civilization, Part III*, followed the lives of a number of Los Angeles crusties and examined their worldview, which is often extremely nihilistic, even for punks.

Crusties in a scene from *The Decline of Western Civilization, Part III.*

DAG NASTY

1985-1988, occasionally thereafter

LINEUP: Dave Smalley (vocals, replaced briefly by Pete Cortner); Brian Baker (guitar); Roger Marbury (bass, replaced by Doug Carrion); Colin Sears (drums, replaced by Scott Garrett)

The melodic Washington, D.C., punk band Dag Nasty was started by Brian Baker, fresh from the demise of **Minor Threat**, after he was inspired by the crop of new bands who sprung up in the mid-1980s. The band originally featured vocalist Shawn Brown, who was replaced by Dave Smalley from **DYS** for their first album, 1986's *Can I Say*. Smalley left after *Can I Say* to accept a graduate studies scholarship at New York University that allowed him to

live in Israel for a year. He was replaced by Pete Cortner for the *Wig Out at Denko's* and *Field Day* albums, which saw the band become more commercial in sound, even recruiting ex-**Descendents** bass player Doug Carrion for his pedigree in pop hooks. After losing their original rhythm section, Dag Nasty split in 1988, and Baker resurfaced (somewhat bizarrely) in the glam-metal band Junkyard with Chris Gates of the **Big Boys**. After the demise of Junkyard, Baker joined **Bad Religion** after Mr. Brett left. Dag Nasty reunited with singer Smalley and the original rhythm section for several reunions over the next two decades and toured sporadically. Smalley sang in the post-Descendents band **All** and formed his own band, **Down by Law**. Although they're credited with being one of the first bands (along with **Rites of Spring**) to pioneer the emotional brand of pop-punk later called **emo**, in reality Dag Nasty had little or nothing in common with modern, ultra-radio-friendly and supposedly "emo" bands like Jimmy Eat World or Dashboard Confessional. While Dag Nasty's music was certainly emotional (the key component in emo), it also served as a midpoint between the hard and fast sound of Minor Threat, and the pop hooks of Southern California bands like the Descendents and Bad Religion. One trivia note: On the 1992 *Four on the Floor* album Baker was unable to contractually appear under his name and instead chose the name Dale Nixon, the pseudonym **Greg Ginn** used when he played bass on the **Black Flag** album *My War*, making Dale Nixon the Alan Smithee of punk.

Discography:
Can I Say (Dischord, 1986; remastered, 2002); *Wig Out at Denko's* (Dischord, 1987; remastered, 2002); *Field Day* (Giant, 1988; Positive, 1995); *Trouble Is...* (Giant, 1988); *85–86* (Selfless, 1991); *Four on the Floor* (Epitaph, 1992); *Can I Say/Wig Out at Denko's* (Dischord, 1995); *Minority of One* (Revelation, 2002). **Junkyard:** *Junkyard* (Geffen, 1989); *Sixes, Sevens & Nines* (Geffen, 1991)

At Berkeley's Gilman Street, the music of Dag Nasty teaches one lucky fan how to fly, 1987.

The Damned lurk outside London's St. Stephen's Church, 1977. (L to R) Captain Sensible, Rat Scabies, Dave Vanian, Brian James.

THE DAMNED

1975-1977, 1978-present

ORIGINAL LINEUP: Dave Vanian (vocals);
Brian James (guitar); Ray Burns, aka
"Captain Sensible" (bass); Chris Millar,
aka "Rat Scabies" (drums)

A prime component of the first wave of English punk and holders of a number of "first" distinctions—first punk band to release a single (their debut "New Rose," the B-side was a cover of the Beatles' "Help", in October 1976 on **Stiff Records**), first British punks to play in the United States (at **CBGB** in April 1977)—the Damned are also quite simply one of the most groundbreaking and resilient bands of any genre. Formed in 1975 by Brian James (who wrote all of the band's original material), along with drummer Rat Scabies (Chris Millar), bassist Captain Sensible (Ray Burns), and singer Dave Vanian (a former grave digger who slicked his hair back and dressed entirely in black, inadvertently creating the look and sensibility of the goth movement), the Damned quickly became one of the most important bands on the punk scene. They were also notable for being on, and getting kicked off of, one of the most famous punk package tours, the legendary "Anarchy Tour" of December 1976.

After the success of their first album, *Damned, Damned, Damned*, the band released a follow-up, *Music for Pleasure*, in November 1977 with second guitarist Lu (Robert Edmunds, now in the **Mekons**). The Damned demonstrated their extreme volatility quite early on by breaking up shortly thereafter for the first of many times. After a few months (of boredom, presumably), the Captain, Rat, and Dave Vanian started playing gigs as the three-piece outfit the Doomed. The Damned properly reunited in December 1978 with Captain Sensible not just replacing Brian James on guitar but also assuming most of the writing duties. They went through a number of bass players in rapid succession, including Henry Badowski and Lemmy Kilmeister from **Motörhead**, before settling on Alistair "Algy" Ward.

With a stable lineup in place, the Damned then produced their most popular album, 1979's *Machine Gun Etiquette*. The album established a new and experimental

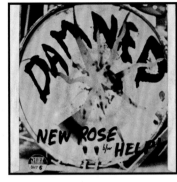

direction for the Damned, and also featured the UK hits "Love Song" and "Smash it Up," parts one and two (part one was an instrumental written by Captain Sensible for the late Marc Bolan of T-Rex, who had championed the Damned by having them open for him on his last tour). Around that time, the extremely prolific Captain Sensible began working on a solo project and had the first of several UK hits with a cover of the show tune "Happy Talk" from the musical *South Pacific* in 1982. Tensions over Captain Sensible's solo success led to his departure from the band in the early-1980s. During the mid-1980s, the Damned shifted in a more gothic direction with the release of the album *Phantasmagoria*. Even without the help of the departed Captain Sensible, they were able to rack up hits on both sides of the Atlantic with "The Shadow of Love." The original Damned reunited in the late-1980s for a tour, but that lineup did not last because of mounting tensions between Scabies and James. Eventually, the Captain agreed to rejoin only if Scabies was asked to leave. James left as well and the band was forced to regroup yet again.

The most current lineup of the band is Vanian, Captain Sensible, and Patricia Morrison (formerly of the **Bags** and goths extraordinaire the Sisters of Mercy), who is also Vanian's wife and the mother of their child. Other new members include Pinch on drums and Monty Oxymoron on keyboards. Rat Scabies coauthored the book *Rat Scabies and the Holy Grail*, a fanciful (but supposedly completely true) version of his quest to find the Holy Grail. James has since played in a reconstituted Lords of the New Church.

Discography:

Damned, Damned, Damned (Stiff, 1977; Demon, 1986; Frontier, 1989); *Music for Pleasure* (Stiff, 1977; Demon, 1986); *Machine Gun Etiquette* (Chiswick, 1979; Big Beat, 1982; Emergo, 1991); *The Black Album* (IRS, 1980); *Friday the 13th EP* (NEMS, 1981); *The Best of the Damned* (Big Beat, 1981; Emergo, 1991); *Strawberries* (Bronze, 1982; Dojo, 1986); *Live at Shepperton 1980* (Big Beat, 1982); *Live in Newcastle* (Damned, 1983); *Damned EP* (Stiff, 1985); *Damned but not Forgotten* (Dojo, 1985); *Phantasmagoria* (MCA, 1985); *Is it a Dream? EP* (MCA, 1985); *Damned Damned Damned/Music for Pleasure* (Stiff, 1986); *The Captain's Birthday Party* (Stiff, 1986); *The Peel Sessions EP* (Strange Fruit, 1986); *Not the Captain's Birthday Party?* (Demon, 1986); *Anything* (MCA, 1986); *The Peel Sessions EP* (Strange Fruit, 1987); *Mindless, Directionless, Energy: Live at the Lyceum 1981* (ID/Revolver, 1987); *The Light at the End of the Tunnel* (MCA, 1987); *The Long Lost Weekend: Best of Volume 1 1/2* (Big Beat, 1988); *Final Damnation* (Restless, 1989); *The Peel Sessions Album* (Strange Fruit, 1990; Strange Fruit/Dutch East India, 1991); *EP* (Deltic, 1990); *Live at the 100 Club* (No Label, 2007).

DANGERHOUSE RECORDS

LOCATION: LOS ANGELES

A bare-bones record label started by Dan Brown, Pat Garrett, and Black Randy to give voice to the artistic and political ambitions of L.A.'s punk bands, Dangerhouse Records released compilations and singles featuring many in the early punk scene during the late-1970s and early-'80s. Some of those who released singles on Dangerhouse included the **Weirdos**, **X**, the Dils, the Alley Cats, the **Avengers**, and the **Bags** as well as lesser-known groups such as the Randoms (led by Pat Garrett, best known for their controversial "Let's Get Rid of NY"), **Black Randy and the Metrosquad**, the Deadbeats, the Eyes, and Rhino 39. Dangerhouse released most of its music between 1977 and 1979 in true **DIY** style, with clear plastic sleeves.

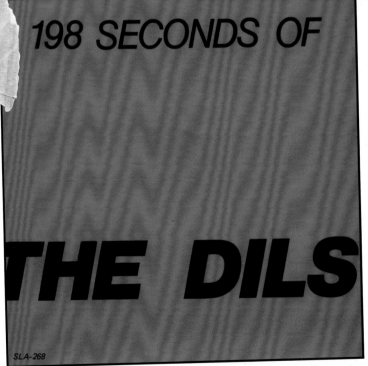

SLA-268

The Dead Boys at CBGB, 1976.

THE DEAD BOYS

1975-1979, 1980s (sporadically), 2005

LINEUP: Stiv (Steve) Bators (vocals); Gene O'Conner, aka "Cheetah Chrome" (guitar); William Wilden, aka "Jimmy Zero" (guitar); Jeff Magnum (bass); John Madansky, aka "Johnny Blitz" (drums)

One of the several bands to grow out of the ashes of classic, early Cleveland proto-punk outfits **Rocket from the Tombs** and **Frankenstein**, the Dead Boys were cornerstones of the first wave of American punk rock, producing one of its landmark singles ("Sonic Reducer") and blazing a path of outrageousness worthy of their English counterparts.

Frankenstein had been playing around Cleveland without much success during the mid-1970s when they met the **Ramones**, who were in town for a show. **Joey Ramone** was instrumental in getting the band a Monday-night audition at **CBGB**, after which things moved with uncommon speed. Following their second gig, CBGB owner **Hilly Kristal** signed on as the band's manager, and within a few weeks they changed their name to the Dead Boys, signed to the Sire label, and were recording their first album, *Young Loud and Snotty*. The Dead Boys sounded a lot like a sped-up version of the 1960s garage rockers that Bators so loved, along with a dollop of Ramones-style guitar (they initially had no bass player, relying on Chrome's and Zero's twin guitars to fill in their sound). They soon gained a following for their onstage antics, which included Nazi paraphernalia, lead singer Stiv Bators hanging himself with a belt, and occasional onstage fellatio from a helpful CBGB waitress. After the first album was released (on which Bob Clearmountain played bass), the band added bassist Jeff Magnum and recorded their second album with Felix Pappalardi (who had produced Cream's *Disraeli Gears* and seemed a poor match for the snotty Cleveland punks). The album is poorly recorded at best, with the guitars mixed way down and the vocals sounding like they were recorded in a garbage can. It captured none of the live Dead Boys sound, and failed to make an impact on the U.S. charts.

Things took a turn for the worse in 1978 when Johnny Blitz got into a fight (alongside **Blondie** roadie Michael Sticca) that resulted in him getting stabbed with his own knife. Afterward, the band organized a series of benefit concerts at CBGB highlighted by appearances from members of Blondie and the Ramones, as well as drag performer Divine and even John Belushi, who briefly played drums with the Dead Boys. The benefits got Blitz back on his feet but the Dead Boys appeared to have crested. The band began to argue more after this, while Sire owner Seymour Stein decided that punk was dead and that the Dead Boys should change their name, look, and image. (By this point, Stein had also sent letters to radio stations asking them to refer to the music coming out of New York as **"new wave"** as opposed to "punk"; he largely attributed the unpleasant connotations and disappointing sales of punk music to the infamy of the **Sex Pistols**.) Between the lack of faith from their label, lackluster sales, and an ugly 1979 incident in which Chrome had a drug-fueled nervous breakdown and had to be dragged away by the NYPD (Chrome later credited Hilly Kristal for getting him into rehab), the Dead Boys finally called it quits in 1979.

Bators recorded a solo album and several singles for Greg Shaw's Bomb label and later formed the Lords of the New Church—a sort of goth-punk supergroup with **Sham 69** bassist Dave Tregunna and the **Damned** guitarist Brian James—who released a few moderately well-received albums throughout the early-1980s. Although Bators's **Iggy Pop**-style onstage self-destruction was a large part of the band's live appeal, the Lords eventually put an ad in the papers looking for a new lead singer, leading to Bators's departure from the group in 1988. While in Paris after the demise of the Lords of the New Church, Bators also attempted to form a group with **Dee Dee Ramone** and **Johnny Thunders**, but tensions split them apart before they could record. Bators was hit by an automobile and died of internal injuries on June 4, 1990. The surviving Dead Boys reunited for a concert to save CBGB in August 2005. Chrome continues to tour on his own and also reunited with Dave Thomas for a Rocket From the Tombs reunion tour.

Discography:

Young Loud and Snotty (Sire, 1977, 1992); *We Have Come for Your Children* (Sire, 1978; Wea International, 2001); *Night of the Living Dead Boys* (live; Bomp!, 1981, 1998); *The Return of the Living Dead Boys* (Revenge, 1987); *Liver Than You'll Ever Be* (live; Pilot, 1988, 2002); *Younger, Louder and Snottier (The Rough Mixes)* (Necrophilia, 1989; Bomp!, 1997); *Twistin' on the Devil's Fork: Live at CBGB* (Bacchus, 1997); *Down in Flames* (Bomp!, 1998); *Magnificent Chaos* (Bomp!, 1998); *All This & More* (Bomp!, 1998); *3rd Generation Nation* (Msi, 1999)

DEAD KENNEDYS

1978-1986

LINEUP: Jello Biafra (vocals, replaced by Brandon Cruz, Jeff Penalty); East Bay Ray (guitar); Klaus Flouride (bass); Ted (drums, replaced by D.H. Peligro)

Although plenty of American punk bands embraced strident political stances, they rarely ran afoul of the authorities in the manner of some of their arguably more activist British brethren; San Francisco's **Dead Kennedys** are one of the biggest exceptions to that rule. Featuring a hard-driving **hardcore** sound and the satirical, biting lyrics of yelping lead singer **Jello Biafra** (aka Eric Boucher), they were one of the few major bands on this side of the pond (particularly on the West Coast) that kept so rigorously to **Crass**-style **DIY** credibility. The Dead Kennedys made it a point to play all-ages shows—the better to inculcate young fans into the mysteries of hardcore and activism—and in order to ensure control of their artistic vision, Biafra formed the **Alternative Tentacles** label with Bill Gilliam to release their albums.

The Dead Kennedys quickly gained popularity and notoriety with their name alone, which in the early years sometimes compelled them to perform under assumed monikers. Their style was pretty well established in the early, take-no-prisoners singles "Holiday in Cambodia" (which struck those who didn't bother to listen carefully as making light of Cambodia's killing fields) and "California, Uber Alles" (an attack on then-governor and liberal sacred cow Jerry Brown). Both singles came out in 1979, the same year that Biafra ran for mayor of San Francisco, and placed a respectable fourth out of 10 candidates. Their classic first album, *Fresh Fruit for Rotting Vegetables*, was released by the **new wave** label IRS in 1980; it was the band's only non-Alternative Tentacles release. Aside from making several musically adventurous albums that helped set the parameters for hardcore punk (as well as

producing one of the greatest punk singles of all time, 1981's self-explanatory "Nazi Punks Fuck Off"), the Dead Kennedys also stirred up their own share of controversy, ultimately due less to Biafra's bridge-burning brand of satire than a "naughty" picture.

The insert poster for the band's 1985 album *Frankenchrist* featured drawings of penises by artist H.R. Giger (who conceptualized the alien in the *Alien* films). This resulted in both the band and their label being charged the following year with distribution of harmful matter to minors, apparently after a 13-year-old girl in Los Angeles bought the record for her little brother. Although the trial ultimately resulted in a hung jury, the whole furor led to the album being banned from many stores nationwide. Biafra was also transformed into one of the more coherent public agitators against Tipper Gore's music censorship movement, the Parents Music Resource Council (PMRC), along with fellow free-speech crusaders Frank Zappa and "Little Steven" Van Zandt.

In 1986, the Dead Kennedys retired after releasing *Bedtime for Democracy*. The other members of the band later reunited without Biafra after wresting control of the Dead Kennedys' catalog on Alternative Tentacles from him in a lawsuit over unpaid royalties. The band continued to tour the United States with new lead singer and former child actor Brandon Cruz, formerly of **Dr. Know**, followed by Jeff Penalty, and after his early-2008 departure, by Skip from the Wynona Riders. Jello Biafra continued his spoken-word performances and kept recording, both on his own and collaborating with bands such as **D.O.A.**

Discography:
Fresh Fruit for Rotting Vegetables (IRS, 1980; Alternative Tentacles, 1993; with extra tracks, Cherry Red, 1999; Manifesto/Cleopatra, 2002); *In God We Trust, Inc.* EP (Alternative Tentacles/Faulty Products, 1981; Manifesto, 2001); *Plastic Surgery Disasters/In God We Trust, Inc.* (Alternative Tentacles, 1982; Manifesto, 2001); *Frankenchrist* (Alternative Tentacles, 1985; Manifesto, 2001); *Bedtime for Democracy* (Alternative Tentacles, 1986; Manifesto, 2001); *Give Me Convenience or Give Me Death* (Alternative Tentacles, 1987, 1990; Manifesto, 2001); *Mutiny on the Bay* (live; Manifesto, 2001); *Live at the Deaf Club 1979* (Manifesto, 2004). **Klaus Flouride:** *Cha Cha Cha with Mr. Flouride* (Alternative Tentacles, 1985); *Because I Say So* (Alternative Tentacles, 1988); *The Light Is Flickering* (Alternative Tentacles, 1991)

The Dead Kennedys, 1984:
(L to R) Jello Biafra, D.H. Peligro, East Bay Ray, Klaus Flouride.

DEAD MILKMEN

1983-1995

LINEUP: Rodney Linderman, aka "Rodney Anonymous" (vocals); Joe Jack Talcum (guitar and occasionally lead vocals); Dave Schultise, aka "Dave Blood" (bass); Dean Sabatino, aka "Dean Clean" (drums)

The Philadelphia wisenheimers in the Dead Milkmen were a snarky reaction to the violence in the **hardcore** scene during the early- to mid-1980s. They utilized messy pop hooks (highlighted by Joe Jack Talcum's jangly guitar) and a sense of humor that veered wildly from the keenly observed to the embarrassingly adolescent. Songs parodied everything from Charles Nelson Reilly to goth wannabes to the punk rock scene itself. The Dead Milkmen toured constantly, playing with a laundry list of bands that included everyone from like-minded absurdists the **Butthole Surfers** and Mojo Nixon to the **Minutemen**, the **Vandals**, and 2 Live Crew. 1988's *Beelzebubba* was probably the artistic and commercial highlight, but things started to go downhill the more Talcum shared vocal duties with Rodney Anonymous (who performed under a variety of different last names, including Mellencamp). After a string of underperforming and poorly received albums, the Dead Milkmen broke up in 1995. Thereafter, several of the members formed various side projects. Tragically, bassist Dave Blood committed suicide in 2004.

As an interesting side note, former Detroit Tigers infielder Jim Walewander was ostracized by fans and team management when he outed himself as a Dead Milkmen fan and the local media portrayed him, essentially, as a crazed lunatic for liking punk rock.

Discography:
Big Lizard in my Back Yard (Fever/Enigma, 1985); *Eat Your Paisley!* (Fever/Restless, 1986); *Bucky Fellini* (Fever/Enigma, 1987); *Beelzebubba* (Fever/Enigma, 1988); *Metaphysical Graffiti* (Enigma, 1990); *Soul Rotation* (Hollywood, 1992); *Not Richard, but Dick* (Hollywood, 1993); *Chaos Rules: Live at the Trocadero* (Restless, 1994); *Stoney's Extra Stout (Pig)* (Restless, 1995)

DEEP WOUND

1982-1984

LINEUP: Charlie Nakajima (vocals); Lou Barlow (guitar); Scott Helland (bass); J. Mascis (drums)

Who would have thought that noisemeister supreme J. Mascis and "wearing-my-heart-on-my-sleeve-is-my-life!" Lou Barlow of legendary indie band Dinosaur were once members of a sloppy, but almost brilliant, early-**hardcore** band? As Deep Wound, Barlow played superfast guitar licks while his high school buddy Mascis blasted the drums with a ferocity he would later transfer to his squalling guitar. After Deep Wound's brief and mostly unremarkable tenure, Barlow and Mascis formed the much more successful band Dinosaur (only the oldtimers remember them before they added the "Jr."). In 2004 a crowd in Northhampton, Massachusetts, was treated to a one-off Deep Wound reunion, though there is no word yet as to whether their dozens of fans have clamored for a full tour.

Discography:
Deep Wound (Damaged Goods, 2005)

THE DESCENDENTS

1978-1982, 1985-1987, 1996-1998, 2004

LINEUP: Milo Aukerman (vocals); Frank Navetta (guitar, replaced by Ray Cooper, Stephen Egerton); Tony Lombardo (bass, replaced by Doug Carrion, Karl Alvarez); Bill Stevenson (drums)

Almost every modern-day **pop-punk** band owes the Descendents a debt, or at the very least, an acknowledgment of stolen sounds. Founded in California by Bill Stevenson as a three-piece with bassist Tony Lombardo and guitarist Frank Navetta, the Descendents released the *Ride the Wild* EP before later wisely adding the scientifically-minded Milo Aukerman on vocals, whose bespectacled visage inspired the band's crude but evocative logo. Stevenson and Aukerman were the mainstays of the band, who went through numerous personnel changes before finally solidifying in the late-1980s with Stephen Egerton on guitar and Karl Alvarez on bass.

A typical Descendents song was a glorification of coffee, girls, being a geek, or a combination of all of the above. (A key part of the band's mythology was their love of caffeine, as epitomized by their legendary pick-me-up, the "Bonus Cup," which featured one-third cup of instant coffee and five spoonfuls of sugar.) The Descendents quickly picked up a strong following, largely thanks to their talent for writing very loud and very poppy **hardcore** songs, Aukerman's personable, dweeby singing (not exactly par for the course in hardcore at the time), and Stevenson's inventive drumming. They went through several lengthy hiatuses, the first when Milo Aukerman left for college in 1982 (to

The Dead Milkmen: (L to R) Dean Clean, Dave Blood, Joe Jack Talcum, Rodney P. Anonymous.

The Descendents insist on rocking hard at all times, even when playing Sun Valley, Idaho, in 1985.

ishing his Ph.D. in biochemistry. Rather than continue the Descendents without Aukerman, Stevenson then formed the similarly spastic **All** with Alvarez, Egerton, and singer Dave Smalley from **Dag Nasty**. Aukerman returned to the new Descendents lineup to record a couple of albums for Epitaph, 1996's *Everything Sucks* and 2004's *Cool to Be You*, which continued in the vein of earlier records but showed increasing subtlety in the Descendents' songwriting, although coffee, food, and girls continued to be their obsessions. Probably the most imitated band in the punk world, the Descendents deserve royalties from any lesser band who copies their formula or drinks too much coffee. You know who you are.

Discography:
Fat EP (New Alliance, 1981; SST, 1988); *Milo Goes to College* (New Alliance, 1982; SST, 1988, 1991); *Bonus Fat* (New Alliance, 1985; SST, 1988, 1991); *I Don't Want to Grow Up* (New Alliance, 1985; SST, 1988, 1990); *Enjoy!* (New Alliance/Restless, 1986, 1991); *All* (SST, 1987, 1990); *Liveage!* (SST, 1987, 1990); *Two Things at Once (Milo Goes to College/Bonus Fat)* (SST, 1988, 1991); *Hellraker* (live; SST, 1989, 1990); *Somery* (SST, 1991); *Everything Sucks* (Epitaph, 1996); *Live Plus One* (Epitaph, 2001); *Cool to Be You* (Fat Wreck Chords, 2004)

pursue a career as a scientist, as immortalized in the classic album *Milo Goes to College*). During the down time, Stevenson played on several **Black Flag** records and toured with the band for several years, leaving acrimoniously in 1985 to re-form the Descendents (minus Navetta, who had moved to Oregon and was replaced by Ray Cooper) for the *I Don't Want to Grow Up* album, which continued the melodic trend of its predecessor. The Descendents continued in the same vein with 1986's *Enjoy!* (which contained the title song, an ode to the joys of releasing gas, captured in full stereo glory) with new bassist Doug Carrion, and then again the following year with te experimental and almost jazzlike *All* record, featuring new guitarist Stephen Egerton and bassist Karl Alvarez. *All* contained the brief title song and an almost as short "No! All!," which introduced the philosophy of *all* (a rather positive-sounding theory that seems to boil down to getting the most out of life, as revealed to Stevenson and friend Pat McCuistion by the "Basemaster General" himself) to the public.

After *All*, in 1987, Aukerman left the band again to concentrate on fin-

THE DEVIL DOGS

1989-1994

LINEUP: Andy Gortler (vocals/guitar); Steve Baise (vocals/bass); Paul Corio (drums, then others)

Obviously influenced by the **Ramones** and the **Dictators** (both of whose music the band covered on their first album), the Devil Dogs played a scuzzy, extremely New York–centric brand of old-school punk rock led by guitarist and singer Andy Gortler, bassist and singer Steve Baise, and a rotating cast of drummers. While they never made a major label album and only left behind a few recordings, many of the later New York scuzpunk bands have the Devil Dogs to thank for keeping things going during a time when lame metal bands from New Jersey dominated the city scene. The Devil Dogs broke up in 1994, after which Baise formed the more melodic Vikings.

Discography:
Devil Dogs (Crypt, 1989); *Big Beef Bonanza* (Crypt, 1990); *The Devil Dogs Live in Tokyo* EP (1+2, 1991); *We Three Kings* (Crypt, 1991); *30 Sizzling Slabs* (Crypt, 1992); *Saturday Night Fever* (Crypt, 1993); *Stereodrive!* (1+2, 1994); *Laid Back Motherfuckers* EP (Headache, 1994). **With the Raunch Hands**: *Sink or Swim* (GaGa Goodies, 1990)

"**Are we not men? We are DEVO.**"

Devo at New York's
Palladium, 1979.

DEVO

1975-present

LINEUP: Mark Mothersbaugh (vocals/guitar/keyboards); Gerald Casale (vocals/bass/synths); Robert Mothersbaugh (guitar); Robert Casale, aka "Bob 2" (guitar); Jim Mothersbaugh (percussion, replaced by Alan Myers, Josh Freese)

Cryptic, hit-making, bizarrely costumed, anarchist spuds from Akron, Ohio, Devo critiqued consumer culture and somehow made a lengthy career out of it. While their techno chops, matching uniforms, and hummable hits like "Whip It" would appear to mark them as little more than inordinately dolled-up new wavers, their caustic social critiques and barely concealed contempt for the mainstream were strictly out of the art-punk playbook. (There are even some anecdotal claims that "Devo" was an unofficial drive-by insult hurled at punks in Los Angeles during the 1980s.)

Devo gelled into their most serious form around 1975 and released several singles on their own Booji Boy label in 1977. The strength of those singles (as well as some championing from proto-punk talent scout **David Bowie**) led to their signing with Warner Bros. in 1978. Their first full-length album, *Q: Are We Not Men? A: We Are Devo*, came out that same year. With Brian Eno producing, the LP vividly showcased Devo's wry commentary on consumer culture. The second album demonstrated more of the band's philosophy, but since there weren't as many chart-ready singles, Devo seemed to be just as unmarketable as Warner Bros. had feared. However, since the band had long been early pioneers of the short-form video, that ability, combined with their pop hooks, gave Devo a major hit in 1980 with the song and video for the inordinately catchy "Whip It," off the self-produced *Freedom of Choice* album (which also showcased some of the band's best material, such as "Girl U Want" and "Gates of Steel"). On some **MTV** or VH1 offshoot somewhere, "Whip It" is probably still playing at any hour of the day or night.

The following records showed less astute social commentary—"Beautiful World" aside—and moved in a more dance-oriented direction. After 1984's *Shout*, the band took a prolonged hiatus to regroup and figure out what Devo stood for in the postmodern world they had been predicting for years, and what it meant to be one of the most commercially successful bands to come out of the punk underground's arthouse wing. In the interim, Mark Mothersbaugh had a lucrative career scoring TV shows such as *Rugrats* and films like *The Royal Tennenbaums*. Devo reunited occasionally after the 1990s, toured to numerous fans who had not been born when the band first released material, and once again spread the cryptic message of devolution.

In 2006, the band launched (with Disney's help) a new offshoot called Devo 2.0, which consisted of a children's version of Devo sung by kids and made to be radio-friendly; presumably and hopefully, irony is the point.

Discography:

Q: Are We Not Men? A: We Are Devo (Warner Bros., 1978); *Be Stiff* EP (Stiff, 1978); *Duty Now for the Future* (Warner Bros., 1979); *Freedom of Choice* (Warner Bros., 1980); *Dev-o Live* EP (Warner Bros., 1981); *New Traditionalists* (Warner Bros., 1981); *Oh No! It's Devo* (Warner Bros., 1982); *Shout* (Warner Bros., 1984); *E-Z Listening Disc* (Rykodisc, 1987); *Total Devo* (Enigma, 1988); *Now It Can Be Told* (Enigma, 1989); *Smooth Noodle Maps* (Enigma, 1990; Dutch East Wax, 1991); *Hardcore Vol. 1, 74–77* (Rykodisc, 1990); *Devo Greatest Hits* (Warner Bros., 1990); *Devo Greatest Misses* (Warner Bros., 1990). **Mark Mothersbaugh:** *Muzik for Insomniaks Volume 1* (Enigma, 1988); *Muzik for Insomniaks Volume 2* (Enigma, 1988)

D GENERATION

1991-1999

CLASSIC LINEUP: Jesse Malin (vocals); Danny Sage (guitar); Todd Youth (guitar); Howie Pyro (bass); Michael Wildwood (drums)

Led by longtime scene members Jesse Malin (formerly of seminal early **hardcore** band Heart Attack) and bassist Howie Pyro of the Blessed, D Generation presented an earnest distillation of New York punk and rock. Bassist Howie Pyro had been an early part of the New York scene along with Malin, and Pyro had been present at a dinner party with Sid Vicious the night before he overdosed. D Generation was signed to a major label but later got dropped when it turned out that punk was not the next big thing after all (another example of a band signed during the post-**Green Day** feeding frenzy when major labels had no idea how to market the music to a mass audience, and little patience to learn how). The band is fondly remembered from the 1990s New York scene, and Jesse Malin still performs as both a solo act and with alt-country rocker Ryan Adams.

Discography:

D Generation (Chrysalis, 1994); *No Lunch* (Columbia, 1996)

D.I.

1982-1990, 1991-1995, 1999-present

LINEUP: Casey Royer (vocals, replaced by Rikk Agnew, others, now Chickn); Alfie Agnew (guitar, replaced by others, now Clinton); John "Bosco" Calabro (bass, replaced by others, now Eddie Tater); John Knight (drums, replaced by others, now Joey Tater)

One of the many great pop-punk bands from Southern California (is there something in the smoggy air?), D.I. (Drug Ideology) had among its ranks members of a number of Los Angeles-area **hardcore** bands, particularly the **Adolescents**. The classic lineup included singer Casey Royer, who had been an excellent and respected drummer (and as it turned out an amazingly poppy vocalist as well), in addition to guitarist brothers Rikk and Alfie Agnew, all from the Adolescents. Tracks such as "Richard Hung Himself" and the (presumably) ironic ode to weapons, "Guns," are just two of the many classics that made the band so memorable, in their L.A. hardcore-meets-the-**Descendents** way. D.I. made a strong impression early in their career in a memorable concert scene from the 1984 film *Suburbia*. A version of D.I. reunited for the benefits to save **CBGB** in August 2005 and released a new album to critical acclaim in 2007.

Discography:

Ancient Artifacts (Reject, 1987); *Horse Bites Dog Cries* (Reject, 1987); *Team Goon* (Reject, 1987); *What Good is Grief to a God?* (Triple X, 1988); *Tragedy Again* (Triple X, 1989); *Live at the Dive* (Triple X, 1993); *State of Shock* (Doctor Dream, 1994); *Caseyology* (Cleopatra, 2002); *On the Western Front* (Suburban Noize, 2007)

THE DICKIES

1977-present

LINEUP: Leonard Graves Phillips
(vocals/mellotron); Stan Lee (guitar);
Billy Club (bass, replaced by many others);
Karlos Kabellero (drums, many others);
Chuck Wagon (keyboards, until 1981)

A goofier Los Angeles version of the early
Ramones, the Dickies' tongue was always
stuck firmly in cheek on songs such as "You
Drive Me Ape (You Big Gorilla)" and "If
Stewart Could Talk" (an ode to the perceived
wisdom of lead singer Phillips's penis; in
concert Leonard Graves Phillips would don
a large penis puppet and channel Stewart).
Although the Dickies were among L.A.'s
longer-lasting punk bands, they were also
regarded as more of a parody of the genre's
conventions than actual punks themselves
(see their recording of the title track to the
1988 film *Killer Klowns from Outer Space*).
Although heroin abuse limited their success,
the Dickies were still one of the best-known
U.S. punk bands from the early years,
famous not just for being the first L.A.
band to be signed by a major label but also
for successfully integrating humor into
what could be a bleak scene. They still tour,
with a changing lineup that always includes
stalwarts Phillips and Stan Lee.

Discography:

Incredible Shrinking Dickies (A&M, 1979); *Dawn of
the Dickies* (A&M, 1979); *Stukas over Disneyland* (PVC,
1983); *We Aren't the World* (ROIR, 1986); *Killer Klowns
from Outer Space* EP (Enigma, 1988); *Great Dictations*
(A&M, 1989); *Second Coming* (Enigma, 1989); *Live in
London—Locked and Loaded* (Taang!, 1991); *Idjit Savant*
(Triple X, 1995)

The Dickies, 1979.

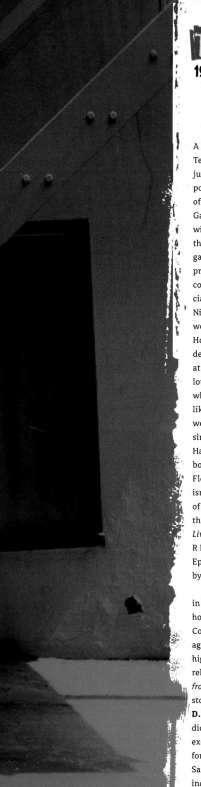

THE DICKS

1980-1986

LINEUP: Gary Floyd (vocals), Glen Taylor (guitar/bass, replaced by Tim Carroll); Buxf Parrot (bass, replaced by Sebastian Fuschs); Pat Deason (drums, replaced by Lynn Perko)

A **hardcore** band raging out of Austin, Texas, the Dicks were instrumental not just in developing the genre's sound and political stance, but also in having one of the few openly gay front men in punk, Gary Floyd. (Interestingly, the two bands with whom the Dicks were most associated, the **Big Boys** and **MDC**, also had openly gay singers.) Floyd was an arresting stage presence, sometimes dressed in elaborate costumes and always provocative, especially during their epic song "Saturday Night at the Bookstore" where Floyd would declare his love for "the Glory Hole" and call out audience members, declaring that they too had been cruising at the bookstore. The Dicks played the fast loud stuff, but could also slow it down when called for (such as when Floyd felt like berating the audience). The Dicks were responsible for one of the great singles of early hardcore, 1980's "Dicks Hate the Police," which ably demonstrated both the band's disdain for authority and Floyd's commitment to smashing capitalism. That same year also saw the release of their first album, the classic live LP they split with the Big Boys, *Recorded Live at Raul's Club*, put out by MDC's R Radical label (their song "Wheelchair Epidemic" was later famously covered by the Jesus Lizard).

The Dicks relocated to San Francisco in late-1982 to find a more hospitable home base for their furiously pro-Commie, pro-gay, **Ronald Reagan**-hating agenda. Although 1983 should have been a high point for the Dicks—what with the release of their first proper album, *Kill from the Heart*, and a slot on the barnstorming Rock Against Reagan tour with **D.R.I.** and MDC—the rest of the band didn't gel in their new surroundings and, except for Floyd, they all soon decamped for Texas. Floyd reformed the band in San Francisco and the new lineup (which included drummer and pianist Lynn Perko, who cofounded the alternative

band Imperial Teen in the mid-1990s) recorded the band's last album, 1985's *These People*. After the Dicks split for good in 1986, Floyd formed the rock group Sister Double Happiness, allowing him to pursue the more blues-influenced musical agenda that had started to alienate some of the Dicks' core punk constituency near the end. He also continued to record under his own name and later played with Black Kali Ma. A version of the Dicks reunited for a few shows in Austin in 2004.

Discography:

Kill from the Heart (SST, 1983); *These People* (Alternative Tentacles, 1985); *Dicks: 1980–1986* (Alternative Tentacles, 1997). **Dicks/Big Boys:** *Recorded Live at Raul's Club* (Rat Race, 1980). **Sister Double Happiness:** *Sister Double Happiness* (SST, 1988); *Heart and Mind* (Reprise, 1991); *Uncut* (Dutch East India Trading, 1992); *Horsey Water* (Sub Pop/EFA, 1994); *A Stone's Throw from Happiness: Live & Acoustic at the Great American Music Hall 6/17/92* (Innerstate, 1999). **Gary Floyd Band:** *Broken Angels* (Glitterhouse, 1995). **Gary Floyd:** *Back Door Preacher Man* (Innerstate, 1999). **El Destroyo:** *The Latest Drag* (Innerstate, 1999). **Black Kali Ma:** *You Ride the Pony (I'll Be the Bunny)* (Alternative Tentacles, 2000). **Imperial Teen:** *Seasick* (Slash/London, 1996); *What is Not to Love* (Slash/London, 1999); *On* (Merge, 2002); *Live at Maxwell's* (DCN, 2002)

THE DICTATORS

1973-1979, 1983, 2000-present

LINEUP: Handsome Dick Manitoba (vocals); Adny (Andy) Shernoff (bass/vocals/keyboards); Ross "the Boss" Friedman (guitar); Scott "Top Ten" Kempner (guitar); Mark Mendoza (bass, replaced by Shernoff; Stu Boy King (drums, replaced by Rich Teeter, Frank Funaro, J.P. Patterson)

One of the key early-New York bands who filled in the gaps between the garage rock of the 1960s, Iggy and the **Stooges**, and early- to-mid-1970s punk, the Bronx-based Dictators started out as a straightforward melodic group led by bassist and multi-instrumentalist Adny (Andy) Shernoff. Later, "secret weapon" Handsome Dick Manitoba (who had previously sung the encores, usually "Wild Thing" by the Troggs) took center stage and became the de facto lead vocalist. In contrast to most 1970s punk bands, the Dictators blended superfast rock covers with originals that were a mix of beautiful ballads, or songs about cars and girls that were as gleefully

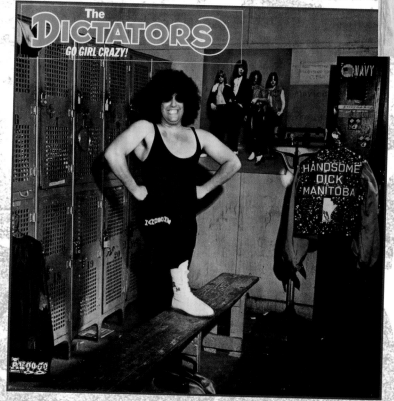

The Dictators find that silly wigs enhance their rocking abilities at the Whisky A Go Go, 1977.

D-U-M-B as anything put out by the **Ramones** (clearly influenced by the Dictators' love of the **MC5** and 1960s girl groups). Their first album, *The Dictators Go Girl Crazy!* from 1975, was not only out well before most of the early punks released anything on vinyl, but also helped inspire **John Holmstrom** and **Legs McNeil** to found *Punk* magazine—in part to meet and hang out with the Dictators.

The Dictators courted controversy in the mid-1970s when Handsome Dick Manitoba was hit on the shoulder with a microphone stand by **Wayne/Jayne County** after Manitoba had heckled her during the concert (see County's entry for the aftermath). The band bounced back from ignominy, however, signing to Elektra Records and putting out several more albums before finally calling it quits. Various members formed bands like the uber-metal Manowar, the Del-Lords, and Handsome Dick's Wild Kingdom; bassist Mark "The Animal" Mendoza even played for a while in Twisted Sister. The Dictators re-formed in the 1990s, releasing several compelling comeback records and touring sporadically. Manitoba opened a bar called Manitoba's on Avenue B in Manhattan, while Shernoff became a respected wine connoisseur. While the Ramones justly deserve the credit for starting the style and sound that defined punk, without the Dictators, there simply would have been no template, and no truly great New York band for everyone else to copy.

Discography:

The Dictators Go Girl Crazy! (Epic, 1975; Sony, 1990); *Manifest Destiny* (Asylum, 1977; Wounded Bird, 2004); *Bloodbrothers* (Asylum, 1978; Dictators Multi/Media, 1998, 2002); *Fuck 'Em if They Can't Take a Joke* (tape; ROIR, 1981, 1995; Danceteria, 1991); *The Dictators Live: New York New York* (ROIR, 1998); *D.F.F.D.* (Dictators Multi/Media, 2001); *Viva Dictators* (live; Escapi Music/New Media Studio, 2005). **Manitoba's Wild Kingdom:** *And You?* (Popular Metaphysics/MCA, 1990)

DIE TOTEN HOSEN

1982-present

LINEUP: Campino (vocals); Breiti (guitar); Kuddel (guitar); Andi (bass); Wölli (drums)

Hailing from Düsseldorf, Die Toten Hosen (the name translates alternately as "the Dead Trousers" or "the Dead Boring") put out a fairly substantial body of work in their native Germany but are best known in America for the 1992 album *Learning English, Lesson One*, which teamed the band with a variety of classic punk vocalists such as **Joey Ramone**, **Johnny Thunders**, and even **Ronnie Biggs**, the Great Train Robber himself. While Die Toten Hosen never had much of a profile in the States, they are still notable for their considerable influence in the UK and Europe, their work as punk archivists (they recorded the last session on which Thunders ever played), as well as their help in reviving public interest in the British class of 1977. Die Toten Hosen are also an example of how punk very quickly mutated from its U.S. and UK roots to spread across the world.

Select Discography:
Learning English, Lesson One (Charisma, 1992); *Love, Peace and Money* (Atlantic, 1995)

THE DILS

1976-1980

LINEUP: Chip Kinman (vocals/guitar); Tony Kinman (vocals/bass); Pat Garrett (drums)

One of the most political, exciting, and yet obscure bands of the original mid-to-late-1970s Los Angeles punk scene, the Dils were led by harmonizing (and Maoist) brothers Chip Kinman on guitar and vocals and Tony Kinman on vocals and bass. They made a brief appearance in a concert scene filmed for Cheech and Chong's *Up in Smoke* in 1978, released a mere three singles (including the much-covered "Class War"), and then broke up in 1980. The Kinman brothers later formed the much less political band Rank and File in the 1980s with Alejandro Escovedo from the **Nuns**. When Rank and File did not achieve the commercial success that the Kinmans and the record company had expected (though the group was later credited with sparking the alt-country movement), the brothers then put together the more experimental BlackBird, and have also performed as a country group, Cowboy Nation.

Discography:
Live! (Iloki-Triple X, 1987); *The Dils* (Lost, 1990). **Rank and File:** *Sundown* (Slash/Warner Bros., 1982); *Long Gone Dead* (Slash/Warner Bros., 1984); *Rank and File* (Rhino, 1987)

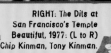

RIGHT: The Dils at San Francisco's Temple Beautiful, 1977: (L to R) Chip Kinman, Tony Kinman.

DIM STARS

1991–1992

LINEUP: Richard Hell (vocals/bass); Robert Quine (guitar); Thurston Moore (guitar); Don Fleming (guitar); Steve Shelley (drums)

A New York punk supergroup comprising **Richard Hell**, **Sonic Youth** members Thurston Moore and Steve Shelley, and producer Don Fleming from Gumball, the Dim Stars released one album (which featured **Voidoids** guitarist Robert Quine on five tracks) and a few singles that demonstrated their improvisational, almost atonal style that combined classic punk with Sonic Youth-level noise stylings. They played a few shows together in the early-1990s, and by all accounts, demonstrated that Hell's more complex version of the Voidoids could have been an ongoing enterprise had Hell decided to keep it going. Dim Stars called it quits in the early-1990s, after which Hell resumed his career writing and performing prose and poetry, while everybody else went back to their day jobs.

Discography:
Dim Stars EP (Ecstatic Peace, 1991); Dim Stars (Caroline, 1992).

The Dim Stars think about what could have been.

DISCHARGE

1977–1987, 1991–1993, 2001–present

LINEUP: Terry "Tezz" Roberts (vocals, replaced by Kelvin "Cal" Morris); Tony "Bones" Roberts (guitar, replaced by Peter Pyrtle, Les Hunt, Stephen Brooks); Roy "Rainy" Wainwright (bass); Tony "Akko" Atkinson (drums, replaced by Mickey Gibson, others)

A great wall of sound broke over the audience, leaving some deaf, some maimed, and the whole crowd clamoring for more—that was the almighty burst of power and speed that was Discharge in their prime. Discharge started in 1977 as a British **hardcore** band often associated with **crust punk**

HEAR NOTHING SEE NOTHING SAY NOTHING

and the anarchist movement. Their longevity is almost as impressive as the depths of their musical rage and perpetual lineup changes. Discharge was among the many punk bands that flirted with heavy metal and influenced the genre crossover of the 1980s; a fact to which Metallica nicely paid tribute by covering two Discharge songs on their *Garage, Inc.* album. However, the crossover they spearheaded, while popularizing their brand of punk, also alienated the band's fan base (on "The More I See" and beyond it almost seems as though Cal is trying to inspire Axl Rose) who just wanted more of the classic Discharge, or "D-Core," sound that had influenced so many other punk bands such as **Broken Bones**, as well as metal bands Anthrax and Slayer. In 2001 Discharge returned to form with their self-titled album. Sadly, though, Cal has vanished and subsequent tours saw Discharge touring with new singer Rat, from equally indelible British hardcore band the **Varukers**.

Discography:
Realities of War EP (Clay, 1980); Fight Back EP (Clay, 1981); Decontrol EP (Clay, 1981); Why (Clay, 1981; Castle, 2003); Hear Nothing, See Nothing, Say Nothing (Clay, 1982; Castle, 2003); Never Again (Clay, 1984; Castle, 2003); Grave New World (Profile, 1986);

Massacre Divine (Clay, 1991, 1995); Shooting Up the World (Clay, 1991, 1995); Live at City Gardens, NJ (Clay, 1995); Clay Punk Singles Collection (Clay, 1995); Live Nightmare Continues (Clay, 1996); Protest & Survive 1980–1984 (Clay, 1996); Vision of War (Recall, 1998); Hardcore Hits (Cleopatra, 1999); Discharge (Sanctuary, 2002); Decontrol: The Singles (Castle, 2002); Society's Victims (boxed set; Castle, 2004); Anthology Free Speech (Castle, 2004); Born Immortal (Rebellion, 2005).

DISCHORD RECORDS

LOCATION: WASHINGTON, D.C.

One of the most influential independent labels in the United States, if not the world, Dischord has stayed true to its mission since being founded in 1980. The label releases only bands from the D.C. area and sells records for much less (including postage-paid) than any other label, major or independent. Major bands on the label over the years have included **Minor Threat**, **SOA**, **Rites of Spring**, **Fugazi**, **Jawbox**, **Beefeater**, **Shudder to Think**, **Dag Nasty**, **Embrace**, the **Faith**, Fidelity Jones, **Government Issue**, the **Nation of Ulysses**, and Q and Not U, to mention but a few.

Dischord was established when **Ian MacKaye**'s original band, the **Teen Idles**, had money left over upon breaking up, and decided to put out a record with the funds. After releasing the Teen Idles' *Minor Disturbance* EP in 1980, MacKaye was inspired by independent record labels, such as Los Angeles's **Dangerhouse Records**, and the vitality of the local scene, which included new bands such as SOA featuring Henry Garfield (later **Henry Rollins**), John Stabb's Government Issue, Ian's brother's band the Untouchables (not to be confused with the later **ska** punk band), as well as D.C.'s **Youth Brigade**, started by Nathan Strejcek, the former lead singer of the Teen Idles. The new label then released records by SOA, Minor Threat, Youth Brigade, and Government Issue.

By the end of 1981, Dischord expanded into a larger operation and moved into the Dischord House in Arlington, Virginia, (whereupon original third founder Nathan Strejcek ceased to be involved in the label). In 1982, Dischord released the classic *Flex Your Head* compilation of 32 songs by a variety of D.C. bands. Records by Void, **Marginal Man**, and Minor Threat followed, but the label almost went under due to a precarious cash flow. This problem was solved through a partnership with John Loder of London's Southern Studios (which had released records by the like-minded band **Crass**), who helped arrange European distribution.

By the mid-1980s, Dischord had become busier, putting out new records by Gray Matter and Ignition. The interesting thing about the Dischord "sound" was that there was no Dischord sound. Although many of the label's early bands pioneered both **hardcore** and **emo**, just as many went in divergent directions, incorporating folk music, free jazz, and other genres into the mix, only sharing a common geographical location and a commitment to **DIY**. Dischord worked closely with the political activists in **Positive Force** D.C. to stage benefit concerts, protests (especially during **Revolution Summer**), and the compilation album *The State of the Union*, which benefited Positive Force. During the late-1980s, the company grew larger and formed Dischord Direct to help in the distribution process.

The 1990s saw a sea change in the popularity of punk and indie rock bands,

and the label had numerous buyout offers during the resultant major-label feeding frenzy, but these were rejected out of hand. Jawbox and Shudder to Think did sign to major labels, but they were never as successful or popular as when they were on Dischord, and both bands broke up not long after leaving. Fugazi, who had quickly become Dischord's flagship band, continued to be a major seller and substantial concert draw.

Because Dischord sees itself not as a record company but as a way to document the music being made by a relatively small geographic community (not every band on the label can even be categorized musically as punk), it is not beholden to standard industry practices and still operates only on handshake deals to release and distribute records. The label is a business, however, and maintains a small and devoted staff who earn a living wage and who receive health benefits, far from the norm of most independent labels. Dischord continues to serve today as an actual viable alternative to the mainstream; that rare true example of the undiluted and uncompromising DIY spirit that epitomizes punk rock.

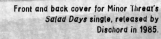

Front and back cover for Minor Threat's *Salad Days* single, released by Dischord in 1985.

DIY

Short for "do it yourself," this aesthetic has long been a key component of the loose aggregation of ideas and ideologies that passes for a coherent philosophy of punk. One example of the DIY movement includes the numerous independent record labels established to bypass the corporate control of the record industry, such as **SST**, **Epitaph**, and **Fat Wreck Chords**. When recording, if a band did have to sign with a major label, the philosophy was extended to control over the selection of producer, songs, and single releases. (A song that epitomizes the difficulties in reconciling the DIY philosophy with corporate culture is the **Clash** song "Complete Control," detailing their frustration at the label's insistence on releasing "Remote Control" as a single from their first album.)

DIY also applies to fashion, such as how a band's members clothe and adorn themselves outside of mainstream fashion outlets. The early punk looks of ripped or altered clothes, such as the homemade "I Hate Pink Floyd" T-shirt worn by Johnny Rotten (**John Lydon**), and the safety pins and ripped clothing worn by the **Electric Eels**, the **Weirdos**, and **Richard Hell** are also key examples of this trend. (Of course, as some early punks have noted when mocking the trend-conscious appearance of latter-day followers, they were using safety pins to keep their clothes together simply because they couldn't *afford* to buy new ones.) The use of alternative or homemade media such as zines is also a key component in DIY. There have been literally thousands of zines produced in the punk community, some of which had little to do with music but covered everything from sports to animal rights to feminism. Although they've declined in popularity in recent years due to the easy availability of online media, print zines—often self-produced and printed on copiers, distributed at shows, sold at independent record stores, or given out for free on the street—were a way to bypass the monolithic media outlets that many punks feel stifle creativity.

Flyers are also a key part of the DIY aesthetic, and because most punk shows cannot rely on traditional means of advertising (due to police regulations, lack of money, or simply because the show is in someone's basement or in a VFW hall), they are either posted on telephone poles or given out at shows.

Although there is no one complete and easy definition of the DIY aesthetic, and many punks disagree among themselves as to what truly constitutes a true DIY initiative, the ethos can be summarized as one of independence from corporate control and emphasis on individual creativity and self-expression. Today, the Internet and cheap computer graphics programs have further led to the expansion of the DIY aesthetic online, where the prohibitive costs of music distribution, pressing, and printing can be largely avoided (although this also disenfranchises anyone without access to computers, which can be a problem in a **squat**). Punk's DIY spirit remains today a crucial part of the movement's drive to wrest control of culture and its production from mainstream society.

(L to R) The Weirdos' Dave Trout, Cliff Roman, and John Denney display their handmade couture at a *Slash* magazine benefit in July 1977.

ANTHOLOGIES

In the 1980s, those prehistoric days before digital file-sharing and the Internet, getting a song on one of the many cassette and LP anthologies that were circulated in the scene was an excellent way for young punk bands who hadn't yet released a record to get exposure to a broader audience than their local clubs afforded. Although a number of these anthologies were stand-alone, many (such as *Blasting Concept* or *Punk and Disorderly*) were released as multi-volume series, acting as a sort of musical periodical for underground music.

PUNK AND DISORDERLY VOLUMES I–III (1982–1983)

This popular Brit-centric series of albums from the early-1980s collected bands such as **Vice Squad**, **Peter and the Test Tube Babies**, the **Exploited**, the Expelled, Abrasive Wheels, the **Partisans**, UK Decay, the **Adicts**, and the **Dead Kennedys**. The compilations were so definitive of the punk scene (with the defiantly mohawked punks on the album covers) that they were even referenced in a song by **NOFX** that celebrates a scenester so punk that he "should have been on the cover of *Punk and Disorderly*."

BLASTING CONCEPT VOLUMES I & II (1983, 1985)

In the old tradition of major labels, who occasionally liked to package their artists together on one album, SST used that concept for this two-volume collection of house bands. Volume I had a strong set of multiple tracks from the **Minutemen**, **Black Flag**, and the **Meat Puppets**, as well as songs from **Hüsker Dü** and Saccharine Trust. Volume II was a decidedly mixed bag, with more songs from the usual suspects, but also too many from the label's lesser talents, including Overkill and Würm, who have since been lost to history.

FLEX YOUR HEAD (1982)

One of the earliest releases from **Dischord Records** was this influential 32-song compilation of early Washington, D.C., **hardcore** bands that serves as a fine historical document for what was happening musically in that scene at that time. Bands with multiple tracks on the album include the **Teen Idles**, **Youth Brigade** (D.C.), **Government Issue**, and the **Untouchables**. The album's title was a clever play on the phrase *flexing your muscles*, in this case, flexing one's mind.

NO NEW YORK (1978)

New York's late-1970s **no wave** movement was given a boost by this helpful anthology, released on Island Records offshoot Antilles and overseen by adventurous producer, former Roxy Music icon Brian Eno. Among the essential no wave artists included are James Chance and the Contortions, DNA (featuring a young Arto Lindsay), Teenage Jesus and the Jerks (featuring a young **Lydia Lunch**), and Mars. An important compilation,

No New York ably documented the reaction to the perceived stagnancy of New York punk, and it inspired a short-lived revolt against musical boundaries that would heavily influence later bands like **Sonic Youth**, of whom Thurston Moore and Lee Ranaldo were already veterans of the scene.

THIS IS BOSTON, NOT L.A. (1982)

In case you hadn't noticed, Boston punks, particularly from the early-1980s, tend to have a chip on their shoulder. Nowhere is their defiant parochialism more evident than within the title of this anthology, which played off the (perceived) overabundance of press about the Los Angeles scene, to the detriment of stories about punks elsewhere in the country, whose scenes were apparently just as lively and engaging as those in bigger cities, thank you very much. The popular Modern Method Records release features the cream of Boston **hardcore**, with songs from **Jerry's Kids**, **Gang Green**, the **F.U.'s**, the **Freeze**, and the Proletariats. The album's title was paid tribute to (and simultaneously parodied) in the late-1990s by the *This is Springfield, Not Shelbyville* anthology that collected punk bands performing tributes to or covers of songs from *The Simpsons* television show.

NOT SO QUIET ON THE WESTERN FRONT (1982)

The first anthology to document the then-burgeoning Bay Area and Northern California scenes, *Not So Quiet on the Western Front* was originally put out by *Maximum RocknRoll* (whose first issue accompanied it), and was later rereleased by punk powerhouse label **Alternative Tentacles**. With 47 bands packed into a mere 74 minutes, the anthology included numerous bands who would become quite well known (**7 Seconds**, **Dead Kennedys**, MDC, and **Flipper**) and many who would never be heard from again (Intensified Chaos). As an attempt to provide listeners of the *Maximum RocknRoll* radio show and a broader audience with an overview of what many of the new and cutting-edge bands sounded like, *Not So Quiet on the Western Front* was more than successful.

NEW YORK CITY HARDCORE—THE WAY IT IS (1988)

Although **Revelation Records** didn't put out this fast and furious 18-song compilation until 1988, well after the heyday of New York **hardcore**, it remains an excellent snapshot of some of the best bands from the scene at that time, such as **Youth of Today**, **Gorilla Biscuits**, **Sick of It All**, and **Nausea**.

D.O.A.'s David Gregg goes airborne while drummer Chuck Biscuits relies on gravity, Los Angeles, 1982.

D.O.A.
1977–present

CLASSIC LINEUP: Joey "Shithead" Keithley, sometimes spelled Keighley (vocals/guitar); Dave Gregg (guitar); Randy Rampage (bass); Chuck Biscuits (drums)

The closest thing that Canada ever had to the **Ramones**, British Columbia's own D.O.A. has been through more lineup changes than most people have hot meals. But after some three decades of nonstop touring and churning out records for limited financial reward, the band has developed an international reputation as the living embodiment of politically aware **hardcore**; their slogan "Talk-Action=0" says it all.

D.O.A. first formed in 1977 as the Skulls and consisted of Joey "Shithead" Keithley, Ken "Dimwit" Montgomery, Gerry "Useless" Hannah, and Brad "Kunt" Kent. After replacing Hannah and Kent with Brian Goble and Simon Werner, the Skulls toured Canada and moved briefly to London to search for success in the British punk scene; instead they moved back to Canada and broke up. Hannah, Mike Graham, Ken Montgomery, and Wimpy put together the rival band **Subhumans**, while Shithead formed D.O.A. with bassist Randy Rampage, drummer Chuck "Biscuits" Montgomery (Ken Montgomery's younger brother), and Brad Kent, and later added second guitarist Dave Gregg. Shithead, along with manager and political activist Ken Lester, wrote numerous songs that openly challenged the political system. D.O.A. cursed out **Ronald Reagan** in many songs ("fucked up Ronnie") and made their disdain for American and Canadian culture (except for hockey and beer) well known. The band toured extensively and released one of the earliest hardcore records, *Hardcore 81*, in 1981 (it may also have been one of the first uses of the term *hardcore* to describe a specific musical style). They received more recognition with the **Alternative Tentacles** release *War on 45* in 1982. (Rock critic Robert Christgau put it nicely: "Hearty, no-bullshit songs for Canadian hardcore to march by.") Although D.O.A. put out many worthwhile records afterwards, *War on 45* is the one with which newbie punk fans should start.

The next two decades saw relentless touring and numerous personnel changes, as well as collaborations with **Jello Biafra** and others. Tragedy struck in 1995 when long-time drummer Ken Jensen was killed in a house fire—the band responded with an album, *The Black Spot*, dedicated to his memory. Keithley, who also operates the Sudden Death label, ran for parliament as a Green Party candidate in the 2001 British Columbia election and received an impressive number of votes. He also released an autobiography *I, Shithead: A Life in Punk*, which detailed the problems inherent in living (and touring) the punk life for 30 years. In 2003, in honor of the band's 25th anniversary, the mayor of Vancouver declared December 21 as "D.O.A. Day"; as it should be.

Discography:

Disco Sucks EP (Sudden Death, 1978; Quintessence, 1978); *Triumph of the Ignoroids* EP (Friend's, 1979); *Something Better Change* (Friend's, 1980; Sudden Death, 2000); *Hardcore 81* (Friend's, 1981; Sudden Death, 2002); *War on 45* (Alternative Tentacles, 1982); *Bloodied but Unbowed* (Alternative Tentacles, 1984; Restless, 1992); *Don't Turn Yer Back (on Desperate Times)* EP (Alternative Tentacles, 1985); *Let's Wreck the Party* (Alternative Tentacles, 1985); *The Dawning of a New Error* (Virus, 1985; Alternative Tentacles, 1992); *True (North) Strong & Free* (Rock Hotel/Profile, 1987, 1990); *Ready to Explode* (Profile, 1987); *Ancient Beauty* (Philo, 1988); *Ornament of Hope* (Philo, 1988); *Talk Minus Action Equals Zero* (Restless, 1988, 1990, 1993); *Murder* (Restless, 1990, 1993); *Last Scream of the Missing Neighbors* (Alternative Tentacles, 1990); *Greatest Shits* (QQRYQ, 1991); *13 Flavours of Doom* (Alternative Tentacles, 1992); *It's Not Unusual... but it Sure is Ugly!* EP (Alternative Tentacles, 1993); *Loggerheads* (Alternative Tentacles, 1993); *Moose Droppings* (Nightmare Music, 1993); *The Black Spot* (Essential Noise/Virgin, 1995); *Festival of Atheists* (Sudden Death, 2000); *Lost Tapes* (Orchard, 2000); *Alive & Kickin'* (Orchard, 2001); *Win the Battle* (Sudden Death, 2002); *Are U Ready* (Sudden Death, 2003); *Live Free or Die* (Sudden Death, 2004); *From Out of Nowhere* (New World, 2004). **Randy Rampage:** *Randy Rampage* EP (Friend's, 1982)

DOC MARTENS

The boot of choice for many punks, particularly **skinheads**, Doc Martens—whose signature thick and cushiony soles were patented by German doctor Claus Maertens in 1959—were manufactured in England's Midlands region and first became attached to punk in the 1960s when British skinheads started wearing them in emulation of working-class style. Soon a codified system was established for how to wear the boots and what the particular styles meant to different punk subcultures. Red laces meant you were a socialist, white equaled **National Front**, and so on (though the symbology became quite arcane and confused over the years and is less adhered to these days). Some racist skins were known for having a policy of standing next to someone wearing the boots, and if their boots looked better and were the right size, the unwary punk might find himself walking home barefoot. Docs, whether the standard eight-eyelet boot or chunky lowtop oxford, became the durable, preferred shoe for non-skin punks throughout the 1980s and 1990s.

Whether Doc Martens are worn by punks today for specific reasons (comfort, a desire for historical continuity, the incongruity of matching them with a skirt, **Riot Grrrl**-style), or just because they're considered part of the uniform remains unclear. In an interesting side note, in 2007 mock-ups of a proposed Doc Martens ad campaign done by venerable agency Saatchi and Saatchi were leaked onto the Internet. The ads featured pictures of Kurt Cobain, **Joe Strummer**, **Sid Vicious**, and **Joey Ramone** as angels in heaven, wearing Doc Martens under their heavenly robes (?!). Not surprisingly, much vitriol and opprobrium was heaped upon the offending parties, and the campaign was quickly disavowed by Doc Martens, who also quickly dumped Saatchi and Saatchi. Joey usually wore Converse, in any case.

JOHN DOE

Leader of Los Angeles punk band **X**, prolific actor, and solo artist John Doe was married for several years to X singer Exene Cervenka and went country in later years (more's the pity). One of the founders and key players in L.A.'s late-1970s and early-'80s punk scene, Doe's savvy songwriting and artistic vision (which incorporated a country and folk-based style into the band's sound) helped X survive the scene's notorious excesses—unlike so many others—and achieve some mainstream success. Doe also toured solo and released a number of roots-rock records. He also infrequently appeared as an actor in musically oriented films, such as *Georgia* or the Jerry Lee Lewis biopic *Great Balls of Fire*. Doe reunited with his other band, the country-based side project the Knitters (along with D.J. Bonebrake, Exene Cervenka, and Dave Alvin), for an album and tour in 2005.

LEFT: An unknown punk gets the boot, 1983.
RIGHT: John Doe performs with X at The Whisky, 1980.

Donna R. in Melbourne, 2003.

THE DONNAS

1993-present

LINEUP: Brett Anderson, aka "Donna A." (vocals); Allison Robertson, aka "Donna R." (guitar); Maya Ford, aka "Donna F." (bass); Torry Castellano, aka "Donna C." (drums)

The women of the Donnas are clearly influenced by the music and look of the **Ramones**, even if their heavy, arena-ready sound and cocky lyrics draw just as much inspiration from hair-metal bands. In true Ramones-style, band members all go by the first name Donna, with only an identifying initial to distinguish them. They formed while attending junior high school in Palo Alto, California, and went through a brief phase during which they played as two entities, the other one called the Electrocutes, before sticking with the Donnas. Early musical efforts were poorly produced and showed a welcome lack of professionalism. Subsequent releases on **Lookout! Records** showed a gradual maturity and the introduction of some metallic crunch. On *Get Skintight*, produced by Steve and Jeff MacDonald from **Red Kross**, the Donnas rock particularly hard on songs like "Skintight" and "Get Outta My Room," which would have felt at home on almost any early Ramones record. The band signed to a major label, made several highly regarded records and were soon showing up in numerous advertisements, on **MTV**, and even as the prom band in the 1999 black comedy *Jawbreaker*. The women in the band subsequently dropped the common Donna first name, the source of much of their initial innocent charm. Later records were more metal-influenced, although why one would want to trade a Ramones influence for that of Motley Crüe is truly mystifying.

Discography:

The Donnas (Super*teem, 1997; Lookout!, 1998); *American Teenage Rock 'n' Roll Machine* (Lookout!, 1998); *Finally a Classy Record From...The Donnas EP* (Kryptonite 1999); *Get Skintight* (Lookout!, 1999); *Turn 21* (Lookout! 2001); *Spend the Night* (Atlantic, 2002); *Gold Medal* (Atlantic, 2004); *Bitchin'* (Purple Feather, 2007)

THE DOUGHBOYS

1986-1997

LINEUP: John Kastner (vocals/guitar); Scott McCullough (guitar, replaced by John Cummings, Wiz, Mark Arnold); John Bondhead (bass/vocals, replaced by Peter Arsenault); Brock Pytel (vocals/drums, replaced by Paul Newman)

The Montreal-based Doughboys (who formed from the ashes of Canada's fondly remembered Asexuals) were one of the most energetic Canadian punk bands of the late-1980s and early-'90s. Their mix of crunchy punk and early metal influences (they frequently covered Alice Cooper's classic "Long Way to Go" during live sets) set them apart during a time when many punk bands were figuratively and literally wandering in the wastelands. Key members came and left, but the classic lineup featured John Kastner on lead vocals, Brock Pytel on drums and vocals, John Bondhead on bass, and John Cummings on guitar. Although they toured constantly and released several well respected albums, they never broke big in the United States. The Doughboys are, however, remembered well by many for their live shows in which they demonstrated enough manic energy that lead singer and guitarist Kastner was later hired to teach rock star poses in Japan. Kastner later founded All Systems Go with members of **Big Drill Car**, which carried on the pop-punk tradition until 2003. Latter-day guitarist Wiz died in 2006.

Discography:

Whatever (Pipeline, 1987; Cargo, 1995); *Home Again* (Restless, 1989, 1993); *Happy Accidents* (Restless, 1991, 1993); *When Up Turns to Down* (Restless, 1992); *Something's Gone Wrong Again— The Buzzcocks Covers* (C/Z, 1992); *Crush* (A&M, 1993); *Fix Me* (Cargo, 1995); *Turn Me On* (Universal/Polygram, 1992; A&M, 1996)

The Doughboys' John Kastner, Gilman Street, 1987.

Down By Law
punkrockacademyfightsong

Down by Law's Dave Smalley, 1994.

DOWN BY LAW

1991-present

LINEUP: Dave Smalley (vocals/guitar); Sam Williams (guitar); Angry John DiMambro (bass, replaced by Keith Davies); Hunter Oswald (drums, replaced by Danny Westman, Milo Todesco)

After he left **Dag Nasty** and **All**, Dave Smalley started up Down by Law with members of the Chemical People. It became something of a one-man outfit as he remained the band's only constant member through numerous lineup changes over the years. Smalley's musical approach in Down by Law can be described as a continuation of the poppy direction he was taking with his previous bands: stripped-down fast guitars and vocals (which well utilized Smalley's pitch-perfect, wide-ranging voice) and thundering drums, but melodic as hell. However, the music didn't always live up to its promise and after Down by Law's first three records the formula started to grow thin. (Although the short hidden tracks on *Punkrockacademyfightsong*, where Smalley calls for the death of the Counting Crows are dead brilliant.) Down by Law were moderately successful for a time with several albums on major indie labels **Epitaph** and Go Kart Records. Smalley later toured as a solo artist and published political commentary that surprised many of his fans, given that it came from a slightly right-of-center perspective.

Discography:
Down by Law (Epitaph, 1991); *Blue* (Epitaph, 1993); *Punkrockacademyfightsong* (Epitaph, 1994); *Down by Law & Gigantor* (Lost & Found, 1995); *All Scratched Up!* (Epitaph, 1996); *Last of the Sharpshooters* (Epitaph, 1997); *Fly the Flag* (Go Kart, 1999); *Split* (with Pseudo Heroes; Theologian, 2000); *PunkRockDays: The Best of DBL* (Epitaph, 2002); *Windwardtidesandwaywardsails* (Union, 2003)

DRAMARAMA

1983-1994, 2004-present

LINEUP: John Easdale (vocals); Peter Wood (guitar); Mark Englert (guitar); Chris Carter (bass); Jesse (drums, replaced by Clem Burke)

An enduring New Jersey outfit, Dramarama best demonstrated the benefits and perils of the commercial record industry. The band started in the early-1980s and combined punk's energy and the pop sound of the Beatles with glam and traditional rock influences (Mott the Hoople is an obvious reference point, with the band covering their "I Wish I Was Your Mother" on one album). Dramarama never identified themselves as particularly punk, but in their garage-rock obsession, they harkened back to the Sonics and other great proto-punk bands who established the musical framework (but not the haircuts) for punk. Despite plugging away for years and garner-ing several minor (though perennial) radio hits such as "Anything, Anything (I'll Give You)," "Last Cigarette," and "Work for Food," Dramarama was forced to call it quits. A worthy band that never quite got a break.

Discography:
Comedy EP (Questionmark, 1984); *Cinema Verite* (New Rose, 1984); *Box Office Bomb* (Questionmark, 1987); *Stuck in Wonderamaland* (Chameleon, 1990); *Live at the China Club* EP (Chameleon, 1990); *Vinyl* (Chameleon/Elektra, 1991); *The Days of Wayne and Roses* (*The Trash Tapes*) (no label, 1992); *Hi-Fi Sci-Fi* (Chameleon/Elektra, 1993); *18 Big Ones: The Best Of* (Elektra/Rhino, 1996); *Everybody Dies* (33rd Street, 2007)

D.R.I.

1982-present

LINEUP: Kurt Brecht (vocals); Spike Cassidy (guitar); Dennis Johnson (bass, replaced by Josh Pappe, John Menor, Chumly Porter, Harald Oimen); Eric Brecht (drums, replaced by Felix Griffin, Rom Rampy)

This Houston **hardcore**-thrash band is better known by their initials, but the name Dirty Rotten Imbeciles has an excellent pedigree: it was what the father of a couple founding band members would call them when throwing them outside for practicing too loud. D.R.I. was one of the fastest of the early hardcore bands, evidenced by their first release, the *Dirty Rotten EP*, which contains 22 songs in 18 minutes, rivaling **Hüsker Dü**'s *Land Speed Record* for brevity. Subsequent albums through the mid-to-late-1980s saw D.R.I. aggressively pioneer-ing the punk-metal crossover sound that became a dominant trend during that time. D.R.I. also was well known for their iconic logo that featured a figure skanking (pre-sumably to the music of D.R.I.). It's clear that the punk-metal crossover, whatever one though of it, would not have been pos-sible without visionary bands like D.R.I., who saw the commonalities between the two genres instead of just the differences. More recently, lead singer Kurt Brecht sang a particularly tasty piece of old school thrash, "Silent Spring," on Dave Grohl's *Probot* tribute to old school thrash and death metal. After a hiatus for Spike to recover from cancer, D.R.I. reportedly went back to recording and touring.

Discography:
Dirty Rotten (Rotten, 1982); *Violent Pacification* EP (Rotten, 1984); *Dealing with It!* (Death/Metal Blade/Enigma, 1985; Rotten, 1991); *Crossover* (Metal Blade/Enigma, 1987; Rotten, 1995); *4 of a Kind* (Metal Blade/Enigma, 1988; Restless, 1993); *Thrash Zone* (Metal Blade/Enigma, 1989); *Dirty Rotten LP/Violent Pacification* (Rotten, 1991); *Definition* (Rotten, 1992); *D.R.I. Live* (Rotten, 1995); *Full Speed Ahead* (Rotten, 1995); *Dirty Rotten Imbeciles* (Cleopatra, 2001)

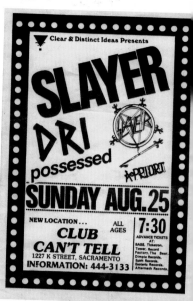

DR. KNOW

1981–1991, 1998–present

CURRENT LINEUP: Brandon Cruz (vocals); Steve Contreras (guitar); Ismael Hernandez (bass); Rick Contreras (Drums)

Although this Los Angeles **hardcore** band featured Brandon Cruz, a former child actor on the 1960s television show *The Courtship of Eddie's Father*, on lead vocals, they're far from the joke that one would imagine them to be. Over the years, Dr. Know actually produced some worthwhile albums, particularly *Wreckage in Flesh* and *This Island*, which show a good grasp of Southern California punk. Originally part of the Oxnard, California "nardcore" scene, Dr. Know (oddly, no intended relation to **Bad Brains**' guitarist Dr. Know) later became more of a punk-metal crossover, keeping the quick drumming, but also adding a crunchier guitar sound and more soloing, before disbanding in 1991. Cruz later joined the reunited **Dead Kennedys** in the early 2000s as a replacement vocalist for **Jello Biafra**. Incidentally, Ismael Hernandez's cartoonist brother Jaime, of *Love and Rockets*, drew the band's vaguely spooky logo.

Discography:

This Island (Death/Restless, 1986, 1993); *Wreckage in Flesh* (Restless, 1988, 1993); *The Original Group* (Mystic, 1995); *Island-Wreckage* (Enigma, 1995); *Valu Pak* (Mystic, 1995); *Habily: What Was Old is New* (Cleopatra, 2001); *Best of Dr. Know* (Mystic, 2003); *Father Son and Holy Shit* (unknown, 2003)

THE DROPKICK MURPHYS

1996–present

LINEUP: Mike McColgan (vocals, replaced by Al Barr); Rick Barton (guitar, replaced by Mark Orrell); Ken Casey (bass); Matt Kelly (drums)

Formed in 1996, the Dropkick Murphys produce a brash and extraordinarily well-marketed brand of Boston **hardcore** fused with traditional Irish music. It's all brawling skinheads and spilled Guinness set to a wall of anthemic guitars and shout-along choruses (being proud of one's Irish roots and Boston upbringing is key), with the occasional sentimental number to get the tear ducts flowing. It's all a very effective mix, if sometimes a little too premeditated. The Murphys' crew has changed quite a bit over the years, with the usual revolving cast of drummers that only stabilized with the addition of Matt Kelly. Considered by some a more raucous U.S. version of the **Pogues**, their music has more in common with poppier punk bands like **Rancid** (except for the bagpipes and mandolin), and in fact several of their albums were released on Hellcat Records, run by Rancid's lead singer. Showing once again an unerring ear for place, time, and music,

ABOVE: The Dropkick Murphys guarding the back alleys of Boston, c.2000.

BELOW: The pit at a Dr. Know show, Emeryville, California, 1986.

director Martin Scorsese chose the Dropkick Murphys' shattering cover of Woody Guthrie's "I'm Shipping Up to Boston" for the opening credits of his Boston mob epic *The Departed*. The Dropkick Murphys have also recently cemented their punk-Gaelic credentials not only by covering Irish classics (such as "Finnegan's Wake" and "(F)lannigan's Ball") but also by bringing on guest stars such as **Shane MacGowan** and Spider Stacy (both from the Pogues), and Luke Kelly from the Dubliners to play on their records.

Discography:

Do or Die (Epitaph, 1998); *The Gang's All Here* (Epitaph, 1999); *Mob Mentality* (Taang!, 2000); *Sing Loud, Sing Proud* (Epitaph, 2001); *Live on St. Patrick's Day from Boston, MA* (Epitaph, 2002); *Blackout* (Hellcat, 2003); *The Warrior's Code* (Hellcat, 2005); *The Meanest of Times* (Born and Bred, 2007)

DUB

In dub—a less commercial and spacier version of **reggae** pioneered by Jamaican innovators such as King Tubby, Scientist, and Lee Scratch Perry—the instruments drop in and out, and echo and reverb are used extensively. Many early British punk bands, such as the **Clash**, the **Ruts**, **Generation X**, and the **Slits**, used dub in their own recordings. Seminal early tracks such as Generation X's "Wild Dub" and the Clash's "Bankrobber Dub" illustrated how an exotic production sound could appeal to the general public (at least in England, where such music was more commonly heard than in America). Later on in the 1980s, American bands such as **Bad Brains** also used dub in their ritualistic praise of Jah Rastafari, the Rastafarian deity. Bad Brains were an exception to the rule, however, dub's use being largely inspired by their religious beliefs. Although **ska** has been quite influential in American punk, in general bands from the States have very little to do with this kind of music, with the exception of **NOFX**, who have dipped their hands into dub from time to time.

THE DWARVES

1986-present

LINEUP: Blag Dahlia (vocals); He Who Cannot Be Named (guitar); Fresh Prince of Darkness (guitar); various bassists and drummers

Filthy scuz-punks from San Francisco (formerly Chicago), the Dwarves made their reputation with outrageous shows that resemble the over-the-top horror-show theatricality of GWAR. The Dwarves' album covers featured copious nudity, but the records themselves did not feature much music. While sometimes the band would play actual songs, most of the time they performed like the quintessential parody of a punk band: loud, tuneless, and violent. Ultimately better known for their offensiveness than their ability to produce music, the Dwarves received some notice for the outrage that erupted when they faked the death of guitarist He Who Cannot Be Named (who normally performs in a jock strap and nothing else), who they alleged was stabbed to death in

"Most offensive album of all time."

—*SPIN* on the Dwarves' "Blood, Guts & Pussy"

Philadelphia in 1993. The sub-**GG Allin** controversy led the Dwarves' label Sub Pop to drop them. But these days the Dwarves soldier on, milking the occasional bit of outrage for whatever it's worth. A recent video for their song "FEFU" features punk strippers the **Suicide Girls** beating the tar out of (the miraculously still alive!) singer. For reasons unknown, the Dwarves get a lot of mileage out of their shtick and are still luring aging punks and pimply teens to the dark side.

Discography:
Horror Stories (Voxx, 1986); *Toolin' for a Warm Teabag* (Nasty Gash, 1988); *Astro Boy* EP (Sub Pop, 1990); *Blood, Guts & Pussy* (Sub Pop, 1990); *Lucifer's Crank* EP (No.6, 1991); *Thank Heavens for Little Girls* (Sub Pop, 1991); *Sugarfix* (Sub Pop, 1993)

DYS

1982–1986

LINEUP: Dave Smalley (vocals); Andy Strahan (guitar); Jon Anastas (bass); Dave Collins (drums)

A metal-punk band that took its name from the Massachusetts Department of Youth Services (which oversees juvenile detention), DYS was fronted by future **Dag Nasty** and **Down by Law** singer Dave Smalley. DYS formed in Boston, inspired by the city's budding **hardcore** scene, particularly bands like **SSD**. DYS promoted the **straight-edge** movement to ridiculous extremes and often confronted audience members about their behavior, sometimes lecturing, sometimes heckling, but luckily never reacting as violently as good friends and straight-edge stalwarts SSD. The band released one significant album and then moved in a more metallic direction, performing heavy power ballads and turning off a lot of fans in the process, although signaling what was to come for many punk bands in the late-1980s (**T.S.O.L.**, for instance) DYS almost signed to major label Elektra before breaking up in 1985. Smalley later went on to Dag Nasty, **All**, and Down by Law, while Anastas put together the popular straight-edge band **Slapshot**.

Discography:
Brotherhood (x-Claim!, 1983); *D.Y.S.* (Modern Method, 1986)

LEFT: Dub producer Lee "Scratch" Perry at his Kingston, Jamaica, studio, in the 1970s.

ABOVE: (L to R) The Dwarves' He Who Canot Be Named, Blag Dahlia, 2005.

EATER

1976-1978, 1996-1997

LINEUP: Ashie Radwan, aka "Andy Blade"
(vocals); Brian Haddock, aka "Brian
Chevette" (guitar); Ian Woodcock (bass);
Social Demise (drums, replaced by Roger
Bullen, aka "Dee Generate"; Phil Rowland)

A first-generation British band famous for
the relative youth of the members, who
considered the **Sex Pistols** to be "too old,"
Eater was composed mostly of 15-year-olds,
with the exception of their particularly
puckish 13-year-old drummer, Dee Generate.
After opening for the **Buzzcocks** in 1976,
Eater gigged around pretty regularly and
notably appeared in **Don Letts**'s 1978 *Punk
Rock Movie*. While Mr. Generate did not last
the entire career of Eater (he was probably
too short to reach the tom-toms), he did
show impeccable taste in drum teachers,
in his case Rat Scabies from the **Damned**.
After numerous personnel changes, the
short-lived band finally called it quits at
the end of 1978. Drummer Rowland later
played with **Slaughter and the Dogs**. A
brief reunion in the 1990s only featured
Blade and Chevette.

Eater remains one of the lesser-known
bands from the classic 1976-77 era, but
some of their singles—"Thinking of the
USA," "Lock it Up," their cover of the **Velvet
Underground**'s "I'm Waiting for the Man,"
or (their best song) "You"—are actually
every bit as good as any punk single pro-

duced that year. Even though they were a
bunch of (literally) snot-nosed kids who
arrogantly dismissed the rest of their
contemporaries like a younger Oasis, Eater
showed that on some level, punk was all
about the kids.

Discography:
The Album (The Label, 1977); *Get Your Yo Yo's Out* EP
(The Label, 1978); *The History of Eater Vol. 1*
(DeLorean, 1985); *All of Eater* (Cargo, 1995, 1997);
The Compleat Eater (Anagram Punk, 1999);
Eater Chronicles 1976-2003 (Anagram Punk, 2003);
Live at Barbarella's 1977 (Anagram Punk, 2004)

THE EFFIGIES

1980-1986, 1987-1990,
1995-1996, 2004-present

LINEUP: John Kezdy (vocals);
Earl Oil Letiecq (guitar, replaced by
Robert O'Conner, Robert McNaughton);
Paul Zamost (bass); Steve Economou (drums)

One of the decade's most popular Chicago-
area punk outfits, the Effigies were a
hardcore band from Evanston, Illinois,
heavily influenced by the British sound
and image of the early-1980s. Particularly
reminiscent of **oi** bands like **U.K. Subs**, the
Effigies also carried on an unfortunate and
acrimonious rivalry with one of the other
big bands in town at the time, **Articles of
Faith**. The Effigies' first songs were included on Autumn Records' *Busted at Oz* compilation of local bands recorded in 1981 at Oz,
the epicenter for Chicago punk at the time.
Later, they put out their own albums via
Ruthless Records, a collaborative effort

The youthful scamps of Eater in London, 1976: (L to R) Andy Blade, Brian Chevette, Dee Generate, Ian Woodcock

between the Effigies and the other big bands on the scene at the time, **Naked Raygun** and **Big Black**. The Effigies experienced bitter deals with various labels and were falsely accused of being Nazis and racists because of their skinhead look, not to mention singer John Kezdy's right-wing views. (For a punk, Kezdy was fairly conservative, challenging the Marxist doctrines of some Chicago punks in interviews with *Maximum RocknRoll*, leading to an infamous 1983 "protest" against the band, when an entire crowd at a club sat on their hands in protest of Kezdy's comments.) The band disbanded in 1986, re-formed with various lineups from 1987 to 1990, and gigged in 1995 and 1996 in the Chicago area to support their reissued material on Touch and Go Records. Starting in 2004, the Effigies sporadically reunited again and began to tour the Midwest (now with hair!).

Discography:

Haunted Town EP (Autumn, 1981; Ruthless, 1984); *We're Da Machine* EP (Ruthless/Enigma, 1983); *The Effigies* EP (Ruthless/Enigma, 1984); *For Ever Grounded* (Ruthless/Enigma, 1984); *Fly on a Wire* (Fever/Enigma, 1985); *Ink* (Fever 1986); *Remains Nonviewable* (Roadkill, 1989; Touch and Go, 1995); *V.M.L. Live Presents the Effigies 12/16/95* (V.M.L., 1996); *Reside* (Criminal IQ, 2007)

EGGHEAD
1994-1998, 2007
LINEUP: Johnny Reno (guitar/vocals); John Ross Bowie (bass/vocals); Mike Faloon (drums/vocals)

Egghead was, as the name might indicate, three rather (intentionally) dorky-looking chaps, who dressed alike in matching uniforms and glasses and sang songs about jet packs, Jackie Chan, and of course, heartbreak and love. The band was instrumental in reviving the New York **pop-punk** scene during the early-1990s after years of domination by more aggressive **hardcore** bands. After touring and putting out several singles, the band finally broke up in 1998. A compilation of their best material was put out by Mutant Pop Records in 1999. After the band's demise, John Ross Bowie became an in-demand actor in commercials and TV shows, Johnny Reno became a screenwriter, and Mike Faloon edited the zines *Go Metric* and *Zisk*. In 2007, Egghead reunited for the Insubordination Fest in Baltimore, as well as a New York gig.

Discography:

Four Headed Beast (Good Guppy, 1995); *Knock off that Evil* EP (Dizzy, 1996); *Trixie Belden vs. Egghead* EP (Dizzy, 1997); *Dumb Songs for Smart People* (Mutant Pop, 1999)

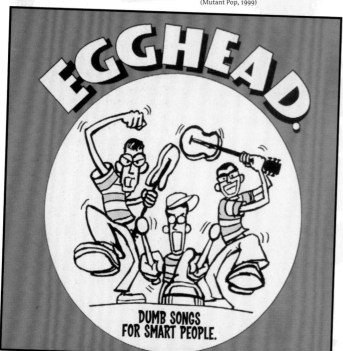

EGG HUNT
1986
LINEUP: Ian MacKaye (vocals/guitar/bass); Jeff Nelson (vocals/drums/gum)

A side project of **Ian MacKaye** and Jeff Nelson after the breakup of **Minor Threat**, Egg Hunt released only one single, the song "We All Fall Down," recorded in England in 1986. Originally written for **Embrace**, MacKaye's post-Minor Threat band, the song was rejected by the other members of the band. Egg Hunt proved to be an important transition between two phases of MacKaye's career, with the loud and abrasive vocals showing that he really was now singing instead of shouting, the atmospheric, almost **reggae**-tinged vibe a forecast of the sound that MacKaye would explore with **Fugazi**. The Egg Hunt project marked the last time that MacKaye and Nelson would collaborate musically, though they worked together via **Dischord Records** for years afterward.

THE ELECTRIC EELS
1972-1975
LINEUP: David "E" McManus (vocals/ percussion); John Morton (vocals/guitar); Brian McMahon (guitar); Nick Knox (drums)

The Electric Eels were one of the few bands who both predated punk (circa 1972) and anticipated most of the early scene's musical, social, and fashion innovations. Although not well known outside of their home base in Ohio, the band not only played **Dead Boys**-style rock that was noisier, more aggressive, and easily identifiable as punk years before the **Ramones** or **Sex Pistols**, but they also dressed in ripped clothing and outlandish outfits long before scenesters in New York and London. The Electric Eels described their music as "art terrorism," wore safety pins, used rude slogans, created outlandish scenes onstage by using things like lawn mowers—in short, the sort of antics that would have barely raised an eyebrow had they been done in performance-art-mad New York.

> ## "The Electric Eels (played) a sociopathic garage-punk mutant that married two-chord frat stomping and atonal free jazz with a real 'fuck you' attitude ...Pale pubescence's poetry was never so beautifully rendered."
>
> —Dave Keenan's review of *The Eyeball of Hell* in *Mojo*, April 2002

The band could only manage a half-dozen gigs (that usually devolved into violent melees) before getting banned at Cleveland-area clubs and disbanding. The proto-punk single "Cyclotron" came out in May 1975, but it was the Electric Eels' "Agitated" which established them as a major force in the United States and abroad, once it was finally released by **Rough Trade** in 1979 at the urging of journalist Jon Savage. Drummer Nick Knox would later join the **Cramps**. Although only briefly on the scene, the Electric Eels were punk legends before the world really knew what punk was, suggesting that punk's origins were less involved in specific geographic scenes and came more from a spontaneous confluence of disgust at the music industry in the 1970s.

Discography:
Having a Philosophical Investigation with the Electric Eels (Tinnitus, 1989); *God Says Fuck You* (Homestead, 1992, 1995); *Beast 999 Presents the Electric Eels in Their Organic Majesty's Request* (Overground, 1998); *The Eyeball of Hell* (Scat, 2001)

THE EMBARRASSMENT
1979–1983, occasional reunions thereafter

LINEUP: John Nichols (vocals/organ); Bill Goffrier (guitar/vocals); Ronnie Klaus, aka "Captain Ron" (bass); Brent "Woody" Giessman (drums)

The Embarrassment was the kind of band who can be described as "quirky" without fear of, well, embarrassment. An art-punk band from Kansas their trademark sound of jangly guitars, anguished throat-clenched vocals, and pseudo-**no wave** rhythms was widely influential on the more introspective punk and alternative American bands of the 1980s and '90s. Known as "The Embos" to some fans, the band was a collection of musicians from Wichita (not exactly the punk capital of the world), most of whom had grown up together, and were all **Sex Pistols** fans. They supposedly just bought one instrument at a time and took it from there. The Embarrassment toured extensively, playing the major clubs in Kansas and New York and performing with everyone from **Iggy Pop** to John Cale and fellow Midwesterner William S. Burroughs, but never made a name for themselves. The Embarrassment first called it quits in 1983 (drummer Brent Giessman played in the Del Fuegos for awhile), though they've reunited several times over the years, and are best remembered for their epic song "Sex Drive." All their records are worth having, but casual fans should probably start with the two-disc anthology, *Heyday 1979-83*.

Discography:
Death Travels West EP (Restless, 1983): *The Embarrassment* (Time to Develop, 1987): *God Help Us* (Bar None, 1990); *Heyday 1979-83* (Bar None, 1995); *Blister Pop* (My Pal God, 2001)

selections from the Bar/None double CD retrospective
heyday • 1979-83

EMBRACE
1985–1986

LINEUP: Ian MacKaye (vocals); Mike Hampton (guitar); Chris Bald (bass); Ivor Hanson (drums)

Embrace is best known for being **Ian MacKaye**'s band after **Minor Threat** and before **Fugazi**, but there was far more substance to them than just serving as a rest stop between two legendary bands. Embrace took MacKaye's ideas and voice in a much more complex, experimental direction, one that presaged many of Fugazi's dabbling with noise and sonic landscapes. The band's members included the instrumental part of the **Faith** (whose singer, at one time, was Ian's brother, Alec MacKaye). Ian also began to develop the signature vocal range with which Fugazi fans became well acquainted. While Embrace only put out an album and a single during their brief existence, they remain noteworthy for expanding the limitations of **hardcore** and experimenting with its key ingredients.

Discography:
Embrace (Dischord, 1987)

EMO

An emotional style of punk developed in the 1980s by bands such as **Dag Nasty** and **Rites of Spring**, *emo* generally refers to bands with confessional lyrics that deal with difficulties in relationships, fitting in, and being honest in a harsh world. Legend has it that people at Rites of Spring shows had been known to burst into tears at their naked, emotional performances. Most of the early emo bands were also extremely devoted to their fans, treating them like family and sometimes even allowing them to share the stage.

However, in the 1990s, the term began to take on different connotations, as pop outfits like Jimmy Eat World, Dashboard Confessional, and Weezer (the last primarily due to their second album, the under-selling, but critically acclaimed, *Pinkerton*) came to be described as emo. Other offshoots created by rock critics include *screamo* and *extremo*, more raucous versions of the same style, as epitomized by bands such as the Used, who scream their confessional lyrics as opposed to singing them melodically. Along the way, an unofficial emo uniform even came about, involving baggy clothing, rumpled hair, and large, nerdy glasses. Many modern bands refuse to be labeled emo, considering the term essentially meaningless and more of a corporate attempt to label music than an honest reaction to a musical style; though some true emo bands are still out there performing under the radar of the cultural mainstream, spawning prolific MySpace pages and zines devoted to their music. Given that the primary audience for emo-style music is composed of those under the age of 21, as long as some bands are able to capture that sense of emotive alienation so attractive to some teenagers, the genre will continue. But it remains to be seen if the success of mall-punk **poseurs** like Fall Out Boy and Panic! At the Disco will further mainstream the term, or kill it off entirely.

The latter-day emo boys of Weezer, 2001. (L to R) Rivers Cuomo, Mikey Welsh.

ENGINE KID

1991-1995

LINEUP: Greg Anderson (vocals/guitar); Brian Kraft (bass); Chris Vandebrooke (drums, replaced by Jade Devitt)

Many have compared Seattle's avant-**hardcore** band Engine Kid to art-punk innovators Slint, which is quite a compliment, but not surprising given how few hardcore bands were trying to work with the kind of musical dynamics Engine Kid did. A better comparison would probably be the **Pixies**, whom Engine Kid also resembled in terms of their loud/quiet/loud song structure. Things got even weirder when the band collaborated with the jazz-punk group **Iceburn**, with whom they recorded a split EP. Engine Kid's final album, *Angel Wings*, takes a startling and interesting, free-jazz direction, including a lengthy John Coltrane cover and a song dedicated to Herbie Hancock. This would have been a great idea to continue with, but the band ran out of steam and broke up in 1995, leaving the ambition of punk-jazz to be taken up by some other brave souls.

Discography:
Astronaut EP (C/Z, 1993); *Bear Catching Fish* (C/Z, 1993); *Angel Wings* (Revelation, 1995). **Iceburn/Engine Kid:** *Iceburn/Engine Kid* EP (Revelation, 1994)

EPITAPH

An enormously successful independent record label started in 1988 by Brett Gurewitz, aka "Mr. Brett" (guitarist for **Bad Religion**), Epitaph released some of the most influential punk records of the 1980s and '90s. Epitaph floundered for some time as Mr. Brett struggled with his heroin addiction, but they scored a major coup with the **Offspring**'s aptly titled 1994 album *Smash*, still one of the best-selling records ever released by an indie label. Bad Religion, was for a time, one of Epitaph's key groups but they perversely (given Mr. Brett's relationships with both the band and the label) left for a major label after the release of *Stranger than Fiction* and only returned after several years of diminishing sales (a common problem for punk bands who depart for the majors). The Epitaph roster is marked by a strong lineup that has included **NOFX**, **Pennywise**, **Agnostic Front**, the **Descendents**, **All**, **Rancid**, **Social Distortion**, **Dropkick Murphys**, and others. More recently they have launched a pair of similarly successful sister labels, the **ska**- and **hardcore**-centric Hellcat, and the less loud but still iconoclastic Anti-, which includes artists Tom Waits and Neko Case.

THE ERGS

2000-present

LINEUP: Mikey Erg (vocals/drums); Jeffrey Erg (guitar/vocals); Joey Erg (bass)

A New Jersey band influenced by the **Descendents**, the **Ramones**, and the Parasites, the admittedly dorky Ergs could be easily slotted into the nerd-rock genre. Led by singing drummer Mikey Erg (formerly of Dirt Bike Annie and other New York **pop-punk** bands), the Ergs alternate their sped-up **hardcore** beat with sweet, almost innocent, songs about (what else?) girls. One of the hardest-touring of the new wave of pop-punk bands, the Ergs were also one of the first to use MySpace. The band also continuously puts out seven-inch singles on a regular basis, confounding those younger punks who only electronically download music.

Discography:
F'N (Frilly Pink, 2000), *Digital Endpoints* (Frilly Pink, 2000); *Three Guys, Twelve Eyes* EP (Whoa Oh, 2001); *Ben Kweller* EP (Fongul 2002); *Dorkrockcorkrod* (Whoa Oh, Don Giovanni 2003, 2005); *Cotton Pickin' Minute* (Prison Jazz 2003), *Jersey's Best Prancers* (Don Giovanni, 2005); *Upstairs/Downstairs* (Dirtnap, 2007)

THE EX

1979-present

LINEUP: G.W. Sok (vocals); Terrie Ex (guitar); Andy Moor (guitar); René (bass, several others, now vacant); Ome Geurt (drums, several others, now Katherina Ex)

An enduring band of Dutch anarchist punks with jazz and improvisational tendencies, the Ex consistently rejected major labels to produce their own product in their own idiosyncratic way. The Ex are among the most important of the European anarchist collectives that flourished during the early-1980s—the British **Chumbawamba**, with whom the Ex have toured, being another prime example—and their unique style and vision have made them one of the most respected of European punk bands.

The band started out with a fairly straightforward musical vision on early releases such as the *All Corpses Smell the Same* EP (which contained the classic punk stompers "Apathy Disease" and "Cells"), but soon the Ex began to mutate, and as members came and went their sonic palette began to expand, incorporating world beat, rap, industrial noise, and dance music, as well as traditional punk rhythms. They also found time to collaborate with like-minded eclectic punks such as the **Mekons** and the Awara, a group of Kurdish refugees from Iraq. Recent collaborations have also led to even more groundbreaking music as the band worked with the African group Konono #1 and legendary saxophone player Getatchew Mekuria. In more recent years, after an experiment with a big band in 2000, the Ex have stripped back down to a four-piece group and range now from playing Mekons-esque folk-type tunes, (about international socialism, of course) to **Fugazi**-style rave-ups. Almost 30 years on, the Ex are as committed to radical politics and music as they were when they started. While the Ex remained unknown to most Americans, their recent releases on Touch and Go—including *Dizzy Spells*, "produced" by Steve Albini—may see them finally get the recognition they deserve.

Discography:
Disturbing Domestic Peace (Verrecords, 1980; Ex, 1994); *History is What's Happening* (More DPM, 1982; Ex, 1994); *Blueprints for a Blackout* (Pig Brother Productions, 1983; Ex, 1992); *Dignity of Labour* (VGZ, 1983; Ex, 1995); *Tumult* (FAI, 1983); *Pokkeherrie* (Pockabilly, 1985; Ex, 1995); *1936, The Spanish Revolution* EP (Ex, 1986, 1997); *Too Many Cowboys* (Ex, 1987, 1993); *Hands Up! You're Free* (Ex, 1988); *Joggers & Smoggers* (Ex, 1989); *Dead Fish* EP (Ex, 1990); *Mudbird Shivers* (Ex/RecRec, 1995)

> **"Let's start a war said Maggie one day
> With the unemployed mass we'll just do away
> They won't mind, like sheep they'll go
> They won't suss us, they'll never know."**
>
> —"Let's Start a War," The Exploited (1983)

THE EXPLOITED

1979-present

LINEUP: Wattie Buchan (vocals); Big John Duncan (guitar, replaced by Karl Morris, others); Gary McCormack (bass, replaced by Billy Dunn, others); Glen Campbell, aka "Dru Stix" (drums, replaced by Danny Heatley, Willie Buchan, others)

One of the most important elements of the second wave of British punk, helping to spawn the notoriously violent and aggressive British **hardcore** scene, the Exploited were founded in Edinburgh, Scotland, in 1979 by Wattie Buchan, and early members included the aptly-named guitarist Big John for the first two records, *Punk's Not Dead*, and *Troops of Tomorrow*. Their third album, *Let's Start a War...*, was a vicious attack on Margaret Thatcher and the Falklands War. By the time of 1985's *Horror Epics*, possibly their best, the Exploited were becoming more metallic and experimental but still included sing-along choruses and socially conscious epics such as the title track, which asserts that compared to the horrors of global starvation, "real life is much more horrible than fiction."

The Exploited continue to record and tour, often with completely new lineups on each record, performing to crowds of variable sizes but consistent dedication. The Exploited's lengthy career is owed partially to the persistence of their fans, aka the "Barmy Army," but largely to the persistence and vision of Wattie. Now, some say that Wattie is a legendary Scottish beast—a sort of Loch Ness monster of punk—only more mythological. But though Wattie's trademark fin mohawk may have been replaced by long pink dreadlocks, it will take more than age to change his angry visage, impenetrable Edinburgh accent, and (as Walt Whitman might have said) "barbaric yawp" of a raspy howl from hell as he races through "Punk's Not Dead" or "Horror Epics" for his devoted followers.

Discography:

Punk's Not Dead (Grand Slamm, 1981); *Troops of Tomorrow* (Grand Slamm, 1982); *Let's Start A War... Said Maggie One Day* (Combat, 1983); *Horror Epics* (Combat, 1985); *Live at the Whitehouse* (Combat, 1985); *Jesus is Dead* (Combat, 1986); *Totally Exploited* (Dojo, 1986); *Death Before Dishonor* (Combat, 1987); *Live and Loud* (Link, 1987); *Punks Alive* (Skunx, 1988); *Massacre* (Rough Justice, 1990); *War Now* (Combat, 1990); *Live in Japan* (Dojo, 1994); *Beat the Bastards* (Relativity, 1996); *Fuck the System* (Import, 2002); *Punk* (Cargo Music, 2002)

LEFT: The Exploited as proof that punk's death has been exaggerated, 1981.

RIGHT: The Exploited, time and place unknown

The Fall's Brix Smith.

and Riddle later joined **No Use For a Name**. Face to Face played a brand of punk so catchy that, by themselves, they illustrate the inherent myopia of a record industry and contemporary radio business that couldn't figure out what to do with them.

Discography:

Don't Turn Away (Dr. Strange, 1992; Fat Wreck Chords, 1992, 1994); *Over It* EP (Victory, 1994); *Big Choice* (Victory, 1995); *Face to Face* (A&M, 1996; Vagrant, 2000); *Econolive* EP (Lady Luck/Victory, 1996); *Live* (Lady Luck/Victory, 1998); *Standards and Practices* (Lady Luck/Victory, 1999; Vagrant, 2001); *Ignorance is Bliss* (Beyond, 1999); *So Why Aren't You Happy?* EP (Atomic Pop, 1999); *Reactionary* (Beyond, 2001); *We Love Gas* (Musea, 2001); *How to Ruin Everything* (Vagrant, 2002)

THE FAITH

1981-1983

LINEUP: Alec MacKaye (vocals); Michael Hampton (guitar); Eddie Janney (guitar); Chris Bald (bass); Ivor Hanson (drums)

The Faith featured **Ian MacKaye**'s brother Alec (from classic Washington, D.C., band the Untouchables) on vocals, along with the other three members of **Henry Rollins'** first band State of Alert, and produced a ferocious and emotionally open style of D.C. **hardcore** (their own unique brand, not as rough and macho as those from Southern California or New York). While MacKaye was somewhat overshadowed by his brother Ian's popularity and guru status, the Faith filled the local scene's void when **Minor Threat** was on hiatus. Alec had all of his brother's charisma, not to mention emotionally honest lyrics, and the Faith, backed by Chris Bald and Ivor Hanson's powerfully complex rhythms, hinted at the **emo** revolution to come in a few years. Eddie Janney, later of **Rites of Spring**, joined the band as a second guitarist for the *Subject to Change* EP. Internal strife eventually doomed the band.

After the Faith broke up, Alec MacKaye played in a variety of bands, including Ignition and continues to work for **Dischord Records**. In 1985, Bald, Hampton, and Hanson later backed up Ian in his first post-Minor Threat band, **Embrace**. Hampton and Hanson later played in the slightly more mainstream Manifesto, and Hanson eventually moved to New York and became a high-rise window washer, later immortalized in his acclaimed memoir of punk window washing, *Life on the Ledge*. One of the best

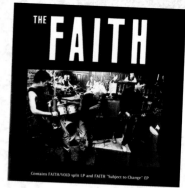

of the early D.C. bands, the Faith deserve recognition for their contribution to the birth of emo, before the name was hijacked by fashionista poseurs.

Discography:

The Faith/Void split (Dischord, 1982); *Subject to Change* EP (Dischord, 1983); *Faith/Void/Faith* (Dischord, 1993)

THE FALL

1977-present

LINEUP: Mark E. Smith (vocals); Brix Smith (guitar 1984-1989, 1994-1996); Martin Bramah (guitar, replaced by Craig Scanlon, others); Tony Friel (bass, replaced by Marc Riley, Steve Hanley, others); Una Baines (keyboards, replaced by Yvonne Pawlett, others); Karl Burns (drums, replaced by Mike Leigh, others)

Long-running British **post-punk** provocateurs the Fall are led by the dour and reclusive Mark E. Smith, who retained their name (which he took from the Camus novel) despite what seemed like several hundred personnel changes. The Fall can be a maddening band to follow because of their long and intricate history of personnel and stylistic changes, which make even the most ardent fan wonder as to whether to enjoy this week's new direction or simply relax and wait for the next about-face. By some estimates nearly 50 musicians have cycled through the band at various times over the past three decades, but that estimate itself may need updating.

Smith himself was a dockworker from Salford (right near the post-industrial musical incubator that is Manchester) who formed the band in 1977 with some like-minded souls similarly into **Can**-style krautrock and the **Velvet Underground**. While their early songs were marked by a somewhat straightforward, repetitious punk sound (including the extremely

FACE TO FACE

1991-2003, 2008-present

LINEUP: Trever Keith (guitar/vocals); Chad Yaro (guitar); Matt Riddle (bass, replaced by Scott Shiflett); Rob Kurth (drums, replaced by Pete Parada)

Victorville, California's Face to Face were best known for their anthem "Disconnected" and the gruff but immensely appealing voice of guitarist Trever Keith, who also possessed a pop sensibility belied by the power of the double guitar attack of Keith and Yaro. Face to Face played the punk circuit for several years and were subsequently signed and dropped by A&M, who could not figure out how to market the band's intricate and hook-driven music. The band strove to write anthems, not just to get radio airplay, but because the scope of their music was actually suited for big arenas, a rare feat for most punk bands. However, said anthems were not able to make it beyond college radio, even when the band recorded "Disconnected" a second time. Face to Face also showed their commitment to the members' punk roots with excellent choices in covers (the **Descendents'** "Bikeage," which they retired from the live set when the Descendents re-formed) and a split EP with **Dropkick Murphys**, which featured some choice cuts such as "The Dirty Glass," "Fortunate Son," and "21 Guitar Salute.") Of course the band eventually ran its course

repetitive "Repetition"), the Fall's musical output—though always reflective of Smith's smart, keenly mordant world-view—soon became much more complex and wide-ranging. The Fall also varied wildly in their sound, sometimes coming off like the Kinks, other times predating electronica, but Smith's desire not to be pigeonholed led to a wide range of styles as he expanded punk's musical repertoire with startling regularity. Early albums like 1979's *Live at The Witch Trials* and 1980's *Grotesque*, were favorites of BBC radio tastemaker **John Peel**, who would be one of the Fall's most vocal champions over the years, helping introduce the band to a certain degree of success in the 1980s (between 1978 and 2004, the Fall recorded over two dozen live "Peel Sessions" for the DJ's show, more are being released on a regular basis). Also helping the Fall find some regularity on the British charts—they would never make much of a dent on American popular music—was when Smith almost simultaneously married and brought into the band "Brix" Smith. An American guitarist nicknamed for her love of the **Clash**'s "Guns of Brixton," Brix brought a more pop-oriented sensibility into the mix, resulting in some odd success like the band's Top 40 cover of the Kinks' "Victoria." Brix and Smith split in both musical and matrimonial terms by the end of the decade, and the 1990s would see the band plumbing some particularly bitter territory. The Fall continued to record and tour with a dark regularity (their flame kept alive by the continual support of Peel until his death in 2004), although their glory days are as long gone as singer Mark E. Smith's original teeth.

There are simply far too many Fall albums to list here, and an entire book could be written about the band's ridiculously prolific output (sometimes as many as five different records coming out each year, many of them pointless live exercises and compilations). Putting that aside, they are, and were, one of the most important of the **post-punk** bands to influence a generation of U.S. bands, most notably **Sonic Youth** and Pavement (Smith has noted that he felt Pavement's Stephen

"If it's me and your granny on bongos, it's still The Fall."

—Mark E. Smith

The Fall's Mark E. Smith and his best mate, sometime in the 1980s.

Malkmus stole the Fall's sound, saying "It's just like listening to the Fall in 1985, isn't it? They haven't got an original idea in their heads.") Beginners are recommended to buy the compilation *50,000 Fall Fans Can't Be Wrong*, which examines the Fall's career from the beginning until about 2004 (meaning that by the time this book finds its way to your hands, there will be approximately another 25 Fall records available).

Essential Discography:
Live at the Witch Trials (StepForward/IRS, 1979); *Dragnet* (Step Forward, 1979); *Bend Sinister* (Beggars Banquet, 1986); *I am Curious Oranj* (Beggars Banquet 1988); *The Frenz Experiment* (Beggars Banquet, 1986); *Middle Class Revolt* (Matador, 1994); *50,000 Fall Fans Can't Be Wrong* (Beggars Banquet, 2004)

THE FASTBACKS
1981–2002
LINEUP: Kim Warnick (vocals/bass); Lulu Gargiulo (vocals/guitar); Kurt Bloch (guitar); Duff McKagan (drums, replaced by innumerable others)

Exceptionally durable pop-punkers, the Fastbacks were led by the versatile songwriting of Kurt Bloch and featured a cast of seemingly thousands of drummers (one of the earliest versions of the band featured a pre-Guns N' Roses Duff McKagan on drums). The Fastbacks were not just a cornerstone of the Seattle musicscape for over 20 years, but also one of the longest-running American indie bands with a female vocalist. Although the Fastbacks first began recording in 1982, with the *Play Five of Their Favorites* EP, they didn't release a full-length album until 1987's *...and His Orchestra*. Playing in a pleasingly **Ramones**-inspired style, lyrics mostly written by Bloch and sung by Kim Warnick, the band built up an extremely loyal local following over the years, despite their low visibility and occasional hiatuses. (Bloch played with the Young Fresh Fellows for a time, and also produced records for French punkers **Les Thugs** and local boys Mudhoney and Tad.) Even with the Fastbacks being a Sub Pop standard during much of the 1990s (Kim Warnick worked for a time at the label), and after being asked by Eddie Vedder to open for Pearl Jam several times, they were never able to cash in on the decade's grunge explosion that lifted so many other Seattle groups to stardom. The Fastbacks called it quits after Warnick left in 2002 to form a short-lived band called Visqueen.

The Fastbacks, a lively bunch.

Fat Wreck Chords' "I'm Not Fat!" Mike, 2001.

Discography:
Play Five of Their Favorites EP (No Threes, 1982); *Every Day is Saturday* EP (No Threes, 1984); *...and His Orchestra* (PopLlama Products, 1987); *Bike-Toy-Clock-Gift* (Bus Stop, 1988); *Very, Very Powerful Motor* (PopLlama Products, 1990); *In America, Live in Seattle* (Lost and Found, 1991); *Never Fails, Never Works* (Blaster, 1991); *The Question is No* (Sub Pop, 1992); *Zucker* (Sub Pop, 1993); *Gone to the Moon* EP (Sub Pop, 1993); *Answer the Phone, Dummy* (Sub Pop, 1994); *New Mansions in Sound* (Sub Pop, 1996)

FAT WRECK CHORDS

One of the few independent punk labels that's not only successful but thriving, San Francisco-based Fat Wreck Chords is run by **NOFX** leader Fat Mike (his wife is the vice president). Started in 1990 because Fat Mike couldn't find anybody to release a NOFX seven-inch single, and now one of the country's biggest indie labels, Fat Wreck's lineup is a high-intensity one, including the boss's own, **Lagwagon**, the **Descendents**, **Subhumans**, **Nerf Herder**, **Against Me**, and **Avail**; many of whom can be sampled on the label's occasional showcase compilations and anthologies like the multi-edition *Fat Music* and *Rock Against Bush*. Fat Wreck Chords is also involved in running the political action website Punkvoter.com, started in 2004. Unlike other labels that expanded too quickly and had to rely on outside investors, Fat Wreck Chords manages to keep itself a lean (unlike its founder) and streamlined organization that actually pays their artists (are you listening, **SST**? **Lookout!**?) and manages to put out consistently high-quality music. Although the anti-**pop-punk** crowd considers them too mainstream, Fat Mike don't care, and that's why he's Fat Mike, and you (most likely) are not.

Fear's Lee Ving plays on while the crowd bays for his blood. Reseda, California, 1982.

FEAR

1977-present

LINEUP: Lee Ving (vocals); Philo Cramer (guitar, replaced by Richard Presley); Derf Scratch (bass, replaced by numerous others, including Flea briefly); Spit Stix (drums, replaced by Andrew Jamiez)

Early Los Angeles punk marauders Fear were led by aggressively abrasive singer **Lee Ving**, who made a career of sorts out of his outrageous stage persona in which he taunted, berated, and castigated members of the audience. The hallmarks of a Fear performance were an ultra-violent **pit** and mocking songs, such as "We Destroy the Family," "Let's Start a War" (where the reasoning included "we need the space"), and "New York's Alright if You Like Saxophones," which put down everyone who was not a current member of Fear. Although often mentioned in the same breath as fellow L.A. trailblazers **Black Flag** and the **Circle Jerks**, Fear was by far the least musically adept of the bunch, using a much more simplistic and metal-tinged **hardcore** template and relying on Ving's penchant for calculated offense to keep people interested. Ving's standard approach was to provoke the crowd with a constant barrage of homophobic epithets and general misogyny (sample line: "Hey, are there any *queers* in the audience tonight?" Cue booing). It was unclear where the joke ended, if Ving was truly a beer-swilling Neanderthaloid stooge of reactionary hatred, just a guy trying to get a rise out of the audience, or both.

Sadly, for a band that is still (technically) in existence, Fear probably peaked around 1981. That was both the year they appeared in the original *Decline of Western Civilization*, and, more infamously, showed up on the Halloween episode of *Saturday Night Live*. The story goes that as a condition

of his final appearance on the show, John Belushi demanded to not only have Fear as the musical guests but that they be allowed to import a bunch of punks into the studio. The result was a pit (led by **Ian MacKaye** and John Joseph McGeown of the **Cro-Mags**) of such ferocious intensity that the *SNL* crew cut the performance off, claiming (falsely) that hundreds of thousands of dollars worth of damage had been done to the studio. The next year saw the release of Fear's first and only worthwhile album, *The Record*.

Fear was inactive for most of the 1980s, due partly to various internal squabbles as well as Ving's acting career—which included a host of minor roles as squint-eyed thugs, most memorably in Penelope Spheeris's *Dudes* (1988), a punk take on *Easy Rider* in which redneck villain Ving kills former bandmate Flea (of Red Hot Chili Peppers fame). After a near 10-year hiatus, Ving re-formed Fear in 1995 with no original members for the heavily suds-centric *Have Another Beer with Fear*. Sporadic tours followed and Fear shows continued to be fun, though the crowd-baiting does grow old after a few decades.

Discography:
The Record (Slash, 1982); *More Beer* (Restless, 1985); *Live…for the Record* (Restless, 1991); *Have Another Beer with Fear* (Sector 12, 1995); *American Beer* (Hall of Records, 2000)

THE FEEDERZ

1977-1987, 2002-2003

LINEUP: Frank Discussion (vocals/guitar); Dan Clark, aka "Clear Bob" (bass); John Vivier, aka "Art Nouveau" (drums)

The Feederz were a punishingly angry gaggle of anarcho-absurdist performance-freak punks formed in the hot sands of Arizona and led by one "Frank Discussion," whose idea of getting attention was encapsulated at their first show, when he sprayed the audience with an assault rifle (firing blanks). Giving one an idea of Discussion's thoughts on the importance of shock value at concerts is an excerpt from the *Weekly World News* describing how he "stunned" fans by showing up with live insects glued to his head; and that was before he started chucking dead animals at the audience. Their first album, the subtly titled *Ever Feel Like Killing Your Boss?*, became an instant punk-novelty collector's item due to it having a square of sandpaper glued to the

front (a telling clue as to what awaited listeners). An example of how the Feederz craved mainstream success is evident in the title of their song, "Jesus Entering Through the Rear" on the **Alternative Tentacles** compilation *Let Them Eat Jelly Beans*. Never quite making the punk mainstream, the Feederz collapsed in the late-1980s, then re-formed just long enough in the new millennium to record *Vandalism: Beautiful as a Rock in a Cop's Face*, before Discussion called it quits again. Rumors persist that Discussion enlisted with the Zapatista rebels in northern Mexico (in other words, putting into practice what Rage Against the Machine always yelled about), though this could simply be mere chicanery on his part, just laying the groundwork for another triumphant return.

Discography:
Ever Feel Like Killing Your Boss? (Flaming Banker, 1984); *Teachers in Space* (Flaming Banker, 1985); *Vandalism: Beautiful as a Rock in a Cop's Face* (Broken Rekids, 2002)

THE FEELIES

1976-1991, 2008

LINEUP: Bill Million (vocals/guitar); Glenn Mercer (vocals/guitar); Keith Clayton (bass, replaced by Brenda Sauter); Dave Weckerman (drums, replaced by Vinny (stet) DeNunzio, Anton Fier); Stanley Demeski (percussion)

During their early punk years (approximately until *The Good Earth* came out in 1986), the Feelies helped redefine the genre in a more intellectual and disjointed way. Named for the multi-sensory films in Aldous Huxley's *Brave New World*, the Feelies were like the New Jersey version of New York's **no wave** movement, with the **post-punk** addition of the Brit-styled herky-rhythms created by their drummer/percussion attack. Although they certainly never conformed to the stereotypical look or sound of punk, bands like the Feelies and the **Embarrassment** started out in the "anything goes" scene of the time, and unlike most other punks, decided that this lack of confinement was a great strategy for their career. A live band par excellence, as shown in their stellar appearance playing at a high school reunion as the Willies in 1986's *Something Wild* (director Jonathan Demme had been a huge fan since seeing them in 1980), the Feelies were also one of the only bands that could ever successfully pull off a fade-out live.

After much critical acclaim and the adoration of fans like R.E.M. (whose Peter Buck produced *The Good Earth*), the on-again, off-again band broke up for good in 1991, and despite the best efforts of their fans, have declined to reunite. Since then, drummer Anton Fier played in his band the Golden Palominos and vocalist/guitarist Glenn Mercer continues to release critically acclaimed solo material that sounds, not surprisingly, quite Feelies-like. In 2008, the Feelies reunited, playing a few dates and stoking rumors of a new album.

Discography:
Crazy Rhythms (Stiff, 1980;Line, 1986;A&M, 1990); *No One Knows* EP (Coyote/Twin/Tone, 1986); *The Good Earth* (Coyote/Twin/Tone, 1986); *Only Life* (Coyote/A&M, 1988); *Time for a Witness* (Coyote/A&M, 1991). **Glenn Mercer:** *Wheels in Motion* (Pravda, 2007)

The Feelies, 1980.

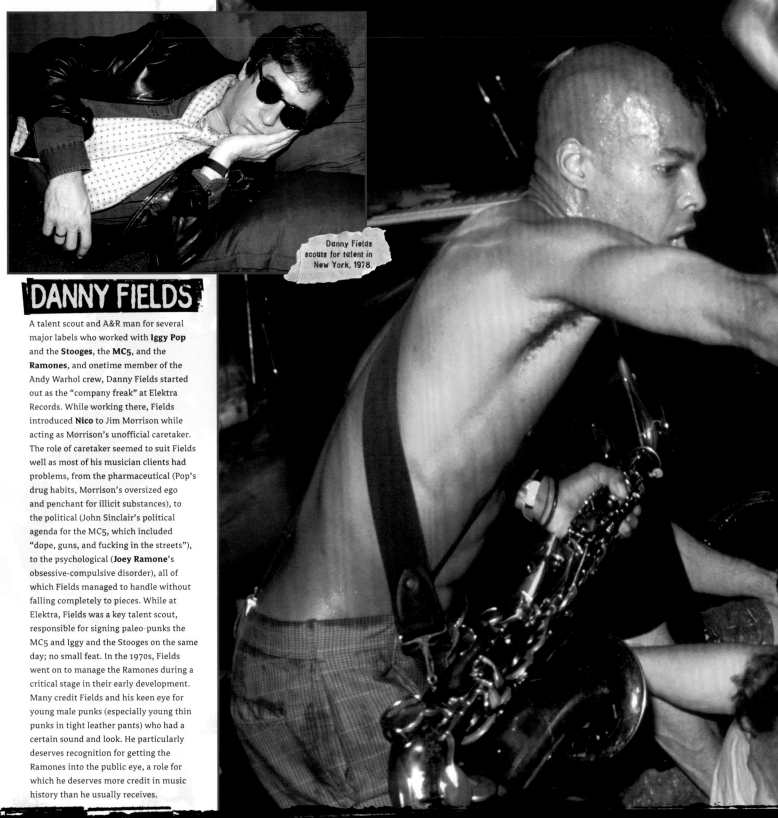

Danny Fields scouts for talent in New York, 1978.

DANNY FIELDS

A talent scout and A&R man for several major labels who worked with **Iggy Pop** and the **Stooges**, the **MC5**, and the **Ramones**, and onetime member of the Andy Warhol crew, Danny Fields started out as the "company freak" at Elektra Records. While working there, Fields introduced **Nico** to Jim Morrison while acting as Morrison's unofficial caretaker. The role of caretaker seemed to suit Fields well as most of his musician clients had problems, from the pharmaceutical (Pop's drug habits, Morrison's oversized ego and penchant for illicit substances), to the political (John Sinclair's political agenda for the MC5, which included "dope, guns, and fucking in the streets"), to the psychological (**Joey Ramone**'s obsessive-compulsive disorder), all of which Fields managed to handle without falling completely to pieces. While at Elektra, Fields was a key talent scout, responsible for signing paleo-punks the MC5 and Iggy and the Stooges on the same day; no small feat. In the 1970s, Fields went on to manage the Ramones during a critical stage in their early development. Many credit Fields and his keen eye for young male punks (especially young thin punks in tight leather pants) who had a certain sound and look. He particularly deserves recognition for getting the Ramones into the public eye, a role for which he deserves more credit in music history than he usually receives.

Fishbone's Angelo Moore solicits audience feedback at CBGB, 1991.

FISHBONE

1979-present

LINEUP: Angelo Moore (vocals/saxophones/theramin); Kendall Jones (guitar, replaced by others); John Norwood Fisher (bass); Phillip "Fish" Fisher (drums, replaced by many); "Dirty" Walter Kibby II (trumpet, replaced by Curtis Storey, Padre Holmes); Chris Dowd (keyboards/trombone, replaced by others)

While in some cases there was mutual derision between the punk and **ska** camps (especially in the post-**Operation Ivy** years), there was one band that could beautifully and spastically meld the two genres: the legendary Fishbone. Relentless in their wonderfully twisted vision, Fishbone has been for some three decades now, a three-ring circus of a punk/**reggae**/metal/ska/funk touring explosion, armed only with their patented mix of musical styles, surrealistic comedy, and dynamic performance style.

Initially formed by a group of junior high school friends from Los Angeles' Watts neighborhood, Fishbone played mostly around Southern California during the early-1980s. Like **Bad Brains**, Fishbone was a bunch of young black musicians who shamelessly professed their love for punk, but at the same time knew that it needed to be shaken up as much as any other genre and so began to write their own material. Their first release, the self-titled 1985 EP, contained catchy, comedic nuggets like "U.G.L.Y." and "Party at Ground Zero" that remain their best-known songs. Although that EP and their next two records, 1986's *In Your Face* and 1988's *Truth and Soul*, were mostly a bouncy blend of funk-tinged ska, these albums were still for years *de rigueur* possessions for many punks (many of whom never went closer to ska than Operation Ivy, much less knew any actual black punks), perhaps due to the presence of freakishly energetic and mohawked singer Angelo Moore. Fellow proto-ska-punkers (who owe a large debt to the trailblazers of Fishbone) such as the Red Hot Chili Peppers and the

Mighty Mighty Bosstones went mainstream in later years, while the more wonderfully weird Fishbone, who never seemed that interested in mainstream success, kept their unique sound intact.

Later albums got louder and more eclectic, pushing ska and funk to the background in favor of a soulful, metal/late-**hardcore** sound that acknowledged their respect for Bad Brains and their approval of the aims of the Black Rock Coalition. In 1991, Fishbone's *The Reality of My Surroundings* LP yielded a couple minor hits (Spike Lee did the video for "Sunless Saturday") and an unforgettable *Saturday Night Live* performance. But despite this flirtation with success and the band's dedicated fanbase (actor John Cusack among them), Fishbone never broke through to the mainstream. Their 2000 album, *The Psychotic Friends Nuttwerx*, featured a bevy of guest performers, includingNo Doubt's Gwen Stefani (who started off in a ska-punk band of her own, after all), Rick James, the Bad Brains' H.R., and assorted Chili Peppers, many of them returning the favor, on what was an otherwise forgettable album.

Over the years Fishbone has toured with hip-hop acts like the Beastie Boys and De La Soul, and performed in any kind of film that would appreciate them (from lip-synching a cover of "Jamaican Ska" in the Frankie Avalon and Annette Funicello comedy *Back to the Beach*, to the OutKast vanity project *Idlewild*, in which they played the house band). Relentless touring, though, has taken its toll and only Moore and bassist John Norwood Fisher remain from the original lineup. If George Clinton and Parliament Funkadelic ever went punk, they would *wish* they could sound half as funky as Fishbone in their prime.

Essential Discography:

Fishbone EP (Columbia, 1985); *In Your Face* (Columbia, 1986); *It's a Wonderful Life (Gonna Have a Good Time)* EP (Columbia, 1987); *Truth and Soul* (Columbia, 1988); *The Reality of My Surroundings* (Columbia, 1991); *Give a Monkey a Brain and He'll Swear He's the Center of the Universe* (Columbia, 1993); *Chim Chim's Badass Revenge* (Arista, 1996); *Nuttasaurusmeg Fossil Fuelin' the Fonkay* (Columbia, 1996); *The Psychotic Friends Nuttwerx* (Hollywood, 2000); *Still Stuck in Your Throat* (Discograph, 2006)

THE FLESH EATERS

1977–1983, occasionally thereafter

LINEUP: Chris D. (vocals); Dave Alvin (guitar); John Doe (bass); D.J. Bonebrake (drums); Steve Berlin (saxophone)

A California band founded by Chris D. (Chris Desjardins), the Flesh Eaters featured a veritable "who's who" of the cream of Los Angeles punk musicians. Among those who played in the Flesh Eaters over the years include John Doe and D.J. Bonebrake from **X**, Stan Ridgeway of Wall of Voodoo, Tito Larriva of the Plugz, and Dave Alvin of the Blasters. Chris D., a poet of doom and gloom who was a high school English teacher when the band first formed, remained the Flesh Eaters' only constant member during their first and most influential spate of existence from 1977 to 1983. The band was one of the most consistently interesting and creepy entities on the scene, with Chris D.'s morbid imagery inspiring a number of proto-goths and some of the gloomier L.A. bands, such as the **Gun Club**, **45 Grave**, and **T.S.O.L.** The Flesh Eaters released new material and toured from 1989 to 1994 and then returned with a new lineup in 1998. Chris D. also played in the band Divine Horsemen.

Discography:

The Flesh Eaters EP (Upsetter, 1978); *No Questions Asked* (Upsetter, 1980; with bonus tracks, Atavistic, 2004); *A Minute to Pray, a Second to Die* (Ruby, 1981; Slash, 1993); *Forever Came Today* (Ruby, 1982); *A Hard Road to Follow* (Upsetter, 1983); *Greatest Hits—Destroyed by Fire* (SST, 1987); *The Flesh Eaters Live* (Homestead, 1988); *Prehistoric Fits,Greatest Hits Vol. 2* (SST, 1990); *Dragstrip Riot* (SST, 1991); *The Sex Diary of Mr. Vampire* (SST, 1992); *Crucified Lovers in Woman Hell* EP (SST, 1993); *Ashes of Time* (Upsetter, 1999, 2001); *Miss Muerta* (Atavistic, 2004); *The Complete Hard Road to Follow Sessions* (remastered; Atavistic, 2004)

FLIPPER

1978–1993, occasionally thereafter

LINEUP: Will Shatter (vocals/bass, replaced by John Dougherty); Bruce Loose (vocals/bass); Ted Falconi (guitar); Steve DePace (drums)

Flipper were an incredibly noisy and bombastic **hardcore** sludge band from San Francisco with a chaotic touring and recording career. Although a couple of the members had played around in Bay Area punk bands like Negative Trend, Flipper's droning sound stood defiantly apart from the quick-and-fast hardcore standard. What recognition Flipper had came from their signature song "Sex Bomb," a seven-minute dirge whose lyrics comprised in total the following: "She's my sex bomb/ My baby/yeah;" that and their strangely ubiquitous logo of a frighteningly fanged fish. Although championed by a number of heavy hitters in the scene such as **Jello Biafra**, Kurt Cobain, and the **Melvins**, as well as the occasional industry type like Rick Rubin (who later signed them to his Def American label), Flipper might have made it to some form of success if not for Shatter dying of a heroin overdose in 1987. The band soldiered on after a brief hiatus with new bassist John Dougherty for the release *American Grafishy*. A reunited Flipper toured with various bands in 2005 and played at the benefit concerts to save **CBGB** that August. The following year they toured briefly with **Nirvana**'s Krist Novoselic on bass.

Discography:

Generic Flipper (Subterranean, 1982); *Blow'n Chunks* (ROIR, 1984); *Gone Fishin'* (Subterranean, 1984); *Public Flipper Limited Live 1980–1985* (Subterranean, 1986); *Sex Bomb Baby!* (Subterranean, 1988); *American Grafishy* (Def American, 1992; Sony, 1993)

Flipper plays CBGB, 2005.

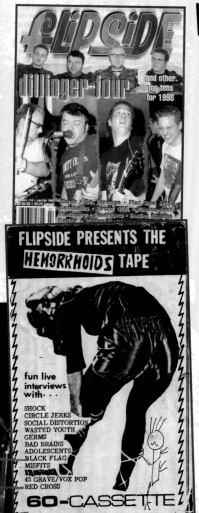

FLIPSIDE

Iconic zine, sadly now defunct, that helped set the standard for California punk in general and **hardcore** in specific, *Flipside* was started in 1977 by a loose cabal of writers. The first issue was a classically rough-looking mash of twenty pages of messy type and smudgy photos—it sold for 25¢ and included album reviews that were essentially nonsensical conversations between writers "Pooch" and "X-8," as well as an up-to-the-minute "Nooze" section (Item: "More than a few unkind words were exchanged between DICK MANITOBA's lady friend and...JOAN JETT at the NUNS/DICTATORS bash at the Whisky."). Although originally designed to cover only the Los Angeles area, *Flipside* quickly grew to include featured reviews, scene reports, and information on regional and international punk scenes. By the early-1990s, the zine had ads and legible typesetting, ran to well over 100 pages in length, and covered bands well outside the punk mainstream (**Shonen Knife**, White Zombie, Gwar). *Flipside* also released record compilations, such as the *Rodney on the ROQ* compilation that came with Issue 21 and included bands from Doggy Style to Beck, and a series of videos of punk bands in the mid-1980s. As with so many other zines, *Flipside* folded in 2001. Todd Taylor, who had worked on *Flipside* in its later years, went on to found **Razorcake** and publish some of the most acclaimed zine writing in the United States.

THE FLOWERS OF ROMANCE

1976-1977

LINEUP: Sid Vicious (vocals); Keith Levene (guitar); Viv Albertine (guitar); Sarah Hall (bass); Palmolive (drums)

An early British supergroup that lasted for about a minute in the tumultuous crash of the 1976-1977 London punk uprising, the Flowers of Romance sounded much better on paper than they did in real life. Naturally, the Flowers of Romance—the name was supposedly suggested by **John Lydon**, who would later use it as the name of a **Public Image Ltd.** single and album, and refer to

the original band as "ponces"—was too much of a clash of divergent personalities to last long. The band did, however, provide the impetus for **Sid Vicious** to become a charismatic, if almost completely musically untalented, stage performer. Their usage of casual blasphemy, attacks on formal religion, and Holocaust references became a fairly well-established part of punk rock during that time period. Vicious was by all means a compelling character, but it soon became apparent to the audience, as well as to the band, that his destiny lay elsewhere. After the Flowers of Romance imploded without ever recording anything, drummer Palmolive and guitarist Viv Albertine would resurface in the **Slits**, guitarist Keith Levene would do stints in the **Clash** and Public Image Ltd., while Vicious joined some band called the **Sex Pistols**.

FLUX OF PINK INDIANS

1980-1987

LINEUP: Colin Latter (vocals); Kevin Hunter (guitar); Derek Birkett (bass); Martin Wilson (drums)

British **hardcore** punks with a distinct anarchist slant, Flux of Pink Indians recorded social-protest songs on the **Crass** record label and later on their own Spiderleg label. Many outlets banned one of their albums, the provocatively named *The Fucking Cunts Treat Us Like Pricks* (subtle lads, they were), and a store was prosecuted for carrying the record. After recording one more record, *Uncarved Block*, simply as Flux in 1986, the band broke up. Derek Birkett went on to found the One Little Indian record label, which released albums by **Chumbawamba** and other bands. Although they may not have been the most musically adept band on earth, their strong anarchist stance and **DIY** commitment, made them one of the best of the British bands who could truly be called "underground."

Discography:
Neu Smell EP (Crass, 1981); *Strive to Survive Causing the Least Suffering Possible* (Spiderleg, 1982); *The Fucking Cunts Treat Us Like Pricks* (One Little Indian, 1984); *Treat* (One Little Indian, 1986); *Uncarved Block* (One Little Indian, 1986); *Not So Brave* (Overground, 1997); *Live Statement* (Overground, 2002); *Fits and Starts* (Dr. Strange, 2003)

4SKINS

1979-1984, 2007-present

LINEUP: Gary Hodges (vocals, replaced by roadie Tony "Panther" Cummins); "Hoxton" Tom McCourt (guitar/bass, replaced on guitar by Steve "Rockabilly" Pear, later Paul Swain); Steve Harmer (bass, replaced by Tom McCourt who switched from guitar); Gary Hitchcock (drums, replaced by John Jacobs)

One of the original **oi** bands, the 4Skins (get it?) were a **skinhead** outfit, connected to the rough and tumble scene of the early-1980s, who went though numerous lineup changes over the years (bassist Hoxton being the most stable member of the band). For a band in such turmoil, the 4Skins put out some consistently enjoyable **ska**-tinged and metal-influenced oi tunes (one critic likened them to "the **Ramones** meeting Black Sabbath") about the plight of the British working class (thus the football-terrace choruses in classics such as "Yesterday's Heroes" and "Low Life"). Controversy struck the 4Skins when a Southall gig was firebombed by Nazi skins just as the band was leaving. Because racist hate flyers were found near the pub, the 4Skins were blamed, much to their chagrin (especially that of Rockabilly Steve, a committed socialist). Like many skinhead bands, violence followed the 4Skins despite their best intentions, and Hoxton was forced to later replace the entire group all over again (new guitarist Paul Swain later disgraced the group's name by joining the neo-Nazi band **Skrewdriver** in 1984. The 4Skins broke up in the early-1980s but reunited in 2007 with original singer Hodges and bassist Harmer.

Discography:
The Good, the Bad and the 4Skins (Secret, 1982); *A Fistful of 4Skins* (Syndicate, 1983); *From Chaos to 1984* (Syndicate, 1984); *Live and Loud!* (Link, 1989); *Clockwork Skinhead* (Harry May, 1999); *One Law for Them* (Cancan, 2000); *Low Life* (Get Back, 2000); *The Secret Life of the 4Skins* (Captain Oi!, 2001)

45 GRAVE
1979-1985, 1989-1990, 2004-present

LINEUP: Mary "Dinah Cancer" Sims (vocals); Paul Cutler (guitar); Rob "Graves" Ritter (bass); Don Bolles (drums)

A death-rock group from Los Angeles who helped put the death-rock scene on the map with their gruesome imagery and mixture of goth, punk, and metal, 45 Grave first appeared on the legendary *Hell Comes to Your House* compilation. They later signed to Enigma, with whom they released their best album, 1983's *Sleep in Safety*, containing their best and most disturbing song, "Partytime," which was used in the punk zombie splatter-comedy *Return of the Living Dead* (1985). Rob Ritter, once of the **Gun Club** and the **Bags**, and ex-**Germs** drummer Don Bolles, inhabited 45 Grave for a while, further cementing the band's punk credentials. Ritter died of an overdose in 1990 and Bolles now plays with a reconstituted Germs. In 2004, Dinah Cancer reformed the band with no other original members and tours as 45 Grave.

Discography:
Sleep in Safety (Enigma 1983); *Autopsy* (Restless, 1987); *Only the Good Die Young* (Restless, 1989);

KIM FOWLEY

Among the most controversial and reviled figures in early U.S. punk, Kim Fowley is best known for masterminding the **Runaways** and putting out the 1960s novelty single "They're Coming to Take Me Away Ha-Ha" as Napoleon XIV. It was the Runaways who cemented Fowley's claim to infamy when he bullied the quintet of teenage girls (including **Joan Jett** and Lita Ford) until the band imploded. Fowley may only have been punk in his mind, but he was able to take advantage of L.A.'s everything-goes period in the 1970s and helped develop the L.A. scene, particularly by being a constant companion of tastemaker **Rodney Bingenheimer**. Fowley later made a notorious appearance on Tom Snyder's *Tomorrow* show wearing a large flower, a cut-up suit, glitter, and the dazed expression of a man long past having gone around the bend. Although Fowley was instrumental in the careers of ex-Runaways Jett and Ford, both would argue (not necessarily incorrectly) that their careers in fact happened *in spite* of him.

FRANKENSTEIN

1975

LINEUP: Steve Bator, aka "Stiv Bators" (vocals);
William Wilden, aka "Jimmy Zero" (guitar);
Gene O'Connor, aka "Cheetah Chrome" (guitar);
John Madansky, aka "Johnny Blitz" (drums)

This early version of the **Dead Boys** was how the legendary Cleveland group served their punk apprenticeships and learned many valuable lessons in what music works in Cleveland, and what is better suited for New York. Frankenstein came together following the demise of **Rocket from the Tombs**, and though too radically nihilistic for Ohio, the band was a proving ground for the charismatic ability of scrawny little Stiv Bators to hold an audience in the palm of his hand. The band honed their punk chops for a while in the friendlier confines of Cleveland until they were effectively banned from most venues; this took about four gigs to accomplish. Frankenstein busted up after about three months, but laid the groundwork for the nucleus that would evolve into the Dead Boys and storm the New York scene.

THE FREEZE

1978–1985, 1991–1995, sporadic reunions

LINEUP: Clifford Croce, aka "Clif Hanger" (vocals); Rob Rosenthal, aka "Rob DeCradle" (guitar); Papa Verje (guitar); Rick Andrews (bass); Scooter Woodless (synthesizers); Kevin Bonelli (drums, replaced by Lou Cataldo, others)

A Boston area **hardcore** band that started in the late-1970s, the Freeze famously appeared on the *This Is Boston, Not L.A.* compilation and for a time comprised the entirety of the Cape Cod scene. The Freeze was notable for being more melodic than most of the Boston hardcore bands, which did not endear them to some of the more aggressive types in the scene. That doesn't mean that the Freeze lacked anger, as is clearly evidenced in their debut single, 1980's "I Hate Tourists." The Freeze was also part of Boston's growing **straight-edge** scene that included bands like **SSD** and **DYS**, with songs like "Idiots at Happy Hour" clearly identifying them as one of the more militant bands in an already militant scene. The Freeze fizzled by 1985 and remained quiet until 1991 when the band was welcomed by German punk label Lost and Found, releasing one live album and recording two more studio records between 1991 and 1995. Lead singer Clif Hanger still sporadically tours with a new version of the band, who played a notable set at **CBGB**.

Discography:

Guilty Face EP (Modern Method, 1982); *Land of the Lost* (Modern Method, 1983); *Rabid Reaction* (Modern Method, 1985); *Misery Loves Company* (Taang!, 1991); *Five Way Fury* (live; Lost and Found, 1992); *Crawling Blind* (Lost and Found, 1994); *Freak Show* (Lost and Found, 1995)

Kim Fowley in his 1970s mad scientist phase.

FUGAZI

1987-present

LINEUP: Ian MacKaye (vocals/guitar);
Guy Picciotto (vocals/guitar); Joe Lally
(bass); Brendan Canty (drums)

Perhaps the most respected band in U.S. punk history, Fugazi was the brainchild of some heavy hitters in the Washington, D.C., scene, including **Ian MacKaye** of **Minor Threat** and **Dischord Records**, and Guy Picciotto and Brendan Canty of **Rites of Spring**. Fugazi was a consistently experimental band who served as a moral benchmark for other punk bands by virtue of the

members taking control of their careers in almost unprecedented ways. The band was legendary for keeping door prices to a reasonable level (usually no more than $5 or $6), not selling merchandise (although there are many "bootleg" T-shirts available with the logo "This is not a Fugazi T-shirt"), touring econo-style, and refusing to be interviewed by magazines that accepted cigarette or alcohol advertisements.

Fugazi (the word is an old Italian slang term for "fake") started out in the late-1980s, at a time when **hardcore** had run into a dead end both musically and politically, and the U.S. punk scene desperately needed a fresh vision. Originally just a three-piece

(Picciotto joined up after their first few live outings), the band's early songs were pretty straightforward, if unusually musically complex and thoughtfully lyrical. As Fugazi grew as a band, the members became more political, and eventually all of the other members adopted MacKaye's dedication to vegetarianism and a substance-free lifestyle, and agreed that the band would not sell merchandise and keep gig prices low. The band also incorporated a more politicized stamp to their music, as seen in a couple of songs from their eponymous 1988 EP: "Suggestion" (a consideration of sexual violence in which MacKaye sang from the woman's perspective) and "Give Me the Cure" (a passionate call to arms regarding the AIDS crisis), which became instant classics and set the bar pretty high for both themselves and other bands to follow.

The mix of intricate musicianship, passionate delivery, and an uncompromising antiauthoritarian fury proved to be a powerfully kinetic concoction, both live and in the studio. Soon Fugazi began incorporating shredding blasts of guitar noise and **reggae** and **dub** rhythms that marked them as musically more akin to British **post-punk** than to U.S. hardcore. Hardcore punks continually flocked to Fugazi shows, however, and a visibly annoyed MacKaye often asked for calm, admonishing the audience when the **pit** had gotten out of control or when the crowd became hostile to female participants; his tongue-lashings of particularly thick-headed crowd members were almost as much a stamp of a typical Fugazi show as the band's astoundingly tight performances.

Although some of the later albums were hit and miss, Fugazi was a relentlessly

FUGAZI
3 SONGS

(L to R) Fugazi's

Fugazi in a rare outdoor sighting, 2000.

aggressive live band (as documented in band friend Jem Cohen's film *Instrument*) whose members were unable to compromise their musical or political vision for mainstream success. Additionally, on albums like 1991's *Steady Diet of Nothing* and 1993's *In On the Kill Taker* they did their level best to remind their fellow lefties that just because the Cold War had ended and **Ronald Reagan** had departed the White House didn't mean that the forces of repression had gone on vacation. After the release of *Argument* in 2001, Fugazi went on an indefinite hiatus that so far has not been determined to mean they have officially broken up. In any case, their towering status as the one true uncompromising U.S. punk band who stuck to their principles and ideals cannot be overestimated.

During Fugazi's indefinite post-2002 hiatus period, Joe Lally has released a couple of solo albums, and MacKaye has continued running Dischord Records. Brendan Canty has been composing soundtrack music for programs on the Discovery Channel, playing drums for Bob Mould, and also producing a series of live music DVDs called *Burn to Shine*. Also, Fugazi has been keeping the flame alive by releasing a series of 30 live concert CDs documenting shows from throughout their history. Ian MacKaye currently tours and plays with acoustic band the Evens with singer/drummer Amy Farina.

Discography:
Fugazi EP (Dischord, 1988); *Margin Walker* EP (Dischord, 1989); *13 Songs* (Dischord, 1990); *Repeater* (Dischord, 1990; plus three songs, 2004); *Steady Diet of Nothing* (Dischord, 1991); *In On the Kill Taker* (Dischord, 1993); *Red Medicine* (Dischord, 1995); *End Hits* (Dischord, 1998); *Instrument* (Dischord, 1999); *Argument* (Dischord, 2001); *Fugazi Live Series, Vols. 1–30* (Fugazi Live Series, 2004). **Joe Lally:** *There to Here* (Dischord, 2006); *Nothing is Underrated* (Discord, 2007). **The Evens:** *12 Songs* (Dischord, 2005); *Get Even* (Dischord, 2006)

FURIOUS GEORGE
1997-1999
LINEUP: George Tabb (vocals/guitar); Evan Cohen (bass); Michael Harper (drums)

Led by prolific writer, musician, and New York scenester George Tabb, Furious George is probably best known for being sued for using the Curious George character in their logo. Furious George could easily be described as a more aggressive version of the **Ramones** (with whom the band were good friends), with Tabb's gruff but evocative voice serving as a counterpoint to his clever lyrics. Typical of Furious George's approach was their best song, "Gilligan" (featuring **Joey Ramone**'s guest appearance), in which the title character, stranded on an island with six other castaways, bemoans his fate and muses that someday he will surely snap and kill the other castaways (who were, after all, only supposed to be gone for a three-hour tour). In addition to losing their 1990s legal fight with *Curious George* publisher Houghton Mifflin, Furious George also gained notoriety of a better sort for serving as actor Adrien Brody's backup band in Spike Lee's *Summer of Sam*.

Discography:
Furious George Goes Ape (7"; Lookout!, 1996); *Furious George Gets a Record* (Recess, 1997); *Bananas* (Recess, 1997); *V.M.Live* (Liberation, 1999)

DON FURY

During the 1980s, when bands in New York's **straight-edge** scene began to record in earnest, many complained of the predatory practices of the various producers running larger recording studios. Don Fury, who ran a studio out of a basement in a small tenement building about five blocks from **CBGB**, was happy to fill in the gap left by the big studios. Rare for a producer, he actually spent time with bands in the CBGB **hardcore** scene, trying to refine and tighten their sound before laying down tracks. Fury's success producing records such as **Agnostic Front**'s *Victim in Pain* led to him becoming sort of a house producer for bands such as **Gorilla Biscuits**, Project X, **Judge**, and **Youth of Today**. If there is a consistent "New York straight-edge hardcore" sound from the mid-to-late-1980s, the credit (or blame) lies at the feet of the talented Fury, who continues to record bands at his Cyclone Sound studio in Coney Island.

THE F.U.'S
1981-1990
LINEUP: John "Sox" Stocking (vocals); Steve Grimes (vocals/guitar); Steve Martin (guitar); Wayne Maestri (bass); Bob "Furapples" Hatfield (drums, replaced by Chris "Bones" Jones)

Boston **hardcore** band the F.U.'s initially started out in the "loud fast rules" style of punk, but as time went on they mellowed their sound, eventually realizing that you can't play ultrafast hardcore forever. They were one of the bands on the crucial 1982 compilation *This is Boston, Not L.A.* and scored a coup by getting Brian "Pushead" Schroeder to do the cover art for their debut *Kill for Christ* album. The F.U.'s got into some hot water with the more political punks after their 1983 *My America* album, which sounded like a hardline nationalistic "love it or leave it" stance that didn't fit in too well with the anti-**Reagan** ethos of most of the contemporary scene (though the band would later claim that most of the lyrics were tongue-in-cheek). Things got worse with a very hostile interview in *Maximum RocknRoll* that tried to paint them (somewhat unfairly) as ultra-patriotic xenophobes, gaining them a certain type of fame in the **Dead Milkmen** song "Tiny Town" ("'Cause we hate blacks and we hate Jews/And we hate punks but we love the F.U.'s"). The F.U.'s eventually went metal and changed their name to the commercially palatable Straw Dogs, which didn't really help them all that much in the long run.

Discography:
Kill for Christ (X-Claim, 1982; Taang!, 2002); *My America* (X-Claim, 1983; Taang!, 2002); *Do We Really Want to Hurt You?* (Gasatanka, 1983; Taang!, 2002). **Straw Dogs:** *Straw Dogs* EP (Restless, 1986); *We Are Not Amused* (Restless, 1986); *Yellow and Blue Attack* (Enigma, 1988); *Your Own Worst Nightmare* (Lone Wolf, 1990)

GANG GREEN

1982–present

CURRENT LINEUP: Chris Doherty (vocals/guitar); Bob Cenci (vocals/guitar); Matt Sandonato (bass/vocals); Walter Gustafson (drums)

A hard-drinking Boston skate-punk outfit fueled by a constant diet of beer and illicit substances, Gang Green could be summed up by their logo: a barely modified Budweiser beer sign with the humble tagline, "King of Bands." Founded by Chris Doherty after he left **Jerry's Kids**, Gang Green originally featured Mike Dean on drums and Bill Manley on bass but shifted to their classic line-up with the addition of the Stilphen brothers, Chuck and Glen, on guitar and bass, and Brian Betzger (also from Jerry's Kids) on drums. Gang Green stood out from the normally **straight-edge** Boston scene because of their irreverence and hard-partying attitude, but nonetheless were one of the most popular Boston bands during the early-1980s. A consistently fun band, Gang Green went so far as to cover the 'Til Tuesday classic, "Voices Carry" (only changing the line "tears are something to hide" to "beers are something to hide"). They made a stunning debut on the classic *This is Boston,*

Gang Green
ANOTHER WASTED NIGHT

CHROME   TAANG 13

OPEN YOUR MOUTH AND SAY...

Gang Green's Chris Doherty in a particularly heavy metal hair moment, Amsterdam, 1988.

Not L.A., compilation, on which their cheeky bursts of sound in songs such as "Kill a Commie" and "Snob" set them apart from the other bands on the album.

Having started out doing short, melodic **hardcore** songs, Gang Green eventually moved in a crunchier, more heavy-metal direction. After several successful releases that celebrated the joys of alcohol, the Stilphen brothers left to form the metal band Mallet-Head, and Gang Green soldiered on for a few years with new bassist Joe Gittleman (who later left to join the Mighty Mighty Bosstones and was replaced by Josh Pappe) and Fritz Erickson on guitar (replaced by Bob Cenci, another alumnus of Jerry's Kids). The band went on hiatus in the 1990s as Doherty and Betzger played briefly in **Klover**, who delivered a catchy brand of mid-1990s **pop-punk**. Doherty re-formed Gang Green in 1996 with their current lineup. They continue to tour, even occasionally outside of Boston.

Discography:
Drunk and Disorderly, Boston, MA EP (Deluxe, 1986); *Another Wasted Night* (Taang!, 1986, 1991); *P.M.R.C. Sucks* 12" EP (Taang!, 1987); *You Got It* (Roadrunner, 1987, 1992); *I81B4U* EP (Roadrunner, 1988, 1990); *Older. . . Budweiser* (Roadrunner, 1989); *Can't LIVE Without It* (live; Roadrunner, 1990); *King of Bands* (Roadrunner, 1991); *Another Case of Brewtality* (Taang!, 1997); *Preschool* (Taang!, 1997); *Back and Gacked* EP (Taang!, 1998); *You Got It/Older. . . Budweiser* (Roadrunner, 2003). **Mallet-Head:** *Mallet-Head* (Old Nick/Frontier, 1988); *Yeah Yeah Yeah* (Frontier/BMG, 1990)

GANG OF FOUR
1977-1984, 2004-present
LINEUP: Jon King (vocals); Andy Gill (guitar); Dave Allen (bass); Hugo Burnham (drums)

One of **post-punk**'s cornerstone bands, Gang of Four was a quartet of British students—out of the same Leeds scene that spawned bands like the **Mekons** and Delta 5—who were excited as much by music as they were by Karl Marx and the **Situationists**. Their combination of leftist politics and spastic funk rhythms would prove extremely influential to **Fugazi**, as well as on the early-2000s post-punk revival, inspiring bands like Bloc Party, Radio 4, Interpol, and Franz Ferdinand, not to mention a whole host of wannabes who invested all their trust-fund money in skinny ties.

Gang of Four set themselves apart from the late-1970s punk sound with their herky-jerky, **reggae**-esque rhythms and singer Jon King's obtuse, socialistic lyrics. Determined not to fall into the same tired clichés about rebellion and anarchy, nor to completely ignore love songs, Gang of Four concentrated instead on making the personal political, and vice versa. Although they were much more politically nuanced than most **hardcore** bands of the 1980s, Gang of Four helped point the way politically (albeit obliquely) for punk to follow in the years to come.

Gang of Four's first single, "Damaged Goods," was released in December 1978. Probably the first punk record to use terms such as *commodity fetishism*, the single also included the classic, "Love Like Anthrax," which combined a metronome-like drumbeat with guitarist Andy Gill's fuzzed-out, choppy spasms of noise-guitar. The band's brilliant follow-up single, "At Home He Feels Like a Tourist," was a subtle critique of the need to substitute entertainment for real thought, but its reference to condoms led to Gang of Four's withdrawal from a coveted slot on *Top of the Pops* when they refused to change the lyric. Following this almost perfect pair of singles, Gang of Four released an equally strong and politically-charged album in 1979, *Entertainment*, which established them firmly in the forefront of post-punk's Marxist wing. Although the 1981 album *Solid Gold* was an altogether solid effort, with songs like "Cheeseburger" and "He'd Send in the Army" that were as good as anything from

"Hard, angular, bold, (Gang of Four was) a pimple on the arse of pop, a corporation of common sense, a smart bomb of text that had me 'at home feeling like a typist.'"
—Bono, liner notes to the reissued *Songs of the Free*

the debut, it was still considered a disappointment by the British music press, who were already looking for the next big thing.

Later albums followed the law of diminishing returns and ultimately called into question the band's ideology and contemporary relevance. Dave Allen left the band after *Solid Gold*, and Hugo Burnham departed after 1982's *Songs of the Free*. This left Andy Gill and Jon King to flounder around in a pedestrian funk—and a **new wave** scene—without much success before they disbanded in 1984. However, later tours with the original members—who reunited a couple of times in the 1990s before officially regrouping in 2004—were reminders of why Gang of Four was regarded as such an indispensable component of post-punk innovation. Inexplicably, the band released an album of rerecorded versions of their early material on 2005's *Return the Gift*; nonetheless, it's nice to have them back.

Discography:
Entertainment (Warner Bros., 1979); *Gang of Four* EP (Warner Bros., 1980); *Solid Gold* (Warner Bros., 1981); *Songs of the Free* (Warner Bros., 1982); *Hard* (Warner Bros., 1983); *The Peel Sessions* (Strange Fruit, 1986); *A Brief History of the Twentieth Century* (Warner Bros., 1990); *Mall* (Polydor, 1991); *Shrinkwrapped* (Castle, 1995); *Return the Gift* (V2, 2005)

Gang of Four play New York, 1979. (L to R) Hugo Burnham, Jon King, Dave Allen, Andy Gill.

GAS HUFFER

1989-2006

LINEUP: Matt Wright (vocals); Tom Price (guitar); Don Blackstone (bass); Joe Newton (drums)

Since the late-1980s, Seattle's Gas Huffer has been managing the impressive feat of constant experimentation with different genres, from **Cramps**-style psychobilly to straight-out punk in the vein of **D.O.A.**, while keeping their original lineup intact. The band's exploration also comes accompanied by a keen feel for the pop hook and an ability to keep a sense of humor while writing songs about love and many other subjects. Gas Huffer's guitarist, Tom Price, came to the band after spending most of the 1980s with beloved local proto-grungers the U-Men (cited as key influences by Soundgarden and **Nirvana**), and then the short-lived Kings of Rock (who paid tribute to little-known Pacific Northwest garage bands of the 1960s). Cramps-loving singer Matt Wright was a U-Men fan and had opened for them with punk band Holy Ghost People (his first band, The Body Bags, "primarily performed in my parents' rec room," he once told a local newspaper).

Gas Huffer's first national tour was opening for Mudhoney in 1991. Over the years that followed, the band busily explored non-punk musical avenues, recording a song for the 1996 Willie Nelson tribute album, *Twisted Willie*, and even spinning off a surf-rock side project, the Del Lagunas. For a number of reasons, including the difficulty Price was experiencing after being diagnosed with Parkinson disease in 2003, Gas Huffer split up after a January 2006 farewell concert in Seattle. Drummer Joe Newton moved back to New York after being hired as a deputy art director by *Rolling Stone*. Although Gas Huffer's version of pop-punk was nicely twisted and melodic, they were never quite able to build the fanbase they definitely deserved.

Discography:
Ethyl EP (Black, 1991); *Janitors of Tomorrow* (Empty, 1991); *Integrity, Technology and Service* (Empty, 1992); *One Inch Masters* (Epitaph, 1994); *The Inhuman Ordeal of Special Agent Gas Huffer* (Epitaph, 1996); *Just Beautiful Music* (Epitaph, 1998); *The Rest of Us* (Estrus, 2002); *Lemonade for Vampires* (Estrus/Touch and Go, 2005)

GAUNT

1991-1999

LINEUP: Jerry Wick (vocals/guitar); Jovan Karcic (guitar); Eric Barth (bass, replaced briefly by Jim Weber, aka "Jim Motherfucker", then Brett Falcon); Jeff Regensburger (drums, replaced by Sam Brown)

Lo-fi Columbus, Ohio, punkers with a raved-up sound courtesy of Jovan Karcic's country-punk guitar, Gaunt formed out of the remains of psychedelic outfit Black Juju and soon became part of one of several intensely real-ized punk scenes (with bands like **New Bomb Turks** and Scrawl) that still occasionally materialize in small Ohio towns. Their sound ranged all over the sonic map, from straight-forward rock shouting to the occasional country twang. Their first full-length album, *Sob Story*, was produced by **Steve Albini** for Thrill Jockey (Gaunt was the label's first signed band). After that, the band soldiered on, putting out great records on Thrill Jockey and Amphetamine Reptile. In 1998 Gaunt released their adventurous major-label record debut, *Bricks and Blackouts*, for Warner Bros. Although the album featured the band's poppier side, right alongside straightforward punk rockers such as "Anxiety" and "97th Tear," it made no dent on the charts and the band was subsequently dropped from the label. Gaunt broke up officially in 1999, after which Sam Brown joined fellow ex-member Jim Weber in the New Bomb Turks. Lead singer Jerry Wick was killed in January 2001 at the age of 33 when a car struck him while he was riding a bike home from his restaurant job late at night. Out of respect for Wick, the band has never reunited.

Discography:
Whitey the Man EP (Thrill Jockey, 1992); *Sob Story* (Thrill Jockey, 1994); *I Can See Your Mom from Here* (Thrill Jockey, 1995); *Yeah, Me Too* (Amphetamine Reptile, 1995); *Kryptonite* (Thrill Jockey, 1996); *Bricks and Blackouts* (Warner Bros., 1998)

G.B.H.

1979-present

LINEUP: Colin "Col" Abrahall (vocals); Colin "Jock" Blyth (guitar); Ross Lomas (bass); Andrew Williams (drums, replaced by Kai Reder, Joseph Montero, Scott Preece)

A respectably long-lived British punk band were started in Birmingham in 1979 (the name comes from the British police term *grievous bodily harm*), G.B.H. made their

reputation both with anthem-heavy albums, such as *City Baby Attacked by Rats*, and their gravity-defying haircuts. Their metal-tinged sound and gruesomely frank lyrics made G.B.H. one of the most relentless and influential bands of the second wave of British punk—a group of various artists sometimes known as "UK82" and better labeled as the first wave of British **hardcore**, which included other permanently pissed-off bands like **Discharge**, the **Exploited**, and the **Varukers**.

Initially known as Charged G.B.H., the band shortened their moniker in 1982 after determining that the London band originally using the name G.B.H. was no longer in existence. G.B.H. started off a little less raucous with the *Leather Bristles, Studs and Acne* EP, but by early-1983, the band had honed their formidable wall of sound—they even had a song called "Wall of Sound"—into a gale-force hurricane. Songs like "Time Bomb" and "Give Me Fire" were as ferocious as anything put out by their friends and frequent tour partners Discharge. G.B.H. continued to tour throughout the 1980s, and even after the British punk scene began to wane, the band continued to spread their message across the country, even getting faster and more aggressive on 1987's *No Need to Panic!*, on which new drummer Kai added a heavy metal sound with his double-bass drums. During the 1990s, G.B.H. slacked off in their output, recording and playing sporadically. But with a new wave of British youth discovering the older bands, G.B.H. continues to tour with three-quarters of the original lineup. Despite the fact that the band's heyday is long gone, the social issues about which they originally sang (poverty, police repression, alcohol abuse) remain sadly just as relevant to the Britain of today as they were more than 25 years ago,

Discography:

Leather, Bristles, Studs and Acne EP (Clay, 1981, 1990, 1995); *Leather, Bristles, No Survivors and Sick Boys . . .* (Clay/Combat, 1982); *City Baby Attacked by Rats* (Clay, 1982; Clay/Combat, 1987; Captain Oi!, 2004); *City Baby's Revenge* (Relativity, 1984; Captain Oi!, 2002); *Midnight Madness and Beyond . . .* (Combat Core, 1986); *Oh No It's G.B.H. Again!* EP (Combat Core, 1986); *Clay Years: 1981-1984* (Clay, 1986, 1995); *No Need to Panic!* (Combat, 1987); *Wot a Bargin'* EP (Combat, 1988); *No Survivors* (Clay, 1989); *A Fridge Too Far* (Rough Justice, 1989; Triple X, 1999); *From Here to Reality* (Rough Justice, 1990; Restless, 1993; Captain Oi!, 2006); *Diplomatic Immunity* (Clay, 1990, 1995); *Clay Punk Singles Collections* (Clay, 1995); *Charged G.B.H: Clay Records* (Clay, 1996); *Celebrity Live Style* (Cleopatra, 1996); *Punk Junkies* (Triple X, 1997); *Live in Japan* (Creative Man, 1998); *Church of the Truly Warped* (Triple X, 1999); *Punk Rock Hits* (Cleopatra, 1999); *The Punk Singles 1981-1984* (Castle, 2002); *Dead on Arrival: A Punk Rock Anthology* (Castle, 2005)

G.B.H., 1982. (L to R)
Ross Lomas, Colin Abrahall,
Colin Blyth, Scott Preece.

GENERATION X

1976-1981

LINEUP: William Broad, aka "Billy Idol" (vocals); Bob "Derwood" Andrews (guitar, replaced by James Stevenson, briefly Steve Jones); Tony James (bass); Mark Laff (drums, replaced by Terry Chimes)

The early Brit-punk group Generation X, best-known for their poppy hits (including the original version of "Dancing with Myself," which eventually became a much bigger hit for former front man Billy Idol), tangential **Bromley Contingent** relationship, and fantastic fashion sense, served as the petri dish in which 1980s megastar extraordinaire, Billy Idol (*née* William Broad), would incubate. Taking their name from a 1964 pop-sociology text about Mods fighting Rockers, Generation X was written off by London punks as a group of mere pretty-boy **poseurs** (particularly sneering front man Idol). A telling account comes from *Regeneration*, photo scenester Ray Stevenson's account of the band's rise: "Since Billy decided he could sing better than tune his guitar, potential guitarists were auditioned but all were ugly or deaf."

Bassist Tony James once supposedly declared that there would never be a fat member of the band. However, for all of their obnoxious boy-band posturing and despite their slim three-album output, Generation X would prove to have a surprisingly deep catalog.

The band signed to Chrysalis Records in July 1977, and in March 1978 released their fantastic, self-titled first album, an unfairly ignored gem that not only contained future classics "Ready Steady Go" and "Your Generation," but also the remix of the song "Wild Youth" into "Wild Dub," one of the first punk attempts at a **reggae** and **dub** crossover. A second, less successful album, *Valley of the Dolls*, produced by Mott the Hoople's Ian Hunter, marked the end of the original lineup. After that, the band began to clash over what musical direction to follow, whether it would be pop, rock, or punk. By the third record, *Kiss Me Deadly* (at which point the boys had shortened the name to just Gen X), they were joined by Terry Chimes from the **Clash** and Steve Jones of the **Sex Pistols**, perversely giving the band an

amount of real punk credibility on the eve of their implosion.

Andrews and Laff formed the standard-issue rock band Empire in 1981 for one album. Tony James later embarrassed himself by forming the late-1980s new wave hit factory Sigue Sigue Sputnik. James tried later to redeem himself by forming the band Carbon/Silicon with the Clash's Mick Jones, but negated that by also reuniting Sputnik.

Discography:

Generation X (Chrysalis, 1978; remastered, EMI International, 2002); *Valley of the Dolls* (Chrysalis, 1979; EMI International, 2002); *Kiss Me Deadly* (Chrysalis, 1981; Capitol, 1990; EMI International, 2005); *Dancing with Myself* EP (Chrysalis, 1981); *The Best of Generation X* (Chrysalis, 1985); *Live* (MBC, 1988); *Perfect Hits 1975-1981* (Chrysalis, 1991; EMI Gold, 2002); *The Gold Collection* (EMI, 2000); *Live at the Paris Theatre, 1978 & 1981* (EMI International, 2000); *Radio One Sessions* (Strange Fruit, 2002); *BBC Live—One Hundred Punks* (Strange Fruit, 2002); *Anthology* (Capitol, 2003); *Sweet Revenge Xtra* (Vivid Sound, 2003; Revel Yell, 2004); *Live at Hatfield Poly 1980* (EMI International, 2005). **Empire:** *Empire* (Dinosaur, 1981)

The pretty lads of Generation X in London, 1979.

THE GERMS

1977–1980

LINEUP: Darby Crash (yowling);
Pat Smear (guitar); Lorna Doom (bass);
Don Bolles (drums, replaced by Rob Henley)

Led by the charismatic and twisted **Darby Crash**, Los Angeles's the Germs are equally remembered for their music and for the myths that surrounded the band and Crash's early, ugly death from a planned heroin overdose. The band was initially started by Crash, a longtime Queen fan who, along with good friend Pat Smear (born Georg Ruthenberg), met future Go-Go Belinda Carlisle and friend Terri Ryan outside the Beverly Hilton while waiting to see Queen. The four formed a band with Carlisle on drums and Ryan (now Lorna

Fowley Presents **new wave** Nights at the **Whisky A Go Go** (where Fowley got on the radio and asked bands from the new scene to just show up and perform) in summer 1977. When the Germs released their single "Forming" on What? Records later that year, it marked a new moment in L.A. punk and clearly foreshadowed the **hardcore** explosion that would take over the city's music scene in a few short years. Although the song's lyrics are quite literate in written form, on record they are almost incomprehensible, with a rhythm differing from the usual blitzkrieg speed of punk of that time. "Forming" was quickly put into heavy rotation by DJ **Rodney Bingenheimer** on his KROQ show, and became a key early U.S. indie release, inspiring many other bands to put out their own records independently.

As Crash's behavior became more erratic and his drug use more problematic, large numbers of L.A. punks decided to emulate him. Crash, unsure of what to write next, embarked on a disastrous project to create new Germs material for use in the Al Pacino film *Cruising*. After those sessions proved particularly uninspired, Crash relocated briefly to England, from which he returned with a **mohawk** and a newfound fascination for Adam and the Ants. Crash then re-formed the Germs for a December 1980 show at the Starwood. Although the concert was an unqualified success, Crash's life had entered a tailspin that ended several days later, when he fatally overdosed on heroin. The remaining Germs disbanded, with guitarist Pat Smear later going on to join **Nirvana** and then

GILMAN STREET

LOCATION: NORTH BERKELEY, CA

Also known as the Alternative Music Foundation, 924 Gilman Street is an all-ages, collective music club in California's East Bay. First opened in 1986 by a group that included *Maximum RocknRoll*'s **Tim Yohannon** who were frustrated by the lack of decent and affordable music venues in the area, it is one of the only clubs in the United States to be run by and for genuine punks who want to see a show without interference from the authorities, drunks, or stoners. All members of Gilman Street are eligible to vote in the operational decision-making process—and everyone

> ## "Fascist is totally extreme right. We're not extreme right. Maybe there's a better word for it that I haven't found yet, but I'm still going to have complete control … One day you'll pray to me."
>
> —Darby Crash, *No* Magazine, 1979

Doom) on bass, but Carlisle was sidelined with mononucleosis and was replaced by Becky Barton (aka Donna Rhia, herself later replaced by Don Bolles and then Rob Henley) for the embryonic version of the Germs.

Fronted by the charismatic and dangerous Crash, the Germs could at first barely play their instruments, but nevertheless became something of a self-destructive cult, with their proto-fascist singer practicing mind-control techniques and initiating people into his circle through the "Germs Burn," a cigarette burn on the arm that followers were then allowed to administer to others as initiation into the "mysteries" of the Germs. The band started gigging around L.A., playing the famous **Kim**

On the first single's success, the Germs signed to the Slash label, and although the ever-contrary Crash wanted Mark Lindsay of Paul Revere and the Raiders to produce their first record, the more sympathetic **Joan Jett** from the **Runaways** was brought in to produce what was quickly hailed as a punk masterpiece: *(GI)*. The Germs' first and only album was loaded with classics like "What We Do is Secret," "Communist Eyes," "Media Blitz," and "Lexicon Devil." Although *(GI)* is not particularly well recorded, even with its somewhat muffled sound the album nonetheless reveals the raw and remarkable talent of the Germs in their prime. Nevertheless, the New York music press largely ignored the effort and the band stayed in a state of limbo, not once playing anywhere outside the state of California.

Foo Fighters. In the end, the twisted legend of Darby, his "Germ burns," and his pitiful attempts at mind control overshadowed the legacy of one of the most literate and interesting bands on the L.A. hardcore scene.

Discography:

Germicide–Live at the Whisky (Mohawk, 1977; tape, ROIR, 1982; Bomp, 1998); *Live from the Masque 1978, Vol. 1* (House of Punk, 1978); *Tooth and Nail* (Upsetter, 1979); *Yes L.A.* (Dangerhouse, 1979); *(GI)* (Slash, 1979); *What We Do is Secret* (Slash, 1981); *What?* (What?, 1982); *Life Is Boring So Why Not Steal This Record?* (New Underground, 1983); *Let the Circle be Unbroken* (Gasatanka, 1985); *Lion's Share* (Ghost o' Darb, 1985); *Rock n' Rule* (XES, 1986); *Media Blitz* (live; Cleopatra, 1993); *Cat's Clause* (Munster/Casatanka, 1993); *Germs (Tribute)–A Small Circle of Friends* (Sony, 1996); *Real Punk! The Nasty Years* (Cleopatra, 1996); *MIA: The Complete Anthology* (Rhino/Slash, 2000)

who shows up there has to buy a membership card to get in ($2 for a year), so theoretically everybody's a member. The club was formed along the same lines as New York's **ABC No Rio**, not allowing alcohol or visibly intoxicated or stoned people on the premises because they distracted from the founding principle of being a band showcase where the police couldn't shut the place down for rowdiness. Over the years Gilman Street has served as the breeding ground for numerous well-known bands, particularly those from the Bay Area such as **Operation Ivy**, **Jawbreaker**, and **Green Day**. The venue continues booking a steady stream of shows these days, mostly of the obscure variety (though they state in no uncertain terms that they will not book any "racist, misogynistic, or homophobic" performers, no exceptions), with door prices still in the $6-7 range. A 1994 incident was instructive in illustrating the depths of the Gilman Street scene's dedication to the **DIY** ethic: While there watching a band, **Jello Biafra** got into an argument with a slam dancer who crashed into him, and was ultimately beaten up by a group yelling "Sellout rock star!," the whole incident resulting in a broken leg for Biafra.

GREG GINN

A remarkably accomplished guitarist and onetime proprietor of an electronics supply store in Hermosa Beach, California, Greg Ginn also just happened to mastermind the creations of **Black Flag** and the **SST** record label, two landmark developments in the history of the 1980s musical underground. Born in 1954, Ginn was a quiet, poetry-reading, ham-radio nut into the Grateful Dead, Motown, and the blues, before being blown away by the **Ramones** and **Television**. He became friends with **Keith Morris** (later of the **Circle Jerks**) in 1976 and they formed the band Panic the following year, changing the name to Black Flag in 1978. Ginn was the impresario who would lead Black Flag through numerous personnel changes in their early stages, especially in the lead singer department. Although Black Flag is regarded by many as the premier, California **hardcore** punk band, in reality their pioneering mixture of hardcore energy and Black Sabbath-style sludge (a large part of which was Ginn's influence) would pave the way for grunge in the 1990s. Almost as important to Ginn's status as a visionary was SST, where he signed an extraordinary and eclectic roster of bands such as **Sonic Youth**, the **Leaving Trains**, **Bad Brains**, **Meat Puppets**, and **Hüsker Dü**. Ginn was also notorious for pouring those groups' profits into other, lesser bands (Lawndale, anyone?) and causing all of those star players to eventually leave the SST roster, often under acrimonious circumstances.

After Ginn ended Black Flag in 1986 (it was his band to end by that point, since for all intents and purposes, he *was* Black Flag),

Greg Ginn leads Black Flag to victory, 1982.

FLIPSIDE INTERVIEWER: Do you make a profit?

obligations), continued running SST, and, with his wife, got heavily involved in rescuing homeless cats. Ginn played benefit shows for cat rescue groups in 2003 as "Black Flag," but (oddly) without **Henry Rollins** and with a computerized bass machine.

One of the most accomplished guitar players in the punk scene, Ginn had a wildly experimental style that expanded the punk-guitar vocabulary beyond the limited palette developed by Johnny Ramone and Steve Jones. The Ginn guitar sound is a mixture of shrieking feedback and dissonance that sometimes sounds as though several people are playing guitar at the same time. His playing, particularly in recent years, could also stray perilously close to jam-band noodling, a fact not at all appreciated by many who came to see Black Flag at the 2003 shows and were instead reportedly treated to extended free jazz solos—but it was all for the cats.

GOBBING

The often-criticized practice of spitting at band members in order to show appreciation or, sometimes, contempt for the music or the performers, gobbing started in England in the late-1970s, becoming the subject of many a shocked mainstream media exposé, but was short-lived even there and never really became a factor in the U.S. version of punk. Many bands, including the **Sex Pistols**, frowned on gobbing, while **John Lydon** (aka Johnny Rotten) and Siouxsie Sioux of **Siouxsie and the Banshees** even blamed it for some of the diseases that they and others contracted during the period when gobbing was at its most prevalent. Gobbing is relatively unknown at punk shows today, although throwing beer and other liquids remains inexplicably popular.

THE GODFATHERS
1985-2000

LINEUP: Peter Coyne (vocals); Chris Coyne (vocals/bass); Mike Gibson (guitar); Kris Dollimore (guitar, replaced by Chris Burrows); George Mazur (drums)

A garage-punk band formed in London in 1985 by brothers Peter and Chris Coyne, previously of the Sid Presley Experience, the Godfathers achieved some fame due to the success of the 1988 single "Birth, School, Work, Death." The band's sound involved taking the first wave of punk and wrapping it up in a mélange of garage rave-up and hard rock (mixed with just a dash of **oi**), and letting it simmer for 15 years or so. The Godfathers stood out at the time not just for eschewing any hint of electronica (practically illegal at the time in the British Isles) but also for being a punk band who showed up onstage and in videos wearing proper suits. Although their sound was tightly constructed, refreshingly loud and basic garage rock, with monstrous guitars and snarled vocals, it was ultimately too limited. After releasing a handful of albums and getting some college radio and **MTV** exposure, the Godfathers couldn't maintain a stable lineup, and after playing to increasingly smaller crowds, they ended up calling it quits in the mid-1990s, although there are some reports that the band was still playing as late as 2000 in a much-changed lineup.

Discography:
Hit by Hit (Link, 1986, 1996); *Birth, School, Work, Death* (Epic, 1988; Sony, 1990); *Cause I Said So* EP (Epic, 1988); *More Songs About Love and Hate* (Epic, 1989); *BBC Radio 1 Live* (Dutch East India/Strange Fruit, 1989); *Out on the Floor* EP (Epic, 1990); *Unreal World* (Epic, 1991); *Afterlife* (Intercord, 1996); *Birth, School, Work, Death: The Best of the Godfathers* (Sony, 1996)

The Godfathers rule London, 1987: (L to R) Chris Coyne, Mike Gibson, George Mazur, Peter Coyne, Kris Dollimore.

GOD IS MY CO-PILOT

1991–present

LINEUP: Sharon Topper (vocals/clarinet/keyboards); Craig Flanagin (guitar); Jer Reid (guitar); Fly (high-end bass); Jason (low-end bass); Fredrik Haake (drums); Gilles (drums)

A noted avant-garde **queercore** band from New York whose lineup never quite seems to remain intact, God is My Co-Pilot started as a way for the openly bisexual husband and wife Craig Flanagin and Sharon Topper to challenge the nature of both punk and gender dynamics. Their chaotic music is more or less uncategorizable, but ranges from bursts of free-jazz noise to Middle Eastern themes to pure rage to **Riot Grrrl**-inflected **hardcore**. Most of the lyrics address themes of sexism and gender constraints, albeit sometimes pedantically. However, God is My Co-Pilot is one of the most exciting and innovative bands active in modern punk, and, needless to say, is much more popular in Europe and Japan than the United States. The band is also prolific to the point of annoyance, sometimes releasing up to 10 records a year, most of them quite worthwhile, though.

Selective Discography:

God Is My Co-Pilot EP (The Making of Americans, 1991); *Gender is as Gender Does* EP (Funky Mushroom, 1992); *On a Wing and a Prayer* EP (Funky Mushroom, 1992); *How I Got Over* EP (Ajax, 1992); *I Am Not This Body* (The Making of Americans, 1992); *When You See This Remember Me* EP (Dark Beloved Cloud, 1993); *Tight Like Fist: Live Recording* (Knitting Factory Works, 1993); *Pissing and Hooting* EP (The Making of Americans/Seze, 1993); *Speed Yr. Trip* (The Making of Americans, 1993; DSA, 1995); *What Doctors Don't Tell You* (tape; Shrimper, 1993); *My Sinister Hidden Agenda* EP (Blackout, 1993; The Making of Americans, 1995); *Getting Out of Boring Time Biting Into Boring Pie* EP 10" (Quinnah, 1993); *Straight Not* (Outpunk, 1993); *Mir Shlufn Hisht* (Avant, 1994); *Kittybait* EP (Ajax, 1994); *How to Be* (The Making of Americans, 1994); *This is No Time to Be Frail* EP 7" (Rough Trade, 1994); *Sharon Quite Fancies Jo* EP 7" (Soul Static Sound, 1994); *The History of Music, Vol. 1* (Meldac, 1995); *The History of Music, Vol. 2* (Meldac, 1995); *Sex is for Making Babies* (Les Disques du Soleil et de L'Acier, 1995); *Puss 02* (Dark Beloved Cloud/The Making of Americans, 1995); *Ootko Sa Poika Vai Tytto?* EP (Trash Can, 1995); *No Fi* (The Making of Americans, 1995); *An Appeal to Reason* EP (Runt, 1995)

Eugene Hutz of Gogol Bordello, London's Brixton Academy, 2006.

Goldfinger, London, 2001.

GOGOL BORDELLO

2000–present

LINEUP: Eugene Hutz (vocals/guitar); Oren Kaplan (guitar); Thomas Gobena (bass/vocals); Eliot Ferguson (drums/vocals); Pamela Jintana Racine (percussion/vocals); Elizabeth Sun (percussion/vocals); Sergey Ryabtzev (violin/vocals); Yuri Lemeshev (accordion/vocals)

One of the most exciting live bands around anywhere, Gogol Bordello have blended the thrash of punk to gypsy music in a sound reminiscent of the **Pogues'** first few records. The band is led by Eugene Hutz, musician, writer, actor (he costarred in the film adaptation of *Everything is Illuminated*), DJ, and the mastermind of the recent explosion of gypsy music in America. Gogol Bordello's freewheeling amalgamation of world music and punk

shows that punk is not only a global phenomenon, but also something that doesn't have to be stuck in the monotonous guitar/bass/drums lineup. The band's crazy and extremely danceable music takes from punk's world-music tradition (as earlier, bands like **Chumbawamba** and the **Mekons** had explored folk and early protest music) and brings it to the next logical step. In short: What could be more punk than mixing **reggae** and Balkan music with a **hardcore** beat?

Gogol Bordello demands that the revolution be frank, open, and danceable (as in songs such as "Think Locally, Fuck Globally"), and offers a stark critique of modern Americans' seeming inability to truly enjoy themselves. As they ask in "American Wedding," when wondering why everyone wants to go home instead of dancing all night long: "Where's the vodka, where's the marinated herring?" Gogol Bordello bring a joyous noise back to

punk's often serious and dour visage while expanding it beyond its American and British roots.

Discography:

Voi-la Intruder (Rubric, 2002); *Multi Kontra Culti vs. Irony* (Rubric/Stinky, 2002); *East Infection* (Rubric, 2005); *Gypsy Punks: Underdog World Strike* (SideOneDummy, 2005); *Super Taranta!* (SideOneDummy, 2007)

GOLDFINGER

1994–present

LINEUP: John Feldmann (vocals/guitar); Charlie Paulson (guitar, replaced by Brian Arthur); Simon Williams (bass, replaced by Kelly LeMieux); "Dangerous" Darrin Pfeiffer (drums)

Slick and high energy, Goldfinger is a Los Angeles, **ska**-influenced punk band that scored a radio hit with "Here in Your Bedroom" in the mid-1990s and tours heavily, particularly on the **Vans Warped** circuit. In general, Goldfinger never quite got their

shot, being mostly ignored for their part in the ska revival (unlike critically lauded **Operation Ivy**), and also missing out on the mainstream success enjoyed by fellow ska-punk bands like Reel Big Fish and No Doubt who later went into straight-ahead pop. One of the reasons may have been that John Feldmann's somewhat strained vocals made the band sound more like **NOFX** than No Doubt. Either way, at this point Goldfinger has put out reliably catchy punk tunes for over a decade now, with 2005's *Disconnection Notice* being among their stronger efforts since their 1996 self-titled album.

Discography:

Richter EP (Mojo/Universal, 1995); *Goldfinger* (Mojo, 1996); *Hang-Ups* (Mojo/Universal, 1997); *Darrin's Coconut Ass* (Mojo/Universal, 1999); *Stomping Ground* (Mojo/Universal, 2000); *Open Your Eyes* (Mojo/Jive, 2002); *Live at the House of Blues* (Kung Fu, 2004); *The Best of Goldfinger* (Mojo/Jive/Legacy, 2005); *Disconnection Notice* (Maverick, 2005)

GOOD CHARLOTTE

1995–present

LINEUP: some poseurs, some wannabes

Is Good Charlotte actually a punk band? The commercially successful band who played the Washington, D.C., club circuit during the mid-to-late-1990s, and achieved heavy radio and **MTV** rotation after their triple-platinum 2002 album *The Young and the Hopeless*, owes their success as much to that album's hook-laden singles as to the assiduous care its members put into their "punk" aesthetic of meticulously-torn clothing and copious amounts of eyeliner. Essentially just a power-pop band (fronted by identical twins Joel and Benji Madden) with a taste for tattoos and a tendency to grace every magazine cover that would have them, Good Charlotte's punk credentials were suspect right from the start, no matter how many times they went on the **Vans Warped** tour, and not just because of their overly glossy music. There was the band's uncomfortably close association with MTV, which featured many of the band's songs (including the inevitable power ballads) and had the Madden brothers work as hosts for several MTV events. Additionally there was the issue of singer Joel Madden's unerring penchant for **poseur**dom, whether it was dating Nicole Richie, launching his own clothing line, or opening for Justin Timberlake.

As Good Charlotte's popular prospects began to dwindle after the release of their fourth album, 2007's *Good Morning Revival*, guitarist-keyboardist Billy Martin tried somewhat defensively to distance the band from ever having claimed to be punk (now that the shtick wasn't working for them anymore), telling a magazine in August 2007 that "I personally can't name one punk band that's been an influence to me. I never listen to that music, I've never been into it, and I was shocked when we started to get lumped in with **pop-punk** bands."

Good Charlotte is ultimately included here as a warning for other bands. Their first two albums actually have a few great pop-punk tunes, some as good as anything **Bad Religion** put on their major label releases. But the music that followed was no more than a crass (unfortunately not *that* **Crass**) attempt to use their Hot Topic look and some ultra-slick production to drag the kids from the Vans Warped tour into dance clubs. Having proved their poseur cred, they also put too much stock in a brief commercial trend that ultimately deserted them. Good Charlotte is the Dorian Gray of punk: they look great, but their now-aged portrait painfully resembles Fall Out Boy.

Discography:
Good Charlotte (Sony, 2000); *The Young and the Hopeless* (Epic, 2002); *The Chronicles of Life and Death* (Epic, 2004); *Good Morning Revival* (Epic, 2007)

Good Charlotte, 2003: grrr!

Gorilla Biscuits' Civ giving a fan the mic at a 2005 "Save CBGB" show, or possibly demonstrating his famous uppercut.

GORILLA BISCUITS

1986-1991, 2005-present

LINEUP: Anthony Civarelli, aka "Civ" (vocals); Walter Schreifels (guitar); Alex Brown (guitar); Arthur Smilios (bass); Luke Abbey (drums, replaced by Sammy Siegler)

Melodic New York **straight-edge** band Gorilla Biscuits unusually played more in the pop style of the **Descendents**. The original lineup varied, but eventually consolidated as a launching ground for bands who would dominate the city's **hardcore** scene for years. Bassist Walter Schreifels occasionally played in **Youth of Today** and later founded the art-punk band **Quicksand**, while drummer Sammy Siegler also played with Youth of Today, **Shelter**, **Judge**, **Bold**, and **Side by Side**. Gorilla Biscuits were signed to **Revelation Records** and first put out a song on the compilation *New York Hardcore—The Way It Is*. In 1989 they released *Start Today*, a pop-infused hardcore classic.

For a while during the late-1980s, during the heady days of all-ages hardcore shows at **CBGB** and the **Anthrax** up in Connecticut, Gorilla Biscuits were the goofier answer to the city's dead-serious, straight-edge bands; even their name was derived from a joking reference to a slang term for drugs (likely unbeknownst to some of their more sincere fans). Certainly the most melodic straight-edge band during the scene's heyday, Gorilla Biscuits had a dedicated following who loved their more inclusive and less violent image. After the straight-edge movement began to decline at the end of the 1980s, and the number of available venues began to decline along with it, Gorilla Biscuits soldiered on before breaking up in 1991. Civ went on to open a tattoo shop and then formed the band **Civ**, who had two successful records before disbanding in the mid-1990s. Gorilla Biscuits were among the bands who reunited for the 2005 save-CBGB shows, occasionally touring thereafter.

Discography:
Gorilla Biscuits EP (Revelation, 1988); *Start Today* (Revelation, 1989). **Civ:** *Set Your Goals* (Revelation/Lava/Atlantic, 1995)

THE GOSSIP

1999-present

LINEUP: Beth Ditto (vocals); Nathan Howdeshell, aka "Brace Paine" (guitar/vocals); Kathy Mendonça (drums, replaced by Hannah Billie)

The Gossip are quite simply one of the most fun and provocative bands in the **queercore** movement. Originally from Arkansas, the band later moved to Olympia, Washington, where they found their niche on the **Kill Rock Stars** label. Akin to similarly minded bands such as **Le Tigre**, the Gossip manage to balance their poppy version of punk with infectious beats. While the band's politics are always evidenced loudly on their sleeves, their songs are meant to not only incite revolutions in gender equity and sexuality, but to also get people up onto the dance floor—the revolution has got to start somewhere, after all.

Discography:
Arkansas Heat (Kill Rock Stars, 2002); *Undead in NYC* (Dim Mak, 2003); *Movement* (Kill Rock Stars, 2003); *Standing in the Way of Control* (Kill Rock Stars, 2006)

GOVERNMENT ISSUE

1980-1989

LINEUP: John Schroeder, aka "John Stabb" (vocals); John Barry (guitar, replaced by Brian Baker, Tom Lyle); Brian Gay (bass, replaced by Lyle, Mitch Parker, Michael Fellows, John Leonard, Jay Robbins); Mark Alberstadt (drums, replaced by Peter Moffett)

Government Issue was among the more influential bands on the Washington, D.C., scene during the 1980s, appearing on one of the most important punk compilations of all time, 1982's *Flex Your Head*. The band started out playing straightforward **hardcore**, but by the *Government Issue* record in 1986 they had begun to experiment, becoming noticeably poppier and more melodic. Singer John Stabb (born John Schroeder) was a flamboyant and provocative presence on the D.C. punk scene, often dressing in loud sportcoats and other garish outfits just to get a rise out of

The Gossip's Beth Ditto becomes one with the crowd at Glastonbury, 2007.

the audience (and occasionally his own band). By 1989, frequent lineup changes and diminishing returns caused Stabb (after a dozen or so members had cycled through, he was the only remaining original member) to break up the band, although he continued to play music under a variety of names. After the demise of Government Issue, bassist Jay Robbins went on to form the impressive **Jawbox**. Stabb was injured during a mugging in July 2007 and benefit shows were organized to pay for his medical bills.

Discography:

Legless Bull EP (Dischord, 1981); *Make an Effort* EP (Fountain of Youth, 1982); *Boycott Stabb* (Dischord/ Fountain of Youth, 1983; Giant, 1988); *Joyride* (Fountain of Youth, 1984); *The Fun Just Never Ends* (Fountain of Youth, 1985); *Give Us Stabb or Give Us Death* EP (Mystic, 1985); *Live on Mystic* (Mystic, 1985); *Government Issue* (Fountain of Youth, 1986; Giant, 1986); *You* (Giant, 1987); *Crash* (Giant, 1988); *Strange Wine* EP (Giant, 1989); *Joyride/The Fun Just Never Ends* (Giant, 1990); *Beyond* (Rockville, 1991)

GREEN DAY

1988-present

LINEUP: Billy Joe Armstrong (vocals/ guitar); Mike Drint (bass); Tré Cool (drums)

One of the more popular and most incorrectly maligned bands of the late-1980s and early-'90s, Green Day was instrumental in helping to finally break punk rock into the U.S. mainstream, indirectly making the music more accessible to those unaware of punk's rich history. Even before their big break, though, singer and guitarist Billy Joe Armstrong had proved himself to be an interesting and varied songwriter, while bassist Mike Drint and drummer Tré Cool proved that a tight rhythm section was half the formula for acceptance in the mass market.

Green Day played their first shows in 1987, when Armstrong and Drint were only 15 years old with original drummer Al Sobrante, under the name Sweet Children. A big part of the **Gilman Street** scene, Green Day recorded several singles and two popular albums on local label **Lookout! Records**, helping create the poppy East Bay sound. Although their Lookout! albums— *1039/Smoothed Out Slappy Hours* and *Kerplunk*—were considerable underground successes, it was when Green Day jumped to major label Reprise in 1994 and released the Grammy-winning, multiplatinum

Green Day's Billy Joe Armstrong about to be engulfed by flame at a festival in Scotland, 2002.

GREEN DAY PRESENTS american idiot

Dookie that everything changed. The album's steady succession of smash singles and near constant radio/**MTV** play—as well as the band's telegenic looks, expressive use of videos, and high-profile touring—made Green Day the first punk band to sell millions of records and also inspired the frantic race that led to so many major indie and punk bands getting signed by, and subsequently dropped from, major labels. Green Day's reputation as being "one to watch" was solidified at the 1994 Woodstock Festival reunion, where the audience complied with a request to shower the band with mud and dirt to hilarious effect. After several more popular albums, a few years' layoff, and some controversy (including the arrest of Armstrong for drunk driving in Los Angeles), a newly politicized Green Day returned with their most audacious concept yet and just in time for a presidential election. The multiplatinum, 2004 rock opera *American Idiot* viciously skewered U.S. voter apathy and media culpability in the dumbing-down of the nation, and corporate culture.

Since they have actually embraced their fame, instead of putting out **DIY** mail-order records, Green Day gets a surprisingly bad rap from some punks, even though they have continued to put out the same type of entertaining and witty music they did when still on Lookout! (which coasted for years on the success of their Green Day backlist, post-*Dookie*). After all, many of the greatest punk bands, from the **Ramones** to the **Clash** and the **Sex Pistols**, recorded with major labels through most of their careers. While *Maximum RocknRoll* is never going to be a fan again, Green Day is more than responsible for introducing a wide variety of fans to punk, and can be thought of as a sort of gateway drug (much like their beloved pot) to stronger stuff; their music being, after all, only a step away from Crimpshine and **Stiff Little Fingers**.

Discography:
1,000 Hours EP (Lookout!, 1989); *39/Smooth* (Lookout!, 1990); *Slappy* EP (Lookout!, 1990); *Sweet Children* EP 7" (Skene!, 1990); *1,039 Smoothed Out Slappy Hours* (Lookout!, 1991); *Kerplunk* (Lookout!, 1992); *Dookie* (Reprise, 1994); *Insomniac* (Reprise, 1995); *Nimrod* (Reprise, 1997); *Warning* (Reprise, 2000); *International Super Hits!* (Reprise, 2001); *Shenanigans* (Reprise, 2002); *American Idiot* (Reprise, 2004)

Green Day, 1994: (L to R) Tré Cool, Mike Drint, Billy Joe Armstrong.

1,000 HOURS

GROOVIE GHOULIES

1989-2007

LINEUP: Kepi (vocals/bass); Roach (guitar); Wendy Powell (drums, replaced by Dan Panic, Scampi)

The jokey and ultra-poppy goth-pop Groovie Ghoulies from Sacramento, California, are almost as influenced by the **Ramones** as they are by comic books, pulp sci-fi, and horror films. Unlike most bands who claim the Ramones as influences, the Ghoulies actually kept things musically as short and sweet as the boys from Queens. When it came to the substance of their songs, the Ghoulies resemble an even goofier version of the **Cramps** or maybe the soundtrack to a zombie movie made by a bunch of smartass teenagers in their basement. A typical Ghoulies song goes something like the lyrics in "'Til Death Do Us Party" from *Go! Stories*: "1, 2, 3, 5, No one here gets out alive! / 6, 7, 9, 10, Reincarnate, do it again!" In 2005, just to prove their versatility, they put out an EP of Chuck Berry covers. A great band with an even better sense of humor, the Ghoulies never got their due; who else would title a song "Freebird" just to get the crowd to call for it at the end of sets? Though the band reportedly broke up, all loyal Ghoulies fans hope for the inevitably ghoulish resurrection someday soon.

Discography:

Appetite for Adrenochrome (Crimson Corpse, 1989; Lookout!, 1996); *Born in the Basement* (Green Door, 1994; Lookout!, 1996; Spring Man, 2004); *World Contact Day* (Lookout!, 1996); *Running with Bigfoot* EP (Lookout!, 1997); *Re-Animation Festival* (Lookout!, 1997; Spring Man, 2004); *Fun in the Dark* (Lookout!, 1999 Spring Man, 2003); *Travels with My Amp* (Lookout!, 2000); *Freaks on Parade* (Stardumb, 2001); *Go! Stories* (Stardumb, 2002); *Monster Club* (Stardumb, 2003; Green Door, 2004); *Berry'd Alive* EP (Green Door, 2005)

BOB GRUEN

Bob Gruen is one of the most respected and most prolific rock photographers of all time. His career, which has included photographing almost every major punk icon as well as the cream of rock royalty (he's probably best known for his John Lennon shots, including the one of him wearing a "New York City" T-shirt), started at the 1965 Newport Folk Festival where he photographed the crowd booing Bob Dylan as he famously went electric. From there Gruen started photographing the hippie scene in New York. In the early-1970s he was the photographer who helped popularize both the drag look of the **New York Dolls** and **David Bowie**'s glam phase. Later, Gruen made his name on the punk scene, taking iconic photographs of the **Ramones** outside **CBGB** and the **Sex Pistols** in various poses, including now-legendary shots of a bare-chested and bleeding **Sid Vicious**, and the Pistols with their faces festooned with straws.

ABOVE RIGHT: Jeffrey Lee Pierce of Gun Club, 1980.

BELOW: Bob Gruen immortalizes the Sex Pistols in Luxembourg, 1977.

GUN CLUB

1980-1996

LINEUP: Jeffrey Lee Pierce (vocals); Ward Dotson (guitar, replaced by Jim Duckworth, Kid Congo Powers, others); Rob Ritter (bass, replaced by Patricia Morrison, others); Terry Graham (drums, replaced by Dee Pop, others)

Gun Club was a blues- and gospel-influenced band led by Jeffrey Lee Pierce, who started out as a Los Angeles punk and ended up as a latter-day bluesman trying to find something primal in U.S. roots music that could resemble punk's fierce energy and integrity. Pierce had a notoriously troubled life, with substance-abuse problems that strained his relationship with collaborators such as Kid Congo Powers (Brian Tristan, formerly of the **Cramps** and future member of the Bad Seeds), as well as onetime **Bags** member Patricia Morrison and Dee Pop from the Bush Tetras, to name but a few. Pierce continued the Gun Club for many years with a variety of lineups that usually contained Kid Congo. He seemed to have gained a handle on the worst of his problems when he suddenly died of a cerebral blood clot in March 1996. Numerous Gun Club albums are spotty, and several live records do not show the band off well.

Yet albums like *Miami*, and particularly *The Las Vegas Story*, show why Pierce's channeling of long-gone bluesmen and the primal swamp of roots music was such a compelling idea in the first place.

Discography:

Fire of Love (Ruby/lash, 1981); *Miami* (Animal, 1982); *Death Party* EP (Animal, 1983); *The Las Vegas Story* (Animal, 1984); *The Birth the Death the Ghost* (ABC, 1984); *Sex Beat 81* (Lolita, 1984); *Two Sides of the Beast* (Castle, 1985); *A Love Supreme* (Offense, 1985); *Danse Kallinda Boom: Live* (Megadisc, 1985); *Mother Juno* (Fundamental, 1987); *Pastoral Hide and Seek* (Fire, 1990); *Divinity* (New Rose, 1991); *In Exile* (Triple X, 1992); *The Gun Club Live in Europe* (Triple X, 1992); *Lucky Jim* (Triple X, 1993)

KATHLEEN HANNA

A brutally honest musician and writer who sang and played in **Bikini Kill** and later joined the more agit-poppy **Le Tigre**, Kathleen Hanna's name is practically synonymous with punk feminism. In the late-1980s, Hanna studied photography at Evergreen College in Olympia, Washington, and ran an art gallery, Reko Muse, which featured art by women. During this period she realized how similarly insular and sexist the art and punk scenes were, and she was inspired to create her own music and art that put gender issues front and center. After some aborted early musical projects (with Amy Carter and Viva Knievel), Hanna assembled Bikini Kill, the band that would assure her legacy in punk history.

In Bikini Kill, Hanna pioneered an extremely confrontational and confessional style in which she sang, wailed, and screamed her intensely personal, politicized lyrics. After moving with the band to Washington, D.C., in 1992, Hanna became one of the pioneers of the feminist-punk **Riot Grrrl** movement, which she helped found with a couple of the members of D.C. band **Bratmobile** who were already putting out the Riot Grrl zine. Hanna's performance style (both musically and lyrically) consisted of an attention-grabbing type of clenched-fist "Take Back the Night" polemic mixed with self-reflexive humor, as well as sometimes overwrought theatrics. An excellent example of Hanna's style and humor can be found on **Mike Watt**'s 1995 solo album, *Ball-Hog or Tugboat?*, on which she leaves a rambling answering-machine message, seemingly furious about being asked to be on the guest-star-heavy record—"I'm just not so sure I wanna be included in your little white rock boy fuckin' hall of shame here, you know?"—before demanding that he return her *Annie* soundtrack. Although the whole thing is a put-on (Hanna later said, "I made that whole thing up, I barely even know him. It's just art."), she still manages to get in some welcome jabs at the white male, rock power structure.

As the 1990s wore on, Hanna increasingly distanced herself from Riot Grrrl for a number of reasons, particularly her growing discomfort with being seen as the leader or mouthpiece of a group that was, by its nature, decentralized and anti-hierarchical. Also, Hanna was tired of the constant misrepresentation of the Riot Grrrl movement by (mostly) male journalists who thought any band with a female member must be emblematic of the entire movement.

Following the demise of Bikini Kill, Hanna moved to Portland, Oregon, and worked on her solo project, Julie Ruin. In Portland, she roomed with zine writer and artist Johanna Fateman, with whom she put together a group called the Troublemakers. After a brief hiatus, Hanna moved to New York, where she again teamed with Fateman along with musician and video artist Sadie Benning, and the three started the Le Tigre project, a queer- and feminist-friendly band that pushed the boundaries of gender norms while still cranking out incredibly dancey songs.

Both idolized and vilified for her aggressive politics, Hanna remains a vibrant example of how women in alternative music can have role models beyond Sarah McLachlan strumming a guitar for dreamy-eyed poets at the Lilith Fair.

"One of the reasons I even got in a band was because I used to go to so many shows and feel so alienated ... There's so much to be had in women working together and completely saying 'fuck it' to the whole male power structure."

—**Kathleen Hanna**, *Ms.*, August/September 2000

Kathleen Hanna performs with Le Tigre in London, 2005.

HARDCORE

A louder, more primitive, and much faster variation of the original punk style, hardcore is largely attributed to bands from New York, Los Angeles, and England who kept punk alive from the late-1970s through the mid-to-late-'80s. Seminal hardcore bands generally include, but are not limited to, the following: **Minor Threat, Black Flag, T.S.O.L.**, the **Circle Jerks, JFA, SSD, Bad Religion, Youth of Today, Agnostic Front, Youth Brigade, 7 Seconds**, and **Bad Brains** on the American side, and the **Exploited, G.B.H., Discharge**, English Dogs, **Vice Squad, Broken Bones**, the **Varukers**, Blitz, and Chaos UK from England.

It is a matter of speculation when hardcore began, although most critics trace its roots, like so many other things, back to the **Ramones**. (Strangely enough, though the Ramones were certainly fast, they did not begin to play hardcore rhythms until the mid-1980s, on songs such as "Warthog" and "Endless Vacation"—attempting to play catch-up to the many bands they inspired.) Steven Blush, in his book *American Hardcore: A Tribal History*, suggests that the first true hardcore punk record might have been the "Out of Vogue" single by Middle Class from Santa Ana, California, or perhaps Bad Brains' lightning-fast single "Pay to Cum." The term itself had become a frequently used phrase by around 1980 or so, though the first use of the term *hardcore* on a record was **D.O.A.**'s *Hardcore 81* album. (Some would argue that hardcore's initial first phase had a shelf life, and although hardcore continues as a style, many critics and members of the punk scene feel its significance in the punk scene was waning by the time **CBGB** ended its hardcore matinees at the end of the 1980s.)

Hardcore as a genre rethought punk to reject the excesses and stylistic dead ends in which the first wave of U.S. punk had seemingly mired itself; in essence it was a wave of kids who were sick of the codified and insular world of the first wave of punks and wanted to kick the door in all over again. The movement also saw a shift in punk demographics from the original larger cities where movements began, such as Boston, L.A., and New York, to the suburbs, where bored kids found an outlet for their aggres-

sions and suspicions about the future in hardcore's lightning-fast rhythms and blunt-force-trauma approach. Like punk rock itself, hardcore should be analyzed not simply as one movement but as a series of overlapping ones that both re-politicized punk and also brought out a sense of resentment and anger that had lurked below the surface for many years, especially among younger suburban punks. Unlike first-wave punk bands from the late-1970s, hardcore groups tended to be much more explicitly political, a result of the growing conservatism of mainstream America highlighted by the 1980 election of **Ronald Reagan** (whose grinning, hated visage adorned countless flyers and album covers). Many first-wave punks may have been revolting out of general societal malaise or dissatisfaction with the musical status quo, but while those concerns were still quite relevant at the dawn of the Reagan era, the hardcore kids felt they had a lot more reasons to be pissed off. After all, the world was supposed to end at any minute, so it made sense to speed up the songs.

In Blush's book—and the excellent documentary of the same name—the end of true hardcore is identified as being around 1986, when many high-profile bands in the movement (such as Minor Threat) had either disbanded or, having run out of steam, started to drift into the heavy-metal camp (as in the case of T.S.O.L.). One of the reasons for the decline of hardcore may have been—somewhat perversely for a genre that was in itself a rebellion against stratified musical style—the reluctance of many in the core audience to accept *any* form of innovation, leading many of hardcore's founding fathers to leave it behind for less hidebound genres. Blush quotes Grant Hart (from hardcore pioneers **Hüsker Dü**, who would themselves rather quickly adopt a more alt-rock style): "I got bored with hardcore very fast. Over time a lot of people started doing what we were doing—it lost its uniqueness." Another reason for hardcore's demise could well have been the steady increase in violence that became a rather unwelcome aspect of the scene over the years. As the bands' music became much faster, and the scene itself became so tribal and fractious (particularly with all the **skinhead** bands prevalent in hardcore), the **pits** turned increasingly violent over the years. Promoters like **Hilly Kristal** of CBGB, who

had for years helped keep the scene going with the club's famous matinee shows, eventually refused to book hardcore bands due to insurance and liability issues.

Although hardcore bands still record and tour (especially on larger tours such as **Vans Warped**, which often features bands including **Pennywise, NOFX, No Use For a Name**, and **Lagwagon**), and new hardcore bands form almost every day, it is clear that the heyday is over. Many newer bands could be labeled as post-hardcore, a style of music that takes the energy of hardcore, and like bands such as **Jawbox** and **Jawbreaker**, channel the music into something more precise and well crafted. Also the trend has increasingly gone away from metal/hardcore crossovers, to intricate, math-rock/jazz stylings in many bands. But then again, the scene keeps reviving itself and by the time of this writing may well have changed again.

The Circle Jerks demonstrate the joys of hardcore in Los Angeles, 1980.

HARE KRISHNA

Oddly enough, Hare Krishna exerted an influence on many members of New York's **hardcore** scene in the 1980s and '90s, most notably on Ray Cappo (formerly of **Youth of Today**), who went on to found the Krishna-core band **Shelter,** and several members of the original **Cro-Mags**. Sometimes branded a cult, the Hare Krishna movement came to the United States in the 1960s and took root in the poor areas of many cities, including New York's Lower East Side, where many young punks in the 1970s and '80s were attracted to the idea of non-Western spirituality. Most punks who embraced Krishna belong to either the International Society for Krishna Consciousness (ISKCON), the largest group working outside of India, or one of its many offshoots. The group is mostly Indian in origin, going back at least 500 years, and primarily was spread in the United States by A.C. Bhaktivedanta Swami Prabhupada, who brought the mission to the West. Krishna devotees are known for their shorn heads and chanting of the mantra "Hare Krishna, Hare Rama," in which *Hare* refers to the energy from God and *Rama* and *Krishna* are two of the Sanskrit words for God.

THE HEARTBREAKERS

1975-1979

LINEUP: Johnny Thunders (vocals/guitar); Walter Lure (vocals/guitar); Richard Hell (bass, replaced by Billy Rath); Jerry Nolan (drums)

One of the most thrilling and self-destructively drug-addled components of early New York punk, the Heartbreakers were a quartet of bad influences led by **Johnny Thunders**, late of the **New York Dolls**, and Jerry Nolan. Their seminal songs like "Born to Lose" and "Chinese Rocks" got them almost as much attention as their seemingly unlimited appetite for drugs and self-destruction. Thunders and Nolan formed the band after becoming dissatisfied with the way the New York Dolls were going under new manager **Malcolm McLaren**, bringing in the important addition of **Television**'s **Richard Hell** on bass (though Hell would later be replaced by Billy Rath after fighting with Thunders; after all, the band was often known as Johnny Thunders and the Heartbreakers). Their blend of early punk and glam (they were one of the few American bands to mix the styles), with a little Chuck Berry-style, blues-based rock tossed into the mix, was brash and electrifying—one more reason they should never be confused with the *other* Heartbreakers, Tom Petty's backup band.

The band split for the first time in late 1977 after releasing their one studio album,

the punk chestnut *L.A.M.F.*, and also taking part in the dismally disastrous Anarchy tour of England with the **Sex Pistols**, the **Clash**, and the **Damned**. The Heartbreakers reunited in 1979 without drummer Nolan for a live album recorded at **Max's Kansas City**. Although it would have been commercially more successful to get the original Heartbreakers back together, in years afterward Thunders proved too erratic or unmotivated to do so and worked on various projects by himself, as did the other members. After years of touring solo, Thunders died of a heroin overdose in 1991. Weakened by years of drug and alcohol abuse, Nolan died of meningitis a few months later. Oddly enough, Walter Lure, who still tours with his band the Waldos, later became a success on Wall Street. A beautiful, wonderful disaster, the Heartbreakers packed a lot of great music (and hard living) into just a few chaotic years.

Discography:

L.A.M.F. (Track, 1977; Jungle, 1984); *Live at Max's Kansas City* (Max's Kansas City, 1979); *D.T.K.—Live at the Speakeasy* (Jungle, 1982). **Johnny Thunders and the Heartbreakers:** *L.A.M.F. Revisited* (Jungle, 1984); *D.T.K. L.A.M.F.* (Jungle, 1984); *Live at the Lyceum Ballroom 1984* (ABC, 1984; Receiver, 1990)

LEFT: Hare Krishna hardcore icon Ray Cappo.
RIGHT: The Heartbreakers, 1977: (L to R) Walter Lure, Johnny Thunders.

Richard Hell's portrait for his
first album cover, 1976.

YOU MAKE ME

Heavens to Betsy play San Francisco, 1992.
(L to R) Corin Tucker, Tracy Sawyer.

HEAVENS TO BETSY

1991-1994

LINEUP: Corin Tucker (vocals/guitar);
Tracy Sawyer (bass/drums)

An all-female band from the fertile breeding
ground of Olympia, Washington, Heavens to
Betsy made some of the most abrasive but
catchy music of the **Riot Grrrl** movement.
They formed when fellow Evergreen College
students guitarist/vocalist Corin Tucker
and bassist/drummer Tracy Sawyer decided
to put together a band for the International
Pop Underground Convention, run by K
Records founder Calvin Johnson of **Beat
Happening**. Over their short existence,
they played with other like-minded bands
like **Bratmobile**, Seven Year Bitch, and
Excuse 17, of whom Carrie Brownstein
was a member. After both Excuse 17 and
Heavens to Betsy fell apart, Brownstein and
Tucker formed the much more aggressive
and popular **Sleater-Kinney** and the rest,
as they say, is history.

Discography:

Bratmobile/Heavens to Betsy (K, 1992); *These Monsters
are Real* EP (Kill Rock Stars, 1992); *Calculated* (Kill
Rock Stars, 1994); *Direction* 7" (Chainsaw, 1994)

RICHARD HELL

A cornerstone player, stylistically and musically, in the formation of New York punk rock during the 1970s, Richard Hell played in the embryonic versions of two famous bands, the **Heartbreakers** and **Television**, before going out on his own with the **Voidoids**. Hell (born Richard Meyers in Lexington, Kentucky, in 1949), along with fellow poets and musicians **Patti Smith** and Tom Verlaine, brought a sense of the doomed poetic to punk, as well as introducing the look of short, spiked hair and ripped clothing, with safety pins as fashion accessories. **Malcolm McLaren** was particularly taken by the look and tried his best to import first Hell and then Hell's stylistic contributions to the early British punk scene.

Hell and Verlaine (born Tom Miller) were schoolmates in Delaware before moving to New York and trying to reinvent themselves in the image of their Parisian poet idols, who had helped start the Romantic movement in poetry. In much the same way, Hell hoped to start a version of the Romantic movement in New York. Aiming to take the machismo out of rock and restore its roots in poetry, they published the poetry book *Wanna Go Out* under the name of fictitious prostitute Theresa Stern. They formed the Neon Boys in 1972, with Verlaine playing guitar and singing, and Hell on bass. After adding guitarist Richard Lloyd and drummer Billy Ficca, the band evolved the following year into Television. A power struggle ensued when Verlaine began to cut Hell's material from the set, eventually causing Hell to leave Television for the Heartbreakers. After fighting the same battle with **Johnny Thunders**, Hell at last went solo, forming his own group, the Voidoids, and releasing the album *Blank Generation* in 1977. The Voidoids put out two more records with only Hell and guitarist Robert Quine before calling it quits in the early-1980s, partly due to Hell's frustrations with rock 'n' roll.

Hell recorded sporadically after the Voidoids' breakup, most notably the **Dim Stars** project with **Sonic Youth**'s Thurston Moore and Don Fleming, and appeared in the occasional film, including Susan Seidelman's 1982 portrait of the New York art-punk scene, *Smithereens*. Hell also continued to write poetry and novels (including *Go Now* in 1997 and *Godlike* in 2005); he served as film columnist for the magazine *BlackBook* from 2004 to 2006 and, perhaps most poignantly, penned the *New York Times'* obituary on the closing of Television's one-time home, **CBGB**.

Discography:
R.I.P. (tape, ROIR, 1984; ROIR/Important, 1990); *Another World* (Overground, 1994); *Go Now* (Tim/Kerr, 1995); *Time* (Matador, 2002); *Spurts: The Richard Hell Story* (Sire/Rhino, 2005). **Richard Hell and the Voidoids:** *Richard Hell* EP (Ork, 1976); *Blank Generation* (Sire, 1977; Sire/Warner Bros., 1990); *Richard Hell/Neon Boys* EP (Shake, 1980); *Destiny Street* (Celluloid, 1982; ID, 1988; Razor & Tie, 1995); *Funhunt: Live at the CBGB & Max's* (tape, ROIR, 1990; ROIR/Important, 1990, 1995). **The Heartbreakers:** *What Goes Around...* (Bomp, 1991); *Live at Mothers* (Fan Club, 1991). **Dim Stars:** *Dim Stars* EP (Ecstatic Peace!, 1991; Caroline, 1992); *Dim Stars* (Caroline, 1992). **Bibliography:** *Artifact* (New York: Hanuman, 1990); *The Voidoid* (UK: Codex, 1996); *Go Now* (New York: Scribner Paperback, 1997); *Weather* (New York: CUZ Editions, 1998); *Hot and Cold: Essays, Poems, Lyrics, Notebooks, Pictures, Fiction* (New York: powerHouse, 2001); *Godlike* (New York: Little House on the Bowery, 2005)

THE HIVES

1993–present

LINEUP: Howlin' Pelle Almqvist (vocals); Nicholaus Arson (guitar); Vigilante Carlstroem (guitar); Dr. Matt Destruction (bass); Chris Dangerous (drums)

Swedish garage-punk revivalists known for their outlandish sense of style, the Hives have a grandiose sense of self, and smart, fast, buzzsaw-style songs whose titles frequently end in an exclamation mark. They have a consistently amusing and musically intense band that, despite frequent airplay on **MTV**, carved their own suavely sartorial niche in the world punk scene. Although occasionally lumped in with that post-millennial spurt of garage rockers like the Strokes and the White Stripes, the Hives have a more distinctively modern take on their image and music. Their mod-suited, fashion-photographer-friendly look harkens back to punk's early days when bands such as the **Ramones** wore distinctive group uniforms, but also to the suit-and-tie look of 1960s bands like the Beatles. After their breakthrough single "Hate To Say I Told You So" (off the 2000 **Epitaph** release *Veni, Vedi, Vicious*) the Hives didn't ever seem poised to truly achieve mainstream success, but they continue recording and touring. Backed by tongue-in-cheek press announcementsabout the inevitability of their future crushing victories over other, lesser bands, the Hives know they are great. They are also convinced that soon, you too, will know of their greatness. The Hives are not afraid to say this to you. You do not believe the Hives? You will, soon. Yes, you will.

Discography:
Barely Legal (Burning Heart, 1997); *Veni, Vedi, Vicious* (Epitaph, 2000); *Your New Favourite Band* (Poptones, 2001); *Tyrannosaurus Hives* (Interscope, 2004); *The Black and White Album* (Interscope, 2007)

The Hives line up for uniform inspection, 2002.

John Holmstrom tries to get Lou Reed's hair just right.

JOHN HOLMSTROM

Artist, writer, designer, visionary, and founding editor of *Punk* magazine, John Holmstrom was closely associated with the **Ramones** and was present at many of the pivotal events in early punk history at **CBGB** in New York. Although the word *punk* itself had been previously associated with bands considered to be particularly disreputable, *Punk* the magazine gave a name and a face to the new movement in New York later in the decade. Holmstrom studied under legendary artist (and inventor of the graphic novel) Will Eisner at the School of Visual Arts (SVA), where he developed the distinctive artistic style that would become so closely associated with the Ramones and punk in general. Holmstrom's look combined hyperrealism (no one could draw a gritty New York brick wall quite like Holmstrom) and a cartoonish visual approach to human subjects (check out the cover of the Ramones' *Road to Ruin*) that would eventually form the recognizable look of early New York punk.

Founded in 1976, Holmstrom's magazine *Punk* featured groundbreaking journalism and design that influenced countless magazines and zines in the punk movement. Holmstrom said he "didn't want to create a magazine about rock and roll, he wanted to do a magazine that *was* rock and roll." Although he made no money from the magazine and helped to finance it through his work as a freelance illustrator, *Punk* was a huge success in terms of sales and particularly, influence. *Punk* served as a crucial source of publicity for early punk rock, with contributions from Mary Harron, **Richard Hell**, Roberta Bayley, **Bob Gruen**, and others who helped establish punk's **DIY** aesthetic.

In addition to the front cover of the Ramones' *Road to Ruin* album, Holmstrom drew the back cover for their *Rocket to Russia* album, taking the Ramones' naturally car-toonish presence and making them into literal cartoons. He also was a prolific editor, and served as the publisher of *High Times* magazine for many years. Along with **Legs McNeil** and Gedd (George Edgar) Dunn, he changed the face of independent publishing and also named and championed the new movement of punk rock in New York. Holmstrom published a new version of *Punk* magazine with several new writers in 2001 and continued to champion New York bands. More recently, Holmstrom worked on a new version of *Punk* magazine, which relaunched in 2006. Holmstrom also created cover art and illustrations for the Kowalskis and **Murphy's Law**.

EDITORIAL PAGE

DEATH TO DISCO SHIT!

LONG LIVE THE ROCK!

KILL YOURSELF. JUMP OFF A FUCKIN' CLIFF. DRIVE NAILS INTO YOUR HEAD. BECOME A ROBOT AND JOIN THE STAFF AT DISNEYLAND. OD. ANYTHING. JUST DON'T LISTEN TO DISCOSHIT. I'VE SEEN THAT CANNED CRAP TAKE REAL LIVE PEOPLE AND TURN THEM INTO DOGS! AND VICE VERSA. THE EPITOME OF ALL THAT'S WRONG WITH WESTERN CIVILIZATION IS DISCO. EDDJICATE YOURSELF. GET INTO IT. READ PUNK.

DRUGS

Initially, many aspects of punk culture served as reactions *against* 1970s arena-rock excess and the perceived drug abuse by hippies, so it would stand to reason that drug abuse would be a behavior that punks could reject collectively. But sadly, the famously addicted Johnny Thunders (of the Heartbreakers and New York Dolls) disproved any such notions early on, even before Sid Vicious became the pathetic junkie he is most remembered as being, and the list of punk's casualties began to mount in the 1970s and '80s.

The roots of punk both in downtown Manhattan glam bands such as the New York Dolls and in blazing Detroit rockers the MC5 and the Stooges practically ensured that many of punk's early practitioners would be drawn to the same level of excess that surrounded those iconic bands. Although tastes varied from scene to scene (with quaaludes, amphetamines, and even glue-sniffing each making a mark), the drug of choice in punk was heroin. The extremely addictive opiate was a favorite early on with Iggy Pop (who became a serious junkie after the Stooges breakup) and the aforementioned Johnny Thunders. Iggy later cleaned himself up, while Thunders—who some considered largely responsible for spreading the drug to England and for introducing it to Vicious (who idolized Thunders) and Dee Dee Ramone—died of a heroin overdose under mysterious circumstances in New Orleans in 1991.

Even more famously addicted to heroin was Vicious, whose habit further damaged his already limited bass-playing ability and was certainly a factor in the stabbing death of his girlfriend (and fellow junkie) Nancy Spungen. Vicious died of an overdose in New York in 1979. Other famous punks who died from heroin over-doses include Dee Dee Ramone, Will Shatter of Flipper, GG Allin, and Darby Crash. Clearly, the cult of the doomed and scrawny addict-artist in the mold of Rimbaud or Thunders was firmly entrenched in punk.

Yet, for all the drug-related deaths, drug use was never universal in punk. In fact, some performers, including childhood friends and punk legends Ian MacKaye (Minor Threat and other bands) and Henry Rollins (Black Flag), went so far as to renounce drug and alcohol use altogether. As the hardcore movement grew in the early-1980s, many younger punks, alarmed by the prevalence of drugs and alcohol in the punk scene, created straight edge, inspired by the Minor Threat song of the same name. Bands in both the straight-edge and Hare Krishna subgenres proselytized to their audiences about the advantages of clean living (abstinence from drugs, alcohol, promiscuous sex, and in some cases, meat). Although their message was sometimes criticized as being anathema to punk's anarchistic tendencies, many in the straight-edge scene (such as SSD) claimed that clean living resulted in even more of a concentrated high than drugs could provide.

Although drug use will likely always be a significant factor in punk rock, serious addiction, while hardly uncommon, is more often the exception than the rule. And though addicts will always find a way to get their fix, punk will most likely never be plagued by drugs quite as much as some other genres are simply because the political and personal reasons behind many punks' involvement can trump the appeal of rock-star excess.

Johnny Thunders, 1979.

Logo of straight-edge band Rabid Lassie.

THE HOMOSEXUALS

1977-1981

LINEUP: Bruno "Wizard" McQuillon (vocals); Anton Hayman, aka "George Harassment" (guitar); Jim "L. Voag" Welton (bass); various (drums)

An obscure British art-punk band dedicated to the **DIY** aesthetic whose legend has only grown over the years, the Homosexuals recorded only sporadically during their brief existence, releasing just one full studio album, but are counted by many as extremely influential on **post-punk** and 1990s indie rock. The Homosexuals predated the indie scene, but their sound, a combination of complex lyrics, spaced-out guitars, and lo-fi production marked them as Sebadoh's unofficial godfathers. Originally named the Rejects, they released numerous singles during their brief time together. The Homosexuals gained a small measure of fame in that time and opened for the **Jam** and the **Damned** at the **Roxy** in 1977, later incorporating styles as diverse as funk, punk, **dub**, and abrasive antipop into a DIY stew. The band never went for glossy production values, proudly maintaining their DIY stance. Their entire recorded output was rereleased on a compilation CD by Morphius.

Discography:
The Homosexuals' Record (Recommended, 1984; Morphius, 2004); *Astral Glamour* (Hyped to Death/ Messthetics, 2004)

TERRI HOOLEY

Proprietor of the Northern Irish record label Good Vibrations, best known for releasing early works by the **Undertones** and others, ex-hippie Terri Hooley was instrumental in recording many early Irish punk bands. Like label owners with a specific "house sound," such as **Greg Ginn**, or producers like Lee "Scratch" Perry who had a magic touch and a similar vibe for every band, Hooley was a remarkably prescient producer and label owner, spotting the embryonic Undertones and helping them to hone their pop-laden sound before they came to the attention of **John Peel**. Although relatively unknown, Hooley had a major hand in shaping one of the most original punk bands of all time.

HOOVER

1992-1994

LINEUP: Joe McRedmond (vocals/guitar); Alex T. Dunham (guitar/vocals); Frederick T. Erskine (bass/vocals); Christopher Farrall (drums/smiley faces)

Hoover was a moody and dramatic Washington, D.C., **hardcore** band from the early-1990s made up of members of well-respected local bands such as Admiral, Hoonah, Fine Day, and Wind of Change. Although most of Hoover's members were not originally from the D.C. area, their introspective music fit in well with the overall sound of other bands on **Dischord Records** at the time. As they never got as much press as the other huge Dischord bands from the label's so-called "second wave" (**Shudder to Think** or **Jawbox**), Hoover stands as one of the great overlooked bands from a label that never suffered from a lack of good music.

Discography:
Lurid Traversal of Rte. 7 (Dischord, 1994)

HUGGY BEAR

1991-1994

LINEUP: Chris Rowley, aka "Morbius" (vocals/trumpet/piano); Jo Johnson, aka "Lionheart" (vocals/guitar); Jon Slade (guitar); Niki Eliot, aka "St. Felony" (vocals/bass); Karen Hill, aka "Kray" (drums/piano)

Although the **Riot Grrrl** movement was associated primarily with the Olympia, Washington, and Washington, D.C., scenes,

Hoover, 1992: (L to R) Alex Dunham, Fred Erskine.

The ladies and gentlemen of Huggy Bear, 1992.

one of its most beloved bands was from Brighton, England. Formed in 1991, Huggy Bear received a lot of buzz early on from the notoriously fickle and trend-mad British music press, but rejected all of the numerous major-label offers hurled their way, eventually signing to indie label Wiiija. The mostly female band, with a (then) anonymous male vocalist, called their members "boy-girl revolutionaries" and laced a sense of anarchic humor through their recordings and performances. Huggy Bear played numerous shows over their relatively short lifespan with other Riot Grrrl-style bands like **Bratmobile** and **Bikini Kill** (another group who featured a stridently pro-feminist agenda while keeping one male in the lineup), releasing a joint album with the latter. Their chaotic and often poppy but ramshackle music was a distinct breath of fresh air during the early-1990s, when every other band was investing heavily in grunge-worthy flannel and heavy rock chords.

Discography:
Rubbing the Impossible to Burst EP (Wiiija, 1992); *Kiss Curl for the Kid's Lib Guerrillas* EP (Wiiija, 1992); *Her Jazz* EP (Catcall/Wiiija, 1993); *Don't Die* EP (Wiiija, 1993); *Taking the Rough with the Smooch* (Kill Rock Stars, 1993); *Long Distance Lovers* EP (Gravity, 1994); *Main Squeeze* EP (Famous Monsters of Filmland/Rugger Bugger, 1994); *Weaponry Listens to Love* (Kill Rock Stars, 1995). **Huggy Bear/Bikini Kill:** *Our Troubled Youth/Yeah Yeah Yeah Yeah* (Catcall/Kill Rock Stars, 1993). **Various Artists:** *Shimmies in Super-8* EP (Duophonic, 1993)

"**Hüsker Dü seemingly defined the punk ethos....without necessarily embracing or endorsing it.**"
—Terry Katzman, band friend and first sound engineer

HÜSKER DÜ

1979-1988

LINEUP: Bob Mould (vocals/guitar); Greg Norton (bass); Grant Hart (drums/vocals)

The rare artistically adventurous but still commercially successful band, Hüsker Dü challenged the orthodoxy of mid-1980s punk by incorporating elements of pure power-pop and psychedelia into their music, Hüsker Dü had numerous minor college radio hits and **MTV** videos before various addictions and tensions between lead singers Grant Hart and Bob Mould boiled over in the mid-to-late-1980s, ultimately destroying the band.

Formed by singer/guitarist Bob Mould, drummer/singer Grant Hart, and bassist Greg Norton in Minneapolis in 1979, Hüsker Dü took their name from a board game popular at the time (it's Danish for "Do You Remember?"). In January 1981, Hüsker Dü released their first single, the superfast

"Statues" EP seven-inch that showed them to be trailblazers for the early **hardcore** sound. The band toured constantly and became friends with the **Minutemen** (who released the first two Hüsker Dü albums on their New Alliance imprint) and **Black Flag** (who released most of the quintessential Hüsker Dü albums of the mid-1980s via Greg Ginn's **SST** label). Later in 1981, SST put out the live *Land Speed Record*, which, though atrociously recorded, became a hardcore landmark because of its raw ferocity. 1983's *Metal Circus* EP contained several brilliant and poppy songs that showed the band's already bristling annoyance at the limitations of hardcore, a genre they'd been so instrumental in establishing. Following the success of *Metal Circus*, Hüsker Dü embarked on its most ambitious project, 1984's *Zen Arcade*. This concept double album covered the musical gamut from Hart's psychedelic pop masterpiece "Pink Turns to Blue," to Mould's subtle hardcore take on relationships on "Pride," to the monumental instrumentals of "Reoccurring Dreams" and "Dreams Reoccurring." A brilliant piece of work—recorded, legend has it, in a mere 40 hours for only $3,200—that was heralded even in some mainstream publications including *Rolling Stone* (which compared it to the **Clash**'s *London Calling*), *Zen Arcade* was a quantum leap for punk equaled only by the Minutemen's *Double Nickels on the Dime* and **Sonic Youth**'s *Daydream Nation*.

The next album, *New Day Rising*, was a powerful but less experimental piece of work that showed Hüsker Dü moving in a more pop direction, which culminated in their next and last record for SST, *Flip Your Wig*. After quarreling with SST house producer Spot over sound (the Hüskers found that their growing pop sensibilities clashed with SST's dynamic and recording ideas), the band signed to Warner Bros., which they defended against the standard cries of "sellout!" by pointing out SST's lax practices and the total artistic freedom given them by the major label.

Hüsker Dü's Warner Bros. debut, 1986's *Candy Apple Grey*, was a crystalline slice of beauty that benefited from better production values and showed off the band members' skill at crafting gorgeous pop tunes. The ambitious though flawed double LP *Warehouse: Songs and Stories*, followed the next year. Although weighted with some good songs, *Warehouse* was too clearly divided between the melancholic songs penned by Mould ("Standing in the Rain," the MTV single "Could You Be the One?") and Hart's more flowery psychedelia ("She Floated Away"), and also illustrated the limitations of the band's increasingly stratified sound.

After the suicide of their manager David Savoy, and amid growing tensions between key songwriters Mould and Hart (exacerbated by Hart's heroin addiction), Hüsker Dü decided to split in 1988. Hart released the autobiographical *2541* record, formed the band Nova Mob, and toured under that name and as a solo artist before taking time off from his music career to deal with various addictions. Mould found more success with his power pop band Sugar as well as with several solo records. He later recorded and wrote music for wrestling programs and video games before returning to solo recording and touring (sometimes with Brendan Canty of **Fugazi**). Norton became a respected chef and started his own restaurant, playing in a couple of bands over the years (most recently the noise/art band the Gang Font with Dave King from

jazz punks the Bad Plus), and, most importantly, keeping his trademark handlebar mustache all the while.

Discography:

Land Speed Record (New Alliance, 1981; SST, 1987); *Everything Falls Apart* (Reflex, 1982); *Metal Circus* EP (Reflex/SST, 1983); *Zen Arcade* (SST, 1984); *New Day Rising* (SST, 1985); *Flip Your Wig* (SST, 1985); *Candy Apple Grey* (Warner Bros., 1986); *Sorry Somehow* EP (Warner Bros., 1986); *Warehouse: Songs and Stories* (Warner Bros., 1987); *The Living End* (Warner Bros., 1994)

Hüsker Dü's Greg Norton.

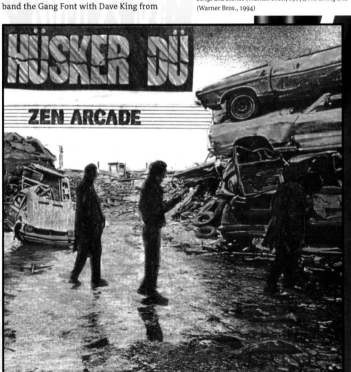

Boredoms, mixed in with Albert Ayers or later John Coltrane. What started as **hardcore** with saxophones quickly became free noise, and the band mutated several times—playing with different configurations ranging up to nine members as Iceburn Collective, all merrily squonking along in an unclassifiable way. Singer/guitarist Gentry Densley went on to play even more atonal/indie rock experiments in Smashy Smashy, but his work with **Engine Kid** is probably his most accessible.

Discography:
Firon (Victory, 1992; Caroline, 1995); *Hephaestus* (Revelation, 1993); *Poetry of Fire* (Revelation, 1994); *Split* (with Engine Kid; Revelation, 1994); *Meditavolutions* (Revelation, 1996); *Power of the Lion* (Iceburn, 1998); *Polar Bear Suite* (Iceburn, 2000)

IGNITE
1993-present

LINEUP: Zoli Teglas (vocals); Brian Balchack (guitar); Brett Rasmussen (bass); Casey Jones (drums, replaced by Craig Anderson)

California's Orange County has been the birthplace of some of the most exciting punk bands of the last 30 years, with the ferocious yet purposeful Ignite being no exception to that rule. Committed to social change and raw, aggressive punk, Ignite is squarely situated in the new leftist/neo-Marxist wave of bands who oppose capitalism and the World Trade Organization (WTO), and are fiercely dedicated to vegetarianism, animal rights, and the environment. Their music is situated somewhere between the hard sound of **straight-edge**, semi-metal bands like Earth Crisis or bands such as **Rise Against** who put the punch of heavy rock back into punk. Singer Zoli Teglas also took over the ever-revolving lead vocal chair for the reunited **Misfits** in 2000 before Jerry Only reclaimed the spot.

Discography:
Scarred for Life (Lost & Found, 1994); *In My Time* (Lost & Found, 1995); *Call on My Brothers* (Conversion, 1995; Revelation, 2000); *A Place Called Home* (TVT, 2000); *Still Screaming for Change/The Lost & Found Years* (Lost & Found, 2001); *Our Darkest Days* (Abacus, 2006)

IRON PROSTATE
1989-1992

LINEUP: Scott Weiss (vocals); George Tabb (guitar); Steve Wishnia (guitar); Charles Young (bass); Mike Linn (drums)

A New York punk band led by rock critics and professional punks (although the difference is sometimes hard to tell) who celebrated the power and finesse of punk's early years, Iron Prostate featured ex-Ed Gein's Car front man Scott Weiss on lead vocals and guitarist George Tabb, who went on to form **Furious George**. Like Weiss and Tabb's other bands, Iron Prostate played a faster version of classic, 1977-era punk, mingled with a dash of 1980s **hardcore**, though with a better-produced guitar sound than most bands from that time period. Iron Prostate also displayed an actual sense of humor, that most of their contemporaries on the late-1980s punk scene distinctly lacked, in songs like "Hell Toupee" (say it a few times fast) . The band was allegedly in the process of recording with Meat Loaf producer Jim Steinman when they dissolved due to the usual creative differences, but not before releasing one of the best and funniest punk singles from the early-1990s: "Bring Me the Head of Jerry Garcia."

Discography:
Loud, Fast and Aging Rapidly (Skreamin' Skull, 1991)

ICEBURN/ ICEBURN COLLECTIVE
1992-present

LINEUP: Gentry Densley (vocals/guitar); James Holder (guitar/saxophone); Doug Wright (bass); Daniel Day (drums)

An intricate math-rock band from Salt Lake City, Iceburn melded elements of punk and the intricacies of jazz into a unique style. Unlike most punk bands who tried to do this in the past, such as Saccharine Trust and the collective free jazz efforts of October Faction (a particularly unlistenable **SST** experiment), the **Minutemen**, or even jazz bands with punk influences like the Bad Plus, the Iceburn guys were equally adept at making punk music for the masses who appreciated the noise and sonic blast of the

Ignite's Zoli Teglas in New York, 2006.

SMALL LABELS

For a time during the late-1970s, a number of mainstream record labels took chances on punk bands, from the **Sex Pistols** to the **Ramones** and even **Suicide**. But after punk proved too threatening to be commercially viable, punk bands were given a choice—to either become **new wave** or be dropped from the label's roster. To make up for the fact that few major labels would take a chance on punk anymore—and since the pre-digital era required physically producing music on vinyl and then distributing it around the world—a number of smaller labels began to spring up, **DIY**-style, during the 1980s as a way of releasing punk music on their own terms. Many of the larger punk labels such as **Slash**, **SST**, **Rough Trade**, **Lookout!**, and **Dischord**, are discussed in individual entries elsewhere in this book. Here are some of the smaller small labels that worked tirelessly over the years, often with scant notice outside of their immediate area, to publicize their respective local scenes.

HELLCAT (Los Angeles)

Back in the late-1990s, Rancid's Tim Armstrong founded this label as an offshoot of larger indie Epitaph. Since then, Hellcat has turned into one of the steadier indie labels, releasing a stream of albums from up-and-coming punk bands, particularly those with musical nods toward ska and reggae. Some of the more established bands on Hellcat include the Dropkick Murphys and Joe Strummer's Mescaleros. Almost every year, Hellcat releases a sampler album, *Give 'Em the Boot*, to highlight their new offerings.

CAPTAIN OI! (High Wycombe, England)

This British label is highly devoted to reissuing out-of-print punk and **oi** records (vinyl and CD), as well as new releases from U.K. Subs, the Cockney Rejects, Angelic Upstarts, and Argy Bargy. Captain Oi! also acts as a distributor for smaller punk labels and even supports teams from the premier division of the Ryman Football League.

K RECORDS (Olympia, Washington)

Some may argue the relative punkness of both the musical output of Beat Happening's Calvin Johnson and his label, but K Records' economic independence, **DIY** aesthetic, and commitment to releasing records by women and the disenfranchised are all indisputable hallmarks of the latter-day punk aesthetic.

GOOD VIBRATIONS (Belfast)

Terri Hooley started this Northern Ireland **pop-punk** label (and record store) back in the mid-1970s. Over the years, Good Vibrations released singles by Rudi, Protex, Outcasts, and, most notably, the Undertones. Before its demise in the early-1980s, Good Vibrations allowed many young Irish bands to release material early in their musical careers and helped establish the Undertones as a band to watch.

EQUAL VISION (Albany, New York)

Founded in the early-1990s by Ray Cappo (of Shelter and Youth of Today fame), Equal Vision started out as a way to release albums by Shelter but soon branched out to become one of the decade's key **hardcore** labels. Over the years, Equal Vision has put out records by Saves the Day, Fivespeed, Seemless, Bane, Modern Life Is War, Converge, and Serpico. These days they've branched out beyond hardcore and also release albums by several experimental, post-hardcore and metal bands.

JADE TREE (Wilmington, Delaware)

This Delaware-based indie—started by musicians and friends Tim Owen and Darren Walters—made a name for itself over the years with a prolific string of popular releases from a wide-ranging list of bands (from melodic punk to post-hardcore to emo) such as Joan of Arc, Pedro the Lion, Jets to Brazil, Trial by Fire, and the Promise Ring.

MR. LADY (Durham, North Carolina / San Francisco)

A queercore-focused, indie record and video distribution label (even punks have to work outside the punk mainstream sometimes), Mr. Lady was started in Durham, North Carolina in 1994 by Kaia Wilson and girlfriend Tammy Rae Carlson. A good sampling of Mr. Lady bands can be found on their *Calling All Kings and Queens* anthology, which included Le Tigre, Sleater-Kinney, and Wilson's band the Butchies.

THE JAM

1972-1982

LINEUP: Paul Weller (vocals/guitar); Bruce Foxton (bass/vocals); Rick Buckler (drums)

Although they would have insisted up and down that they were not punk, the Jam was indeed one of the most energetic and polished punk bands from the British punk movement of the mid-1970s. Originally the Jam were the leaders of the mod revival that coincided and overlapped with punk in England during the 1970s, and which led to the rebirth of the parka, the Vespa, and the Edwardian suits so beloved by the fashion-conscious sector of the British public at the time.

Led by controversial singer and guitarist Paul Weller (who identified as a member of the conservative Tory Party early on, much to his eventual regret), the Jam applied punk energy to a revival of the classic mod sound and image as epitomized by the early Who, and it proved to be an electrifying combination. Early albums such as *In The City* and *This is the Modern World* are just as important as political protests against the lack of jobs and opportunities for British youth in the 1970s than anything on the **Sex Pistols'** *Never Mind the Bollocks*, and just as brilliantly recorded. Although the Jam was just a three-piece band, the frenetic energy of Weller's guitar, along with the steady rhythm section of Bruce Foxton and Rick Buckler, showed that relatively complex songs such as "All Around the World" and "Bricks and Mortar" could be as effective as any pop masterpiece from the 1960s, yet still sound remarkably contemporary. Some punks were unimpressed though, and the **Exploited** famously railed against the mods, leading to clashes between mods and punks that were reminiscent of the *Quadrophenia*-style clashes between mods and rockers during the 1960s.

As the Jam members grew older, Weller showed less inclination to play straight rock 'n' roll, and later material began to go in a more R&B direction, much to the dismay of many fans (stylistic experimentation being a cardinal sin to some punks, while monotony from record to record is a cardinal sin to others). Chafing under the musical restrictions inherent in a three-piece lineup, Weller experimented by adding additional instruments and more of a soul flavor to the band, a sound he would pursue to more success in his next band, the Style Council.

Weller maintained an active solo career and as of 2006, was beginning to finally incorporate more Jam songs into his live sets. Bass player Foxton has been a member of the reconstituted **Stiff Little Fingers** since the late-1980s. The Jam's music, unlike some of the early forefront of 1977 punk, has aged as well as any bona fide pop and rock classics, and their surprisingly rich and deep catalog is highly recommended. From their early cover of the *Batman* theme, to the later and more

The Jam practice the mod hop, London, 1977: (L to R): Paul Weller, Rick Buckler, Bruce Foxton.

THE·JAM

The Jam's Paul Weller tames his unruly guitar, 1977.

GOING UNDERGROUND

complex classics like "Town Called Malice," the Jam showed a depth and diversity that still rings strong today.

Discography:

In the City (Polydor, 1977); *This is the Modern World* (Polydor, 1977); *All Mod Cons* (Polydor, 1978); *Setting Sons* (Polydor, 1979); *Sound Affects* (Polydor, 1980); *The Jam* EP (Polydor, 1982); *The Gift* (Polydor, 1982); *The Bitterest Pill (I Ever Had to Swallow)* EP (Polydor, 1982); *Beat Surrender* EP (Polydor, 1982); *Dig the New Breed* (Polydor, 1982); *Snap!* (Polydor, 1983); *The Peel Sessions* (Strange Fruit, 1990); *Greatest Hits* (Polydor, 1991); *Extras* (Polydor, 1992); *Live Jam* (Polydor, 1993); *The Jam Collection* (Polydor, 1996); *Direction, Reaction, Creation* (Polydor, 1997); *The Very Best of the Jam* (Polydor, 1997); *This is the Modern World and All Mod Cons* (Collector's Choice Music, 2000); *45 RPM: The Singles 1977–79* (Polydor, 2001); *45 RPM: The Singles 1980–82* (Polydor, 2001).

Bruce Foxton: *Touch Sensitive* (Arista, 1984). **The Style Council:** *A Paris* EP (Polydor, 1983); *Introducing the Style Council* EP (Polydor, 1983); *Café Leu* (Polydor, 1984); *My Ever Changing Moods* (Geffen, 1984); *Our Favourite Shop* (Polydor, 1985); *Internationalists* (Geffen, 1985); *The Lodgers* EP (Polydor, 1985); *Home & Abroad: Live!* (Geffen, 1986); *The Cost of Loving* (Polydor, 1987); *Confessions of a Pop Group* (Polydor, 1988); *The Singular Adventures of the Style Council (Greatest Hits Vol. 1)* (Polydor, 1989); *Here's Some That Got Away* (Polydor, 1993); *The Style Council Collection* (Polydor, 1996); *The Style Council in Concert* (Polydor, 1997); *The Complete Adventures of the Style Council* (Polydor, 1998)

JAWBOX

1989-1997

LINEUP: J. Robbins (vocals/guitar); Bill Barbot (guitar/vocals); Kim Coletta (bass); Adam Wade (drums, replaced by Zach Barocas)

An aggressive Washington, D.C., band led by J. Robbins (formerly of **Government Issue**), who was known for his blistering and crunchy guitar-driven songs, Jawbox released several consistently powerful albums on **Dischord Records** that helped define (along with **Jawbreaker**) the early-1990s style of gruff and aggressive, but heartfelt and slowed-down **hardcore**. Jawbox later jumped to a major label, Atlantic, where they had a minor hit with the song "Savory" in 1994. The band didn't survive the transition from indie to major label very well, though, and split up in 1997, with Robbins going on to form Burning Airlines. Jawbox's music has aged well over the years, despite some overproduction on the final Atlantic records; their first three albums are highly recommended.

Discography:
Jawbox EP (DeSoto/Dischord, 1990); *Grippe* (Dischord, 1991); *Novelty* (Dischord, 1992); *Savory + 3 EP* (Atlantic, 1994); *For Your Own Special Sweetheart* (Atlantic, 1994); *Jawbox* (Tag/Atlantic, 1996); *My Scrapbook of Fatal Accidents* (DeSoto, 1998). **Jawbox/Leatherface:** *Your Choice Live Series* (Your Choice, 1995)

JAWBREAKER

1988-1996

LINEUP: Blake Schwarzenbach (vocals/guitar); Chris Bauermeister (bass); Adam Pfahler (drums)

Jawbreaker's lead singer Blake Schwarzenbach didn't just wear his heart on his sleeve, he used that sleeve to dry the many tears he cried during the many, many great Jawbreaker songs about lost love and missed chances. The Berkeley-based band with roots in New York (they formed after meeting as students at NYU) helped serve as a template for much of the early-1990s punk scene, which was greatly in need of inspiration. Along with **Jawbox**, Jawbreaker slowed down the **hardcore** beat, but kept its intensity and raw guitar sound, while lyrically inspiring a new generation (who had evidently missed the memo about **Dag Nasty** and **Rites of Spring**) to write short and emotive songs. That the modern and

decidedly non-punk **emo** movement is influenced by Jawbreaker is no reason to avoid them, however, as their music is miles better both lyrically and musically than later emo imitators like Saves the Day and Jimmy Eat World.

Jawbreaker's sound was marked by an extremely tight and constantly shifting, stop-and-start musical approach, created by Schwarzenbach's scratchy, distinctive vocals and the ultratight rhythm section of bassist Chris Bauermeister and drummer Adam Pfahler. Their first two records, *Unfun* and *Bivouac*, were extremely influential, as Schwarzenbach's highly personal lyrics addressed issues of loss and authenticity with a candor rarely seen in the punk scene. Their breakthrough record, *24 Hour Revenge Therapy* (1994), established Jawbreaker as one of the most important punk bands of the 1990s, alongside **Fugazi**, and added a new dimension of sophisticated pop on songs such as "The Boat Dreams from the Hill" and "Do You Still Hate Me?" Jawbreaker was signed to DGC Records in the post-**Green Day** years and released one more album, the underrated but criminally overproduced *Dear You*, before calling it quits in 1996. After Jawbreaker's demise, Schwarzenbach formed the stranger but compelling **Jets to Brazil**, and began teaching writing at Hunter College in New York after that band broke up.

Discography:
Unfun (Shredder, 1990); *Bivouac* (Tupelo Communion, 1992); *24 Hour Revenge Therapy* (Tupelo Communion, 1994); *Dear You* (DGC, 1995)

J CHURCH

1992-2007

LINEUP: Lance Hahn (vocals/guitar); Ben White (bass); Chris Pfeiffer (drums)

The three-piece J Church were led by vocalist/guitarist Lance Hahn, who moved from Hawaii and started the band with Cringer cofounder and bassist Gardner Maxam. Hahn was a punk archivist who wrote for **Maximum RocknRoll** and also worked on a book on the British anarchist bands of the 1970s, of which he had a legendry encyclopedic knowledge. In addition, the multitalented Hahn played in Monsulo and ran the Honey Bear Records label. J Church has gone through an almost Spinal Tap level of turnover since 1992,

with recent members of the band including, but not limited to, Ben White (of the diary comic *Snakepit*) on bass, David DiDonato on guitar, and Chris Pfeiffer on drums (Adam Pfahler of **Jawbreaker** was also a drummer for some time).

J Church has toured extensively and released as many as 10 records per year due to Hahn's prodigious talents as a songwriter. While amazingly prolific, Hahn was also extremely consistent as a writer, constantly cranking out **pop-punk** classics and playing with an onstage ferocity that belied his considerable girth. Hahn also stuck exclusively to indie labels, despite the cashing-in trend of the 1990s, and maintained his integrity as leader of one of the last, great independent American bands, content to live within the punk world all his life. Tragically, longtime health problems led to Hahn's death in October 2007. Fans wishing to find out how impressive J Church was should seek out some of the hundreds of seven-inch splits they did; almost all are well worth tracking down.

Essential Discography:
Quetzalcoatl (Allied, 1993); *Nostalgic for Nothing* (Broken Rekids, 1995); *Yellow Blue* (Allied, 1995); *Cat Food* (Damaged Goods, 1998); *One Mississippi* (Honest Don's Hardly, 2000); *Meaty, Beaty, Shitty Sounding* (Honey Bear, 2001); *Palestine* (Honey Bear, 2002); *Society is a Carnivorous Flower* (No Idea, 2004)

JERRY'S KIDS

1981-1987, 2004-present

LINEUP: Bryan Jones (vocals, replaced by Rick Jones); Rick Jones (vocals/bass); Bob Cenci (guitar); Dave Aronson (guitar, replaced by Chris Doherty); Brian Betzger (drums, replaced by several)

A first-wave Boston **hardcore** band, Jerry's Kids helped develop the city's scene and was one of the most original and fastest bands of the 1980s. Jerry's Kids' original lineup included Bryan Jones on lead vocals, Chris Doherty on guitar, and Bryan's brother Rick Jones on bass. Like many of the hard/fast bands on the crucial compilation, *This is Boston, Not L.A.*, Jerry's Kids proved to be as volatile as their music was aggressive and they soon broke up, with Bryan Jones and original guitarist Aronson leaving and Rick Jones taking over on vocals. After breaking up for a second time, Doherty and Betzger left to form **Gang Green**. After some time off, Jerry's

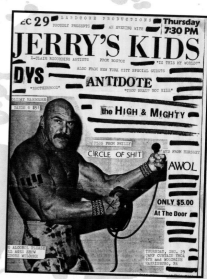

Kids got back together and the 1987 lineup featured Bob Cenci and Dave Aronson back on guitar. They later veered in a more metallic direction for *Kill Kill Kill* before retiring again. Jerry's Kids have reunited for several shows since 2004 and have played around mostly in the Boston area.

Discography:
Is This My World? (XClaim, 1983; Taang!/Funhouse, 1987; Taang!, 2002); *Kill Kill Kill* (Taang!, 1989)

JERSEY BEAT

Jersey Beat is a long-running **zine** started in 1982 and published by rock writer Jim Testa, an insurance salesman from Weehawken, New Jersey, who occasionally performs as a musician, playing his own compositions at clubs and open-mic nights. The zine is one of the best and longest-running publications devoted to punk and indie music, having covered almost every movement in punk since the heyday of 1980s **hardcore**. While many zines, such as *Maximum RocknRoll*, function as a sort of punk police, *Jersey Beat* was always ecumenical in its tastes, covering bands as diverse as the Chills, T.Rex, and the Flaming Lips. Testa's devotion to covering good music before (and even after!) it bubbles up to the mainstream marks him as one of the most influential East Coast zine-makers of the last quarter-century.

Jets to Brazil play
Charlotte, N.C., 2001.

JETS TO BRAZIL

1997-2003

LINEUP: Blake Schwarzenbach (vocals/
guitar); Bryan Maryansky (guitar
2000–2003 only); Jeremy Chatelain (bass);
Chris Daly (drums)

A melodic punk band started by Blake
Schwarzenbach after the demise of the
much-beloved **Jawbreaker**, Jets to Brazil
was a sort of latter-day **hardcore** supergroup. The band was, however, firmly
under Schwarzenbach's vision, featuring
him on lead vocals, guitar, *and* keyboards.

Jets to Brazil can be seen as a natural
extension of where Jawbreaker was going
before their dissolution. Schwarzenbach's
voice is in fine form, and although intricate,
the guitar and bass lines are more straightforward pop than those of Jawbreaker,
leaving lots of room for **effects** and even

the occasional keyboard part. In 2003 the
band disbanded without a major announce-
ment and Schwarzenbach went back to
teaching writing.

Discography:
Orange Rhyming Dictionary (Jade Tree, 1998); *Four
Cornered Night* (Jade Tree, 2000); *Perfecting Loneliness*
(Jade Tree, 2002)

JOAN JETT

Joan Jett (born Joan Larkin) started absurdly young, even for a punk, playing in her first band while still a teenager, and remains likely to keep performing until punk rock Social Security kicks in. In the 1970s, Jett, a young and androgynously striking guitarist, was noticed by professional creep/svengali **Kim Fowley** and recruited for his new project the **Runaways**. Soon they were one of the most popular bands on Los Angeles' Sunset Strip, to some degree for their catchy mixture of proto-punk and glam, but more compellingly because they were all teenage girls. The Runaways were playing **CBGB** by 1977. With the band's ambiguously sexual presence, and singles like the churning, rebel-girl anthem "Cherry Bomb," Jett and her bandmates were unknowingly laying the groundwork for a future generation of **Riot Grrrls**, who would realize that punk didn't have to be an all-boys club.

Fed up with Fowley's manipulation and abuse, Jett eventually went solo, and soon became a fixture on the L.A. punk scene, which led to her "producing" (some reports suggest she mostly showed up and drank with the band) the **Germs**' 1979 album *(GI)*. While most of Jett's solo career with the Blackhearts in the 1980s and '90s produced a string of straightforward, three-chord rock singles ("I Love Rock 'n' Roll," for instance), her history with the Runaways and the Germs, and her generally inestimable punk cred (Steve Jones and Paul Cook of the **Sex Pistols** played on her first album) gave her stature in the eyes of bands like **Bikini Kill**, who would credit her as an influence. Jett also later collaborated with Seattle punks the Gits after their singer Mia Zapata was raped and murdered in 1993, sang a duet with Paul Westerberg of the **Replacements**, produced Bikini Kill's *New Radio* EP (also singing backup and playing guitar), and signed smaller punk bands to her own Blackheart label. Surprisingly, Jett's 2006 album *Sinner* is as good as most of her early-1980s work.

Essential Discography:
Joan Jett (Ariola, 1980); *I Love Rock 'n' Roll* (Boardwalk, 1981); *Glorious Results of a Misspent Youth* (Blackheart, 1984); *Hit List* (Epic, 1990); *Pure and Simple* (Warner Bros., 1994); *Sinner* (Blackheart, 2006).

Joan Jett in 1976: punk before you even knew what that meant.

JFA

1981-1988, 1998-present

LINEUP: Brian Brannon (vocals); Don "Redondo" Pendelton (guitars); Corey Stretz (bass, briefly replaced by Alan Bishop); Mike Sversvold (drums, replaced by many)

A **hardcore** band from Phoenix, Arizona, JFA's name was short for Jodie Foster's Army, after the actress about whom John Hinckley (who shot **Ronald Reagan**) obsessed. One of the first bands to sing about the **skateboarding** lifestyle—in the way that bands like the Surf Punks and **Bl'ast!** sang—about surf culture, JFA was led by vocalist Brian Brannon (who also

wrote for *Thrasher* magazine). The band, which would only accept members who could skate, released several great punk singles on *Blatant Localism* (which includes the classic tracks "Beach Blanket Bong Out" and "Out of School"), but they really came into their own with the *JFA* record in 1984. Subsequent releases were good, but the band ran out of steam in the late-1980s, not releasing any more records until *Only Live Once* in 1999.

Discography:

Blatant Localism EP (Placebo, 1981); *Valley of the Yakes* (Placebo, 1983); *JFA* (Placebo, 1984); *Mad Garden* EP (Placebo, 1984); *JFA Live* (Placebo, 1985); *Nowhere Blossoms* (Placebo, 1988); *Only Live Once* (Rotz, 1999); *We Know You Suck: Blatant Localism/Valley of the Yakes* (Alternative Tentacles, 2003)

JFA's Brian Brannon (left) and Alan Bishop, 1984.

JOY DIVISION

1976-1980

LINEUP: Ian Curtis (vocals); Bernard Sumner (guitar/keyboards); Peter Hook (bass); Stephen Morris (drums)

An increasingly influential **post-punk** band led by the tragic and brooding epileptic Ian Curtis, Joy Division composed much of the sonic palette for the post-punk and **new wave** scenes. Curtis, a frustrated poet and songwriter from Manchester, England, is said to have been inspired by the **Sex Pistols**' legendary concert at the Lesser Free Trade Hall in Manchester on July 20, 1976. Following several abortive attempts to get a band going, Curtis hooked up with bass player Peter Hook and guitarist Bernard Sumner. After trying in vain to find a drummer open to playing in something besides 4/4 time, the band finally completed the lineup with Stephen Morris, giving birth to the band Warsaw (its name taken from **David Bowie**'s Berlin-period song "Warsawza"). Unlike the deep melodic voice that Curtis used on Joy Division songs, early Warsaw material found Curtis singing in a higher register and the band playing in a faster punk style than most Joy Division fans would have recognized in retrospect.

After some experimentation, with the members agreeing that their sound needed to expand, the band changed tactics by going back to their original idea of recreating the sparse and minimalist soundscapes that Bowie had crafted during his Berlin years, allowing Curtis' natural voice (a deep and creepy croon unheard in punk music of that time) to emerge on his Bowie-esque lyrics about death and alienation. Seeing their greatness, influential television journalist Tony Wilson signed Joy Division to his embryonic Factory label in a contract reportedly written in Wilson's blood, setting up the band for a larger recording budget and more time to work on their signature sound. As Curtis developed as a singer and a musician, the band also expanded musically, creating a sound greatly aided by producer and mad genius Martin Hannett, who sometimes would force a long-suffering Morris to play the same metronomic beat over and over again for hours. With sparse guitars and a bass that emulated a guitar, the Joy Division sound, oft-imitated but never equaled, was born.

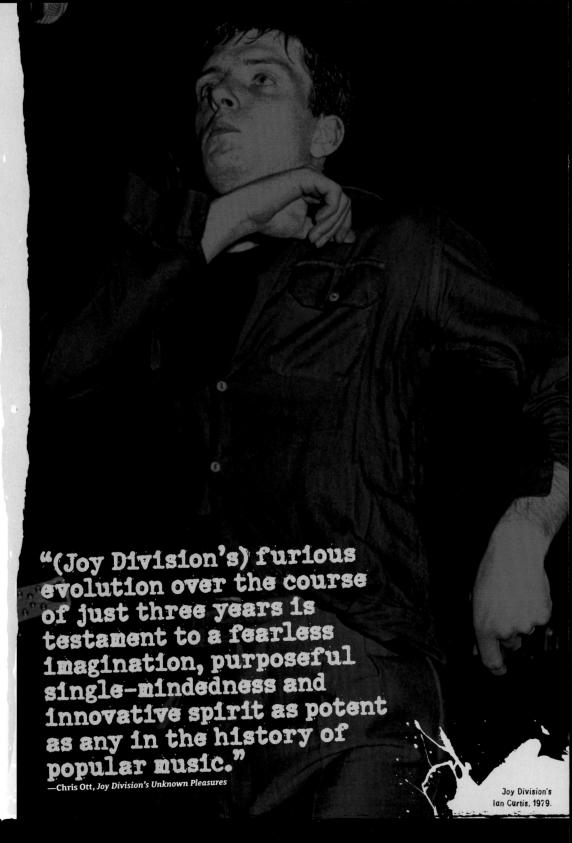

"(Joy Division's) furious evolution over the course of just three years is testament to a fearless imagination, purposeful single-mindedness and innovative spirit as potent as any in the history of popular music."
—Chris Ott, *Joy Division's Unknown Pleasures*

Joy Division's Ian Curtis, 1979.

Joy Division in 1979, preparing to spread cheer and good will to all mankind.

JUDGE

1987–1991

LINEUP: Mike "Judge" Ferraro (vocals); John "Porcell" Porcelly (guitar); Jimmy Yu (bass, replaced by Matt Pincus); Luke Abbey (drums, replaced by Sammy Siegler)

The prolific Mike Judge (Mike Ferraro), who formerly played drums with **Youth of Today** and Death Before Dishonor (who later became Supertouch), led this definitive New York **straight-edge hardcore** band. After touring with Youth of Today on the *Break Down the Walls* tour, Judge decided that he would rather sing and express himself rather than remain hidden behind the drums. Judge started to collaborate with John Porcell of Youth of Today, Jimmy Yu of Death Before Dishonor on bass (later replaced by Matt Pincus), and Luke Abbey from **Warzone** (later replaced by Sammy Siegler). They released several records and became a major touring attraction. Even though Mike Judge was a militant straight-edge activist during that time period, he also took the name as an ironic joke on his own judgmental attitudes. Despite the goofiness of the name, Judge *was* an extremely confrontational straight-edge band, and *Bringin' it Down* and *No Apologies* are ferocious records that still hold up. Judge broke up in 1991, after which Mike Judge formed an acoustic project called Mike Judge & Old Smoke.

Discography:

Bringin' it Down (Revelation, 1989); *Storm* (Revelation, 1994); *No Apologies* (Lost & Found, 1995); *What We Said & Where it Went* (Lost & Found, 1996); *Judge This* (Executive Thug, 2002); *What it Meant: The Complete Discography* (Revelation, 2005)

By this time, depressed by his recurring epilepsy (not at all helped by his alcohol and drug problems), Curtis slipped into a deep depression. He ultimately committed suicide on May 18, 1980, just before setting out on what would have been a lucrative North American tour. The rest of the band eventually regrouped as New Order, one of the most successful new wave bands. The illuminating 2007 biographical film, *Control*, was based on the book *Touching from a Distance* by Curtis' widow Deborah and directed by Anton Corbijn, a photographer who had taken several evocative portraits of Joy Division.

Curtis remains, for many, the poet laureate of the punk and post-punk movement, and his tragic early death doomed him to be a romantic figure, sadly emulated by many in the goth scene that he helped to inspire. But there was just as much storytelling and introspection as there was nihilism in Joy Division's work. When Curtis sang "She's Lost Control" he was not just chronicling a grim story, but making oblique references to himself. Joy Division's legacy left an indelible stamp on goth and post-punk music that endures today, with modern bands such as Interpol probably owing the band's management royalty checks.

Discography:

An Ideal for Living EP (Enigma, 1978; Anonymous, 1978); *Unknown Pleasures* (Factory, 1979; Qwest, 1989); *Closer* (Factory, 1980; Qwest, 1989); *Still* (Factory, 1981; Qwest, 1990); *The Peel Sessions* EP (Strange Fruit, 1986, 1987, 1993); *Substance* (Qwest, 1988, 1990); *The Peel Sessions Album* (Strange Fruit, 1990); *Permanent Joy Division 1995* (Qwest, 1995); *All the Lyrics* (Ei, 1998); *Preston 28 February 1980* (live; Factory, 1999); *Complete BBC Recordings* (live; Varese, 2000); *Heart and Soul* (box set; Rhino, 2001); *Les Bains Douches 18* (live; Factory, 2001); *Before and After/BBC Sessions* (live with New Order; Varése, 2002); *Refractured Box One* (Phantom, 2003); *Les Bains Douches, Vol. 1* (live; Get Back, 2004); *Les Bains Douches, Vol. 2* (live; Get Back, 2004)

"I think maybe I took it a little too far on the first record. I made more enemies than I did friends."

—Mike Judge

NICK KENT

British journalist and rock critic Nick Kent played a key part in early punk rock both as a writer and as a member of the embryonic, pre-Johnny Rotten version of the **Sex Pistols**. While working as a journalist Kent—who was enamored of the **Stooges**, the **MC5**, and the **New York Dolls**—met both **Malcolm McLaren** and Glen Matlock, who invited him to join their band Q.T. Jones and the Sex Pistols. This early edition consisted of Paul Cook on drums, Glen Matlock on bass, Wally Nightingale on guitar, and Steve Jones on vocals. Kent replaced Nightingale and (according to Kent) introduced the band to the music of the **Modern Lovers** and the Stooges. McLaren eventually fired Kent from the Sex Pistols before Rotten was inducted into the band—Kent had by then developed a serious drug habit, as he freely admits in his articles on the Pistols. Sacking notwithstanding, Kent maintained a relationship with the band until he was attacked at a Sex Pistols show by a bicycle-chain-swinging **Sid Vicious** and a knife-wielding Jah Wobble. He continues working as a writer, having written extensively on his days in the punk scene for *MOJO* magazine.

KILLING JOKE

1979–1988, 1990, 1994–present

LINEUP: Jeremy "Jaz" Coleman (vocals/keyboards); Geordie Walker (guitar); Martin "Youth" Glover (bass, replaced by Paul Raven, others); Paul Ferguson (drums, replaced by Jimmy Copley, Martin Atkins, others including Dave Grohl)

A proto-industrial London punk band best known for their anthem "Eighties," Killing Joke was one of the more aggressive entities of the **post-punk** era and became a touchstone for many of the industrial bands who followed in their wake. In the beginning, Killing Joke was more abrasive than almost any band out there, mixing punk and **reggae**

Killing Joke in Cologne, Germany, 1982. (L to R) Big Paul Ferguson, Geordie Walker, Martin "Youth" Glover, Jaz Coleman.

on tracks such as "Turn to Red," one of the most potent punk-**dub** mixes. Other early-1980s singles such as "Wardance" (which **John Peel** promoted on his radio show) and "Follow the Leaders" put them in the forefront of the British post-punk movement and led many to believe that Killing Joke could keep post-punk music viable in a **new wave**-driven marketplace. However, the band's increasing paranoia and infatuation with the occult took its toll as did the many rhythm section replacements that have plagued the band to the present day.

Killing Joke meandered their way through the late-1980s and early-'90s, coming back strong with the album *Pandemonium* and subsequent tour in 1994. Although the band continues to tour and record to this day, various members now also do production work, leading these preachers of darkness to enter into strange collaborations, such as when bassist Martin "Youth" Glover worked with Paul McCartney, and Youth and Coleman teamed up to record a symphonic Pink Floyd record with the London Philharmonic Orchestra. Longtime bassist Paul Raven died of a heart attack in 2007.

Discography:

Almost Red EP (Malicious Damage, 1979; Island, 1981; EG, 1990); *Killing Joke* (Malicious Damage/EG, 1980, 1990; Red International, 2003; resissue with bonus tracks, Virgin, 2005); *What's This For?* (Malicious Damage/EG, 1981, 1989; reissue with bonus tracks, Virgin, 2005); *Revelations* (Malicious Damage/EG, 1982; reissue with bonus tracks, Virgin, 2005); *Ha!* EP (live, Malicious Damage/EG, 1982; EMI, 2005); *Fire Dances* (Malicious Damage/EG, 1983, 1987; remastered with bonus tracks, EMI, 2008); *Night Time* (EG/Malicious Damage, 1985; EG, 1987); *Brighter Than a Thousand Suns* (EG/Virgin, 1986, remastered with bonus tracks, EMI, 2008); *Outside the Gate* (EG/Virgin, 1988; remastered with bonus tracks, EMI, 2008); *An Incomplete Collection* (EG, 1990); *Extremities, Dirt and Various Repressed Emotions* (Noise International/RCA, 1990, 1997); *Laugh? I Nearly Bought One!* (EG/Caroline, 1992); *Pandemonium* (Big Life/Zoo, 1994); *Jana Live* EP (Butterfly Records/Big Life, 1994); *Millennium* (Zoo, 1994); *BBC in Concert* (Windsong, 1995); *Wilful Days* (Blue Plate, 1995); *Democracy* (Zoo, 1996); *No Way Back but Forward Go!* (live; Pilot, 2001); *Love Like Blood* (Brilliant, 2002); *The Unperverted Pantomime* (Pilot, 2003); *Chaos for Breakfast* (box set; Malicious Damage, 2004); *Killing Joke For Beginners* (Caroline, 2004). **Anne Dudley and Jaz Coleman:** *Songs from the Victorious City* (China/TVT, 1991). **Murder, Inc.:** *Murder, Inc.* (Invisible, 1992; Futurist/Mechanic, 1993); *Corpuscle* EP (Invisible, 1992). **Fireman (pseudonym for Youth and Paul McCartney):** *Strawberries Oceans Ships Forest* (Parlophone, 1993; Capitol/EMI, 1994). **Us and Them:** *Symphonic Pink Floyd* (Point Music, 1995)

KILL ROCK STARS

LOCATION: OLYMPIA, WASHINGTON

Started in 1991 by Slim Moon, Kill Rock Stars (KRS) remains today one of the most crucial indie/punk/eclectic record labels in the United States; the closest thing that the West Coast has to a still-extant, scene-defining landmark like **Dischord** on the East. Kill's first full-length release was a star-studded compilation (heavy on Pacific Northwest locals) that featured everyone from **Nirvana** to the **Melvins** to **Nation of Ulysses** and **Bikini Kill**. Just as Dischord is most identified with the musical output of founder and punk icon **Ian MacKaye** (despite the many other excellent bands the label has released over the years), the Olympia, Washington-based KRS is similarly known in the punk canon for their role in putting out albums by female-led and queer-friendly bands like early **Sleater-Kinney**, **Bratmobile**, and Bikini Kill. However, their slate has also included a wide range of other groups, from indie rockers **Huggy Bear** and **Unwound** to easygoing popsters the Decemberists. KRS spun off a sister label 5 Rue Christine (5RC) in 1997 to release more experimental bands like Xiu Xiu and Deerhoof. In 2006, Moon shockingly left KRS to work for world-music label and Warner Bros. subsidiary Nonesuch Records, his wife Portia Sabin taking over his duties at KRS and 5RC. KRS has accumulated enough indie cred in the punk rock community to survive Moon's departure, but it remains to be seen if the label will continue to have as strong a catalog as it had in the mid-to-late-1990s.

KLEENEX

1978–1983

LINEUP: Regula Sing (vocals, replaced by Chrigle Freund, Astrid Spirit); Marlene Marder (guitar); Klaudia Schifferle, also known as Klaudia Schiff (bass); Lislot Hafner, also known as Lislot Ha (drums, replaced by Beat Schlatter); Angie Barrack (saxophone, replaced by Christoph Herzog)

An all-female band from Zurich who helped define the **post-punk** sound with their off-kilter songs, Kleenex played in a frenetically catchy but dissonant style that challenged the listener to follow the complexity of the music and lyrics on early singles such as "Madness" and "Krimi." Other tracks such as "Hedi's Head" showed that the Swiss band's choice to sing in English was not just a commercial consideration, but also an aesthetic direction in which they could choose words not so much for their meaning, but for their sound, forming brilliant non sequiturs that were funny and engaging at the same time. Using everything from bird noises, whistles, wails, and sometimes a bass being played with tom-tom mallets, Kleenex were true originals. Along with bands such as the **Raincoats** and the Au Pairs, Kleenex showed how women could break apart definitions of punk music. Eventually, the band was forced to change its name to Liliput in 1980 after the Kleenex company threatened litigation. Kleenex/Liliput later expanded their sound with a saxophone player before eventually calling it quits in 1983. Guitarist Marlene Marder went on to form the band Danger Mice in the 1980s.

Discography:
Liliput (Rough Trade, 1982); *Some Songs* (Rough Trade, 1983); *LiliPut* (2-CD retrospective; Kill Rock Stars, 2001). **Danger Mice:** *Sound Session* EP (Swiss Sounds!, 1989)

KLOVER

1995

LINEUP: Mike Stone (vocals/guitar); Chris Doherty (guitar); Darren Hill (bass); Brian Betzger (drums)

A short-lived offshoot of **Gang Green**, Klover featured Chris Doherty and Brian Betzger on guitar and drums, respectively, abetted by newcomer Mike Stone's abrasive but radio-friendly punk vocals, to create a generally more pop sound than that of Gang Green. Although Klover lasted only for about a minute, they did manage to secure one of the major label contracts being hurled about during the mid-1990s by record company executives desperate not to miss out on the next **Green Day**. Klover's one album, 1995's *Feel Lucky Punk*, was generally well-regarded and showed its Boston roots by including a cover of Beantown proto-punkers the Real Kids' "All Kinds of Girls." Nevertheless, Klover soon closed up shop thereafter in order to revive Gang Green for more tours, records, skateboarding, and above all, more beer.

Discography:
Feel Lucky Punk (Mercury, 1995)

KRAUT

1981–1985, sporadic reunions

LINEUP: Davey Gunner (vocals); Doug Holland (guitar, replaced by Chris Smith); Don Cowan (bass); John Koncz, aka "Johnny Feedback" (drums)

Early New York **hardcore** band Kraut played a critical role in the metamorphosis of the local scene from punk to hardcore. They got their first gig opening for the **Clash** during their legendary series of shows at Bond's Casino in the hot, wet summer of 1981 by sending a demo tape to the band on a whim. Although young at the time (drummer "Johnny Feedback" was only 13 in 1981), Kraut quickly became fixtures on the New York scene, releasing the popular "Kill for Cash" single later that year. Kraut were one of the first New York bands to speed up their sound like their contemporaries **Bad Brains**, while keeping the melodic feel of punk. In 1983, Kraut scored a couple of rare feats for a punk band: first getting former **Sex Pistol** Steve Jones to play on their debut album, and even more astoundingly landing in rotation on the nascent **MTV** network with their video for "All Twisted." As was common in the 1980s, Kraut later began to slow down and add more metallic solos to their sound. Guitarist Doug Holland left not long after to join the **Cro-Mags** and was replaced by Chris Smith from **Battalion of Saints**. The band broke up after Smith died in a tragic drowning; Feedback and Gunner went on to form Gutterboy. Kraut reunited for shows in 1991, 2001, and 2002.

Discography:
An Adjustment to Society (Cabbage, 1982); *Whetting the Scythe* (Cabbage, 1984); *Night of Rage* (New Red Archives, 1986, 1989); *The Movie* (New Red Archives, 1990); *Complete Studio Recordings* (New Red Archives, 1995); *Live at CBGB* (New Red Archives, 2002). **Gutterboy:** *Gutterboy* (DGC, 1990; Mercury, 1992)

HILLY KRISTAL

Onetime manager of legendary Greenwich Village jazz nightclub the Village Standard, in 1973, Hilly Kristal started a new club at 315 Bowery that he hoped to turn into a center of bluegrass and country, his favorite kinds of music. Of course that club, **CBGB**, didn't do much for bluegrass but would later become the incubator of the East Coast punk revolution. In the divey, Hell's Angels atmosphere of the early CBGB (where a quarter purchased a pitcher of beer and bikers were much more likely to congregate than bluegrass aficionados), Kristal was unable to make ends meet until **Television** and other like-minded bands started playing there in March 1974. The club soon became world-famous, hosting the first real appearances of such iconic artists as the **Ramones**, **Talking Heads**, **Blondie**, **Richard Hell**, and countless others. All throughout, Kristal was an omnipresent figure at the door, watching with some bemusement the various bands and audience members who tried to slip in for free or claim they were with the band. Kristal also tried his hand at managing groups, including the **Dead Boys** and latter-day punk group Reconstruction.

Although by the new millennium Kristal had started to rake in serious money licensing the CBGB name and logo, he was unable to keep the club open against the pressures of rapid gentrification and that pesky back rent. Efforts to open a version of the club in Las Vegas were discussed, but hadn't come to fruition by the time Kristal died from lung cancer in 2007, at the age of 75. Kristal, although not a musician himself, was one of the most influential figures in the American punk scene, and it is difficult to imagine punk developing without the friendly confines of CBGB to nurture the scene when it was struggling to find an audience. Kristal also befriended many in the punk scene, and was renowned for paying bands when money was tight, and even for getting the more addicted punks (such as the Dead Boys) to clean up.

"Other clubs were all about models and beautiful people, and (Hilly Kristal) was about letting the musicians in for free, to hear music and get cheap beers... It automatically created a scene, and we'd just hang out all night."

—David Byrne,
quoted by the Associated Press, 8/26/07

Hilly Kristal helpfully escorts Legs McNeil off the premises, 1976.

LAGWAGON

1990–present

LINEUP: Joey Cape (vocals); Chris Flippin (guitar); Chris Rest (guitar); Jesse Buglione (bass); Dave Raun (drums)

Originally formed under the name Section 8, this melodic band from Goleta, California, has toured and recorded with a determined regularity over the years (showing up on the **Vans Warped** tour multiple times), and is widely considered one of the best of the **Fat Wreck Chords** groups. While some bands with this catchy a sound can end up veering dangerously close to **emo** territory, Lagwagon has managed to keep their focus clear and consistent. Songs like the pun-filled "Violins" and "Falling Apart" are as good as anything from the Fat Wreck Chords stable. Pretty much every one of Lagwagon's albums are worth owning, though the best album (outside of *Hoss*) is *Live in a Dive*, which manages to capture some of the energy of their amazing concerts.

Discography:
Duh (Fat Wreck Chords, 1992); *Trashed* (Fat Wreck Chords, 1994); *Hoss* (Fat Wreck Chords, 1995); *Double Plaidinum* (Fat Wreck Chords, 1997); *Let's Talk About Feelings* (Fat Wreck Chords, 1998); *Let's Talk about Leftovers* (Fat Wreck Chords, 2000); *Blaze* (Fat Wreck Chords, 2003); *Resolve* (Fat Wreck Chords, 2005); *Live in a Dive* (Fat Wreck Chords, 2005)

Lagwagon in San Francisco, 2002. Chris Flippin (airborne), Jess Buglione.

LA MERE VIPERE

LOCATION: CHICAGO

The short-lived but historic "punk dance club" (America's only!) La Mere Vipere, formerly the Snake Pit, was originally just another gay bar on Chicago's North Side. In 1977, the owners, trying to enliven their normally dead Sunday nights, began holding "Punk Nights" (or "Anarchy Nights," the record is unclear) to try and cash in on what many thought at the time as a viable new scene. After popular response, those themed music nights gave birth to a "Punk-O-Rama" weekend and then a complete overhaul of the DJ's previously disco-heavy record stash. Gawkers, "scene tourists," the occasional confused local, and people desperate for a place to listen to new music (as well as the fanatic **Ramones**-lovers of Mary Alice Ramel's *Gabba Gabba Gazette* zine crew, who reportedly were later bounced from the club for fighting) went there in droves, making La Mere for a brief time the city's hottest club.

La Mere Vipere burned down on April 27, 1978, amid a welter of rumors about police collusion and political pressure. Fittingly, the second night of a benefit concert series at an American Legion hall to raise money for the owners was cancelled because, as the *Chicago Reader* put it, "the sudden appearance of spray paint in the bathrooms and on the outside walls was more than the Legion had bargained for." The short heyday of La Mere Vipere is not just a blip in early punk history, but also an indication of how early punk clubs struggled with political and civic pressure to keep punks from "ruining" various good neighborhoods.

> "So they burned it down, so build another one. Don't go on to me that they burned it down, BUILD ANOTHER ONE. YOU'RE THE ONLY ONES THAT ARE GONNA DO IT!"

—Patti Smith, April 28, 1978, at a Lincoln Park concert the day after La Mere Vipere burned down

THE LEAVING TRAINS

1980-2006

LINEUP: "Falling James" Moreland (vocals/guitar); Manfred Hofer (guitar, replaced by Mike Barnett, others); Tom Hofer (bass, replaced by Eric Stringer, others); Hunter Crowley (drums, replaced by Hilary Laddin, Lenny Montoya, others); Sylvia Juncosa (keyboards)

An extraordinarily long-lived squadron of Los Angeles punks, the Leaving Trains were led in loose and ever-shifting formation by their transvestite singer, "Falling James," better known as either a) James Moreland, or b) Courtney Love's first husband. While Moreland gets most of the press for the Leaving Trains—he launched a quixotic presidential campaign in 1996 under a platform of giving the land back to Native Americans and moving everyone else to Greenland—they've also gathered a number of fans along the way through their chaotic shows, brilliantly off-kilter songwriting, and noisy rave-ups. The thing about the Leaving Trains is that the band didn't really know whether they wanted to be noise provocateurs or serious songwriters and it showed after the *Kill Tunes* and *Fuck* albums, when quality varied wildly from record to record. Early members of the pre-Leaving Trains band the Mongrels included future **Circle Jerks** and **Bad Religion** guitarist Greg Hetson. The Leaving Trains are an example of how focus almost always helps punk rock bands with idiosyncratic visions.

Discography:
Well Down Blue Highway (Beemisbrain/Enigma, 1984); *Kill Tunes* (SST, 1986); *Fuck* (SST, 1987); *Transportational D. Vices* (SST, 1989); *Sleeping Underwater Survivors* (SST, 1990); *Loser Illusion Pt. o* EP (SST, 1991); *The Lump in My Forehead* (SST, 1992); *The Big Jinx* (SST, 1994); *Drowned and Dragged* EP (SST, 1995); *Smoke Follows Beauty* (SST, 1996); *Favorite Mood Swings (Greatest Hits 1986–1995)* (SST, 1997); *Emotional Legs* (Steel Cage, 2001)

TED LEO

Ted Leo first started playing in bands while in high school in New Jersey during the 1980s, later joining the neat and tidy punk group Chisel as singer/guitarist while at Notre Dame in 1993. After graduation, Chisel spent a few years on the Washington, D.C., scene, releasing a few albums to moderate reward before disbanding in 1997. Leo then made a name for himself with projects like Citizens Arrest and Ted Leo and the Pharmacists (aka Ted Leo/Pharmacists), whose sound evoked both the **Clash** and the righteousness of early punk (the latter probably influenced by Leo's **DIY** attitude and vegan lifestyle), with an extra dash of mod attitude via the **Jam**. The band gained greater exposure after the Pharmacists signed with **Lookout! Records** in 2001. That year's album, *The Tyranny of Distance*, resulted in Leo being compared by critics to sardonic singer-songwriters with a political bent such as Elvis Costello and Billy Bragg. After a string of successful Lookout! releases, Leo and his band achieved an impressive level of indie success (such as an appearance on *Late Night with Conan O'Brien* and opening for Death Cab for Cutie). Leo is well-regarded as being one of the few punk singer-songwriters who was able to gain national exposure without substantially changing his sound.

Ted Leo in New York, 1999.

Discography:
Chisel: *Nothing New* EP (Gern Blandsten, 1995); *8 A.M. All Day* (Gern Blandsten, 1996); *Set You Free* (Gern Blandsten, 1997). **Ted Leo/Pharmacists:** *Tej Leo (?) Rx/Pharmacists* (Gern Blandsten, 1999); *The Tyranny of Distance* (Lookout!, 2001); *Hearts of Oak* (Lookout!, 2003); *Tell Balgeary, Balgury is Dead* EP (Lookout!, 2003); *Shake the Sheets* (Lookout!, 2004); *Living with the Living* (Touch and Go, 2007)

LES THUGS

1983-1999

LINEUP: Eric Source (vocals/guitar); Thierry Meanard (guitar); Pierre-Yves Source (bass); Christophe Source (vocals/drums)

One of the only French punk bands to make any sort of impression on the U.S. (besides **Metal Urbain** in the 1970s), Les Thugs were one of Sub Pop's first signings. The band, whose name comes not in homage to football hooligans but from the legendary Indian assassins who worshipped the goddess Kali, was started in 1983 by the Source bothers and soon made a reputation for their fiery political lyrics. Songs like "Dirty White Race," with lyrics such as "Tell me how can you be so proud, proud of your dirty white race ?/... you killed the Indians, the Jews... / Destroyed and plundered 'round the world," showed that the band's hearts were in the right place. Sadly, Les Thugs never sold many records in the U.S. and finally called it quits in 1999.

Discography:
Frenetic Dancing (Gougnaf Mouvement, 1985); *Radical Hystery,* (Closer, 1986); *Electric Troubles* (Closer, 1987; Sub Pop, 1989); *Dirty White Race* (Vinyl Solution, 1988) *Still Hungry, Still Angry* (Vinyl Solution, 1989; Sub Pop, 1990); *I.A.B.F* (Vinyl Solution, 1991; Sub Pop, 1991); *As Happy As Possible* (Sub Pop, 1993); *Strike* (Sub Pop, 1996); *Nineteen Something* (Sub Pop 1998); *Tout Doit Disparaitre* (EMI, 1999); *Road Closed 1983–1999* (Sub Pop, 2004)

"If it wasn't for the fact that he was Courtney Love's first husband, Falling James might be just another aging punk transvestite running for president."

—David Grad, *New York Press*

HOMOSEXUALITY

Although punk began, like most revolutionary movements, as liberation from restrictive societal norms, that doesn't mean that it left all the problems of mainstream society behind. This is particularly true in regards to homosexuality, with which punk has had a long and fairly troubled relationship. There were a few openly gay or bisexual performers in punk's early years, with the leaders of bands such as the **Big Boys** and the **Dicks** being as out and proud as possible. (*Maximum RocknRoll* famously hailed the latter group as "A Commie Faggot Band!") Oddly, both those bands hailed from the repressive state of Texas, while in enlightened New York—where pre-punks like the **New York Dolls** flirted with glitter-rock pseudo-drag— one night at **CBGB** in 1976 transsexual **Wayne/Jayne County** was heckled in such a purported, homophobic fashion by the **Dictators'** Dick Manitoba that County sent Manitoba to the hospital with a broken collarbone. For his part, **Dee Dee Ramone** sang in the autobiographical song about drug hustling, "53rd and 3rd," about stabbing a prospective john in order to prove he was "no sissy."

Over the years there were several openly (or heavily closeted) gay members of punk bands—including Grant Hart and Bob Mould of **Hüsker Dü** and **Darby Crash** of the **Germs**—but in general their sexuality was rarely directly addressed. MDC's Dan Dictor was one of the few gay punks who made an open issue of the fact. Most likely this was due, at least in part, to the intolerance many punks still demonstrated during the 1970s and '80s toward homosexuality. **Bad Brains**, particularly lead singer H.R., were the most famously intolerant punks in the scene during the 1980s, which made many punks turn against the band. (The **Dead Kennedys'** Jello Biafra said that the homophobia of a band he loved caused him "heartbreak.") While the punk scene certainly showed itself willing to castigate some of its leaders for their openly homophobic stances (unlike, for instance, contemporaneous rock or heavy metal bands or rappers), there were many punk fans who were just as intolerant as the bands themselves. This intolerance was particularly evident in the more testosterone-pumped **hardcore** and **skinhead** scenes, where rampant machismo and gay-bashing were sadly not uncommon.

The 1990s also saw the rise of **queercore** punk and bands such as Sta-Prest, **Team Dresh**, **Tribe 8**, **Pansy Division**, and other bands, particularly on the **Outpunk Records** label, the first record label devoted exclusively to queer punk bands. (Outpunk had risen out of the influential zine published by Matt Wobensmith.) Many of the bands on Outpunk and other labels are much more outspoken than the earlier generation of punks who were largely closeted. For example, bands such as Tribe 8 openly question traditional ideas of gender and homosexuality by performing sex acts on stage using strap-ons and experimental straight boys, while Pansy Division celebrates gay male sexuality with anthems such as "Smells Like Queer Spirit." Many openly gay punks also reject traditional labels such as *gay* or *lesbian* as too confining and politically charged and prefer the term *queer* as being more inclusive.

This is not to say that all of the punk scenes are equally open about their sexuality or that all scenes are equally inclusive (it is doubtful that a skinhead scene would be welcoming to queer punks, although there certainly are subdivisions within skinhead culture that are more queer-identified). Nor is it true that gay, lesbian, and transgender punks are absolutely and always accepted. But based upon the current openness not expressed during the early days of punk rock, there are certainly signs that the punk community is far more accepting of differences in gender and sexuality than it had been in the past. That acceptance includes bands like the gay, **straight-edge** band Limp Wrist and, for better or for worse, Black Fag (who cover Black Flag songs like a group of high-camp Weird Al Yankovics).

Darby Crash on Sunset Boulevard, 1977.

Hüsker Dü, 1985.

LETCH PATROL

1988–early-1990s

LINEUP: Harris Pankin (vocals); George Tabb (guitar); John Rinaldi (guitar); Pete Marshall (bass); Chuck Clearwater (drums)

New York anti-**hardcore** band Letch Patrol founded the so-called "scum rock" movement, which combined heavy metal and punk with a generous amount of outrageous behavior, bodily fluids, and abuse of the crowd (think Gwar and the **Butthole Surfers** meet the **Ramones** and **GG Allin**). Led by vocalist Harris Pankin, a former squatter from Detroit by way of San Francisco, and a rotating cast of musicians, Letch Patrol—their name indicating their favorite proclaimed activity: spying on women—released only one seven-inch during their brief existence. At a prominent television appearance of Letch Patrol during the Tompkins Square Park riots in New York, viewers were treated to the sight of ugly, bitter punks such as Pankin complaining loudly about police brutality, confirming the worst fears of American parents about the dangers of the punk scene. Little was known of the band after they broke up until 2005, when the *New York Press* reported that the then-homeless Pankin had played for the New York City Grand Central Neighborhood Services soccer team at the Homeless Cup of Soccer in Graz, Austria.

Discography:
Love is Blind/Axe to Grind 7" (Electric Shaman, 1988)

LE TIGRE

1998–present

LINEUP: Kathleen Hanna (vocals/guitar/various); Johanna Fateman (vocals/various); Sadie Benning (films/audio/visual, replaced by JD Samson)

Feminist **queercore** dance band Le Tigre was led by former **Bikini Kill** singer **Kathleen Hanna** and played a subversively poppy and poppily subversive combination of **new wave** dance rhythms, furious beats, and sometimes-punk guitars accompanied by Hanna's always-punk vocals. Most of their incredibly bouncy songs dealt with the impermanence of gender and normative assumptions about classifications of straight and gay. Although they started out on indie Mr. Lady Records, Le Tigre signed with Universal in 2004 for their *This Island* album, a typically eclectic mix of dance-bop electronica goofiness (the Ric Ocasek-produced "Tell You Now," plus a cover of the Pointer Sisters' "I'm So Excited") and strident anti-war slogan-chanting ("New Kicks"). Perhaps not surprisingly for a band with such a complicated approach to mass culture—love of pop music, hatred of the conformist mind-set—Le Tigre allowed several of their catchier songs to be used in commercials, films, and even reportedly the Boston Red Sox radio broadcasts. Le Tigre announced they were taking "an extended break" in 2007 though refrained from declaring the band's official break-up.

Discography:
Le Tigre (Mr. Lady, 1999); *Feminist Sweepstakes* (Mr. Lady, 2001); *This Island* (Strummer/Universal 2004)

DON LETTS

Erstwhile punk renaissance man Don Letts has contributed much to punk over the years, not only by documenting the early scene with his ever-present camera, but also by introducing many of punk's key players to **dub** and **reggae**. Letts was born to Jamaican parents in London in 1956 and during the mid-1970s started working at **Acme Attractions**, one of the early, punk fashion shops on King's Road. While employed there, Letts played dub for all the punks (including the **Clash** and the **Sex Pistols**) who hung around the place. After the store shut down, Letts left to manage the **Slits**, helping them evolve beyond just being a noisy punk band by encouraging them to listen to the reggae that influenced their records, taking them on the White Riot tour with the Clash.

Although he later joined Mick Jones' Big Audio Dynamite as an amateur keyboardist (in one interview, Letts said the keys had colored stickers on them to guide his playing), Letts's most significant contribution to his many friends in the scene was as a filmmaker. Over the years, Letts directed music videos for the Clash, the Slits, **Public Image Ltd.**, and numerous reggae bands, as well as a couple of notable feature documentaries. *Punk Rock Movie* (1978) was a dynamic and mostly handheld collection of Super-8 footage Letts shot in 1977 at the **Roxy**, where he was resident DJ, featuring many of the key bands of the time and early scenesters such as **Shane MacGowan** (with teeth!). *Westway to the World* (2000), meanwhile, stands as the signature documentary on the Clash. More recently, the wide-ranging *Punk: Attitude* (2005) featured interviews with many of punk's original founders, particularly members of the New York scenes, including Arthur Kane from the **New York Dolls** (just before his death), **Legs McNeil**, **Henry Rollins**, and members of the Sex Pistols, **Bad Brains**, and **Agnostic Front**. Letts was not just lucky enough to be present with camera in hand during punk's birth, but was a formative presence, turning on the mostly white street punks to ganja, reggae, and dub and helping to lay the path for **post-punk**'s direction in the following years.

Le Tigre says "cheese," 2003. (L to R) JD Samson, Kathleen Hanna, Johanna Fateman.

LIFETIME

1990-1997, 2005-present

LINEUP: Ari Katz (vocals); Dan Yemin (guitar); Peter Martin (guitar); Dave Palaitis (bass); Scott Golley (drums)

New Jersey band Lifetime released several important records, such as *Background* and *Hello Bastards*, that stood out in the early-1990s scene for their clear, concise, punchy version of **hardcore**; singer Ari Katz ensuring that they would sound nothing like the hard/fast bands prevalent in the New Jersey scene at the time. After Lifetime broke up in 1997, Yemin joined Kid Dynamite, while Katz, Palaitis, and Golley formed Zero Zero. Lifetime got back together to do a few shows starting in 2005 and gradually discovered that they had disbanded before accomplishing all that they could. So, in 2007 they released a self-titled album that picked up quite nicely where they had left off in the late-1990s.

Discography:

Lifetime EP (New Age, 1991); *Background* (New Age, 1993); *Hello Bastards* (Jade Tree, 1995); *The Seven Inches* (Glue, 1996); *Jersey's Best Dancers* (Jade Tree, 1997); *Lifetime* (Fueled by Ramen, 2007)

LARRY LIVERMORE

Zine publisher, writer, and founder of **Lookout! Records**, Larry Livermore was one of the most influential people involved in the **DIY** movement, responsible for signing many important bands. Livermore took a gamble long before many others did in the belief that punk could be accessible. He thought **hardcore** did not have to be simply mindlessly loud, but could also be incredibly moving and articulate as exemplified by Lookout! stalwarts such as the **Mr. T Experience** and even the young **Green Day**, who arguably produced their best record (*Kerplunk*) while on his label. Although Livermore eventually distanced himself from the label (which fell into its demise thereafter), his keen eye for talent and influential writing on the punk scene in zines such as *Maximum RocknRoll* ensure his place in the history of West Coast punk.

LONDON SS

1975–1976

LINEUP: Mick Jones (guitar); Brian James (guitar); Tony James (bass); Roland Hot (drums)

This rough-sounding early version of the **Clash** that also featured future members of **Public Image Ltd.**, the Pretenders, the **Damned**, and **Generation X**, served as a sort of punk proving ground for the London scene. The musical style of London SS, however, was closer to glam rock or the **MC5** than to the sound that would make the Clash famous. Managed during their brief life by Bernie Rhodes, the theorist and professional agitator who also worked extensively with the Clash later on, London SS briefly featured Chrissie Hynde of the Pretenders as a member, along with Brian James before he left to form the **Damned**. When Rhodes assumed greater control of the band and recruited **Joe Strummer**, the band mutated into the Clash. London SS never officially recorded (although the Clash song "Protex Blue" was reputedly written during this time period) and is primarily remembered for the numerous groups spawned by its members. Today, Mick Jones and Tony James play together in Carbon/Silicon, a band who (luckily) in no way sound like the London SS.

LOOKOUT! RECORDS

LOCATION: BERKELEY

One of the cornerstone independent punk labels, Lookout! has released records by **Green Day**, the **Donnas**, the **Mr. T Experience**, **Operation Ivy**, the **Queers**, **Avail**, the Hi-Fives, and many others. Founded by **Larry Livermore** and David Hayes in Berkeley in 1987, Lookout! has gravitated toward local California bands and those at the poppier end of the punk spectrum (Green Day and the **Groovie Ghoulies**), in essence helping to create what became known as the "East Bay sound." Hayes left in 1989 to form Very Small Records and Too Many Records, and Livermore ran the label for most of the 1990s, later turning over control to onetime mailroom employee Chris Appelgren.

Since Lookout! had had the superb good taste and luck to sign Green Day, later on, when the band signed to major label Reprise and went multiplatinum with 1994's *Dookie*, their Lookout! releases then also went platinum. After that, between Green Day's catalog and Operation Ivy's steady-selling 1990 album *Energy*, Lookout! was awash in more cash than most indie labels ever see. But then expensive promotional campaigns for the **Donnas** and **Pansy Division** didn't pan out and numerous releases by lesser-selling bands ate up much of the money that Lookout! had saved over the years. After some problems in paying royalties on time, a number of bands (angry over accounting sloppiness) charged breach of contract and took back their master recordings. Avail reissued their albums on Jade Tree Records, **Screeching Weasel** took theirs to Asian Man, Pansy Division to **Alternative Tentacles**, and Operation Ivy to Hellcat. But most importantly, Green Day rescinded their masters in August 2005 (later reissuing the albums on Reprise), apparently forcing massive layoffs of Lookout! staff. Although the label's future seemed uncertain for a time, with artists like **Ted Leo** and the Donnas still on their backlist, Lookout! seemed able to weather the storm.

LOS CRUDOS

1991–1998

LINEUP: Martin Sorrondeguy (vocals); Jose (guitar); Juan (bass); Ebro (drums)

When the Latino **hardcore** band Los Crudos (the "Crude Ones") started performing in the early-1990s, doing shows in Chicago's Latino-populated Pilsen neighborhood, they made, through their defiantly politicized, Spanish-language punk rock, a radical statement in a scene that had almost no Latino representation (with the notable exception of the Plugz). Like many of the proto-**emo** bands that came out of Washington, D.C., in the 1980s, Los Crudos wanted their listeners to *consider* the lyrics, often pausing to pass out lyric sheets and to try and explain the nuances of the songs. (This rarely appealed to the bozo elements of Chicago's punk scene, who would sometimes yell, "Shut up and play!") Los Crudos released a number of rapid-fire punk singles on their own Lengua Armada label, but never got major indie distribution and only recorded one full album. Although they toured the world and were the subject of some rabid zine reviews, Los Crudos weren't able to break through to the punk mainstream and played their last show on October 17, 1998. Uruguayan singer Martin Sorrondeguy later joined up with the **queercore**, **straight-edge** band Limp Wrist and directed *Beyond the Screams: A U.S. Latino Hardcore Punk Documentary*. Los Crudos are a little-known, but welcome counterpoint to the usual sea of white faces prevalent at many punk shows even to the present day.

Discography:
Canciones Para Liberar Nuestras Fronteras (Lengua Armada, 1997)

LOST LOCKER COMBO

2007–present

LINEUP: Bill Florio (vocals); Hallie Bullets (vocals/tap dancer); Jonnie Whoa Oh (bass); Stephanie (cheerleader); Scotty (drums); Frank (guitar); Julie Ruiz (xylophone); Joe Bruiser (guitar); Oliver (drums)

The New York-based Lost Locker Combo uses the theme of high school as a starting point for some of the most raucous **pop-punk** that the East Coast has heard in many years. Members dressed as cheerleaders preside over group chants and throw cake into the audience, while performing songs about geography, grammar, and—of all things—scoliosis. Lost Locker Combo reimagines high school as a much better place than it was, with punks as the dominant clique and where everyone is free to let their freak flag fly (in a stylish school uniform, of course). The band is also somewhat of a punk super-group, with members of bands such as **Egghead**, the Unlovables, the **Shemps,** and others playing at various points.

Discography:
Freshman Orientation (Whoa Oh, 2007)

LOVE AND ROCKETS

An underground comic book created in 1982 by "Los Bros. Hernandez"—Gilbert and Jaime trade off duties and storylines, while third sibling Mario has contributed on occasion—*Love and Rockets* is not, repeat not, to be confused with the identically named **new wave** band featuring former members of Bauhaus (though some say that they got their name from the comic).

The Oxnard, California-raised Jaime and Gilbert started out doing a goofy comic that was equal parts science fiction and

> **"Resistance, reaction, unrest—that's what Latin America and punk are about."**
> —Los Crudos' Martin Sorrondeguy, *OC Weekly*, Nov. 15, 2001

Lydia Lunch, the dark, beckoning siren of no wave.

comedic romance. But *Love and Rockets* quickly evolved into the sprawling, multi-headed opus readers have followed for over two decades, a narrative that mixes themes of Latino heritage, lesbian culture, and punk rock attitude into its lovesick, nostalgic story-lines. With their beloved bisexual Latina heroines Maggie and Hopey, and somewhat fantastical but generally dead-on represen-tations of the Los Angeles punk scene, Los Bros. Hernandez were among the most influential artists in underground comic books during the 1980s and '90s.

Love and Rockets stopped publication in 1996 but resumed in 2001 after the brothers had a chance to recharge their creative juices. Like underground bands who changed their sound or upgraded their production equip-ment, the Hernandez brothers also had to face charges of "selling out" from under-ground purists because the artistic style of *Love and Rockets* kept improving. Also, as the comic continued to garner acclaim and attention it was considered too mainstream

by some of the more elitist punks (though it continued being published by small comic house Fantagraphics). But with the 2003 publications of the mammoth collections *Palomar* and *Locas*, the scope of the series' ambitions became truly clear, rendering any complaints from purists nearly irrele-vant. A monumental work on the under-ground community, *Love and Rockets* is not just one of the most epic comic series in the genre's history, but the only consistently punk comic to survive as long as it has.

LYDIA LUNCH

New York singer and poet Lydia Lunch worked and collaborated with Teenage Jesus and the Jerks, 8 Eyed Spy, **Sonic Youth**, and many others over the years. A key member of New York's **no wave** movement in the early-1980s, Lydia Lunch (born Lydia Koch) left an abusive home in Rochester, New York, became part of the punk scene at an early age, and began working as a waitress at **CBGB**. She formed her first band, Teenage Jesus and the Jerks, with notoriously con-frontational saxophone player James Chance and drummer Bradley Field to create a chal-lenging wall of noise. Chance later left to found James Chance and the Contortions (later James White and the Blacks), while Lunch brought in various bass players to play the music she labeled *no wave*. The band barely recorded, but managed to get several tracks included on the scene-defining *No New York* compilation.

In 1980, Lunch disbanded the Jerks and started a solo career with her pseudojazz

album *Queen of Siam*. She returned to her own abrasive form with the formation of 8 Eyed Spy, along with drummer Jim Sclavunos (later a member of Nick Cave's Bad Seeds) and bassist George Scott, who would die of a heroin overdose before the band became popular. Lunch went on to collaborate with a dizzying array of musicians and writers, including Nick Cave, Michael Gira (of the Swans), Jim Thirwell (Foetus), Sonic Youth, **Henry Rollins**, and Exene Cervenka of **X**, as well as appear in the films of Richard Kern and in Asia Argento's *The Heart is Deceitful Above All Things* (2004). For the past several decades, Lunch concentrated mostly on writ-

ing and spoken word, in which her emotionally naked performances were extremely challeng-ing and difficult to witness, as was the point.

Discography:

Queen of Siam (ZE, 1980; Widowspeak, 1985; Triple X, 1991); *13.13* (Ruby, 1982; Widowspeak, 1988); *The Agony Is the Ecstacy* EP (4AD, 1982); *In Limbo* EP (Doublevision, 1984; Widowspeak, 1986); *The Uncensored Lydia Lunch* (tape; Widowspeak, 1985); *Hysterie* (Widowspeak, 1986; CD Presents, 1986); *Honeymoon in Red* (Widowspeak, 1987; Atavistic 1996); *Drowning in Limbo* (Widowspeak, 1989; Atavistic 1995); *Oral Fixation* (Widowspeak, 1989); *Conspiracy of Women* (Widowspeak 1990); *Crimes Against Nature* (Triple X, 1993); *Universal Infiltrators* (Atavistic, 1995); *Transmutation/Shotgun Wedding: Live* (Insipid Vinyl, 1996). **With Thurston Moore:** *The Crumb* EP (Widowspeak, 1988). **With Exene Cervenka:** *Rude Heiroglyphics* (Rykodisc, 1995)

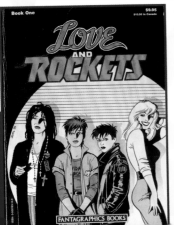

THE LURKERS

1976-1980, 1982-1984, 1987-1995, 2001-present

LINEUP: Howard Wall (vocals); Pete Stride (guitar); Arturo Bassick (bass); Manic Esso (drums, replaced by Pete Hayes)

An English band from Uxbridge in the loud and fast pop style of the **Ramones**, the Lurkers were and are dedicated to beer, girls, and generally having a good time. The band started in the summer of 1976 (opening for proto-punk and perennial political candidate Screaming Lord Sutch) as punk began to sweep Britain. Although the Lurkers honestly wanted to play the sort of punk that they loved as a reaction to the period's bloated art rock, they were mostly dismissed by the music press (*NME* called them "the ultimate in pre-packaged instant punk"), much to the chagrin of the hardworking band. Although they released numerous, classic 1977-style punk singles such as "Shadow" and "Freak Show," the Lurkers were still substantially less-known than many of their contempo-

raries, although a 1977 Peel Session helped increase their visibility. The first two albums are classic punk and well worth owning, but soon after the rot set in as the band went through numerous personnel changes and several breakups. A reunited version of the Lurkers with only original bassist Bassick (on vocals and bass) has toured in recent years.

Discography:
Fulham Fallout (Beggars Banquet, 1978; Captain Oi!, 2000); *God's Lonely Men* (Beggars Banquet, 1979, 2000); *Shadow* (Beggars Banquet, 1979); *Greatest Hit: Last Will and Testament* (Beggars Banquet, 1980, 1998); *Final Vinyl* EP (Clay, 1983); *This Dirty Town* (Clay, 1983, 1990, 1997); *Wild Times Again* (Weser, 1988, 1998); *King of the Mountain* (Link, 1989); *Live and Loud!!* (Link, 1990); *Totally Lurkered* (Dojo, 1992); *Ripped n' Torn* (Step 1, 1995); *Live in Berlin* (Released Emotions, 1995); *Non-Stop Nitropop* (Weser, 1996, 1998); *Take Me Back to Babylon* (Receiver, 1997); *Last Will & Testament (Greatest Hits)* (Beggars Banquet, 1997); *Beggars Banquet Singles Collection* (Anagram Punk UK, 1999); *Ain't Got a Clue* (Mayo, 1999; Takoma, 2000); *BBC Punk Session* (live; Captain Oi!, 2000); *Wild Times Again/ Non-Stop Nitropop* (Captain Oi!, 2001); *Powerjive/King of the Mountain* (Anagram Punk, 2002); *The Punk Singles Collection* (Captain Oi!, 2002); *On Heat* (Ataque Frontal, 2002); *26 Years* (Ahoy, 2003); *Lurkin' Aboot* (live; Bassick Productions, 2004); *Live Freak Show* (Kotumba, 2004). **Pete Stride/John Plain:** *New Guitars in Town* (Beggars Banquet, 1980)

JOHN LYDON

The former lead yowler of the **Sex Pistols** (as Johnny Rotten), singer for **Public Image Ltd.** (under his own name), and generally scampish hellraiser, John Lydon was born in 1956 to Irish parents and raised in a scrubby north London housing estate. The legend goes that at some point during London's punk tumult, Lydon—who had been scavenging work as a ratcatcher, among other things—was spotted by punk impresario Bernie Rhodes walking down King's Road with chopped, dyed-green hair and a home-made "I Hate Pink Floyd" T-shirt. After that, Rhodes' associate **Malcolm McLaren** got Lydon to audition for his new band, which would become the Sex Pistols, and for whom he would become Johnny Rotten. The nickname was originally given to Lydon to highlight his disregard for dental hygiene but soon also became appropriate as a description of his withering sarcasm and biting comments and lyrics. With his ever-present sneer, hunched-back demeanor, seemingly universal contempt

"They all bitched at the first rehearsals (for the Sex Pistols) about how I couldn't sing, which was true. I still can't, and I don't really want to."

—John Lydon, *Rotten: No Irish, No Blacks, No Dogs*

for everything and everybody, and the roaring sound of the Sex Pistols behind him, Rotten proved to be the perfect face of England's punk revolution.

In Lydon's autobiography *Rotten: No Irish, No Blacks, No Dogs*, he presents his response to McLaren's allegations (both in print, in litigation, and in the movie *The Great Rock 'n' Roll Swindle*) that the Sex Pistols were merely puppets for the purported Svengali. Not long after the Pistols' self-immolation, in 1978 Lydon put together the forward-looking Public Image Ltd., the adventurous **post-punk** outfit that utilized his wide-ranging music tastes (he owned a formidable **reggae** and **dub** collection), and serves as his real legacy in the music world.

From the 1990s onward, Lydon seemed to have decided that his contributions to new music were mostly behind him, instead serving as a perpetually sardonic guest on the odd TV show (such as a 1997 episode of *Judge Judy*) or fronting the occasional Sex Pistols reunion tour to mock and harangue all within range. These days, Lydon is quite well known in Britain for his nature shows (*John Lydon Goes Ape, John Lydon's Shark Attack*, etc.), sarcastic appearances on various vacuous celeb-reality shows, and unrepentant ability to flog the Sex Pistols' dead horse for more of that lovely, filthy lucre.

The Lurkers pose in between breakups.

John Lydon between Steve Jones' legs in Amsterdam, 1977.

Shane MacGowan, 19, in the swank London editorial offices of his magazine, *Bondage*, 1976.

SHANE MACGOWAN

If Shane MacGowan was merely known for being an influential member of the early London punk scene circa 1977 (that's him at the start of **Don Letts**'s *Punk Rock Movie*, slamming in his Union Jack coat) and a member of the Nipple Erectors (later the **Nips**), one of the first UK bands to fuse punk and **rockabilly**, he would have more than earned an entry here. But in addition to all that, MacGowan also went on to form the most influential melding of Irish and punk music ever, the legendary **Pogues**. Despite his (very) drunken bravado, trademark mumbled vocals, and easily parodied lack of dental hygiene, MacGowan also proved to be an unusually gifted poet, sort of a modern-day Brendan Behan or a gutter-oriented Yeats, who could sum up the sheer futility of a life in which drink—and possibly love—is the only chance for redemption. MacGowan's repute as a writer grew throughout the Pogues' success of the early-1980s, but many (caught up in the myth of the hard-drinking "paddy") never gave him his due as a poet for lines such as the following from "A Rainy Night in Soho": "We watched our friends grow up together/And we saw them as they fell/Some of them fell into heaven/Some of them fell into hell."

Although MacGowan's work with his post-Pogues band the Popes had its flashes of brilliance, it seemed that dissolute living had finally caught up with him. A restored sense of purpose as part of an ongoing reunion with the Pogues, though, found MacGowan creatively reinvigorated, even singing his heart out from a wheelchair after a nasty fall in March 2006. When critics dismiss punk as simplistic or unoriginal, Shane MacGowan may be the best example of how pure lyrical poetry, strong drink, and a gift for melody can combine for some of the most ferocious music ever created.

MABUHAY GARDENS

LOCATION: SAN FRANCISCO

One of the key punk clubs on the San Francisco scene for years, Mabuhay Gardens rivaled anything in New York or Los Angeles. Located at 443 Broadway in the North Beach neighborhood, the club evolved from a Filipino restaurant into a club run by the durable Ness Aquino with punk booker Dirk Dirksen during the 1970s and '80s. During its heyday from 1976–1983, however, bands such as the **Avengers**, the **Dead Kennedys**, **Black Flag**, **Iggy Pop**, the **Feederz**, and even **Devo** helped turn "The Fab Mab" into the **CBGB** of San Francisco. After 1983, the club made concessions to changing tastes by hosting numerous heavy metal bands and closed a few years later. An effort was made to reopen the club in October 2007, but in a typical case of punk disorganization, the club closed in early November just a month later.

"I was talking to a business guy once, an accountant, and he said, 'They should invite you to come speak at Harvard Business School,' And I said, 'Well, I don't give a fuck about business.' I reject the whole notion."

—Ian MacKaye, interviewed by *Salon.com*, January 8, 2001.

Ian MacKaye, 1996.

IAN MACKAYE

Longtime advocate of radical causes, vegetarianism, **DIY** culture, and the **straight-edge** lifestyle, and one of the most visible and admired people in punk rock, Ian MacKaye started out as a teen skateboard fanatic in Washington, D.C., who inexplicably loved the music of Ted Nugent (it also is possible, though unlikely, that the "Nuge" inspired MacKaye to start the straight-edge movement because of Nugent's notorious aversion to drugs and alcohol). It was, however, the **Cramps** and especially **Bad Brains** (a band whom MacKaye championed for many years) that transformed the clean-living young man into a young punk.

MacKaye formed an early band called the Slinkees in 1979 with three other friends from Woodrow Wilson High School, and used the group to humorously espouse his clean-living lifestyle (a typical Slinkees song was called "I Drink Milk"). The Slinkees then evolved into the **Teen Idles** with the addition of singer Nathan Strejcek and toured cross-country with roadie Henry Garfield (who later changed his name to **Henry Rollins** before joining **Black Flag**). During the tour, MacKaye devised his famous *X* on the hand to signify that the punk bearing the mark was at a show to listen to music and not drink.

In 1980, MacKaye and Teen Idles drummer Jeff Nelson used a few hundred dollars of the band's savings to form **Dischord Records** in order to release the eight-song, seven-inch "Minor Disturbance," whose cover depicted two hands crossed with *X*s on them. MacKaye and Nelson ran Dischord from then on, putting out not only their own music but also albums of bands (regardless of genre) from the D.C. area. At the end of 1980, MacKaye, tired of not singing, broke up the Teen

Idles and formed **Minor Threat**, which quickly became one of the most important bands in **hardcore** history. However, MacKaye (who eventually became a vegetarian in 1984) was also increasingly alienated from the band because of his bandmates' reluctance to embrace the didactic lyrics he was writing, as they wanted the band to be more commercial.

Although MacKaye would later become famous for advocating a **pit** that was fun instead of violent, as a young and impressionable punk, he was notorious for instigating numerous fights. Steven Blush quoted MacKaye in his book *American Hardcore*, almost bragging about how tough he and his crew were in the D.C. scene circa 1981, stating that, "We were gonna be the worst motherfuckers—we wanted to scare people. It was a form of intimidation backed up by the threat of unpredictableness."

When Minor Threat broke up in 1983, MacKaye concentrated on running Dischord Records for a while before forming **Embrace**, which featured three-fourths of Alec MacKaye's band **Faith**. The short-lived Embrace created innovative music radically different from the Minor Threat sound, a shift that confused many of MacKaye's earlier fans. By this time, however, with the D.C. core fragmenting into subgenre cliques, MacKaye was less concerned with commercial success and more focused on political and social change. In 1985 he was a major participant in the famous **Revolution Summer** movement of bands that, despite its name, tried not so much to foster armed revolution but rather to create a more inclusive and politically motivated D.C. scene. Even if their political goals were not met, the Revolution Summer groups (like Embrace, **Beefeater**, Gray Matter, and others) did create a large catalog of music, including Embrace's sole album, released in 1986.

After the demise of Embrace, amidst internal dissension and musical differences, MacKaye worked at Dischord and released the *Egg Hunt* single, his last collaboration with Jeff Nelson, before forming **Fugazi** in 1987. This would be MacKaye's third great musical innovation in punk: Having played a key role in establishing both straight edge and hardcore as subgenres, with his electrifying new band he would help lead punk out of the creatively stunted, sectarian repetition much of it had fallen into. As a guitarist and vocalist in Fugazi, MacKaye became one of the most audible voices in punk's DIY underground. He and the band became legendary for their marathon shows, and anticonsumerist attitude ($5–6 door prices, all ages shows, and no merchandise of any kind).

Ian MacKaye, performing with Fugazi in 2002.

As the leader of Fugazi, MacKaye became even more outspoken in both his music and his public statements, challenging both mainstream society and the punk community's insularity. Even though Fugazi sold quite a respectable number of records for a punk band, since the band never cashed in on the lucrative marketplace of T-shirt/poster merchandising or overpriced concert tickets (in addition to maintaining their ideology and passing up free publicity by refusing to be interviewed by magazines that contained alcohol or cigarette ads), the band hardly made MacKaye into the punk millionaire some of his detractors have strangely called him. The overstated caricature of MacKaye as the stern-voiced, monastic didact—stopping a show, for instance, if the pit became too violent or not female-friendly—took on ludicrous status over the years, perhaps due to the simple fact that as one punk icon after another went on to big-time media exposure (as in the case of his old comrade in arms Henry Rollins), MacKaye's simple lifestyle and consistent beliefs seemed inexplicable to a generation accustomed to their idols eventually selling out.

Fugazi went on indefinite hiatus after their last studio album, 2001's *The Argument*. For his follow-up project the Evens, MacKaye went lo-fi and minimalist as a guitarist and vocalist joining with drummer/vocalist Amy Farina. MacKaye has stayed politically active, with news outlets reporting in May 2007 that he had helped clean up and digitally enhance a recently released audiotape from the 1970 Kent State shootings in which the Ohio National Guard can supposedly be heard being ordered by superiors to open fire on students. MacKaye was also the subject of rumors maliciously spread online in 2007 saying that he had been killed by a hit-and-run driver at a Fugazi show in Pittsburgh, (thankfully false as, sadly, were the rumors about a Fugazi reunion).

Although many see MacKaye's community-oriented, DIY, no-frills lifestyle and career hard to emulate, MacKaye remains an elder statesman for the punk community. As **Joe Strummer** reportedly once said of MacKaye, "Ian's the only one who ever did the punk thing right from day one and followed through on it all the way."

MADAME WONG'S

LOCATION: LOS ANGELES

In 1978, hoping to attract more customers, the owner of a Los Angeles Chinatown restaurant, Esther Wong, decided to try booking something different from the Polynesian bands she usually hired for live entertainment. Almost instantly, her restaurant became the epicenter of the L.A. scene, with hundreds of customers packing in to hear punk and (later) **new wave** bands who had almost nowhere else to play. The original Madame Wong's closed in 1985. A second location in Santa Monica, Madame Wong's West—opened to accommodate the second tier of bands she couldn't fit on the bill at the original restaurant—operated from 1978 to 1991. The notoriously picky and dictatorial Wong earned herself the nickname "godmother of punk" even though the most adventurous bands she booked were probably Oingo Boingo and the Plimsouls, with new wave stars like the Police and the Go-Go's dominating. Wong

also loses punk points for allegedly stopping a **Ramones** show (minus 20 points right there) until the band cleaned up graffiti they'd supposedly written in the bathroom. (Minus another 1,000 for destroying valuable Ramones graffiti!) Still, though, her heart was in the right place. Wong died in 2005 at the age of 88.

MAGAZINE

1977-1981

LINEUP: Howard Devoto (vocals); John McGeoch (guitar, replaced by Robin Simon, Bob Mandelson); Barry Adamson (bass); Martin Jackson (drums, replaced by John Doyle); Bob Dickinson (keyboards, replaced by Dave Formula)

After Howard Devoto founded and rapidly departed Manchester punk legends the **Buzzcocks**, he together this early **post-punk** outfit. Magazine left behind the Buzzcocks' revved-up, three-chord-style punk, and opted for a leaner, more angular style, reminiscent of American bands like the **Embarrassment** and the early **Feelies**, but with Devoto's inscrutable lyrics adding a sense of mystery. They put out several remarkable records, such as the classic single "Shot by Both Sides" (written with Buzzcock bandmate Pete Shelley) and a truly unique first album, *Real Life*. Their Martin Hannett-produced third album, *The Correct Use of Soap*, was a promising step toward fusing the early Magazine sound with **Joy Division**-type soundscapes. But Magazine started to splinter when John McGeoch played with **Siouxsie and the Banshees** during that band's hiatus in the late-1970s; he quit Magazine in 1980 to continue playing with the Banshees. Devoto left in 1981, later founding Luxuria and playing with old friend Pete Shelley in the Buzzkunst. Adamson later performed with Nick Cave and the Bad Seeds, and McGeoch went on to play with **Public Image Ltd.** before his death in 2004.

Discography:
Real Life (Virgin, 1978); *Secondhand Daylight* (Virgin, 1979); *The Correct Use of Soap* (Virgin, 1980); *Play* (IRS, 1980); *Magic Murder and the Weather* (Virgin, 1981)

Sting at Madame Wong's, 1979.

Berlin Brats guitarist Keith Hages at the Masque, January 1978.

MARGINAL MAN

1982-1988

LINEUP: Steve Polcari (vocals); Kenny Inouye (guitar); Peter Murray (guitar); Andre Lee (bass); Mike Manos (drums)

Marginal Man were one of the great Washington, D.C., punk bands during the glory days of the **Dischord** scene. The band debuted at the legendary "555" show on January 2,1983, along with **Faith** and **Minor Threat** (the "555" referred to the fact that all three bands had five members; unusual for the scene at the time). Marginal Man's first two records are among the finest examples of politically aware D.C. punk. Songs like "Friends" and the anti-**Ronald Reagan** rant "Pandora's Box" showed the band developing a more melodic brand of **hardcore**, a style that many later D.C. bands would emulate. After releasing some records on larger indie Giant, Marginal Man felt that the scene had splintered and the band fractured over song topics (singer Steve Polcari distanced himself from the radical politics of the band's early years). After some dissension and a feeling that the band had run its course, guitarist Peter Murray instigated a final breakup in late 1988. (Note of trivia: Guitarist Kenny Inouye's father is the long-serving senator from Hawaii, Daniel Inouye.)

Discography:
Identity (Dischord, 1984); *Double Image* (Giant, 1985); *Marginal Man* (Giant, 1989)

THE MASQUE

LOCATION: LOS ANGELES

An illegal club and performance space run in a 10,000-square-foot basement in the Hollywood Center building on North Cherokee Avenue by Los Angeles scenester **Brendan Mullen**, the Masque is considered by many to be the birthplace of the L.A. scene. Mullen was aided in opening the Masque in 1977 by Fluxus artist Al Hansen, the grandfather of singer Beck Hansen. It started out as a rehearsal space where many bands practiced, but then Mullen realized that he could also use it as a performance venue at a time many punks could not get a show at one of the major clubs on the Sunset Strip. The Masque, like **CBGB**, was run-down and filled with empty bottles and passed-out patrons, but was beloved by many in the L.A. scene for the bands it hosted. A short list of the punk legends who played their first shows at the Masque include: the **Dickies**, **X**, the **Bags**, the **Skulls**, the Go-Go's, and **Fear**. The Masque was forced to close in 1979 due at least in part to police harassment.

The Eyes play the Masque, November 1977: (L to R) Charlotte Caffey (Go-Go's), D.J. Bonebrake (X), Joe Nardini.

MAXIMUM ROCKNROLL

The be-all and end-all of punk zines, and by far the most consistent in terms of release schedule and political and musical commentary, *Maximum RocknRoll* started out in 1977 as a punk radio show on KPFA in Berkeley, California. In 1982, the show inspired the print zine of the same name, which accompanied **Alternative Tentacles'** *Not So Quiet on the Western Front*, one of the key early punk compilation albums. For most of its existence *MRR* was led by collective leader **Tim Yohannon** (who sadly passed away of lymphoma in 1998 at the age of 52).

Over the years *MRR* provided an outlet for punks around the globe to communicate with each other, read scene reports, find out about new bands and zines, and keep up with new releases from small independent labels that could not afford to advertise outside of *MRR*. A good review from the notoriously picky record reviewers could also double or triple a band's sales, and *MRR*'s classified ads allowed bands (years before the Internet) to book tours, find places to crash, and sell and trade records with a community base bound not by geography, but by a communal spirit and shared interests.

MRR's stance as an uncompromising arbiter of what was truly "punk" caused a lot of controversy over the years. For its many supporters, *MRR* was an oasis that refused to work with major labels or run ads for bands that signed with them and sold out the **DIY** aesthetic. But to its detractors, *MRR* can be insufferably elitist and snobbish, obsessed with decreeing who is and is not punk, all due to the zine's own insular criteria. Despite these often-valid criticisms, the importance of *MRR* to the international punk scene cannot be overestimated and to this day the collective that publishes the zine remains true to the original mission of its founders.

MAXIMUM ROCKNROLL NO.96 MAY 1991 $2.00

SPECIAL SOVIET PUNK ISSUE!

Debbie Harry leads Blondie at Max's Kansas City (where she once waitressed), 1976.

MAX'S KANSAS CITY

LOCATION: NEW YORK

Located at 213 Park Avenue South, Max's Kansas City was the unlikely spot where many influential punk predecessors and early punk bands played before the New York scene finally coalesced around **CBGB**. Max's Kansas City was opened in 1965 by entrepreneur and art connoisseur Mickey Ruskin. He gave the place its name on the advice of writer Joel Oppenheimer, who reasoned that it brought to mind cuts of steak from Kansas City.

Max's was as exclusive as it was visionary; there was a strict door policy with a velvet rope (years before Studio 54 thought of the same trick), and artists such as Robert Rauschenberg, John Chamberlain, and, most especially, Andy Warhol called the club home. Warhol was an ardent customer during the late-1960s (his "HQ," the Factory, was located practically around the corner), holding court in the (in)famous back room with his entourage of drag queens, junkies, and superstars (such as Sugar Plum Fairy, Jackie Curtis, and Candy Darling, all later immortalized in **Lou Reed**'s "Walk on the Wild Side"). Members of the **Velvet Underground**, **Iggy Pop**, and Alice Cooper were also early patrons who relied heavily on the notoriously uncollectible tabs given out by the ever-generous Ruskin to artists and performers he judged worthy of his indulgence. Other notable habitués included **Leee Black Childers**, the famous punk rock photographer and manager; **Patti Smith**, the punk poet; singer Cherry Vanilla; members of the **New York Dolls**; and noted punk transsexual **Wayne/Jayne County**, who was a DJ upstairs at Max's for several years.

Max's became known as a mecca for live music, often booking bands that no one else would take a chance on. The Velvet Underground had a lengthy residence here that led to a famous live album and ended with the band imploding onstage and the final departure of Lou Reed. During the early-1970s, the nascent glitter scene was represented by Iggy Pop, Alice Cooper (who performed in a dress with cones to simulate breasts), and others (all of whom despised the glitter label). The New York Dolls played Max's several times a week in their early incarnation.

Ruskin closed Max's in 1974, though in 1975 it was reopened by Tommy Dean, who made it a prime breeding ground for punk bands during the mid-to-late-1970s. In 1976, the album *Max's Kansas City 1976* was released, featuring Cherry Vanilla and her Staten Island Band, **Suicide**, **Pere Ubu**, the Fast, and Wayne County and the Back Street Boys. There was an informal rivalry between the upscale and "uptown" Max's Kansas City and CBGB, although many bands such as the **Heartbreakers** (who released a live album recorded at Max's Kansas City), **Television**, the **Ramones**, and the Sic Fucks played both clubs. The **Sex Pistols** referenced the place in their song "New York": "Think it's swell playing Max's Kansas / You're looking bored and you're acting flash." **Sid Vicious** was also a regular during the late-1970s and played at Max's with various pickup bands to varying degrees of success. Later on, members of the **no wave** scene, including **Lydia Lunch** and James Chance, played the club in its last incarnation. Max's closed in 1981, though it was briefly revived in the 1990s; a deli currently occupies the space.

Discography:
The Velvet Underground Live at Max's Kansas City (Cotillion, 1972); *Max's Kansas City 1976* (ROIR, 1976); *Live at Max's Kansas City* (Max's Kansas City, 1979)

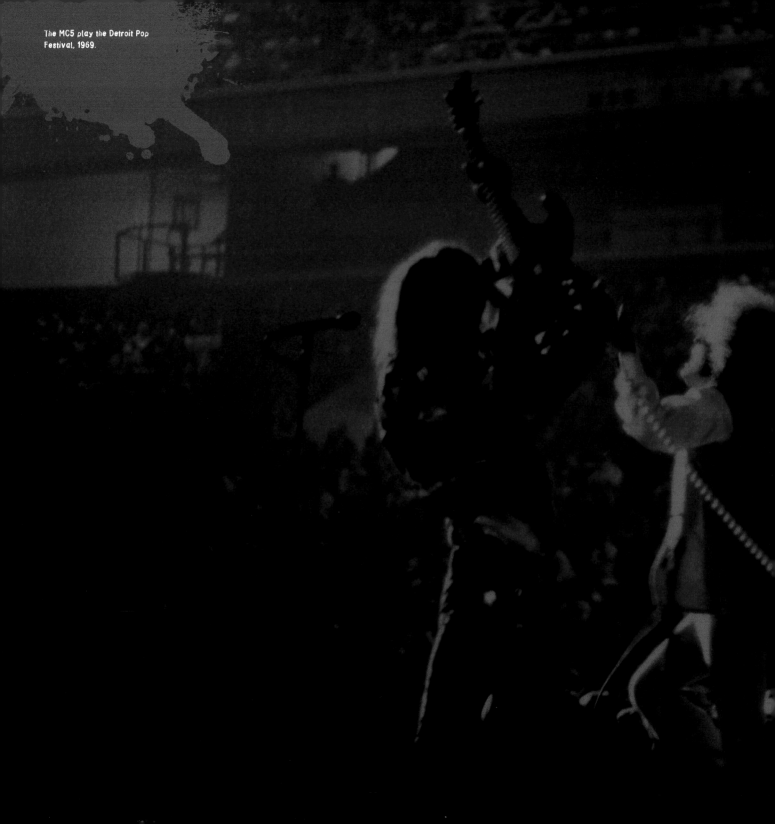

The MC5 play the Detroit Pop
Festival, 1969.

THE MC5

1964–1972

LINEUP: Rob Tyner (vocals); Fred "Sonic" Smith (guitar); Wayne Kramer (guitar); Michael Davis (bass); Dennis Thompson (drums)

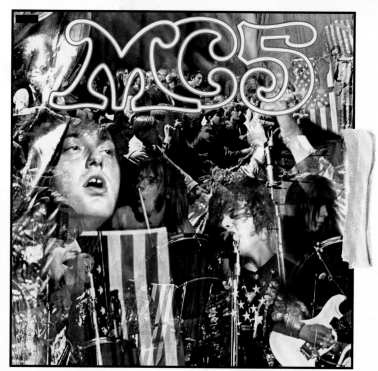

The ultimate proto-punk band from the late-1960s, the MC5 made their reputation with the anthem "Kick Out the Jams" and their signature mixture of jazz riffs and brutal feedback-laden guitar sound. The MC5 (aka the "Motor City Five") were an explosively talented band, led by manager and radical activist John Sinclair. But Sinclair, a professional agitator, saw in the MC5 the potential to use their music to rouse the masses to revolution; he believed this despite not even caring for their sound (he was a jazz and blues aficionado). Given that most record industry executives prefer not to market the radical overthrow of the state—not to mention the constant conflict between Sinclair and almost anyone in a position of authority—the band's initial promise seemed doomed from the start.

In 1966, the MC5 were more or less a house band at Detroit's Grande Ballroom, where Sinclair produced projected light shows to go along with the longer more psychedelic songs in the band's early repertoire. The MC5 were as ferocious a band as any in the mid-1960s and should have been due for superstardom but were sidetracked by their association with Sinclair's White Panther Party. Another pseudo-revolutionary group with unrealistic goals, the White Panthers' stated goals were first to be in full allegiance with the Blank Panthers. Perhaps more important was their plan—number two in the 10-point program that Sinclair announced in 1968—for "total assault on the culture by any means necessary, including rock 'n' roll, dope, and fucking in the streets." While further points called for the abolition of money and the brilliant recognition that "leaders suck," point number two was what probably attracted many to finally hear what the MC5 actually sounded like; they were not disappointed.

The MC5 played for protestors at the 1968 Democratic National Convention in Chicago; in the audience were Yippies (adherents of the Youth International Party) and Elektra A&R man **Danny Fields**, who

signed the band. The MC5's first album was recorded live at the Grande Ballroom in 1968 and released the following year amid controversy due to the first line of "Kick Out the Jams": "Kick out the Jams, Motherfuckers!" When Detroit retailer Hudson's refused to stock the record, the always-cautious MC5 took out an ad in an underground paper saying "Fuck Hudson's," using the Elektra logo. Following that, the MC5 were banned from a number of venues, making finding gigs a difficult task. After Elektra dropped them, the MC5 signed to Atlantic and dropped Sinclair, who was subsequently sentenced to 10 years in jail for a pot arrest. The band released two more albums, *Back in the USA* and *High Time*, each one less political, before getting dropped by Atlantic, after which the members scattered.

Vocalist Rob Tyner died in 1991. Guitarist Fred Smith later married punk poet **Patti Smith**, and the two retired into relative obscurity to raise a family before Fred's untimely death in 1994. Guitarist Wayne Kramer did a stint in prison, later played in the band Gang War with **Johnny Thunders**, and now tours on his own and with the rhythm section of the MC5, with special guests taking over for the late Rob Tyner and Fred Smith. The remaining members

of the band tour with a changing roster of lead singers, billing themselves as DKT (the initials of the three surviving members) MC5, along with guest singers such as Mark Arm from Mudhoney. Despite the group's obscurity during their era and their often lengthy and intricate jamming, the MC5 is still regarded as very influential on the early punk and heavy metal scenes. Almost any band from Mudhoney to the Reigning Sound who combines copious amounts of noise, distortion, and free jazz, owes a debt to the MC5.

Discography:

Kick Out the Jams (Elektra, 1969, 1983); *Back in the USA* (Atlantic, 1970; Rhino, 1992); *High Time* (Atlantic, 1971; Rhino, 1992); *Babes in Arms* (ROIR, 1983, 1997; Danceteria, 1990); *Do It* (Revenge, 1987); *Live Detroit 68/69* (Revenge, 1988); *Kick Out the Jams* (live; Elektra, 1991); *Power Trip* (Alive, 1994); *Black to Comm* (Receiver, 1994); *Looking at You* (Receiver, 1994); *American Ruse* (Total Energy, 1995); *Live 1969/70* (New Rose, 1995); *Teenage Lust* (live; Total Energy, 1996); *Phun City, UK* (Sonic, 1996); *Starship: Live at Sturgis Armory June 1968* (live; Total Energy, 1998); *Ice Pick Slim* EP (live; Alive, 1997); *Thunder Express* (Cleopatra, 1999); *'66 Breakout* (Total Energy, 1999); *Greatest Hits Live* (Cleopatra, 1999); *The Big Bang: The Best of the MC5* (Rhino, 2000); *Motor City is Burning* (live; Trojan, 2001); *Human Being Lawnmower: The Baddest and Maddest of MC5* (Total Energy, 2002); *Extended Versions* (BMG Special Products, 2003); *Take 2: High Time/Back in the USA* (WEA International, 2004); *Purity Accuracy* (box set; Easy Action, 2004); *Are You Ready to Testify: Live Bootleg Anthology* (Castle/ Ryko, 2005)

Although there is some disagreement about the exact year of decade in which punk rock began, most scholars date it from the early-to-mid-1970s, and refer to bands and movements that preceded that period as *proto-punk*. Prime examples of this genre would be Iggy and the **Stooges**, the **MC5**, the Monks, the Seeds, the Music Machine, the Sonics, and many other bands that are often today called *garage* (although some had called that brand of music "punk" during the late-1960s). The *Nuggets* album series of 1960s garage rock anthologies (curated by **Patti Smith** guitarist Lenny Kaye) is regarded as a particularly rewarding treasure trove of proto-punk, along with other major collections such as the *Pebbles* series.

Most critics and scholars identify the two primary 1960s proto-punk bands as the Stooges and the MC5—although some also note the key influence of the Doors, and admittedly **Iggy Pop** owes much of his early image and look to Doors singer Jim Morrison—certainly two of the bands most cited in interviews by such early punks as the **Ramones** and the **Sex Pistols** when they were asked who influenced their musical direction. The Stooges album *Raw Power* is regarded as a proto-punk trailblazer, leading to many punk bands covering the anthemic "Search and Destroy." Also sometimes lumped under the proto-punk label are bands as diverse as the **Velvet Underground**, Frank Zappa and the Mothers of Invention, Jonathan Richman and the **Modern Lovers** (the Sex Pistols were known to cover "Roadrunner"), and the **Dictators**, who were a clear stepping-stone between garage rock and punk.

THE SEEDS

A proto-punk garage and psychedelic 1960s band led by the enigmatic Sky Saxon, the Seeds were best known for the song "Pushing Too Hard." The band was remarkably different and much more abrasive than many of their contemporaries and is considered, along with the Sonics and the Music Machine, to be the band who most inspired punk rock years later. Sky Saxon still tours with a reconstituted Seeds to this day, further spreading his blessedly warped vision to a new generation.

ZOLAR X

This Los Angeles band from the early-1970s had members who dressed in elaborate and bizarre space alien costumes and played the Sunset Strip clubs. Their use of props, space images, and extravagant getups—as well as their habit of staying in character as aliens on, and offstage—made them stand out from the early L.A.

scene. Although they dissolved later in the decade, they heavily in—————— art punks and epitomized the contention that the American scene was largely an artistic one as opposed to the United Kingdom's more working-class movement. An album of their material was released by **Alternative Tentacles** in 2005, around the same time that a new version of the band, minus jailed lead singer Zory Zenith, was touring.

THE SONICS

One of the little-known but often-cited progenitors of 1960s garage rock, who later provided inspiration for many in the 1970s punk scene, the Sonics' best-known songs, "Strychnine" and their epic track "The Witch," showcased lead singer Gary Roslie's manic singing for a small and appreciative group of dissatisfied youths looking for better music in the 1960s.

THE MONKS

This group of U.S. servicemen stationed in Germany during the early-1960s distinguished themselves first with their distorted guitar sound and amateurish punk vocals, but also by wearing monks' robes onstage and shaving the crowns of their heads in monks' tonsures. Their debut album, *Black Monk Time*, originally released in 1966, was reissued in the 1990s and led to a revival of interest in the band that sporadically re-formed for tours. A book chronicling the band's 1960s exploits, *Black Monk Time: Coming of the Anti-Beatle*, by Thomas Edward Shaw and Anita Klemke, was published in 1995.

THE STANDELLS

A 1960s band from Los Angeles (although they did claim in their most famous song that Boston was their home) whose raw sound made them early proto-punk standard-bearers (particularly for Boston bands). They were best known for the hit single "Dirty Water" and an appearance on the TV show *The Munsters*; that, and opening for the Rolling Stones. **Minor Threat** later paid the Standells a tribute by covering "Sometimes Good Guys Don't Wear White."

THE MUSIC MACHINE

One of the key 1960s proto-punk bands, the Music Machine is considered to have anticipated punk's energy and style many years before the movement became formalized. The band formed as the Ragamuffins in 1965 but mutated into the Music Machine by 1966. Most famous for the classic "Talk Talk" (a song that predates **hardcore** but nonetheless shows how music can be sped up to ridiculous speeds and still be urgent and vital), the Music Machine's Farfisa organ style placed them on the garage and psychedelic side of the music scene. Had they formed in 1976 as opposed to 1966, the Music Machine would have just been called punk instead of proto-punk.

THE FUGS

This band of pranksters and musicians were kings of New York protest music during the 1960s. Like proto-punk Yippies with a less destructive bent than the MC5, the Fugs (their name taken from a certain obscene euphemism in the censored version of Norman Mailer's book *The Naked and the Dead*) can be seen as forerunners to the early-1970s pre-punk performers like Patti Smith who mixed the personal and the political. At least one writer later noted a lyrical similarity between the Fugs and the **Dead Kennedys**. Founded in 1965, the Fugs went on several lengthy hiatuses and re-formed sporadically for benefits and protest concerts.

The Fugs, circa 1970.

Situationist, entrepreneur of the influential shop **Sex,** and manager and alleged Svengali behind the **Sex Pistols** (as well as early versions of Adam and the Ants, Bow Wow Wow, and the last incarnation of the **New York Dolls**), Malcolm McLaren has an undeniable position in punk history, although what that position is, remains a subject of fierce debate.

A onetime art student fixated on Situationist politics and performance-art spectacle, McLaren was responsible, along with his partner and ex-wife **Vivienne Westwood**, for introducing punk fashion to Britain in the mid-1970s at their notorious London shop Sex. Of course, the bondage clothing and ripped T-shirts sold at Sex were heavily inspired by the look of New York punks like **Richard Hell** and the New York Dolls (whom McLaren briefly managed in 1974–75), but McLaren of course claimed that it had all sprung fresh from his brain, an attitude that would eventually lead to decades of lawsuits.

The amount of credit that McLaren deserves for the creation, sound, and look of the Sex Pistols, whom he managed until their 1978 breakup, has been debated for years. He claims that the Pistols were solely his idea, while the band themselves (particularly **John Lydon**) believe otherwise. Strangely enough, film director Julien Temple presented both sides of the argument in his dueling Pistols documentaries *The Great Rock 'n' Roll Swindle* and *The Filth and the Fury*. The answer is unclear, but the look and marketing of the Sex Pistols (much of the latter being ingeniously disastrous) owed much to McLaren's fashion sense and his collaboration with **Jamie Reid**. While

Malcolm McLaren cocks a
saucy eyebrow in Paris, 1979.

the Sex Pistols gave McLaren much more publicity and notoriety than he could ever have dreamed , the recriminations, lawsuits, and financial turmoil that embroiled him and his management company, Glitterbeast, lasted for years and eventually took a large financial toll on all parties involved. (When McLaren finally sat down for an interview on former Pistol Steve Jones's radio show in Los Angeles a few years ago, Jones's first question was "WHERE'S THE FUCKING MONEY?")

During the 1980s, McLaren moved his music impresario business from the world of punk to that of **new wave**, managing the careers of several groups and releasing albums of his own music. His well-known eye for talent enabled him to develop careers for both Adam Ant and Bow Wow Wow before they decided he was too controlling and slipped from his clutches. McLaren successfully experimented with other musical genres in his solo career and produced a number of hits that were ahead of their time, including "Double Dutch," a British Top-10 hit in 1983, and the forward-looking "Buffalo Gals," which essentially introduced hip-hop to Britain. Subsequent albums saw McLaren experimenting with African music, funk (with Bootsy Collins), and opera (his 1984 version of *Madame Butterfly* was an inexplicable Top-20 hit in the UK). McLaren returned to the Svengali business in 1998 with JUNGK, an all-Asian version of the Spice Girls. At this point, however, he seemed to lose interest in his project, and an attempt to run for mayor of London in 2000 also went nowhere.

Discography:
Duck Rock (Charisma, 1983); *D'Ya Like Scratchin'* EP (Island, 1984); *Fans* (Island, 1984); *Swamp Thing* (Island, 1985); *Paris* (No!/Vogue/Gee Street/Island, 1995); *Buffalo Gals Back to Skool* (Priority, 1998). **Malcolm McLaren and the Bootzilla Orchestra:** *Waltz Darling* (Epic, 1989). **Malcolm McLaren Presents the World Famous Supreme Team Show:** *Round the Outside! Round the Outside!* (Virgin, 1990).

LEGS McNEIL

Gonzo-style journalist, author, and cofounder of *Punk* magazine in the mid-1970s, Legs McNeil was present at the ground zero of New York punk, helping to name the movement and to create its aesthetic by championing musicians such as the **Dictators**, the **Ramones**, and **Lou Reed**. After McNeil's older friends **John Holmstrom** and Ged Dunn had settled on becoming, respectively, editor and publisher of *Punk*, it was left to Legs to become the magazine's "resident punk." McNeil used his youthful exuberance (and a love of mind-altering substances) to write surrealistic interviews with real punk rockers and with cartoon characters such as Boris and Natasha (from the *Rocky and Bullwinkle* television show) and Sluggo (from the comic strip *Nancy*). After *Punk* folded in the late-1970s, McNeil worked as a journalist and editor for magazines such as *Spin* (he once famously went down the Mississippi River with old friend **Richard Hell**) and eventually turned to book writing, coauthoring (with Gillian McCain) in 1996 the definitive book about the punk revolution (in New York, at least), *Please Kill Me*.

Legs McNeil, getting wine all over somebody's floor, 1978.

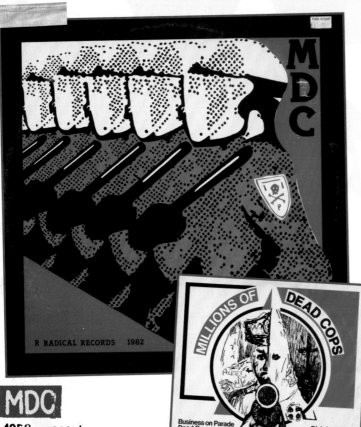

R RADICAL RECORDS 1982

MDC

1978-present

LINEUP: Dave Dictor (vocals); Eric Mucho (guitar, many others, now Ron Posner); Matt Van Curra (bass, replaced by many others, including Mikey Donaldson); Al Batross (drums, many others, now two drummers, Al Schvitz and Dejan Poda)

A radical band whose moniker stands for either "Millions of Dead Cops" or "Multi-Death Corporation" (or "Millions of Dead Christians" or "Marine Death Corps" or "Male Dominated Culture" or...), MDC was relentless in their full-on attack on capitalism, homophobia, police brutality, racism, and other ills of the American system. The band formed as the Stains in 1978 in Austin, Texas, and released the "John Wayne Was a Nazi" seven-inch in 1981 before changing their name to Millions of Dead Cops.

Among the most militant of the 1980s **hardcore** bands (exemplified in their cover depiction on the first issue of *Maximum RocknRoll* in 1982), MDC played music as uncompromising and fierce as their name. Their first several albums were released on their own label, R Radical Records, which also put out records by bands like the **Dicks**,

D.R.I., **Reagan Youth**, and the Offenders. Over the years, the band went through multiple personnel changes, with singer Dave Dictor the only consistent member (Matt Freeman from **Rancid** played bass in one version of the band). MDC continue to record and tour, and in August 2005 played at the benefit concerts to save **CBGB**. Bassist Mikey Donaldson died of unknown causes in September 2007.

Discography:

Millions of Dead Cops (R Radical, 1982; MDC, 1995); *Multi-Death Corporations* (R Radical, 1983); *Chicken Squawk 7"* (Boner Records, 1984); *Smoke Signals* (R Radical, 1986); *This Blood's for You* (R Radical/ Boner, 1987; MDC, 1995); *More Dead Cops 1981–1987* (R Radical/Boner, 1988); *Metal Devil Cokes* (R Radical, 1988; Goldar, 1994); *Elvis In the Rheinland: Live in Berlin* (live; Destiny, 1989); *It's the Real Thing* (Boner, 1989, 1995); *Hey Cop, If I Had a Face Like Yours* (R Radical, 1991; MDC, 1995); *Shades of Brown* (New Red Archives, 1993); *Thanks for Giving Me What I Didn't Want* (New Red Archives, 1993); *Now More Than Ever* (Beer City, 2002; Cleopatra, 2002); *Magnus Dominus Corpus* (Sudden Death, 2004)

THE MEATMEN

1980-1997

LINEUP: Tesco Vee, aka Robert Vermuellen (vocals); Greg Ramsey (guitar, replaced by Rich Ramsey, Brian Baker, Stuart Casson, others); Lyle Preslar (guitar); Rich Ramsey (bass, replaced by Mike Achtenburg, Graham McCullough, others); Jim Forsey (drums, replaced by Eric Rachtman, Mr. X, Todd Swalla, others)

Notorious for their scatological lyrics and obsession with all things relating to bodily functions and perversion, the Meatmen were led by singer Tesco Vee (born Robert Vermuellen), who toured for years with various incarnations of the band. (Vee had originally run a fanzine called *Touch and Go* and later founded the label **Touch and Go**. Their first album, *We're the Meatmen... and You Suck,* featured their trademark song "Crippled Children Suck" and an ode to the recently passed John Lennon, "One Down Three to Go." Vee followed up the first record with *War of the Superbikes*, which had Brian Baker and Lyle Preslar from **Minor Threat** on guitars. Subsequent albums were less popular, and recordings grew more sporadic as the 1990s wore on. Vee, who was once pictured in a gay porn magazine with a dog bone stuck up his ass, and who wrote songs such as "Blow Me Jah" and "Mr. Tapeworm," is one of the most relentlessly vulgar and yet jolly punk songwriters on record—not bad for an ex-fourth grade teacher.

Discography:

Blud Sausage EP (Touch and Go, 1982); *Crippled Children Suck* EP (Touch and Go, 1982); *We're the Meatmen...and You Suck!* (Touch and Go, 1983); *War of the Superbikes* (Homestead, 1985, 1994); *Rock 'n' Roll Juggernaut* (Caroline, 1986, 1994); *We're the Meatmen...and You Still Suck!* (live; Caroline, 1989); *Crippled Children Suck* (Touch and Go, 1990); *Stud Powercock: The Touch and Go Years 1981–1984* (Touch and Go, 1990, 1991); *Pope on a Rope* (Pravda, 1995); *War of the Superbikes, Vol. 2* (Go Kart, 1996); *Evil in a League with Satan* EP (Go Kart, 1997). **Tesco Vee and the Meat Crew:** *Dutch Hercules* EP (Touch and Go, 1984)

THE MEAT PUPPETS

1980-present

LINEUP: Curt Kirkwood (vocals/guitar); Cris Kirkwood (vocals/bass); Derrick Bostrom (drums, now Ted Marcus)

The Meat Puppets are an Arizona power trio who melded punk and country into a unique sound. Among their fans was **Nirvana**'s Kurt Cobain, who covered three of the band's songs on the *Nirvana Unplugged* album and video with support from the Meat Puppets' Curt and Cris Kirkwood. Although the Meat Puppets were originally part of the early **hardcore** scene, and some of the band's early music was quite fast and aggressive, they were better known for slow, drug-fueled material. This marked them as outsiders to the mid-1980s hardcore scene, which looked upon long hair and musical experimentation as anathema. The band was undaunted, however, and they responded with some of the most challenging music of their career, releasing the trilogy of *Meat Puppets*, *Meat Puppets II*, and *Up on the Sun*.

The Meat Puppets were one of the **SST** label's staples for many years, but eventually decided to move to the majors thanks to SST's notorious lack of skill in promoting bands (or successfully accounting for their money). Recording on the London Label, they landed a 1994 hit with "Backwater" off *Too High to Die*. Drummer Derrick Bostrom and Cris Kirkwood left the band after the *No Joke!* album. Curt Kirkwood formed a new band called the Royal Neanderthal Orchestra in Austin, Texas, but later changed the name of the band to Meat Puppets for several new releases. Cris Kirkwood went through several stints in rehab for heroin addiction and was arrested in December 2003 for attacking a security guard at a post office; he would eventually serve 18 months in prison. The Kirkwoods reunited in 2007 to record a new album, *Rise to Your Knees*, with drummer Ted Marcus replacing Bostrom.

Discography:
In a Car EP (World Imitation, 1981; SST, 1985; Rykodisc, 1999); *Meat Puppets* (Thermidor/SST, 1982; Rykodisc, 1999); *Meat Puppets II* (SST, 1984; Rykodisc, 1999); *Up on the Sun* (SST, 1985; Rykodisc, 1999); *Out My Way* EP (SST, 1986; Rykodisc, 1999); *Mirage* (SST, 1987; Rykodisc, 1999); *Huevos* (SST, 1987; Rykodisc, 1999); *Monsters* (SST, 1989; Rykodisc, 1999); *No Strings Attached* (SST, 1990); *Forbidden Places* (London, 1991); *Too High to Die* (London, 1994); *No Joke!* (London, 1995); *Live in Montana* (Rykodisc, 1999); *Golden Lies* (Atlantic, 2000); *Live* (DCN, 2002); *Classic Puppets* (Rykodisc, 2004); *Rise to Your Knees* (Anodyne, 2007)

The Meat Puppets, 1984: (L to R) Cris Kirkwood, Derrick Bostrom, Curt Kirkwood.

The Mekons, cowboys
of the 1980s.

> ## "We're the only band that has been together for the whole 30 years of punk. And that simultaneously makes us the best and worst punk band ever."
>
> —Jon Langford at a Mekons concert in Milwaukee, September 2007

THE MEKONS

1977–present

LINEUP: Jon Langford (guitar/vocals); Tom Greenhalgh (guitar/vocals); Sarah Corina (bass); Sally Timms (vocals); Susie Honeyman (violin/vocals); Robert "Lu" Edmunds (oud/saz); Rico Bell (accordian/vocals); Steve Goulding (drums); Kevin Lycett (vocals/guitar, departed early-1980s); Dick Taylor (guitar, dates unclear)

One of punk's strangest and most long-lived bands, the Mekons experimented in almost every musical genre from country and western to **dub**, and probably also invented some along the way. The original Mekons were started by art students in Leeds, England (much like **Gang of Four**), during late-1977. In January 1978, they released their brilliant first single, "Never Been in a Riot," which parodied both the **Clash** single "White Riot" and punk's halfhearted commitment to revolutionary politics. After numerous personnel changes—including the departure of founder and vocalist Kevin Lycett, and sometime member Dick Taylor (whose credits include the Pretty Things and a brief sting with the very early vintage Rolling Stones)—the band solidified with Jon Langford and Tom Greenhalgh playing guitars and singing most of the songs. They were abetted by Sally Timms on vocals and, occasionally, violinist Susie Honeyman and multi-instrumentalist Robert "Lu" Edmunds, an ex-member of the **Damned**, and an ever-evolving rhythm section, which eventually settled with ex-Graham Parker and the Rumour drummer Steve Goulding and bassist Sarah Corina.

The Mekons released a staggering number of records in their 30-plus-year career, most created outside of the machinery of major labels. Their 1985 album *Fear and Whiskey* is often looked upon as one of the first alt-country records and certainly one of the first attempts to fuse punk's attitude with country music's swagger. Despite years of acclaim and consistent touring (and far too many solo and side projects to be mentioned here), the Mekons were rarely on a major label (an EP on A&M being the exception in 1990), but that did not slow their remarkable output or put a damper on their revolutionary politics. The Mekons at their best made the personal seem intensely political, as in "He Beat Up His Boyfriend" and "(Sometimes I Feel Like) Fletcher Christian"; or an attack on U.S. imperialism such as "Ghosts of American Astronauts" seem as longing and romantic as any keyboard-driven **new wave** dance classic of the 1980s.

Cofounder Jon Langford now lives in Chicago. In between frequent Mekons tours he works on various art projects and records under the names Waco Brothers, Pine Valley Cosmonauts, and his own. In 2005, Langford was commissioned by the Walker Arts Center in Minneapolis and Alverno College to create a multimedia version of his Pine Valley Cosmonauts record *The Executioner's Last Songs* for a stage tour.

Discography:

The Quality of Mercy Is Not Strnen (Virgin, 1979; Blue Plate, 1990); *Devils Rats and Piggies: A Special Message from Godzilla* (Red Rhino, 1980; Quarterstick, 2000); *It Falleth Like the Gentle Rain from Heaven—The Mekons Story* (CNT Productions, 1982; Feel Good All Over, 1993); *The English Dancing Master* EP (CNT Productions, 1983); *Fear and Whisky* (Sin, 1985); *Crime and Punishment* EP (Sin, 1985); *Edge of the World* (Sin, 1986; Quarterstick, 2000); *Slightly South of the Border* EP (Sin, 1986); *Honky Tonkin'* (Sin/Twin/Tone, 1987); *New York* (tape, ROIR, 1987; ROIR/Important, 1990); *So Good It Hurts* (Sin/Cooking Vinyl/Rough Trade, 1988); *Original Sin* (Sin/Twin/Tone, 1989); *The Dream and Lie of . . .* EP (Blast First, 1989); *The Mekons Rock 'n' Roll* (Twin/Tone/A&M, 1990); *F.U.N. '90* EP (Twin\Tone/A&M, 1990); *The Curse of the Mekons* (Blast First, 1991); *Wicked Midnite/All I Want* EP (Loud Music, 1992); *I (Heart) Mekons* (Quarterstick, 1993); *Millionaire* EP (Quarterstick, 1993); *Retreat from Memphis* (Quarterstick, 1994); *Mekons United* (Touch and Go, 1996); *I Have Been to Heaven and Back: Hen's Teeth and Other Lost Fragments of Unpopular Culture, Vol. 1* (Quarterstick, 1999); *Where Were You? Hen's Teeth and Other Lost Fragments of Unpopular Culture, Vol. 2* (Quarterstick, 1999); *Journey to the End of the Night* (Quarterstick, 2000); *Oooh! (Out of Our Heads)* (Quarterstick 2002), *Punk Rock* (Quarterstick, 2004), *Natural* (Quarterstick, 2007). **Mekons/Kathy Acker:** *Pussy, King of the Pirates* (Quarterstick, 1996)

MELODY MAKER

This British music magazine extensively covered the punk movement, though not always in positive terms. *Melody Maker* was cofounded in 1926 by Michael Giles and Ian McDonald and originally focused on outsider music such as jazz, although in the 1950s the publication gradually shifted focus to rock 'n' roll. The focus on rock made *Melody Maker* more popular than ever, and at its peak the circulation was more than 250,000 copies per week. During its mid-to-late-1970s heyday, *Melody Maker* featured a few writers, such as Caroline Coon (who later managed the **Clash**) and *Punk* magazine's Mary Harron, who quite astutely covered the punk revolution. For quite a few years, the magazine was close to a bible for music lovers in the UK and around the world. Poor circulation, a changed format, and a reluctance to adapt to new musical movements led to *Melody Maker*'s demise in 2000, when it was forced to merge with *NME (New Musical Express)*, leaving the world of music journalism much the poorer.

THE MELVINS

1986–present

LINEUP: Roger "Buzz" Osborne, aka "King Buzzo" (vocals/guitar); Matt Lukin (bass, replaced by Lori Black, Mark Deutrom, Kevin Rutmanis, David Scott, Jared Warren); Dale Crover (drums)

A sludge-rock band from Aberdeen, Washington, who heavily influenced **Nirvana** (among others), the Melvins pioneered the fusion of Black Sabbath-style heavy metal riffs with punk's energy, although played at a glacial pace. The band was briefly signed to Atlantic Records, no doubt because of their relationship with Nirvana, but returned to independent labels a few years later. The Melvins continued to tour and record, and were enormously influential on grunge (bassist Matt Lukin would later join Mudhoney), **post-punk**, and modern experimental heavy metal. The daughter of former child star Shirley Temple, Lori Black, was even a member for a short period. The Melvins continue to work in their own sludgy way toward one day recording rock's slowest record, even if it takes them 10,000 years.

Discography:

Melvins EP (C/Z, 1986); *Gluey Porch Treatments* (Alchemy, 1987; Ipecac, 2000); *Ozma* (Boner, 1989); *Eggnog* EP (Boner, 1991); *Eight Songs* EP ((C/Z, 1991); *10 Songs* (C/Z, 1991); *Your Choice Live Series, Vol. 12* (Your Choice, 1991); *Bullhead* (Boner, 1991); *Melvins* (Boner/Tupelo, 1992); *Houdini* (Atlantic, 1993); *Stoner Witch* (Atlantic, 1994); *Live* (X-mas, 1996); *Stag* (Mammoth/Atlantic, 1996); *Honky* (Amphetamine Reptile, 1997); *Singles 1–12* (Amphetamine Reptile, 1997); *Alive at the Fucker Club* (Amphetamine Reptile, 1998); *The Maggot* (Ipecac, 1999); *The Bootlicker* (Ipecac, 1999); *The Crybaby* (Ipecac, 2000); *Melvins at Slim's on 8-Track 6.17.99* (8-track; Life Is Abuse, 2000); *The Trilogy on Vinyl* (Ipecac, 2000); *Electroretard* (Man's Ruin, 2001); *Colossus of Destiny* (Ipecac, 2001); *Hostile Ambient Takeover (H.A.T.)* (Ipecac, 2002); *26 Songs* (Ipecac, 2003); *Melvinmania: The Best of the Atlantic Years 1993–1996* (Atlantic, 2003); *Pigs of the Roman Empire* (Ipecac, 2004); *Mangled Demos from 1983* (Ipecac, 2005); *(A) Senile Animal* (Ipecac, 2006). **Snivlem:** *Prick* (Amphetamine Reptile, 1994). **FantomasMelvins Big Band:** *FantomasMelvins Big Band* (Ipecac, 2002). **King Buzzo:** *King Buzzo* EP (Boner/Tupelo, 1992). **Dale Crover:** *Dale Crover* EP (Boner/Tupelo, 1992). **Joe Preston:** *Joe Preston* EP (Boner/Tupelo, 1992). **Melvins with Jello Biafra** *Never Breathe What You Can't See* (Alternative Tentacles, 2005); *Sieg Howdy!* (Alternative Tentacles, 2006)

The Melvins break for it, 1993.

THE MEMBERS

1977-1983

LINEUP: Nick Tesco (vocals); Gary Baker (guitar, later Nigel Bennett); Jean-Marie Carroll (guitar); Steve Morley (bass); Adrian Lillywhite (drums)

An obscure but worthy British band from Camberley, Surrey, the Members were one of the earlier punk bands to discover **reggae** and pop. Initially playing straight-forward punk rock, the Members debuted in July 1977 at the **Roxy** in London and soon found themselves playing alongside most of the key bards at the time. Looking high and low for a producer, they finally settled on the drummer's brother, producer Steve Lillywhite (later of U2 fame) and released the classic single "Feat on the Streets" (an anti-**National Front** song). After determining that punk had reached a dead end, the Members added reggae and dance touches to their music, but when they failed to chart, the band called it quits in late 1983.

Discography:
At the Chelsea Night Club (Caroline, 1979); *The Choice is Yours* (Virgin, 1980); *Uprhythm, Downbeat* (Arista, 1982); *Going West* (Albion, 1983)

METAL URBAIN

1976-1982, 1984, 1987, 2003-present

LINEUP: Claude "Clode" Panik (vocals, replaced by Eric Debris); Pat Luger (guitar, until 1980); Rikky Darling (guitar, replaced by Herman Schwartz); Zip Zinc (synthesizer, until 1977); Eric Debris (synthesizer, later lead vocals with Charlie H on synthesizer)

An example of how quickly the punk impulse spread throughout the world, this French punk band was one of the first to play in the United Kingdom, and was best known for their anarchic combination of brash guitar and electric drums. Metal Urbain's first single—"Panik"—in October 1977, was the first single released by quintessential **post-punk** label **Rough Trade**. Although the band sang entirely in French, Metal Urbain was still quite successful in the early British punk scene, with their use of a synthesizer instead of a drummer making them stand out even more. They later reunited for several world tours, and various members

have continued in this same vein over the last three decades. The best entry point for newcomers to their music is the *Chef D'Oeuvre* compilation, which contains early singles like "Panik" and "Lady Coca Cola" that demonstrate Metal Urbain's early bridging of punk and industrial music.

Discography:
Tokyo Airport (Celluloid, 1979); *Les Hommes Mort Sont Dangereux* (Byzz, 1981); *Chef D'Oeuvre* (EMI, 2004); *J'irai Chier Dans Ton Vomi* (Warner, 2006)

MINOR THREAT

1980-1983

LINEUP: Ian MacKaye (vocals); Lyle Preslar (guitar); Brian Baker (bass, replaced by Steve Hansgen briefly when Baker moved to second guitar); Jeff Nelson (drums)

Perhaps the single most legendary **hardcore** band in America, Minor Threat produced a ferocious sound that energized the entire Washington, D.C., scene. They jump-started the **straight-edge** movement, and even helped plant the root of **Dischord Records**. There is in fact almost no way to sum up just how important Minor Threat was to countless punks on a political, social, and philosophical level.

Singer **Ian MacKaye** and drummer Jeff Nelson started Minor Threat in November 1980 after the demise of their previous band, the **Teen Idles**, when MacKaye wanted to sing more and develop his new ideas about living straight and rejecting the false promises of drugs and alcohol. (In fact, Minor Threat was almost called Straight.) With their electric shows featuring Ian flailing about onstage and the band's sonic assault of anger, they were a quick success in the D.C. scene. The band's initial EPs, *Minor Threat* and *In My Eyes* put MacKaye and Nelson's start-up label Dischord on the map as a source of imaginative and aggressive new music. Although the first EP established Minor Threat's penchant for angry diatribes (the alarmingly self-righteous "Straight Edge" gave the name to the burgeoning, clean-living movement in punk), *In My Eyes* showed the band's sense of humor

"I'm a person just like you
But I've got better things to do
Than sit around and fuck my head
Hang out with the living dead
Snort white shit up my nose
Pass out at the shows
I don't even think about speed
That's something I just don't need
I've got the straight edge."
—Minor Threat, "Straight Edge"

MINOR THREAT

$3.50
Postpaid from Dischord

OUT OF STEP

by ending with a comical but reverent cover of the Monkees' "(I'm Not Your) Steppin' Stone." That EP also included the particularly angry "Guilty of Being White," in which MacKaye, who had elsewhere described getting attacked in D.C. for being white, refused to accept that his race made him complicit in crimes (such as slavery) that were committed a hundred years before his time. Sadly, years later the song would be taken up by white-power bands who (absurdly) saw it as an endorsement of racism; Slayer infamously changed the lyrics once to "guilty of being *right*."

Minor Threat broke up for a time in 1981 when guitarist Preslar went to Northwestern University and Baker joined **Government Issue** on guitar. It wasn't long before Preslar abandoned his college career, and Minor Threat reunited in March 1982 to even greater acclaim and national touring. Some fans cried "sell-out," leading Minor Threat to pen the hilarious song "Cashing In," a joking assertion that they were reuniting only for the money. Minor Threat then added bassist Steve Hansgen as Baker moved to second guitar for the *Out of Step* EP. Hansgen did not gel well with the band and was asked to leave, but the damage had been done, and Minor Threat was almost through. With Baker and Preslar trying to write more commercial songs, MacKaye decided to leave the band after recording the three-song *Salad Days* EP, which ended with a cover of the Standells' "Good Guys Don't Wear White"— possibly a veiled allusion to how Minor Threat was being perceived in the D.C. scene. Ian MacKaye went on to play in the short-lived **Embrace** and **Egg Hunt** projects before founding **Fugazi**. Nelson continued to work with MacKaye at Dischord and tried his hand at graphic design, most notably the "Meese is a Pig" signs that seemingly sprouted out of thin air during **Revolution Summer**. After briefly collaborating with Glenn Danzig of the **Misfits**, Preslar and Baker joined the **Meatmen**. Baker founded **Dag Nasty**, briefly played in the heavy metal band Junkyard, and also toured and performed with **Bad Religion**.

The importance of Minor Threat can hardly be overestimated, with their influence still resonating both in and out of the punk scene. Minor Threat not only recorded their own music, distributed their own records, and booked their own shows, they were also one of the few bands at that time to tour outside their local fan base, conducting two major tours, playing New York numerous times, and even making it as far as California. The band also helped spread the emerging straight-edge scene to cities completely unaware of the idea. Although Minor Threat's output was primarily via singles and EPs, Dischord (always attuned to economic realities) compiled all of their material onto the 26-song *Complete Discography*; an essential purchase, to say the least.

Discography:
Minor Threat EP (Dischord, 1981); *In My Eyes* EP (Dischord, 1981); *Out of Step* (Dischord, 1983); *Minor Threat* (Dischord, 1984); *Complete* (Dischord, 1988). **Embrace:** *Embrace* (Dischord, 1987). **Teen Idles:** *Minor Disturbance* EP (Dischord, 1981)

"We were liberated by punk class rebellion."
—Mike Watt interviewed in *Flipside*, 1985

The Minutemen, 1980: (L to R) D. Boon, Mike Watt, George Hurley.

THE MINUTEMEN
1980-1985

LINEUP: D. Boon (vocals/guitar); Mike Watt (bass); George Hurley (drums)

One of the ultimate **DIY** bands and light-years ahead of their time, the Minutemen left behind a musical and cultural legacy that was matched by few bands from the 1980s. Although the Minutemen started off as a punk band, they quickly went beyond the genre in jazz- and funk-influenced jams that expanded punk's musical boundaries. In terms of talent, the members had eclipsed many of their punk brethren at the time, but made sure not to show off by keeping their songs short and to the point—sometimes clocking in at only a few seconds.

The Minutemen—who originally formed in 1980 as a four-piece called the Reactionaries—consisted of the larger-than-life D. Boon, who played guitar and sang, Mike Watt on bass and vocals, and George Hurley on drums. Self-described "corndogs from [San] Pedro," they were all working-class guys who stood in stark contrast to the many slumming middle- and upper-class kids making up much of Southern California's punk scene at the time. The Minutemen borrowed from the best of British **post-punk** in ideological commitment and focus as well as in musical experimentation, with D. Boon's jagged polemics and Watt's precision bass keeping things focused. The Minutemen evolved even further by the time of the release of 1983's *What Makes a Man Start Fires?* and began to explore more of a loose, jazzy feel, perfected by Hurley's drumming, which could be a thundering gallop or a slow, swing-time waltz.

With the 1984 double-album *Double Nickels on the Dime*, one of the best-selling records at the time on **SST** (where the band members actually worked for a time), the Minutemen also showed that the three-piece lineup was not inherently limiting musically. The members experimented with bizarre juxtapositions of politics and popular culture in songs such as "Political Song for Michael Jackson to Sing." An answer of sorts to their Minnesota buddies **Hüsker Dü**, whose similarly adventurous concept album *Zen Arcade* was released at around the same time, *Double Nickels* was a defining achievement for both American punk and the Minutemen, standing as the signature triumph of their extremely prolific recording period. *Project: Mersh*, the Minutemen's joking salute to selling out, added more instrumentation but did little to bring the band in an actual commercial direction, nor did the almost unlistenable daylong jam with members of **Black Flag** that was released as the *Minuteflag* EP.

D. Boon was killed in a van accident in December 1985 right around the release time of their last album, *3-Way Tie (for Last)*. The band had included a ballot on the last record, and the results of the fan voting led to the excellent posthumous *Ballot Result*.

After Boon's death, Watt and Hurley formed the adventurous fIREHOSE with guitarist and singer Ed from Ohio (later of Whiskeytown, whose singer, Ryan Adams, would go on to a successful solo career) and released several records in the late-1980s and early-'90s. After fIREHOSE ran its course, Watt sporadically released solo records with various friends, such as Eddie Vedder of Pearl Jam, and later played bass and recorded with the reconstituted Iggy and the **Stooges**. The Minutemen's legacy of thrilling music and DIY-style production and touring was immortalized in the 2005 documentary *We Jam Econo*.

Discography:
Paranoid Time EP (SST, 1980, 1990); *The Punch Line* (SST, 1981, 1992); *Bean-Spill* EP (Thermidor, 1982); *What Makes a Man Start Fires?* (SST, 1983, 1991); *Buzz or Howl Under the Influence of Heat* (SST, 1983, 1991); *Double Nickels on the Dime* (SST, 1984, 1990); *The Politics of Time* (New Alliance, 1984, 1990); *Tour-Spiel* EP (Reflex, 1985); *Just a Minute, Men* (Virgin Vinyl, 1985); *My First Bells 1980–1983* (tape; SST, 1985); *Project: Mersh* EP (SST, 1985, 1993); *3-Way Tie (for Last)* (SST, 1985, 1990); *Ballot Result* (live; SST, 1987, 1990); *Post Mersh, Vol. 1* (SST, 1987, 1990); *Post Mersh, Vol. 2* (SST, 1987, 1990); *Post Mersh, Vol. 3* (SST, 1989, 1991); *Introducing the Minutemen* (SST, 1998). **Minuteflag:** *Minuteflag* EP (SST, 1986)

THE MISFITS

1977–1983, 1996–present

LINEUP: Glenn Danzig (vocals, replaced in reunion by Michale Graves, Jerry Only); Frank Licata, aka "Franché Coma" (guitar, replaced by Bobby Steele, others); Paul Caiafa, aka "Doyle Wolfgang Von Frankenstein" (guitar, replaced by Dez Cadena); Jerry "Only" Caiafa (bass, now lead vocals); James "Mr. Jim" Catania (drums, later Joey Image, Arthur Googy, Dr. Chud, Marky Ramone, presently Robo)

A horror-punk band from Lodi, New Jersey, originally led by vocalist Glenn Danzig (a sort of satanic Elvis figure who later went on to front Samhain and Danzig), the Misfits drew inspiration from a macabre mix of the supernatural and science-fiction films, even though their name was reputedly (and oddly) taken from Marilyn Monroe's last film. Formed in the mid-1970s by Danzig, who at that time played keyboards through a fuzzbox, the band didn't seriously take shape until 1977. The Misfits first recorded the *Static Age* album (which would not be released until 1995) and numerous singles on their own Plan 9 label. Named after the Ed Wood cult film *Plan 9 from Outer Space*, the label was originally called Blank Records until Mercury bartered for the name to be used for their own sub-label).

After gigging around, the band changed lineups, adding guitarist Bobby Steele and drummer Joey Image. Following their success opening for the **Damned** at Hurrah in New York, the Misfits showed up almost literally on the Damned's doorstep in late 1979 and asked to be added to their tour. Charmed by the Misfits' chutzpah, the Damned agreed to take the young Americans with them, but after squabbles over pay, the Misfits left the tour and drummer Image quit. After a fight, Steele and Danzig also spent a night in jail in London, leading the Misfits to write the song "London Dungeon." Returning to the U.S., Steele was bounced from the band and replaced by Caiafa's

younger brother Paul "Doyle" Caiafa on guitar, and Arthur Googy was put on drums.

By this time, the band members had already spent quite a bit of time and money developing a unique look, dressing in black leather, chains, and spikes, and gelling their hair down past their eyes in a sort of reverse mohawk referred to as a "devilock." Their supernatural Satanisms were pronounced enough to have drawn the ire of Tipper Gore and the Parents Music Resource Center (PMRC) during the 1980s. The Misfits released their clearest and most concise mixture of pop and punk gloom in 1982 with the *Walk Among Us* album. After Googy departed, the band hired former **Black Flag** drummer Robo (the band members were good friends with Black Flag and **Henry Rollins**, who has a prominent Misfits tattoo on his arm) and recorded the faster and darker *Earth A.D.* album. After fighting with Danzig, Robo left the band and was replaced by Todd Swalla of the **Necros** for a few final shows, after which the Misfits disbanded in late 1983.

Danzig then formed the more gothic Samhain for several records before turning to a more commercial, heavy-metal sound with his titular band Danzig, scoring a minor radio and **MTV** hit with the song "Mother." Danzig resisted efforts at a true Misfits reunion and later achieved some infamy for an Internet video clip from July 2004 in which he was knocked out by a

Misfit Michael Graves sweats through his makeup, 1997.

MISFITS — WALK AMONG US

SHED

musician with whom he had been feuding backstage at a concert. Doyle and Jerry formed the hair metal band Kryst the Conqueror in 1987, and in 1995 the two re-formed the Misfits with new singer Michale Graves and drummer Dr. Chud for several tours and new records. When that lineup dissolved, the Caiafa brothers recruited former **Ramones** drummer Marky Ramone, and former Black Flag and DC3 guitarist and singer Dez Cadena to put together a reconstituted Misfits. Bobby Steele formed the Misfits-influenced Undead. Shortly after, Robo rejoined the Misfits in time to play a save **CBGB** benefit show in August 2005 and continued on in the band. Despite numerous calls for it, the closest the original Misfits have come to a genuine reunion were several shows where Doyle joined Danzig onstage for a few encores.

Discography:
Bullet EP (Plan 9, 1978); *Beware* EP (Cherry Red, 1979); *Evilive* EP (Plan 9, 1982, 1986); *Walk Among Us* (Ruby, 1982, 1988); *Earth A.D./Wolf's Blood* (Plan 9, 1983); *Earth A.D./Die Die My Darling* (tape; Plan 9, 1984); *Legacy of Brutality* (Plan 9/Caroline, 1985); *Misfits* (Plan 9/Caroline, 1986); *Static Age* (Caroline, 1995); *Collection II* (Caroline, 1995); *Box Set* (Caroline, 1996); *American Psycho* (Geffen, 1997); *Famous Monsters* (Roadrunner, 1999); *Cuts from the Crypt* (Roadrunner, 2001); *12 Hits from Hell* (Caroline, 2001). **Undead:** *Nine Toes Later* EP (Stiff, 1982); *Never Say Die!* (Rebel, 1986); *Act Your Rage* (Post Mortem, 1989); *Live Slayer* (Skyclad, 1991); *Dawn of the Undead* (Shagpile/Post Mortem, 1991; Shock/Post Mortem, 1997); *Evening of Desire* EP (Overground, 1992); *Til Death!* (Underworld/Post Mortem, 1998). **Samhain:** *Intium* (Plan 9, 1984; Plan 9/Caroline, 1986); *Unholy Passion* EP (Plan 9, 1985; Plan 9/Caroline, 1986); *November-Coming-Fire* (Plan 9/Caroline, 1986); *Final Descent* (Plan 9/Caroline, 1990); *Box Set* (E-Magine, 2000); *Samhain Live, 85–86* (E-Magine, 2002). **Kryst the Conqueror:** *Deliver Us from Evil* EP (Cyclopean, 1989)

MISSION OF BURMA

1979-1983, 2002-present

LINEUP: Roger Miller (vocals/guitar); Clint Conley (bass); Peter Prescott (drums); Martin Swope (other sounds/tape loops, now Bob Weston)

A short-lived but influential band from Boston, best known for the songs "That's When I Reach for My Revolver" (later covered by Moby) and "Academy Fight Song," Mission of Burma was founded in 1979 by guitarist and singer Roger Miller after the breakup of his band Moving Parts. After a few gigs as a three-piece, the band decided to expand its sound by adding Martin Swope, who "played" a tape machine that added tape loops and effects to the band's live sound. After playing around Boston for several years, Mission of Burma released an EP and their first complete album, *Vs.*, in 1982. They were forced to call it quits relatively early due to the chronic tinnitus of guitarist Roger Miller (later to join the Alloy Orchestra and provide live soundtracks to silent films). Mission of Burma re-formed without Swope and with new member Bob Weston (of **Steve Albini**'s Shellac) in 2002, and toured and released the album *OnOffOn* on Matador Records to critical acclaim in 2004. Prescott also played in the Volcano Suns, Kustomized, and Peer Group. After the success of *OnOffOn*, the band re-formed again to release the highly acclaimed, studio album *The Obliterati* in 2006 on Matador, and they have been touring ever since.

Discography:
Signals, Calls and Marches EP (Ace of Hearts, 1981); *Vs.* (Ace of Hearts, 1982); *The Horrible Truth About Burma* (Ace of Hearts, 1985); *Peking Spring* (Taang!, 1987); *Forget* (Taang!, 1987); *Mission of Burma* (Rykodisc, 1988); *OnOffOn* (Matador, 2004); *The Obliterati* (Matador, 2006)

THE MODERN LOVERS

1970-1973

LINEUP: Jonathan Richman (vocals); John Felice (guitar); Ernie Brooks (bass); David Robinson (drums); Jerry Harrison (keyboards)

Proto-punk folk band the Modern Lovers was led in its brief but important existence by Jonathan Richman, the gangly, awkward, light-hearted troubadour who mixed his sardonic sense of comedy with a deeply-felt appreciation of the **Velvet Underground** and a genuine innocence. The Modern Lovers' only official release was recorded in 1972 as a collection of demos (one, fittingly, produced by John Cale of the Velvet Underground) but not released until 1976. The album was extremely influential on many punk bands who, although normally attracted to louder material, plugged into the Modern Lovers' authenticity and rawness. The **Sex Pistols**, among others, covered the song "Road Runner." The group disbanded in 1973, after which Richman embarked on a long and prolific solo career (reinvigorated in recent years thanks to a memorable role as a singing narrator in the film *There's Something About Mary*). Keyboard player Jerry Harrison later joined a little outfit called the **Talking Heads**, while drummer David Robinson signed up with the Cars.

Discography:

Jonathan Richman and the Modern Lovers: *Jonathan Richman and The Modern Lovers* (Beserkley, 1977; Beserkley/Rhino, 1986); *Rock 'n' Roll with the Modern Lovers* (Beserkley, 1977; Beserkley/Rhino, 1986); *Back in Your Life* (Beserkley, 1979; Beserkley/Rhino, 1986); *The Jonathan Richman Songbook* (Beserkley, 1980); *Jonathan Sings!* (Sire, 1983; Sire/Blue Horizon/Warner Bros., 1993); *Rockin' and Romance* (Twin/Tone, 1985); *It's Time for Jonathan Richman and the Modern Lovers* (Upside, 1986); *Modern Lovers 88* (Rounder, 1987); *The Beserkley Years: The Best of Jonathan Richman and the Modern Lovers* (Beserkley/Rhino, 1987); *Jonathan Richman* (Rounder, 1989); *Jonathan Goes Country* (Rounder, 1990); *23 Great Recordings by Jonathan Richman and the Modern Lovers* (Beserkley/Essential/Castle Communications, 1990); *Having a Party with Jonathan Richman* (Rounder, 1991); *I, Jonathan* (Rounder, 1992); *¡Jonathan, Te Vas a Emocionar!* (Rounder, 1994); *You Must Ask the Heart* (Rounder, 1995); *A Plea for Tenderness* (Nectar Masters, 1995); *Surrender to Jonathan!* (Vapor, 1996); *I'm So Confused* (Vapor, 1998); *Her Mystery Not of High Heels and Eye Shadow* (Vapor, 2001). **Modern Lovers:** *The Modern Lovers* (Beserkley, 1976; Beserkley/Rhino, 1986); *Live* (Beserkley, 1977); *The Original Modern Lovers* (Bomp!, 1981); *Live at the Long Branch Saloon* (New Rose, 1992); *Precise Modern Lovers Order: Live in Berkeley and Boston* (Rounder, 1994); *Live at the Long Branch and More* (Last Call, 1998)

The Modern Lovers' Jonathan Richman in later times, 1985.

MOHAWK

Also known as the "mohican," this distinct hairstyle, based on a Native American ritual haircut, involved a variation on shaved sides, sometimes with the liberal use of gel and hairspray to elevate hair to spikes. In England, *Sounds* magazine reported the use of mohawks in bands as early as April 1979, perhaps inspired by the movie *Taxi Driver*, in which Robert De Niro's character Travis Bickle wears a short one. Britain, however, often saw mohawks that were six inches tall or taller in a large symmetrical fin that cov-

ered the whole head. Some famous examples of punks with mohawks—at least some of the time—included the gents of **G.B.H.**; Wattie Buchan from the **Exploited**; Lars and Tim from **Rancid**; Richie Stotts, Jean Beauvoir, and Wendy O. Williams from the **Plasmatics**; **Joe Strummer** during the later days of the **Clash** (though, oddly, not in their earlier days when the band was arguably much more punk); and numerous punks in pictures and on television. The covers of the *Punk and Disorderly* compilations also showed numerous punks with mohawks.

The mohawk was one of punk's most expressive forms of resistance to the fashion

and cultural norms of society, and in the early days of punk, wearing a mohawk (as well as sporting visible tattoos) made mainstream employment a difficult task. The more elaborate variations include the liberty spikes or crown styles, which involved a specific configuration of spikes. A "reverse" version was the devilock, worn by the members of the **Misfits**, in which the hair was grown long and pulled into a lock on the forehead.

In the early years, it was quite common to see groups of punks with mohawks at shows, but things began to change once

Mr. T. (of TV's *The A-Team*) also wore a mohawk, after which it began to be caricatured in mainstream media. Aside from certain British **hardcore** bands, the mohawk largely fell out of favor in the late-1980s and early-'90s. With the punk revival of the 1990s and the emergence of fashion-heavy trends, however, the mohawk started to become more permissible in mainstream culture. This led to the unfortunate introduction of the "faux hawk," which didn't involve completely shaving the sides of the head and so could conceivably be worn on the job.

Assorted anarchists with London bobby, 1985.

KEITH MORRIS

Lead singer of the **Circle Jerks** and the original lead singer of **Black Flag**, Keith Morris was one of the first to sing in what would be known as the West Coast **hardcore** style, marked by vocals that were fast and furious, but still followed a legible melody with pop hooks buried in the mix. Well known for his excessive lifestyle, a cleaned-up Morris sporadically re-forms the Circle Jerks for occasional tours and in the meantime works as an A&R scout for a small record label. Morris was a trailblazer of the early hardcore sound and his stage antics and frequent dives into the audience inspired numerous younger punks to follow his footsteps. Although the classic years of the Circle Jerks and Black Flag are long behind him, Keith Morris remains one of the key punk innovators of the West Coast scene.

Keith Morris performing with the Circle Jerks in California, 2002.

Uncle Motörhead: (L to R) Nancy Spungen, Sid Vicious, Lemmy Kilmister.

MOTÖRHEAD

1975–present

LINEUP: Ian "Lemmy" Kilmister (vocals/bass); "Fast" Eddie Clarke (guitar, replaced by Brian Robertson, Wurzzel, Philip Campbell); Phil "Philthy Animal" Taylor (drums, replaced by, Pete Gill, now Michael Delaouglou, aka "Mikkey Dee")

Motörhead is a near-indestructible wild beast whose furious roar heavily influenced the early punk scene, in particular, the **Damned**, who Lemmy briefly joined. Former Hendrix roadie, gravel-voiced "Lemmy" Kilmister started Motörhead after falling out with the more lysergic elements of the space-rock band Hawkwind (something about drug possession and jail). Kilmister named the band after a song he'd written for Hawkwind, which the band recorded (they had otherwise rejected Lemmy's songwriting contributions).

While Motörhead's music is one of the templates for modern metal, the band's dedication to fast, loud, and aggressive music (the term is British slang for a speedfreak) set them well apart from the mid-1970s metal scene. In fact, Motörhead's music anticipated many of the stripped-down innovations later picked up by punks, many of whom considered Motörhead to be among the only heavy-metal bands a self-respecting punk could consider worth a listen, and whose crowds could mingle safely at shows and pubs. Lemmy was also a huge **Ramones** fan, penning the tribute song "R.A.M.O.N.E.S." for Motörhead's 1916 album (which the Ramones later covered). Still going today at the age of 217, Lemmy is a punk original, warts and all.

Essential Discography:
Motörhead (Chiswick, 1977; Big Beat, 1978; Roadracer Revisited, 1990); *Overkill* (Bronze, 1979; Profile, 1988);

Bomber (Bronze, 1979; Profile, 1988); *Ace of Spades* (Mercury, 1980; Profile, 1988); *No Sleep 'til Hammersmith* (Mercury, 1981; Profile, 1988); *Iron Fist* (Mercury, 1982; Roadracer Revisited, 1990); *Another Perfect Day* (Mercury, 1983); *No Remorse* (Bronze, 1984; Roadracer Revisited, 1990); *Orgasmatron* (GWR/Profile, 1986); *Rock 'n' Roll* (GWR/Profile, 1987); *No Sleep at All* (GWR/Enigma, 1988); *1916* (Epic, 1991); *March or Die* (Sony, 1992); *Bastards* (ZYX, 1993); *Sacrifice* (CMC, 1995); *Overnight Sensation* (CMC, 1996); *Snake Bite Love* (CMC, 1998); *Everything Louder than Everyone Else* (CMC, 1999); *We Are Motörhead* (CMC, 2000); *Hammered* (Castle, 2002); *Inferno* (SPV, 2004). **Motörhead and Girlschool:** *St. Valentine's Day Massacre* EP (Bronze, 1980)

THE MR. T EXPERIENCE

1985-present

LINEUP: Frank Portman, aka "Dr. Frank" (vocals/guitar); Jon Von Zelowitz (guitar, replaced by Ted Angel, also keyboards); Byron Stamatatos (bass, replaced by Aaron Rubin, Joel Reader, Gabe Meline, now Bobby); Alex Laipeneiks (drums, replaced by Jim "Jym" Ruzicka)

Currently known by the less dated—and less embarrassing—moniker MTX, the Mr. T Experience was, for a time one, of the most lyrically confident and musically adventurous bands on the West Coast scene. The East Bay-centered band started in October 1985, and was led from their inception by the one constant member, "Dr. Frank" (real name Frank Portman, a onetime student of Greek and history at UC-Berkeley). They first released the fairly pedestrian *Everybody's Entitled to Their Own Opinion* in 1986 but soon branched out. After going through numerous lineup changes and surviving the departure of

co-leader Jon Von Zelowitz, Dr. Frank is the only original member at this point and has taken the band into a resolutely power-pop direction with shimmering 1960s harmonies and occasional keyboards, much to the chagrin of a minority of fans and the delight of the rest who followed along with the natural evolution of the band. Dr. Frank released an eclectic solo record *Show Business is My Life* in 1999 and has recently become an acclaimed author of a book for young adults (albeit a book for young adults who are in to the **Ramones** and the **Stranglers**) called *King Dork*.

Discography:

Everybody's Entitled to Their Own Opinion (Disorder, 1986; Lookout!, 1990); *Night Shift at the Thrill Factory* (Rough Trade, 1988; Lookout!, 1996); *Big Black Bugs Bleed Blue Blood* (Rough Trade, 1989; Lookout!, 1997); *Making Things with Light* (Lookout!, 1990); *Milk Milk Lemonade* (Lookout!, 1992); *Our Bodies, Ourselves* (Lookout!, 1993); *Taping Up My Heart* EP (Lookout!, 1995); *. . . And the Women Who Love Them* EP (Lookout!, 1994, 2002); *Alternative is Here to Stay* EP (Lookout!, 1995); *Love is Dead* (Lookout!, 1996); *Revenge is Sweet and So Are You* (Lookout!, 1997); *Road to Ruin* (Skull Duggery, 1998); *Alcatraz* (Lookout!, 1999); *Songs About Girls, Etc.* (Lookout!, 1999); *The Miracle of Shame* EP (Lookout!, 2000); *Yesterday Rules* (Lookout!, 2003).
Dr. Frank: *Show Business is My Life* (Lookout!, 1999)

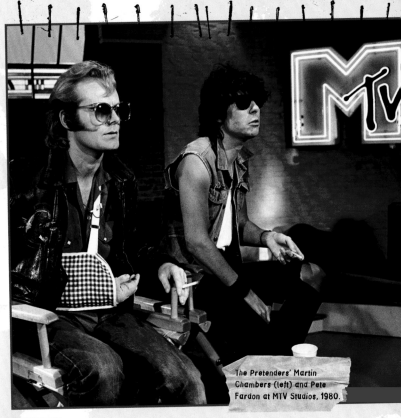

The Pretenders' Martin Chambers (left) and Pete Fardon at MTV Studios, 1980.

MTV

When the Music Television Network started broadcasting in 1980, it played the promotional music videos of songs provided by record companies bracketed by commentary by VJs or Video jockeys (you couldn't call them disc jockeys). The musical experiment soon became a crown jewel of the Viacom empire and a trendsetting cornerstone of the modern music industry. Despite its cultural prevalence today and obsession with the equivalent of punk rock boy-bands, MTV was shunned by most punks for the majority of its history. The **Dead Kennedys** even wrote a song called "MTV Get Off the Air" to critique the mindless images of consumer culture and anti-intellectualism that dominated the channel. During the late-1980s and early-'90s, MTV's "alternative" music show *120 Minutes*—though it focused mostly on videos by and interviews with indie rock artists such as the Church, R.E.M., and XTC—would also sometimes play videos from bands like **Hüsker Dü**, **Sonic Youth**,

the **Replacements**, the **Pogues**, the **Descendents**, and **Killing Joke**.

In later years, **Henry Rollins** (whose video for the **Rollins Band**'s "Liar" was a brief hit) occasionally popped up on MTV to provide commentary. Although some **pop-punk** bands, such as Sum 41 and Blink-182, later benefited from heavy exposure on MTV, many bands, such as **NOFX**, refused to have anything to do with the mega-conglomerate. Given that MTV now concentrates primarily on nonstop reality programming with only occasional musical content, it seems likely that the channel's involvement with punk will be even more nonexistent in the future. MTV has several sister stations, though, and before a format change M2 was once a more free-form version of MTV that occasionally played videos by punk bands, such as **Black Flag**'s "TV Party." Now MTV's sister channel VH-1 Classic has adopted some of the videos cast off by MTV and sometimes broadcasts original *120 Minutes* programs randomly, mixing Black Flag, Sonic Youth, and Haircut 100, all in the same program.

MUDD CLUB

LOCATION: NEW YORK

A popular New York venue for punk bands during the late-1970s and early-'80s, the Mudd Club was immortalized in the **Talking Heads** song "Life During Wartime." The club itself, located at 77 White Street in downtown Manhattan, was known for its stringent door policy and for letting people in based on looks and perceived hipness—as opposed to simply letting in punk and **new wave** kids—while also catering to underground celebrities such as painter Jean-Michel Basquiat and **Lydia Lunch**. In 1980 John Rockwell observed in the *New York Times* that "this club's small size and elitist attitude make it the rock equivalent of Studio 54, at least insofar as despairing crowds left standing on the street are concerned." Today the club is long gone, although there is a plaque at the building, commemorating a memorable historical nexus for in New York nightlife.

BRENDAN MULLEN

A Scottish immigrant and Los Angeles resident, Brendan Mullen played a major role in the early L.A. scene with his legendary underground club the **Masque**, which served as a centerpiece of the scene during its short lifespan (1977–79). After the Masque shut down, Mullen worked as a promoter, booking some of the era's greatest punk groups, from **Sonic Youth** and the **Butthole Surfers** to **Lydia Lunch** and the first L.A. performances by the **Replacements**. Later, seeing the new hip-hop scene as exciting as early punk, Mullen booked some of L.A.'s first hip-hop shows. (Legend has it that at one early South Bronx-style hip-hop show, an underage Dr. Dre was in the crowd.) Mullen later co-wrote the definitive account of the L.A. scene in his 2001 book *We Got the Neutron Bomb* (named after a famous song by local punks the **Weirdos**) with coauthor Marc Spitz. In 2008, he followed it up with *Live at the Masque: Nightmare in Punk Alley*, a 300-page photo album of the club's "golden years."

"This ain't no Mudd Club / or CBGB / I ain't got time for that," now."

—Talking Heads,
"Life During Wartime"

Unnamed couple at the Mudd Club, 1980.

Mudd Club 1979: Victoria Geldis and writer-musician Lance Loud

MURPHY'S LAW
1983-present

LINEUP: Jimmy Drescher, aka "Jimmy Gestapo" (vocals); Alex Morris (guitar, replaced by many); Pete Martinez (bass, replaced by many); Petey Hines (drums replaced by many)

This New York **hardcore** band, fronted by "Jimmy Gestapo" (Jimmy Drescher), were at the height of their popularity during the late-1980s scene but never seemed to stop touring. Murphy's Law released their first, self-titled album in 1986 and then went on a tour with the Beastie Boys, exposing New York hardcore to mainstream audiences across the United States. Murphy's Law was different than many on the NYHC scene of the early-to-mid-1980s; unlike bands such as **Youth of Today**, they were certainly not **straight edge**, nor did they project the air of menace that bands like the **Cro-Mags** did. Despite his name, Jimmy Gestapo sang about partying, having a good time, and hanging with his fellow punks on the scene, and what could be wrong with that? Although certainly a **pit** at a Murphy's Law show was no less dangerous than that of any other New York hardcore band at that time. (Murphy's Law, however, did possess a sense of humor their contemporaries mostly lacked, as in songs like "Crucial Bar-B-Q" or "Cavity Creeps," where the band resolutely chanted "We Make Holes in Teeth!") Problems with their record label and internal band conflict hurt Murphy's Law's chances for success, and the band went through several lineup changes until only longtime scene stalwart Jimmy Gestapo remained.

Discography:

Murphy's Law (Rock Hotel/Profile, 1986); *Back with a Bong!* (Profile, 1989, 1992); *The Best of Times* (Relativity, 1991); *Murphy's Law/Back with a Bong!* (Another Planet, 1994); *Good for Now* EP (We Bite, 1995); *Dedicated* (Another Planet, 1996); *The Party's Over* (Artemis, 2001); *Beatles Karaoke* (Castle/Pulse, 2002); *Covered* (NYHC Tattoo Records, 2005)

Murphy's Law plays the final hardcore matinee at CBGB, October 8, 2006.

NAKED RAYGUN

1981–1991, 2006–present

LINEUP: Jeff Pezzati (vocals); Santiago Durango (guitar, replaced by John Haggerty, Bill Stephens); Marko Pezzati (bass, replaced by Camilo Gonzalez, Pierre Kezdy); Eric Spicer (drums)

A Chicago band who cared little for punk's rules, Naked Raygun was a cross between **post-punk** and **hardcore** (original guitarist Santiago Durango and singer Jeff Pezzati were also members of Chicago noise-rockers **Big Black**), with acknowledged influences from **Gang of Four** and **Mission of Burma**. In their sporadic career they made some of the most intense music of the Midwest scene. With their tight rhythmic approach, hardcore ferocity, occasionally metallic guitar edge, and unique pop sensibility, Naked Raygun stood out in a scene dominated by bands such as the **Effigies** who were much more straightforward with their music. Relentless touring and the loss of all original members except for singer Jeff Pezzati put a strain on the band, causing them to quit for the first time in 1991, despite critical acclaim and a loyal fanbase. Guitarist John Haggerty later formed the successful Pegboy in the 1990s, and Pezzati played for a time with the Bomb in the late '90s. Naked Raygun re-formed for the 2006 Riot Fest in Chicago, and toured afterward, a welcome comeback for a band who was never really recognized for their genius the first time around.

Discography:

Basement Screams (Ruthless, 1983; Quarterstick/Touch and Go, 1999); *Throb Throb* (Homestead, 1985; Quarterstick/Touch and Go, 1999); *All Rise* (Homestead, 1985; Quarterstick/Touch and Go, 1999); *Jettison* (Caroline, 1988; Quarterstick/Touch and Go, 1999); *Understand?* (Caroline, 1989; Quarterstick/Touch and Go, 1999); *Raygun...Naked Raygun* (Caroline, 1990; Quarterstick/Touch and Go, 1999). **Pegboy:** *Three-Chord Monte* EP (Quarterstick/Touch and Go, 1990); *Strong Reaction* (Quarterstick/Touch and Go, 1991); *Fore* (Quarterstick/Touch and Go, 1993); *Earwig* (Quarterstick/Touch and Go, 1994). **The Bomb:** *Torch Songs* (Jettison Music, 2001); *Indecision* (Thick, 2005)

NAPALM DEATH

1982–present

LINEUP: Lee Dorrian (vocals, replaced by Mark "Barney" Greenway); Justin Broadrick (guitar, replaced by Mitch Harris); Bill Steer (guitar, replaced by Jesse Pintado); Jim Whitely (bass, replaced by Shane Embury); Mick Harris (drums, replaced by Danny Herrera)

Begun in Birmingham, England, Napalm Death's brand of heavy metal (or grindcore, or noisecore, or speedcore; it is hard to categorize) was initially influenced by the speed of thrash and **hardcore**, but was taken to extremes in which songs became mere blurs of sound. Although the band's songs were often accompanied by copious lyrics—often fairly well-constructed bits about vegetarian issues or animal rights—the vocals often came out sounding like prolonged screams of agony. Napalm Death's trends toward the metal side of the equation, the band's strong anti-war and animal rights viewpoints illustrate their punk point of view. The records *Scum* and *The Peel Sessions* highlight the band at their early best, before they slowed down to a more conventional style after weathering repeated personnel changes, leading ultimately to a band with no original members. One of Napalm Death's key members, drummer Mick Harris, went on to more experimental music, most notably the acclaimed **dub** group Scorn, and he also collaborated with avant-jazz artists such as John Zorn and former Faith No More singer Mike Patton.

Discography:

Scum (Earache, 1987); *From Enslavement to Obliteration* (Earache, 1988); *Napalm Death* EP (Rise Above, 1989); *Mentally Murdered* EP (Earache, 1989); *The Peel Sessions* (Strange Fruit/Dutch East India Trading, 1989); *Harmony Corruption* (Earache/Combat, 1990); *Suffer the Children* EP (Earache, 1990); *Mass Appeal Madness* EP (Earache/Relativity, 1991); *Death by Manipulation* (Earache/Relativity, 1992); *Utopia Banished* (Earache/Relativity, 1992; Earache, 1996); *The World Keeps Turning* EP (Earache, 1992); *Nazi Punks Fuck Off* (Earache, 1993); *Fear, Emptiness, Despair* (Earache/Columbia, 1994); *Greed Killing* EP (Earache, 1996); *Diatribes* (Earache, 1996); *Inside the Torn Apart* (Earache, 1997); *Bootlegged in Japan* (live; Earache, 1998); *Leaders Not Followers* EP (Relapse, 1999); *The Complete Radio One Sessions* (BBC/Fuel 2000/Varèse Sarabande, 2000); *Enemy of the Music Business* (Spitfire, 2001); *Order of the Leech* (Spitfire, 2002); *Leaders Not Followers: Part 2* (Century Media, 2004); *The Code is Red...Long Live the Code* (Century Media, 2005); *Smear Campaign* (Century Media, 2006)

Napalm Death asks,
"What's in your future?"

> # "Punk ain't no religious cult
> # Punk means thinking for yourself
> # You ain't hardcore 'cause you spike your hair
> # When a jock still lives inside your head"
> —Dead Kennedys, "Nazi Punks Fuck Off!"

Neo-Nazi skinhead rests up, 2001.

THE NECROS

1979–1989

LINEUP: Barry Henssler (vocals); Andy Wendler (guitar); Corey Rusk (bass, replaced by Ron Sakowski); Todd Swalla (drums)

The Necros were a straightforward **hardcore** band, hailing from Maumee, Ohio, who veered into heavy metal in the mid-1980s. While the Necros never quite became hair-metal sellouts, they nonetheless attempted to expand the limited palette to which hardcore had confined itself for several years, suggesting that sometimes a slower tempo or the addition of a solo were not acts of heresy. Original bassist Corey Rusk was replaced by Ron Sakowski in 1983 after Rusk broke his leg. Rusk later become proprietor of the **Touch and Go** label and got entangled in an acrimonious fight with the band over their early Touch and Go material. Despite their lack of national attention, the Necros were an influential band (counting **Sonic Youth** as longtime fans) who are probably more popular today, due to reissues, than during their heyday.

Discography:
Necros EP (Dischord/Touch and Go, 1981); *Conquest for Death* (Touch and Go, 1983); *Tangled Up* (Restless, 1987); *Live or Else* (Medusa, 1989); *Tangled Up/Live or Else* (live; Restless, 2005). **Necros/White Flag:** *Jail Jello* EP (Gasatanka, 1986).

NAZI PUNKS

The American version of England's **National Front** was an extremely loose and disorganized agglomeration of **skinheads** and their allies in the Aryan Nation and White Brotherhood, generically referred to as "Nazi punks," who occasionally participated in riots inside and outside shows and periodically attacked or taunted minorities and gays in the scene. Some of the more daring ones boldly displayed their swastika tattoos in public, as a brazen challenge to anyone who wanted to pick a fight with a gang of angry skins by challenging this provocation. New York and Los Angeles seemed to have particularly large contingents of racist punks in the early-1980s, inspiring the **Dead Kennedys** to write their anthem "Nazi Punks Fuck Off!" (later covered by **Napalm Death**). The movement mostly faded during the 1990s, though the growth of the Internet allows it to continue in diminished form to this day. Even though few punks now (openly) identify themselves with racist or Nazi movements, some skinheads (especially in the South) are still allied with various white-power movements and can be identified by buttons and other paraphernalia that celebrate either the Aryan Nation or white power.

> # "Punk ain't no religious cult
> # Punk means thinking for yourself
> # You ain't hardcore 'cause you spike your hair
> # When a jock still lives inside your head"

—Dead Kennedys, "Nazi Punks Fuck Off!"

Neo-Nazi skinhead rests up, 2001.

THE NECROS

1979-1989

LINEUP: Barry Henssler (vocals); Andy Wendler (guitar); Corey Rusk (bass, replaced by Ron Sakowski); Todd Swalla (drums)

The Necros were a straightforward **hardcore** band, hailing from Maumee, Ohio, who veered into heavy metal in the mid-1980s. While the Necros never quite became hair-metal sellouts, they nonetheless attempted to expand the limited palette to which hardcore had confined itself for several years, suggesting that sometimes a slower tempo or the addition of a solo were not acts of heresy. Original bassist Corey Rusk was replaced by Ron Sakowski in 1983 after Rusk broke his leg. Rusk later become proprietor of the **Touch and Go** label and got entangled in an acrimonious fight with the band over their early Touch and Go material. Despite their lack of national attention, the Necros were an influential band (counting **Sonic Youth** as longtime fans) who are probably more popular today, due to reissues, than during their heyday.

Discography:

Necros EP (Dischord/Touch and Go, 1981); *Conquest for Death* (Touch and Go, 1983); *Tangled Up* (Restless, 1987); *Live or Else* (Medusa, 1989); *Tangled Up/Live or Else* (live; Restless, 2005). **Necros/White Flag:** *Jail Jello* EP (Gasatanka, 1986).

NAZI PUNKS

The American version of England's **National Front** was an extremely loose and disorganized agglomeration of **skinheads** and their allies in the Aryan Nation and White Brotherhood, generically referred to as "Nazi punks," who occasionally participated in riots inside and outside shows and periodically attacked or taunted minorities and gays in the scene. Some of the more daring ones boldly displayed their swastika tattoos in public, as a brazen challenge to anyone who wanted to pick a fight with a gang of angry skins by challenging this provocation. New York and Los Angeles seemed to have particularly large contingents of racist punks in the early-1980s, inspiring the **Dead Kennedys** to write their anthem "Nazi Punks Fuck Off!" (later covered by **Napalm Death**). The movement mostly faded during the 1990s, though the growth of the Internet allows it to continue in diminished form to this day. Even though few punks now (openly) identify themselves with racist or Nazi movements, some skinheads (especially in the South) are still allied with various white-power movements and can be identified by buttons and other paraphernalia that celebrate either the Aryan Nation or white power.

SKANK-O-ZINE HARDCORE FOR CENTRAL PA. #5

FROM OHIO AT LONG LAST TOUCH AND GO RECORDING ARTISTS

NECROS

NECROS

$5

WITH: THE OUTRAGE
3 D.C. MEDIA DISEASE
BANDS UNDERGROUND SOLDIER
PENN. STATE
AND SPECIAL GUESTS: WASTED TALENT
AND THE DAY I LOST MY VIRGINITY

ALL AGES SHOW

7:30
LIL JO'S
7430 DERRY ST.
HARRISBURG, PA.

MAKE PLANS NOW FOR WEDNESDAY

SEPT. 7TH

NO BOOZE PLEASE

NEGATIVE APPROACH

1981-1985, 2006-present

LINEUP: John Brannon (vocals); Rob McCulloch (guitar, replaced by Harold Richardson); Graham McCulloch (bass, replaced by Ron Sakowski); Chris "O.P." Moore (drums)

The Detroit-based Negative Approach was a key component in the first wave of aggressive, American **hardcore** bands in the early-1980s, and one of the only groups to come out of the Midwest. While their roots were in hometown music like the **Stooges**, Negative Approach was also heavily influenced by California skate bands, hardcore outfits like the **Necros** and **Black Flag**, and British **oi** bands like Blitz and the **4Skins**. The band had one of the more relentless live shows around, and although they were impressively aggressive on record, the live material captures their spirit of confrontation better than any of their singles or studio records. After Negative Approach's 1985 demise, singer John Brannon formed the band Laughing Hyenas. In 2006 the band (with original singer John Brannon and drummer Chris Moore) reunited for the 25th anniversary **Touch and Go** show, and have toured subsequently.

Discography:
Tied Down (Touch and Go, 1983, 1988, 1991); *Live Your Life for You* (bootleg; no label, 1992); *Total Recall* (live; Touch and Go, 1992, 1994); *Ready to Fight, Demos Live and Unreleased 1981–83* (Reptilian, 2005)

> "Any Negative Approach show was a testosterone cocktail in a dirty glass."
> —Tesco Vee

NEGATIVE FX

1982

LINEUP: Jack "Choke" Kelly (vocals); Patrick Raftery (guitar); Rich Collins (bass); Bass Brown (drums)

Even though they only played a handful of shows during their very short but intense lifespan (possibly six, although some die-hard fans contend there were seven, but one may have been a rehearsal confused with an actual show), **Negative FX** made a huge impact on the Boston **hardcore** scene in their time. By all accounts, the band played as hard, fast, and loud as was humanly possible, putting as much sheer aggression into their short bursts of noise/songs as possible. Although the lyrics were actually pretty good, you naturally couldn't make them out under the layers of noise, which may be why during a coveted slot opening for **Mission of Burma**, the band had the plug pulled after one song, leading to a near riot. Not surprisingly, Negative FX was a focal point for the Boston crew of militant **straight-edge** types. Negative FX leader and scenester Jack "Choke" Kelly, later formed the bands Last Rites and **Slapshot**, and unsurprisingly kept the whole militant straight-edge thing going long past its expiration date.

Discography:
Negative FX (Taang!, 1984)

NERF HERDER

1994-2003, 2005-present

LINEUP: Parry Gripp (vocals/guitar); Dave Ehrlich (guitar); Charlie Dennis (bass, replaced by Pete Newbury, Marko 72, Justin Fischer, Ben Pringle); Steve "the Cougar" Sherlock (drums)

This melodic nerd-punk band from Santa Barbara, California—who took their name, appropriately enough, from an insult Princess Leia hurled at a Han Solo in *The Empire Strikes Back*—made songs for the ironic geek faction of punks who began to make their presence known in the 1990s. Nerf Herder's catchy hooks and pop-culture references made them the ideal choice for providing the intro music to the TV show *Buffy the Vampire Slayer*. Second guitarist Dave Ehrlich was added to beef up the band's sound in 1998. They briefly disbanded in 2003, during which time singer/guitarist Parry Gripp found time to knock out a 51-song solo album called *For Those About to Shop, We Salute You*, supposedly inspired by an offer to write a jingle for frozen waffles. Nerf Herder's refusal to take themselves seriously (writing an entire song critically evaluating the recorded output of Van Halen, or apologizing to a girlfriend with the lyric, "I'm sorry I crashed through your window on acid...") mark them as one of the few bands to realize that punk can occasionally be fun?

Discography:
Nerf Herder (My Records, 1995; Arista, 1996); *Foil Wrapped for Freshness* (self-release, 1995); *How to Meet Girls* (Honest Don's, 2000); *High-Voltage Christmas Rock* (self-release, 2000); *My* EP (My Records, 2001; Honest Don's, 2003); *American Cheese* (Honest Don's, 2002); *Nerf Herder IV* (Oglio, 2008)

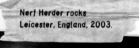

Nerf Herder rocks Leicester, England, 2003.

NEUROSIS

1985-present

LINEUP: Scott Kelly (vocals/guitar); Steve Von Till (vocals/guitar); Dave Edwardson (bass); Jason Roeder (drums); Noah Landis (keyboards, replaced by Simon McIlroy); Adam G. Kendall (visual media, replaced by Pete Inc.)

California **hardcore** band Neurosis turned dark metal/industrial group by adding doomful and atmospheric keyboards, crunchy guitars, and manic tom-tom drumming (sounding as though several drummers are playing simultaneously). Neurosis is one of the few bands who followed the hardcore-to-metal trajectory not to make a few bucks, but in order to actually expand themselves musically. Harsh, moody, and not for the faint of heart.

Discography:

Pain of Mind (Alternative Tentacles, 1988); *The Word as Law* (Lookout!, 1990); *Souls at Zero* (Virus, 1992); *Enemy of the Sun* (Alternative Tentacles, 1994); *Through Silver in Blood* (Relapse, 1996); *Times of Grace* (Relapse, 1999); *A Sun that Never Sets* (Relapse, 2001); *Live in Lyons* (Howling Bull, 2002); *Live in Stockholm* (Neurot, 2003); *Neurosis and Jarboe* (Neurot, 2003); *The Eye of Every Storm* (Neurot, 2004); *Given to the Rising* (Neurot, 2007)

NEW BOMB TURKS

1994-1999, occasionally thereafter

LINEUP: Eric Davidson (vocals); Jim "Motherfucker" Weber (guitar); Matt Reber (bass); Sam Brown (drums)

Named for a character in the little-seen and hardly remembered 1980 comedy *The Hollywood Knights*, the New Bomb Turks are a Columbus, Ohio, outfit who've been proudly flying the punk flag off and on since the 1990s. Known for their fast-paced sound, off-kilter humor, and particularly ferocious energy, the band plays a combination of garage rock and punk that's equally inspired by the former's monster riffs as it is by the latter's manic energy. New Bomb Turks were inexplicably overlooked in the massive, major label sweep of the punk underground in the early-1990s, but would have sold about eight gazillion records had they gotten any radio play. *Scared Straight* is probably their best record, but even the last official release *The Night Before the Day the*

Earth Stood Still shows the band still cranking out sheer garage brilliance.

Discography:

So Cool, So Clean, So Sparkling Clear EP (Datapanik, 1992); *!!Destroy-Oh-Boy!!* (Crypt, 1993); *Drunk on Cock* EP (Engine, 1993); *Information Highway Revisited* (Crypt, 1994); *Pissing Out the Poison* (Crypt, 1995); *Scared Straight* (Epitaph, 1996); *At Rope's End* (Epitaph, 1998); *The Blind Run* EP (Epitaph, 2000); *Nightmare Scenario* (Epitaph, 2000); *The Big Combo* (Dropkick, 2001); *The Night Before the Day the Earth Stood Still* (Gearhead, 2002)

NEW WAVE

The much-derided term *new wave* was not so much a genuine musical movement as it was an attempt by the music industry to try and repackage punk in a more friendly way for an American audience who never really embraced any of the first wave of punk bands. Even after the music industry had moved on from its brief flicker of interest in punk (not being satisfied with record sales in the thousands as opposed to the hundreds of thousands or millions), they were faced with a plethora of traditionally unclassifiable and critically beloved, but low-selling new music that could be marketed in a less threatening way than punk.

Wanting to avoid punk's stigma, Sire Records' Seymour Stein (who signed everyone from the **Ramones** to Madonna) openly campaigned in the late-1970s for the label *new wave*, which he thought would be more accessible to a general public. Originally the term was used to describe bands out of the **CBGB** scene who seemed more quirky than they were abrasive—such as **Blondie**, **Devo**, the **Talking Heads**, or underground pop acts like the Police and Elvis Costello. But by the 1980s, new wave had become the more commonly understood catchall description for all the radio-friendly, synthesizer-driven bands like Flock of Seagulls and Culture Club who meshed New Romantic baroque costumes with disco's danceability. (Purists would argue this was all hardly new wave; in fact, *New York Rocker*'s September 1978 issue was largely devoted to discussing whether or not new wave was already dead.) It wasn't long before most punk music and early, artier new wave, was marginalized, with desperate record labels encouraging punk acts on their roster to put out more danceable, radio-friendly singles. Soon,

New wave superheroes Blondie, 1980.

bands as disparate as the **Clash** and New Order could be heard on the same radio stations and at the same dance clubs.

Ultimately, the term *new wave* did more than anything else to sink the chance for commercial change that punk had seemed to promise. The huge success enjoyed by bands later marketed as new wave—Blondie is one example—helped convince many punks by the early-1980s that the movement was dead. The atten-

dant rise of **hardcore** in the U.S. and the UK during this same time period was at least partially a backlash against the compromises many once-underground bands made to gain radio play and be considered new wave. Although some in the scene embraced new wave, there were just as many who found it (at least the later, industry-friendly version) to be nothing more than a dilution of punk's revolutionary promise.

The New York Dolls'
David Johansen (left)
and Johnny Thunders
perfect their back-to-
back rock stance.

THE NEW YORK DOLLS

1971-1977, 2004-present

LINEUP: David Johansen (vocals); John Genzale, aka "Johnny Thunders" (guitar); Rick Rivets (guitar, replaced by Sylvain Sylvain); Arthur "Killer" Kane (bass); Billy Murcia (drums, replaced by Jerry Nolan)

One of the last missing links between punk, glam, and 1960s garage rock, the New York Dolls were nothing short of a rock 'n' roll legend during their early-1970s heyday, but their influence had greater, far-reaching consequences that continue to reverberate today. Formed in 1971 out of a band named Actress, the Dolls were a good-looking group of boys influenced equally by Mick Jagger's swagger and sneer, **Iggy Pop**'s theatrics, 1960s girl groups, and...drugs, lots of drugs.

The Dolls debuted in March 1972, quickly making a name for themselves playing around New York wherever they could get a gig, including gay bath houses. But they gained real notoriety when they established a residency at the Mercer Arts Center in the Oscar Wilde Room, where they performed alongside bands such as **Suicide**. Later graduating to playing **Max's Kansas City**, the Dolls began to draw a crowd of celebrities, including **Lou Reed** and **David Bowie** (who had been known to wear a dress or two in his time), and finally were signed to a management contract by Marty Thau.

Seeking to drum up interest in the band, the Dolls undertook a tour of England in 1972, opening for Rod Stewart and the Faces at a Wembley Pool concert, where a young Glen Matlock (later of the **Sex Pistols**) was inspired by the Dolls to start dreaming of his own musical future. The Dolls drew a following, but tragedy struck that November in London when original drummer Billy Murcia overdosed on barbiturates and was placed in a bathtub to recover, whereupon he promptly drowned. The Dolls returned to New York discouraged, but after a few weeks Murcia was replaced by former gang member Jerry Nolan. With Nolan in the band, the Dolls tightened up musically and signed a deal with Mercury Records.

The New York Dolls' self-titled, Todd Rundgren-produced debut album was released in 1973 to little commercial success but international critical acclaim, catching the notice of a young **Malcolm McLaren**. After their follow-up album, the all-too-aptly named *Too Much Too Soon* (produced by girl-group producer George "Shadow" Morton), failed to make a dent on the charts in 1974, Mercury dropped the band. The Dolls attempted to keep going, but Nolan's and Thunders's growing addictions to heroin, and bassist Arthur Kane's drinking problem, complicated the band's woes. In an attempt to change their image, the Dolls decided to sign up with McLaren, who did a complete makeover, first clothing the band in red leather outfits and placing a huge Communist hammer-and-sickle flag behind them, and then taking them on a disastrous tour of Florida, where they were chased by locals unimpressed by their sartorial splendor. Nolan and Thunders then left the band, and, despite guitarist Sylvain Sylvain's and Johansen's best attempts (including firing McLaren, who'd replicate his genius for sensationalistic branding and poorly planned tours

with the Sex Pistols), the Dolls definitively fell apart by 1977.

After the collapse, Nolan and Thunders put together the **Heartbreakers** with **Richard Hell** and guitarist Walter Lure. David Johansen went on to a solo career of some success (with Sylvain as his guitarist for a time), scoring several chart hits during the 1980s after transforming himself into the sperplexingly popular Buster Poindexter lounge-lizard caricature, before returning to his blues roots and touring with the Harry Smiths. Thunders died of drug-related causes in New Orleans in 1991. Kane, meanwhile, converted to Mormonism and struggled with addiction and poverty, as related in Greg Whiteley's 2005 documentary *New York Doll*. Johansen, Sylvain, and Kane brought the band back together in 2004 for a series of concerts, though Kane would die of leukemia halfway through.

The New York Dolls' legacy of hard-rocking androgyny can be felt throughout punk, **post-punk**, and heavy metal. In fact, it was one of their biggest fans, the Smiths' Morrissey (once president of a Dolls fan club), who convinced them to reunite in

2004. In 2006 the Dolls returned as if they had never left with *One Day It Will Please Us To Remember Even This*, featuring just Johansen, Sylvain, and a group of sidemen including former Hanoi Rocks bass player Sam Yaffa. *One Day* reveals a band of glam-rockers who had grown up but still looking for their next beer, their next frock, their next kiss. Older, but much wiser, the Dolls improbably returned to form over 30 years after their initial dissolution.

Discography:

New York Dolls (Mercury, 1973, 1977); *Too Much Too Soon* (Mercury, 1974; Mercury/Hip-O Select; 2005); *Lipstick Killers: The Mercer Street Sessions 1972* (tape, ROIR, 1981; CD, ROIR/Important, 1990; ROIR, 2000); *Red Patent Leather* (Fan Club, 1984); *Best of the New York Dolls* (Mercury, 1985); *Night of the Living Dolls* (Mercury, 1986); *Personality Crisis* EP (Kamera, 1986); *Morrissey Presents the Return of the New York Dolls Live From Royal Festival Hall*, 2004 (Attack/Sanctuary, 2004); *One Day It Will Please Us To Remember Even This* (Roadrunner, 2006). **David Johansen and Sylvain Sylvain:** *Tokyo Dolls Live!* (Fan Club, 1986). **The Original Pistols/New York Dolls:** *After the Storm* (Receiver, 1985)

NEW YORK ROCKER

Started in 1976 by Alan Betrock as a rival to **John Holmstrom**'s *Punk*, *New York Rocker* covered much of the same music, but without the unique cartoon style of *Punk*. For a time in the late-1970s, it, along with *Creem* and *Trouser Press*, showcased some of the best rock journalism in the U.S. *New York Rocker* covered the **CBGB** scene pretty extensively (putting **Television**, **Patti Smith**, and **Blondie** on the cover long before they appeared in the mainstream press) and featured writers and photographers Steven Meisel, Roberta Bailey, Duncan Hannah, and Lester Bangs. Publisher and editor Betrock left in late-1977, after which his successor, Andy Schwartz, expanded the magazine's scope to include (shockingly) bands from outside the Big Apple. Starting in 1979, Betrock put out music on the Shake Records label, including releases by **Richard Hell**, the DBs, and the Smithereens. After struggling financially, *New York Rocker* finally shut down for good in 1982, the same year that Betrock's critically lauded book, *Girl Groups: The Story of a Sound,* was published. Betrock died of cancer in April 2000.

NICO

Born Christa Päffgen in Cologne, Germany, in 1938, the ethereal beauty and husky-voiced Nico became a model while still a teenager, her name supposedly given to her by a photographer while on location in Ibiza, Spain. Nico first made her mark with a haunting cameo in Federico Fellini's 1960 classic film *La Dolce Vita* before becoming a Euro-supermodel with aspirations of becoming a pop singer (she released a little-heard, seven-inch single in 1965 that featured the Rolling Stones' Brian Jones and a pre-Led Zeppelin Jimmy Page).

In the mid-1960s, Nico made her way into Andy Warhol's inner circle, appearing in his film *Chelsea Girls*. She also joined an experimental band Warhol was managing called the **Velvet Underground**, who were part of a touring Warhol performance group, with dancers and a light show, called the Exploding Plastic Inevitable. Nico sang the vocals on three of the most memorable songs from the band's first album, *The Velvet Underground and Nico*: "All Tomorrow's Parties," Femme Fatale," and "I'll Be Your Mirror." Though her haunting, Ute Lemper-style drone gave the material a welcome note of vampiric Weimar decadence, **Lou Reed** soon tired of sharing the spotlight with another singer and she left the Velvet Underground in 1967.

After leaving the Velvet Underground, Nico began a career as a solo artist. Apparently, however, her departure from the Velvets wasn't as acrimonious as it appeared, as John Cale, Reed, and Sterling Morrison all showed up (along with her then-boyfriend Jackson Browne) to play on her first album, the almost universally acclaimed, 1968 atmospheric masterpiece *Chelsea Girl*, featuring songs written by Browne, Reed, Cale, and Bob Dylan. (Nico surrounded herself with talented collaborators, just as she accrued liaisons with enigmatic up-and-comers such as Browne, **Iggy Pop**, and actor Alain Delon, with whom she had a child.) Cale also worked with Nico on her next record, the equally influential but more minimalist **post-punk** precursor *The Marble Index*, which showcased Nico's songwriting. Her first two records and unique vocal stylings would, quite correctly, be cited

by critics years later as being predecessors of goth music and the drone-rock experiments of post-punk.

After *The Marble Index*, however, Nico's solo career entered a long, rocky period marred by her struggle with heroin addiction, as well as a more tepid response to her later work. She became a virtual recluse, rarely touring and recording only sporadically. She died in 1988 of a cerebral hemorrhage after falling from a bicycle in Ibiza.

Essential Discography:
Chelsea Girl (Verve, 1968); *The Marble Index* (Elektra, 1968); *Desertshore* (Reprise, 1970); *The End* (Island, 1974); *Drama of Exile* (Aura, 1981); *Live in Denmark* (VU, 1983); *Camera Obscura* (Beggar's Banquet, 1985, 1996); *Behind the Iron Curtain* (Dojo, 1986). **The Velvet Underground:** *The Velvet Underground and Nico* (Verve, 1967)

999 in London, late-1970s: (L to R) Pablo Labritain, Nick Cash, Guy Days, Jon Watson.

999

1976-present

LINEUP: Nick Cash (vocals); Guy Days (guitar); John Watson (bass, replaced by Arturo Bassick); Pablo Labritain (drums)

An unusually long-lived punk band from the UK first wave, who never quite made a name in the States, 999 flirted with **new wave** keyboards at various points, and with different names (the Fanatics, 48 Hours). Also, they auditioned nearly everyone in the scene at some point, from the Pretenders' Chrissie Hynde to **Generation X**'s Tony James (both of whom were also going through the revolving door of the pre-**Clash** band **London SS**). 999's first single, "I'm Alive," was released in 1977 on their own label, Labritain Records. On the strength of that single and their electrifying live shows (lead singer Nick Cash was a maniac onstage), the band was able to sign with United Artists, who put out their first two albums. Released in February 1978, *999*, was good enough to make the charts, but it was *Separates*, which came out later the same year, that featured the band's most popular song (and one of the most common inclusions on punk compilations), "Homicide," which later climbed up the UK Top 40 with no radio play. Other hits soon followed, such as the infectious "High Energy Plan." A 1979 tour of the U.S. was a disappointment, demonstrating 999's frustrating inability to crack the American market. The band's lineup remained relatively stable over the years, with drummer

Ed Case briefly replacing an injured Pablo Labritain and original bassist John Watson leaving to be replaced by Arturo Bassick (born Arthur Billingsley) of the **Lurkers**.

Discography:
999 (United Artists, 1978); *Separates* (United Artists, 1978); *High Energy Plan* (PVC, 1979); *The Biggest Prize in Sport* (Albion, 1979; Anagram, 1995); *The Biggest Tour in Sport* (Polydor, 1980); *Concrete* (Albion, 1981); *13th Floor Madness* (Albion, 1984); *Identity Parade* (Albion, 1984); *Face to Face* (Labritain, 1985); *In Case of Emergency* (Dojo, 1986); *Lust, Power and Money* (ABC, 1987); *Live and Loud!* (Link, 1989); *The Cellblock Tapes* (Link, 1990); *You Us It!* (Anagram Punk, 1993); *Live in L.A. 1991* (Triple X, 1994); *Scandal in the City* (Line, 1997); *Live at the Nashville* (Anagram, 1997, 2002); *Takeover* (Abstract, 1998); *Slam* (Overground, 1999); *English Wipeout: Live* (Overground, 1999)

THE NIPS

1977-1980

LINEUP: Shane MacGowan (vocals); Adrian Thrills (guitar); Roger Towndrow (guitar, replaced by Gavin "Fritz" Douglas, many others); Shanne Bradley, aka "Dragonella" (bass); Arcane Vendetta (drums, replaced by many)

While **Shane MacGowan** would later go on to much renown in the **Pogues**, in the mid-1970s he was just another happily pogo-ing punk kid and amateur, drunken Irish poet who fell in love with the **Sex Pistols** and decided he should start his own band. The Nips were less a straight-ahead punk band and more a bracing, punk-**rockabilly** combo that gave no indication of how radically and powerfully MacGowan would switch directions in later years. Although the Nips received some critical attention from their first couple of energetic singles, their original name of the Nipple Erectors caused a

wee bit of a problem, leading them to shorten it to the simpler (but probably no-less-offensive) Nips in 1978. The major labels never came calling but the Nips were nevertheless able to tour with everyone from the **Damned** to Dexy's Midnight Runners to the **Jam** (whose Paul Weller produced one of their singles). While the band's lineup would change with a baffling regularity over the few short years they were together, the core remained MacGowan and bassist Shanne Bradley, who later changed her name to "Dragonella" so that people would stop confusing her with MacGowan. The band was over by 1980, but MacGowan was already planning his next project, a little something called the Pogues that would cast such an enormous shadow that MacGowan's punk roots with the Nips were widely and shamefully forgotten.

Discography:
Only at the End of the Beginning (live; Soho, 1980); *Bops, Babes, Booze & Bovver* (Big Beat, 1987, 2000)

London, 1977: The Nips' Shane MacGowan teaches his mic who's boss.

NIRVANA

1987–1994

LINEUP: Kurt Cobain (vocals/guitar);
Krist Novoselic (bass); Pat Smear
(live guitar); Dave Grohl (drums)

To put it simply: Nirvana was the most popular and biggest-selling band ever associated even remotely with punk. Although many in the punk community discounted the band for breaking out of their original fanbase, Nirvana still kept true (or at least paid lip service) to punk ideals of authenticity and attitude, while producing music that was much closer to punk in sound and spirit than bands in the grunge wave like Soundgarden or Tad. Also, Nirvana (particularly lead singer and guitarist Kurt Cobain) went out of their way to use the visibility from their success to champion punk bands like the Vaselines, the **Raincoats**, the **Melvins**, and the **Meat Puppets**. It's possible to say that if

Nevermind had never broken through in 1991, helping bring Nirvana's fusion of heavy metal, punk, and underground into the mainstream, bands such as **Green Day** might never have made it to the majors.

Cobain was a confused, misanthropic delinquent from the small logging town of Aberdeen, Washington, who had been going to punk shows in Seattle and later playing in a band called Fecal Matter (with one of the members of the Melvins, his idols). In 1985 he met bassist Krist (Chris) Novoselic, who had a similar record collection and love of punk and early metal. Over the next few years, the musical duo of Cobain (originally as drummer) and Novoselic would constantly change styles, names (the Stiff Woodies and Skid Row being only a couple of the awful early choices), and drummers once it was decided Cobain should be singer and guitarist. With drummer Chad Channing on board, they began building a reputation

in the Pacific Northwest scene for their live shows. Nirvana's first single, "Love Buzz," was released on Sub Pop in 1988, followed by the band's first national tour and a brief period with a second guitarist, Jason Everman, who would later join Soundgarden.

Nirvana's first album, 1989's *Bleach*, was a milestone, because although it resembled some of the other records put out by other bands within the embryonic grunge scene of the time (such as the Melvins and Green River), it showed Nirvana busily perfecting their twisted combination of Black Sabbath sludge-metal, **Black Flag**, and cynical lyrics that not only helped set the musical template for the 1990s but also demonstrated to many punks that they did not have to reject every band that was on a major label. Due to the success of Nirvana's touring and the steady airplay *Bleach* was getting on college radio, when in 1990 the band started shopping around a slick, six-

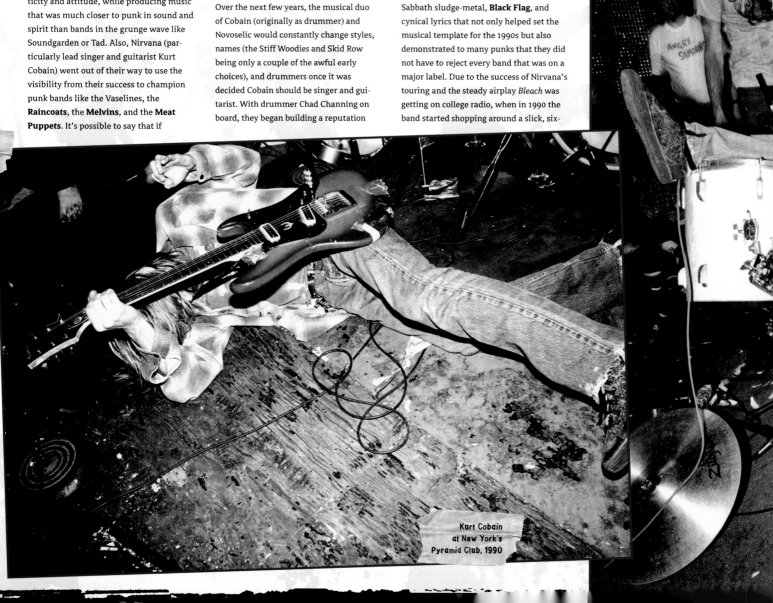

Kurt Cobain
at New York's
Pyramid Club, 1990

NIRVANA

"BLEACH"

song demo produced by Butch Vig, it led to a glut of major labels (who could sense that hair metal was running its course) starting a bidding war. DGC Records (reputedly on the advice of **Sonic Youth**, who had toured with Nirvana and tried to mentor the younger band) signed them just as Channing was replaced on drums by Dave Grohl, previously of the Washington, D.C., punk band Scream. Nirvana's major-label debut, *Nevermind*, was released in the summer of 1991, and although Nirvana (especially Cobain) was not entirely happy with its overly polished sound, by the end of the year the album was selling hundreds of thousands of copies every week—in large part thanks to **MTV**'s constant rotation of the video for the single "Smells Like Teen Spirit." This all led to *Nevermind* going multiplatinum and starting a rush on flannel shirts and Converse Chuck Taylor sneakers.

Naturally, with success came scrutiny, and Nirvana made good copy for the rock press, as well as the mainstream news media, confused by the success of this new, almost uncategorizable band's success. In particular, there was media frenzy surrounding Cobain's relationship with his new headline-grabbing wife Courtney Love (who had a cameo in the punk-themed film *Sid and Nancy*, appeared along with **Shane MacGowan** and the **Clash**'s **Joe Strummer** in *Straight to Hell*, and helped to form the Minneapolis pseudo-**Riot Grrrl** group Babes in Toyland), with rumors persisting about their heroin abuse.

The band's ambivalence about their newfound fame began to show during this period, such as when they were featured on the cover of *Rolling Stone* in January 1992 with Cobain wearing a homemade T-shirt that read, "Corporate Magazines Still Suck" (playing off **SST**'s "Corporate Rock Still Sucks" slogan).

In 1993, Nirvana released their third and final studio album. *In Utero* was simultaneously a return to form and a look forward, with a sound that was both more raw and powerful than *Nevermind* but with a cleaner, less-radio friendly sound, courtesy of engineer **Steve Albini**. On that year's tour, Nirvana added Pat Smear of the **Germs** as a second guitarist (Smear would later play in Grohl's post-Nirvana pop-rock band the Foo Fighters). Near the end of the year, Nirvana performed a stunning and unexpectedly moving acoustic set on MTV's show *Unplugged*, covering songs by the Vaselines, Leadbelly, **David Bowie**, and several by the Meat Puppets (with the Kirkwood brothers sitting in for three songs); the live recording was released in April 2004. That same month, after several previous attempts, Cobain committed suicide at his home in Seattle; he was 27 years old. His troubled lyrics, contradictory attitude toward fame, and early death ensured that Cobain would be immortalized in the public's mind as a doomed romantic poet, unable to stand the slings and arrows of outrageous fortune.

Although the following years haven't been kind to the band's memory, with swirling conspiracy theories about Cobain's death (see Nick Broomfield's 1998 documentary *Kurt & Courtney* for one of the more sensational ones), and ugly battles over the band's recorded legacy with Love on one side and Grohl and Novoselic on the other. Whether read as a musical success story marred by personal tragedy, or a sad example of the dangers facing underground musicians who get signed to a major label, Nirvana will long be remembered as one of the only punk-oriented bands to ever cross over into the mainstream.

Discography:

Blew EP (Sub Pop/Glitterhouse, 1989); *Bleach* (Sub Pop, 1989, 1992); *Sliver* EP (Sub Pop, 1990); *Nevermind* (Sub Pop/DGC, 1991); *Hormoaning* EP (DGC, 1992); *Incesticide* (Sub Pop/DGC, 1992); *In Utero* (Sub Pop/DGC, 1993); *MTV Unplugged in New York* (DGC, 1994); *Singles* (Geffen, 1995); *From the Muddy Banks of the Wishkah* (DGC, 1996)

No For An Answer at Berkeley's Gilman Street.

NO FOR AN ANSWER

mid-1980S-1990

LINEUP: Dan O'Mahony (vocals); Gavin Oglesby (guitar); John Mastropaolo (bass, replaced by Sterling Wilson); Casey Jones (drums, replaced by Chris Bratton)

One of the first West Coast **straight-edge** bands, No For An Answer was formed by lead vocalist Dan O'Mahony, who had been inspired by **7 Seconds** and **Minor Threat** to form a that would promote antichemical and pro-youth messages. O'Mahony later formed the progressive **hardcore** band 411 and published the books *Three Legged Race* and *Four Letter World*, both dealing with his years in the hardcore and straight-edge movements. While many considered the straight-edge hardcore scene to be an East Coast phenomenon confined to Washington, D.C., New York, and Boston, No For An Answer showed that the movement's positive message could be brought to the jaded, hedonistic scenes of Orange County as well. Lead singer Dan O'Mahony was also one of the most articulate and straightforward interview subjects of the 1980s hardcore scene.

Discography:
You Laugh (Revelation, 1988, 1997); *A Thought Crusade* (Roadrunner, 1989)

NOFX

1983-present

LINEUP: "Fat Mike" Burkett (vocals/bass); Eric Melvin (guitar); Aaron Abeyta, aka "El Hefe" (guitar/trumpet); Erik Sandin (drums, replaced briefly by Scott Sellers)

NOFX—a play on **Negative FX**—started out as a Berkeley, California-based power trio led on bass and vocals by "Fat Mike" Burkett, who also runs the very successful indie punk label **Fat Wreck Chords** with his wife, Erin. They played their first gig at the **Cathay de Grande** in Hollywood. In 1986, the band experimented briefly with a new lead singer, Dave Allen (he later died in a car crash). More fruitfully, they added a second guitarist (Dave Casillas, who was replaced by Steve Kidwiller for the band's first album, *S&M Airlines*). The lineup stabilized with the addition of guitarist and horn player El Hefe (Aaron Abeyta), who was a major reason for the band's incorporation of **ska**, **reggae**, and **dub** into their often humorous songs.

Later relocating to Los Angeles, NOFX became one of the most successful punk bands of the 1990s, touring successfully on their own and on the **Vans Warped** tour. Their records on Epitaph continued to sell well, and the 1994 album *Punk in Drublic* was certified gold in the U.S., a rarity for a punk album. During the 2004 elections,

NOFX surprised many by bringing politics to the forefront of their message and founding Punkvoter.com. Despite the members' often cheerfully tasteless humor, NOFX has remained one of the most consistent bands in underground music for more than two decades.

Discography:
Liberal Animation (Fat Wreck Chords, 1988; Epitaph, 1991); *S&M Airlines* (Epitaph, 1989); *Ribbed* (Epitaph, 1991, 1993); *The Longest Line* EP (Fat Wreck Chords, 1992); *Maximum Rocknroll* (Mystic, 1992); *White Trash, Two Heebs and a Bean* (Epitaph, 1992); *Don't Call Me White* EP (Fat Wreck Chords, 1992); *Punk in Drublic* (Epitaph, 1994); *I Heard They Suck Live* (Fat Wreck Chords, 1995); *Heavy Petting Zoo* (Epitaph, 1996); *Eating Lamb* (Epitaph, 1996); *HOFX* EP (Fat Wreck Chords, 1996); *So Long and Thanks for All the Shoes* (Epitaph, 1997); *Pump Up the Valuum* (Epitaph, 2000); *The Decline* EP (Fat Wreck Chords, 2000); *45 or 46 Songs That Weren't Good Enough to Go on Our Other Records* (Fat Wreck Chords, 2002); *War on Errorism* (Fat Wreck Chords, 2003); *The Greatest Songs Ever Written (By Us)* (Epitaph, 2004); *Wolves in Wolves' Clothing* (Fat Wreck Chords, 2006); *They've Actually Gotten Worse Live!* (Fat Wreck Chords, 2007)

NOFX in San Francisco, 2002. (L to R) El Hefe, Fat Mike, Eric Melvin.

NOMEANSNO

1979-present

LINEUP: Rob Wright (vocals/bass); Andy Kerr (guitar, replaced by Tom Holliston); John Wright (drums/keyboards)

These veteran musicians from Vancouver, British Columbia, dabble in a variety of styles and rely more on noise, progressive rock, and free jazz than traditional punk bombast. In many cases they more closely resemble New York loft jazz, or later-period Miles Davis (the band once covered part of *Bitches Brew*) via early Hawkwind, than four-on-the-floor punk. But because of a special dispensation developed by the Canadian government (who actually *subsidize* their nation's punk bands to tour) NOmeansno have been officially deemed more punk than the **Sex Pistols**. The Wright brothers—Rob on vocals and bass, John on drums and keyboards—also play in the **Ramones**-esque band the Hanson Brothers. According to NOmeansno's website, former guitarist and vocalist Andy Kerr suffered for quite some time with a serious addiction to crossword puzzles, which is thankfully now under control.

Discography:

Mama (Wrong, 1984); *Sex Mad* (Psyche Industry, 1987); *Small Parts Isolated and Destroyed* (Virus, 1988); *Wrong* (Alternative Tentacles, 1989); *0+2=1* (Virus, 1991); *Live & Cuddly* (Virus, 1991); *You Kill Me* (Alternative Tentacles, 1991); *Why Do They Call Me Mr. Happy?* (Alternative Tentacles, 1993); *Mr. Right & Mr. Wrong* (Wrong, 1994); *The Worldhood of the World (As Such)* (Alternative Tentacles, 1995); *Dance of the Headless Bourgeoisie* (Alternative Tentacles, 1988); *No One* (Alternative Tentacles, 2000); *Generic Shame* (Wrong, 2001); *All Roads Lead to Ausfahrt* (AntAcidAudio, 2006)

NO TREND

1982-1988

LINEUP: Jeff Menteges (vocals); Dean Evangelista (guitar, replaced by Buck Parr, Frank Price); Robert "Smokeman" Marymont (bass, replaced by Jack Anderson); James Peachey (drums); Eric Leifert (saxophone, replaced by Brian Nelson)

A caustic, quasi-**hardcore** band formed in Ashton, Maryland, who played extensively in the Washington, D.C., punk scene, No Trend was known for attacking movements such as the local **straight-edge** scene with a subversive wit that went against the punk political orthodoxy of the time. No Trend was generally anti any kind of movement, particularly the

The grey-haired eminences of NOmeansno at London's Underworld, 2007.

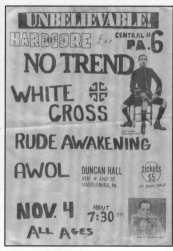

UNBELIEVABLE!
HARDCORE for CENTRAL #6 PA.
NO TREND
WHITE CROSS
RUDE AWAKENING
AWOL   DUNCAN HALL
        2981 N. 2ND ST.
        HARRISBURG, PA.
tickets $5
AT DOOR ONLY
NOV. 4 ABOUT 7:30 PM
ALL AGES

behavioral and dress codes that D.C. straight-
edgers had taken to their extremes, and used
to post flyers reading "No Trend, No Scene,
No Movement." Bassist Jack Anderson was
once quoted as saying that the band "taunted
punk rockers, who were essentially conform-
ists within their own scene." Both in music
and temperament, the provocateurs in No
Trend—who wore ludicrous outfits and
incorporated everything from funk and
new wave to lounge and **ska** into their
riotous sound, even having **no wave** star
Lydia Lunch sing on their song "A Dozen
Red Roses," had much more in common
with jokey noisemakers **Butthole Surfers**
and **Flipper** than they did with D.C. bands
like **Minor Threat**. Although No Trend was
quite successful for a time, the band could
only keep it going for so long. (Their last
album, the long-unreleased *More*, featured
an 18-minute song, "No Hopus Opus" that
included a 40-piece orchestra and plenty of
free jazz.) After tremendous turnover and
a half-dozen years of disturbing the peace,
they decided to call it quits in 1988. While
not well-remembered today, No Trend was
nevertheless important for demonstrating
that not all hardcore bands were as hidebound by tradition as some would have
wanted them to be.

Discography:

Teen Love EP (No Trend, 1983); *Too Many Humans*
(No Trend, 1984); *A Dozen Dead Roses* (No Trend, 1985);
Heart of Darkness EP (Widowspeak, 1985); *When
Death Won't Solve Your Problems* (Widowspeak, 1986);
Tritonian Nash—Vegas Polyester Complex (Touch and
Go, 1986); *More* (described as their "lost" album;
unknown label, 2001)

NO USE FOR A NAME

1987-present

LINEUP: Tony Sly (vocals/guitar); Chris Dodge (guitar, replaced by Chris Shiflett, Dave Nassie, others); Steve Papoutsis (bass, replaced by Matt Riddle, others); Rory Koff (drums)

A pop-**hardcore** band from California's San Jose skate scene, No Use For A Name has a revolving lineup centered around the founding core of singer/guitarist Tony Sly and drummer Rory Koff. Other members over the years have included bassist Matt Riddle, formerly of **Face to Face**, guitarist Chris Shiflett (who went on to join the Foo Fighters), and guitarist Dave Nassie, previously with **Suicidal Tendencies** and the dance-punk band Infectious Grooves. No Use For A Name play a contagious style of melodic hardcore that is reminiscent of **Bad Religion** and **NOFX**. (The latter band's "Fat Mike" runs the **Fat Wreck Chords** label on which NUFAN records.) In 2005 the band played the main stage on the **Vans Warped** tour, one of the surest signs of modern punk success. While NUFAN is one of the poppiest West Coast punk bands, no one could accuse them of selling out—they have sounded the same since the late-1980s.

Discography:

No Use for a Name EP (Woodpecker, 1989); *Let 'Em Out* EP (Slap a Ham, 1990); *Incognito* (New Red Archives, 1990); *Don't Miss the Train* (New Red Archives, 1992); *The Daily Grind* (Fat Wreck Chords, 1993); *¡Leche Con Carne!* (Fat Wreck Chords, 1995); *Making Friends* (Fat Wreck Chords, 1997); *More Betterness!* (Fat Wreck Chords, 1999); *The NRA Years* (Golf, 2000); *Live in a Dive* (Fat Wreck Chords, 2001); *Hard Rock Bottom* (Fat Wreck Chords, 2002); *Keep Them Confused* (Fat Wreck Chords, 2005); *All the Best Songs* (Fat Wreck Chords, 2007); *The Feel Good Record of the Year* (Fat Wreck Chords, 2008)

No Use For A Name, 2005: Tony Sly (left), Rory Koff.

No wave champions Lydia Lunch (left) and James Chance at Max's Kansas City, 1978.

NO WAVE

As music critics and early punks began to abandon the slowly dying original New York punk scene, many became alarmed by the corporate-sounding and keyboard-driven rhythms of **new wave**. Sure, the punks loved to dance but not necessarily to what was being marketed as *new wave* or the glittering decadence that was the New York disco scene. As new arrivals on the scene began to look for a space to experiment while keeping punk's energy alive, a new musical movement began to appear in the performance spaces of downtown Manhattan. The founders of this often atonal and abrasive form of punk were soon lumped under the anti-catch phrase, *no wave*. A series of formative shows at the Artists' Space in Soho and at other locations in 1978 included performances by Teenage Jesus and the Jerks (with **Lydia Lunch**), James Chance, DNA, and the Theoretical Girls (with avant-garde guitarist Glenn Branca). After those shows, musician and producer Brian Eno, always on the lookout for something that challenged the dominant dogma of popular music, persuaded several of the bands to perform on the definitive anthology album *No New York*, which came out later that year

on Island's Antilles label. Other important no wave artists included Jim Thirlwell (later of the various Foetus projects), **Suicide** (who predated the no wave movement by at least a decade, but were lumped into it for their terrifying performances and refusal to be melodic), and the Swans, all of whom are featured in the 2004 documentary *Kill Your Idols*.

No wave was in some sense a reaction to the failed, revolutionary promise of punk's early, free-form, "anything goes" attitude, but it was also an artistic movement in its own right. Seeking to merge the avant-jazz freedom of composition with a full-on assault on their audiences, the chief no wave bands tended to produce a shrieking wall of dissonant noise meant to challenge the expectations of uptown "tourists" still hoping to see some spiky-haired clowns playing **Ramones**-type riffs. No wave was, by its nature, abrasive and experimental, and many of its proponents were known for their aggressive stage performances and challenges to the audience. Some artists, such as James Chance, would sometimes physically, as well as verbally, abuse those who had come to see the band perform. Others, like Lydia Lunch, no wave's dark queen, engaged in "performance art" (based on her troubled childhood and

problems with her family) that challenged the audience's expectations of not only what a performance was, but of where the performer ended and the audience began.

No wave was more or less over by 1982, though Lunch would go on to a long-lasting solo career, as did Glenn Branca, who carved out a niche as a well-respected, avant-garde, minimalist composer. The most famous progeny of the scene, however, would be Thurston Moore and Lee Ranaldo, whose pivotal art-punk band **Sonic Youth** adapted

the techniques learned at Branca's side to figuratively detune punk rock to its most pleasantly atonal core, and then reinvent it for a new generation of younger punks, eager for both ferocity and jazz-like innovation.

THE NUNS
1976-present

LINEUP: Jennifer Miro (vocals); Alejandro Escovedo (guitar); Delphine Neid (bass)

An early, female-led, U.S. punk group from San Francisco, the Nuns were fronted by platinum-blonde chanteuse Jennifer Miro and indie guitarist Alejandro Escovedo (supposedly he first put the group together to play "the worst band in the world" for a student film he was shooting). The Nuns had a dissonant and abrasive sound similar to **no wave**, but by the time they put out their first album in 1980, they had become quite proficient at their own unique style. The Nuns cemented their status in legend when they opened for the **Sex Pistols** at the Pistols' last concert ever, in 1978 at San Francisco's Winterland. Although they were one of the key, early Bay Area punk bands, the Nuns broke up in the mid-1980s, after which Escovedo formed Rank and File with Chip and Tony Kinman, formerly of the **Dils**. They have reformed intermittently in later years for more goth-tinged albums that play up Miro's vampiric chanteuse side.

Discography:
The Nuns (Posh Boy/Bomp!, 1980);
Rumania (PVC, 1986)

The Nuns, circa late-1970s.

THE OFFSPRING

1987–present

LINEUP: Bryan "Dexter" Holland (vocals); Kevin "Noodles" Wasserman (guitar); Greg "K" Kriesel (bass); Ron Welty (drums, replaced by Adam Willard, Pete Parada)

One of the most successful punk bands of the 1990s, the Offspring were formed in the late-'80s in California's Orange County after a pair of high school cross-country teammates tried to form a band called Manic Subsidal following a **Social Distortion** show. The band later formed into its current incarnation (including guitarist "Noodles," the school custodian), and named themselves the Offspring in 1986, going on to play numerous shows with many of the period's key punk groups. The Offspring self-released a single in 1987, and put out their self-titled, debut album on Nemesis in 1989, later signing to indie label **Epitaph**.

Already known for their energetic concerts, the Offspring were perfectly ready and willing to capitalize on the surprise success in 1994 of the "Come Out and Play (Keep 'em Separated)" single off the album *Smash*—in heavy rotation on the radio and **MTV** for months. *Smash* eventually sold some 11 million copies, setting a record for an indie release and establishing Epitaph as a "major" punk label. Strangely, the Offspring then left Epitaph a couple years later for Columbia, a move that seriously alienated many of their fans. While none of the Offspring's subsequent major label albums achieved the success of *Smash*, the band has continued to play and record with an enviable regularity, encouraging up-and-coming bands through their label Nitro. Lead singer Bryan "Dexter" Holland joins the exclusive club of punk lead singers with Ph.D.s (which also includes Milo Aukerman of the **Descendents** and Greg Graffin of **Bad Religion**).

Essential Discography:
The Offspring (Nemesis, 1989; Nitro, 1990); *Baghdad* EP (Nemesis, 1990); *Ignition* (Epitaph, 1992); *Smash* (Epitaph, 1994); *Ixnay on the Hombre* (Columbia, 1997); *Americana* (Columbia, 1998); *Conspiracy of One* (Columbia, 2000); *Splinter* (Columbia, 2003); *Greatest Hits* (Columbia, 2005)

The Offspring in
Melbourne, 2001.

Oi-boys the Angelic Upstarts.

"We stand for punk as bootboy music. Oi! is working-class, and if you're not working-class you'll get a kick in the bollocks."

—Stinky Turner, the Cockney Rejects

OI

A term generally attributed to music critic Gary Bushell, *oi* is a British movement originating in the late-1970s that mixed **skinhead**, street punk, and working-class music and culture. The original bands lumped into the oi scene included **Slaughter and the Dogs**, the **Cockney Rejects**, the **Angelic Upstarts**, **Skrewdriver**, and, most importantly, **Sham 69**. All of the key oi bands use anthemic, sing-along choruses that were probably derived from the chants heard at

English football games (including the chant "Oi! Oi! Oi!" or some variation of the word *oi*), with large contingents of working-class fans. Although the movement did include a fair number of skinheads in the early years, early oi was not inherently racist. By the early-1980s, however, oi bands like Skrewdriver were openly identifying themselves as racist and allied with the **National Front**, and some members of the oi scene also identified with, or at least did not condemn, the racist elements within the punk, skinhead, and oi movements.

A second generation of primarily skinhead oi bands formed in the early-1980s and included the Business, **4Skins**, Combat 84, and others. The movement spread throughout the world, including the United States, and although it was never as popular outside of England, numerous bands from the early years and more contemporary bands such as the Templars keep the spirit of oi alive (not to mention the numerous compilations like *Strength Thru Oi!*, *Oi! The Album*, and *Addicted to Oi!*, all released on—what else?—Captain Oi! Records

It remains to be seen if oi music will ultimately be more associated with the racist followers, who were some of its biggest proponents, or the majority (who likely skew to the right of the political spectrum) who appreciated catchy music and a sense of unity. Oi certainly did indicate that a large section of working-class fans needed music that dealt with everyday working-class life, not just songs about rebellion and anarchy.

100 CLUB

LOCATION: LONDON

Although it later became a punk landmark, London's 100 Club was originally a restaurant that began hosting jazz performances during World War II. In the postwar years, the club booked mainstream acts such as Rod Stewart, the Who, and B.B. King, but by the 1970s business was waning. Things took a turn on the nights of September 20 and 21, 1976, when the old jazz haunt became the site of the 100 Club Punk Festival, where **Subway Sect** and **Siouxsie and the Banshees** made their debuts. The more established bands that played in the festival included the **Clash,** the **Damned,** French punk band Stinky Toys, the **Vibrators** with guest guitarist Chris Spedding, the **Buzzcocks**, and, most notably, the **Sex Pistols**. This was also the night when Sex Pistols fan and future bassist **Sid Vicious** (he was drumming for the Banshees at the time) allegedly threw a glass into the crowd, causing a mini-riot, and later that evening attacked journalist **Nick Kent** with a chain. Although bands like the **Exploited** and **Discharge** would later play the 100 Club, the violence at the 1976 Punk Festival led to most punk bands being banned from the club thereafter; **Alternative TV** was the last punk band to play there in April 1978 before the club's demise as a rock venue. In the mid-1990s the 100 Club played host to alternative bands such as Suede and Cornershop, as well as a number of world music performers.

John Lydon at the 100 Club, 1976.

ZINES

Even though *zines*—the term is a contraction of "fanzines," itself a shortening of "fan magazines," produced for and circulated by science-fiction fans for decades—predate the punk movement and have been around in some form or another for at least 50 years, they became extremely popular during the early days of punk as a noncorporate way for punks to communicate with one another and the outsider community. As some of the last examples of the underground press (which in the United States flourished during the 1960s and early-'70s, only to have most of the publications ultimately go out of business or be bought up by a number of "alt-weekly" chains in the new millennium), zines usually have no financial backing and are produced by small groups of individuals, or occasionally just one person, to a set of criteria determined not by ad sales but instead by what the editor(s) deem worth writing about.

The quintessential zine "look" was established pretty early on in the punk days and it generally involved the taping down of ribbons of roughly typed text over some sort of image (usually borrowed from the public domain, some comic strip, or movie still) and photocopying it hundreds of times as quick as possible late-night at Kinko's. Later, the pages would be stapled together and the whole rough-and-ready publication shipped off to a few lucky subscribers or the generous bookstores and record stores that had available space for zines. Zines were also frequently given out during shows or sold from small stands (along with seven-inch singles and pins), or occasionally swapped or traded. Although most started out as on-the-fly, pirate publications, a number of zines evolved into many different forms and looks, with a number approaching a level of graphic sophistication and professionalism of mainstream magazines.

Early British and European punk zines included Mark Perry's *Sniffin' Glue*, *Bondage* (created by **Shane MacGowan** of the **Pogues**), as well as *Ripped and Torn* from Glasgow, and *I Wanna Be Your Dog* from Paris. Key American zines from the early days include **John Holmstrom** and **Legs McNeil**'s seminal *Punk*, as well as Greg Shaw's *Who Put the Bomp* (later shortened to just *Bomp!*). Punk's mid-period produced a flurry of important and long-lived zines, including *Maximum RocknRoll*, *Flipside*, *Punk Planet*, and *Profane Existence*. The number of zines made by these collectives must number in the thousands, though most have never been collected or cataloged, despite the best efforts of *Factsheet 5* and others who try to cover the world of alternative publishing. In 1990 *Factsheet 5* founder Mike Gunderloy wrote in the *Whole Earth Catalog* (a sort of hippie zine precursor) that since the late-1970s he had collected some 10,000 zines, which he estimated was only about 10 percent of all American zines (this number may now be suspect as the number of low-budget zines since then has grown exponentially). There are major collections of zines kept at the State University of New York at Albany, Duke University, and the **ABC No Rio** collective in New York.

Although many of the zines published over the last three decades have been dedicated to punk rock or music within the larger context of popular culture (like *Go Metric*, *Chunklet*, and *Law of Inertia*), not all zines are specifically about music. Some zines chronicle local movements or the artistic endeavors of a local community, while many others espouse a particular political agenda. There are **queercore** zines, such as *Slander* (which offers a queer Asian-American perspective on punk), zines devoted to vegans, radical politics, anti-corporate behavior, or even, in the case of *Chin Music* and *Zisk*, sports (albeit from a punk rock perspective).

One very popular subgenre is the category of personal or autobiographical zines, which inspired and sometimes evolved into the current vogue for blogs (which require no postage or clever, copy-theft stratagems), most notably Aaron Elliott's idiosyncratic, handwritten travelogue *Cometbus*. Other zines are more closely

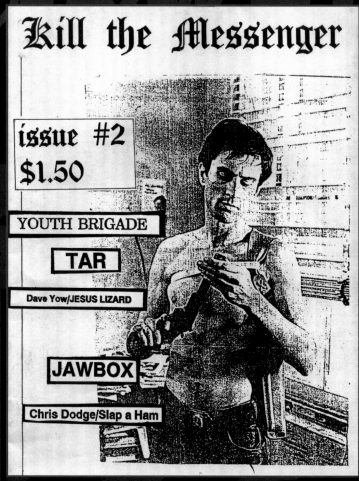

Kill the Messenger

issue #2
$1.50

YOUTH BRIGADE

TAR

Dave Yow/JESUS LIZARD

JAWBOX

Chris Dodge/Slap a Ham

related to comic books as more and more cheap graphic design and photo programs are available, which enable artists to more fully express their vision in zine format. An excellent example of a comic collection is Ben Snakepit's *Snakepit* strip, which chronicles in three panels his adventures (or lack thereof) of the day.

While some zines are supported by advertising and others by sales, the vast majority (even the ones with copious advertising) rarely make any kind of profit and are supported simply by the wallet of the zine editor, sometimes supplemented by the resale of review CDs sent by record companies. Financially insolvent, with limited readerships and no business plans, zines are one of the clearest manifestations and continuing examples of the DIY movement in action, existing only at the whim of their creators and audience. With the advent of new technology and website hosting, many zines have either migrated onto the Internet or at least have an online presence; this has led many to question the future of paperbound zines. But the Internet just does not have the "feel" that many old punks have come to covet in zines, nor does the Internet allow one to collect or trade zines. Like it or not, in the quasi-anarchist world of punk, ownership is as important as ever, with some zine collectors as rabid about their collections as comic book fans. But whether produced online or on paper, zines will continue as long as independent publishing exists.

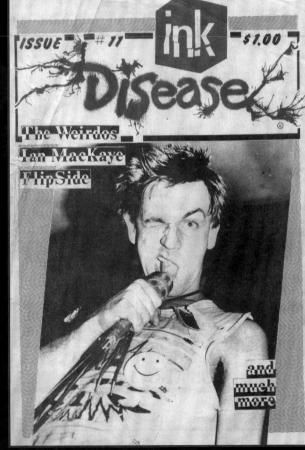

THE 101'ERS

1974–1976

LINEUP: Joe "Woody" Strummer (vocals/guitar); Clive Timperley (guitar); "Desperate" Dan Kelleher (bass/keyboards); Richard Dudanski (drums); Simon "Big John" Cassell (alto sax); Alvaro Peña-Rojas (tenor sax)

The 101'ers were quintessential London pub-rockers who would go down in history as the starting point for their singer, future **Clash** leader **Joe Strummer**. The 101'ers played a combination of covers, original R & B-influenced material, and some future Clash songs in their embryonic forms. The band formed in September 1974 and took the name from a squat at 101 Walterton Road in north-west London, where several of its members then lived. One of their most popular songs, the finger-snapping "Keys to Your Heart," was apparently inspired by Strummer's relationship with Paloma Romero, who'd soon become better known as Palmolive of the **Slits**.

The 101'ers were quite popular during the pub-rock scene of the mid-1970s but once punk rock grew in popularity and the **Sex Pistols** arrived on the scene (they were frequently in the crowd for the 101'ers and opened for them at least once), pub rock was rendered as redundant as art or prog rock. In 1976, Strummer left the 101'ers and joined the embryonic version of the Clash. A long-awaited CD version of the 101'ers' session was finally released in 2005 after years of only poor-quality bootlegs available to the general market. It includes 21 tracks of originals and alternative mixes as well as rare live and studio material, personally supervised by drummer Richard Dudanski with the cooperation of Strummer's widow. Dudanski later played with the **Raincoats** and **Public Image Ltd.**

Discography:
Elgin Avenue Breakdown Revisited (Astralwerks, 2005)

THE ONLY ONES

1976–1981

LINEUP: Peter Perrett (vocals/guitar); John Perry (guitar); Alan Mair (bass); Mike Kellie (drums)

A poppy band lumped in with the early punks for commonality of style as opposed to ideological or sociological reasons, the Only Ones knocked out a couple of fantastic singles like "Lovers of Today" and "Another Girl, Another Planet," which would be covered by multiple bands over the next several decades. The Only Ones dissolved after three studio records in 1981. After that, Singer Peter Perrett recorded sporadically after that, occasionally as "the One," but to little success. In 1989, an album of demos from Perrett's early 1970s pseudo-**Velvet Underground** band England's Glory were released. The band was enormously influential on the indie rock scene, particularly on the work of Paul Westerberg and the **Replacements** (whose killer cover of "Another Girl, Another Planet" became one of their most popular tunes).

Discography:
The Only Ones (CBS, 1978); *Even Serpents Shine* (CBS, 1978); *Special View* (Epic, 1979); *Baby's Got a Gun* (Epic, 1980); *Remains* (Closer, 1984); *Alone in the Night* (Dojo, 1986); *Live* (Skyclad, 1989); *The Peel Sessions Album* (Strange Fruit, 1989). **England's Glory:** *Legendary Lost Recordings* (Skyclad, 1989). **The One:** *Woke Up Sticky* (Demon, 1996)

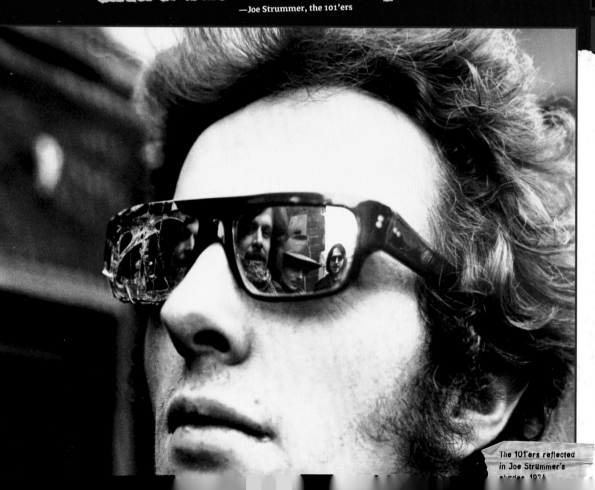

"We were the latecomers, more like the dirty cousins, because we were squat-rockers and a bit younger and a bit more incapable."
—Joe Strummer, the 101'ers

The 101'ers reflected in Joe Strummer's shades, 1974

Operation Ivy's Jesse Michaels (Left) jumps off the drum kit while Matt Freeman plays on in Davis, California, 1987.

OPERATION IVY

1987-1989

LINEUP: Jesse Michaels (vocals); Tim Armstrong (guitar); Matt Freeman (bass); Dave Mello (drums)

One of the best examples of a band who were far more influential after their demise than during their lifetime, Operation Ivy was the vanguard of the new **ska** revival in the United States, which followed their brief run during the late-1980s. During their heyday in the Berkeley, California, scene, Operation Ivy was extraordinarily popular for their powerful sense of authenticity and their anthems of punk integrity.

Operation Ivy often played at **Gilman Street** in Berkeley, where their themes of unity against the outside world struck a responsive chord with the local punk community, as did the sheer emotive power of their playing. The members of **Green Day** were huge fans of Operation Ivy during this period, later covering the song "Knowledge," both live and on *1,039/Smoothed Out Slappy Hours.* Although Operation Ivy had only one official full-length album—a later CD rerelease would add the eight-song EP *Hectic* and a couple of songs from compilations. They were little known outside Berkeley during their existence, but their one release is a punk-ska masterpiece, and they are now widely acknowledged as being one of the most influential bands of the late-1980s. Guitarist Tim Armstrong and bassist Matt Freeman went on to form the far more successful **Rancid** several years after the demise of Operation Ivy.

Discography:
Hectic EP (Lookout!, 1988); *Energy* (Lookout!, 1989)

THE OUTCASTS

1977-1985

LINEUP: Greg Cowan (vocals/bass); Martin Cowan (guitar); Colin "Getty" Getgood (guitar); Gordy Blair (bass); Colin Cowan (drums); Raymond Falls (second drums)

Despite its relative isolation (and very real dangers of simply walking down the wrong street), the Belfast scene was one of the most vibrant and aggressive within the borders of the United Kingdom during the late-1970s. One of the bands who best reflected that scene's particular desperation and black sense of humor were the Outcasts, who were legendarily banned from five different pubs in the period of one week. Astutely noticing that Northern Ireland did not have much of a scene, the Outcasts decided to create one of their own, along with similar minded bands such as **Stiff Little Fingers** and the Defects, opening for acts like the **Clash** and the **Radiators from Space**. Early singles such as "Teenage Rebel" got the band airplay on the **John Peel** show. The Outcasts then took advantage of their resulting fame to draw even larger crowds of brawling hooligans to their shows and, in a punk first, added a second drummer to their already thunderous live sound. Drummer Colin Cowan's death in a 1981 car crash ended that phase of the band, which then changed directions in a mishmash of **hardcore** and psychobilly styles. The Outcasts finally called it quits in 1985, victims of the decline of commercial airplay for punk in the UK. Never a very political band, the Outcasts demonstrated punk's ability to serve as a release from the very real horrors of growing up in a war zone.

Discography:
Self Conscious Over You (Good Vibrations, 1979; Captain Oi!, 2004)

OUTPUNK RECORDS

LOCATION: SAN FRANCISCO

An independent U.S. record label specializing in **queercore** bands, Outpunk Records was started by zine publisher and onetime *Maximum RocknRoll* staffer Matt Wobensmith, who also wrote a zine called *Outpunk.* The label started off by releasing the influential compilations *There's a Faggot in the Pit* and *There's a Dyke in the Pit.* Between 1992 and 1997, Outpunk released music by prominent queer, or queer-friendly, bands such as **Bikini Kill**, **Tribe 8**, Swine King, and **Pansy Division**. Wobensmith ended Outpunk in the late-1990s and started the short-lived Queercorps label before going on to found the queer hip-hop label A.C.R.O.N.Y.M. Records.

There's a DYKE in the Pit

featuring **Bikini Kill**   **Tribe 8**
Lucy Stoners   **7 Year Bitch**

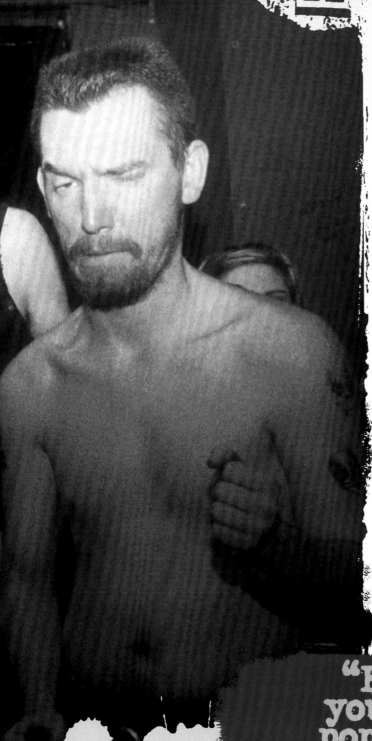

Pansy Division, 1998.

THE PAGANS
1977–1979, occasional reunions

LINEUP: Mike Hudson (vocals/bass); Mike "Tommy Gunn" Metoff (guitar); Tim Allee (bass); Brian Hudson (drums)

Cleveland punks the Pagans started out in 1974 as the Mad Staggers and later Venus in Furs, playing **Velvet Underground** and **New York Dolls** covers. They evolved into their Pagans lineup by 1977, becoming bona fide members of the late-1970s U.S. punk wave, even though they never quite received due credit. The Pagans fell apart a couple of years later, in the midst of recording an album, due to various financial and drug-fueled problems. Although the band never quite managed to record a proper album during their brief existence, they did release numerous singles (later collected, along with what studio work existed, on a of couple posthumous CDs). Among the most memorable was the romantic ballad, "What's This Shit Called Love," later covered in a particularly moving version, by those quintessential romantics the **Meatmen**. The 2001 CD *Shit Street* contains a number of live recordings, including a couple that feature fellow Ohio punks Cheetah Chrome and Jimmy Zero from the **Dead Boys**. The band reunited a handful of times in recent years with a shifting lineup for live shows, including a performance at Cleveland's Rock 'n' Roll Hall of Fame in 2005. Following the death of his brother Brian in 1991, Mike Hudson spent six years recording a highly personal solo record, *Mike Hudson Unmedicated*. Hudson's memoir, *Diary of a Punk*, chock-full of Pagans history, was published in March 2008.

Discography:
Buried Alive (Treehouse, 1986); *Shit Street* (Crypt, 2001); *The Pink Album* (Crypt, 2001). **Mike Hudson:** *Mike Hudson Unmedicated* (Sonic Swirl, 2006)

PANSY DIVISION
1991–present

LINEUP: Jon Ginoli (vocals/guitar); Patrick Goodwin (guitar, replaced by Joel Reader); Chris Freeman (bass); Dustin Donaldson (drums, replaced by Luis Illades)

A central and founding band of the **queercore** movement, Pansy Division sound like the **Ramones** but sing about the joys of sodomy, oral sex, and young, fem boys. They started out as a trio, but added a second guitarist later on. Pansy Division first appeared on the *Outpunk Dance Party* compilation, and between 1993 and 1998 released albums annually on **Lookout! Records** for six years. The band also released a record of mostly covers that included the **Nirvana** parody "Smells Like Queer Spirit." In 1994, **Green Day** asked Pansy Division to open for them on their *Dookie* arena tour, throwing a monkey wrench at a mainstream audience expecting *straight* songs about masturbation. Pansy Division has also made their own, albeit somewhat tongue-in-cheek, attempts at a breakthrough, recruiting Metallica's Kirk Hammett as a guest star for a solo on the song "Headbanger" and collaborating with Rob Halford of Judas Priest for a cover of "Breaking the Law" at a gay pride event.

Discography:
Smells Like Queer Spirit EP (Lookout!, 1992); *Undressed* (Lookout, 1993); *Deflowered* (Lookout!, 1994); *Pileup* (Lookout!, 1995); *Wish I'd Taken Pictures* (Lookout!, 1996); *More Lovin' From Our Oven* (Lookout!, 1997); *Absurd Pop Song Romance* (Lookout!, 1998); *Total Entertainment!* (Alternative Tentacles, 2003); *The Essential Pansy Division* (Alternative Tentacles, 2006)

> "By 1990, it seemed like you could do anything in popular music but be gay. It seemed like the last taboo."
>
> —Pansy Division's Jon Ginoli

THE PARTISANS

1978–1985, 1999–present

LINEUP: Rob "Spike" Harrington (vocals);
Andy Lealand (guitar); Louise Wright (bass,
replaced by Dave Parsons, others);
Mark "Shark" Harris (drums)

A second-wave punk band from the wonderful world of Wales, the Partisans got tossed in with the **oi** boys after music critic Gary Bushell included them on the 1981 *Carry On Oi!* compilation. While the Partisans were never really part of the oi scene—particularly once violence started getting out of control due to fans of rival British football clubs instigating fights—they soon joined the anarcho-punk movement, opening for **Conflict** to reaffirm their street cred. Eventually the band began to slow down their sound in the early-1980s as they tried to make sense of the new British music scene. But despite becoming more melodic while retaining their punk edge, the Partisans ran out of steam and called it quits in 1985. They were in limbo until 1999, when Harrington and Lealand got back together for reunion gigs, which continued sporadically thereafter. Parsons eventually joined Transvision Vamp and later signed up with Brit-grunge band Bush.

Discography:
The Partisans (No Future, 1983); *The Time Was Right* (Cloak and Dagger, 1984); *Police Story* (Anagram Punk, 2000); *Idiot Nation* (Dr. Strange, 2004)

JOHN PEEL

The single most influential advocate for new and emerging bands in British radio history, John Peel was born John Robert Parker Ravenscroft in Heswall, England, in 1939. Peel began his career spinning British Invasion records in America during the mid-1960s in Dallas, San Francisco, and Oklahoma City. In 1965, he moved back to the UK, briefly deejaying for a pirate radio station, and then starting a lengthy career at the BBC's Radio One. In the roughly four decades to follow, Peel recorded live performances of almost every major band of the punk, rock, **reggae**, hip-hop, and electronic music movements, creating a historical music database almost without equal. Despite his signature boast of being "the most boring man in Britain," he had

an uncanny sense of what the next exciting band or genre was going to be, and his instincts and taste led to the exposure of some vital and exciting bands.

John Peel's show aired on BBC Radio One until his death from a heart attack in October 2004 while vacation in Peru. Not long before his death, Peel interviewed the recently re-formed **Undertones**, who had written what he considered to be "the best song in the world," "Teenage Kicks." (Peel had often said he wanted the line "Teenage Kicks So Hard to Beat" inscribed on his tombstone.) Peel's legacy lives on today in the numerous volumes of *Peel Sessions*, recorded live during his radio program and popular as both bootlegs and legitimate releases. Some of these live sessions, such as the ones by **Siouxsie and the Banshees**, the Undertones, and **Napalm Death**, are in fact just as essential as anything in the artists' catalogs. For many early bands, including those without recording contracts, this was also a convenient way to release material and gain publicity.

Although some U.S. DJs (such as **Rodney Bingenheimer** in Los Angeles) had been sympathetic to punk rock, it was John Peel whose broad and eclectic tastes contributed more than any other radio personality in disseminating punk to a wider audience.

> "I've always imagined I'd die by driving into the back of a truck while trying to read the name on a cassette, and people would say, 'he would have wanted to go that way.' Well, I want them to know that I wouldn't."
> —John Peel

John Peel, 1968.

PENETRATION

1976–1979, 2002–present

LINEUP: Pauline Murray (vocals); Gary Chaplin (guitar, replaced by Neale Floyd); Fred Purser (guitar/keyboards); Robert Blamire (bass); Gary Smallman (drums)

A legendary, female-fronted punk band from Durham, England, Penetration were inspired by a **Sex Pistols** gig to form their own punk band (although they named themselves after a **Stooges** song). They soon became popular based on an opening set for **Generation X** in 1977, leading to a deal with Virgin Records and the "Don't Dictate" single. The band continued in their own idiosyncratic way for another two years before calling it quits in late 1979. (The band got back together in 2002 for the reunion circuit.) Penetration's legacy is relatively minor, despite their brilliant songwriting, and although Siouxsie Sioux arguably remains the most influential woman in punk, Pauline Murray more than gives her a run for her money.

Discography:
Moving Targets (Virgin, 1978, 1990); *Coming Up for Air* (Virgin, 1979); *Race Against Time* (Clifdayn, 1979)

PENNYWISE

1988–present

LINEUP: Jim Lindberg (vocals); Fletcher Dragge (guitar); Jason Thirsk (bass, replaced by Randy Bradbury); Byron McMackin (drums)

Hailing from Hermosa Beach, California, Pennywise has played ultra-fast, melodic punk for some two decades and remains one of the most popular **hardcore** bands on the scene today. Two years after the release of the EP *A Word from the Wise*, Pennywise released their self-titled debut album on **Epitaph** in 1991. On *Pennywise* the band finally distinguished themselves from the other punk bands crowding the Southern California scene at the time. Numerous other albums followed in the same dynamic and powerful formula, and the band's repu-tation grew as extensive touring created a large and diverse fanbase. Pennywise was courted heavily in the 1990s by major labels during the post-Green Day acquisition frenzy but decided they were better off sell-ing hundreds of thousands of records on Epitaph rather than being mismarketed, and eventually dropped, by a major label. Tragedy struck in 1996 with the suicide of longtime bassist Jason Thirsk, to whom the band paid tribute on the song "Bro Hymn Tribute" from the 1997 *Full Circle* album.

Discography:
A Word from the Wise EP (Theologian, 1989); *Pennywise* (Epitaph, 1991); *Wild Card* EP (Theologian, 1992); *Wild Card/A Word from the Wise* (Theologian, 1992); *Unknown Road* (Epitaph, 1993); *About Time* (Epitaph, 1995); *Full Circle* (Epitaph, 1997); *Straight Ahead* (Epitaph, 1999); *Live @ the Key Club* (Epitaph, 2000); *Land of the Free?* (Epitaph, 2001); *From the Ashes* (Epitaph, 2003); *The Fuse* (Epitaph, 2005); *Reason to Believe* (Epitaph, MySpace, 2008)

LEFT: Penetration's Pauline Murray at London's Roundhouse, 1978.

RIGHT: Jim Lindberg of Pennywise at New York's Irving Plaza, 2002.

PERE UBU

1975-present

LINEUP: Dave Thomas (vocals); Tom Herman (guitar); Tony Mamione (bass); Scott Krauss (drums); Allen Ravenstine (keyboards)

This enduring art-punk band from the fertile Cleveland scene has been led since the mid-1970s by singer Dave Thomas, who had formerly fronted the influential (but hardly prolific) **Rocket from the Tombs** with guitarist Peter Laughner. Thomas formed Pere Ubu as a self-described "avant garage" group in 1975 (naming the band after a character from the Alfred Jarry play *Ubu Roi*) following the demise of Rocket from the Tombs. Their original lineup included keyboard genius Allen Ravenstine and guitarist (and former steel worker) Tom Herman, who helped create the unique soundscapes that were Pere Ubu's signature.

In 1975, Pere Ubu released their first single (and one of the first independent punk singles), "30 Seconds Over Tokyo." Their popular though somewhat controversial single "Final Solution" followed in 1976. (That year also saw Laughner leave the band due to his problems with addiction; he died in 1977.) Pere Ubu's debut album, *The Modern Dance*, came out in 1978, with several equally adventurous releases following soon after, including *Dub Housing*. Pere Ubu's music remains almost uncategorizable to this day, and new albums can be infuriatingly spotty as well as challenging. In leading the artier wing of American punks, Pere Ubu may be one of the few bands who lived up to punk's promise of limitless creativity and experimentation. Pere Ubu's enigmatic lyrics also made for interesting listening, because (at times) they were written from the perspective of Thomas's lifelong devotion to the Jehovah's Witnesses. In 2003, Thomas re-formed Rocket from the Tombs with Cheetah Chrome and Richard Lloyd (from **Television**), for tours and an album. Even after too many personnel changes to keep track of, Pere Ubu still tours and records with Thomas and numerous new musicians.

Essential Discography:
The Modern Dance (Blank, 1978); *Datapanik in the Year Zero* EP (Atlantic, 1978); *Dub Housing* (Chrysalis, 1978); *U-Men Live at the Interstate Mall* (Tricity, 1979); *New Picnic Time* (Chrysalis, 1979)

"Pere Ubu is totally inconsequential and irrelevant. That is the power of Cleveland. Embrace, my brothers, the utter futility of ambition and desire. Your only reward is a genuine shot at being the best. The caveat is that no one but your brothers will ever know it."
—David Thomas

Pere Ubu in New York, 1988.

PETER AND THE TEST TUBE BABIES

1978-present

LINEUP: Peter Bywaters (vocals); Derek "Del" Greening (guitar); Chris "Trapper" Marchant (bass, numerous others); Nicholas "Ogs" Loizides (drums, numerous others)

English punks of surprisingly creative longevity, Peter and the Test Tube Babies were fronted by the so-called "first punk in Peacehaven," Peter Bywaters, and debuted on the *Vaultage 1978* compilation. The Test Tube Babies' oeuvre from the late-1970s includes the (unrecorded) classic that gave the **Sex Pistols** "God Save the Queen" a run for its money in terms of regal offensiveness: "The Queen Gives Blow Jobs." Thanks to their inclusion on the compilation *Oi! The Album*, the Test Tube Babies were lumped into the **oi** genre, leading to a **skinhead** following that the band hardly expected, or wanted. Nevertheless, their goofy antics and classic, comedic tunes (including "Banned from the Pubs") made them one of the more memorable bands on the scene.

Discography:
Pissed and Proud (No Future, 1982; Century Media, 1994); *Mating Sounds of South American Frogs* (Trapper, 1983; Dr. Strange, 1997; Dojo, 1999; Inandout, 1999); *Soberphobia* (Hairy Pie, 1986; Castle, 1994; Captain Oi!, 2002); *Peter and the Test Tube Babies* (Rock Hotel, 1991); *Shit Factory* (Rebel, 1990; Triple X, 1994; Goldar, 1999); *Loud Blaring Punk Rock* (Hairy Pie, 1994; Dr. Strange, 1997; Captain Oil, 2002); *Rotting in the Fart Sack* EP (We Bite, 1995); *Journey to the Centre of Johnny Clarke's Head* (Dr. Strange, 1997); *Test Tube Trash* (Dr. Strange, 1997); *Supermodels* (Dr. Strange, 1997); *Alien Pubduction* (Pub City Royal, 1998; Cargo, 2002); *Cringe* (Rebel, 1999); *Schweinlake* (We Bite, 1999); *The Punk Singles Collection* (Anagram Punk, 2000); *Best of Peter and the Test Tube Babies* (Anagram Punk, 2001); *Live and Loud* (Step-1, 2003)

RAYMOND PETTIBON

The graphic artist whose work would come to define the look and attitude of the 1980s' American **hardcore** scene, Raymond Pettibon was born Raymond Ginn in Tucson, Arizona, in 1957, and is the brother of **Black Flag** guitarist and **SST** founder **Greg Ginn**. As SST's house artist, his artwork became ubiquitous on albums and flyers for SST bands like Black Flag (for whom Pettibon designed a famous logo, and briefly played bass) and the **Minutemen**. Always challenging, a typical Pettibon cover was the album art of Black Flag's *Slip It In*, which featured a nun holding on to a muscular man's leg. Although a prolific designer of punk album covers, Pettibon was also a serious artist and later became disillusioned because most punks did not appreciate his work as art, but simply as something to slap onto the front of an album or copy onto a flyer. More recently, Pettibon designed the covers of **Mike Watt**'s solo album *Ball-Hog or Tugboat?* and **Sonic Youth**'s *Goo*. Today, Pettibon's work is shown in major galleries and museums across the United States including the Whitney Museum of American Art.

PINHEAD GUNPOWDER

1990-present

LINEUP: Billie Joe Armstrong (vocals/guitar); Mike Kirsch (guitar, replaced by Jason White); Bill Schneider (bass); Aaron Cometbus (drums)

Green Day's prolific songwriter Billie Joe Armstrong formed Pinhead Gunpowder with guitarist Mike Kirsch (from Fuel), and Crimpshrine drummer and *Cometbus* zine writer/publisher Aaron Cometbus. The side project started originally as a goof, with the band members rehearsing at House-O-Toast, the Berkeley, California, hangout where Aaron lived. Pinhead Gunpowder played just a few shows, primarily in the Bay Area, mostly because of Green Day's heavy touring schedule. Being in the band allowed Armstrong to play the melodic and simple pop-punk that Green Day abandoned as they "grew" as artists. Pinhead Gunpowder concentrated on singles and compilation cuts for several years, and didn't get around to releasing a full-length album until *Goodbye Ellston Avenue* in 1997. They continue to record sporadically today and remain an outlet for both Armstrong and Cometbus.

Discography:
Jump Salty EP (Lookout!, 1994); *Carry the Banner* (Lookout!, 1995); *Goodbye Ellston Avenue* (Lookout!, 1997); *Shoot the Moon* (Adeline, 1999); *Compulsive Disclosure* (Lookout!, 2003)

Pinhead Gunpowder in San Francisco, 2002.

PIT

The term *pit*—one of the many names applied to the area where ritualistic dancing occurs during many punk shows, usually the space directly in front of the stage—is primarily a North American invention, possibly native to California, and not in use everywhere else in the world. Dancing in the pit was originally typified by the pogo, a dance some claim **Sid Vicious** invented (though **Shane MacGowan** was a vigorous early practitioner), which involved hopping up and down without much contact with other dancers. Later on, *slamming*, in which dancers deliberately bumped each other, became the norm at most punk shows, with the advent of **hardcore** leading to a more violent style. Many pits were hostile to women, and some were dominated by the more violent **skinheads**, who would use the cover of dancing in the pit to start fights and settle scores.

After the punk-metal crossover of the late-1980s, the term *moshing* became more prevalent as a way to describe activity on the floor. Many older punks angrily decried the violence in the pit, and bands such as **Fugazi** often stopped shows that were too violent or too aggressive toward women. By the late-1980s, there was increasing concern about violence and antisocial behavior in the pit, and even **CBGB**, home of the famous hardcore matinee, eventually decided to ban most hardcore bands from the venue due to pit-related violence. After numerous lawsuits in various towns, many clubs stopped allowing pits to form or put up signs warning patrons that they danced at their own risk. Meanwhile, many women, especially in the Washington, D.C., scene, were eventually disgusted by the sexist groping and violence allowed in the pit. (This became part of the genesis for the **Riot Grrrl** movement in the 1990s, in which women in the scene started fighting back, sometimes forming a human chain around the pit to keep men out and provide a safer space for dancing.) These days, pits are fairly commonplace at many mainstream metal and hard rock shows, and less a part of the punk scene.

THE PIXIES

1986-1993, 2004-present

LINEUP: Charles Thompson, aka "Black Francis" (vocals/guitar); Joey Santiago (guitar); Kim Deal (bass); David Lovering (drums)

The noisy and raucous Pixies were a staple of the late-1980s and early-'90s American indie music scene, laying the groundwork for '90s indie music and serving as a prime influence on **Nirvana** and Radiohead, among many others. Initially a punk band along the lines of **Hüsker Dü**, the Pixies went on to become more melodic, but also more twisted than most of their punk brethren. The Pixies were led by the enigmatic Black Francis—real name Charles Thompson (he later went by Frank Black in his post-Pixies solo career—and Kim Deal (who early on was known as Mrs. John Murphy, her then-husband's name), along with guitarist Joey Santiago, and drummer (now magician) David Lovering.

In the mid-1980s, Black Francis was a UFO and sci-fi nut whose fervent, almost preacherlike, vocals could be attributed to the fact that his entire family became born-again Christians when he was 12. At the University of Massachusetts, Black Francis and his roommate Santiago decided to form a band. The Dayton, Ohio-raised Kim Deal, who had previously (and again after the Pixies' demise) played in the Breeders with her twin sister Kelley Deal, answered an ad "seeking a female bass player who liked Hüsker Dü and Peter, Paul & Mary." After adding Lovering, a friend of Deal's husband, the band began playing as the Pixies.

The Pixies quickly established a style of their own with Thompson's lyrics (a bizarre mixture of David Lynch, biblical metaphor, and sci-fi allusions), Santiago's innovative guitar playing, and the band's patented "whispered then shouted vocals" that demonstrated a complete disregard for what was occurring in the music scene during the late-1980s. Working with producer Gary Smith, the Pixies recorded what was then called the "Purple Tape," a collection of early songs that became *Come On Pilgrim*, the group's first EP for 4AD Records. Their first full-length album, *Surfer Rosa*, recorded by antiproducer **Steve Albini**, was immediately hailed as a minor masterpiece upon its release in March 1988. After touring to enormous success (and causing friction with headlining band Throwing Muses when the Pixies' fans far outnumbered theirs), the band turned to English producer Gil Norton, to helm their breakthrough record, *Doolittle*, one of the most crucially important U.S. indie records of the decade. The Pixies scored minor radio and video hits with the songs "Monkey Gone to Heaven" and "Here Comes Your Man" and even cracked the UK Top 10 chart; the album ultimately went gold.

Tensions arose between Black Francis and Deal over her intake of drugs and alcohol, as well as over her side project the Breeders, formed, ironically, with Throwing Muses' Tanya Donelly. The next album recorded with Norton, 1990's *Bossanova*, took the Pixies in a more surf-guitar direction, which lost them some of their fanbase. After more infighting, the rest of the band went to Los Angeles to work on their next record without telling Deal, who later was reluctantly asked to rejoin them for *Trompe le Monde* in 1991. After supporting U2 on a U.S. tour, the Pixies were unilaterally dissolved by Black Francis, who allegedly fired Deal by fax and the others via a BBC radio interview about his first solo project. After the Pixies' dissolution, Deal went on to commercial success with the Breeders before her drug and alcohol abuse sidelined her career. The Pixies reunited for a hugely successful string of shows in the United States and Europe in 2004 and continued to tour afterwards.

Discography:

Come on Pilgrim EP (4AD, 1987; 4AD/Rough Trade, 1988; 4AD/Elektra, 1992); *Surfer Rosa* (4AD/Rough Trade, 1988; 4AD/Elektra, 1992); *Gigantic* EP (4AD, 1988); *Doolittle* (4AD/Elektra, 1989); *Monkey Gone to Heaven* EP (4AD/Elektra, 1989); *Here Comes Your Man* EP (4AD/Elektra, 1989); *Bossanova* (4AD/Elektra, 1990); *Velouria* EP (4AD, 1990); *Dig for Fire* EP (4AD, 1990); *Trompe le Monde* (4AD/Elektra, 1991); *Planet of Sound* EP (4AD, 1991); *Death to the Pixies* (4AD/Elektra, 1997); *At the BBC* (4AD/Elektra, 1998); *Complete B-Sides* (4AD, 2000); *Pixies* (SpinArt, 2002); *Wave of Mutilation: Best of The Pixies* (4AD, 2004)

The Pixies backstage at Washington, D.C.'s 9:30 Club, 1988: (L to R) Kim Deal, David Lovering, Black Francis, Joey Santiago.

The Plasmatics getting wacky, 1981.

THE PLASMATICS

1978–1983

LINEUP: Wendy O. Williams (vocals); Richie Stotts (guitar); Wes Beech (guitar); Osao Chosei Funahara (bass, replaced by Jean Beauvoir); Stu Deutsch (drums)

Although the Plasmatics were one of the most notorious "punk" bands of the late-1970s and early-'80s, they also had little to do with punk rock except for stylistic connections like the **mohawks** sported by guitarist Richie Stotts (a true punk), Jean Beauvoir, and singer Wendy O. Williams. Williams's outrageous antics, such as smashing televisions with a sledgehammer and exploding cars onstage while wearing little more than whipped cream or masking tape on her breasts, made the Plasmatics famous but also a bit of a joke to both punks and mainstream critics who used them to illustrate the argument that punk bore no real message other than nihilism, crass acts of autodestruction, and publicity stunts.

The Plastmatics were managed by Williams's companion Rod Swenson, who wrote many of their lyrics and helped the band generate controversy. Beauvoir left in 1981, and Stotts followed him after the *Metal Priestess* EP, after which the newly reconstituted band recorded *Coup d'État* and then dropped the Plasmatics name and even recorded an ill-advised rap album. After several unsuccessful solo records, Williams retired from music to work for animal rights. She died of a self-inflicted gunshot wound in 1998.

Discography:

New Hope for the Wretched (Stiff America, 1980); *Beyond the Valley of 1984* (Stiff America, 1981; PVC, 1991); *Metal Priestess* EP (Stiff America, 1981); *Coup d'État* (Capitol, 1982). **Wendy O. Williams**: *W.O.W.* (Passport, 1984); *Kommander of Kaos* (Gigasaurus, 1986); *Maggots: The Record* (Profile, 1987).

PLASTIC BERTRAND

1978–1982, 2001–present

LINEUP: Roger Jouret (vocals); Lou Deprijck (various instruments)

Roger Jouret first put together the Belgian punk rock band Hubble Bubble in the mid-1970s, but soon became bored with punk's formalities. Plastic Bertrand was Jouret's tongue-in-cheek, two-man take on punk and **new wave**, Belgian-style, whose biggest hit, "Ça Plane Pour Moi," now receives its most consistent play at American sporting events, oddly enough. The other member of the "band" was songwriter and producer Lou Deprijck. Plastic Bertrand sang silly, infectious, pop songs with French lyrics, an early example of punk-styled new wave not taking itself all that seriously and somehow achieving chart success. These days a constant presence on the European art/celebrity scene, Jouret toured as Plastic Bertrand again in 2001.

Discography:

Plastic Bertrand AN1 (Sire, 1978); *Ça Plane Pour Moi* (Sire, 1978); *J'te Fais un Plan* (RKM, 1979); *L'Album* (Attic, 1980); *Grands Succés/Greatest Hits* (Attic, 1981); *Plastiquez Vos Baffles* (Attic, 1982); *L'Essentiel: Best of Plastic Bertrand* (EMI, 2002); *King of the Divan: Best of Plastic Bertrand* (EMI, 2003); *Ultraterrestre* (Xxi-21, 2004)

THE POGUES

1982–1996, periodic reunions thereafter

LINEUP: Shane MacGowan (vocals); Philip Chevron (guitar); Jem Finer (guitar/banjo); Cait O'Riorden (bass, replaced by Darryl Hunt); Andrew Ranken (drums); James Fearnley (accordion/other); Spider Stacy (tin whistle); Terry Woods (guitar, citern)

Irish folk-punks the Pogues combined raucous punk energy with traditional Gaelic tunes, led for most of their history by noted writer, singer, scenester, and original **Sex Pistols** fan **Shane MacGowan**. The Pogues combined a love of traditional Irish music with the frantic energy of punk rock, and the haunting, often brilliant, lyrics of the alcohol-fueled MacGowan (one of the finest songwriters in the Irish tradition, even though he was born in Kent, England, and spent most of his life in London).

The Pogues started playing in the early-1980s as MacGowan's first band the **Nips** were winding down. MacGowan put himself at the mic to sing/mumble his lyrics, backed up by drummer Andrew Ranken, bassist Cait O'Riorden (who would leave the band to marry Elvis Costello), Spider Stacy on tin whistle, banjo player and guitarist Jem Finer, and accordionist and multi-instrumentalist James Fearnley. It wasn't long before the Pogues (originally known as Pogue Mahone, Gaelic for "kiss my ass") became a major force in both the Irish and punk scenes.

In 1984, the Pogues released their first album, *Red Roses for Me*, a mix of traditional Irish ballads and original material. MacGowan's raucous composition "Boys of the County Hell," in particular, indicated greater triumphs to come. The band added more members, including guitarist Philip Chevron, previously of the Irish punk band **Radiators from Space**. The Elvis Costello-produced 1985 followup *Rum, Sodomy, and the Lash* (named for a famous joke about the British naval tradition, long falsely attributed to Winston Churchill), featured the hauntingly beautiful ballads "A Pair of Brown Eyes" and "The Sick Bed of Cuchulainn," which showed the depth of MacGowan's songwriting. The next year's *Poguetry in Motion* EP contained one of MacGowan's finest moments, the ballad "A Rainy Night in Soho," and showed that his songwriting talents were growing by leaps and bounds.

The promise of "A Rainy Night in Soho" was further confirmed by the Pogues's 1988

The Pogues in Bourges, France, 1987.

breakthrough masterpiece *If I Should Fall from Grace with God*, which featured a dizzying variety of songs, from the rave-up title song to the party anthem "Fiesta" to their best-known song, "A Fairy Tale of New York" (this sarcastic, romantic duet paired MacGowan with Kirsty MacColl, daughter of Irish songwriter Ewan MacColl, whose "Dirty Old Town" the Pogues had earlier covered). The Pogues had also expanded in numbers, replacing the departed O'Riorden with bassist Darryl Hunt and adding folk veteran Terry Woods on mandolin and other instruments. By 1989's *Peace and Love*, MacGowan's throat problems and excessive drinking had gotten out of control, leading to him writing fewer songs and the band adding more contributions from Woods and Finer to the songwriting mix. An EP yielded the successful single "Yeah, Yeah, Yeah, Yeah," but the next album, the mostly excellent **Joe Strummer**-produced *Hell's Ditch*, which runs the gamut of styles from Irish to world music, found MacGowan becoming increasingly erratic, and he was asked to leave the band following the album's release.

After touring with Strummer as a lead vocalist, the Pogues regrouped with Spider Stacy on lead vocals for the mediocre *Waiting for Herb*, whose few good numbers included the lively "Tuesday Morning." The subsequent *Pogue Mahone*, without Woods, Chevron, or Fearnley, showed a lack of inspiration, and the band subsequently retired. MacGowan landed on his feet, first dueting with Nick Cave on the old standard "What a Wonderful World" and then starting a new band, Shane MacGowan and the Popes. MacGowan toured and recorded sporadically with the Popes when alcohol or heroin didn't impair him. After 2001, MacGowan reunited with the Pogues for a number of successful tours.

Discography:

Red Roses for Me (Stiff, 1984; Stiff/Enigma, 1986); *Rum, Sodomy, and the Lash* (Stiff/MCA, 1985); *Poguetry in Motion* EP (Stiff/MCA, 1986; WEA, 1991); *St. Patrick's Night* EP (Pogue Mahone, 1988); *If I Should Fall from Grace with God* (Stiff/Island, 1988); *Peace and Love* (WEA, Island, 1989); *Misty Morning, Albert Bridge* EP (WEA, 1989); *Yeah Yeah Yeah Yeah* EP (Island, 1990); *Hell's Ditch* (WEA, Island, 1990); *Essential Pogues* (Island, 1991); *The Best of the Pogues* (Warner Music, 1991); *The Rest of the Best of the Pogues* (Warner Music, 1992); *Waiting for Herb* (Chameleon/Elektra, 1993; Elektra, 1993); *Pogue Mahone* (Warner Music, 1995; Mesa, 1996); *The Very Best of the Pogues* (Warner Music, 2001)

Poison Idea at London's Garage, 2003.

THE POISON GIRLS

1977-1989

LINEUP: Vi Subversa (vocals/guitar); Richard Famous (guitar); Bernhardt Rebours (bass/keyboard); Lance D'Boyle (drums); Nil (electric violin)

Inspired by the radical aspect of punk politics, female vocalist Vi Subversa founded British anarchist band the Poison Girls in 1977. The band worked closely with fellow musical anarchists **Crass**, particularly drummer Penny Rimbaud, who produced the Poison Girls' first two albums, while Crass singer Eve Libertine lent guest vocals to the first album. The Poison Girls will be remembered not just for their attacks on the hypocrisy of social norms, but for showing that punk wasn't just for the young— Vi Subversa was already a middle-aged mom when she started up the band.

Discography:

Hex (Xntrix-Small Wonder, 1979; Crass, 1981); *Chappaquiddick Bridge* (Crass, 1980); *Total Exposure* (live; Xntrix, 1981); *Where's the Pleasure?* (Xntrix, 1982); *I'm Not a Real Woman* EP (Xntrix, 1983); *Seven Year Scratch* (Xntrix, 1984); *Songs of Praise* (CD Presents, 1985); *Statement: The Complete Recordings 1977–1989* (Cooking Vinyl, 1996); *Real Woman* (Cooking Vinyl, 1997); *Poisonous* (Recall, 1998)

POISON IDEA

1980-1993

LINEUP: Jerry Lang (vocals); Tom Roberts, aka **"Pig Champion"** (guitar); Glen Estes (bass); Dean Johnson (drums)

A phenomenally nihilistic **hardcore** band from Portland, Oregon, Poison Idea's sound and attitude were heavily inspired by **Discharge** and the **Germs**. During the late-1980s and early-'90s, Poison Idea stood out in the Pacific Northwest scene for their brash and abrasive brand of hardcore, best realized on the classic EP *Record Collectors Are Pretentious Assholes*, which showcased the band at their loudest and fastest. Led by the aptly named "Pig Champion" (Tom Roberts) on guitar, the band made poorly produced and self-destructive songs that celebrated epic substance abuse and gluttonous eating. You really had to be there to appreciate Poison Idea in their prime, but without them and the Fartz, the scene in that part of the country was pretty bleak indeed—unless you count **D.O.A.**, and they were Canadian.

Discography:

Pick Your King EP (Fatal Erection, 1983; Taang!, 1992); *Record Collectors Are Pretentious Assholes* EP (Fatal Erection, 1984; Taang!, 1992); *Kings of Punk* (Pusmort, 1986; Taang!, 1992); *War All the Time* (Alchemy, 1987; Tim/Kerr, 1994); *Filthkick* EP (Shitfool, 1988); *Darby Crash Rides Again* EP (American Leather, 1989); *Getting the Fear* (Rockport, 1988); *Ian MacKaye* EP (In Your Face, 1989); *Feel the Darkness* (American Leather, 1990; Tim/Kerr, 1994); *Official Bootleg* EP (American Leather, 1991); *Live in Vienna* EP (American Leather, 1991); *Dutch Courage* (Bitzcore, 1991); *Blank Blackout Vacant* (Taang!, 1992); *Pajama Party* (Tim/Kerr, 1992); *We Must Burn* (Tim/Kerr, 1993); *Religion & Politics Parts 1 & 2* EP (Tim/Kerr, 1994); *Your Choice Live Series* (Your Choice, 1994); *The Early Years* (Tim/Kerr, 1994); *Dysfunctional Songs for Codependent Addicts* (Tim/Kerr, 1994); *Pig's Last Stand* (Sub Pop, 1996). **Jeff Dahl and Poison Idea:** *Jeff Dahl...Poison Idea* (Triple X, 1993)

THE POP GROUP

1977–1980

LINEUP: Mark Stewart (vocals); Gareth Sager (guitar/saxophone); John Waddington (guitar); Simon Underwood (bass, replaced by Dan Catsis); Bruce Smith (drums)

Formed in Bristol, England, in late 1977, the Pop Group was one of the first and most strident **post-punk** bands, incorporating funk and **dub** into their incendiary attacks on capitalism and consumer culture. Heavily influenced by both the avant-garde work of composer John Cage and the anger of early punk, the Pop Group made noisy, aggressive, and pioneering post-punk music, particularly on their first album, *Y*, and several subsequent classic singles, including the split "Where There's a Will" with the **Slits**. Like many bands of the time, the Pop Group took a hardline political stance, challenging not only Britain's Tory government and Prime Minister Margaret Thatcher, but also directly attacking the hypocrisy of punks who preached revolution but remained silent on social issues. After the band broke up in 1980, lead singer Mark Stewart went on to form Mark Stewart and the Maffia, Gareth Sanger formed the band Rip Rig & Panic, and Simon Underwood (who left after the first album) put together the **new wave** jazz-funk outfit Pigbag.

Discography:

Y (Radarscope, 1979; WEA, 1996); *For How Much Longer Do We Tolerate Mass Murder?* (Y/Rough Trade, 1980); *We Are Time* (Y/Rough Trade, 1980); *We Are All Prostitutes* (Radarscope, 1998). **Pigbag:** *Dr. Heckle and Mr. Jive* (Stiff, 1982); *Lend an Ear* (Y, 1983); *Pigbag Live* (Y, 1983); *Favourite Things* (Y, 1983); *Discology: The Best of Pigbag* (Kaz, 1987); *Pigbag: The BBC Sessions* (Strange Fruit, 1998). **Rip Rig & Panic:** *God* (Uh Huh/Virgin, 1981); *I Am Cold* (Virgin, 1982); *Attitude* (Virgin, 1983). **Mark Stewart and the Maffia:** *Learning to Cope with Cowardice* (Plexus, 1983). **Mark Stewart:** *As the Veneer of Democracy Starts to Fade* (Mute, 1985); *Mark Stewart + Maffia* (Upside, 1986); *Mark Stewart* (Mute, 1987); *Metatron* (Mute/Restless, 1990); *Control Data* (Mute, 1996); *Kiss the Future* (Soul Jazz, 2005); *Edit* (Crippled Dick Hot Wax, 2008)

Pop Group's Mark Stewart in 1978.

IGGY POP

Iggy Pop (born James Osterberg in 1947), along with his band the **Stooges**, is considered the godfather of punk rock, particularly for his work with the Stooges in the 1960s and '70s and for creating such iconic songs as "Search and Destroy," "I Wanna Be Your Dog," "Loose," "Lust for Life," and the theme song for the 1984 film *Repo Man*. Since his start as a drummer in the mid-1960s, Iggy Pop (his nickname came from his first band the Iguanas) has remained a true original, influencing generations of punks and countless front men who usually emulate his earlier excessive behavior (rolling in glass and peanut butter, fighting with the audience, etc.) as opposed to his creativity and electric dynamism as a front man.

Iggy's unbridled approach to music has been cited by numerous early punks as a direct influence on important bands like the **Dictators**, the **Ramones**, and the **New York Dolls**. After one of his many epic battles with heroin, he reappeared in the late-1970s to provide creative inspiration for not just punk, but also the **new wave, no wave**, heavy metal, and even krautrock movements. Albums like *The Idiot* and *Lust For Life*—created along with collaborator and keyboard player **David Bowie**, who took Iggy under his wing for a time—indicates the hybrid of punk and krautrock that exemplify Bowie's Berlin/Brian Eno period.

Never content to coast on his legacy, Iggy flirted with commercial success on later albums such as the over-produced but still excellent *Blah-Blah-Blah* and even pedestrian heavy metal on *Instinct*. Although *Brick By Brick* (1990) yielded a commercial hit in Iggy's duet with Kate Pierson of the B-52's on "Candy," the 1990s were mostly years of downtime for Iggy, with misguided attempts at everything from punk/metal mishmashes to poetry(!) and spoken word(!!) on 1999's *Avenue B*. Iggy came back strong in the new millennium by collaborating with the surviving Stooges, Ron and Scott Asheton, along with ex-**Minutemen** bassist **Mike Watt**, for some cuts on the hard-edged *Skull Ring*, and later a full reunion for several tours in 2007.

Still presenting a buff physique and now a wine connoisseur instead of a junkie (Iggy is a Bordeaux aficionado) Iggy Pop remains a monumental figure in rock and punk, and is still just about as exciting to watch (as of 2007 he was still inviting fans at concerts to invade the stage) and listen to as he was back in his prime.

Essential Discography:

The Idiot (RCA, 1977; Virgin, 1990); *Lust for Life* (RCA, 1977; Virgin, 1990); *New Values* (Arista, 1979; Buddah, 2000); *Soldier* (Arista, 1980; Buddah, 2000); *Party* (Arista, 1981; Buddah, 2000); *Zombie Birdhouse* (Animal, 1982; IRS, 1991); *I Got a Right* (Invasion, 1983; Enigma, 1985; Revenge, 1987); *Choice Cuts* (RCA, 1984); *Blah-Blah-Blah* (A&M, 1986); *Instinct* (A&M, 1988); *Brick by Brick* (Virgin, 1990); *Livin' on the Edge of the Night* EP (Virgin, 1990); *American Caesar* (Virgin, 1993); *Naughty Little Doggie* (Virgin, 1996); *King Biscuit Flower Hour* (King Biscuit Flower Hour, 1997); *Avenue B* (Virgin, 1999); *The Heritage Collection* (Arista, 2000); *Beat Em Up* (Virgin, 2001); *Skull Ring* (Virgin, 2003).

ABOVE LEFT: Iggy on the North American *The Idiot* tour, 1977.

RIGHT: Iggy expresses his opinions at Rodney Bingenheimer's English Disco, 1975.

POP-PUNK

A term with multiple meanings, some of them derisive, *pop-punk* is a fairly self-defining sub-genre of melodic punk. Contrary to much initial public perception, punk was not universally abrasive and rejective of traditional rock 'n' roll conventions. Many bands, especially early on, were trying to return to a more pop-based form of music that they felt had been rejected by the pomposity of 1970s prog rock and arena bands. A number of punk bands swore their allegiance to the quick and clever two- to three-minute pop song. Early bands such as the **Ramones**, the **Descendents**, and **Bad Religion** were extremely indebted to harmony bands such as the Beach Boys, Big Star, and even the Brill Building songwriters and classic girl groups produced by Phil Spector during the early-1960s. (The Ramones were later to work with Spector on the ill-fated *End of the Century* album.)

Many West Coast pop-punk bands such as Bad Religion and **Green Day** used harmonies and smoother, less aggressive vocals than their East Coast brethren like **Agnostic Front**, who would have decried the music as "too soft." Although the pop-

Green Day in Dallas, 2001: (L to R) Tré Cool, Billie Joe Armstrong, Mike Drint.

The Ramones in London, 1976: (L to R) Johnny, Tommy, Joey, Dee Dee.

punk movement could more or less be traced back to the Ramones, the **Dictators**, and other like-minded bands, the Ramones also played much harder, more metallic-tinged songs in their later years (and even embraced **hardcore** punk to a limited extent), with numerous bands following in their wake. Green Day is a good example of a band who actually paid their dues on the punk scene while remaining very poppy. The bands who imitated Green Day's style (who were themselves imitating the Ramones, the Descendents, Bad Religion, the **Clash**, **Stiff Little Fingers**, and so on), such as Blink-182, Sum-41, **Good Charlotte**, and their ilk, have little connection to punk other than some fashion accoutrements and the peppy sound fostered by the earlier, overly produced bands.

Generally speaking, pop-punk is a U.S. phenomenon. While there were numerous bands from the United Kingdom, such as **Generation X** and the **Undertones**, who could also have fit the definition, British punk generally tried to reject the trappings of the pop song. Today, the term is largely used as a pejorative by many in the punk community, with most bands disputing that description, in much the same way that most bands who are saddled with the **emo** label also now reject that description. Although some punk songwriters (such as the late **Joey Ramone**) were not ashamed to mention their love of pop music, the classification of "pop-punk" is nevertheless far from universally accepted.

POSEURS

Since punk began, a *poseur* (or *poser*) could be defined variously as somebody who thinks "Sk8tr Boy" singer Avril Lavigne is "punk" and wears mall-bought studded belts and new Converse All Stars; goes to the **Vans Warped** tour because Yellowcard is playing and ignores the **Damned**; is **straight edge** for all the wrong reasons; identifies as punk but is scared of the **pit**; listens to **emo** convinced that men with slicked-down bangs and lyrics about trivial high school crushes are huge emotional dramas; and so on. While the term is useful in delineating fake punks from those who make an effort to really live a **DIY** lifestyle, ultimately, *everyone* is a poseur, especially anyone

who preaches tolerance while judging who is punk and who is not, makes arbitrary judgements based on a zine's recommendation, or, God forbid, reads about punk in a book.

POSITIVE FORCE

A political movement started by Reno, Nevada, band **7 Seconds** during the early-1980s and quickly adopted by punks in numerous other cities (most famously in Washington, D.C.), Positive Force worked closely with many in the punk community (including **Ian MacKaye** and Jeff Nelson from **Minor Threat** and **Dischord Records**) to combat the evils of weapons proliferation and the **Ronald Reagan** administration. Kevin Seconds, the cofounder of Positive Force and lead singer of 7 Seconds, and the original Reno organization would book local shows and bands who wanted to play in Reno. The group had its heyday in D.C. during the mid- to late-1980s, but internal fighting and pressures soon led many of the largest local "chapters" to cease functioning or revamp themselves to operate as smaller, more effective coalitions.

The best book-length account of the Washington, D.C., Positive Force scene is found in *Dance of Days: Two Decades of Punk in the Nation's Capital*, by Mark Andersen (who remains a member of Positive Force D.C.) and journalist Mark Jenkins. It details the intricacies and changes within the scene and within Positive Force. The D.C. version eventually had less to do with punk and more to do with community service, including grocery deliveries to the elderly and the development of local groups and community centers. Mark Andersen eventually wrote another book about the movement called *All the Power: Revolution Without Illusion*.

the slits

Cut

POST-PUNK

Although any music after the initial wave of early- to mid-1970s punk could be labeled *post-punk*, the term specifically refers to a genre that grew out of frustration with the genre's musical "formula," which many punks felt was far too restricting for a movement purportedly based on experimentation. The term is usually applied to the music produced in the late-1970s and early-'80s by bands such as **Public Image Ltd.**, **Joy Division**, **Gang of Four**, the **Pop Group**, the **Slits**, and others who expanded the musical palette of punk rock beyond three-chord simplicity.

This push for a new direction in underground music came about once many of those who had first followed punk realized that new generations of fans and bands within the second wave of punk and **hardcore** had come to the punk scene less to celebrate difference and revolution than to play dress up and sing along. Other bands realized that the sonic experimentation of European bands such as Kraftwerk, Neu,

and **Can** had shown the possibility of incorporating instruments outside of the typical guitar, bass, and drums lineup that dominated the punk scene.

The other clear change brought about by post-punk was the influence of musical styles such as **ska**, **reggae**, and disco, elements of which were incorporated by many of the more adventurous of the post-punk bands. The **2 Tone** scene that dominated British music for a few years in the late-1970s and early-'80s can also be seen as a post-punk reaction to punk's political and musical limitations. The term *post-punk* did not really get as much use in the United States as it did in England, and the term **new wave** was largely (and wrongly) used to describe the more electronic types of music that proliferated in the late-1970s and early-'80s in the United States. For years, post-punk was used as a catchall to describe underground bands whose music seemed otherwise unclassifiable. These days, there are any number of bands from Erase Errata to Interpol, who seek to re-create the post-punk sound and image.

PROFANE EXISTENCE

An influential and long-lived **crust-punk** zine created by the anarchist collective of the same name from Minneapolis (motto: "Making punk a threat again!"), *Profane Existence (P.E.)* also runs a record label and distributes other small labels. The zine deals with **DIY** issues, punk social movements, direct action against the system, and advocation for social change. The collective also collaborated to establish and run nonprofit anarchist institutions in Minneapolis like the Emma Center, a gathering space and punk music venue in the early 1990s, and Extreme Noise Records. First formed in 1989, the zine, label, and collective went on hiatus in 1998, though by 2002 most facets of *Profane Existence* resurfaced. Current issues can be obtained for free, and the zine also has a website. A small but influential presence in punk culture, *Profane Existence* made great contributions to the DIY and punk communities both in the U.S. and across the world.

THE PROFESSIONALS

1979-1982

LINEUP: Steve Jones (vocals/guitar); Andy Allen (bass, replaced by Paul Myers); Paul Cook (drums)

Comprised of musicians Steve Jones and Paul Cook and bassist Andy Allen (later replaced by Paul Myers from **Subway Sect**), the Professionals may have seemed a cheesy attempt to cash in on the **Sex Pistols** legacy, the band actually was a convincing punk/pub-rock hybrid who played well beyond their means. Jones persuasively demonstrated that his guitar work had not (unlike that of **Sid Vicious**) been overdubbed and Cook was his usual magnetic self, but the band never really gelled. They only recorded one full album before Jones relocated to the United States after being arrested for possession of heroin, essentially ending the band.

Discography:
Didn't See It Coming (Virgin, 1981)

THE PROMISE RING

1995-2002

LINEUP: Davey VonBohlen (vocals/guitar); John Gnewikow (guitar); Scott Beschta (bass, replaced by Tim Burton, Scott Schoenbeck); Dan Didier (drums)

This Milwaukee-based quartet of affable and talented young musicians was one of the most prominent **emo** bands of the late-1990s, and helped—along with bands like Sunny Day Real Estate and Jimmy Eat World—to popularize the genre for a new generation of more mainstream fans (though this may be something to hold against them). The Promise Ring, particularly on the *Horse Latitudes* EP, demonstrated that emo is more than whining—one actually needs a subject to whine *about* (and some hooks; hooks are good). The band went through various tragedies, including a near-fatal van crash and a benign brain tumor for singer Davey VonBohlen. They broke up soon after releasing the more indie-rock-oriented *Wood/Water* in 2002.

Discography:
30 Degrees Everywhere (Jade Tree, 1996); *The Horse Latitudes* EP (Jade Tree, 1997); *Nothing Feels Good* (Jade Tree, 1997); *Very Emergency* (Jade Tree, 1999); *Electric Pink* EP (Jade Tree, 2000); *Wood/Water* (Anti, 2002)

PROPAGANDHI

1986-present

LINEUP: Chris Hannah (vocals/guitar); Scott Hopper (bass, replaced by Mike Braumeister, John K. Samson, Todd Kowalski); Jord Samoesky (drums)

In the mid-1980s, when Manitoban punks Chris Hannah and Jord Samoesky were looking for a bass player, they put up a flyer defining themselves as a "progressive thrash band." No one really knew what this meant, including Hannah and Samoesky, but the group that resulted from that flyer became one of the more literate and politically active bands of the 1990s, with its members supporting a variety of causes, including vegetarianism and animal rights. A sample song title that demonstrated their commitment was: "Apparently I'm a P.C. Fascist (Because I Care About Both Human *and* Non-Human Animals)." With their slight pop edge and compelling hooks, Propagandhi were one of the better and tighter **Fat Wreck Chords** bands. Propagandhi formed the label G7 Welcoming Committee Records, which in 1997 released an album by the Weakerthans, a soon-to-be popular band formed by ex-Propagandhi bassist John Samson.

Discography:
How to Clean Everything (Fat Wreck Chords, 1993); *Less Talk, More Rock* (Fat Wreck Chords, 1996); *Where Quantity is Job #1* (G7 Welcoming Committee, 1998); *Today's Empires, Tomorrow's Ashes* (G7 Welcoming Committee/Fat Wreck Chords, 2001); *Potemkin City Limits* (G7 Welcoming Committee, Fat Wreck Chords, 2005)

PUBLIC IMAGE LTD.

1978-1993

LINEUP: John Lydon (vocals); Keith Levene (guitar); John Wardle, aka "Jah Wobble" (bass); Jim Walker (drums, replaced by many)

John Lydon's post-**Sex Pistols** band, named for the 1968 Muriel Spark novel, featured original punk scenemaker Jah Wobble (John Wardle), Keith Levene (formerly of the **London SS** and an early incarnation of the **Clash**), and conceptual artist Jeanette Lee. Public Image Ltd.'s debut album, *Public Image*, was released in December 1978 and reflected Lydon's disillusionment with the recording industry, organized religion, and the former management of the Sex Pistols. Although the first record was received by critics with mixed reviews, most were astonished by the second release, *Metal Box*, which came out as three 12-inch records inside a tin box, hence the title (subsequent editions as well as reissues on CD were renamed *Second Edition*). The sound of *Metal Box* was as radical in its way as the original Sex Pistols sound, with its combination of punk, funk, **dub**, **reggae**, and abrasive noise helping to essentially found the **post-punk** genre.

In a particularly bizarre moment for American television, Public Image Ltd. (PiL) appeared on Dick Clark's *American Bandstand* in May 1980 to lip-sync to the songs "Careering" and "Poptones," but, instead, a bored John Lydon waded into the audience, and the show nearly became a riot. Despite television promotions and critical acclaim, *Metal Box* did not break the band in the United States, although it did make them a critical success. The band went through numerous personnel changes early on, with Wobble eventually being asked to leave the band in a controversy over ownership of several music tracks. Levene departed as well during the 1984 production of *This Is What You Want...This Is What You Get*, and subsequent albums such as *Album* (also released in the same no-frills style as *Tape* and *CD*) found Lydon working with a diverse group of musicians, including former Cream drummer Ginger Baker and metal guitar virtuoso Steve Vai. PiL remained a draw in Europe and the

John Lydon at his
Notting Hill apartment,
1979.

United States and had several minor video
and radio hits, but the band was never as
inspired as they were for the first several
groundbreaking records.

Lydon soldiered on for years in PiL
with various sidemen (1987's *Happy?* featured John McGeoch from **Siouxsie and
the Banshees** and **Magazine**, along with
Lu Edmonds from the **Damned**) until he
dissolved the last version of the band in
the late-1990s. The work of PiL is still considered as distinctive and influential as
it was in the beginning, and even if they
didn't live up to their ultimate potential,
the band paved the way for the experimentation of indie and underground music
from the 1980s to the present.

Discography:
Public Image (Virgin, 1978); *Metal Box* (Virgin, 1979);
Second Edition (Island, 1980); *Paris au Printemps*
(Virgin, 1980); *Flowers of Romance* (Warner Bros.,
1981); *Live in Tokyo* (Virgin, 1983; Elektra, 1986);
Commercial Zone (PiL, 1983); *This Is What You Want...
This Is What You Get* (Elektra, 1984); *Album* (Elektra,
1986); *Cassette* (tape; Elektra, 1986); *Compact Disc*
(CD; Elektra, 1986); *Happy?* (Virgin, 1987); *9* (Virgin,
1989); *The Greatest Hits So Far* (Virgin, 1990); *That
What Is Not* (Virgin, 1992); *Plastic Box* (box set; Virgin,
1999). **John Lydon:** *Psycho's Path* (Virgin, 1997)

PUNK

The New York magazine that gave a name to the movement was started in late 1975 by illustrator and super music fan **John Holmstrom** along with his friends **Legs McNeil** and Ged Dunn. Holmstrom and company had been looking for a project to work on, and after rejecting the idea of starting a movie company, Holmstrom found a furnished storefront that was perfect for working on a magazine. In the debut issue, Holmstrom and his crew of writers made a case for a new brand of underground rock 'n' roll that challenged the mainstream music clogging the airwaves in the early-1970s. Disillusioned with most of contemporary rock, Holmstrom had seen the **Ramones**, and approved of other bands such as the **Dictators**, the **Stooges**, and Alice Cooper, and was known for his ability to find music worthy of attention at a time when the music scene in the United States was dominated by corporate rock bands. Aware that rock fans at the time were craving more involvement with their music, Holmstrom convinced McNeil, who really wanted to be a publicist, to be the "resident punk" of the magazine (due to his lack of rock critic credentials), and with several others helping out, the magazine was born.

Punk showed that it wanted to be something different when its first issue (December 1975) featured an interview with the Ramones and a cartoon cover of, and interview with, **Lou Reed**. Although the name *Punk* had been used in various permutations prior to the start of the magazine (Lenny Kaye, of the **Patti Smith** band, had used "punk" to describe garage rock bands; Holmstrom himself recalls first seeing the term in *Creem Magazine*), Holmstrom's magazine was the first to use the term to describe the music scene at **CBGB**. Holmstrom had wanted to name the publication after a **New York Dolls** song, but McNeil had suggested that the term *punk* would better sum up their philosophy.

The magazine was an instant success, with the first print run of some 4,000 copies selling out quickly and becoming an instant collector's item. (Complete sets are now available on eBay for several hundred dollars.) *Punk* gained immediate acclaim from the *Village Voice* and other "downtown" newspapers that seemed to recognize Holmstrom's crew "got" what was going on in new music and culture. The next few issues were equally innovative and tried a variety of different forms, such as Fumetti issues (in which photos were assembled together to tell a story), which unfortunately were the least popular of *Punk*'s run. Subsequent issues highlighted the new bands around CBGB and also featured the magazine's version of journalism, which included McNeil's "interviews" with "celebrities" such as the cartoon characters Sluggo

and Boris and Natasha. Holmstrom was essentially trying to re-create the sense of urgency for music that had dominated the best pre-punk and garage rock of the 1960s and that was reborn in New York in the '70s.

Punk ended far before its time (issue 18 was completed but never saw the light of day), owing to several factors, including the demonization of punk by the media. Other magazines also sprang up that were inspired by punk, such as *Sniffin' Glue* in England, which feuded with *Punk*, not realizing that the Americans were at least partially parodying what they celebrated. The magazine ultimately made celebrities of McNeil and Holmstrom and established them as key commentators on punk rock. Ironically, though, the best-selling issue of *Punk* was in fact issue 16, the "disco issue."

PUNK PLANET

Punk Planet was started by Daniel Sinker in 1994 as a bimonthly, Chicago-based zine out of frustration with the orthodoxy of modern punk rock and to give exposure to bands and **DIY** activity that **Maximum RocknRoll** would not cover. Less concerned than some of the more parochial zines were with settling scores and laying down the punk law, *Punk Planet* was more interested in publishing unusually excellent and in-depth interviews, many of which have been collected in book form. *Punk Planet* remains one of the most highly respected zines in the history of punk rock, and its influence can be felt in how much more inclusive modern punk has become in terms of music and ideology. Unfortunately, the magazine ceased publication in 2007, though the website and book publishing imprint remain active.

QUEERCORE

A movement originally designed to highlight one of the most ill-kept secrets in punk rock—the prevalence of gay men and lesbians as members and innovators of the scene—queercore also demonstrates the discontent and anger felt by gay punks against the mainstream gay society, sometimes considered as dogmatic and unaccepting as the insular punk community. Some of the more important queercore bands (although not all of them accepted this label) included **Pansy Division** and **Tribe 8**.

Many punks in the early Los Angeles, Bay Area, and New York scenes were openly gay (although certainly not always accepted as such), however, this was not the case everywhere in the U.S., with antigay slurs and violence cropping up regularly. Even though members of **hardcore** bands such as the Texas-based **MDC**, the **Big Boys**, and the **Dicks** were openly gay, the 1980s were not the most progressive years in the U.S. punk community, which could often be just as homophobic as mainstream society (though the approving cover of the May/June 1983

issue of *Maximum RocknRoll* read: "The Dicks: A Commie Faggot Band!??!"). By the 1990s, however, things had changed somewhat on the grassroots level, due at least in part to the revolutionary gender politics of the **Riot Grrrl** movement. By that time, many bands such as the extremely political Tribe 8 and **Team Dresch** were not only openly out but also fiercely confrontational about their sexual identity (or their rejection of the notion of a fixed sexual identity).

The term *queercore* can most likely be traced back to the zine *J.D.s,* started by G. B. Jones and Bruce LaBruce (the infamous **DIY** art-punk, porno auteur) in 1985. *J.D.s* (for "juvenile delinquents") helped kick-start the whole movement, originally using the descriptive *homocore*, and when that was considered too limiting, replacing it with the more inclusive *queercore* appellation. Among the more notable contributors were novelist (and huge **Hüsker Dü** fan) Dennis Cooper and performance artist and writer Vaginal Davis. In 1989, Jones and LaBruce published a wake-up call of a manifesto in *Maximum RocknRoll* about the marginalization of gays within the punk scene entitled "Don't Be Gay." *J.D.s* later inspired the zines *Holy Titclamps* by Larry-bob,

The queercore pioneers of
Tribe 8: (L to R)
Trantrum, Slade Bellum,
Silas Howard, Leslie Mah,
Lynn Breedlove.

THE QUEERS

QUEERS

later days and better lays

THE QUEERS

1982-present

LINEUP: Wimpy Rutherford (vocals/guitar, replaced by Joe King, aka "Joe Queer"); Dangerous Dave (guitar/vocals); "B-Face" (bass, replaced by Ben Vermin); Hugh O'Neill (drums, replaced by Matt Drastic)

A catchy (and despite the name, non-**queercore**) band from Portsmouth, New Hampshire, with a very obvious debt to the Beach Boys and the **Ramones** (they once covered the entire Ramones record *Rocket to Russia*), the Queers have been touring in one incarnation or another since 1982 and making remarkably consistent music the entire time. However, the Queers only started to take themselves seriously when original lead singer Wimpy Rutherford left and Joe King (aka "Joe Queer," another assumed nod to the Ramones) took over lead vocal and guitar duties. After signing to **Lookout!** during the 1990s, the classic line-up of King, Hugh O'Neill on drums, and "B-Face" on bass released numerous albums of remarkably poppy and energetic (some critics would say derivative) music in a never-ending quest to create (first) the ultimate Ramones homage and (later) the ultimate Beach Boys homage. Although not a joke band per se, the Queers' music tends to be dominated by a gleefully demented sense of humor, in which the preferred topics are girls ("Ursula Finally Has Tits," "She's a Cretin"), alcohol ("Next Stop Rehab," "I Only Drink Bud"), and the Ramones (almost every song). Hugh and B-Face were gone by the late-1990s (Hugh died from brain cancer in 1999), while King now tours with assorted sidemen under the Queers name.

Discography:

Love Me EP (Doheny, 1982); *Kicked out of the Webelos* EP (Doheny, 1984); *Grow Up* (Shakin Street, 1990; Lookout!, 1994); *A Proud Tradition* EP (Doheny, 1992; Selfless, 1993); *Too Dumb to Quit* EP (Doheny, 1993; Selfless, 1993); *Love Songs for the Retarded* (Lookout!, 1993); *Rocket to Russia* (Selfless, 1993; Liberation, 2001); *Look Ma, No Flannel* EP (Clearview, 1994); *Beat Off* (Lookout!, 1994); *Surf Goddess* EP (Lookout!, 1994); *Shout at the Queers* (Selfless, 1994); *Suck This* (Clearview, 1994, 1996); *The Queers Move Back Home* (Lookout!, 1995); *Surf Goddess* EP (Lookout!, 1995); *My Old Man's a Fatso* EP (Wound Up, 1995); *A Day Late and a Dollar Short* (Lookout!, 1996); *Bubblegum Dreams* EP (Lookout!, 1996); *Don't Back Down* (Lookout!, 1996); *Everything's O.K.* EP (Hopeless, 1998); *Punk Rock Confidential* (Hopeless, 1998); *Later Days and Better Lays* (Lookout!, 1999); *Beyond the Valley of the Assfuckers* (Hopeless, 2000); *Today* EP (Lookout!, 2001); *Live in West Hollywood* (Hopeless, 2001); *Pleasant Screams* (Lookout!, 2002); *Weekend at Bernie's* (live: Doheny, 2006); *Munki Brain* (Asian Man, 2007)

Homocore by Deke Nihilson, *Outpunk* by Matt Wobensmith, and *Chainsaw* by Donna Dresch, all of which helped establish a uniquely queer punk DIY aesthetic.

The first queercore compilation, *J.D's Top Ten Homocore Hit Parade Tape*, was released on cassette and included bands like Fifth Column, Nikki Parasite, the Apostles, and Academy 23, some of whom were not necessarily queer but were supportive of queercore's politics. This inclusivity could cause problems, however, as queercore-identified bands with straight members sometimes received a cold shoulder from more doctrinaire queer punks. *J.D.s* ceased publication soon after the tape's release, but the movement spread regardless, with other bands such as **God Is My Co-Pilot**, Pansy Division, Team Dresch, Tribe 8, and Fifth Column demonstrating queercore's musical breadth.

Although many queercore bands had to either form their own labels or join with friends' labels, such as Chainsaw Records and **Candy Ass Records**, soon indie labels such as **Lookout!**, **Kill Rock Stars**, and **Alternative Tentacles** also began to show-case queercore bands. As a matter of course, queercore embraced different musical styles and was not limited to hardcore. This openness was reflected in newer bands such as Addicted 2 Fiction, Ninja Death Squad, and Excuse 17, who were far more musically diverse than the earlier bands; there are even queercore, **straight-edge** bands such as Limp Wrist. Recently, festivals like Homo a Go Go, held yearly in Olympia, Washington, have provided a showcase for queer zines, bands, music, and films and acted as a gathering place for like-minded activists.

QUICKSAND

1990–1995, 1998

LINEUP: Walter Schreifels (vocals); Tom Capone (guitar); Sergio Vega (bass); Alan Cage (drums)

Rising out of the rapidly dissolving New York **hardcore** scene in the late-1980s, experimental hardcore band Quicksand had solid punk bona fides, featuring former members of **Gorilla Biscuits** and **Youth of Today**. The band took a more innovative and melodic approach to punk than many of their former scenemates (some would later file Quicksand into the decidedly miniscule genre of post-hardcore). Guitarist Tom Capone (who also played in **Bold** and **Shelter**), laid down crunchy metallic riffs over which lead vocalist Walter Schreifels screamed out lyrics. Quicksand put out two highly acclaimed (but poor-selling) albums and an EP before they broke up in 1995. Although numerous bands were later influenced by them, Quicksand never had the impact that their raw, powerful sound deserved. The band reunited briefly for a 1998 North American tour alongside the Deftones and Snapcase, and thereafter, retreated into what appears to be a permanent state of dissolution; the members have since gone on to various side projects and reunions with their former bands.

Discography:
Quicksand EP (Revelation, 1990); *Slip* (Polydor, 1993); *Manic Compression* (Island, 1995)

Quicksand displays their calm, quiet side, 1993.

rewarding years with the Pogues until their chaotic dissolution. He later rejoined the Pogues for their 2004 reunion and remains in the band to the present day, except for a leave of absence to treat a brain tumor. The Radiators got back together for an AIDS benefit in 1987 and a **Joe Strummer** benefit concert in 2003. They seriously reunited in 2004—with Cait O'Riorden, who also played bass in an earlier version of the Pogues and who later married and divorced Elvis Costello—and toured and recorded sporadically over the following years, returning to their original name in 2007.

Discography:

TV Tube Heart (Chiswick, 1977; Big Beat, 2005); *Ghostown* (Chiswick, 1979, 1989); *Buying Gold in Heaven: The Best of the Radiators (from Space) 1977–1980* (Hotwire, 1985); *Dollar for Your Dreams: The Radiators Live!—Aid to Fight AIDS Benefit, Dublin, September 13th, 1987* (Comet, 1988); *Cockles and Mussels: The Very Best of the Radiators* (Chiswick, 1995); *Alive-Alive-O! Live in London (1978) + Rare Studio Tracks* (Chiswick, 1996); *Live at the Southend Kursaal 1977* (Rejected, 2005); *The Midnite Demos* (Rejected, 2005); *Trouble Pilgrim* (625, 2006)

RADIO BIRDMAN

1974-1978, 1996-present

LINEUP: Rob Younger (vocals/guitar); Deniz Tek (guitar); Chris Masuak (guitar); Carl Rorke (bass, replaced by Jim Dickson); Ron Keeley (drums, replaced by Russell Hopkinson); Phillip "Pip" Hoyle (keyboards)

A seminal Australian punk band led by vocalist and onetime surfer Rob Younger and Michigan-born guitarist Deniz Tek, who played in a style reminiscent of the **Stooges** (the band's name comes from the Stooges' 1970 song), Radio Birdman influenced a brand of raw guitar rock that both predated and anticipated punk. The original band only lasted about four years, after which Younger and Tek put together a new one, the New Race, with ex-members of the Stooges and the **MC5**. After that outfit's dissolution, its members went to work with straight-up rock outfits like the Lime Spiders and the Hoodoo Gurus, while guitarist Chris Masuak reportedly worked as a surgeon in the U.S. Navy. A 1996 reunion led to Radio Birdman's re-formation and occasional tours. Although bad timing kept Radio Birdman from the international attention many felt they deserved during their initial run, after Sub Pop reissued their music in 2001, appreciation for their brand of early, raw Stooges-style punk has grown considerably.

Discography:

Burn My Eye EP (Trafalgar, 1976); *Radios Appear* (Trafalgar, 1977; Sire, 1978); *Living Eyes* (WEA, 1981); *More Fun!* EP (WEA, 1988); *Under the Ashes* (WEA, 1988); *Ritualism* (live; Crying Sun, 1996); *Radio Birdman: The Essential 1974–1978* (Sub Pop, 2001)

THE RAINCOATS

1977-1984, 1994-1996, sporadically thereafter

LINEUP: Ana Da Silva (vocals/guitar); Gina Birch (vocals/bass); Paloma Romero, aka "Palmolive" (drums, replaced by Ingrid Weiss); Vicky Aspinall (violin/guitar)

Although mostly known as one of the favorite bands of Nirvana's Kurt Cobain (who helped inspire their comeback and subsequent reissues of their records), the Raincoats were an all-female, London-based quartet who produced some of the earliest art/noise versions of **post-punk**. Like the **Slits** (with whom they shared drummer Palmolive), but less messy, the Raincoats believed that women intrinsically performed more naturally when working by themselves than they would with male musicians. Their wonderfully raw music was a chaotic mess at a time when the punk scene was being co-opted by the music industry into a slightly more contrived and marketable combination of power pop and nihilistic anger.

However, after Kurt Cobain's relentless name-checking, the Raincoats reformed in 1994 with **Sonic Youth**'s Steve Shelley briefly on drums. (Palmolive had left music before the Raincoats broke up becoming a born-again Christian in 1985 after dabbling in New Age spirituality.) They then opened for **Nirvana** on that band's final, ill-fated tour. The Raincoats released an album in 1996 (produced by Shelley) to critical acclaim but meager sales. Like **Kleenex** and the Slits, the Raincoats were a pivotal band in the evolution of women fighting for a place in the testosterone-filled world of punk.

Discography:

The Raincoats (Rough Trade/DGC, 1979); *Odyshape* (Rough Trade/DGC, 1981); *The Kitchen Tapes* (cassette; ROIR, 1983); *Moving* (Rough Trade/DGC, 1984); *Looking in the Shadows* (Rough Trade/DGC, 1996)

THE RADIATORS FROM SPACE

1976-1981, 2004-present

LINEUP: Stephen Averill, aka "Steve Rapid" (vocals); Philip Chevron (guitar); Peter Holidai (guitar); Mark Megaray (bass, replaced by Neil Whiffen, Cait O'Riorden, Jesse Booth); Jimmy Crashe (drums, replaced by Johnny Bonnie)

One of the very first punk bands from Ireland, the Radiators from Space were originally formed by guitarist Philip Chevron—a brilliant songwriter who later joined the **Pogues**—in Dublin in 1975 as Greta Garbage and the Trash Cans. Their debut single "Television Screen" came out in early 1977 and actually cracked the Irish Top 20 (perhaps the first time a punk single accomplished that anywhere in the world). In June 1977, the band played one of the first major Irish punk festivals (with the Vipers and the **Undertones**) in Dublin. At the festival, an 18-year-old fan was stabbed to death; saddling the band with an undeserved reputation for violence.

After that tragic event, the Radiators from Space found themselves not so welcome in their native land. Shortening their name to the less tongue-tripping Radiators, they moved to the more punk-friendly confines of London, though without founding singer Steve Rapid (who stayed behind in Dublin and became friendly with the early version of U2, eventually becoming their graphic designer). In July 1977, the Radiators' debut album, *TV Tube Heart*, was released. Two years later the critically acclaimed but slightly slick and underselling *Ghostown* (whose mood was regarded by Chevron as being akin to a "midnight walk through Dublin with the ghosts of the city's past") followed.

The Radiators first split up in 1981, after which Chevron spent a number of

The Raincoats, 1979.

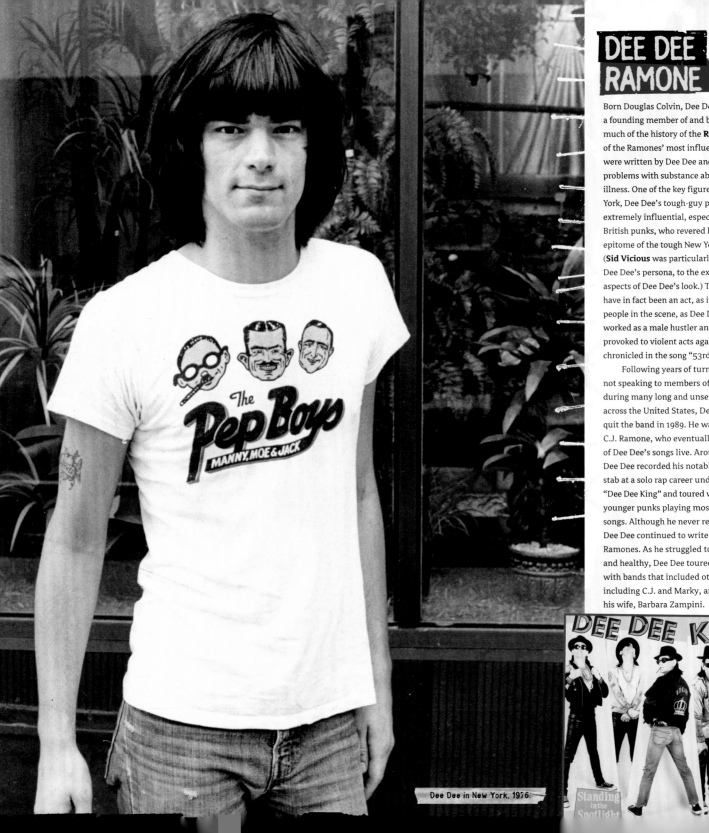

DEE DEE RAMONE

Born Douglas Colvin, Dee Dee Ramone was a founding member of and bass player for much of the history of the **Ramones**. Many of the Ramones' most influential songs were written by Dee Dee and referenced his problems with substance abuse and mental illness. One of the key figures in early New York, Dee Dee's tough-guy persona was extremely influential, especially among British punks, who revered him as the epitome of the tough New York street punk. (**Sid Vicious** was particularly taken with Dee Dee's persona, to the extent of imitating aspects of Dee Dee's look.) This may not have in fact been an act, as it was with many people in the scene, as Dee Dee had actually worked as a male hustler and may have been provoked to violent acts against his johns (as chronicled in the song "53rd and 3rd").

Following years of turmoil, and after not speaking to members of the Ramones during many long and unsettling van drives across the United States, Dee Dee finally quit the band in 1989. He was replaced by C.J. Ramone, who eventually sang several of Dee Dee's songs live. Around this time, Dee Dee recorded his notably embarrassing stab at a solo rap career under the moniker "Dee Dee King" and toured with a variety of younger punks playing mostly Ramones songs. Although he never rejoined the band, Dee Dee continued to write songs for the Ramones. As he struggled to stay clean and healthy, Dee Dee toured sporadically with bands that included other Ramones including C.J. and Marky, and occasionally his wife, Barbara Zampini.

Dee Dee in New York, 1976.

Shortly after the Ramones were inducted into the Rock and Roll Hall of Fame in 2002, Dee Dee Ramone died of a heroin overdose in California. He was featured in the documentary *Hey Is Dee Dee Home?*, which played to some acclaim. A pioneer of punk whose songs were essential to the Ramones' success, Dee Dee was also in many ways the classic image of the rock star as dissolute artist.

Discography:
Standing in the Spotlight (Sire Records, 1989)

JOEY RAMONE

The founder and lead singer of the **Ramones** was a gaunt and gangly guy from Queens, who started out playing the drums for **Dee Dee Ramone**'s band but switched to singing only a couple months after their first show. A legendary front man and gentle soul who loomed large across both the concert stage and punk history, Joey (born Jeffrey Hyman) was as rooted in 1960s garage rock as he was in the intricacies of Phil Spector's "wall of sound" style prevalent in the girl groups records he enjoyed so much. It was his unique voice (along with Johnny Ramone's mighty guitar) that made the Ramones the enormously influential band that they were.

Joey never enjoyed good health, and after falling in New York, his lymphoma resurfaced and eventually caused his death in 2001 at the age of 49. After his death, a solo record was released (one he had been working on for several years with frequent collaborator Daniel Rey) that highlighted his health crisis and his love of girl groups, pure pop songs, and even TV stock market analyst Maria Bartiromo. The album fittingly contained a version of the Louis Armstrong classic "What a Wonderful World" that demonstrated Joey's place in the pantheon of U.S. singer-songwriters.

In 2003, the City of New York named the corner of Bowery and 2nd Street "Joey Ramone Place," the site of the now-defunct **CBGB** music club at which Joey Ramone's legend began.

Discography:
Don't Worry About Me (Sanctuary Records, 2002)

Joey in London, 1977.

THE RAMONES
1974–1996

LINEUP: Jeffrey Hyman, aka "Joey Ramone" (vocals); John Cummings, aka "Johnny Ramone" (guitar); Douglas Colvin, aka "Dee Dee Ramone" (bass, replaced by C.J. Ramone); Tamas Erdelyi, aka "Tommy Ramone" (drums, replaced by Mark Bell, aka "Marky Ramone," Richie Reinhardt, aka "Richie Beau" or "Richie Ramone")

One of the two most important bands in punk rock history (the other being the **Sex Pistols**), the Ramones are arguably the band who created, or at least first articulated, the 1970s version of punk. The influence of the Ramones is vast, with almost every punk band out there having at some point learned or stolen ideas from the "brothers" from Queens, New York.

The Ramones' first gig was on March 30, 1974. After that, the band played around the city for a few months before learning about the new scene that was developing at **CBGB**, where the Ramones quickly started a residency. Audiences were first repelled, and then enraptured, by the band's energetic new sound and lightning-speed sets, punctuated by shouting matches between the Ramones about what song to play next. A key moment in early punk rock history occurred on July 4, 1976, the date of the Ramones' legendary performance at London's Roundhouse: In the audience that night were members of the **Clash**, the **Damned**, the Sex Pistols, and many others who later indicated that seeing that show inspired them to form punk bands.

The Ramones were signed by Seymour Stein to Sire Records in 1976 and recorded their first, self-titled album the same year. The album was laid down in record time and with a low budget but still accurately reflected the Ramones' ideas about sound and velocity, which led to numerous instances of DJs playing the record for a few seconds and then flinging it across the room. Several other records followed, but, despite critical acclaim and extremely devoted fans in the major cities, the Ramones could not find a home on radio,

even when producing incredibly poppy songs. The Ramones were consistently popular in New York, but the rest of the United States proved a harder nut to crack, even with their renowned cross-country tours in a small van—a disciplined but nerve-racking practice that would see the band playing thousands of shows before finally retiring in 1996.

The Ramones were given some exposure in the U.S., most notably in the film *Rock 'n' Roll High School*. Roger Corman, the king of the B-movie industry, set out to make a film that capitalized on the disco craze but was eventually dissuaded from this idea and decided to film a movie about rebellion at a high school in Los Angeles instead. After going through several titles, concepts (from "Heavy Metal High School" to "Disco High School"), and bands (Todd Rundgren and Cheap Trick were both considered), the Ramones were chosen to become punk movie stars. In late 1979, the Ramones filmed their scenes in California, arriving onscreen singing "I Just Wanna Have Something to Do" in a convertible driven by **Rodney Bingenheimer**. During filming, the band, needing more tour money than the $5,000 Corman was paying for their time, played three disastrous gigs with Black Sabbath, whose fans were hostile, to say the least. More trouble ensued when **Dee Dee Ramone** had to be taken to the hospital after he swallowed pills that fans were throwing at the band on set.

Following the completion of *Rock 'n' Roll High School*, the Ramones embarked on their most ambitious, doomed project to date, recording the album *End of the Century* with legendary producer Phil Spector. The sessions proved disastrous, with Spector spending 10 hours listening just to the opening chord of *Rock 'n' Roll High School* and eventually threatening the band with a loaded pistol. Even with Spector's glossy production, and its selling more copies than any other prior Ramones album, the record did not enter the U.S. Top 40, although it did spawn their first British Top 10 single—a cover of the Ronettes' "Baby I Love You."

After the disappointing Spector sessions, the Ramones returned to their relentless touring schedule and continued to produce records, always with diminishing returns. The band went through several painful

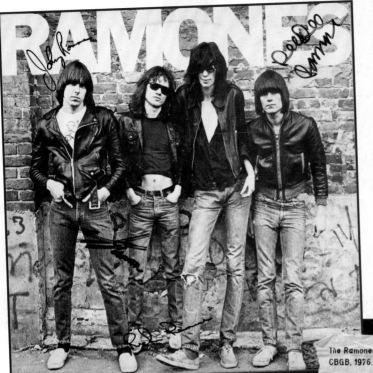

packed stadiums to screaming fans who later mobbed their cars as though they were the Beatles. The official final Ramones concert (the last of some 2,263 shows) took place on August 6, 1996, at the Palace club in Hollywood and was recorded for posterity.

After the Ramones retired, Johnny Ramone sold his legendary Mosrite guitar and moved to California, while Joey became a vocal supporter of numerous bands in the New York scene. The story of the Ramones was ably chronicled in the 2004 documentary *End of the Century*. The film was an open and frank account of the dissension within the band precipitated by Johnny Ramone marrying Joey's girlfriend, Johnny's role as the taskmaster of the group, Dee Dee Ramone's drug problems, and Joey's struggles with obsessive-compulsive disorder. Many of the band members died young: Joey from lymphoma in 2001, Dee Dee from a

heroin overdose in June 2002, and Johnny from cancer in September 2004.

Like too many punk bands, the Ramones were much more popular in the United States after they broke up. Their once obscure (to the mainstream, at least) songs are now heard in movies, commercials, and in baseball stadiums across the country. Despite the vast numbers of their imitators, the Ramones have an enduring legacy in punk history that remains uniquely their own.

Discography:

Ramones (Sire, 1976); *Leave Home* (Sire, 1977); *Rocket to Russia* (Sire, 1977); *Road to Ruin* (Sire, 1978); *It's Alive* (Sire, 1979); *Rock 'n' Roll High School* (Sire, 1979); *End of the Century* (Sire, 1980); *Pleasant Dreams* (Sire, 1981); *Subterranean Jungle* (Sire , 1983); *Too Tough to Die* (Sire, 1984); *Animal Boy* (Sire, 1986); *Halfway to Sanity* (Sire, 1987); *Ramones Mania* (Sire, 1988); *Brain Drain* (Sire, 1989); *All the Stuff (And More) Volume I* (Sire, 1990); *All the Stuff (And More) Volume II* (Sire, 1991); *Loco Live* (Sire, 1991); *Mondo Bizzaro* (Radioactive, 1992); *Acid Eaters* (Radioactive, 1993); *Adios Amigos* (Radioactive, 1995); *Greatest Hits Live* (Radioactive, 1996)

The Ramones at home.
CBGB, 1976.

personnel changes, first in 1978 with the retirement of original drummer and band visionary Tommy Ramone, who desired to work more in production and songwriting for the band (a notion quickly shot down by the band's stern taskmaster, Johnny Ramone). Then replacement drummer Marky Ramone (Mark Bell, the original drummer for the **Voidoids**) left in 1983 due to problems with alcoholism, and was replaced by Richie Ramone (Richie Beau), who departed after three years because he was not paid the same salary as the other band members. Marky returned in 1987 and stayed with the band until the Ramones disbanded.

Many fans were disappointed when founding member Dee Dee Ramone quit in 1989 and was replaced by C.J. Ramone, who (somewhat perversely) adopted Dee Dee's look and even sang some of his songs in concert. Due to **Joey Ramone**'s failing health and the general rigors of touring, the band decided to hang it up in 1996 after several farewell tours that saw packed houses of rapturous fans. In particular, the band had become enormously popular in Latin and South America, where they played in

Rancid in Salt Lake City, 1995. (L to R) Lars Frederiksen, Tim Armstrong, Matt Freeman.

RANCID

1991-present

LINEUP: Tim Armstrong (vocals/guitar); Lars Frederiksen (guitar/vocals); Matt Freeman (bass/vocals); Brett Reed (drums, replaced by Branden Steineckert)

Rancid was one of the few punk bands of the mid- to late-1990s to achieve major commercial success while still being regarded by their fans as having integrity. Led by a couple of longtime constituents of the East Bay scene and former key members of **Operation Ivy**, Matt Freeman and Tim Armstrong, Rancid took Operation Ivy's catchy, brash energy and mashed it up with obvious influences from late-1970s punk to create a commercially viable brand of punk.

Rancid started as a trio in 1991, a few years after Operation Ivy's demise. Armstrong (who had previously played under the name "Lint" and was the ex-husband of Brody Dalle from the Distillers), Freeman, and drummer Brett Reed released their heavily **Clash**-influenced, self-titled debut album in 1993 on **Epitaph** after an EP on **Lookout!** caught the ear of Epitaph founder/**Bad Religion** guitarist Brett Gurewitz. After the first record's surprise success, Rancid decided to augment their sound with second guitarist and vocalist Lars Frederiksen (previously of British punk stalwarts the **UK Subs**) in 1993. Their next record, 1994's *Let's Go*, was one of the few punk crossover records to gain exposure on both major radio stations and **MTV**. The next year, the huge hit album *...And Out Come the Wolves* showed Rancid experimenting with **ska**, **reggae**, and **dub** on hits like "Roots Radicals," "Ruby Soho," and "Time Bomb," songs that established Rancid as one of the most popular punk bands in the world. *Life Won't Wait* continued the formula to more artistic, but less commercial, success. The following record, *Rancid*, was a return to the band's **hardcore** roots but seemed to put them in a creative holding pattern that would last for the next four years.

When Rancid finally returned with a new album in 2003, *Indestructible*, the band had lived though the deaths of close friends, Armstrong's messy divorce, and bouts with alcoholism. The renewed energy, diverse musical styles and arrangements, and the theme of the record—Rancid as a community—reestablished them as one of the best bands in the United States. Although the band faced continual criticism for being on a major label and overtly copying the Clash, Rancid remained one of the most vital and imaginative musical forces on the contemporary American scene. Armstrong also ran Hellcat Records and played in the joke punk/rap band the Transplants.

Discography:
Rancid (Epitaph, 1993); *Let's Go* (Epitaph, 1994); *...And Out Come the Wolves* (Epitaph, 1995); *Life Won't Wait* (Epitaph, 1998); *Rancid* (Hellcat/Epitaph, 2000); *Indestructible* (Hellcat, 2003). **Lars Frederiksen and the Bastards:** *Lars Frederickson and the Bastards* Hellcat, 2001); *Viking* (Hellcat, 1004)

RAR (ROCK AGAINST RACISM)

The one punk-affiliated political movement that made a difference, Rock Against Racism (RAR) raised awareness of racist and Nazi movements in England in the late-1970s, hosting several benefit concerts, mostly in and around London in 1977 and 1978, at which many punk bands played. Started by the Socialist Workers Party, RAR grew out of a general revulsion toward the white-power and anti-immigrant sentiments that had been growing in England since the late-1960s. Oddly enough, RAR was primarily inspired to action after a couple members of British rock royalty apparently made racist comments from the stage: **David Bowie** had supposedly been spouting bizarre pro-fascist statements (he may or may not have been acting in character), while a drunken Eric Clapton made a soon-infamous rant at a 1976 Birmingham, England, concert that implored the crowd to "Stop Britain from becoming a black colony" and to "get the foreigners out."

On May Day, 1977, the RAR house zine summarized the movement's intent by proclaiming "We want rebel music. Crisis Music. Now Music. Music that knows who the real enemy is. Rock Against Racism." The movement's biggest event was held in April 1978, when approximately 100,000 people marched six miles from Trafalgar Square to East London for a "Carnival Against the Nazis" featuring the **Clash**, **X-Ray Spex**, and British **reggae** band Steel Pulse. The British police often used heavy-handed tactics against members of the organizations that sponsored Rock Against Racism, as documented in the **Ruts** song "Jah War." It is unclear how many punk bands in Britain supported RAR, but what is clear is that the massive response to its anti-racism message played a major role in publicizing and turning back the tide of racist hate that had been building to critical mass in Britain at the end of the 1970s.

Joe Strummer (Left) and Mick Jones of the Clash at the July 14, 1979, RAR show in London.

THE RAT

LOCATION: BOSTON

While the Boston scene never gets its due in the annals of punk history, and many of its members can endlessly argue the merits of **SSD** versus Willie "Boom Boom" Alexander to the present day, the one thing no Boston punk worth their salt can deny is the importance of the Rat. Officially the Rathskeller, the Rat opened in 1974 on Kenmore Square and was known as the club where many of the early Boston punk bands such as **Unnatural Axe** played during the scene's early heyday. The club persisted long into the age of **new wave** with bands as diverse as **Talking Heads**, **Black Flag**, the **Dead Boys**, the Proletariat, and even REM playing there. A dive bar that all Boston fans—from **straight-edge** kids to **ska** and **hardcore** fans—called their own, the Rat continued to showcase Boston's best groups as well as touring bands until its demise in 1997.

RAZORCAKE

One of the most popular and influential zines in the United States, the Los Angeles-based *Razorcake* covers punk and pop culture via the musings of contributors like Nardwuar and Rev. Norb. Founded in 2001 by Sean Carswell and former *Flipside* copublisher Todd Taylor, *Razorcake* is notable for not playing the punk litmus-test game so common to other punk zines. While other zines are often subject to haphazard production schedules and shoddy design, *Razorcake* looks and feels a lot like a typical magazine that would appear in an ideal world where

bands such as the Mormons, Pink Razors, and the Love Me Nots got the acclaim they so richly deserve. The zine also features some of the best cartoonists working in the punk underground, such as Kiyoshi Nakazawa and the ever-entertaining Ben Snakepit. *Razorcake* also sponsors an independent book publisher, Gorsky Press.

RONALD REAGAN

The focal point for incessant outpourings of punk outrage during the 1980s, U.S. president Ronald Reagan, the perennial B-list actor-turned-Cold-Warrior, seemed to symbolize everything that was wrong with America during that decade. Reagan's combination of relentless cheeriness and Commie-hating militarism was a constant irritant to many teens growing up in suburban America, so it naturally followed that punk would use Reagan for creative target practice.

The ever-amiable Reagan was referenced in a slew of punk songs from "I Shot Reagan" by **Suicidal Tendencies** to the **Ramones'** "Bonzo Goes to Bitburg" (written and produced with the help of the **Plasmatics'** Jean Beauvoir) to "Fucked Up Ronnie" by **D.O.A.**, while his cheaply photocopied (and often defaced) visage leered out from at least half of the band flyers taped up on club walls.

In the early-1980s a group of anarchistic punks took the name **Reagan Youth** from the president, and in 1983 bands like the **Dicks** and the **Crucifucks** toured on the Rock Against Reagan tour. Additionally, in the mid-1980s a campaign of civil disobedience by Washington, D.C., punks vehemently opposed Reagan's foreign and domestic policies through protests, benefit concerts, creative graffiti, and posters that decried various members of the Reagan administration. An effort was made to replicate the anti-Reagan consensus during the 2004 election with the Rock Against Bush tour, organized by **Fat Wreck Chords'** Michael "Fat Mike" Burkett. While George W. Bush may have finally surpassed Reagan in the amount of rage and venom aimed against him, there's just no replacement for the Gipper.

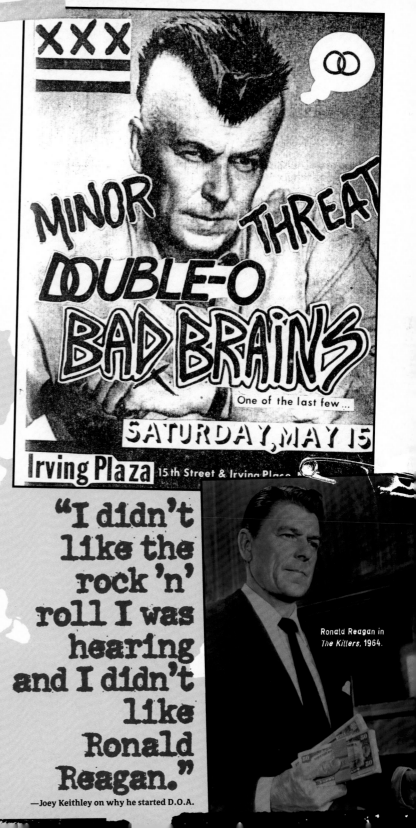

XXX

MINOR THREAT
DOUBLE-O
BAD BRAINS
One of the last few...
SATURDAY, MAY 15
Irving Plaza 15th Street & Irving Place

"I didn't like the rock 'n' roll I was hearing and I didn't like Ronald Reagan."

—Joey Keithley on why he started D.O.A.

Ronald Reagan in *The Killers*, 1964.

REAGAN YOUTH

1980–1989, 2007–present

LINEUP: Dave Insurgent (vocals); Paul Cripple (guitar); Andy Apathy (bass, replaced by Al Pike, replaced by Vic Venom); Charley Tripper (drums, replaced by "The Steve," replaced by Johnny Aztec)

Your quintessential New York **hardcore**, anarchist **crust-punk** band, Reagan Youth really, *really* couldn't stand the president. Singer Dave Insurgent (Dave Rubenstein) and guitarist Paul Cripple (Paul Bakija) started the band while still in high school, quickly making their mark on the scene alongside bands such as **Agnostic Front** and the **Cro-Mags**, with whom they played many Sunday afternoon **CBGB** hardcore matinees during the 1980s. In all the years they were together, Reagan Youth only released one album, possibly as a result of some of the members' drug addictions. The band broke up in the late-1980s after their nemesis **Ronald Reagan** left office and the band's name became obsolete. Various members played together in loose aggregations after the band's demise but never had the level of success enjoyed by Reagan Youth. Rubenstein fell prey to drug addiction along with his prostitute girlfriend Tiffany Bresciani. In 1993, after his mother died in a car accident and Tiffany was murdered by Long Island serial killer Joel Rifkin, Rubenstein subsequently committed suicide. Rubenstein's friend Jesse Malin later formed **D Generation**, who often closed their shows playing the Reagan Youth song "Degenerated," and dedicating it to Rubenstein. Bassist Al Pike later played in the post-**Misfits** band Samhain. In 2007, Reagan Youth regrouped without Insurgent and toured again with new vocalist Pat Distraction.

Discography:
Reagan Youth Volume 1 (New Red Archives, 1989); *Reagan Youth Volume 2* (New Red Archives, 1990); *A Collection of Pop Classics 1984* (New Red Archives, 1994); *Live and Rare* (New Red Archives, 1998); *Punk Rock New York* (LoveCat Music, 2004)

REDD KROSS

1980–1987, occasionally thereafter

LINEUP: Jeff McDonald (vocals); Greg Hetson (guitar, replaced by others); Steve McDonald (bass); John Stielow (drums, replaced by others)

The McDonald brothers, Jeff and Steve, formed Los Angeles's Redd Kross in 1978 when Jeff was 14 and Steve was 11, originally calling themselves the Tourists and then Red Cross (the name later modified after a threatened lawsuit by the International Red Cross). Their first public performance was at an eighth-grade graduation party, which also starred an embryonic **Black Flag**. The original band featured the McDonald brothers, along with Greg Hetson on guitar and John Stielow on drums (replaced soon by Ron Reyes, who replaced **Keith Morris** in Black Flag). Numerous personnel changes shook the band (including Dez Cadena, pre-Black Flag, on guitar) before settling on a lineup of Tracy Marshak on guitar and Janet Housden on drums (a rare example of female representation in an early **hardcore** band) for the *Born Innocent* record. Even though the band appeared on the cover of *Flipside*, Redd Kross later abandoned hardcore for a more melodic, hippie-inspired, psychedelic sound that was epitomized on their 1987 album *Neurotica*. Redd Kross also worked as the hardcore parody band Anarchy 6.

Discography:
Red Cross EP (Posh Boy, 1980, 1987); *Born Innocent* (Smoke 7, 1982; Frontier, 1986); *Teen Babes from Monsanto* (Enigma, 1984); *Neurotica* (Big Time, 1987; Five Foot Two/Oglio, 2002); *Third Eye* (Atlantic, 1990); *Phaseshifter* (This Way Up/Mercury, 1993); *2,500 Redd Kross Fans Can't Be Wrong* EP (Sympathy for the Record Industry, 1994); *Show World* (This Way Up, 1997). **Anarchy 6:** *Hardcore Lives!* (Gasatanka/Giant, 1988); *Live Like a Suicidal* (tape; Dutch East Tapes, 1991)

Redd Kross c.1993: (L to R) Jeff McDonald, Gere Fennelly, Eddie Kurdziel, Steve McDonald, Brian Reitzel.

LOU REED

Regarded as one of the founding fathers of punk rock for his groundbreaking work with the **Velvet Underground** and for his decadent and adventurous work in the early-1970s, it is hard to imagine punk existing without Lou Reed, whom almost every early punk cites as an inspiration.

A prolific pop songwriter and student of poet Delmore Schwartz, Reed formed the Velvet Underground in 1965. After the band's demise, Reed took several of their songs and recorded his first solo album with Rick Wakeman and Steve Howe (both of art rock band, Yes) as session musicians. The *Lou Reed* album, however, was a constrained continuation of the work Reed had been doing with the Velvet Underground, and it wasn't until the **David Bowie**-produced *Transformer*, that Reed reached his full potential on songs such as "Vicious," "Perfect Day," and the radio hit "Walk on the Wild Side," all of which celebrated the decadence of the New York glam and downtown scenes. (Most of the characters in the song "Walk on the Wild Side" were members of Andy Warhol's entourage.) With the 1973 song cycle *Berlin*, Reed turned more somber, perhaps reflecting his own personal disintegration into drug and alcohol dependency. But he proved his vitality the following year with the aggressive live album *Rock n Roll Animal*, cementing his position as a proponent of what would soon be called punk rock.

Reed was on the cover (via a **John Holmstrom** illustration) and the subject of a feature story in the first issue of *Punk* magazine, demonstrating the large debt that the scene owed to him. After *Rock n Roll Animal*, however, Reed's work became much less inspired and deliberately difficult, as in the case of the notoriously unlistenable *Metal Machine Music*, which Reed supposedly recorded in an attempt to get out of his contract with RCA Records.

Solid work followed on *The Blue Mask* and *The Bells*, but Reed settled into apparent artistic complacency for most of the 1980s. He returned to form with the dark, 1989 concept album *New York* and his collaboration the following year with old pal John Cale on the apologetic Warhol tribute *Songs for Drella*. Reed continued to experiment

LEFT: Lou Reed goes Bowie in Brussels, 1974.

RIGHT: Lou Reed in his signature garb, undated.

and even re-formed the Velvet Underground for a tour and live record in 1996, the same year the group was inducted into the Rock and Roll Hall of Fame. He continues to release challenging, if noncommercial, music to a rabid fan base.

Discography:

Lou Reed (RCA, 1972); *Transformer* (RCA, 1972, 1981); *Berlin* (RCA, 1973, 1981); *Sally Can't Dance* (RCA, 1974); *Rock n Roll Animal* (RCA, 1974, 1981); *Lou Reed Live* (RCA, 1975); *Metal Machine Music: The Amine B Ring* (RCA, 1975; Buddah, 2000); *Coney Island Baby* (RCA, 1976); *Rock and Roll Heart* (Arista, 1976); *Walk on the Wild Side: The Best of Lou Reed* (RCA, 1977); *Street Hassle* (Arista, 1978); *Live: Take No Prisoners* (Arista, 1978); *The Bells* (Arista, 1979); *Growing Up in Public* (Arista, 1980); *Rock and Roll Diary 1967–1980* (Arista, 1980); *The Blue Mask* (RCA, 1982); *I Can't Stand It* (RCA, 1982); *Legendary Hearts* (RCA, 1983); *Live in Italy* (RCA, 1984); *New Sensations* (RCA, 1984); *City Lights: Classic Performances* (Arista, 1985); *Mistrial* (RCA, 1986); *New York* (Sire, 1989); *Retro* (RCA, 1989); *Magic and Loss* (Sire, 1992); *Between Thought and Expression: The Lou Reed Anthology* (RCA, 1992); *Set the Twilight Reeling* (Warner Bros., 1996); *Different Times: Lou Reed in the '70s* (RCA, 1996); *Perfect Night: Live in London* (Warner Bros., 1998); *The Definitive Collection* (Arista, 1999); *Ecstasy* (Warner Bros., 2000); *NYC Man: The Collection* (BMG Heritage/RCA, 2003); *The Raven* (Warner Bros., 2003). **Lou Reed/John Cale:** *Songs for Drella* (Sire/Warner Bros., 1990)

REGGAE

Reggae has had an enormous impact on punk rock both in England and in the United States, with numerous bands like the **Clash, Public Image Ltd.**, and the **Slits** frequently drawing on its rhythms and lyrical content. In the United States, bands such as **Bad Brains** (whose members actually converted to Rastafarianism), **Operation Ivy**, **Rancid**, and **NOFX** also draw upon reggae's rhythms and subject matter.

The history of punk and reggae can be traced to England, where disaffected Caribbean immigrants settled in mostly urban areas rife with police harassment. Their resistance to the discrimination they faced inspired a punk community looking for other outlaw figures to identify with in a culture that marked both themselves and Rastafarians as outsiders. Dedicated genre fans such as Paul Simonon and **Joe Strummer** of the Clash helped incorporate reggae rhythms into their music. The Clash went on to cover numerous reggae songs, such as "Police and Thieves" by Junior Murvin and "Pressure Drop" by Toots and the Maytals, and also worked with reggae producers Mikey Dread and Lee "Scratch" Perry. The Clash also tried to articulate how they were inspired by Rastafarian resistance to authority in the songs "White Riot" and "White Man in Hammersmith Palais," which expressed their frustration about how white punks were not as unified or as politically active as Rastafarians.

Around the same time, other punks such as **John Lydon** (who allegedly had the largest reggae collection in England in the 1970s) spent time in Jamaica with reggae heroes like Dr. Alimantado. **Don Letts** played reggae and **dub** music during his DJ sets at **Acme Attractions** and the **Roxy**, partly because of the lack of acceptable punk singles to play during the mid-1970s but also because of the antiauthoritarian affinity he perceived between punk and reggae. In a display of solidarity among dispossessed peoples, Bob Marley wrote a song called "Punky Reggae Party," in which he noted the "Slits, the Clash, and the Feelgoods" would be there alongside the Wailers in a party at which all men are "rejected by society, treated with impunity,

Bob Marley performing in the 1970s.

protected by their dignity." The implicit connections between Rastafarians and punks in England were key to early punk and the development of punk into **post-punk**, and the revolutionary advances made by bands such as Public Image Ltd. and the Slits cannot be imagined without the influence of reggae bands. English punk's resistance to the norms of society was clearly influenced by the ready-made antiestablishment views espoused by reggae artists. Later, the **2 Tone** movement led by the **Specials**, the Beat, the Selecter, and Madness—bands mostly influenced by reggae's predecessors, **ska,** and rock steady—helped fuse a black-and-white coalition in an effort to fight racism and the **National Front**.

Although some American bands are and were influenced by reggae, many ultimately drew more from ska than reggae, although there are several important exceptions. Bad Brains, credited with introducing reggae to most U.S. punks, were militant Rastafarians torn between the desire to play punk and the need to reconcile their religion with a largely antireligious scene. Bad Brains' powerful fusion of punk and reggae influenced countless bands, most notably **Fugazi**. Unfortunately, Bad Brains also absorbed some of the less open-minded aspects of the Rastafarian religion, such as its intolerance of homosexuality. Other American bands like Operation Ivy, Rancid, and NOFX also used reggae and ska rhythms, although the former owed a particular debt to the Clash's use of reggae. (NOFX's guitarist El Hefe has acknowledged how the resistance to modern society embedded in reggae was critical to the band's political awakening.)

Although numerous bands still try to fuse the aggression of punk with reggae's musical and ideological approach, which in its purest form is a positive step, the less savory aspects of Rastafarian culture (their apocalyptic nature, homophobia, and some sects' reverse racism) brings into question whether reggae's ideology can be separated from the music.

JAMIE REID

Situationist and conceptual artist Jamie Reid (born in 1947) is best known for his early cut-and-paste montage work on the flyers and graphic design for the **Sex Pistols**. Reid helped define the punk appropriation of disparate images that would symbolize the **DIY** art style used by numerous punk bands. Reid's connection with punk began when he met **Malcolm McLaren** in 1968 (a particularly significant year for the Situationist movement) while organizing a student protest at Croydon Art College. After college, Reid founded Suburban Press in 1970, where he worked to develop his unique cut-and-paste style that turned advertisements from images of suburban society into something much more sinister and subversive.

When McLaren needed help in getting the Sex Pistols a unique design style, he turned to Reid, who reworked the ripped-up punk style in new ways that emphasized the music's political and tribal nature, placing it in firm opposition to popular culture.

Reid's most prominent work for the Sex Pistols included the album cover for *Never Mind the Bollocks, Here's the Sex Pistols* and the sleeves for the singles "Anarchy in the UK," "God Save the Queen," "Holidays in the Sun," and "Pretty Vacant." Reid is now a world-famous artist who exhibits his work in major museums such as the Centre Pompidou in Paris and the Victoria & Albert Museum in London. He also worked on the Ten Year project at the Strongroom Recording Studios in London, which celebrated Reid's anarchist and Druidic beliefs.

NEVER MIND THE BOLLOCKS HERE'S THE SEX PISTOLS

Jamie Reid, 1990.

"No one dramatized the limits of freedom better than the Replacements, whose youthful violence was always directed at themselves."

—Peter S. Scholtes, *City Pages*, September 5, 2001

ONLY D·C· APPEARANCE!!!!!!!!!

THE

REPLACEMENTS

AT TICKETRON
$12.00/$9.00 W.GWID
ON SALE NOW

WEDNESDAY
Feb. 5th
8:00pm

GEORGE WASHINGTON UNIV.
MARVIN CENTER
800 21ST. STREET N. W.

The 'Mats take San Francisco, 1987.

THE REPLACEMENTS

1979-1990

LINEUP: Paul Westerberg (vocals/guitar);
Bob Stinson (guitar, replaced by Slim
Dunlap); Tommy Stinson (bass); Chris Mars
(drums, replaced by Steve Foley)

A bratty and shambolic punk, pop, classic rock, and ultimately indefinable band of misfits led by master songwriter Paul Westerberg, the Replacements started doing sloppy **hardcore** before shifting course radically and becoming one of the most important bands in 1980s and '90s alternative rock.

The Stinson brothers of Minneapolis started the Replacements in the late-1970s as the Impediments, with Bob on guitar, Tommy (who was only 14 when the band began) on bass, and Chris Mars on drums. They were joined by Westerberg, who apparently heard the band rehearsing through a basement window and asked if he could join as guitarist and singer. He soon became chief songwriter as well. The band's first album, 1981's *Sorry Ma, Forgot to Take Out the Trash*, was a messy thrasher that featured numerous, jokey hardcore songs (including "Something to Du," a nod to fellow Minneapolis punks **Hüsker Dü**), many clocking in at only a minute or so. The hardcore phase didn't last too long, though, as the Replacements had already begun to mature musically by the second EP, *The Replacements Stink*, which contained a number of slower and more melodic songs along with a few powerful anthems like "Dope Smokin' Moron" and "Fuck School." The two albums that followed (1983's

Hootenanny and 1984's *Let It Be*) were hailed as instant classics upon their release, and the Replacements legend continued to grow.

If the Replacements (or the 'Mats, as their die-hard fan called them) were maturing musically, they were also de-volving into a drunken and stoned mess onstage, with gigs a haphazard prospect at best as members wandered drunkenly on- and offstage or took audience requests to play songs they barely knew. (This is captured in all its debauched glory on the cassette-only release *The Shit Hits the Fans*.) Bob Stinson was the biggest offender, even-tually becoming too much for even the heavy-drinking Westerberg to take. After the band decamped from their longtime label Twin/Tone for major label Sire—yielding the more commercial release *Tim*—Bob was fired. After releasing *Pleased to Meet Me* as a trio, guitarist Slim Dunlap joined the band. Westerberg began to chafe under the limitations of the group, and the last record, *All Shook Down*, was essentially a Westerberg solo record featur-ing limited contributions from the rest of the Replacements. By the last tour, Mars had been sacked and replaced by drummer Steve Foley. Their last show was a free con-cert in Chicago's Grant Park on July 4, 1991.

After the breakup of the Replacements, Westerberg sobered up and started a semi-successful and critically acclaimed solo career. Bassist Tommy Stinson later joined the latter-day version of Guns N' Roses and somehow managed to put out several solo records at the same time. Mars put out sev-eral solo records with album covers that illustrated his abilities as a painter. Bob Stinson tried to start a variety of new bands before his career of substance abuse caught up with him; he died in 1995. Despite the legends and hyperbole that surrounded the Replacements, at their best they were one of the greatest and most brutally honest bands in American music.

Discography:

Sorry Ma, Forgot to Take Out the Trash (Twin\Tone, 1981); *The Replacements Stink* EP (Twin\Tone, 1982, 1986); *Hootenanny* (Twin\Tone, 1983); *Let It Be* (Twin\Tone, 1984); *The Shit Hits the Fans* (tape; Twin\Tone, 1985); *Tim* (Sire, 1985); *Boink!!* (Glass, 1986); *Pleased to Meet Me* (Sire, 1987); *Don't Tell a Soul* (Sire/Reprise, 1989); *All Shook Down* (Sire/Reprise, 1990)

REVELATION RECORDS

LOCATION: NEW HAVEN, CONNECTICUT; HUNTINGTON BEACH, CALIFORNIA

First started in Connecticut in 1987 by Jordan Cooper and Ray Cappo of **Youth of Today**, Revelation Records' catalog certainly reflects the taste of the founders. The label began with a **Warzone** seven-inch single in 1987 and has since released more than 120 records by artists such as **Civ**, **Sick of It All**, **Dag Nasty**, Youth of Today, **Bold**, **Supertouch**, **Gorilla Biscuits**, **Judge**, and **Ignite**; not to mention the scene-defining compilation *New York Hardcore—The Way It Is*. Although many of the records released by Revelation (especially during the early years) were by **straight-edge** bands, they never turned into a completely straight-edge label. Cappo left Revelation in 1988 to concentrate more on his work with Krishna Consciousness. The label later relocated to Huntington Beach, California.

REVOLUTION SUMMER

The term *Revolution Summer* was first used by Washington, D.C., scene stalwart Amy Pickering (later of **Dischord Records**), who was working a job at the Neighborhood Planning Council in the U.S. capital when she decided to create an uprising against an unpopular supervisor. Pickering started sending notes reading, "Be on your toes... this is Revolution Summer," to a variety of Georgetown punks, who became energized by the potential of real revolutionary change. The term became a self-fulfilling prophecy that was later used to describe the political and social protests led by punks and **Positive Force** in D.C. during the summer of 1985. During this time, many punks engaged in resistance actions against the **Ronald Reagan** administration, with Dischord cofounder and former **Minor Threat** drummer Jeff Nelson famously placing numerous signs and posters around

town that described Attorney General Edwin Meese as "a pig." Summer 1985 also saw the rise of a new generation of more emotionally mature and politically active bands such as **Rites of Spring** and **Beefeater**. Although there were no long-lasting political ramifications of the Revolution Summer, it demonstrated how punks could, with proper mobilization, organize to demand change.

THE RICH KIDS
1977-1979

LINEUP: Midge Ure (vocals/guitar); Glen Matlock (vocals/bass); Steve New (guitar); Rusty Egan (drums); Ian "Mac" McLagan (keyboards)

Saying later he had gotten sick of "all the bullshit," bassist Glen Matlock was unceremoniously ousted from the **Sex Pistols** in 1977 (he was replaced by **Sid Vicious**), after that he set up this poppy, **new wave**-influenced band. They released only one album, *Ghosts of Princes in Towers*, produced by former **David Bowie** collaborator Mick Ronson and featuring Ian McLagan from the Small Faces/Faces on keyboards. After the Rich Kids' brief tenure, singer-guitarist Midge Ure went on to the popular, electro-new wave group Ultravox. Matlock continued to record and argue his importance in the Sex Pistols story, publishing his memoir *I Was a Teenage Sex Pistol* in 1990 and rejoining the band for their various reunion tours.

Discography:
Ghosts of Princes in Towers (EMI, 1978; Fame, 1983)

RIOT GRRRL

One of the only punk movements that actually made waves in mainstream society, Riot Grrrl was an anarchistic collection of like-minded individuals working through low-budget labels, zines, and spoken word to reenergize punk, if only for a few glorious years.

Although many women were considered key figures in the early days of Riot Grrrl, the primary instigators were Allison Wolfe and Molly Neuman (later of **Bratmobile**) from the zine *Girl Germs*, who had met in Olympia, Washington, in 1989. The two of them, along with **Kathleen Hanna** of **Bikini Kill**, produced a manifesto that celebrated a hypothetical

"girl riot." The manifesto noted the lack of encouragement women faced in a boy-band-dominated atmosphere, proclaimed their refusal to quietly accept the male status quo, and, while denying they were reverse sexists, laid claim to being the "TRUEPUNKROCKSOULCRUSADERS THAT WE KNOW we really are." The Riot Grrrl label stuck and was applied to bands such as Bratmobile and Bikini Kill, who wore the title proudly. But it was also universal enough in the true spirit of **DIY** to encourage females across the country and the world to make the term their own and start their own bands, zines, or other outlets for artistic expression.

Although there was a manifesto, there was no dogma, so Riot Grrrl was free to be whatever combination of feminism and self-expression that could be created outside the standards of the male-dominated punk rock scene. The idea that punk didn't have to be a boys-only club proved infectious, and it spread to scenes around the world, establishing particularly strong roots in England with bands like **Huggy Bear**.

With the media primed in 1991 to look for the next big underground movement after grunge, Riot Grrrl made for great copy. A positive story in the short-lived, feminist-lite magazine *Sassy* that year was followed by a veritable media onslaught,

Riot Grrrls at the Supreme Court, 1992.

Riot Grrrls protest at the Supreme Court, 1992.

RISE AGAINST

1999–present

LINEUP: Tim McIlrath (vocals); Dan Precision (guitar, replaced by Todd Mohney, Chris Chasse, Zach Blair); Joe Principe (bass); Brandon Barnes (drums)

The Chicago-based punks of Rise Against (including two former members of the much-beloved Windy City **pop-punk** outfit 88 Fingers Louie) started in 1999 to make more politically aware, **hardcore** punk defined by the harshness of lead singer Tim McIlrath's powerful vocals. Originally named Transistor Revolt, they released a self-produced demo under that name in 2000 and played numerous times on the **Vans Warped** tour. After releasing two albums on **Fat Wreck Chords**, they bolted for Geffen in 2004. There, Rise Against's use of the classic production duo of Bill Stevenson and Stephen Egerton (of the **Descendents** and **All**) beefed up their sound to an almost metallic sheen on *Siren Song of the Counter-Culture*, but captured the band at their creative peak on the 2006 album, *The Sufferer & the Witness*. Along with frequent tour mates **Against Me**, Rise Against demonstrates that taking on the mainstream can be done within the confines of a major label.

Discography:
The Unraveling (Fat Wreck Chords, 2001); *Revolutions per Minute* (Fat Wreck Chords, 2003); *Siren Song of the Counter-Culture* (Geffen, 2004); *The Sufferer & the Witness* (Geffen, 2006); *This is Noise* EP (Geffen, 2008)

Rise Against convinces the crowd that they haven't sold out.

particularly during the summer 1992 Riot Grrrl convention in Washington, D.C. Magazines and newspapers such as *Newsweek* and *Rolling Stone* weren't sure what to make of Riot Grrrl, with a *USA Today* story including this condescending bit: "From hundreds of once pink, frilly bedrooms comes the young feminist revolution. And it's not pretty. But it doesn't wanna be. So there!" All this attention by a part-titillated and part-disgusted mainstream media increasingly categorized Riot Grrrl as either "man-hating" or as a fad embraced by mostly middle-class white girls working through their issues.

Due to the unsolicited overexposure and snarky comments from high profile "allies" (including Courtney Love), an unofficial media blackout was put in place by 1993. Many of the central Riot Grrrl groups dissolved not long thereafter, with the exception of Bikini Kill. The legacy of Riot Grrrl lives on in many of the **queercore** bands (the sleeve of Huggy Bear's split album with Bikini Kill reads "Queercore for the Queercorps") and in subsequent projects of its founders, such as Hanna's band **Le Tigre**.

RITES OF SPRING

1984-1986

LINEUP: Guy Picciotto (vocals/guitar); Eddie Janney (guitar); Michael Fellows (bass); Brendan Canty (drums)

Before Jimmy Eat World/Yellowcard/The Used/My Chemical Romance, a band defined the emotional and expressive side of punk rock: Washington, D.C.'s Rites of Spring. A **hardcore** band who slowed down the tempo and wrote about the personal in increasingly obtuse ways, Rites of Spring made fans feel as though the band had been reading their diaries (years before Dashboard Confessional apparently decided to literally do this).

With Guy Picciotto's raw and strained vocals about lost potential and unrequited love, Rites of Spring created not merely a slower version of punk, but one that emphasized saving one's self before saving the world. Sure, the bombs and **Ronald Reagan** would always be there, but would the scene? Allegedly, the band's mix of slowly building dynamics and crescendos made more than one fan cry, although most likely the tale of countless weeping punks is more urban legend than fact. In any case, like their **Dischord** label mates **Embrace**, Rites of Spring brought something new and exciting to a D.C. scene that was already fraying at the edges in the mid-1980s.

Rites of Spring began to play together seriously in March 1984, started by classmates Picciotto and drummer Brendan Canty (who had already played in a couple of short-lived bands together), as well as guitarist Eddie Janney (previously of D.C. stalwarts Untouchables and the **Faith**) and bassist Mike Fellows. One reason Rites of Spring made such a strong impact had to do with the shifting landscape of 1980s punk, with hardcore becoming increasingly restricted and many scenes falling into petty squabbles. The year 1985 saw a reimagining of the punk scene in direct action and defiance during **Revolution Summer**, with Rites of Spring providing a powerful soundtrack to the demonstrations marking the politicization of the D.C. scene. The band's full-length album, *End on End*, was released that year, and even today still withstands the test of time, despite less than stellar production values.

A four-song EP, *All Through A Life*, was recorded in January 1986, but Rites of Spring broke up later that winter. In a strange, "only in D.C." twist, the full lineup re-formed as a completely different band, Happy Go Licky. They played with limited success until 1988 without much recorded output, although **Ian MacKaye** later remastered a recording compiling 21 tracks from seven of their local D.C. live shows and released it as the *Will Play* live album through Dischord. After that, Picciotto and Canty joined Joe Lally and Ian MacKaye in **Fugazi**, and the rest as they say, is history. Guitarist Janney went into production work and also played with soulful New York punks Girls Against Boys. Bassist Fellows worked with both **Royal Trux** and Air Miami, and later recorded under the name Mighty Flashlight.

Discography:
End to End (Discord, 1985); *All Through A Life* EP (Dischord, 1986). **Happy Go Licky**: *Will Play* (Dischord, 1997)

THE RIVERBOAT GAMBLERS

1997-present

LINEUP: Mike Wiebe, aka "Teko" (vocals); Fadi El-Assad, aka "Freddy Castro" (guitar); Colin James, aka "Colin Ambulance" (guitar, replaced by Ian MacDougall); Pat Lillard, aka "Spider" (bass, replaced by Rob Marchant); Jesse Hamilton, aka "Jesse 3X" (drums)

One of the great modern punk bands, Riverboat Gamblers formed in the college town of Denton, Texas. They are particularly renowned for their energetic live performances during which front man Teko rolls around, climbs on gear, and generally demolishes the stage, the band's equipment, and occasionally the rest of the band and the audience. Despite entreaties by major labels following a particularly compelling show at the 2003 South by Southwest festival in Austin, Texas, the Riverboat Gamblers remained true to their indie roots, a tactic that has proven successful for their expanding fanbase. Over the last few years the Riverboat Gamblers have been steadily touring, with the likes of the **Rollins Band**, **X**, **Against Me**, and the **MC5**. While the records are always engaging, the band keeps their following based on the energy of their live shows, which rival the intensity of an **Iggy Pop** performance.

Discography:
Riverboat Gamblers (Vile Beat, 2001); *Something to Crow About* (Gearhead, 2003); *To the Confusion of Our Enemies* (Volcom, 2006)

THE RIVERDALES

1995-present

LINEUP: Ben Foster, aka "Ben Weasel" (vocals/guitar); Dan Schafer, aka "Dan Vapid" (bass/vocals); Dan Sullivan, aka "Dan Panic" (drums, replaced by Dan Lumley)

A **Ramones**-esque side project that featured three of the four members of **Screeching Weasel**, Chicago's Riverdales followed the same sonic template as Screeching Weasel but in an even poppier style. While their music is undeniably catchy, the Riverdales' close approximation of the Ramones template has been criticized by some as making them a veritable cover band. (But then again, if one is going to start a cover band, one may as well cover the Ramones.) The

Riverdales' debut, self-titled 1995 album was produced by Screeching Weasel's Mass Giorgini and Billie Joe Armstrong from **Green Day;** the Riverdales later opened for Green Day and continued in their own idiosyncratic way, as is typical of a Ben Weasel band.

Discography:

Riverdales (Lookout!, 1995); *Storm the Streets* (Honest Don's, 1997); *Phase Three* (145, 2003). **Ben Weasel and His Iron String Quartet:** *These Ones Are Bitter* (Mendota, 2007)

TOM ROBINSON

Although much of Tom Robinson's work (especially after the late-1970s and early-'80s) was tangential to punk rock, his first two records with the Tom Robinson Band (which he formed after being inspired by a **Sex Pistols** show) and his influence on the late-'70s scene were quite substantial. The Tom Robinson Band performed, along with the **Clash**, **X-Ray Spex**, and **Generation X**, at the famous 1978 **RAR (Rock Against Racism)** concert in London's East End. Staunchly political (his band's logo copied the clenched-fist design used by the International Socialists), Robinson was also notable as one of the foremost openly gay musicians in the early English punk scene, a fact he celebrated in the controversial 1978 single "Glad to be Gay," eventually banned by the BBC. Robinson's music comes across today as better than average pub rock, but it was performed at a time when British punk had yet to settle on a single musical style. Robinson's introduction of the political as personal marked him as one of the few early punks not to merely scream for revolution, but also to come up with a platform for political change.

Discography:

Tom Robinson Band: *Rising Free* EP (EMI, 1978); *Power in the Darkness* (Harvest/Capitol, 1978; Razor & Tie, 1993); *TRB Two* (Harvest, 1979; Razor & Tie, 1993); *Tom Robinson Band* (EMI, 1981; Fame, 1982); *Rising Free: The Very Best of TRB* (EMI Gold, 1997). **Tom Robinson:** *North by Northwest* (IRS, 1982); *Cabaret '79: Glad to Be Gay* (Panic, 1982; Castaway Northwest, 1997); *Atmospherics* EP (Panic, 1983); *Hope and Glory* (Geffen, 1984; Castaway Northwest, 1997); *Still Loving You* (Castaway Northwest, 1986; Blueprint, 1998); *The Collection 1977–1987* (EMI, 1987); *Last Tango: Midnight at the Fridge* (Dojo, 1987; Castaway Northwest, 1997); *Back in the Old Country* (Connoisseur Collection, 1989); *Living in a Boom Time* (Cooking Vinyl, 1992); *Love Over Rage* (Rhythm Safari/Priority, 1994); *Having It Both Ways* (Cooking Vinyl, 1996); *The Undiscovered* (Cooking Vinyl, 1998); *Home from Home* (Oyster, 1999)

Tom Robinson, who has a band, 1982.

ROCKABILLY

Both in its original 1950s form and also through its frequent revivals during the '60s and '70s, rockabilly was a key (although often unsung) influence on punk both musically and stylistically, as well as an inspiration for punk's ever-present sneer. Rockabilly inspired much of the fashion choices for British Teddy Boys and, later, punks—particularly the uniform of boots, bandanas, and slick-backed hair. In his duck-tailed days, **Joe Strummer** adopted a rockabilly look and showed his allegiance to the genre in **Clash** songs such as their cover of "I Fought the Law." (In 2003, several bands recorded a Clash tribute album called *This Is Rockabilly Clash*.) Bands such as the **Cramps** make the influence of rockabilly on punk particularly obvious, while the likes of the Reverend Horton Heat and the Supersuckers attracted a crossover of punk and rockabilly fans that eventually formed into a mutant crossbreed known as *psychobilly*. In 2006, Rhino Records released a huge 101-song anthology titled *Rockin' Bones: 1950s Punk and Rockabilly* that made the connection even more explicit.

ROCKET FROM THE CRYPT

1990-2005

LINEUP: John "Speedo" Reis (vocals/guitar); Andy "The Notorious N.D." Stamets (guitar); Pete Reichert, aka "Petey X" (bass); Adam "Atom" Willard (drums, replaced by Ruby Mars); Paul "Apollo 9" O'Beirne (sax/percussion); Jason "JC 2000" Crane (trumpet/percussion)

Following the breakup of San Diego **hard-core** band Pitchfork, John Reis (aka Speedo) decided to form a new band who would pay tribute to one of the great proto-punk bands, the short-lived, Cleveland super-group **Rocket from the Tombs**. At the same time Reis was playing in the similarly supercharged and intricately chaotic, post-hardcore band Drive Like Jehu (who broke up in 1995). Rocket from the Crypt, however, spent a decade and a half putting out oddly complex punk rock with the unique addition of a two-man horn section who doubled as extra percussionists.

After several years of touring and garnering a substantial indie following (one can still see their logo tattooed on the arms and backs of many fans), in 1995 Rocket from the Crypt released an EP and two albums—*Hot Charity* on small label Elemental, and their major label debut, *Scream, Dracula, Scream!*. The records were hailed by critics for their clear connection to the raw garage and proto-punk sound of their aforementioned heroes. For their efforts Rocket from the Crypt achieved **MTV** airplay, as well as an opening slot on tour with **Rancid**. After the typical lineup changes, Rocket from the Crypt finally broke up following a farewell concert on Halloween 2005. Drummer Ruby Mars was for a time a pro skateboarder, competing as Mario Rubalcaba, while band mastermind Reis put together a new band, the Night Marchers.

Discography:

Paint As a Fragrance (Headhunter, 1991); *Circa: Now!* (Headhunter, 1992; Interscope, 1993); *All Systems Go* (Headhunter, 1993; Sympathy for the Record Industry, 1998); *Hot Charity* (Elemental, 1995); *Scream, Dracula, Scream!* (Interscope, 1995); *RFTC* (Interscope, 1998); *All Systems Go II* (Swami, 1999); *Group Sounds* (Vagrant, 2001); *Live from Camp X-Ray* (TVT, 2002)

ABOVE: Rockabilly revivalists the Reverend Horton Heat, 2001.

RIGHT: Rocket from the Crypt, 1996.

ROCKET FROM THE TOMBS

1974–1975

LINEUP: David Thomas, aka "Crocus Behemoth" (vocals); Peter Laughner (guitar); Gene O'Connor, aka "Cheetah Chrome" (guitar); Craig Bell (bass); Johnny "Madman" Madansky (drums)

The ultimate 1970s Ohio proto-punk band Rocket from the Tombs was influenced just as much by the raw rock of the **Stooges** and bleak lyrics of **Lou Reed** as they were by the absurdist music and humor of Frank Zappa. The band was legendary on the Cleveland scene during their short life span, but internal tension over the role of singer David Thomas (a local reporter also known as "Crocus Behemoth") and his unique voice soon split the band into different camps. After trying out a young Stiv Bators (later of the **Dead Boys**) on vocals and having different members of the band individually singing their songs, the band decided to break up.

Members of Rocket from the Tombs would later go on to form **Pere Ubu** and the Dead Boys, changing their names along the way: Guitarist Gene O'Connor to Cheetah Chrome and drummer Johnny "Madman" Madansky to Johnny Blitz. In 1977, 25-year-old guitarist Pete Laughner (who had spent time in Pere Ubu, as well as a few other bands, and who had befriended *Creem* writer **Lester Bangs**) died of liver failure brought on by chronic substance abuse. Several surviving members, including Thomas and Chrome, along with **Television** guitarist Richard Lloyd, reunited for reunion tours as Rocket from the Tombs almost 30 years after the band's demise. In 1990 a group of San Diego punks would pay the band the ultimate compliment by naming themselves **Rocket from the Crypt**.

Discography:
The Day the Earth Met the Rocket from the Tombs (Smog Veil, 2002)

ROIR RECORDS

LOCATION: NEW YORK

An eclectic and powerfully influential label, ROIR Records (Reach Out International Records) released seminal music from **Bad Brains** and **Suicide**, as well as numerous dub and reggae classics. ROIR was initially founded by Neil Cooper as a cassette-only label, devoted to an eclectic mix of what would later be referred to as world music and specializing in dub, reggae, and punk music. Other bands who have released records on ROIR include the Skatalites, the **MC5**, the **Raincoats**, the **New York Dolls**, Suicide, and **Television**. The label also released the 1982 compilation *New York Thrash*, which included **Adrenaline O.D.**, **Kraut**, and the first recorded material by those Bad Brains-loving kids, the Beastie Boys. Due to declining sales of cassettes, the label eventually sold LPs and CDs as well.

ROLLINS BAND

1987–2003, 2006

LINEUP: Henry Rollins (vocals); Chris Haskett (guitar); Andrew Weiss (bass, replaced by Marcus Blake, Melvin Gibbs); Sim Cain (drums)

The less-than-creative name for **Henry Rollins'** band after he left **Black Flag** in the late-1980s, the Rollins Band toured relentlessly through the '80s and '90s, showcasing Rollins' new stage persona—equal parts singer, screamer, and actor. A typical show would start in chaos and end with Rollins rolling around the stage in his shorts.

The Rollins Band went through various permutations and lineup changes over the years, all the while keeping to the same structurally complex and punk-influenced but heavy sound that hearkened back to the music of Rollins' youth. He described the band's sound to *Rolling Stone* as "definitely the six-guitars-blazing-per-song, rock-and-roll-Motor-City-madness kind of vibe." The Rollins Band toured and recorded on a regular basis before getting their big break after proving a surprise success as the opening band on the first Lollapalooza tour in 1991. Following that, the Rollins Band had several semi-successful singles, such as "Low Self Opinion" and "Liar," the latter of which was in constant **MTV** rotation.

Originally featuring rhythm section Sim Cain and Andrew Weiss, from Gone and

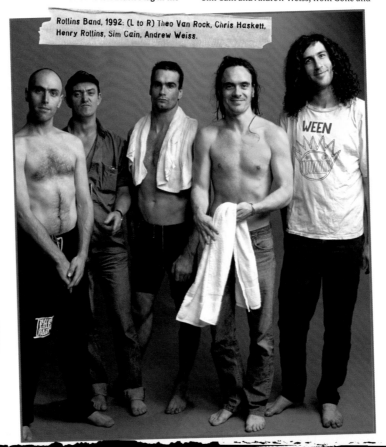

Rollins Band, 1992: (L to R) Theo Van Rock, Chris Haskett, Henry Rollins, Sim Cain, Andrew Weiss.

Regressive Aid, along with guitarist Chris Haskett, the band went through the usual personnel changes in the late-1990s. Rollins later reconstituted the band (without Haskett, Cain, and Weiss) in a more hard rock direction, to diminishing returns, and thereafter concentrated primarily on his spoken-word tours and other ventures. The original lineup returned in 2006 for a few concerts, including a performance on Rollins' show on the IFC cable channel.

Discography:
Life Time (Texas Hotel, 1988; Buddha, 1999); *Do It* (Texas Hotel, 1989); *Hard Volume* (Texas Hotel, 1989; Buddha, 1999); *Turned On* (Quarterstick, 1990); *The End of Silence* (Imago, 1992; NMC, 2002); *Electro Convulsive Therapy* EP (Imago, 1993); *Weight* (Imago, 1994); *Come In and Burn* (DreamWorks, 1997); *Insert Band Here: Live in Australia 1990* (Buddha, 1999); *Get Some Go Again* (DreamWorks, 2000); *Nice* (Sanctuary, 2001); *The Only Way to Know For Sure: Live in Chicago* (Sanctuary, 2002); *Weighting* (2.13.61, 2003); *Come In and Burn Sessions* (2.13.61, 2004)

HENRY ROLLINS

Punk vocalist, writer, TV personality, character actor, and spoken-word artist, Henry Rollins (born Henry Garfield) started as a skinny Washington, D.C., punk in the late-1970s, who rebelled against his family and military school to achieve fame and fortune managing the Georgetown Häagen-Dazs. Rollins soon gravitated toward the budding punk scene along with friend **Ian MacKaye**, becoming a roadie for the **Teen Idles**, and briefly serving as front man for **hardcore** band **SOA**. Rollins made his reputation by becoming the fourth and best-known vocalist for **Black Flag** in 1981 (replacing Dez Cadena). Although Black Flag was guitarist **Greg Ginn**'s pet project, it was Rollins who either put them on the map, or ruined them, depending on your point of view. Either way, Rollins' wild man stage persona and heavily tattooed body made him among the most compelling front men in punk.

In 1984, Rollins, who had always been a writer (his tour diaries were known for their literary flair and meticulous detail), founded the company **2.13.61** to publish his own collections of shorter prose pieces, poetry, and journal entries like *Pissing in the Gene Pool* and *Adventure in the Great Outdoors*. What initially seemed simply a vanity press, though, grew over the years to become one of the more important punk publishing houses, releasing the music and

Henry Rollins, whose
eyes can see into your
very soul, 1982.

writing of people whom Rollins admired, from dark luminaries William S. Burroughs, Nick Cave, and **Lydia Lunch**, to free-jazz master Charles Gayle.

Not long after leaving Black Flag, in 1987 Rollins started up the solo music band for which he would become famous on a mainstream level, the hard rock outfit **Rollins Band**. Through the late-1980s, he mixed Rollins Band performances with his spoken-word performances, which alternated between ribald storytelling and deeply personal reflection. In December 1991, Rollins' best friend and housemate Joe Cole was murdered during a botched robbery, an episode that afterward informed some of Rollins most powerful and tragic spoken-word performances. Rollins' musical profile grew after the band's 1991 slot on the Lollapalooza tour, which garnered them some notoriety. Major label albums, videos on **MTV**, guest VJ appearances, and a writing gig with *Details* magazine, all followed.

Starting in 1994, Rollins—who had previously performed in underground filmmaker Richard Kerns' *The Right Side of My Brain* (1985)—was cast in mainstream films like *Heat* and *Lost Highway*; ironically, for the man who sang "Police Story," he was often cast as a police officer. After years of keeping tour diaries, in 1994, Rollins finally published *Get in the Van*, a copiously illustrated memoir of his years of touring with Black Flag. The book's audio version won a Grammy the following year, and it served as one of the first serious accounts of the hardcore movement in America, opening the door for many books and documentaries that would follow. To this day, Rollins remains one of the most sought-after commentators for documentaries on punk, showing up in films like *American Hardcore* and **Don Letts'** *Punk: Attitude*, confirming his stature as the face of American punk rock.

In recent years, Rollins has concentrated more on his publishing venture, spoken-word tours (including multiple tours on overseas military bases with the USO), and media appearances such as his radio show *Harmony in my Head* or his IFC series *The Henry Rollins Show* (which serves essentially as an opportunity for Rollins to showcase his favorite bands, from Slayer to **Sleater-Kinney**, and also to interview

Henry Rollins croons for the masses somewhere, sometime in the early-1990s.

his favorite musicians, actors, and directors). Rollins has also remained politically active and in 2003 he toured with his band to raise money for the defense fund of the West Memphis Three, the trio of teenage heavy metal fans from Arkansas convicted in 1993 on allegations of ritualistically murdering three children—a case later seen as being almost entirely circumstantial. Rollins also released an album of Black Flag covers (recorded with the Rollins Band and guests like **Iggy Pop** and Lemmy from **Motörhead**) whose proceeds also went to the defense fund.

Discography:
Hot Animal Machine (Texas Hotel, 1987; Buddha, 1999); *Big Ugly Mouth* (Texas Hotel, 1987; Quarterstick, 1992); *Sweatbox* (Texas Hotel, 1989; Quarterstick, 1992); *Live at McCabe's* (Texas Hotel, 1990; Quarterstick, 1992); *Human Butt* (Touch and Go/Quarterstick, 1992); *The Boxed Life* (Touch and Go/Quarterstick, 1992; Imago, 1993); *Get in the Van* (Time Warner, 1994); *In Conversation* (Tabak, 1995); *Everything* (2.13.61/Thirsty Ear, 1995); *Black Coffee Blues* (2.13.61/Thirsty Ear, 1997); *Think Tank* (Touch and Go/Quarterstick, 1998); *A Rollins in the Wry* (Quarterstick, 2001). **Henrietta Collins and the Wifebeating Childhaters:** *Drive by Shooting* EP (Texas Hotel, 1987). **Henry Rollins/Gore:** *Live* (Eksakt, 1987). **Lydia Lunch/Henry Rollins/ Hubert Selby Jr./Don Bajema:** *Our Fathers Who Aren't in Heaven* (Widowspeak, 1992). **Wartime:** *Fast Food for Thought* EP (Chrysalis, 1990).

"When you say, 'Be all you can be,' I know you're not talking to me, motherfucker. I know I'm not joining the navy and I know your laws don't mean shit to me because the hypocrisy that welds them all together, I cannot abide. There's a lot of people with a lot of fury in this country— America is seething at all times. It's like a Gaza Strip that's three thousand miles long."

—Henry Rollins, quoted in Michael Azerrad's *Our Band Could Be Your Life*

ROUGH TRADE

LOCATION: LONDON

What eventually became one of the most crucial punk and post-punk labels was originally started in 1976 by Geoff Travis as a specialty import record store in London's Notting Hill neighborhood. The store soon became a gathering place for those eager to find out what new punk and **reggae** releases were coming out. In 1978, Travis was inspired to start his own label to showcase some of the new music that other labels would not touch. The first Rough Trade release was the seven-inch "Paris Marquee" by French punks **Metal Urbain**. This classic debut was soon followed by innovative records by **Stiff Little Fingers**, then later the Smiths and the **Raincoats** as Rough Trade became almost synonymous with British post-punk. Since then, the label has proved eclectic in its tastes, releasing music by bands as diverse as They Might Be Giants, Mazzy Star, Arcade Fire, and Lucinda Williams. Sadly, this good taste did not prove enough to keep the label in business and Rough Trade was acquired by Zomba in the late-1990s, then again in 2007 by the mega-indie Beggars Group (who also had purchased Matador and 4AD).

Current artists on Rough Trade include twisted folk troubadour and ex-Moldy Peaches Adam Green, British Sea Power, the Libertines, Babyshambles, Cornershop, Belle and Sebastian, and the Unicorns. The Rough Trade shop in London's East End still features the famous ceiling signed by dozens of visiting bands, including **Sonic Youth**.

The Rough Trade shop in London, c.1978.

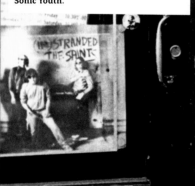

THE ROXY
LOCATION: LONDON

The legendary London club where many of the original punk bands played during the mid- to late-1980s, the Roxy was one of the few places to allow such bands to play on a regular basis, serving as a de facto head-quarters for the first wave of Brit-punk. Aware of the new music sweeping London, a trio of entrepreneurs (including a former manager of the **Damned** and then-manager of **Chelsea**) located a gay nightclub called Chaguarama's in the then-rundown Covent Garden neighborhood and decided it was perfect to showcase the burgeoning genre, despite its size and questionable acoustics.

The Roxy officially opened on January 1, 1977, with the **Clash** headlining. A quick succession of early British punk tastemak-ers followed, including the Damned, the **Adverts**, **Eater**, the **Jam**, **Wire**, **Slaughter and the Dogs**, the **Stranglers**, **Siouxsie and the Banshees**, **Sham 69**, **G.B.H.**, the **Heartbreakers**, and the **Slits**. This early gestation period of punk was captured on the classic *Live at the Roxy* album, released in 1977. During this same time, resident Roxy DJ **Don Letts** was playing a big role in intermixing punk and **reggae** with his voluminous collection of both commercial and rare reggae and **dub** vinyl, while also filming a scene at the Roxy that would later appear in *The Punk Rock Movie*.

Don Letts and cohort in front of the Roxy, 1978.

"I never much liked playing there anyway"

—Crass, "Banned from the Roxy"

Royal Trux's
Jennifer Herrema, 2000.

ROYAL TRUX

1985–2001

LINEUP: Jennifer Herrema (vocals);
Neil Hagerty (vocals/guitar); Dan Brown
(bass); Chris Pyle (drums); Rob Armstrong
(percussion)

Originally formed as an offshoot of indie/
noise band Pussy Galore, Royal Trux soon
took on a life of its own, with records
such as *Twin Infinitives* and *Cats and Dogs*
demonstrating the twisted vision of
singer Jennifer Herrema and guitarist
Neil Hagerty—bandmates and a romantic
couple—at their best. The band's untitled
second *Royal Trux* record, however, is either
the most compelling piece of disturbing

noise music ever recorded outside of the
Boredoms, or just completely unlistenable, depending on one's taste. Eventually
Herrema and Hagerty broke up and the
band dissolved in 2001, although each one
continued in the aftermath of Royal Trux.
Today Herrema tours with the similar
sounding RTX while Hagerty records as
the Howling Hex.

Discography:

Royal Trux (Drag City, 1988); *Twin Infinitives*
(Drag City, 1990); *Royal Trux Untitled* (Drag City,
1992); *Cats and Dogs* (Drag City, 1993); *Thank You*
(Virgin, 1995); *Sweet Sixteen* (Virgin, 1996); *Accelerator*
(Drag City, 1998); *Veterans of Disorder* (Drag City,
1999); *Pound for Pound* (Drag City, 2000); *Hand of
Glory: Recordings From 1985–89* (Drag City, 2002).
RTX: *Transmaniacon* (Drag City, 2004); *Speed to
Roam EP* (Drag City, 2005); *Western Xterminator*
(Drag City, 2007)

RUDIMENTARY PENI

1981–present

LINEUP: Nick Blinko (vocals/guitar); Grant
(Mathews) Bland (bass); Jon Grenville (drums)

During the tail end of the first punk era,
numerous punks who were either too young
to have participated in the 1977 scene, or who
were simply not interested in music at the
time, began forming their own bands, influenced by the new **hardcore** musical and political stance epitomized by bands such as the
Exploited and **Discharge**. However, many of
those bands took the clichéd political postur-

ing of bands such as the **Sex Pistols** and the
Clash and applied real live anarchy and col-
lectivism to their own purposes. After the
example set by true anarchist punks **Crass**,
Rudimentary Peni decided to form their own
band dedicated to political change and anarchist principles. Initially they recorded on the
Crass Records label before leaving to work
on their own. Despite the lack of sales and
exposure in the United States, Rudimentary
Peni has long been one of the most important
anarchist bands on the English punk scene.

Discography:

Farce (Crass, 1982); *Death Church* (Corpus Christi,
1983); *The EPs of RP* (Corpus Christi, 1987); *Cacophony*
(Outer Himalayan, 1988); *Pope Adrian the 37th
Psychristiatric* (Outer Himalayan, 1995); *Echoes of
Anguish* (Outer Himalayan, 1988); *The Underclass*
(Outer Himalayan, 2000)

The Runaways invent the
triple power-stance at
CBGB, 1976.

THE RUNAWAYS

1975-1978

LINEUP: Michael "Micki" Steel (vocals/bass, replaced on vocals by Cherie Currie, on bass by Jackie Fox); Joan Jett (guitar); Lita Ford (guitar); Sandy West (drums)

Los Angeles Svengali **Kim Fowley** created this 1970s band who played raw rock 'n' roll very reminiscent of early punk, and featured future superstar **Joan Jett** and future heavy metal vixen Lita "Kiss Me Deadly" Ford well before their successful solo careers of the '80s. The Runaways were first formed in 1975, and members over the years also included Cherie Currie, Sandy, and Micki Steel (who later went on to considerably more success in the Bangles, and who was subsequently replaced by Jackie Fox and later by Peggy Foster and Laurie McCallister).

Fowley, who had previously worked as a songwriter and performer, deliberately organized and marketed the Runaways as a girl group, albeit a tougher one than had previously been seen in music. He recruited Kari Krome to write songs for the Runaways, wanting to create a raw, sexualized, all-female band that could rock as hard as any male band but still remain firmly under his control. Following grueling world tours and several years of abuse by Fowley, Jackie Fox quit, followed shortly by Cherie Currie. After Jett sang for a spell, the band finally dissolved amid much acrimony. Although talented, and responsible for the bratty, rebellious pre-punk classic "Cherry Bomb" (a sound emulated by some bands of the **Riot Grrrl** movement in the 1990s and covered by **Bratmobile**), the Runaways were still best known for the careers launched by members after the band's final concert at Cow Palace in San Francisco on New Year's Eve, 1978. Jett later had a successful solo career, forming the Blackhearts in 1979, producing the first and only **Germs** album, and working with Riot Grrrl bands like **Bikini Kill**.

Discography:

The Runaways (Mercury, 1976; Cherry Red, 2003); *Queens of Noise* (Mercury, 1977; Cherry Red, 2003); *Live in Japan* (Mercury, 1977; Cherry Red, 2004); *Waitin' for the Night* (Mercury, 1977; Cherry Red, 2004); *And Now … the Runaways* (Cherry Red, 1978; Cherry Red, 1999); *Flaming Schoolgirls* (Cherry Red, 1980; Cherry Red, 2004); *Little Lost Girls* (Rhino, 1981; Rhino, 1990); *The Best of the Runaways* (Mercury, 1982; Mercury/Universal, 2005); *I Love Playing with Fire* (Laker/Cherry Red, 1982); *Born to Be Bad* (Marilyn, 1991)

THE RUTS

1977-1980

LINEUP: Malcolm Owen (vocals); Paul Fox (guitar); John "Vince Segs" Jennings (bass); Dave Ruffy (drums)

Hailing from the London suburb of Southall, the Ruts were a heavily **reggae**-influenced early punk band formed, somewhat strangely, by two members—guitarist Paul Fox and singer Malcolm Owen—of the prog-rock group Aslan. Another band that can credit influential disc jockey **John Peel** with introducing them to a wider audience, the Ruts were known for their social conscience, playing many **RAR (Rock Against Racism)** gigs and working with the People Unite offices, which were attacked during a police action (an event that inspired the **dub** song "Jah War"). Through their extensive involvement in RAR, the Ruts met the reggae band Misty in Roots, who released the Ruts' first single, "In a Rut," on their People Unite record label in 1978, leading to the band being signed by Virgin the next year. A number of popular singles followed, the best known of which is the hyper-political "Babylon's Burning," which hit the Top 10 chart in England. While getting ready for a new album, the band briefly fired Owen in an attempt to get him to tackle his heroin addiction. But after Owen's reinstatement in the band and the release of their debut, *The Crack*, he fatally overdosed in July 1980.

The Ruts toured without Owen after his death, replacing him with saxophone player and keyboardist Gary Barnacle and renaming themselves Ruts DC (from the Italian *da capo*, which translates as "from the beginning"). As Ruts DC, the band went on several tours and released two dub- and reggae-inspired albums and a collaboration with dub hero Mad Professor before calling it quits in 1983. Numerous live albums and collections were released after the demise of the Ruts, making their catalog look much more extensive than it actually was during the band's brief existence.

In July 2007, **Henry Rollins** joined the surviving three members of the original Ruts for a benefit concert whose proceeds went to cancer research and to guitarist Paul Fox, who had been recently diagnosed with lung cancer. **UK Subs** and **Tom**

The Ruts' John Jennings (Left) and Malcolm Owen.

Robinson also performed at the show, described later by the *Times of London* as "one of the great punk shows of all time." Fox succumbed to cancer in October 2007 at the age of 56.

Discography:

The Crack (Virgin, 1979, 1988; Blue Plate, 1991); *Grin & Bear It* (Virgin, 1980); *The Peel Sessions* EP (Strange Fruit, 1986); *The Ruts Live* (Dojo, 1987); *Live and Loud!!* (Link, 1987); *You Gotta Get Out of It* (Virgin, 1987); *The Peel Sessions Album* (Strange Fruit, 1990). **Ruts DC:** *Animal Now* (Virgin, 1981); *Rhythm Collision* (Bohemian, 1982). **Ruts DC and the Mad Professor:** *Rhythm Collision Dub, Vol. 1* (tape; ROIR, 1987)

Afterward, singer Chris Bailey kept the Saints going through the 1980s with a revolving cast of musicians and a direction change toward more straight-ahead, blues-based rock 'n' roll. Bailey revived the Saints name in the late-1990s, toured again under that moniker, and did occasional solo projects. In the early-1990s, Kuepper also formed the Aints (originally with fellow Australian and **Celibate Rifles** member Kent Steedman) as a Saints cover band for one live record, then put out '60s-based, raucous rock 'n' roll for a time, and recorded his own material in a variety of styles and formats. After spending some time collaborating and touring with Nick Cave and the Bad Seeds, Chris Bailey revived yet again a new incarnation of the Saints in 2005, releasing a couple of studio albums and embarking on several world tours.

Essential Discography:
(I'm) Stranded (Sire, 1977); *Eternally Yours* (Sire, 1978); *Prehistoric Sounds* (Harvest, 1978); *Prehistoric Song* (Harvest, 1978); *Nothing Is Straight in My House* (Cadiz, 2005); *Imperious Delirium* (Wildflower, 2006)

SCENES

The word *scene* is usually associated with regional punk movements, commonly based around large urban centers. Some of the most frequently cited examples are the early scenes of London, Manchester, New York, Washington, D.C., Los Angeles, and Cleveland. Although it is impossible to list the variety of scenes and different permutations of punk that existed from city to city, from suburb to suburb, and in towns throughout the world, it is important to note that scenes varied dramatically from one time and place to the next. This was particularly true with the New York, L.A., and D.C. scenes, where the music evolved

from the earlier, artier punk to the later permutations of **hardcore** that became predominant within just a few years. Some scenes were more political than others and a few more **straight-edge**. A number of scenes, Seattle for instance, became breeding grounds for major label bands and have been well chronicled in various books and articles, whereas other scenes were largely ignored, except in local lore, oral tradition, and perhaps in the regional scene reports published by major zines such as *Maximum RocknRoll*.

There were often disputes between various scenes that were geographically close, such as the feuds that erupted between Boston and New York bands (particularly during the straight-edge, hardcore days), and between the D.C. and New York scenes over issues such as straight edge, vegetarianism, and conduct in the **pit**. Additionally—as **Henry Rollins** chronicles in his autobiographical book *Get in the Van*—there were serious rivalries between the English and American scenes. American bands touring Europe during the early-1980s could sometimes expect verbal as well as physical abuse not only from the more boisterous audience members but also from the bands with whom they supposedly shared a common philosophy. Much of the history of regional scenes is unwritten, and it will remain to be seen if many of them in the United States (not to mention the rest of the world) are ever fully documented. Some indications of the diversity of current scenes can be found in the regional reports in *Maximum RocknRoll* and in a variety of zines and websites that detail local events.

THE SAINTS

1974-1989, 2005-present

LINEUP: Chris Bailey (vocals); Ed Kuepper (guitar); Kym Bradshaw (bass, replaced by Caspar Wijnberg); Ivor Hay (drums, replaced by Peter Wilkinson)

Not all of the quintessential punk bands of the first wave were from England or the United States. In particular, Australia's Saints demonstrated that punk was not just a regional phenomenon, and had more to do with attitude than the British preoccupation with class struggle. Essentially a sped-up rock 'n' roll band with a long history and a vast catalog, the Saints were best known for their blistering self-financed single and debut 1977 album *(I'm) Stranded*. Guitarist Ed Kuepper, who wrote many of the Saints' classic songs, left in 1978 to form his own band, Laughing Clowns (he later released several dozen solo records in short order).

> **"Everybody's talking about their hometown scenes And hurting people's feelings in their magazines You want to know what it all means? It's nothing."**
> —Fugazi, "Song #1"

THE SCREAMERS

1975-1981

LINEUP: David Harrigan, aka "Tomata du Plenty" (vocals/keyboards/percussion); Melba Toast, aka "Tommy Gear" (keyboards); David Braun (keyboards); K.K. Barrett (drums);

Although the performance-artist collective the Screamers were certainly one of the most vital bands on the early Los Angeles scene, their legendary influence has to be taken in large part on oral reports and faith, as they never made a proper recording of their music (except for some poorly recorded live tracks). The Screamers were mostly the brainchild of Tomata du Plenty, a young actor and artist who had been a superstar (in the Warholian sense of the word) in the renowned Bay Area drag troupe the Cockettes back in the late-1960s. He later performed in underground theater before going to punk shows at **CBGB** and becoming enthralled with the new art form. Du Plenty and fellow drag artist Melba Toast put together an outfit called the Tupperwares, who could now be classified as proto-**new wave**, before heading out to L.A. and putting together the Screamers with K.K. Barrett and David Braun.

For a few short years, the Screamers were so far ahead of their time that many bands today still have not caught up. They defined a West Coast style of **no wave** dissonance that mixed performance art with drag spectacle and fringe theatricality along with heavy distortion from two keyboards and almost no guitar. Sadly, the only non-bootleg of the Screamers at their best comes from a VHS tape of a concert released by Target Video in 1986. A rarely seen avant-garde film called *Population 1*, which featured the band, made a brief round of the festival circuit in 1986 and 1987 before going out of print.

After their 1981 breakup, Barrett began a career doing production design for films such as *Lost in Translation* and *Adaptation*, and was interviewed by **Don Letts** for the 2005 documentary *Punk: Attitude*. Du Plenty returned to his roots in the underground L.A. theater scene and worked on underground films while continuing as a full-time painter, before his death from cancer in 2000. Although they never influenced punk's second wave, the experimentation and anything-goes attitude of the early L.A. scene can be traced back to the legendary theatrics of the Screamers.

SCREAMERS
X ALLEY CATS
& FLESHEATERS
MARQUEE WED.
WEST 213-445-5552 MAR.
30 S.FIRST, ARCADIA 15

The Screamers, 1977: (L to R) Tommy Gear,
KK Barrett, Tomata du Plenty.

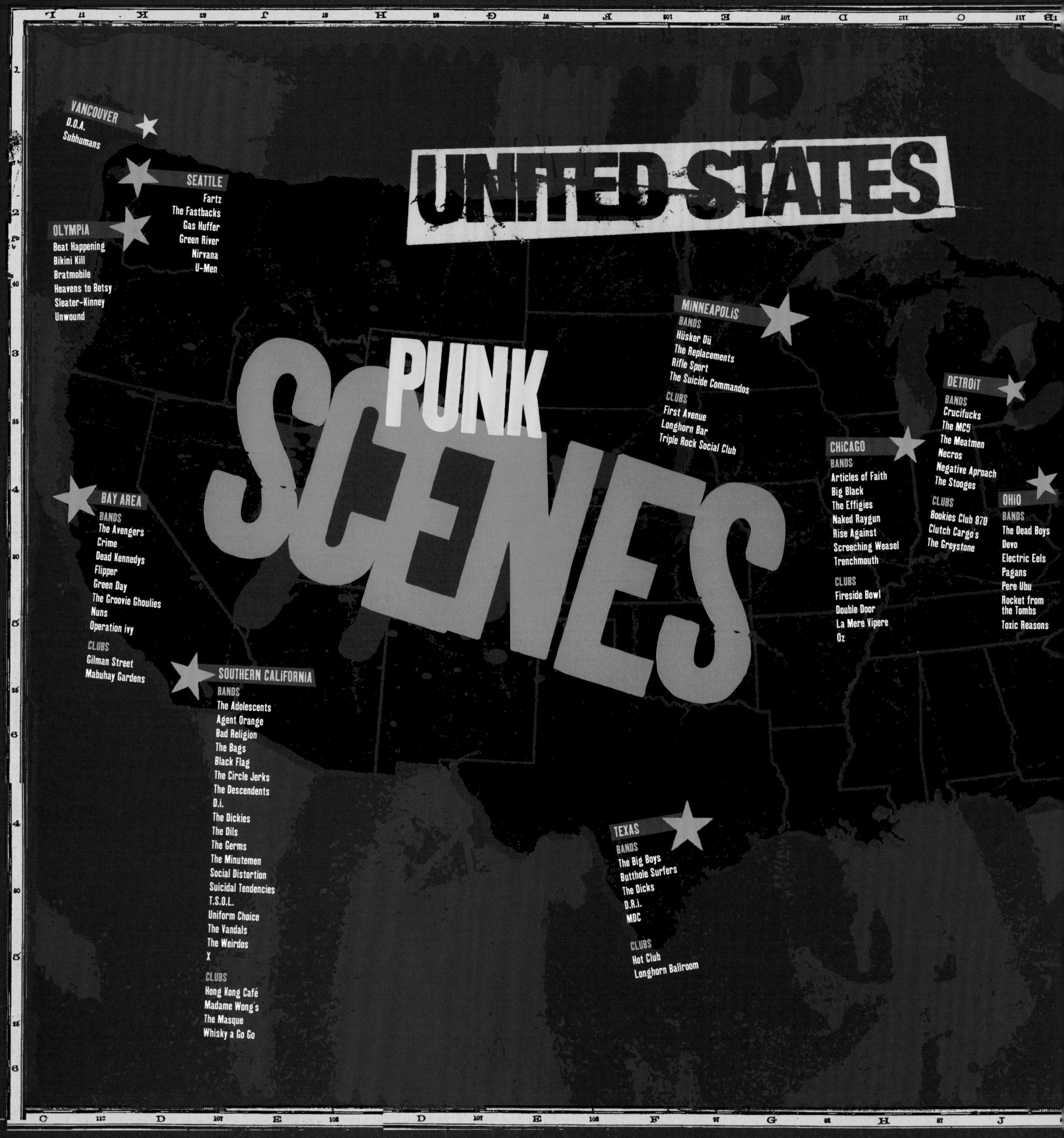

PUNK SCENES

VANCOUVER
D.O.A.
Subhumans

SEATTLE
Fartz
The Fastbacks
Gas Huffer
Green River
Nirvana
U-Men

OLYMPiA
Beat Happening
Bikini Kill
Bratmobile
Heavens to Betsy
Sleater-Kinney
Unwound

BAY AREA
BANDS
The Avengers
Crime
Dead Kennedys
Flipper
Green Day
The Groovie Ghoulies
Nuns
Operation Ivy

CLUBS
Gilman Street
Mabuhay Gardens

SOUTHERN CALIFORNIA
BANDS
The Adolescents
Agent Orange
Bad Religion
The Bags
Black Flag
The Circle Jerks
The Descendents
D.i.
The Dickies
The Dils
The Germs
The Minutemen
Social Distortion
Suicidal Tendencies
T.S.O.L.
Uniform Choice
The Vandals
The Weirdos
X

CLUBS
Hong Kong Café
Madame Wong's
The Masque
Whisky a Go Go

MiNNEAPOLiS
BANDS
Hüsker Dü
The Replacements
Rifle Sport
The Suicide Commandos

CLUBS
First Avenue
Longhorn Bar
Triple Rock Social Club

CHiCAGO
BANDS
Articles of Faith
Big Black
The Effigies
Naked Raygun
Rise Against
Screeching Weasel
Trenchmouth

CLUBS
Fireside Bowl
Double Door
La Mere Vipere
Oz

DETROiT
BANDS
Crucifucks
The MC5
The Meatmen
Necros
Negative Aproach
The Stooges

CLUBS
Bookies Club 870
Clutch Cargo's
The Greystone

OHiO
BANDS
The Dead Boys
Devo
Electric Eels
Pagans
Pere Ubu
Rocket from
the Tombs
Toxic Reasons

TEXAS
BANDS
The Big Boys
Butthole Surfers
The Dicks
D.R.I.
MDC

CLUBS
Hot Club
Longhorn Ballroom

UK & IRELAND

BOSTON

BANDS

Dropkick Murphys
DYS
The Freeze
The F.U.'s
Gang Green
Jerry's Kids
Mission of Burma
The Modern Lovers
Negative FX
Pixies
Slapshot
SSD
Unnatural Axe

CLUBS

Cantone's
Gallery East
Maverick's
The Paradise
The Rat
The Underground

NEW YORK

BANDS

Agnostic Front
Blondie
Cro-Mags
The Dictators
Gorilla Biscuits
Heartbreakers
Kraut
Murphy's Law
New York Dolls
The Ramones
Richard Hell
and the Voidoids
Sick Of it All
Patti Smith
Sonic Youth
Talking Heads
Television
Velvet Underground

CLUBS

171A
A7
CBGB
Max's Kansas City
Mudd Club
Pyramid Club

WASHINGTON, D.C. AREA

BANDS

Bad Brains
Beefeater
Dag Nasty
Embrace
The Faith
Fugazi
Government Issue
Iron Cross
Jawbox
Marginal Man
Minor Threat
Nation of Ulysses
No Trend
Rites of Spring
SOA
Teen Idles
Youth Brigade

CLUBS

The Bayou
The Chancery
D.C. Space
9:30 Club
Space ii Arcade

NORTHERN IRELAND

The Defects
The Outcasts
Stiff Little Fingers
The Undertones

LEEDS

Delta 5
Gang of Four
The Mekons

MANCHESTER

Buzzcocks
John Cooper Clarke
The Fall
Joy Division
Magazine
Slaughter and the Dogs

LONDON AND ENVIRONS

BANDS

The Cockney Rejects
Chumbawamba
The Clash
Crass
The Damned
Eater
Generation X
The Jam
The Sex Pistols
Sham 69
Siouxsie and the Banshees
The Slits
Throbbing Gristle
UK Subs
Wire
X-Ray Spex

CLUBS

100 Club
Roxy

THE REST OF THE WORLD

PARIS/FRANCE

BANDS

Les Thugs
Metal Urbain
Stinky Toys

JAPAN

The Blue Hearts
The Boredoms
Shonen Knife
Teengenerate

AUSTRALIA

Celibate Rifles
Saints
Radio Birdman

NEW ZEALAND

Masochists
Scavengers
Suburban Reptiles

SCREECHING WEASEL

1986-1994, 1996-2001

LINEUP: Ben Foster, aka "Ben Weasel" (vocals/guitar); John Pierson, aka "Johnny Jughead" (guitar); Vince Vogel, aka "Vinne Bovine" (bass, replaced by Danny Vapid); Steve Cheese (drums, replaced by Danny Panic)

The extremely prolific Chicago punks in Screeching Weasel cranked out a relentless stream of catchy **pop-punk** tunes, led by **Ramones** fan and singer Ben Weasel. The band went through various permutations and short breakups over the years, with their most stable lineup being the early-1990s version consisting of Danny Vapid (Dan Schafer) on bass and Danny Panic (Dan Sullivan) on drums. A restless creator of new music, Weasel started the **Riverdales** (also with Vapid and Panic), *another* Ramones-influenced band, frequently collaborates with the **Queers**, and has also recorded several solo records. In addition, Weasel is a prolific writer and columnist for zines such as *Maximum RocknRoll*; although according to legend he was axed from the publication after committing the cardinal sin of having the Riverdales open for **Green Day** (Mike Dirnt had played bass for Screeching Weasel's 1993 album *Anthem for a New Tomorrow*). Ben Weasel was controversial to some, but due in large part to his talents as musician, scenester, and songwriter, Screeching Weasel became one of the key bands to keep the pop-punk flag flying.

Discography:

Screeching Weasel (Underdog, 1987); *Boogadaboogadaboogada* (Roadkill, 1988); *My Brain Hurts* (Lookout!, 1991); *Ramones* (Selfless, 1992); *Wiggle* (Lookout!, 1993); *Anthem for a New Tomorrow* (Lookout!, 1993); *How to Make Enemies and Irritate People* (Lookout!, 1995); *Kill the Musicians* (Lookout!, 1995); *Bark Like a Dog* (Fat Wreck Chords, 1996); *Television City Dream* (Fat Wreck Chords, 1998); *Emo* (Panic Button, 1999); *Thank You Very Little* (Panic Button/Lookout!, 1999); *Weasel Mania* (Fat Wreck Chords, 2005).

SEPTIC DEATH

1981-1986

LINEUP: Brian "Pushead" Schroeder (vocals); Jon Taylor (guitar); Mike Matlock (bass); Paul Birnbaum (drums)

Inspired by British anarchist punk bands like **Rudimentary Peni**, and just as fast and aggressive as the best of the anarcho-core English punks, Septic Death was led by the controversial but brilliant artist, writer, and musician Brian "Pushead" Schroeder. They were one of the most extreme of the thrash/punk crossover bands of the 1980s, creating a gory and nihilistic style that would be popularized in later years and much imitated by **crust punks**, and later grindcore fans. From the band's home base in Boise, Idaho, Schroeder did artwork for Metallica and a number of punk bands like the **Necros** and the **F.U.'s** (as well as the cover for the classic 1982 **Better Youth Organization** compilation *Someone Got Their Head Kicked In*), and wrote extensively in zines and magazines such as the **skateboarding** magazine *Thrasher*, for which he was the music editor and wrote the "Puszone" column about **hardcore** and heavy metal music. Pushead's view on life and mortality was summed up in the name of the band, as he was quoted by the *Flex Your Head* zine: "Septic Death represents when you die, you are dead... You are deceased, your body rots away." The cheerful Pushead also created the labels Pusmort and Bacteria Sour.

Discography:

Barricaded Suspects (Toxic Shock, 1983, 1994); *Empty Shells* (cassette; self-release, 1983); *Need So Much Attention... Acceptance of Whom* (Pusmort, 1984); *P.E.A.C.E.* (R Radical, 1984); *Now That I Have Your Attention What Do I Do With It* (Pusmort, 1984); *Time Is the Boss Aaarrggh It's Live* (Deluxe, 1984); *Live Dirt up a Side Track Carted Is a Putrid Evil Flexi* (Kalv and Dig, 1985); *Cleanse the Bacteria* (Pusmort, 1985); *Burial Mai So* (Pusmort, 1987); *Kichigai* (Pusmort, 1988); *Nightmare Takes a Nap Box Set Volume 1* (Pusmort, 1990); *Attention* (Pusmort, 1991); *Theme from Ozo Bozo* (Toy's Factory, 1992); *Nightmare Takes a Nap Box Set Volume 2* (Pusmort, 1993); *Decade of Disaster* (Toxic Shock, 1994); *Taste* (Pushead Bacteria Sour, 1995); *Somewhere in Time* (Lost and Found, 1997); *Nightmare Takes a Nap Box Set Volume 3* (Pusmort, 1998); *Desperate for Attention* (Flex 16, 1998); *Crossed Out Twice* (Bacteria Sour, 1999); *Uncontrollable Proof* (Sourpus, 1999); *Victim of a Thought Crime* (Sourpus, 2000); *Septic Death* (Pusmort, 2000); *Chumoku* (Prank, 2002).

SERPICO

1991-1998

LINEUP: John Telenko (vocals, replaced by John Lisa); Sal Cannestra (guitar); Hobi Klapuri (guitar, replaced by Michael DeLorenzo); Lew Dimmick (bass, replaced by Marc Treboschi); T.J. Quatrone (drums, replaced by Chris "Niser" Guardino)

One of the mid- to late-1990s New York bands who were considerably more popular in Europe than at home, Serpico originally called themselves Sleeper, but a British band bought the name from band leader John Lisa in 1994 and the Americans changed their name to Serpico (after one of their better-known songs). Originally hailing from Staten Island, Serpico lasted from 1991 (the year they released their debut, seven-inch record on John Lisa's homegrown Tragic Life label) until their ugly and embarrassing death in September 1998.

Typical band problems, ranging from temper tantrums to creative differences to laziness, led to nearly a dozen lineup changes, shaky flights to Europe, onstage nudity, phlegm, blood, and a ton of hard feelings and irreparable damages to previously solid friendships. Guitarist Michael Thomas DeLorenzo, bassist Marc Treboschi (later of In Crowd), and drummer Chris "Niser" Guardino joined the fold after most of the original lineup left. Sal Cannestra of In Crowd also played guitar on several records but got kicked out, much to Lisa's later regret as he added a sense of rare calm to the band. Still, despite all the instability, Serpico was one of the few New York **hardcore** bands to reinvigorate the European tour circuit in the early-1990s.

Rumble, Serpico's final Equal Vision CD and swan song, cost the label thousands to record but only brought in two-fifths of the initial investment, prompting Equal Vision's Steve Reddy to proclaim, "That's the *LAST* fucking time I sign a non-Krishna band." Serpico called it quits shortly after the *Rumble* tour and re-formed only temporarily with the help of Darien's Greg Swanson and Murdock's Rob Marinelli. John Lisa's very latent homosexuality

(at 30 years old) came to full bloom in 1998 when he left the European farewell tour because he missed his Mexican boyfriend back in New York. Easily the best of Serpico's output was their 1996 single "I'm Not Dead," which was released by C.I. records and hand-numbered to 1,000. Powerful, raw, and melodic, they finally got to where they wanted to be, even if only 1,000 people listened globally.

Discography:

Sleeper: *Display Debut 7"* (Tragic Life, 1991); *Time and Tide* (42, 1993); *Splinter 7"* (Allied, 1993); *Preparing Today for Tomorrow's Breakdown* (Excursion; also released as *Serpico* on CD, 1994). **Serpico:** *Feel Bad Rainbow* (Equal Vision, 1995); *They Shoot Babies Don't They? 7"* (Day After, 1995); *Rumble* (Equal Vision, 1996); *I'm Not Dead 7"* (C.I., 1996); *The Weakest Boy in the Troop Award Singles Collection* (Excursion, 1996); *Heroes of the Bomb Scare 7"* (Day After, 1998).

7 SECONDS

1979-present

CLASSIC LINEUP: Kevin Marvelli, aka "Kevin Seconds" (vocals/guitar); Steve Youth (bass/guitar); Troy Mowat (drums)

Led by the charismatic singer/guitarist Kevin Seconds along with long-term members Steve Youth (Kevin's brother) and drummer Troy Mowat (along with a variety of other bass and guitar players, most notably Bobby Adams), 7 Seconds have been together in some form for over 25 years, and rank as one of the most influential and melodic **hardcore** bands around. The band originally formed as a reaction to the conservative nature of their hometown of Reno, Nevada, exchanging letters with **Ian MacKaye** and **Henry Rollins**. 7 Seconds pioneered the so-called "skeeno sound"—named for the Nevada area encompassing Reno, Lake Tahoe, and Sparks; a scene that Kevin Seconds wrote about for **Maximum RocknRoll**—and developed a distinctive look by drawing black lines below their eyes, much like athletic sun protection or Indian tribal paint. After playing some shows with **Minor Threat**, 7 Seconds began to tour outside their home base and started mentoring other bands such as **Youth of Today**. They worked with punks around the country to provide information on venues at which touring bands could play, and they created a network of activist punks who could work on social and political issues.

Although 7 Seconds did not necessarily identify themselves as a **straight-edge** band, the members did reject drugs and alcohol and dedicated themselves to clean living. The band also helped punks through their record label **Positive Force**, which grew to a national organization dedicated to political and social change. 7 Seconds put out some of the fastest, yet most accessible music of the early-1980s and covered both Nena's "99 Red Balloons" and Nancy Sinatra's "These Boots Are Made for Walking." After several classic records like the ode to unity *Walk Together, Rock Together* and the soaring *New Wind*, 7 Seconds mutated in the 1980s, with the members growing their hair and changing their style of music to a glossier alt-pop sound reminiscent of U2 or REM, as documented on the live record *Live: One Plus One*. Kevin Seconds later also released work under various other names, including his own name, Drop Acid (provocative name for a onetime straight-edge icon), Five Foot Ten, and Mustard. More recently, 7 Seconds toured with their classic lineup and continues to record.

Discography:

Socially Fucked Up (tape; Vicious Scam, 1981); *3 Chord Politics* (tape; Vicious Scam, 1981); *Skin, Brains, and Guts* EP (Alternative Tentacles, 1982); *Committed for Life* EP (Squirtdown, 1983); *The Crew* (B.Y.O., 1984, 1994); *Walk Together, Rock Together* (Positive Force/B.Y.O., 1985, 1994); *Blasts from the Past* EP (Positive Force, 1986); *New Wind* (Positive Force/B.Y.O., 1986, 1994); *Praise* EP (Positive Force/B.Y.O., 1987); *Live: One Plus One* (Positive Force/Giant, 1987, 1995); *Ourselves* (Restless, 1988, 1993); *Soulforce Revolution* (Restless/Roadrunner, 1989, 1993); *Old School* (Headhunter/Cargo, 1991); *Out the Shizzy* (Headhunter/Cargo, 1993); *Alt.Music.Hardcore* (Headhunter/Cargo, 1995); *The Music, the Message* (Immortal/Epic, 1995); *7 Seconds* (B.Y.O., 1997); *Good to Go* (SideOneDummy, 1999); *Scream Real Loud . . . LIVE!* (SideOneDummy, 2000); *The Better Youth Years* (Golf, 2001); *Take It Back, Take It On, Take It Over* (SideOneDummy, 2004). **Jackshit:** *Hicktown* EP (Squirtdown, 1984). **Drop Acid:** *Making God Smile* (Restless, 1991); *46th & Teeth* EP (Headhunter/Cargo, 1992). **Kevin Seconds/5'10":** *Rodney, Reggie, Emily* (Earth Music/Cargo, 1994). **Kevin Seconds:** *Stoudamire* (Earth Music/Cargo, 1997); *Heaven's Near Wherever You Are* (Headhunter/Cargo, 2001). **Mustard:** *Mostaza* (Sunspot, 1996)

Kevin Seconds spreads the hardcore gospel in San Francisco, 2004.

"Why do you have to go heavy metal to prove you're a good musician?"

—Kevin Seconds, interviewed in *Suburban Voice*, Issue no. 13, 1984.

76% UNCERTAIN

1983-1989, 2002-present

LINEUP: Bones (vocals); Jeff Roberts (guitar, replaced by Ed Winnick); Mike Spadaccini (guitar); Kenny (guitar); Dave (bass); Chip Moody (drums, replaced by others)

Connecticut **hardcore** band 76% Uncertain was formed out of two other bands, CIA and Reflex from Pain. At their best they were the smartest, brattiest punk group from Connecticut, even though they violated a cardinal punk rule by having three guitarists at one point. Numerous personnel changes and lack of recording support led to 76% Uncertain calling it quits by the end of the 1980s. After the death of Jeff Roberts in a car accident, the band reunited in 1997 for benefit shows for his family and continue to reunite sporadically.

Discography:
Estimated Monkey Time (Shmegma, 1984); *Nothing But Love Songs* (Shmegma, 1986); *Hunka Hunka Burnin' Log* (Wishingwell/Giant, 1989)

SEX

LOCATION: LONDON

Malcolm McLaren and partner **Vivienne Westwood**'s London fashion boutique, Sex, at 430 Kings Road in Chelsea was a punk landmark where the **Sex Pistols** first formed and where most of punk fashion in Britain was developed. The store started out in 1971 as Let It Rock, a place for McLaren and a partner to sell Teddy Boy gear and 1950s records. The store quickly mutated into Too Fast to Live Too Young to Die, wherein the entrepreneurial owners sold motorcycle jackets and paraphernalia, and zoot suits. At this point the store attracted a clientele that included Alice Cooper, **Lou Reed**, and the **New York Dolls**, whom McLaren managed in 1974. Although McLaren all but ruined the Dolls' career, he returned from the United States ready to cash in on the punk style.

In 1974 McLaren rechristened the shop Sex and stocked it with bondage gear and leather and rubber costumes, sold by shop assistants such as Chrissie Hynde (later of the Pretenders) and a pre-Pistols Glen Matlock. Another Sex employee, the enigmatic Jordan, later became one of the most

famous faces of British punk rock, later starring in *Jubilee*. (Director Derek Jarman described her look as "the face that launched a thousand tabloids...art history as makeup.") Almost all of London's first-wave punks were regulars, including Siouxsie Sioux and Mick Jones. The Sex Pistols formed at the shop after an 18-year-old **John Lydon** performed to an Alice Cooper record and passed the audition. **Don Letts** was a regular as well but apparently fell out of favor after he went to work at the only other real rival shop, **Acme Attractions**. Never one to hang on to a trend too long, in December 1976 McLaren got bored and changed the shop into Seditionaries: Clothes for Heroes (the design elements included large "tasteful" photographs of the firebombing of Dresden), and it outfitted most of the class of 1977. The store transitioned into Westwood's signature fashion emporium World's End in 1980, which it remains today.

Sid Vicious (left) and Johnny Rotten in Penzance, 1977.

Sex's Vivienne Westwood (right) with employees; Chrissie Hynde extends a middle finger to fashion.

THE SEX PISTOLS

1975-1978, occasionally thereafter

LINEUP: John Lydon aka "Johnny Rotten" (vocals); Steve Jones (guitar); Glen Matlock (bass, replaced by Sid Vicious); Paul Cook (drums)

Besides being the most important band in 1970s punk (next to the **Ramones**), the Sex Pistols pioneered an aesthetic that would prove incalculably influential on both the British and American scenes. Along the way they created a tabloid shocker of a media storm that, for better or for worse, defined how the mainstream public would view punk rock for years to come.

The Sex Pistols started as a Roxy Music- and **David Bowie**-inspired group called the Strand or the Swankers (composed of Steve Jones, Warwick "Wally" Nightingale, and Paul Cook) who'd been rehearsing together since 1972. Eventually they came into contact with **Malcolm McLaren** who was looking to form a band inspired by the experiences he had managing the **New York Dolls** and the exotic look he had seen on New York punk pioneer **Richard Hell**. McLaren sacked Nightingale (even though he'd provided the rehearsal space), added Glen Matlock (a clerk at Sex), and shifted Jones from "singer" to guitarist. (British journalist **Nick Kent** was also an early member but soon left due to his growing drug problem.) After McLaren spent fruitless months searching for a lead singer, asking at different points the Dolls' Sylvain Sylvain and **Johnny Thunders** to front his new group, he eventually found the proper singer in the misanthropic but compelling **John Lydon**. After auditioning with his

back to the band, singing along to Alice Cooper's "Eighteen," the charismatic Lydon (soon to change his name to Johnny Rotten, partially due to his problems with basic dental hygiene) was asked to join the band, and the Sex Pistols were born.

The Sex Pistols' first gig was on November 6, 1975, at St. Martin's Art College (where Matlock was a student), and they soon began playing art colleges such as St. Albans and Chelsea School of Art, often under assumed names. Soon the band graduated to larger clubs like the Marquee, supporting bands such as Eddie and the Hot Rods, a gig that was reviewed by the *New Music Express (NME)* and started a string of positive press that McLaren expertly manipulated into gigs at larger

venues like the **100 Club**. After fans Howard Devoto and Pete Shelley of the embryonic **Buzzcocks** organized a show at the Manchester Free Trade Hall in June 1976, a flock of bands inspired by the Sex Pistols' look and attitude started to form. Early fans included the members of **Joy Division**, Morrissey of the Smiths, and Tony Wilson of Factory Records. By July 1976, the Pistols had already worked out many of their best-known songs, such as "Anarchy in the U.K.," "Pretty Vacant," and "Seventeen." Their music was utterly unlike anything in England at the time, a mix of Jones' and Cook's early rock 'n' roll influence, Matlock's love of the Beatles and good pop melodies, and Lydon's preference for dissonance,

reggae, kraut-rock, and primal screaming. Somehow it all worked.

From that point on, the Sex Pistols' notoriety spread via word of mouth and a few rave reviews in the British press, which was much more open to punk rock than its U.S. counterparts would later prove to be. On December 1, 1976, thanks to the band Queen canceling at the last minute, the

January 14, 1978:
The Sex Pistols' final show.

The Sex Pistols: (L to R)
Paul Cook, Steve Jones,
Glen Matlock, John Lydon.

Sex Pistols were booked on Bill Grundy's TV show *Today*. The band, accompanied by friends and various **Bromley Contingent** hangers-on (including Siouxsie Sioux and Sue Catwoman), drank heavily before the cameras rolled. The subsequent profanity-laced furor led to tabloid headlines screaming "The Filth and the Fury," Grundy being suspended for two weeks, and the cancellation of many dates for the Sex Pistols' upcoming tour of the United Kingdom with the **Heartbreakers**, the **Damned**, and the **Clash**. The Damned were kicked off the tour for offering to play a show at which the other bands had declined to perform, as they were protesting the Sex Pistols being asked to give an audition performance for the approval of the local town council. The tour ended acrimoniously, with most dates canceled and great financial loss by the band. After returning from a brief tour of Holland in 1976, they were unceremoniously dumped

from their label EMI due to allegations of improper behavior in the airport en route to Holland. The Sex Pistols signed shortly thereafter to A&M Records and were subsequently dumped again after yet another violent debacle featuring the irrepressibly untalented but charismatic **Sid Vicious** (who had taken over on bass after Matlock had been sacked, supposedly for his secret love of the Beatles).

The Sex Pistols signed to Virgin Records and released the "God Save the Queen" single in May 1977, leading to an almost immediate ban from the airwaves. On June 7, the band embarked on a cruise down the River Thames, during which they played a seven-song set before being asked to dock by police, who arrested eleven people, including McLaren. That same month, despite an almost complete lack of airplay, "God Save the Queen" went to number one on the British charts. The Sex Pistols' first (and to some minds, only real) album

Never Mind the Bollocks, Here's the Sex Pistols was released in England in October 1977; notoriety and controversy immediately followed. In late-1977, a shopkeeper was brought to court for displaying a mock-up of the album cover, but after testimony, including some by professors on the origins and common usage of the word *bollocks*, the case was dismissed.

After much discussion and many aborted attempts, the Sex Pistols started a truncated tour of the United States in January 1978 that skipped the major venues in Los Angeles and New York but concentrated on the Deep South. They started at the Great Southeast Music Hall in Atlanta and worked their way west, stopping at venues more accustomed to country music tours. (McLaren hadn't learned his lesson from touring the New York Dolls in unfriendly territories.) To no avail, Vicious was given a babysitter by the label, but his continued search for heroin in an unfamil-

iar country led to frequent fights and childish behavior. The fractious tour ended a mere two weeks later at the Winterland Ballroom in San Francisco on January 14, 1978. Johnny Rotten ended the chaotic show by taunting the audience with the now-classic line "Ever get the feeling you've been cheated?" This would be the last live performance of the Sex Pistols for almost two decades.

Following the Winterland show, Vicious found solace with some fans who scored him heroin, leading to an overdose. The band effectively ended when Steve Jones and Paul Cook informed Rotten that they no longer wanted to work with him. Rotten flew to New York to release some steam, while Jones and Cook flew down to Rio de Janeiro, Brazil, to record with noted English fugitive **Ronnie Biggs**. Rotten, along with **Don Letts**, went off in February to sign bands for Richard Branson of Virgin Records. Sid Vicious went to Paris to film the video for his cover of the Frank Sinatra standard "My Way." Shortly after Vicious and and his American girlfriend Nancy Spungen returned to the U.S., she was found dead of a stab wound at the Chelsea Hotel in New York, and Sid Vicious was arrested and charged with the killing. He overdosed in a Greenwich Village apartment and died on February 2, 1979.

John Lydon (he ditched the Rotten not long after the band's dissolution) sued Malcolm McLaren to dissolve the Sex

Pistols' assets, and in February 1979 the judge ruled against McLaren. Part of the lawsuit's resolution was the quick release of the soundtrack to the upcoming Sex Pistols' film. *The Great Rock 'n' Roll Swindle* was put into theaters quickly to recoup any money owed the group. Like the somewhat grab-bag film, the album was a collection of odds and ends and new recordings made by various permutations of the band without Lydon, who launched a lawsuit against McLaren and his company Glitterbeast that would last for eight years. Lydon went on to make **post-punk** history with his band **Public Image Ltd.**, Cook and Jones formed the **Professionals**, and McLaren kept on looking for the next big thing.

The Sex Pistols reunited with Lydon, Jones, Cook, and original bassist Matlock for tours in 1996 (appropriately titled the "Filthy Lucre Tour"), 2003, and 2007. They were inducted into the Rock and Roll Hall of Fame in 2005 but declined to attend, instead posting a handwritten note on their website that read, in part, "We're not your monkeys, we're not coming. You're not paying attention."

Despite constant debate over the relative control of the band by McLaren (as epitomized in the dueling Julien Temple films *The Great Rock 'n' Roll Swindle* and *The Filth and the Fury*), the cultural and social influence of the Sex Pistols cannot be underestimated. Although most punk bands (including the Sex Pistols) borrowed musically from the **Ramones**, the Sex Pistols have had more demonstrable influence than any other band on punk's look and attitude. Despite their brief life span, the Sex Pistols' legacy is almost unequalled.

Discography:
Spunk (Blank, 1977); *Never Mind the Bollocks, Here's the Sex Pistols* (Warner Bros., 1977); *The Great Rock 'n' Roll Swindle* (Virgin, 1979); *Some Product: Carri On Sex Pistols* (Virgin, 1979); *Flogging a Dead Horse* (Virgin, 1980); *The Heyday* (tape; Factory, 1980); *The Mini Album* EP (Chaos, 1985; Restless, 1988); *The Original Pistols Live* (Receiver, 1985); *Live Worldwide* (Konexion, 1985); *Best of the Sex Pistols Live* (Bondage, 1985); *Where Were You in '77* (77, 1985); *Power of the Pistols* (77, 1985); *We Have Cum for Your Children (Wanted: The Goodman Tapes)* (Skyclad, 1988); *Better Live Than Dead* (Restless, 1988); *The Swindle Continues* (Restless, 1988); *Anarchy Worldwide* (Specific, 1988); *Cash for Chaos* EP (Specific, 1988); *Pirates of Destiny* (I Swirled, 1989); *The Mini Album Plus* (Chaos, 1989); *Live and Loud!!* (Link, 1989); *No Future, U.K.?* (Receiver, 1989); *Live at Chelmsford Top Security Prison* (Restless, 1990). **The Original Pistols/New York Dolls:** *After the Storm* (Receiver, 1985). **Sid Vicious:** *Sid Sings* (Virgin, 1979); *Love Kills NYC* (Konexion, 1985)

SHAI HULUD

1995-present

LINEUP: Damien Moyal (vocals, replaced by Chad Gilbert, Matt Mezzale, Eric Dellon); Matt Fox (guitar); Oliver Chapoy (guitar, replaced by Greg Thomas, Ryan Burns); David Silber (bass, replaced by Matt Fletcher); Steve Kleisath drums (replaced by Tony Tintari, Brian Go)

One of the most primal and ferocious metal/ **hardcore** crossover bands in recent years, Shai Hulud makes music that effectively evokes their namesake, the sandworms in Frank Herbert's sci-fi epic *Dune*, in sheer massive size and impact. Their blistering vocals, barrage of noisy guitars, and expertly played drums belie the band's supposed influences of **JFA** and **NOFX**, and demonstrate an engaging merger of metal and hardcore that bands like Earth Crisis never did as well. After going through various drummers and vocalists, the band almost changed their name to The Warmth of Red Blood before wisely going back to Shai Hulud. They remain today one of the most primal bands of the hardcore-metal reemergence of the late-1990s.

Discography:
A Profound Hatred of Man (Crisis, 1997); *Hearts Once Nourished with Hope and Compassion* (Crisis, 1997); *That Within Blood Ill-Tempered* (Revelation, 2003); *Misanthropy Pure* (Metal Blade, 2008)

SHAM 69

1975-1980, occasionally thereafter

LINEUP: Jimmy Pursey (vocals); Johnny Goodfornothing (guitar, replaced by Dave Parsons); Neil Harris (guitar); Albert Maskell (bass, replaced by Dave Treganna); Billy Bostick (drums, replaced by Mark Cain, Rick Goldstein)

Roaring out of the gutters of Hersham, England, in 1975, Sham 69 played music with loud, football-stadium choruses and unfortunately, due to their general **oi** appeal, attracted a large and unwanted contingent of fans from the racist, fascist **National Front**. The band's name came from graffiti in their home neighborhood that read "Hersham 69," but the first three letters "H-E-R" eventually faded, so the band adopted the remaining scrawl as their name. Sham 69 was plagued by personnel changes early on, with singer/ shouter Jimmy Pursey being the only one of the old Hersham lads who stuck it out.

Their first album, 1978's *Tell Us the Truth*, featured one live side and one side of studio recordings. Although Sham 69 wished to focus on the music, this became nearly impossible due to the band's working-class credentials, which brought **skinheads** (often National Front members) to their shows in swarms, and violence usually followed.

Although Sham 69 never declared themselves as followers of the National Front (and in fact played a number of **RAR** shows), they also (along with more avowedly anarchist bands such as **Crass**) refused to bar racist skinheads from their shows. This preference for audience freedom didn't prevent them from being unfairly lumped in with other, racist, oi bands.

Sham 69 struggled on but eventually broke up in 1980 after four records. Pursey and guitarist Dave Parsons reunited every now and again over the years and toured to celebrate the band's 30th anniversary. Bassist Dave Treganna later went on to form the Lords of the New Church with Stiv Bators from the **Dead Boys** and Brian James from the **Damned**. Recently, Parsons and Pursey disputed the Sham 69 legacy and Pursey left to form the new band Sector 27 while Parsons soldiered on with a new lead singer, begging the question: When exactly did punk bands start making 1960s-style legacy tours?

Discography:
Tell Us the Truth (Sire, 1978); *That's Life* (Polydor, 1978; Dojo, 1996; Captain Oi!, 2005); *The Adventures of the Hersham Boys* (Polydor, 1979; Dojo, 1996; Captain Oi!, 2005); *The Game* (Polydor, 1980; Dojo, 1996; Captain Oi!, 2005); *Information Libre* (Creative Man, 1995); *Kings and Queens* (Dojo, 1995); *Soapy Water and Mister Marmalade* (Plus Eye, 1995); *The A Files* (Cleopatra, 1997); *Direct Action: Day 21* (Resurgent, 2001); *Live at CBGB* (Dojo, 1991; Harry May, 2002)

Sham 69 in London, 1977.

GREG SHAW

The publisher of groundbreaking music fanzines *Mojo Navigator* (from 1966) and *Who Put the Bomp* (from 1970, later shortened to *Bomp!*), the much-beloved Greg Shaw hired writers such as **Lester Bangs** and Greil Marcus, and is credited by some with fathering the modern style and substance of serious rock journalism. Over the next several decades Shaw also ran a group of interconnected businesses (record label, store, zine), mostly under the *Bomp!* name, in order to promote artists whom he liked—usually well ahead of their time—such as the Flaming Groovies, **Iggy Pop**, Stiv Bators (between the **Dead Boys** and the Lords of the New Church), the Plimsouls, and the notable series of *Pebbles* anthologies of 1960s pop nuggets. Shaw died of a heart attack in October 2004 in Los Angeles.

SHELTER

1990-present
LINEUP: Ray Cappo (vocals); John "Porcell" Porcelly (guitar, replaced by others); Graham Land (guitar, replaced by others), Chris Interrante (bass, replaced by others); Sam Dirksz (drums, replaced by others)

Among the more famous bands of the Krishna-core scene, Shelter was a New York group led by the formidable pair of vocalist Ray Cappo and guitarist John "Porcell" Porcelly, later of the influential **straight-edge** band **Youth of Today**. After cofounding **Revelation Records**, and following the breakup of Youth of Today, Cappo struggled for some time to determine if music and a spiritual life were mutually incompatible, and Shelter was the compromise in which music and spirituality were mixed with

equal fervor. Cappo and Porcell's Shelter was a natural (to them anyway) progression from Youth of Today to the doctrines of the **Hare Krishna** sect, with most of their lyrics reflecting their commitment to Krishna Consciousness. The band survived a close call in 1997 when touring with the *Beyond Planet Earth* album: Their tour van went off a cliff in Colorado leaving most of the members without serious injury but extraordinarily rattled. Eventually, Porcell left the band, and Shelter went on for a while without him, calling it quits in the early-1990s for a time before the inevitable reunion. Several of the members (apparently some 42 musicians have at one time or another been part of Shelter) subsequently reunited for new albums. Cappo has worked with numerous other bands and released a few solo recordings, Porcell went on to found a record label and to record with **Bold**.

Discography:
Perfection of Desire (Revelation, 1990); *Quest for Certainty* (Equal Vision, 1991; Revelation, 1998); *Attaining the Supreme* (Equal Vision, 1993); *Mantra* (Supersoul/Roadrunner, 1995); *Beyond Planet Earth* (Supersoul/Roadrunner, 1997); *Chanting, Prayers, and Meditations* (Son of Yashoda, 1997); *When 20 Summers Pass* (Victory, 2000)

SHEMPS

2002-present
LINEUP: Artie Philie (vocals); "Squeaky" Dave Wilentz (guitar); Neil Halpin (guitar); Bill Florio (bass); Matt Longoria (drums); Neil Callahan (keyboards)

Despite coming from musical backgrounds as diverse as Milhouse, Dick Army, and Indecision (all monstrously loud and superb in their own ways), the Shemps continue in the vein of those bands, but add to the mix a much-needed dose of melody, garage rock, and humor that never came across

as well in their previous bands. For his part, vocalist Artie Philie shouted like a glorious, tortured loon in earlier bands, whereas in the Shemps he restrains his sound to good effect. Bassist Bill Florio, for his part, pens the occasional column for *Maximum RocknRoll*. Along with bands like the Ergs, Steinways, Groucho Marxists, and others, the Shemps are making **pop-punk** sound as fresh and reinvigorated as it has in at least 20 years—and not a moment too soon.

Discography:
To Hell and Back 7" (Gloom, 2003); *Spazz Out with the Shemps* (Reservation, 2004)

SHONEN KNIFE

1981-present
LINEUP: Naoko Yamano (vocals/guitar); Michie Nakatani (vocals/bass, replaced by Atsuko Yamano); Atsuko Yamano (drums, replaced by Mana "China" Nishiura)

With a name that can literally be translated as "boy's knife," Shonen Knife was for a time the most popular Japanese band to tour the West. The Osaka band's founders—Michie Nakatani, and sisters Naoko and Atsuko Yamano—drew heavily from their love of the **Ramones** and American **pop-punk**, as well as straight Western pop music like the Beatles (they later covered the song "Rain").

Shonen Knife was quickly championed in America by bands such as **Redd Kross** and **Sonic Youth**, both of whom—along with L7, **Mr. T Experience**, **Government Issue**, and Lunachicks—covered the band's songs for the 1989 tribute album *Every Band Has a Shonen Knife Who Loves Them*. Kurt Cobain was a huge fan, asking the band to open for **Nirvana** on the UK leg of the *Nevermind* tour. Shonen Knife's first release in America was 1990's self-titled album, followed by the popular 1992 major-label debut *Let's Knife* (whose cover featured the band in full, perky retro '60s mod attire). The following year's album *Rock Animals* spawned a single ("Tomato Head") whose video got into heavy rotation on **MTV**. In 1994, Shonen Knife's alterna-cred peaked with their inclusion on that year's Lollapalooza tour. After that high-water mark, the band returned to releasing records via indie labels.

Nakatani retired from Shonen Knife in June 1999 and was replaced on bass by Atsuko, with new drummer Mana "China" Nishiura later stepping in to complete the group. Nishiura left in 2004 to join the Japanese metal band DMBQ, and in November 2005 was killed in an auto accident in New Jersey while touring with them. DMBQ and Shonen Knife performed a tribute concert for Nishiura in Kyoto during the spring of 2006. Shonen Knife now tours with new drummer Etsuko. (Atsuko is currently in semi-retirement.)

Although Shonen Knife had numerous songs that sound (and very often are) peculiar to American ears, they are actually very challenging in the ways that they deal with consumer culture and maintaining the balance of being female in a male-dominated industry (especially in Japan, where, traditionally, few women hold positions of authority) and playing an American art form in a culture that has its own unique take on rebellion. The band also makes a strong effort to preserve the **DIY** aesthetic, taking control of their image, for instance, through drummer-turned-bassist Atsuko Yamano's designs for the band, which mark them as being quite far removed from the Japanese mass-produced *idoru* (female idols, mostly manufactured in the manner of boy bands in the United States).

Discography:
Burning Farm (Japan Zero, 1983; cassette; K, 1985); *Yama No Attchan* (Zero, 1984; MCA Victor, 1995); *Pretty Little Baka Guy* (Subversive, 1986; Oglio, 2004); *Shonen Knife* (Gasatanka/Giant, 1990); *Pretty Little Baka Guy + Live in Japan!* (Gasatanka/Rockville, 1990); *712* (Gasatanka/Rockville, 1991); *Let's Knife* (Virgin, 1992); *Rock Animals* (Creation, 1993; Virgin, 1994; EMI Special Markets, 1998); *Brown Mushrooms and Other Delights* EP (Virgin, 1993); *We Are Very Happy You Came* (Creation, 1993); *Favorites* EP (MCA, 1993); *Greatest History* (MCA, 1995); *The Birds and the B-Sides* (Virgin, 1996); *Super Mix* (MCA Victor, 1997); *Brand New Knife* (Big Deal, 1997); *Explosion!* EP (Big Deal, 1997); *Ultra Mix* (MCA Victor, 1998); *Happy Hour* (Big Deal, 1998); *Strawberry Sound* (Japan Universal Victor, 2000); *Millennium Edition* (Universal Victor, 2001); *Heavy Songs* (Confidential, 2003); *Genki Shock* (Oglio/Glue Factory, 2006); *Fun! Fun! Fun!* (Blues Interactions, 2007)

Shelter, 1997: Ray Cappo on the right, John Porcell shirtless to his left.

Shonen Knife explores the East Village in New York.

"When I finally got to see (Shonen Knife) live, I was transformed into a hysterical nine-year-old girl at a Beatles concert."
—Kurt Cobain

Shudder to Think, 1998.

SHUDDER TO THINK

1986-1998

LINEUP: Craig Wedren (vocals/guitar); Chris Matthews (guitar, replaced by Nathan Larson); Stuart Hill (bass); Mike Russell (drums, replaced by Adam Wade, Kevin March)

The Washington, D.C., **hardcore** and post-hardcore scenes had many components—integrity, dedication, emotion, and talent—but what they may have lacked until the advent of Shudder to Think was that most critical element of all for major label success: style. With mastermind Craig Wedren running the band, Shudder was one the most engaging bands of the late-1980s **Dischord Records** stable. Similar to **Jawbox** in their intense dynamic, Shudder was also distinctive for Wedren's unique falsetto, which marked the band as more of a throwback to classic rock and glam (which helped when the band played on the ultra-glam *Velvet Goldmine* soundtrack). Despite Shudder's keen sense of style and general coolness, Sony couldn't sell them to the masses, and the band broke up in 1998. Both Larson and Wedren have since written music for films. Wedren released solo album in 2005 and the two, along with Larson's wife, the Cardigans' Nina Persson, played together live in New York in 2007.

Discography:
Curse, Spells, Voodoo, Mooses (Sammich, 1989); *Ten Spot* (Dischord, 1990); *Funeral at the Movies* (Dischord, 1991); *Get Your Goat* (Dischord, 1992); *Pony Express Record* (Epic, 1994); *50,000 B.C.* (Epic, 1997); *First Love, Last Rites: The Soundtrack* (Sony, 1998). **Craig Wedren:** *Lapland* (Team Love, 2005)

SICK OF IT ALL

1985-present

LINEUP: Lou Koller (vocals); Pete Koller (guitar); Rich Cipriani (bass, replaced by Craig Setari); Armand Majidi (drums)

A New York **hardcore** band with a ferocious, raw, and aggressive sound, Sick Of It All was founded in 1985 by brothers Lou and Pete Koller and proved a massive draw in the city's hardcore scene during the 1980s and '90s due to their über-aggressive sound. The band found themselves the subject of unwanted controversy in 1992 when teenager Wayne Lo murdered several classmates at his Massachusetts prep school while wearing a Sick Of It All T-shirt. Although some in the mainstream media reported that Lo had been influenced by the band, the *New York Times* actually provided a forum for the band to explain why their lyrics were not about violence and that Lo had willfully misinterpreted their music's philosophy. (A rare example of a band getting a chance to defend itself from mainstream suspicions about the links between punk and violence.) SOIA continues today as one of the flagship acts of New York hardcore.

Discography:
Sick of It All (Revelation, 1987, 1997); *Blood, Sweat, and No Tears* (Relativity, 1989); *We Stand Alone* EP (Relativity, 1991); *Just Look Around* (Relativity, 1992); *Scratch the Surface* (EastWest, 1994); *Live in a World Full of Hate* (Lost & Found, 1995); *Spreading the Hardcore Reality* (Lost & Found, 1995); *Built to Last* (Elektra, 1997); *Call to Arms* (Fat Wreck Chords, 1999); *Yours Truly* (Fat Wreck Chords, 2000); *Live in a Dive* (Fat Wreck Chords, 2002); *Relentless Single* (Bridge Nine, 2003); *Life on the Ropes* (Fat Wreck Chords, 2003); *Outtakes for the Outcast* (Fat Wreck Chords, 2004); *Death to Tyrants* (Abacus, 2006)

Sick Of It All,
keeping American
hardcore alive, 1989.

SIDE BY SIDE

1987-1990

LINEUP: Jules Massey (vocals);
Eric Fink (guitar); Alex Brown (guitar);
Billy Bitter (bass); Sammy Siegler (drums)

One of the many unheralded bands who soldiered on during the crucial years of the New York **hardcore straight-edge** scene in the late-1980s, Side by Side played alongside bands such as **Youth of Today**, although they were much less doctrinaire than most of that scene's bands at the time. Although generally acknowledged as straight edge, they were somewhat reluctant to take on the movement's mantle because of all the attendant baggage and presumed promises that accompanied such a label. Their music now sounds a bit dated, but still has some great moments that will bring any old New York hardcore straight-edge kid from the 1980s right back to the Pyramid Club on Avenue A. Side by Side recorded an EP and a full-length album for **Revelation Records** before hanging it up at the end of the decade. Following the demise of Side By Side, singer Jules Massey formed the band Alone in a Crowd.

Discography:
You're Only Young Once EP (Revelation, 1988);
You're Only Young Once LP (Revelation, 1997).
Alone in a Crowd: *S/T* (Flux, 1989)

SIOUXSIE AND THE BANSHEES

1976-1996

LINEUP: Susan Dallion, aka "Siouxsie Sioux" (vocals); John McKay (guitar, replaced by Robert Smith, others); Steve Severin (bass); Kenny Morris (drums, replaced by Budgie, others)

Siouxsie and the Banshees have been claimed by both the punk and goth camps—although lead singer Siouxsie Sioux has long been uncomfortable with both of those labels. Regardless of the band's ultimate identity, the Banshees created some of the moodiest and most starkly atmospheric music of the early punk scene. The Banshees—led by stalwarts Siouxsie Sioux and bassist Steve Severin—created a unique sound and look that inspired many young men and women to experiment with gender, identity, and copious amounts of makeup.

Lovers of all things shocking and **David Bowie**-esque, Siouxsie and Severin first got into the London punk scene via the **Bromley Contingent**. This led to a close association with the **Sex Pistols**, and a starring role for Siouxsie, who was sitting behind the Pistols during their infamous appearance on Bill Grundy's *Today* show, lending her an inestimable amount of punk historical credibility.

The Banshees were formed in September 1976 by Siouxsie and Severin after the breakup of their short-lived first group, the **Flowers of Romance**. Their show at that year's **100 Club** punk festival—with drummer **Sid Vicious** (who refused to play cymbals) and guitarist Marco Perroni (later of Adam and the Ants)—was an unqualified attention-getter that revealed Siouxsie's electrifying stage presence. The entire show, in fact, was an improvisational 20-minute version of The Lord's Prayer (they would record it later for their second album).

After Vicious and Perroni left the band, Siouxsie and the Banshees decided to take themselves more seriously and in 1977, the group solidified into its first real lineup with the addition of John McKay on guitar and Kenny Morris on drums. Early gigs were rife with controversy as Siouxsie sometimes wore a swastika onstage (apparently to demystify it, but both she and Severin often gave contradictory accounts of this in interviews at the time) and sang about there being "too many Jews for my liking" in the song "Love in a Void" (which she later re-recorded as meaning "too many fat businessmen"). These and similar statements, as well as Siouxsie's love of bondage clothing, guaranteed the band attention.

Siouxsie and the Banshees became known in the London scene as the longest-running, unsigned punk band, but after months of gigging without success, they finally managed to score a record deal at Polydor. Their first LP, *The Scream*, came out in October 1978 and received wide critical acclaim. By then, the band had honed their skills and stripped down their sound to minimalist punk-influenced, eerie-rock wails that presaged the goth scene.

Siouxsie and the Banshees' second album, *Join Hands*, was released the following year, but the band splintered when Morris and McKay abruptly quit shortly before a gig in 1979. Siouxsie and Severin

soldiered on with replacements, including the **Slits'** Budgie (who would remain a member until the band's demise) on drums and Robert Smith on guitar, performing double duty with his "real" band, the Cure, until the mid-'80s.

Siouxsie and the Banshees grew in popularity as the 1980s went on, with Siouxsie toning down her image (slightly) for mass consumption as the band moved into a more sophisticated musical phase. Along the way, the band became so identified with the goth movement that they were name-checked in the **Dead Milkmen**'s satirical "You'll Dance to Anything" a certain kind of punk immortality. The Banshees's 1988 album *Peepshow* delivered the band's first U.S. chart hit: the poppy "Peek-a-Boo." In 1991, the spookily romantic "Kiss Them For Me" from the album *Superstitious* became Siouxsie and the Banshees' only American Top 40 hit. That same year, Siouxsie and Budgie got married, and the band played on the first Lollapalooza tour, along with **Henry Rollins** and **Butthole Surfers**.

Although Siouxsie and the Banshees have had sporadic reunions since the mid-1990s, Siouxsie now largely tours and records either by herself or as part of the Creatures with Budgie (the two divorced in 2007). One of the first female punk originals, Siouxsie paved the way for women in punk.

Discography:

The Scream (Polydor, 1978; Geffen, 1984); *Join Hands* (Polydor, 1979; Geffen, 1984); *Kaleidoscope* (PVC, 1980; Geffen, 1984); *Juju* (PVC, 1981; Geffen, 1984); *Arabian Knights* EP (PVC, 1981); *Once Upon a Time/The Singles* (PVC, 1981; Geffen, 1984); *A Kiss in the Dreamhouse* (Polydor, 1982; Geffen, 1984); *Nocturne: Live* (Wonderland/Geffen, 1983); *Hyaena* (Wonderland/Geffen, 1984); *The Thorn* EP (Wonderland/Polydor, 1984); *Cities in Dust* EP (Geffen, 1985); *Tinderbox* (Wonderland/Geffen, 1986); *Through the Looking Glass* (Wonderland/Geffen, 1987); *The Peel Sessions* EP (Strange Fruit, 1987); *Peepshow* (Wonderland/Geffen, 1988); *The Peel Sessions* EP (Strange Fruit, 1988); *The Peel Sessions* (Strange Fruit/Dutch East India Trading, 1991); *Superstition* (Wonderland/Geffen, 1991); *Twice Upon a Time—The Singles* (Wonderland/Geffen, 1992); *The Rapture* (Wonderland/Geffen, 1995). **Creatures:** *Wild Things* EP (Polydor, 1981); *Feast* (Wonderland/Polydor, 1983); *Boomerang* (Geffen, 1989). **The Glove:** *Blue Sunshine* (Wonderland/Polydor, 1983; Rough Trade, 1990). **Siouxsie:** *Mantaray* (Decca, 2007)

Siouxsie Sioux and a few Banshees play Devon, England, in the late-1970s.

THE SITUATIONISTS

A subversive, French social and political movement, which originally formed in 1957, the Situationists were extremely influential on the first wave of British punk. While some doubted the intellectual breadth of the punk movement, many of the more revolutionary figures in the scene were drawn to the ideas of the Situationists' leading theorist Guy Debord, author of *The Society of the Spectacle*, who coined such provocative statements as "The art of the future will be the overturning of situations or nothing."

Many scholars, such as Greil Marcus in his book *Lipstick Traces: A Secret History of the Twentieth Century*, have found a link between **Malcolm McLaren**'s work with the **Sex Pistols** and his interest (from his art school days) in the Situationsists. **Jamie Reid** was certainly influenced by the Situationists in his cut-and-paste artwork for the Sex Pistols in which different images and words were juxtaposed, often in a manner that evoked a ransom note. Although the individual members of the Sex Pistols would later deny both the extent of McLaren's control and their involvement in any movement (most especially Situationism), it is difficult to deny the connection, both on a stylistic and ideological level, between certain anarchist collectives and **squats** in England (see **Crass**) during punk's first wave of the 1970s and the French Situationists.

Other punk bands over the years have appropriated the Situationists' provocative antiauthoritarian stance and adapted it to the punk scene's design. The liner notes of the **Feederz**'s 1984 album *Ever Feel Like Killing Your Boss?* offer Situationist pamphlets for sale via mail order. That same year, *Maximum RocknRoll* published a lengthy essay entitled, "An Introduction to the Situationist International" that referenced the Feederz and others. **Unwound**'s singer Justin Trosper said that he had been "under the influence of Situationism" when making the 1995 album *The Future of What*. Even more recently, the Minneapolis punks of the Dillinger Four recorded an album for **Fat Wreck Chords** in 2002 entitled

> "(The Situationist International) understood, as no one else of their time did, why major events…arise out of what are, seemingly, the most trivial provocations. (P)eople were bored, they were not free, they did not know how to say so. Given the chance, they would say so."
> —Greil Marcus, *Village Voice Literary Supplement*, 1982.

The Situationist Comedy, a brilliant and subversive record that must have made both the Sex Pistols and the late Debord proud.

SKA

Ska is a Jamaican precursor to **reggae** that achieved great popularity in England during the early-1960s, and since then has left its mark on numerous punk bands on both sides of the Atlantic. Epitomized by bands and musicians such as the Skatalites and Desmond Dekker. ska was faster than its successors rock steady and reggae, which slowed the beat down while keeping ska's basic, peppy syncopations. The use of ska was a recurring motif in many punk scenes, from the **2 Tone** movement in England in the late-1970s and early-'80s to the American scenes of the '80s and the '90s. The English version of ska, however, at least in the 2 Tone days, was much more overtly political than most of the American bands who jumped on the bandwagon in the 1990s.

The popularity of ska in England also reflected British societal problems with racism and cultural assimilation, which had been inflamed after a large number of Caribbean immigrants moved into some of the poorer neighborhoods in London and other major cities, bringing a fascinating new kind of music with them. Many of the original members of ska bands were also influenced by the early, non-racist **skinhead** scene in which young, disaffected British men and women adopted the uniform of the working class and listened to imported ska and reggae records from Jamaica. (One can see a particularly vivid portrait of this scene in Shane Meadows' 2006 film *This is England*.)

The rise and influence of movements such as **RAR (Rock Against Racism)**, the demise of the first wave of punk in England, and the fact that many bands (such as the **Clash** and the **Ruts**) were already playing or adapting reggae music, led to a generation of new punk musicians who were looking for a new creative direction. Ska then became a powerful force for social commentary in the hands of British bands such as the **Specials**, the Selecter, and the English Beat, most of whom recorded for 2 Tone, the record label started by Specials keyboard player Jerry Dammers.

Although it didn't last long, the British ska scene also influenced numerous American bands. Most American ska bands came out of California, by far the most prominent of them being **Operation Ivy**. Although the band's time on the Berkeley

The Selecter in New York, 1980: (L to R) Ned Davies, Charley Anderson, Pauline Black, Arthur "Gaps" Hendrickson.

scene was relatively truncated, their legacy led to the formation of many ska bands in the United States in the late-1980s to mid-'90s, including far less political bands such as Reel Big Fish, **Goldfinger**, the Mighty Mighty Bosstones (the rare East Coast exception to the California ska rule), and No Doubt. While their sound was too omnivorous to categorize, **Fishbone**'s music was particularly ska-heavy during their early years in the 1980s, and their sound would be echoed by outfits like Red Hot Chili Peppers. While ska in the U.S. could have a political element, as demonstrated by Operation Ivy, it largely lacked the intense edge that the best of British ska possessed.

SKATEBOARDING

Skateboard enthusiasts and punk culture have a long and varied relationship, with most of the earliest alliances coming from California's Orange County scene. Many of the early West Coast bands were skateboard aficionados, and the 1970s *Lords of Dogtown*-style outlaw culture that went along with skateboarding fit in well with the early **hardcore** punk scenes.

During the early-1980s, many skaters and surfers in California became interested in punk bands like **Black Flag**, the **Circle Jerks**, **Suicidal Tendencies**, and **JFA**, some of whom also skated themselves. The young skaters found punk's energy and aggression to be the perfect background music for their intense but generally antiauthoritarian athleticism (as expressed in the popular sticker: "Skateboarding is Not a Crime"). Later on, the connection became even tighter, with bands such as the **Big Boys** launching their own line of skateboards. *Thrasher* magazine also highlighted the connection in their pages throughout the 1980s, even releasing popular skate videos with punk soundtracks. Photographer Glen Friedman was one of the most famous chroniclers of the skate-punk scene, with his shots of both skaters and hardcore bands holding an almost iconic status today.

Skate-punk as a musical genre remains enormously popular in the United States today, with venues from television to live tours (such as the **Vans Warped** tour) that feature skate-punk bands as well as skateboarding demonstrations.

TOM GROHOLSKI INTERVIEW
PHILLY STREET SHREDDING
TEXAS COVERAGE
PLUS— RECORDS, GRINDERS, CARTOONS AND OTHER NEAT STUFF!

THIS END

PRICE: JUST ONE STAMP YOU LAME-OS!

ZINE

Vol. 1 No. 4

SKINHEADS

Although as a subculture they actually predate punk, skinheads are nevertheless one of the most controversial and sometimes reviled groups in punk, mostly due to their (not always justified) reputation for violence and racism. The skinhead movement traces its roots back to 1960s British working-class culture. Initially, it was not racist, and the members were fans of **reggae, ska**, and rock steady music who wore exaggerated variations on the traditional outfits of factory workers, including steel-toed boots, suspenders, straight-legged denim jeans, and extremely short hair. This movement coalesced around the clubs where performers such as **Symarip** and Judge Dread played for racially mixed audiences united by their class backgrounds more than they were divided by race. Different skinheads began associating themselves in a tribal style by adopting variations in dress and hairstyle, with shorter-haired "suedeheads" and "smoothies" adopting their own distinct looks under the skinhead umbrella. Although the open exhibitions of racism didn't erupt until later, by the end of the 1960s some groups of particularly xenophobic skinheads were attacking Pakistani immigrants with weapons, clubs, and their boots; in 1970 thousands of Pakistanis marched on the prime minister's residence at 10 Downing Street in London to protest these assaults.

By the 1970s, when punk was becoming popular in England, the "skins" began to divide into more specialized subgroups. A large contingent joined forces with militant football fans and right-wing, nationalistic movements such as the **National Front**, whose brand of jingoism attracted many skinheads. The widespread violence that was common at shows by **Skrewdriver** and other right-wing bands (not to mention **Sham 69**, who didn't want the skins there but felt obligated to allow them in) caused the media to demonize skins and to create the monolithic, stereotypical image prevalent today.

In the United States, many were first introduced to the skinhead look through the music of underground **hardcore** bands and the shaved heads of many of their fans.

British skinheads on parade, 1983.

The shaved head, however, was not automatically a skinhead identifier in the U.S., as it was often associated with other movements such as **straight-edge** punk or simply hardcore rejection of the excesses of punk fashion. Many skinheads, alarmed by the bad publicity the movement was receiving from the media—which was particularly negative in the U.S., where the association between skinhead and racism was much more absolute—formed groups such as SHARP (Skinheads Against Racial Prejudice) in the late-1980s.

Modern skinhead dress styles include dress shirts (Ben Sherman the preferred label), suspenders, flight jackets, jeans rolled at the cuff for men, and boots (**Doc Martens** in particular) with laces indicating one's support of white power or racial unity or even communism. Men's hair is generally shorn close but not always completely off, while the women usually sport a fringe on the front and back.

Musically, most British skins listened to a variant of 1970s **oi** music as epitomized by the likes of Sham 69, **Angelic Upstarts**, and Blitz, whereas many American skinheads identified with bands such as **Agnostic Front**, **Warzone**, and the **Cro-Mags**. Today, bands such as the Templars, Anti-Heroes, and Niblick provide much of the modern skinhead soundtrack.

SKREWDRIVER
1977-1979, 1982-1993
LINEUP: Ian Stuart Donaldson (vocals); Phil Walmsley (guitar); Ron Hartley (guitar); Kevin McKay (bass); John "Grinny" Grinton (drums)

Notorious white-power band Skrewdriver had its roots in the original punk movement, but quickly embraced a **skinhead** look and the racist Nazi philosophy epitomized by the **National Front**. Having originally started out in Blackpool, England, as a Rolling Stones cover band called the Tumbling Dice, Skrewdriver played as a rather pedestrian punk band in their first incarnation (once opening for **Sham 69** at the **Roxy**). However, in 1982, lead singer and white-power agitator Ian Stuart Donaldson re-formed the band, greeting his audience with a Nazi salute to indicate Skrewdriver's new direction and also his involvement with the National Front, the

British white-power, anti-immigrant political group. In 1983, Skrewdriver released the "White Power" single, which definitively established the band's new focus on racist heavy metal, as did the album *Hail the New Dawn*. Despite setbacks (such as Donaldson being sentenced to a year in jail for a racially motivated beating in the 1980s), the band soldiered on, *sans* talent by most any standards that matter. Donaldson later formed an umbrella racist music organization called Blood and Honour and a **rockabilly** band called the Klansmen, and kept up a steady stream of new Skrewdriver material, even including a racist reworking of Lynyrd Skynyrd's "Sweet Home Alabama." In 1993, Donaldson died in car crash that his Blood and Honour followers claimed was a government assassination, and Skrewdriver ended with his death. While clearly not all skinheads were racist thugs, bands like Skrewdriver did nothing to soften this reputation.

Essential Discography:
Skrewdriver (Chiswick, 1977); *Hail the New Dawn* (ISD/Blood and Honour, 1984)

SLAPSHOT
1985-2002
LINEUP: Jack Kelly (vocals); Steve Risteen (guitar); Jordan Wood (second guitar, replaced by Jonathan Anastas, Darryl Sheppard); Jamie Sciarappa (bass, replaced by Chris Lauria); Mark McKay (drums, replaced by Barry Hite)

A Boston-based, **straight-edge**, **hardcore** band with an aggressively straightforward sound, Slapshot was formed in the mid-1980s by former members of **DYS** and **Negative FX** in a perhaps quixotic attempt to combine straight edge with a love of hockey. The band was originally called Straight Satan, named after the motorcycle gang associated with Charles Manson, until the sports theme became more dominant later on. They quickly became one of the key bands in the Boston **scene**. Eventually guitarist/bassist Jonathan Anastas left the band to return to college (he now works for an advertising agency in Los Angeles), and he was replaced by **SSD's** Jamie Sciarappa.

Slapshot's sound became more heavy metal-oriented as the years went by, much as DYS's sound had before them. After 1997 the band went on semi-hiatus, playing some

shows in Europe but none in the United States for years, and they officially broke up in the new millennium.

Discography:
Back on the Map EP (Taang!, 1986); *Step on It* (Taang!, 1988, 1991); *Sudden Death Overtime* (Taang!, 1989); *Live at South 36* (We Bite, 1993); *Blast Furnace* EP (We Bite, 1993); *Unconsciousness* (We Bite, 1994); *16 Valve Hate* (Taang!, 1995); *Old Tyme Hardcore* (Taang!, 1996); *Greatest Hits: Slashes and Crosschecks* (Century Media, 2001; Bridge Nine, 2003); *Digital Warfare* (Bridge Nine, 2003); *Tear It Down* (Thorp, 2005)

SLASH/SLASH RECORDS
LOCATION: LOS ANGELES

The Los Angeles-based zine *Slash*, and the related label Slash Records, were essential in both the promotion and release of pivotal music from bands in the L.A. scene. *Slash*, one of the first punk-related zines in the United States, was founded in 1977 by Philomena Winstanley and Claude "Kickboy Face" Bessy, who had previously worked on several **reggae**-related zines. *Slash* focused mostly on L.A. acts such as the **Screamers**, the **Weirdos**, and **X**, as well as bands the editors admired, like the **Damned**. The zine helped expose many of the early L.A.

bands to readers outside of the immediate geographic area, letting people around the world find out about the thriving punk seeds germinating there.

Although *Slash* folded in 1980, two years prior the zine's publisher Bob Biggs had founded Slash Records to release music by the local bands covered in the zine; their slogan was "Small enough to know the score, big enough to settle it." Slash Records featured an impressive roster of acts from **Fear**, X, the Plugz, **Gun Club**, and the **Germs** as well as national acts such as Violent Femmes, Los Lobos, L7, the **Misfits**, and Faith No More. For many years Slash Records' albums were distributed by Warner Bros., making them one of the first indie labels with major distribution. Biggs sold Slash Records to London Records in 1996 and continued to work there for several years thereafter. In 2003, the label was revived by Biggs as Slash/BiggMassive.

SLAUGHTER & THE DOGS

1976–1979, occasionally thereafter

LINEUP: Wayne Barrett (vocals); Mick Rossi (guitar); Howard "Zip" Bates (bass); Brian "Mad Muffet" Grantham (drums)

Starting out as a Manchester pub cover band whose repertoire featured songs by **David Bowie** and **Lou Reed**, Slaughter & the Dogs were early punk pioneers reminiscent of the **Sex Pistols** and the **Damned**. They started playing gigs at London clubs like the **Roxy** (and were featured in **Don Letts**'s *Punk Rock Movie*) and put out sporadic singles like the classic "Cranked Up Really High" on the pioneering Manchester label, Rabid. The band's major contribution to the development of early punk was the 1978 release of their album *Do It Dog Style* on major label Decca Records. Slaughter & the Dogs broke up not long after but would sporadically re-form in subsequent decades with various lineups including Billy Duffy (later of the Cult) and, according to rumor, the Smiths' Morrissey briefly on vocals. Some members later formed a band called the Studio Sweethearts with Billy Duffy. These days, Slaughter & the Dogs continue to tour on the punk circuit.

Discography:

Do It Dog Style (Decca, 1978; Damaged Goods, 1989); *Live Slaughter Rabid Dogs* (Rabid, 1979); *Live at the Factory* (Thrush, 1981); *Rabid Dogs* (Receiver, 1989); *The Slaughterhouse Tapes* (Link, 1989). **Slaughter: Bite Back** (DJM, 1980)

Slaughter & the Dogs at the Roxy, undated.

"(Sleater-Kinney) came from the Pacific Northwest, from the land of hemp and used bookstores, and they conquered the world."

—Rick Moody

NEW YORK UNIVERSITY
Doors Open At 8PM
$5 w/NYU ID
Must have valid NYU ID for entry • No Cameras

Thursday at 8:00PM

OCT **17** 2002

NYU Program Board Presents
SLEATER-KINNEY

General Admission

Irving Plaza, 17 Irving Pl. btwn 15 and 16 Sts.

Sleater-Kinney, 2005: (L to R) Carrie Brownstein, Janet Weiss, Corin Tucker.

SLEATER-KINNEY

1994-2006

LINEUP: Corin Tucker (vocals/guitar);
Carrie Brownstein (vocals/guitar); Lora
MacFarlane (drums, replaced by Janet Weiss)

An all-female trio from Olympia, Washington, Sleater-Kinney became one of the most commercially successful punk bands in the United States during the 1990s. Although their clean-cut demeanor was more librarian than punk, their music was a riveting noise-punk assault of atonal guitars and an intricate snarl of heartfelt lyrics.

Sleater-Kinney was started after the demise of earlier bands who had been lumped into the **Riot Grrrl** movement, with Corin Tucker from **Heavens to Betsy** and Carrie Brownstein (a classically trained pianist) from Excuse 17 joining forces as twin guitarists/singers. Tucker and Brownstein (who had originally met while at Evergreen College in 1992), felt that their sound was perfect the way it was and boldly decided to go where no one in punk (except for the **Cramps**) had gone before, *sans* bassist. The ladies simply tuned their guitars lower and then went through a few drummers for the first couple of years before settling in 1996 on Janet Weiss, who also played in the band Quasi with her former husband, Sam Coomes.

Sleater-Kinney's eponymous debut record was released on Donna Dresch's Chainsaw label in 1995 and caused a minor sensation, but the band hit their stride with the electrifying *Call the Doctor* in 1996, which featured the song "I Wanna Be Your Joey Ramone," situating the band as direct challengers of not just the punk status quo but also of any preconceptions about what all-female punk bands should sound like or sing about. After moving up to major indie label **Kill Rock Stars**, with the demise of Brownstein and Tucker's relationship and the addition of Weiss, the next record, *Dig Me Out*, was even more emotionally charged, and one of the decade's most successful indie label releases.

In 2001, Tucker and her husband had their first child—the aptly named Marshall Tucker Bangs—and this newfound sensibility as a mother and feminist icon gave added depth to their subsequent album, *One Beat*, in 2002. Sleater-Kinney then opened for longtime fans Pearl Jam on their 2003 tour. They left Kill Rock Stars for Sub Pop for the 2005 album *The Woods*, an album that sounded closer to classic rock and, though it baffled some longtime fans, received nearly unanimous critical approval. Sleater-Kinney announced an "indefinite hiatus," leaving a legacy as one of the most politically articulate and musically powerful bands in modern punk rock.

Discography:

Sleater-Kinney (Chainsaw, 1995); Villa Villakula, 1995); *Call the Doctor* (Chainsaw, 1996); *Dig Me Out* (Kill Rock Stars, 1997); *The Hot Rock* (Kill Rock Stars, 1999); *All Hands on the Bad One* (Kill Rock Stars, 2000); *One Beat* (Kill Rock Stars, 2002); *The Woods* (Sub Pop, 2005)

The Slits prepare to terrorize the men of England, 1977.

THE SLITS

1976-1981

LINEUP: Arianna "Ari-Up" Foster (vocals); Vivian Albertine (guitar); Tessa Pollitt (bass); Paloma "Palmolive" Romero (drums, replaced by "Cut" Budgie, Bruce Smith)

One of the earliest and most important all-female punk groups, the Slits were also famous for their forward-thinking experiments with **reggae,** funk, and **dub** music. The original lineup consisted of drummer Palmolive (the Spanish-born Paloma Romero, who lived with **Joe Strummer** for two years, and got her punk name from the **Clash**'s bassist Paul Simonon), guitarist Kate Korus, bassist Suzy Gutsy, and the impressively dreadlocked 14-year-old Arianna "Ari-Up" Foster on vocals. (Ari-Up's mom later married **John Lydon**, making him perhaps the scariest, or coolest, step-dad in history.) Before the band was a few weeks old, Gutsy and Korus left and were replaced by Vivian Albertine on guitar and bassist Tessa Pollitt, who had previously played in the **Flowers of Romance.**

The Slits started off as a rather primitive punk band, but soon were playing opening gigs for the Clash, the **Buzzcocks,** and others. The band waited a long time to record their first album, and in that time their raw sound evolved into a fusion of reggae, funk, and dub that had little to do with the loud and fast punk rock being made around them. The Slits made a conscious decision to play music that was more organically "female" as opposed to the inherently male music that dominated most of punk and rock 'n' roll. When the band began to record its first record, Budgie (later of **Siouxsie and the Banshees**) replaced Palmolive (who later went on to play with the **Raincoats**) and played on most of the tracks.

The first Slits album, *Cut*, was released in 1979 with a provocative cover showing the band's women posing topless and covered with mud, which both parodied and debunked the notion of using women's bodies as tools to sell a record. After touring, replacing Budgie with drummer Bruce Smith from the **Pop Group**, and putting out the harder and more dub-inflected album *Return of the Giant Slits*, the Slits broke up at the end of 1981. Ari-Up moved to Jamaica, recorded solo records, worked with the likes of reggae producer/legend Lee "Scratch" Perry, and performed in Adrian Sherwood's New Age Steppers with Albertine. In 2005, Ari announced a Slits reunion that featured her and bassist Tessa Pollitt (as well as Pollitt's daughters), the **Sex Pistols'** Paul Cook, and Mick Jones of the Clash.

The Slits were not only the most important all-female punk band of the 1970s, but their experimental use of mixed musical genres also paved the way for the **post-punk** experimentation of the '80s and '90s.

Discography:
Cut (Island, 1979); *Untitled (Retrospective)* (Rough Trade, 1980); *The Return of the Giant Slits* (CBS, 1981); *The Peel Sessions* (Strange Fruit, 1989)

PATTI SMITH

Iconic punk poet, singer, writer, and performer Patti Smith was the queen of the early New York scene, serving as inspiration in later years to singers like P.J. Harvey. With her band, the Patti Smith Group, she brought (along with **Richard Hell** and Tom Verlaine of **Television**) a poetic and

romantic sensibility to New York punk that helped distinguish it from the (sometimes) more working-class British version that tried hard to disassociate itself with anything romantic or poetic.

Born in Chicago in 1946, Smith later moved to the wilds of New Jersey, where she gave birth to a child given up for adoption and worked in a factory (later dramatized in her first single, "Piss Factory"). She moved to New York in fall 1967, where she met photographer Robert Mapplethorpe (who would later create the stark black-and-white photographic portraits of Smith that helped define her image), and quickly made a name for herself on the Bowery poetry scene during the early-1970s. The established poets on the scene, like **Jim Carroll**, were surprised

by the intensity and rock 'n' roll edge (borrowed from her hero Keith Richards) that Smith brought to her readings with guitarist (and rock critic) Lenny Kaye. Smith also became involved with playwright Sam Shepard, writing and performing in the play *Cowboy Mouth* with him in 1971.

At that time, Smith was unsure about becoming a rock star, and, inspired by the French poet Arthur Rimbaud, began to concentrate more on her writing, releasing the book of poems *Seventh Heaven* in 1972. Her performances with Kaye began to resemble songs more than they did poems set to music, and soon the possibility of playing at rock clubs and making albums was taken much more seriously. Eventually, to augment their sound, Kaye and Smith added

keyboard player Richard Sohl and then solidified what would be the band's classic lineup with the addition of Ivan Kral on bass and Jay Dee Daugherty on drums.

The 1975 album *Horses* was produced by the **Velvet Underground**'s John Cale and released by Clive Davis' Arista label. (Davis had taken note of the band during their early 1975 stint at **CBGB**.) The first record from a member of the New York punk scene, *Horses* was an instant classic and a powerful indication that Smith's artistic coconspirators were as influenced by the romantic poets as they were by the grime and nihilism of their beloved Lower East Side neighborhood. After touring and solidifying as a band, the Patti Smith Group returned to the studio in late 1976 to record

> ## "Genius is dangerous. Those that think it can be packaged are fools."
> —Patti Smith

Patti Smith at New York's Bottom Line, 1975.

Radio Ethiopia, which took the band further in an almost mystical direction. Aided by Smith's dynamic stage presence and manic intensity, Radio Ethiopia found her sometimes chanting and sometimes singing her lyrics, depending on the way in which the band took the song musically. The Patti Smith Group toured to support the record, but disaster loomed. While on the road with Bob Seger in 1977, Patti Smith fell onstage and cracked a vertebra in her neck, forcing her to withdraw from making music for a year, just as the band was poised for success. In 1978, the Patti Smith Group released Easter, which contained their biggest hit, "Because the Night," cowritten with Bruce Springsteen, but by then Sohl had been replaced by Bruce Brody, and some of the magic was gone.

Following the release of the Todd Rundgren-produced Wave in 1979, and after a final performance in Florence, Italy, for 70,000 fans, Patti Smith decided to retire and marry Fred "Sonic" Smith (of the **MC5**), move to Detroit, and raise a family. She briefly came out of retirement in the late-1980s with her album Dream of Life, which included the anthemic "People Have the Power," and then went back on hiatus for several more years until the 1996 release of Gone Again, which marked her return to music following years of immense personal tragedy. Mapplethorpe, who had become one of her closest friends, died in 1989; longtime collaborator Sohl passed away in 1990; and both her husband, Fred Smith, and brother Todd Smith, died in 1994. Afterwards, Smith continued to tour and record with a reconstituted band that featured Kaye and Daugherty, putting out music that justified her vision as the "poet laureate" of punk rock.

In 2005, to mark the album's 30th anniversary, Patti Smith performed Horses in its entirety both at London's Royal Festival Hall and New York's Brooklyn Academy of Music (BAM). She also performed at the last-ever CBGB concert in 2006 and was, fittingly, inducted into the Rock and Roll Hall of Fame in 2007.

Discography:
Horses (Arista, 1975); Dream of Life (Arista, 1988); Gone Again (Arista, 1996); Peace and Noise (Arista, 1997); Gung Ho (Arista, 2000); Trampin' (Sony, 2004); Twelve (Sony, 2007). **Patti Smith Group:** Radio Ethiopia (Arista, 1976); Easter (Arista, 1978); Wave (Arista, 1979)

WINSTON SMITH

Notorious graphic artist and designer Winston Smith (born Patrick Morey) pioneered a style of deconstructionist art that was evocative of the collage work of American masters like Romare Bearden, or even the animation that artist Terry Gilliam contributed to Monty Python. Smith's album cover design is best exemplified by the disturbing collages of classic suburbia and Americana that he created for the **Dead Kennedys**. He also worked for the American version of **RAR (Rock Against Racism)** and created album covers for various punk bands (including **Green Day**'s Insomniac album), as well as penning a political column for Spin magazine in the 1990s. Smith continues to design album covers and exhibit his work to increasing critical acclaim.

SMOKEWAGON

2001-present
LINEUP: Kevin Omen (vocals/guitar); Pat Fondiller (bass); Jesse James Howard (drums)

A Brooklyn-based trio influenced by Johnny Cash, Nick Cave, Ennio Morricone, and other outlaws, Smokewagon is known for their evocative lyrics; a musical mix of punk, blues, goth, country, and **post-punk**; and invariably smart choices in covers (including a slower, country version of the **Misfits**' "Skulls"). Although the band dresses in the prerequisite black and constantly references dark and brooding neo-Western imagery, there is a stark sense of twisted humor beneath the surface. Singer/guitarist Kevin Omen's bitter wail of a voice also marks Smokewagon as natural successors to the melding of post-punk (bassist Pat Fondiller frequently plays with ex-Swan Michael Gira's band Angels of Light) and the bitter, resigned country of Johnny Cash's last few Rick Rubin-produced records. At their best, Smokewagon elicits a giddy sort of depression.

Discography:
Smokewagon (Three Bullets, 2002); Deuce (Phantom, 2006)

SNIFFIN' GLUE

The intentionally low-tech and quite popular British zine Sniffin' Glue—inspired (not surprisingly) by the **Ramones**' song "Now I Wanna Sniff Some Glue"—was started in mid-1976 by Mark Perry (while working a day job as a bank clerk) as a photocopied handout, and lasted a mere dozen issues before closing shop in 1977. The first issue included the following opinion by Perry, which pretty much encapsulates the zine's ultimate thesis: "The Ramones are what 1976 punk rock is all about. They are kids, I'm a kid and you are kids—you must be if you are reading this shit."

Sniffin' Glue's look epitomized the **DIY** zine movement with bizarrely scribbled covers and rough blocks of interior typescript. Perry was uncomfortable being considered part of the mainstream rock press and encouraged readers to start their own zines. In 1977, he started the Step Forward Records label with Miles Copeland; they released records by the **Fall**, **Sham 69**, and **Chelsea**. That same year, Perry played his first show with **Alternative TV** and included a flexi-disk of their single in the final issue of Sniffin' Glue in August 1977.

In 2000, he released Sniffin' Glue: The Essential Punk Accessory, a compilation of original writings from the zine.

SOA

1980-1981
LINEUP: Henry Rollins (vocals); Michael Hampton (guitar); Wendel Blow (bass); Simon Jacobsen (drums, replaced by Ivor Hanson)

The early Washington, D.C., **hardcore** outfit SOA (State of Alert) was fronted by an 18-year-old kid named Henry Garfield (later **Henry Rollins**), who used his time with the band as a period of self discovery. This is where he found his lyrical point of view and holler of a voice, which he would use to perfection in his next band, **Black Flag**. The members of SOA were all formerly in the Extorts, which featured a pre-**Minor Threat** Lyle Preslar. They then teamed up with Henry, and played their first show (with Minor Threat) at a December 1980 house party, where they opened for D.C. stalwarts Black Market Baby, the Untouchables, and **Bad Brains**. SOA put out only a single EP, 1981's No Policy. The second-ever **Dischord** release, No Policy is as rawly produced as it is

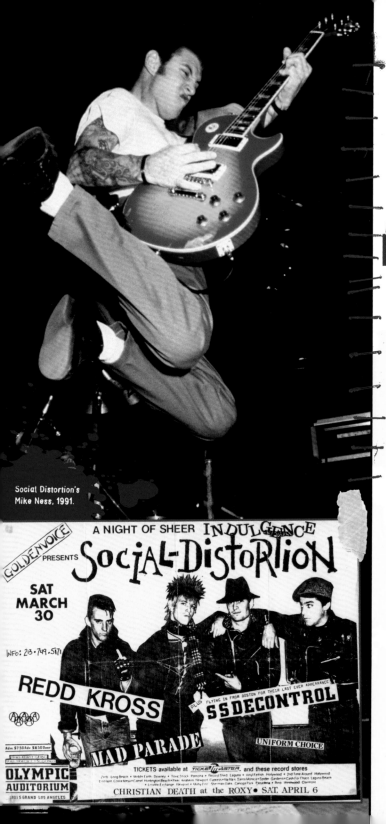

Social Distortion's Mike Ness, 1991.

A NIGHT OF SHEER INDULGENCE

GOLDENVOICE PRESENTS

Social Distortion

SAT MARCH 30

INFO: 213·749·5171

REDD KROSS

PLUS FLYING IN FROM BOSTON FOR THEIR LAST EVER APPEARANCE

SS DECONTROL

MAD PARADE

UNIFORM CHOICE

TICKETS available at TICKET MASTER and these record stores

Adm $7.50 Adv $8.50 Door

OLYMPIC AUDITORIUM
1801 S GRAND LOS ANGELES

CHRISTIAN DEATH at the ROXY · SAT. APRIL 6

---

performed, essentially a crazed summation of Rollins's views on life (ambiguous) and work (horrific), providing a keen glimpse into why Rollins would later become a punk voice for the ages. SOA's last show was opening for Black Flag in Philadelphia in June 1981, just a few days before Rollins went on to front the headliner. SOA's last drummer, Ivor Hanson, later played in **Embrace** and **Faith**.

Discography:
No Policy EP (Dischord, 1981)

SOCIAL DISTORTION

1979-present

CLASSIC LINEUP: Mike Ness (vocals/guitar); Dennis Danell (bass); Casey Royer (drums)

One of the classic, first-wave Orange County **hardcore** bands, Social Distortion later adapted their sound into a punk-**rockabilly** hybrid, with the heavily tattooed and gutter-voiced Mike Ness remaining the only constant.

A catalyst for the late-1970s California scene, Social Distortion originally featured Ness backed by brothers Rikk and Frank Agnew. (They would soon depart to form the **Adolescents** and **D.I.**) Social Distortion's early sound was straightforward, melodic hardcore, albeit with slightly more personal lyrics than was common at the time. **Rodney Bingenheimer** started playing some of their songs on his radio show and in 1981 Social Distortion released their first single, "Mainliner/Playpen." The high point of Social Distortion's first incarnation came in 1983, when they released the classic album, *Mommy's Little Monster*. That same year the band appeared in the film *Another State of Mind*—an indelible snapshot of the early-1980s American punk scene that documented their troubled and drug-fueled national tour with **Youth Brigade** (L.A.) in a breakdown-prone school bus.

Afterwards, Ness' drug use became increasingly problematic, leading to several stints in jail and rehab and the band's first major break up in the mid-1980s. Then, with a sober Ness backed up by a new rhythm section, Social Distortion came back strong in 1988 with the album *Prison Bound*,

which combined Ness' punk roots with an overt debt to the Hank Williams- and George Jones-style country and rockabilly he had always loved. The next record, the eponymous *Social Distortion*, yielded several hugely successful singles including "Ball and Chain" and "Story of My Life." Longtime Guitarist Dennis Danell died from heart failure in 2000 at the age of 38. After a brief hiatus, the band continued with guitarist Jonny Wickersham.

Discography:
Mommy's Little Monster (13ᵗʰ Floor, 1983; Triple X, 1990; Time Bomb, 1995); Prison Bound (Restless, 1988; Time Bomb, 1995); Social Distortion (Epic, 1990); Story of My Life . . . and Other Stories EP (Epic, 1990); Somewhere Between Heaven and Hell (Epic, 1992); Mainliner (Wreckage from the Past) (Time Bomb, 1995); White Light, White Heat, White Trash (550 Music/ Epic, 1996); Live at the Roxy (Time Bomb, 1998); Sex, Love and Rock 'n' Roll (Time Bomb, 2004). **Mike Ness:** Cheating at Solitaire (Time Bomb, 1999); Under the Influences (Time Bomb, 1999)

S.O.D.

1985-2001

LINEUP: Billy Milano (vocals); Scott Ian (guitar); Dan Lilker (bass); Charlie Banante (drums)

S.O.D. (Stormtroopers of Death) started out as a something of a joke version of **hardcore** for members of thrash band Anthrax in 1985. Guitarist Scott Ian and drummer Charlie Banante added former Anthrax bassist Dan Lilker (then playing with Nuclear Assault) and then-roadie Billy Milano as singer for an album that produced a parody of thrash metal and hardcore that was just as good as many of the "serious" practitioners of the genre. Their debut record, *Speak English or Die*, had crossover appeal, and became a major influence on metal fans who had previously hated punk, convincing them to embrace the emerging thrash/hardcore scene; it went on to eventually sell over a million copies. The album did have its un-PC moments ("Fuck the Middle East," for instance, or the title song's anti-immigrant rant) that led some to question the extent to which the band and their fans were joking. In any event, S.O.D. continued to tour and record sporadically over the following years, and Milano often toured with his more metal-oriented band, M.O.D.

Discography:
Speak English or Die (Megaforce, 1985, 2000, 2005); Live at Budokan (Megaforce, 1992); Bigger Than the Devil (Nuclear Blast, 1999)

"There are few greater sights in rock than watching Lee Ranaldo and Moore hammering the hell out of their guitars to Kim Gordon's raspy voice."

—*New Music Express*, February 26, 2001

LEFT: Sonic Youth blast away at CBGB, 1986. (L to R) Lee Ranaldo, Kim Gordon, Steve Shelley, Thurston Moore.

BELOW: The famous *Daydream Nation* cover, art by Gerhard Richter.

SONIC YOUTH

1981–present

LINEUP: Thurston Moore (vocals/guitar); Lee Ranaldo (guitar); Jim O'Rourke (guitar); Kim Gordon (bass); Steve Shelley (drums)

Formed in New York during the early-1980s **no wave** movement, Sonic Youth has spent well over two decades as the reigning lords of avant-garde art-punk. They create a unique squall of noise with their alternative forms of tuning and intentional dissonance, sometimes created via the use of drum sticks or screwdrivers applied to guitars. (Sonic Youth often used as many as 20 back-up guitars, each with its own tuning.)

Sonic Youth formed in 1981 as an offshoot of the work that guitarists Thurston Moore and Lee Ranaldo had been doing with composer Glenn Branca in the late-1970s and early-'80s; bassist Kim Gordon (who married Moore in 1984) and drummer Richard Edson completed the original lineup. The first, self-titled EP (released on Branca's label Neutral) was as noisy and dissonant as anything on Manhattan's no wave scene, but few of its pieces actually had anything like tradi-tional song structures. After Edson left to pursue acting (*Stranger Than Paradise*, *Ferris Bueller's Day Off*, *Platoon*), Bob Bert took over on drums for the next few albums; he would later play for Pussy Galore. With the 1983 album *Confusion is Sex*, Sonic Youth began to find a middle ground between the seemingly competing drives toward noise experimentation and their love of pop and punk. The band's creation of an entirely new form of pul-sating **post-punk** or post-no wave would become incredibly influential on indie

bands throughout the 1980s and '90s. *Bad Moon Rising* (1985) took a step closer to conventional rock and provided a look back at Sonic Youth's past. (The song "Death Valley 69" featured no wave lumi-nary **Lydia Lunch** singing with Gordon; the two would later form a side project named after the author Harry Crews.)

With *EVOL*, Sonic Youth added drummer Steve Shelley (formerly of the **Crucifucks**) and signed to **SST**, home to the cream of the mid-1980s indie music crop. At SST, Sonic Youth produced some of its most compelling music, including the epic "Expressway to Yr Skull," which on the 12-inch single has a listed time of infin-ity, thanks to a well-placed flaw in the record that keeps the final drone playing in a continuous skip. At around the same time, Sonic Youth showed their love for pop culture by forming (with friend **Mike Watt**) the goofy side-project Ciccone Youth, as an off-kilter homage to Madonna (Ciccone being her original last name); they later released *The Whitey Album* in 1988. After the *Master-Dik* EP and the phe-nomenal 1987 album *Sister*, Sonic Youth jumped to Enigma for their breakthrough: the double-LP *Daydream Nation*. That record established them as one of the most important bands in the independent music scene and led to them being signed to major label DGC (later home of Sonic Youth fans **Nirvana**).

Their 1990 DGC debut *Goo* was a very hook-driven work that still had its epic washes of classic Sonic Youth guitar noise and fragmented poetry. However, better production and some catchier songs led to the band gaining more popularity through **MTV**, particularly via the album's single "Kool Thing" and its video (featuring Chuck D. of Public Enemy). Sonic Youth appeared in the film *1991: The Year That Punk Broke*—which documented the increasing popularity of bands such as Nirvana (shown in the film as a little-known band opening for Sonic Youth on a European tour). In 1992, they released the popular album *Dirty*, which, though given plenty of gloss by Nirvana producer Butch Vig, featured an uncharacteristically raw cover of the **Untouchables**' "Nic Fit," and some ripping guitar work by **Ian MacKaye** on "Youth Against Fascism," a com-

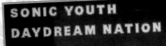

SONIC YOUTH
DAYDREAM NATION

mentary on the Supreme Court justice Clarence Thomas confirmation hearings.

During the mid-1990s, Sonic Youth started working on more obtuse and experimental records that lost them a considerable share of their growing fanbase even as it allowed them to both expand musically and return to their orchestrated-noise roots. As the decade wore on, Sonic Youth became less concerned with success and more interested in the experimentations of their youth, leading to a host of collaborations and an adventurous series of compositions that they released via their own label, SYR. The band flowered creatively when frequent collaborator Jim O'Rourke joined as a third guitarist in 2002, contributing to the albums *Sonic Nurse* and *Murray Street* (the latter named for the downtown Manhattan location of their recording studio, almost destroyed in the 9/11 attacks); he left in 2005. With their boundless innovation and penchant for championing obscure bands, Sonic Youth serve today as the revered elders of an increasingly fragmented scene, their contributions to modern atonal music almost too numerous to catalog.

Select Discography:

Sonic Youth EP (Neutral, 1982; SST, 1987); *Confusion Is Sex* (Neutral, 1983; SST, 1987; DGC, 1995); *Kill Yr Idols* EP (Zensor, 1983, 1987); *Sonic Death: Live* (cassette; Ecstatic Peace!, 1984; SST, 1988); *Bad Moon Rising* (Homestead, 1985; DGC, 1995); *Death Valley 69* EP (Homestead, 1985); *EVOL* (SST, 1986; DGC, 1994); *Sister* (SST, 1987; DGC, 1994); *Master-Dik* EP (SST, 1988); *Daydream Nation* (Blast First/Enigma, 1988; DGC, 1993); *Daydream Nation* EP (Blast First/Enigma, 1988); *Goo* (DGC, 1990); *Dirty* (DGC, 1992); *Experimental Jet Set, Trash and No Star* (DGC, 1994); *Made in USA* (Rhino, 1995); *Screaming Fields of Sonic Love* (DGC, 1995); *Washing Machine* (DGC, 1995); *SYR1: Anagrama* EP (Sonic Youth, 1997); *SYR2: Slaapkamers Met Slagroom* EP (Sonic Youth, 1997); *A Thousand Leaves* (DGC, 1998; Sonic Youth, 1998); *Hold That Tiger* (Goofin, 1998); *Silver Session for Jason Knuth* (Sonic Knuth, 1998); *SYR4: Goodbye 20ᵗʰ Century* (Sonic Youth, 1999); *NYC Ghosts & Flowers* (Geffen, 2000); *Murray Street* (DGC/Geffen, 2002); *Sonic Nurse* (Geffen, 2004); *SYR6: Koncertas Stan Brakhage Prisiminumui* (Sonic Youth, 2005); *Rather Ripped* (Geffen, 2006); *The Destroyed Room: B-Sides and Rarities* (Geffen, 2006). **Sonic Youth/Jim O'Rourke:** *SYR3: Invito al Cielo* (Sonic Youth, 1998). **Ciccone Youth:** *The Whitey Album* (Blast First/Enigma, 1988; DGC, 1995). **Sonic Youth/Eye Yamatsuka:** *TV Shit* EP (Ecstatic Peace!, 1994). **Lee Ranaldo:** *From Here to Infinity* (SST, 1987); *Scriptures of the Golden Eternity* (Father Yod, 1993; Father Yod/Drunken Fish, 1995); *Broken Circle/Spiral Hill* EP (Starlight Furniture Company, 1994); *East Jesus* (Atavistic, 1995). **Jim Sauter/Don Dietrick/Thurston Moore:** *Barefoot in the Head* (Forced Exposure, 1990). **Thurston Moore:** *Psychic Hearts* (DGC, 1995). **Kim Gordon/D.J. Olive/Ikue Mori:** *SYR5* (Sonic Youth, 2000)

The Specials, 1980. Lynval Golding (foreground), Terry Hall.

THE SPECIALS

1979-1985

ORIGINAL LINEUP: Neville Staple (vocals); Terry Hall (vocals); Lynval Golding (guitar); Roderick James Byers, aka "Roddy Radiation" (guitar); Horace Panter, aka "Sir Horace Gentleman" (bass); John Bradbury (drums); Emmanuel "Rico" Rodriguez (trombone); Jerry Dammers (keyboards)

The original **2 Tone** band, the Specials started playing together in Coventry, England, in 1977 as the Automatics and later as the Special AKA, getting their first exposure to the public while opening for the **Clash** on their summer 1978 tour. Originally designed to bridge the gap between punk and **reggae**, the Specials shifted courses—and their name—around 1979, evolving into their proper **ska** format and pioneering the British ska revival that quickly swept the nation. They scored numerous hits between 1979 and 1981, including "Too Much Too Young," "Ghost Town," and "Free Nelson Mandela." Essentially a vehicle for the political and social views of keyboardist and songwriter Jerry Dammers—a former mod and **skinhead** who in 1979 started up the 2 Tone record label, which would prove crucially important to the ska revival in both England and the United States—the Specials would go through various permutations and lineups over the years after essentially disbanding in the early-1980s. Singers Neville Staple and Terry Hall, and guitarist Lynval Golding, left for the more pop-oriented Fun Boy Three.

In the 1990s and 2000s, various conglomerations of ex-members—without Dammers—would tour under the name the Specials or the Special Beat. Although largely ignored by many today, the Specials are primarily responsible for the great ska revival in England during the early-1980s.

Discography:

The Specials (2 Tone/Chrysalis, 1979); *More Specials* (2 Tone/Chrysalis, 1980); *Ghost Town* EP (2 Tone/Chrysalis, 1981); *The Peel Sessions* EP (Strange Fruit, 1987); *The Singles Collection* (Chrysalis, 1991). **Special AKA:** *The Special AKA Live!* EP (2 Tone, 1980); *In the Studio* (2 Tone/Chrysalis, 1984)

PENELOPE SPHEERIS

In the 2000s, documentaries on punk would become almost as ubiquitous as **Green Day** imitators. But when Penelope Spheeris' grotty look at the Los Angeles scene, *The Decline of Western Civilization*, hit theaters in 1981, it stood nearly alone in a media landscape that had essentially consigned punks to freakshow status. A UCLA film major who started out producing comic shorts for Albert Brooks and his first feature *Real Life* (1978), Spheeris turned down a different road with *Decline*, which made her name as one of the foremost cinematic chroniclers of the punk world. Three years later she directed and co-wrote *Suburbia*, a fictional tragedy about homeless L.A. punks that was heavily informed by her documentary experience. In 1987 she made *Dudes*, a more mainstream comedy about New York punks on a harrowing cross-country road-trip in which **Fear**'s **Lee Ving** played their redneck adversary. Spheeris spent some years writing for *Roseanne* (a good match for her working-class feminist pugnacity) and making comedies like *Wayne's World*. She later returned to punk subjects with 1998's *The Decline of Western Civilization, Part III*, a look at **crust punks** in the contemporary L.A. scene, and developing a film version of **John Lydon**'s autobiography *Rotten*.

SQUATS

Loosely defined as any semi-abandoned building or farmhouse where punks would live together, usually illegally, without paying rent (the idea being that if a building is abandoned, it effectively becomes property of the people), squats have been an important element in punk culture, often serving as laboratories for methods of living in systems organized by anarchist or communal principles of mutual self-interest. The styles and sizes of squats vary widely from city to city and country to country, with famous punk squats being located in Amsterdam; Minneapolis (the Big House); London; Manchester, England; New York; and Washington, D.C., to name a few. Punk squats are differentiated from the more

established residences like the Dial House farmhouse in Essex, England—the base of operations for **Crass** and their assorted community, which still operates on anarchist principles despite the fact that it is owned legally. As a general rule, long-term, organized, punk squats are more common at this point in Europe, due in some part to the European punk scene's more stridently anarchist tendencies. The 2007 book *Punk House: Interiors in Anarchy* is a fascinating photographic record taken during 2004 by Abby Banks in some 65 punk houses, some of them squats, in smaller American cities and towns such as Chattanooga, Tennessee, Gainesville, Florida, and New Orleans.

> "Living together is a punk rock rite of passage into responsibility in complete disregard of social standards."
>
> —Thurston Moore, from *Punk House*

Some jolly lads facing eviction from their alternative housing arrangements in London's King's Cross neighborhood, 1979.

SSD

1981-1985

LINEUP: Phil "Springa" Springs (vocals); Alan "Lethal" Barile (guitar); Jamie Sciarappa (bass); Chris Foley (drums)

Also known as Society System Decontrol or SS Decontrol, Boston's first and most important 1980s **hardcore straight-edge** band was one of the more vocal straight-edge proponents and also one the most ferocious metal-tinged bands of the time. Led by guitarist Alan "Lethal" Barile, SSD pioneered Boston hardcore (particularly its heavy metal influences) and allowed the scene to grow—even though a number of the other bands playing around town at the time (like **Jerry's Kids**) were hard drinkers with little use for SSD's devotion to straight edge. SSD had a loose aggregation of 20 or so superfans known as the Boston Crew, all of whom were recognizable by their shaved heads, straight-edge militancy, and ferocity in the **pit**. The band released their first EP, *The Kids Will Have Their Say!*, in 1982, on their own XClaim! label, founded that same year. After SSD broke up a few years later, bassist Jamie Sciarappa played in **Slapshot** for a time before joining My Eye. Drummer Chris Foley was in a variety of bands, including Crime and Punishment. The meat-eating and brawny brand of straight edge practiced by SSD stood in stark contrast to the more ascetic vegan style that later became synonymous with straight edge.

Discography:
SS Decontrol: *The Kids Will Have Their Say!* EP (XClaim!, 1982); *Get It Away* (XClaim!, 1983). **SSD:** *How We Rock* (Modern Method, 1984); *Break It Up* (Homestead, 1985); *Power* (Taang!, 1992)

SST RECORDS

LOCATION: LOS ANGELES

In the 1970s, when future punk legend **Greg Ginn** was a ham radio aficionado in Hermosa Beach, California, he started a company dealing with ham radio equipment called SST Electronics. In 1978, Ginn and Chuck Dukowski of **Black Flag** morphed the company into SST Records as a way to release Black Flag albums and singles. SST Records grew quickly after a few years and in a short period of time put out

seminal records from almost every major punk, indie, and experimental band of the 1980s. The list of bands who recorded some of their best material for SST—particularly during the golden period of the mid-1980s—reads like an American punk hall of fame: Black Flag, the **Minutemen**, **Sonic Youth**, **Bad Brains**, **Meat Puppets**, **Hüsker Dü**, and the **Descendents**. Although SST was, for a time, one of the most influential, underground record labels, its talent roster became depleted during the late-1980s, as many bands departed for bigger labels where they hoped the financial record-keeping would be better. In later years, the label became an outlet for Ginn's solo work and avant-jazz artists; the results were not pretty. Many of the best bands from SST's golden age, such as the **Meat Puppets**, later had their catalogs rereleased by other record labels. SST had the potential to be one of history's great punk labels, but due to Ginn's idiosyncratic nature—and lax accounting—it never fulfilled that promise.

STAGE-DIVING

Stage-diving at a show—the process of being hoisted up onstage by members of the audience, possibly making a brief statement either into the mic or into empty air, and diving off the stage—is a long-standing punk ritual related to the **pit**, slam-dancing, and crowd-surfing. Although the custom started at punk shows, it made its way into heavy metal culture and is now mainstream behavior at most thrash metal shows. Although an old tradition at punk shows, stage-diving is considered a nuisance by some bands (like **Fugazi**), many of whom hire extra security to keep non-band members off the stage. There are bands who embrace stage-diving, however, and openly encourage their fans to come onstage, usually during the encores. There is an inherent danger to stage-diving ("will anybody catch me?"), but that is of course part of the thrill.

The ever-popular backward stage-dive, performed here at a 1982 Fear show in California.

THE STEINWAYS

2003-present

LINEUP: Grath Madden (vocals/guitar); Ace (guitar); Michelle Shirelle (bass/vocals); Chris Grivet (drums)

One of the best developments in the New York/New Jersey area during the 2000s was the resurgence of the **pop-punk** scene, in which bands such as the **Ergs** and The Groucho Marxists keep alive the spirit of the 1990s bands like **Egghead**. Among the most exciting of this newer breed are the Steinways, hailing from that legendary bastion of punk: Queens (birthplace of the **Ramones**). With songs like "I Wanna Kiss You on the Lips" and "Carrie Goldberg," the Steinways sound like some gorgeous and yearning mixture of the Ramones, **Screeching Weasel**, and classic Brill Building songs. Recognizing their creative limitations by titling the final song on their *Missed the Boat* album, "How to End a Steinways Song," the Steinways stand as proof to jaded types, who have long since decided that the scene was over and done, that punk is not only still viable but can also be goofy, and even innocent.

Discography:
Missed the Boat (Cold Feet, 2007); *Gorilla Marketing* (Cold Feet, 2008)

STIFF LITTLE FINGERS

1977-1982, occasionally thereafter

LINEUP: Jake Burns (vocals/guitar); Henry Cluney (guitar); Ali McMordie (bass); Brian Faloon (drums, replaced by Jim Reilly, Brian "Dolphin" Taylor)

Northern Ireland's Stiff Little Fingers laid down a harsh and angular musical trail for generations of political **pop-punks** and **post-punks** to follow. They started out as a Deep Purple cover band called Highway Star before being inspired by the emerging sound of punk and changing their name to Stiff Little Fingers (after a song by the **Vibrators**). Stiff Little Fingers released their first record, the incendiary single "Suspect Device," in March 1978 (it was a favorite of **John Peel**, who gave it heavy play on his radio show), but did not release a proper

Stiff Little Fingers in Belfast, 1977.

material. Even though they are senior citizens by punk standards, Stiff Little Fingers' certainly stands the test of time and their first four studio records are indispensable for a punk record collection.

Discography:
Inflammable Material (Rough Trade, 1979; Restless, 1990, 1993, 2005); *Christmas Album/Live in Sweden* (bootleg/unknown label, 1979); *Broken Fingers/Live in Aberdeen* (bootleg/unknown label, 1979; EMI, 2002); *Nobody's Heroes* (Chrysalis, 1980; Restless, 1990, 2005); *Hanx!: Live* (Chrysalis, 1980; Restless, 1990, 2005); *Go for It* (Chrysalis, 1981; Restless, 1990; EMI, 2004); *Now Then . . .* (Chrysalis, 1982; EMI, 2004); *All the Best* (Chrysalis, 1983; One Way, 1995); *The Peel Sessions* EP (Strange Fruit, 1986); *Live and Loud!!* (Link, 1988); *No Sleep 'til Belfast* EP (Skunx, 1988; Castle, 1994; Kaz, 1988); *See You Up There!* (Caroline, 1989); *The Last Time* EP (Link, 1989); *The Peel Sessions* (Strange Fruit, 1989, 2002); *Flags and Emblems* (Castle, 1991, 2004); *Fly the Flags: Live* (Castle, 1991; Snapper, 1998); *Get a Life* (Castle, 1994, 2004); *BBC Radio 1 Live in Concert* (Windsong, 1993; Griffin, 1995); *Pure Fingers Live: St. Patrix 1993* (Original Masters, 1995, 1999); *Tinderbox* (Taang!, 1997; EMI, 2002); *And Best of All . . . Hope Street* (EMI, 1999); *Hope Street: Greatest Hits Live* (Oxygen, 1999); *Tin Soldiers* (Harry May, 2000); *Live Inspiration* (Recall, 2000); *Anthology* (EMI, 2002); *The Radio One Sessions* (Strange Fruit, 2003); *From the Front Row Live* (Silverline, 2003); *BBC Live in Concert* (Strange Fruit, 2003); *Guitar and Drum* (Kung Fu, 2004); *Backs Against the Wall* (EMI, 2004); *Song By Song* (Phantom, 2004); *Wasted Life: Live* (Phantom, 2004); *Fifteen and Counting . . . Live at the Barrowland* (unknown label, 2006)

album until February 1979. That year's *Inflammable Material* contained one of the best and most hopeful calls for political and social change in punk history, "Alternative Ulster." Led by charismatic singer and guitarist Jake Burns, Stiff Little Fingers blasted out a series of songs—most written by *Daily Express* journalist Gordon Ogilvie—that reflected the harsh realities of turbulent and violent everyday life in Northern Ireland.

The group officially called it quits in 1983 but re-formed in 1987 with a new lineup featuring Burns, Cluney, and former **Jam** bassist Bruce Foxton. A revised lineup including Burns and (for a while) Foxton still tours and consistently releases new

STIFF RECORDS
LOCATION: LONDON

London's Stiff Records secured its place in history when the label released the first English punk seven-inch single. The **Damned**'s "New Rose" came out in October 1976, beating the **Sex Pistols**' debut by two months. Stiff also unleashed records by eclectic artists such as Elvis Costello, the **Adverts**, Wreckless Eric, Madness, Dave Edmunds, and Graham Parker. Started by Dave Robinson and Jake Riviera in July 1976, Stiff originally put out records by pub-rock entrepreneurs Dave Edmunds and Nick Lowe and had an early distribution deal with Island Records, which allowed their material a wider release than most small labels. Known for their cheeky slogans—"If It Ain't Stiff, It Ain't Worth A Fuck," for example—Stiff also released the first Damned album, *Damned, Damned, Damned* (produced by Nick Lowe, who did the same for many Stiff releases), **Richard Hell**'s "Blank Generation" single, and Elvis Costello's first records and singles. Riviera left in 1984 to form Radar Records, and Stiff Records was eventually acquired by Island and then ZTT.

THE STIMULATORS
1978–1981
LINEUP: Patrick Mack (vocals); Denise Mercedes (guitar); Anne Gustavsson (bass, replaced by Nick Marden); Harley Flanagan (drums)

An early New York **hardcore** band that featured a young Harley Flanagan, later of the **Cro-Mags**, on drums (he was only 11 years old when the band started), the Stimulators were quickly eclipsed by other bands playing around the city, particularly **Bad Brains**. This is a shame, as the Stimulators' only record, 1982's *Loud Fast Rules!*, stands the test of time as one of the great unsung New York classics. The band was more or less gone from the scene by 1981, however, due mostly to the changing nature of the local scene to the more aggressive hardcore style. The Stimulators' lead singer, Patrick Mack, died of AIDS in 1983. A version of the band played at one of the final **CBGB** shows in 2006, on the same bill with Bad Brains.

Discography:
Loud Fast Rules! (ROIR, 1982)

THE STOOGES

1967–1974, 2003–present

LINEUP: Iggy Pop (vocals); Ron Asheton (guitar); David Alexander (bass, replaced by James Williamson); Scott Asheton (drums)

Iggy Pop (born James Osterberg), often called the "godfather of punk," made his early fame with the dark and dangerous, proto-punk rock madness that was the Stooges (aka Iggy and the Stooges), a band that would influence countless punk and heavy metal bands over the following four decades. In Ann Arbor, Michigan during the late-1960s, guitarist Ron Asheton and bassist Dave Alexander decided to form a band after being inspired by an electrifying Who concert in England. Iggy Pop, who was at the time drumming for a blues-rock band called the Prime Movers, decided to team up with the Asheton brothers and Alexander. They played their first show at a Halloween party in 1967 as the Psychedelic Stooges.

The Stooges (the name was soon shortened) quickly became well known across the Midwest for their raucous shows and Iggy Pop's Jim Morrison-inspired persona. While the Stooges played their drone-like trance music, Iggy Pop, sometimes dressed in glitter and body paint, writhed around the stage and contorted his body into various positions, sometimes smearing himself in peanut butter, rolling in broken glass, or simply antagonizing the audience. The Stooges were friends with the **MC5** (who considered the Stooges their "baby brother" group) and through their connections were signed along with the MC5 by **Danny Fields** to Elektra Records in 1968. John Cale of the **Velvet Underground** (another band who similarly bucked the era's mellow musical trend) produced the Stooges' first record, containing the classics "I Wanna Be Your Dog" and "No Fun," which would both be covered by many punk bands later in the 1970s.

When *The Stooges* was released in August 1969, although it did not make much of an impression on the general public, many future punk pioneers took notice, including **Patti Smith**, Alan Vega of **Suicide**, and Scott Kempner of the **Dictators**. The **Ramones** and **Sex Pistols** would also look to the early Stooges for

inspiration—the Pistols' **Sid Vicious** and **John Lydon** were clearly influenced by Iggy Pop's wicked stage persona, and their band would later cover "No Fun." The second record, *Fun House*, was as revolutionary as the first, incorporating jazz riffs courtesy of saxophone player Steve MacKay (Miles

Davis had played with the Stooges before and was a fan), and even more intense songs such as "TV Eye." At the same time, the Stooges were introduced to heroin by road manager and ex-junkie John Adams, who showed the band how to snort and shoot up the drug, leading to a lengthy addiction for Iggy Pop. At this point, Dave Alexander had been replaced by James Williamson, and Danny Fields became the Stooges' de facto manager after leaving

Elektra. Unfortunately for the band, Elektra declined to pick up the option on the Stooges' third album, and Fields left after becoming frustrated with the band's constant drug abuse.

After signing a deal with Clive Davis at CBS Records, Iggy Pop began to record with Williamson on guitar and, after auditioning others, invited the Asheton brothers back, this time with Ron on bass, to record the seminal *Raw Power* album in England. *Raw Power* featured the powerful title song and the instant classic "Search and Destroy." The record typically failed to make a dent in the charts, however, and Iggy and the Stooges decamped to the Beverly Hills Hotel, where they, along with **Leee Black Childers,** descended into a pit of debauched behavior and drug addiction.

Iggy (Right) and assorted Stooges, c.late-1960s.

After CBS dropped the group, Iggy Pop went on to work with **David Bowie** on several critically acclaimed solo records, becoming even more legendary in the process. The Asheton brothers went on to a variety of different projects, most notably New Order (*not* the **new wave** dance band featuring former members of **Joy Division**).

In 2004, the Stooges reunited for several tours with **Mike Watt** from the **Minutemen** playing bass, alongside the Asheton brothers and saxophonist Steve MacKay. In 2007, a reconstituted Stooges recorded and toured with the new record *The Weirdness*, with live shows that demonstrated that even a 60-year-old Iggy was a more formidable performer than almost anyone on the scene, inviting rapturous audiences to "invade the stage" in a love fest 30 years in the making.

Discography:

The Stooges: *The Stooges* (Elektra, 1969, 1977, 1982); *Fun House* (Elektra, 1970, 1977, 1982); *No Fun* (Elektra, 1980); *Rubber Legs* (Fan Club, 1987); *What You Gonna Do* EP (Revenge, 1988); *Live 1971* (Starfighter, 1988); *Live at the Whisky a Go Go* (Revenge, 1988); *My Girl Hates My Heroin* (Revenge, 1989); *1970: The Complete Fun House Sessions* (Elektra/Rhino Handmade, 1999); *Skull Ring* (Virgin, 2003); *The Weirdness* (Virgin, 2007). **Iggy and the Stooges:** *Raw Power* (Columbia, 1973; Columbia/Legacy, 1997); *Metallic K.O.* (Import, 1976); *I'm Sick of You* EP (Bomp!, 1977); *(I Got) Nothing* EP (Skydog, 1978); *I'm Sick of You* (Line, 1981, 1987); *Death Trip* EP (Revenge, 1987); *Pure Lust* EP (Revenge, 1987); *Raw Power* EP (Revenge, 1987); *Gimme Danger* EP (Revenge, 1987); *She Creatures of Hollywood Hills* (Revenge, 1988); *The Stooges* (Revenge, 1988); *Metallic 2xKO* (Skydog, 1988); *Raw Stooges Vol. 1* (Electric, 1988); *Raw Stooges Vol. 2* (Electric, 1988); *Search and Destroy—Raw Mixes Vol. III* (Curtis, 1989); *Iggy and the Stooges* (Revenge, 1991); *I Got a Right* EP (Bomp!, 1991). **Iggy Pop & James Williamson:** *Jesus Loves the Stooges* EP (Bomp!, 1977); *Kill City* (Bomp!, 1978)

STRAIGHT EDGE

A punk movement whose adherents did not drink, take drugs, have promiscuous sex, or, in many cases, eat meat or other animal products, straight edge was unofficially founded and given its name by the 1981 **Minor Threat** song "Straight Edge" (as well as other songs, such as "Out of Step With the World"), which calls those who use chemicals to alter their consciousness essentially "the living dead." Although Minor Threat's singer and songwriter **Ian MacKaye** had not meant to start a movement—and became in fact publicly ambivalent toward straight edge in subsequent

> "For people with a tendency to veer to fundamentalism, Straight Edge is a perfect vehicle. But for people who are healthy-minded, it's also worked out well. I think people have done some good things with it. And some dumb shit, too."
>
> —Ian MacKaye, quoted in Steven Blush's *American Hardcore*

years—many other bands of a similarly fast and loud **hardcore** demeanor took up the banner, including **Youth of Today**, **SSD**, **7 Seconds**, **Gorilla Biscuits**, **Bold**, **Uniform Choice**, and Straight Ahead.

The first wave of straight edge, epitomized by MacKaye's first band, the **Teen Idles**, came up with the idea to allow underage punks into bars by marking an *X* on their hands to indicate that they were there for the music, not the intoxicants. The movement soon spread, with the *X* becoming the unofficial symbol of straight edge. Other symbols, such as the *XXX*, also indicated that a punk was *extremely* straight edge, and the "True Till Death" tattoo that many straight-edge punks wore indicated that they had not merely jumped on a trend but had dedicated their lives to the ideology.

As often happens with such ideology-driven subcultures, there appeared many divisions in the community as to what actually constitutes straight edge, with a particularly ardent and prolonged debate over whether someone could be straight-edge if he or she consumed or used animal products. Many straight-edge punks either became strict vegans or at least stopped using animal products (particularly those in New York and Washington, D.C.). Although many older and more traditional punks raised in the drug-and-alcohol-filled scenes of major cities rejected straight edge, many younger punks—especially during the second generation of straight edge from the mid-to late-1980s—saw straight edge not only as a way of standing out from the non-punk crowd but also as a rebellion against the codified culture that the older punks had embraced. In her book *All Ages: Reflections on Straight Edge*, Beth Lahickey notes that "Straight edge provided an untraditional form of rebellion—rebelling against traditional forms of rebellion."

Although the straight-edge scene continued after the late-1980s, it never again had the prominence or exposure of the glory days of the New York and D.C. scenes, where bands like Youth of Today played numerous shows that provided a primer to young punks regarding the positive outcome of leading a clean lifestyle. A number of bands considered to be straight-edge, such as 7 Seconds, never really used the term, while other bands, including **Crucial Youth**, seemed much more like a parody of straight edge. Some straight-edge followers, such as Ray Cappo of Youth of Today, later moved on to become followers of Krishna Consciousness, which they saw as a natural step in furthering the movement's ideals for clean living.

THE STRANGLERS

1974–present

LINEUP: Jean-Jacques Burnel (vocals/bass); Hugh Cornwell (vocals/guitar); Brian Duffy, aka "Jet Black" (drums); Dave Greenfield (keyboards)

Originally named the Guildford Stranglers, this English band was as famous for their members' paranoia (fueled by misogyny and a love of science fiction) and punk feuds as they were for their ferocious and sometimes bizarre music. The Stranglers even had a sort of gang of followers, known as the Finchley Boys, while singer and bassist Jean-Jacques Burnel, a martial arts expert, was well known for his fights with **Clash** bassist Paul Simonon and writer Jon Savage.

By 1976, the Stranglers had shortened their name, lost some of their pub-rock stylings, and garnered enough attention to warrant opening for the **Ramones** at their first concert in London (a highly contested slot that **Malcolm McLaren** had supposedly tried to procure for the **Sex Pistols**). Mark Perry's *Sniffin' Glue* zine raved, "Sometimes they sound like the Doors, other times like **Television**, but they've got an ID of their own." The Stranglers's first album, 1977's *Rattus Norvegicus*, made a big splash on release, not least for including "Peaches," a strange and sexist Top 10 hit whose lyrics are inconsequential ("Looks like I'm gonna be stuck here the whole summer / What a bummer") when they're not sarcastically nudge-nudge, wink-wink ("Walkin' on the beaches / Lookin' at the peaches").

By the time the Stranglers' third album, *Black and White*, came out in 1978 the band had descended into utter paranoia, worrying about the "men in black" (secret government operatives who supposedly silenced those who knew too much about UFOs), and delving into some heavy drug use. Women's groups began to picket the Stranglers' performances because of the alleged misogyny of their lyrics (and because of the strippers occasionally featured in the band's live shows). In November 1979, singer/guitarist Hugh Cornwell was arrested and spent some time in jail for possession of heroin. The band members found themselves again in trouble after a riot at a French gig led to a brief stay in jail.

The Stranglers continued on to diminishing returns, although they did manage to release several singles and videos that charted in the United States, including "Skin Deep." But the band's drug addictions and paranoia kept them from releasing material on a consistent basis. After fighting with his bandmates for almost 15 years, Cornwell left in 1990, but the Stranglers continued to record and tour with Burnel, drummer Brian Duffy ("Jet Black"), keyboardist Dave Greenfield (notorious for having a mustache, an egregious punk rock fashion faux pas), and new singer Paul Roberts.

Discography:

Rattus Norvegicus (A&M, 1977); *No More Heroes* (A&M, 1977, 1991; Fame, 1987); *Black and White* (A&M, 1978); *Live X-Cert* (UA, 1978); *The Raven* (UA, 1979; EMI, 1985); *Don't Bring Harry* EP (UA, 1979); *IV* (IRS, 1980); *The Gospel According to the Meninblack* (Stiff, 1981; Fame, 1988); *La Folie* (Liberty, 1981; Fame, 1983); *The Collection 1977–1982* (Liberty, 1982; Fame, 1989); *Feline* (Epic, 1983); *Aural Sculpture* (Epic, 1984); *Off the Beaten Track* (Liberty, 1986); *Dreamtime* (Epic, 1986); *All Live and All of the Night* EP (Epic, 1987); *IV Rattus Norvegicus* (A&M, 1988; Fame, 1982); *All Live and All of the Night* (Epic, 1988); *Rarities* (Liberty, 1988); *The Evening Show Sessions* (Nighttracks/Strange Fruit, 1989); *Singles (The UA Years)* (Liberty, 1989); *10* (Epic, 1990); *Greatest Hits 1977–1990* (Epic, 1990). **Hugh Cornwell and Robert Williams:** *Nosferatu* (Liberty, 1979). **J.J. Burnel:** *Euroman Cometh* (UA, 1979; Mau Mau, 1987); *Un Jour Parfait* (CBS, 1989). **Dave Greenfield and J.J. Burnel:** *Fire and Water (Ecoutez Vos Murs)* (Epic, 1983). **Hugh Cornwell:** *Wolf* (Virgin, 1988); *Another Kind of Love* EP (Virgin, 1988); *Hi Fi* (Koch Progressive, 2001)

JOE STRUMMER

The lead singer of both the **Clash** and the Mescaleros, and one of the founders of British punk, so-called "punk warlord" Joe Strummer was not the poor busker he initially claimed to be, but in fact a well-raised diplomat's child who did his best later in life to look past his privileged upbringing to highlight injustices and oppression through song. Born John Graham Mellor in 1952, Strummer's musical career started in the mid-1970s with London pub-rockers the **101'ers**, a band he mostly shunned after he heard the abrasive but thrilling new sound of punk. Although Strummer (who had been calling himself "Woody") dropped for a time his Woody Guthrie-esque love of folk, world, and roots music when he joined the Clash, he did his best to expand the musical palette of the Clash to eventually embrace **reggae**, **ska**, and other world music genres, particularly in the band's middle and later years.

Always politically minded, Strummer turned his social outrage into musical inspiration after Margaret Thatcher became England's prime minister and **Ronald Reagan** was elected president of the United States. Both elections served to galvanize his political view and inform his songwriting on Clash albums—especially *London Calling*.

After spending many years as the leader of "the only band that mattered," when the Clash finally dissolved, largely due to Strummer's mistrust of long time musical comrade Mick Jones and his foolish re-embracement of ex-manager Bernie Rhodes in 1986, Strummer spent some time

The Stranglers in London, 1976: (L to R) Hugh Cornwell, Dave Greenfield, J.J. Burnell.

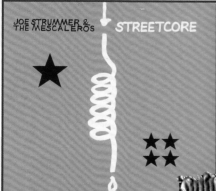

JOE STRUMMER & THE MESCALEROS STREETCORE

in the creative wilderness, looking for a new outlet. His sporadic solo career—sometimes with a backing band called the Latino Rockabilly War—led to a solo album, 1989's *Earthquake Weather*, that was received in lukewarm fashion and possibly had been created only to fulfill contractual obligations. Strummer also did some soundtrack work during this period for director Alex Cox, contributing music to *Sid and Nancy* (1986), the surrealist epic *Walker* (1987), and the spaghetti western goof *Straight to Hell* (1987). He also acted in a number of Cox's films during this period, but more notably in Jim Jarmusch's *Mystery Train* (1989).

After an almost decade-long hiatus from music, Strummer formed a new band, the Mescaleros, and released several albums that were amalgamations of world music, funk, punk, and reggae. During the 1990s he also deejayed on the BBC radio program *London Calling*.

Strummer died of a heart attack in December 2002 at the age of 50, leaving behind a musical and political reputation as influential as anyone in punk rock. His life and art have inspired several posthumous works, including the compilation *Let Fury Have the Hour: The Punk Rock Politics of Joe Strummer*, edited by Antonino D'Ambrosio. Julien Temple's 2007 documentary on Strummer, *The Future is Unwritten*, is an excellent starting point for the uninitiated. Today, Strummer's inspirational legacy is that of a man who tried to stretch punk to its fullest potential and actually live a life worth living.

Discography:
Walker (Virgin Movie Music, 1987); *Earthquake Weather* (Epic, 1989); *Gangsterville* EP (Epic, 1989); *Island Hopping* EP (Epic, 1989). **Joe Strummer and the Mescaleros:** *Rock Art and the X-Ray Style* (Mercury, 1999); *Global a Go-Go* (Hellcat, 2001); *Streetcore* (Hellcat, 2003).

Joe Strummer with the Clash in Holland, 1978.

SUBHUMANS (CANADA)

1978-1982, occasionally thereafter

LINEUP: Brian "Wimpy-Roy" Goble (vocals); Mike Graham (guitar); Gerry Hannah, aka "Gerry Useless" (bass, replaced by Ron Allan); Ken "Dimwit" Montgomery (drums, replaced by Randy Bowman)

While many punk bands preached revolution and activism, the Vancouver-based Subhumans (a different entity entirely from the British band of the same name) took it to another level. Originally an offshoot of the Skulls (which also included future members of **D.O.A.**), the Subhumans played their first show at an anarchist-sponsored "Anti-Canada Day" celebration on July 1, 1978. They released their first single in 1978, "Death to the Sickoids" (a rant against the mainstream press), and followed up with their self-titled debut album the following year. The band was determined to get their fiercely political and powerfully performed message out to a wider audience on tours in which they played with everyone from **Black Flag** to **Bad Brains**. After the usual number of personnel changes, the Subhumans broke up in late 1982 after singer Brian Goble (aka "Wimpy-Roy") joined up with D.O.A.

In 1983, the Subhumans' original bassist, Gerry Hannah (aka "Gerry Useless," sometimes also called "Nature Punk"), made the news after having hooked up with the militant group Direct Action, who engaged in bombings and acts of civil disobedience. Hannah was charged in the bombing of a Litton Industries factory near Toronto that made parts for U.S. cruise missiles and served five years in jail for conspiracy, which led to the group's demise. Hannah was later the subject of the documentary *Useless* in 2004. The Subhumans re-formed briefly in 1995 and then again in 2005 to tour and record new material.

Discography:
The Subhumans EP (Quintessence, 1979); *Incorrect Thoughts* (Friends, 1980); *No Wishes, No Prayers* (SST/Enigma, 1983); *Pissed Off...With Good Reason!* (Essential Noise/Virgin, 1996); *New Dark Age Parade* (Alternative Tentacles, 2006)

The Subhumans' Brian Goble in Seattle, 1981.

SUBHUMANS (ENGLAND)

1980-1985

LINEUP: Dick Lucas (vocals); Bruce (guitar); Phil (bass); Trotsky (drums)

The *other* Subhumans were English, though they shared many of the principles of the similarly named band from Vancouver, Canada. Anarcho-punks from Wiltshire, the Subhumans came together after singer Dick Lucas and guitarist Bruce met at a 1980 **Angelic Upstarts** show, and mined the same vein of anti-Thatcher rage as **Crass** and **Rudimentary Peni**. Originally discovered by **Flux of Pink Indians**, the Subhumans released several early singles before forming their own label, Bluurg, which put out most of their subsequent albums. Lucas went on to form the **ska**-punk band Citizen Fish. The Subhumans reunited for several tours in later years. Still one of the better of the anarchist bands, their music, particularly on the first two records, sounds as vital and engaging today as it did 25 years ago.

Discography:
The Day the Country Died (Bluurg, 1982); *From the Cradle to the Grave* (Bluurg, 1983); *Worlds Apart* (Bluurg, 1985); *Alive in a Dive* (Fat Wreck Chords, 2004); *Unfinished Business* (Bluurg, 2004); *All Gone Live* (Cleopatra, 2004)

FROM ENGLAND   WRCT PRESENTS:

SUBHUMANS

MAY 9TH

FROM D.C.

SCREAM

HALF LIFE

THE BANANA
3887 Bigelow Blvd

ALL AGES

SUBWAY SECT

1976-1980, 2002

LINEUP: Vic Godard (vocals); Paul Packham (guitar, replaced by Rob Marche); Paul Myers (bass, replaced by Chris Bostock); Barry "Baker" Auguste (drums, replaced by Sean McLusky)

Also known as Vic Godard and the Subway Sect, this band was part of punk's first wave in England. Originally just some soul boys from South London who liked to hang out at **Sex Pistols** shows, they were led by the artistic Vic Godard, pushed into existence by **Malcolm McLaren**, and influenced less by punk than by traditional pop, French music, swing bands, Frank Sinatra, and **rockabilly**. Subway Sect was more musically ambiguous than most of their peers at the time, and although they were part of the 1976 punk festival at the **100 Club**, and toured with the **Clash** on the 1977 White Riot tour, it was clear that they would not be constrained by punk's limitations. Thanks to their manager Bernie Rhodes and Godard's changing whims, Subway Sect

Subway Sect harmonizes in London, 1977.

Suicidal Tendencies, 1990.

broke up in the late-1970s but re-formed in 1980 with a new lineup that added a keyboardist, Dave Collard. Godard went solo in 1982 and continued to put out music, also founding the Motion Records label, when not working his day job as a postman in London. A new Subway Sect returned briefly in 2002.

Discography:
What's the Matter Boy? (Oddball/ MCA, 1980, 1982; Demon, 1996; Universal, 2000; PolyGram, 2001); *Songs for Sale* (London, 1982); *A Retrospective (1977–81)* (Rough Trade, 1985); *Holiday Hymn* (MCA, 1985); *Twenty Odd Years: The Best of Vic Godard and the Subway Sect* (Motion Pace, 1999); *Sansend* (Motion Pace, 2002); *Singles Anthology* (Motion Pace, 2005). **Vic Godard:** *T.R.O.U.B.L.E.* (Upside, 1986); *The End of the Surrey People* (Postcard, 1993); *We Oppose All Rock and Roll* (Overground, 1996); *In T.R.O.U.B.L.E. Again* (Tugboat, 1998); *The Long Term Side Effects* (Tugboat, 1998)

SUICIDAL TENDENCIES

1982-1995, 1998-present

ORIGINAL LINEUP: Mike Muir (vocals); Grant Estes (guitar); Mike Clark (guitar); Louiche Mayorga (bass); Amery Smith (drums)

Suicidal Tendencies started out in the early-1980s as a Los Angeles **hardcore** band with a sense of humor that helped win them legions of fans with their classic, self-titled 1983 debut album. One of the better-selling hardcore albums of all time, *Suicidal Tendencies* included the eternal classic "Institutionalized" (widely known thanks to **MTV** and the *Repo Man* soundtrack) as well as the hyperfast "I Shot the Devil" and "I Won't Fall in Love Today." Suicidal Tendencies stood out from much of the rest of the hardcore scene at the time due to their purported gang affiliations—rumors which, whether true or not, were fueled by the band's *cholo* fashion style, frequent flashing of "V13" hand signals, and graffiti for a Venice Beach gang with whom

the band was supposedly connected.

By the time their second album, *Join the Army*, came out in 1987, Suicidal Tendencies had begun their long, slow, painful descent into heavy metal and funk-rock. By the time *Lights…Camera…Revolution!* came out in 1990, the band had gone almost entirely mainstream metal. Suicidal Tendencies even made an ill-advised song-for-song remake of their first record, *Still Cyco After All These Years*, because singer Mike Muir was apparently upset at no longer owning the rights to the original. They broke up a few times over the years and went through a lengthy cycle of personnel changes but always got back together for more lucrative tours. Muir also found some success with the funk band Infectious Grooves and had a solo career as the slightly more punk Cyco Miko.

Select Discography:
Suicidal Tendencies (Frontier, 1983); *Join the Army* (Caroline, 1987); *How Will I Laugh Tomorrow When I Can't Even Smile Today* (Epic, 1988); *Feel Like Shit Déjà Vu /Controlled by Hatred* (Epic, 1989); *Lights…Camera… Revolution!* (Epic, 1990); *FNG* (Virgin, 1991); *The Art of Rebellion* (Epic, 1992); *Still Cyco After All These Years* (Epic, 1993); *Suicidal for Life* (Epic, 1994); *Prime Cuts: The Best of Suicidal Tendencies* (Epic, 1997)

PUNK AND MASS MEDIA

As in the relationship of mass media to most subcultures, the media usually gets it completely wrong at first, then starts highlighting negative elements, and goes on to exploit it for camp value or to sell products. Welcome to capitalism! The first time most people were made aware of punk was the day after the Sex Pistols' now legendary appearance on Britain's *Today* TV show in 1976. The guests' seemingly bizarre appearance, coupled with their obscene language, caused a sensation, with the next day's tabloids screaming outrage about the "foul-mouthed yobs" and dubbing the whole scene "the filth and the fury."

As with most media frenzies, it was over quickly—not before the Pistols and other punk bands were banned by panicky town councils who had either read the tabloids or seen the scandalous reports on the nightly news. It was also likely to do with the gobbing, pogo-ing, and other uncouth rituals in which the punks partook. However, by the time Malcolm McLaren engineered a worthy publicity stunt the following year on a boat in the Thames River that coincided with the Queen's jubilee and resulted in a few arrests, the circus had moved on; coverage was minimal, and the media needed a new source of sustenance.

The American media's reaction to punk was first attributed mostly to the Sex Pistols and their disastrous January 1978 tour of the United States. The domestic version of punk was actually somewhat tamer, didn't garner much media frenzy, and therefore didn't warrant the coverage the Sex Pistols took for granted. This changed somewhat in the early-1980s, when the rise of the Los Angeles scene (which sprouted clubs where freaky drug addicts listened to sheer noise and bashed into each other like ping-pong balls) brought about a spate of paranoid news coverage, laced with "where are your children tonight?" messages. Fuel was added to the fire by the L.A. police department using ham-fisted, riot-control tactics on young punks at shows. Although the fright passed quickly to the next perceived outrage of youth culture, the damage had been done and punk was saddled with the nihilistic reputation that would stop it from getting any substantial radio play. Prior to these incidents, punk might have been considered an amusing oddity, but eventually many saw it as a legitimate threat to the nation's youth. Probably not coincidentally, it was during this time of full-fledged Reagan-era conformity that punks began to appear in film and TV shows as villains.

This stereotyping was used to hilarious effect in "Next Stop, Nowhere," a 1982 episode of the medical whodunit series *Quincy,* in which the doctor investigates a murder at a "punk" club where kids high on quaaludes with Day-Glo hair slam-danced to the nihilistic

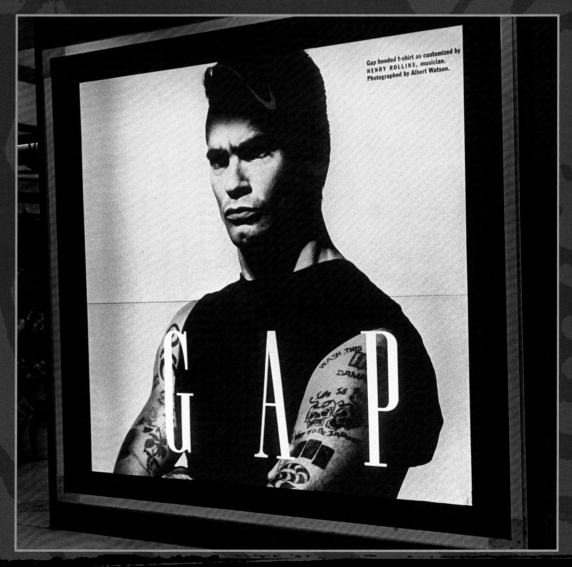

Gap hooded t-shirt as customized by HENRY ROLLINS, musician. Photographed by Albert Watson.

lyrics of the house band, Mayhem. 1982 also saw the exploitation flick *Class of 1984*, about a high school held hostage by a violent gang of mohawked misanthropes. While wildly off the mark (most punks can attest they spent high school in the 1980s getting beat up by jocks), the film at least had the sense to put a couple of Fear songs on the soundtrack. By the time of *Star Trek IV* in 1986—wherein Spock uses the Vulcan neck pinch on a punk who flips off Captain Kirk—just giving a cast member a mohawk, some piercings, a leather jacket, and an angry glare had become Hollywood shorthand for "violent delinquent."

Throughout the 1980s, there was next to no realistic examination of punk by the mainstream media. For many punks, who had built an alternate media of zines and small labels, this was perfectly fine. But time changes everything, of course, and most counter-cultural artifacts once considered frightening are eventually absorbed back into the mass culture. After grunge and indie-rock broke into the mainstream in the early-1990s (and many

former metalhead bands boasted about their punk influences), punk began to be seen as more relevant by an increasingly interested marketing culture. At the same time, many fans of the genre had gone into advertising and it was almost inevitable that eventually they would start using the music of their youth in major campaigns.

In the early- and mid-1990s, a number of iconic punk songs, from the Stooges' "Search and Destroy" to the Clash's "London Calling" and the Ramones' "Blitzkrieg Bop," were sold for commercial usage (the latter now almost as ubiquitous at baseball stadiums as peanuts and Cracker Jacks). The Buzzcocks and Black Flag have allowed their songs to be used in commercials, and in 1991 Subaru famously tried to sell a car as being "like punk rock."

This absorption of punk into mass culture has made for some strange frisson—bands like Devo licensed and created music for a consumer culture it had once artfully satirized, and Iggy Pop's ode to heroin injection ("Lust for Life") was used to promote cruise line vacations. Punk's growing visibility in

mainstream culture was abetted by phenomena such as the Vans Warped tour, which started in 1995 and quickly became a lucrative merchandising venue as well as a way for old-timer punk bands to make a living. The following year, the Sex Pistols got back together for their first of several reunion tours, starting a trend among other early punk groups who decided to give it one more go in a seemingly friendlier media environment. (Not to mention the chance to occasionally play at larger, nicer venues where the bathrooms weren't like hazardous waste dump sites.)

Many punks were furious about this change of attitude in which advertising and media entities dug deeper and deeper into underground culture for some "authentic" bit of rebellion, whether fashion or music, that could be used to market a product. To some punks, though, this didn't present a problem, just an opportunity to make a buck and gain exposure.

The use of punk music in mass advertising campaigns led to some controversies, such as when a 2005

Nike-sponsored skateboard tour used an ad campaign explicitly modeled on the first Minor Threat EP's iconic cover. Although Nike claimed they were simply fans and thought people at skate shows would be as well, Ian MacKaye—famously opposed to any kind of marketing, merchandising, or any association with corporate entertainment, as Nike should clearly have known—summed up his position rather succinctly to MTV: "What the hell were they thinking?" (The whole controversy and its attendant issues of mass media co-option of the underground are well covered in *Punk Planet* editor Anne Elizabeth Moore's 2007 book *Unmarketable: Brandalism, Copyfighting, Mocketing, and the Erosion of Integrity*.)

The issue of DIY purity, whether it's possible or even desirable, continues to plague punk today, and will not be resolved anytime soon. Although there's no definitive way to tell whether punk's greater exposure these days will result in more fans or just the music being used as another way to sell soap, the latter seems more likely. Given that history has shown mass media's tendency toward the easy stereotype, it's safe to assume that the usage of "London Calling" in a car commercial will ultimately *not* lead toward any greater understanding of punk by the society at large. But if even one more young life is saved from mediocrity by his or her first exposure to the Clash, it just might be that some good will come of the use of punk in advertising.

Suicide, 1980: Martin Rev (left), Alan Vega.

SUICIDE

1971–1981, occasionally thereafter

LINEUP: Alan Vega (vocals); Martin Rev (synthesizer)

Early New York band and performance-art duo Suicide had an aggressive, abrasive sound that influenced not only the nascent punk movement (barely a glimmer in the **Ramones'** eyes back in 1971) but also the industrial and goth scenes. Suicide may even be among the earliest bands to use the word *punk*—in the title of a performance-art piece in 1971, "Punk Rock Mass." Founded by artist Alan Vega and free-jazz guitarist Martin Rev, the band took inspiration from both **Iggy Pop**'s assaultive stage persona and the experimental music of the late-1960s psychedelic electronica group Silver Apples. Starting as a four-piece, Suicide pared themselves down to a mean and minimalist duo, fronted by Vega who shouted at and menaced the audience, often with a weapon such as a bike chain.

Suicide often played at the Mercer Arts Center in New York with like-minded bands such as the **New York Dolls** before the (literal) collapse of that venue. The proto-**no wave**rs did not really gel with the other bands in the New York scene at **CBGB** or **Max's Kansas City**, but still managed to get themselves signed by Marty Thau to his fledgling Red Star label. Their first album, *Suicide*, was released in 1977 and still feels years ahead of its time, at once minimalist and at other times as daunting as anything produced by a full band. Suicide was clearly influential on numerous young bands of the time, including even the Cars, who actually brought Suicide on tour. (Cars' singer Ric Ocasek produced Suicide's second record.) None of Suicide's albums were ever popular, but they left their mark on countless bands from Soft Cell to Depeche Mode. Suicide went on frequent hiatuses and released records sporadically during the 1980s and '90s, continuing to tour all the while.

Discography:
Suicide (Red Star, 1977); *Alan Vega and Martin Rev: Suicide* (Restless, 1980); *Half Alive* (ROIR, 1981); *Ghost Riders* (ROIR, 1986); *A Way of Life* (Wax Trax!, 1989); *Why Be Blue* (Brake Out/Enemy, 1992); *American Supreme* (Mute, 2002); *Attempted: Live at Max's Kansas City* (Sympathy for the Record Industry, 2004)

THE SUICIDE COMMANDOS

1974–1978

LINEUP: Chris Osgood (vocals/guitar); Steve Almaas (bass); Dave Ahl (drums)

In the cold, dark, pre-punk era of the early-1970s, a Minneapolis trio started making some furious, distorted music that somehow never really made much of an impact past the borders of the Twin Cities. But the Suicide Commandos proved to be one of the most forward-thinking of the early American and Midwest punk bands. Sadly, they only released one full-length album, 1977's *Make a Record*, a fast-paced and lean piece of work, with ear-blasting guitars and shouted vocals on classics like "Mosquito Crucifixion" and "Attacking the Beat" that would have made the band quite well-known had they been playing in London or New York instead of the doldrums of the Midwest. The band did their best to tour before the circuit had established itself, opening for the **Ramones** and Cheap Trick. The Suicide Commandos also helped to lay the foundation for future Twin Cities punk bands like the **Replacements** and **Hüsker Dü**. A live album, *The Commandos Commit Suicide Dance Concert*, hit the stores in 1979, but by then the band had already broken up. The last Suicide Commandos show was in late November 1978, with nearly a thousand frenzied fans filling the (sadly long-since defunct) punk-friendly Minneapolis bar the Longhorn, one fan apparently shouting, "The Commandos are the Beatles breaking up in '62!" Bassist Steve Almaas went on to form the country-influenced Beat Rodeo where he let his soulful, melancholic vision blossom.

Discography:
Make a Record (Blank, 1977); *The Commandos Commit Suicide Dance Concert* (Twin/Tone, 1979)

SUICIDE GIRLS

Not a band or movement so much as a marketing ploy, the Suicide Girls are essentially a group of heavily tattooed punk and goth girls who strip for a variety of print and web-based promotions, as well as the occasional live performance. As many

An assortment of Suicide Girls strike a pose, 2004.

things in the new millennium do, the Suicide Girls started out as just a website. In 2001, Portland punks Sean "Suicide" and his friend "Missy" decided (supposedly) as a lark to start up a website that would show naked women (one of the primary motivators for the Internet, after all), but they would be dedicated to the notoriously picky (but presumably still porn-hungry) young punk demographic. In practice, this meant that the viewers would be more likely to see Bettie Page haircuts, curled lips, tattoos, and black nail polish on the naked ladies than blonde hair extensions and Stepford Wife smiles. Little more than a cheap ploy, relentless press coverage (sadly, from some of the same publications that had drooled over the very *idea* of **Riot Grrrl**) ensured more popularity and soon the Suicide Girls were hitting the road on live burlesque tours, stripping to the sounds of Ministry, **Joy Division**, and **Killing Joke**; turning punk into a traveling porn road show. Somewhere, hopefully, the **Slits** and the **Raincoats** are plotting their revenge.

SUPERCHUNK

1989–present

LINEUP: Mac McCaughan (vocals/guitar); Jack McCook (guitar, replaced by Jim Wilbur); Laura Ballance (bass); Chuck "Chunk" Garrison (drums, replaced by Jon Wurster)

One of the most successful American indie/**pop-punk** bands of the 1990s, the powerfully engaging Superchunk hails from the fertile musical ground of Chapel Hill, North Carolina. They started out as simply Chunk (after the drummer's nickname) but changed it in time for their first album. *Superchunk*, released on influential indie label Matador in 1990, ably demonstrated the band's raucous poppy punk as orchestrated by lead singer and guitarist Mac McCaughan. The *Foolish* album (1994) was their slowest and most reflective, devoted thematically to the romantic breakup of bassist Laura Ballance and McCaughan. Subsequent records saw the band refining their sound and expanding their musical breadth, but never straying far from the Superchunk style. In their prime, Superchunk produced some of the most

imaginative and wistful music of the 1990s. Most of the band's albums have been released on Merge Records, a label that McCaughan and Ballance started in 1989, which features a sterling lineup of bands ranging from the Arcade Fire and the **Buzzcocks** to Dinosaur Jr. and the Magnetic Fields. Superchunk only plays limited tours today, with McCaughan performing in Portastatic, a side project he started back in 1992.

Discography:

Superchunk (Matador, 1990; Merge, 1999); *The Freed Seed* EP" (Merge, 1991); *No Pocky for Kitty* (Matador, 1991; Merge, 1999); *Tossing Seeds (Singles 89–91)* (Merge, 1992); *Hit Self-Destruct* EP (Hippy Knight, 1992); *On the Mouth* (Matador, 1993; Merge, 1999); *Foolish* (Merge, 1994); *Driveway to Driveway* EP (Merge, 1994); *On Paper It Made Perfect Sense* EP (Fellaheen, 1994); *Incidental Music 1991–95* (Merge, 1995); *Here's Where the Strings Come In* (Merge, 1995); *The Laughter Guns* EP (Merge, 1996); *Indoor Living* (Merge, 1997); *Hello Hawk* EP (Merge, 1999); *Come Pick Me Up* (Merge, 1999); *1,000 Lbs.* EP (Merge, 2000); *Late-Century Dream* EP (Merge, 2001); *Here's to Shutting Up* (Merge, 2001). **Portastatic:** *I Hope Your Heart Is Not Brittle* (Merge, 1994); *Scrapbook* EP (Merge, 1995); *Slow Note from a Sinking Ship* (Merge, 1995); *The Nature of Sap* (Merge, 1997); *De Mel, del Melão* (Merge, 2000); *Looking for Leonard* (Merge, 2001); *The Perfect Little Door* EP (Merge, 2001); *The Summer of the Shark* (Merge, 2003); *Bright Ideas* (Merge, 2005)

SYMARIP

1969–1983

LINEUP: Johnny Orlando (vocals); Roy Ellis (vocals); Josh Roberts (guitar); Michael Thomas (bass); Frank Pitter (drums); Montgomery "Monty" Naismith (keyboards/organ); Roy "Bug" Knight (saxophone); Johney Johnson (trumpet); Carl Griffith (tenor/alto saxophone)

The British-West Indian **ska-reggae** band Symarip (also known as the Pyramids) made history when they released the infectious and oft-covered *Skinhead Moonstomp* single and album loosely based on Derrick Morgan's classic "Moon Hop" in 1969. Symarip is generally known as the first **skinhead** band and skinheads were increasingly attracted to their shows back when they were primarily fans of rock steady and ska music. Skinhead icons from the early years, before the corrupting influence of the **National Front** and other vile scum, Symarip demonstrated the more positive side of the skinhead movement, which emphasized camaraderie and dancing to fantastic music as opposed to boot-boy violence spurred by crappy pub-rock bands.

Discography:

The Pyramids (President, 1969); *Skinhead Moonstomp: The Album* (Trojan, 1969, 2003); *Skinhead Moonstomp: The Best of Symarip* (Trojan, 2004)

SUPERCHUNK

TALKING HEADS

1975–1991

Lineup: David Byrne (vocals/guitar);
Tina Weymouth (bass); Chris Frantz
(drums); Jerry Harrison (keyboards)

The Talking Heads were a central part of the early **CBGB** scene—back when the definition of punk was much broader and more inclusive than it would later become. Along with **Blondie**, Talking Heads would go on to become one of the most commercially successful bands from the early punk scene.

Led by the prolific songwriter and multi-talented musician David Byrne, the band was formed in 1974 by Rhode Island School of Design students Byrne (whose quavery, distinctive vocal style nearly defined nerd art-punk-funk), Tina Weymouth (bass), and Chris Frantz (drums). They started gaining notice after moving to New York and playing gigs at CBGB in 1975, soon augmenting their sound with the addition of Jerry Harrison (formerly of Jonathan Richman's **Modern Lovers**) on keyboards. Following early successes such as "Psycho Killer" (the still-popular deadpan single from their first album, *Talking Heads '77*—one of several produced by Brian Eno), the band began to further augment their sound with backup singers and additional percussionists, becoming arguably the most funk-oriented CBGB alumni. By the end of the 1970s, the

Talking Heads had moved on and became considered more of a **new wave** band.

Although the Talking Heads never had the aggression or raw power of the many punk bands who played with them at CBGB (famously, they opened for the **Ramones** in 1975), their brand of polyrhythmic music and arcane lyrics set the standard for American art-punk, preceding the more adventurous stylings that would arrive with the 1980s' American **post-punk** movement. The Talking Heads made early use of **MTV** to promote their music in a series of distinctive and striking videos for songs such as "Burning Down the House" and "Nothing But Flowers." Jonathan Demme's 1984 live concert film *Stop Making Sense* (filmed during the band's last tour, when they were at the height of their commercial success), featured lead singer Byrne in a much celebrated (and mocked) oversized suit, helping to cement his reputation as an eccentric genius with a flair for the theatrical.

After several hit records (including 1988's *Naked*, which they recorded in Paris with African musicians), the Talking Heads broke up in 1990. Byrne went on to a wide-ranging solo career, which found him further exploring his interest in non-Western music genres. Frantz and Weymouth, who are married, record with their side project, the dance-rock band Tom Tom Club. The Talking Heads were inducted into the Rock and Roll Hall of Fame in 2002, reunited for the induction ceremony, and parted ways again.

Discography:

Talking Heads: 77 (Sire, 1977); *More Songs about Buildings and Food* (Sire, 1978); *Fear of Music* (Sire, 1979); *Remain in Light* (Sire, 1980); *The Name of This Band Is Talking Heads* (Sire, 1982); *Speaking in Tongues* (Sire, 1983); *Stop Making Sense* (Sire, 1984); *Little Creatures* (Sire, 1985); *True Stories* (Sire, 1986); *Naked* (Fly/Sire, 1988)

The Talking Heads in New York,
1978: (L to R) Jerry Harrison,
Chris Frantz, David Byrne,
Tina Weymouth.

punk into their extraordinarily loud and potent musical assault—think maybe a snottier **Radio Birdman** mixed with the aggression of Guitar Wolf—Teengenerate was, for a time in the 1990s, one of the most popular Japanese punk bands to play around the world. They broke up in the mid-1990s but crosspollinated with bands Tweezers and Raydios and also reunited for several shows in mid-2005.

Discography:
Audio Recording (Cruddy Record Dealership, 1993; Pop Llama, 1995); *Get Action!* (Crypt, 1994); *Smash Hits!* (Estrus, 1995); *Savage!!!* (Sympathy for the Record Industry, 1996); *Live at Shelter* (Target Earth, 2001))

TEEN IDLES

1979-1980

LINEUP: Nathan Strejcek (vocals); Geordie Grindle (guitar); Ian MacKaye (bass); Jeff Nelson (drums)

One of the earliest **hardcore** bands in Washington, D.C., the Teen Idles were also one of the first to tour outside the District, and served as the impetus for the founding of **Dischord Records**. Formed in the late-1970s out of a band called the Slinkees (made up of a number of friends from Woodrow Wilson High School), the Idles featured future **Minor Threat** members Ian MacKaye on bass and Jeff Nelson on drums, and Nathan Strejcek (who would later form the D.C.-based **Youth Brigade**) on vocals. Rounding out the lineup was youthful roadie Henry Garfield (who later went on to fame and glory as one **Henry Rollins**). The Idles were equally impressed by and terrified of fellow D.C. punks **Bad Brains**, whose unimaginable energy and power served as inspiration to the fledgling Idles. A West Coast tour in 1980 was also inspiring to the band, giving them the idea of marking their hands with large X's (which later became the ultimate signifier of the **straight-edge** movement). After breaking up later that year, the Idles put $600 of savings toward the release of their sole EP, *Minor Disturbance*, which became Dischord release No. 1—essentially kick-starting the D.C. **hardcore** scene.

Discography:
Minor Disturbance EP (Dischord, 1980); *Anniversary* (Dischord, 1996)

Personal Best

TEAM DRESCH

1993-1996

LINEUP: Jody Bleyle (vocals/bass); Kaia Wilson (guitar/vocals); Donna Dresch (guitar/bass); Marci Martinez (drums, replaced by Melissa York)

A Portland, Oregon-based outfit named after guitarist and local inspiration Donna Dresch (who was also responsible for Chainsaw Records and had even briefly been a member of Dinosaur Jr.), Team Dresch were one of the most energetic bands in the **queercore** movement. Their first record, 1995's *Personal Best* (with a classic cover that satirized the notorious kitsch film) was a mere 24 minutes long but got the point across with such edgy, **Ramones**-style pop-punk songs as "Fagetarian and Dyke" and "Hate the Christian Right!" After *Personal Best*, drummer Marci Martinez was replaced by Melissa York. Team Dresch broke up not long after their second album, 1996's *Captain My Captain*. Following that, guitarist Kaia Wilson went on to form the queercore band the **Butchies**, one of the groups that drew younger members of the queer community to punk rock.

Dresch turned her attention to Chainsaw Records, releasing **Sleater-Kinney**'s first two albums.

Discography:
Personal Best (Chainsaw/Candy-Ass, 1995); *Captain My Captain* (Chainsaw/Candy-Ass, 1996). **Kaia:** *Kaia* (Chainsaw/Candy-Ass, 1996); *Ladyman* (Mr. Lady, 1997); *Oregon* (Mr. Lady, 2002). **Butchies:** *Are We Not Femme?* (Mr. Lady, 1998); *Population 1975* (Mr. Lady, 1999); *3* (Mr. Lady, 2001). **Infinite X's:** *The Infinite X's* (Chainsaw, 2001). **Adickdid:** *Dismantle* (G, 1993)

TEENGENERATE

1993-1995

LINEUP: Fink (vocals/guitar); Fifi (guitar/vocal); Sammy (bass); Shoe (drums, replaced by Suck)

Starting out as the American Soul Spiders, this group of Japanese noise-punks took the name Teengenerate from a **Dictators** song. Incorporating elements of garage and proto-

TELEVISION

1973–1978, occasionally thereafter

LINEUP: Tom Verlaine (vocals/guitar); Richard Lloyd (guitar); Richard Hell (bass); Billy Ficca (drums)

One of the first New York "punk" bands to coalesce in the mid-1970s, Television blazed a trail for many bands to follow—though they did so in a manner that was far from stereotypically punk. Television convinced **CBGB** owner **Hilly Kristal** to let new bands play there on nights when nothing else was going on; an action that by itself earns them a place in punk history.

Television began in the early-1970s as the Neon Boys, an early pre-punk group featuring singer and guitarist Tom Verlaine (Tom Miller), **Richard Hell** (Richard Meyers, an old boarding-school friend of Verlaine's) on bass, and Billy Ficca on drums. Not long after forming, the Neon Boys dissolved and re-formed in 1973 as Television, with Richard Lloyd on second guitar. Yet after Hell and Verlaine fell out over "creative control" issues,, Hell left Television (he was replaced by ex-**Blondie** bassist Fred Smith), and went on to join the **Heartbreakers** with **Johnny Thunders** in 1975 before forming Richard Hell and the **Voidoids**.

In August 1975, Television released their first single, "Little Johnny Jewel," which hinted at the dual guitar experimentation for which Television would eventually become recognized. On their first two albums in particular, they pioneered a unique twin-guitar attack that has been a major influence on New York bands, from the chiming-bells sound of **Sonic Youth**'s double guitars all the way to the Strokes, who borrow freely from the band's rhythmic experiments and singer Tom Verlaine's vocal style. The first album, 1977's *Marquee Moon*, was a critical smash hit, though ultimately underselling in the U.S. (it performed relatively well in the UK). The album's epic title track, and such other classics as "Venus De Milo" and "Friction," all demonstrated the vitality and fluidity of Lloyd and Verlaine's dueling guitars, something relatively unheard of in the early punk scene

After releasing *Adventure* in 1978, Television split due to conflicts between Verlaine and Lloyd. Both went on to solo careers of varying success, with Lloyd eventually becoming a session guitarist for artists such as Matthew Sweet and Rocket from the Tombs. Ficca played drums with various bands, most notably the Waitresses, who had a minor hit with "I Know What Boys Like." Television reunited in 1992 and recorded a self-titled third album to (again) critical acclaim, but poor sales. The band continued to regroup and tour sporadically, based mostly on the worshipful respect *Marquee Moon* still engenders in Television fans.

Discography:

Marquee Moon (Elektra, 1977); *Adventure* (Elektra, 1978); *The Blow-Up* (cassette; ROIR, 1982; CD; Danceteria, 1992); *Television* (Capitol, 1992). **Tom Verlaine:** *Tom Verlaine* (Elektra, 1979); *Dreamtime* (Warner Bros., 1981; Infinite Zero, 1994); *Words from the Front* (Warner Bros., 1982); *Cover* (Virgin/Warner Bros., 1984); *Flash Light* (IRS, 1987); *The Wonder* (Fontana, 1990); *Warm and Cool* (Rykodisc, 1992); *The Miller's Tale* (Virgin, 1996)

Television at CBGB, 1977.

TELEVISION PERSONALITIES

1977-1998, 2004-present

LINEUP: Dan Treacy (vocals); Ed Ball (keyboards)

A quirky and loosely-formed British punk band that veered off into left field after a number of early **Jam**- and punk-influenced singles, Television Personalities were started by keyboardist Ed Ball and singer-songwriter (and only consistent member) Dan Treacy (whose mother apparently ran a dry-cleaning shop across King's Road from Malcolm McLaren's shop **Sex**) in the late-1970s. Their first song, "14th Floor," was a jokey punk-rock parody that attracted the attention of British DJ **John Peel** and was quickly followed by their scathing critique of **poseurs** in the hit "Part-Time Punks" from the 1978 EP *Where's Bill Grundy Now?* During the 1980s, Television Personalities became more of a psychedelic group, heavily influencing the UK's explosion of trippy neo-hippie bands—but still working as outsiders, thanks largely to Treacy's drug-addled

visions and his knack for fashioning them into stunning pop gems. By the late-1990s Treacy had fallen into serious drug addiction and spent time in prison. After several years in creative hibernation, he was released from prison in 2004, then reunited with Ball and recorded *My Dark Places* in 2006, perhaps the best record by a recovering addict with mental problems since the last Roky Erickson record.

Discography:

Where's Bill Grundy Now? EP" (Kings Rd., 1978; Rough Trade, 1979; Overground, 1992); *...And Don't the Kids Just Love It* (Rough Trade, 1981; Fire, 1991; Razor and Tie, 1995); *Mummy Your Not Watching Me* (Whaam!, 1982; Dreamworld, 1987; Fire, 1991); *They Could Have Been Bigger than the Beatles* (Whaam!, 1982; Dreamworld, 1986; Fire, 1991); *The Painted Word* (Illuminated, 1985; Fire, 1991); *Chocolat Art* (Pastell, 1985, 1991); *Privilege* (Fire, 1990); *Camping in France* (Overground, 1991); *How I Learned to Love the Bomb* EP (Overground, 1992); *Closer to God* (Fire/Seed, 1992); *Not Like Everybody Else* EP" (Little Teddy, 1993); *You, Me and Lou Reed* EP (Fantastic Plastic, 1993); *The Prettiest Girl in the World* EP" (Overground, 1994); *Yes Darling, But Is It Art? (Early Singles and Rarities)* (Fire/Seed, 1995); *I Was a Mod before You Was a Mod* (Overground, 1995); *Top Gear* (Overground, 1996); *Paisley Shirts & Mini Skirts* (no label/unofficial CD, 1996); *Made in Japan* (Little Teddy, 1996); *Mod Is Dead* (Teenage Kicks, 1996); *Prime Time Television Personalities 1981–1992* (Nectar Masters, 1997); *Don't Cry Baby...It's Only a Movie* (Damaged Goods, 1998); *Part-Time Punks: The Very Best of Television Personalities* (Cherry Red, 1999); *Conscious* (Little Teddy, 2001)

> ## "I'm shocked, I suppose, by the fact that I'm even alive."
> —Genesis P-Orridge, RE/Search #4/5

Throbbing Gristle's Genesis P-Orridge at London's YMCA, 1980.

Dan Treacy of Television Personalities, 2006.

THROBBING GRISTLE

1975-1980, occasionally thereafter

LINEUP: Genesis P-Orridge (vocals/bass/noise); Cosey Fanni Tutti (guitar); Peter "Sleazy" Christopherson (tapes); Chris Carter (synthesizer)

The first industrial noise band to raise the ante on punk's abrasiveness, Throbbing Gristle essentially created industrial music as it led punk to become even more noisy and experimental. Fronted by the chameleon-

like Genesis P-Orridge (originally named Neil Megson, he took his new moniker from a school nickname and the food on which he survived while starting his career), the London-based band grew out of the COUM Transmissions Group, a confrontational performance art collective to which P-Orridge and Cosey belonged.

Early Throbbing Gristle shows were timed to a punch clock and featured art exhibits alongside the music and P-Orridge's provocative performances. Their plan was to shock audiences not through mindless slogans and punchy guitars, but by way of disquieting lyrics and musical soundscapes. Throbbing Gristle produced consistently alarming music such as "Hamburger Lady" (about a burn victim) and quietly subversive titles like *20 Jazz Funk Greats*, which disguised itself as a relatively pleasant-looking album, but was sure to thoroughly shock any listener who had bought it under false pretenses. To release their work when no other record company would sign them, Throbbing Gristle formed Industrial Records.

After releasing *Heathen Earth* in 1980, Throbbing Gristle decided to break up; many live albums, reissues, and compilations followed, most of dubious quality. Carter and Fanni Tutti began a new project as Chris and Cosey, while P-Orridge and Christopherson went on to form the even more shocking Psychic TV before Christopherson left to create the slightly more accessible Coil. P-Orridge remains the most active of the group, playing under a variety of new names, working in magic rituals to disrupt complacency, and apparently well on his way to creating an entirely new gender. P-Orridge was also one of the first punks to practice body modification through scarring, tattoos, and piercing, including several weighty piercings on his genitals.

A link between the art communes of the 1960s and punk rock, Throbbing Gristle may also have been more powerful and subversive than any of the punk groups of the 1970s who espoused anarchy without ever having truly experienced it. Sure to be regarded one day as important as the art world's Dadaist or surrealist movements were in their time, Throbbing Gristle pushed the boundaries of music and art so far that most bands are still playing catch-up 30 years later.

Discography:

The Second Annual Report of Throbbing Gristle (Mute, 1977); *DOA: The Third and Final Report of Throbbing Gristle* (Mute, 1978); *Throbbing Gristle* (Fetish, 1978); *20 Jazz Funk Greats* (Industrial, 1979); *First Annual Report* (Industrial, 1979); *At the Factory, Manchester (Live)* (Industrial, 1980); *At Sheffield University (Live)* (Industrial, 1980); *Heathen Earth* (Industrial, 1980); *Beyond Ja Funk* (Rough Trade, 1981); *Funeral in Berlin (Live)* (Zensor, 1981); *Mission of Dead Souls (Live)* (Mute, 1981); *Rafters/Psychic Rally* (World, 1981); *Live at Death Factory* (no label, 1982); *Thee Psychick Sacrifice* (Illuminated, 1982); *Editions . . . Frankfurt . . . Berlin . . . (Live)* (Illuminated, 1982); *Furher Dermenscheit* (American Phono, 1983); *Once upon a Time (Live at the Lyceum)* (Casual Abandon, 1983); *Nothing Short of a Total War* (cassette; Cause for Concern, 1984) *Live at Heaven* (Rough Trade, 1985); *Live Vol. 1* (Grey Area, 1996); *Live Vol. 4* (Grey Area, 1996); *Grief* (Thirsty Ear, 2001); *The First Annual Report of Throbbing Gristle* (Thirsty Ear, 2001); *TG Now* (Mute, 2004)

JOHNNY THUNDERS

The brilliant but hopelessly drug-addicted guitar player for the **New York Dolls** and his own band, the **Heartbreakers**, Johnny Thunders helped determine the musical and stylistic directions that punk took in the mid-1970s. Born John Gezale, Thunders joined the embryonic New York Dolls in the early-1970s and quickly helped them establish their reputation as stylishly glam proto-punk pretty boys ready to do anything in the service of rock 'n' roll (excess). When the Dolls splintered in 1975 after their disastrous Florida tour, Thunders, along with drummer Jerry Nolan, left to concentrate on their shared tastes for more aggressive music and heroin. They returned to New York, gathered up guitarist Walter Lure and bassist **Richard Hell** (recently booted from the art punks in **Television**), and formed the Heartbreakers. Marketed by manager **Leee Black Childers** as out-of-control lunatics (using the catch phrase "catch them while they're still alive"), the Heartbreakers did their best to live up to their reputation, playing around New York unsuccessfully for a time before briefly joining the **Sex Pistols**, the **Damned**, and the **Clash** on the ill-fated 1976 Anarchy tour. Although most of the gigs were canceled, Johnny Thunders was credited with one lasting effect of the tour: introducing British punks to heroin.

After the demise of the Heartbreakers, Thunders recorded sporadically as a guest artist and worked on his own music. His first solo album, 1978's *So Alone*, was a haunting, melancholic piece of work that contains the signature tune, "You Can't Put Your Arms Around a Memory." The album featured guest appearances from Thin Lizzy's Phil Lynnott, the Damned's Paul Grey, and Peter Perrett from the **Only Ones** (not to mention contributions from Steve Jones and Paul Cook, fresh from the ashes of the Sex Pistols). Thunders toured and recorded sporadically throughout the 1980s with different aggregations of musicians—most notable were collaborations with Wayne Kramer of the **MC5** on the *Gang War* sessions and Patti Palladin of Snatch on the *Copy Cats* album, developing an increasingly damaging addiction to hard drugs all the while.

An ill-fated attempt by Thunders in 1990 to form a punk supergroup in Paris with Stiv Bators (**Dead Boys** and Lords of the New Church) and **Dee Dee Ramone** ended in acrimony when Dee Dee accused Thunders of theft, throwing bleach over Thunders' clothing and smashing his guitar. Thunders returned to the United States, and moved to New Orleans, where he died under mysterious circumstances, apparently of a heroin overdose, in 1991.

Discography:

So Alone (Real Music, 1978; Sire/Warner Bros., 1992); *In Cold Blood* (New Rose, 1983); *Diary of a Lover* EP (Jem, 1983); *Too Much Junkie Business (New)* (cassette; ROIR, 1983; ROIR/Important, 1990); *Hurt Me* (New Rose, 1983); *Que Sera, Sera* (Jungle, 1985); *Stations of the Cross* (cassette; ROIR, 1987; ROIR/Important, 1990); *Bootlegging the Bootleggers* (Jungle, 1990). **Jimmy K:** *Trouble Traveller* (Meldac, 1986). **Johnny Thunders & Patti Palladin:** *Copy Cats* (Restless, 1988). **Johnny Thunders & Wayne Kramer:** *Gang War* (Zodiac/DeMilo, 1990). **Heartbreakers:** *L.A.M.F.* (Track, 1977; Jungle, 1984); *Live at Max's Kansas City* (Max's Kansas City, 1979); *D.T.K.: Live at the Speakeasy* (Jungle, 1982). **Johnny Thunders & the Heartbreakers:** *L.A.M.F. Revisited* (Jungle, 1984); *D.T.K. L.A.M.F.* (Jungle, 1984); *Live at the Lyceum Ballroom 1984* (ABC, 1984; Receiver, 1990)

Johnny Thunders shows off his sneer in London, 1973.

Token Entry in New York, 1988.

TOUCH AND GO

LOCATION: CHICAGO

Beginning as a zine run by **Meatmen** singer Tesco Vee, *Touch and Go* evolved into a record label with an impressive pedigree run by Corey Rusk (former bassist for the **Necros**). Originally based in Detroit, Touch and Go relocated to Chicago, later helping to put that city's punk scene on the map. Worthy bands that have appeared on Touch and Go include the **Butthole Surfers**, the **Jesus Lizard**, **Big Black**, and (more recently) **post-punk** veterans such as the **Ex** and the **Mekons**. In 1990, Touch and Go started up a subsidiary label, Quarterstick, whose artists include **Henry Rollins**, Rodan, and Pegboy. Although their position in the punk world is well established, Touch and Go should probably be most commended for reissuing the **Naked Raygun** catalog, which in itself should earn them a form of punk sainthood.

TOKEN ENTRY

1980-1990

LINEUP: Anthony Comunale (vocals); Mickey Neal (guitar); Arthur Smilios (bass); Ernie Parada (drums)

A key skate-punk band and fixture on the New York **hardcore** scene during the mid-1980s, Token Entry started out as the unfortunately named Gilligan's Revenge in 1980; the band (inspired by the city transit system) changed their name to Token Entry in 1984. Token Entry were originally a fairly interesting New York hardcore band, and later added touches of funk to their sound in a more **Fishbone**-like style. Some of their later recordings were produced by **Bad Brains** guitarist Gary "Dr. Know" Miller (who was able to notably increase the shredding quality of Token Entry's guitar sound. After Token Entry's breakup, bassist Arthur Smilios went on to play with **Gorilla Biscuits** and **Civ**, while drummer Ernie Parada went on to form **Black Train Jack**.

Discography:
Ready or Not Here We Come EP (Turnstyle Tunes, 1985); *From Beneath the Streets* (Positive Force, 1987); *Go Kart*, 1998); *Jaybird* (Hawker, 1988; Go Kart, 1998); *The Weight of the World* (Emergo, 1990)

TOO MUCH JOY

1981-1996

LINEUP: Tim Quirk (vocals); Jay Blumfeld (guitar); Sandy Smallens (bass, replaced by William Whitman); Tommy Vinton (drums)

The in-jokey punks of Too Much Joy hailed from Scarsdale, New York, having apparently formed in 1981 to play **Clash** covers at high school dances—only to find out that nobody in their suburban high school even knew who the Clash were. Too Much Joy toured with admirable energy over the years, releasing several respectable albums, such as *Cereal Killers* and *Son of Sam I Am*. Even so, the band never saw much success in the marketplace, though they did achieve notoriety in other ways. Not long after rap group 2 Live Crew was faced with obscenity charges for their lyrics, Too Much Joy performed a set of the hip-hop group's songs in Florida as a protest and ended up getting arrested (all except for drummer Tommy Vinton, who, perhaps not coincidentally, was once a New York policeman). Too Much Joy also became known for inadvertently inspiring the Republican revolution of the mid-1990s when a fan and staffer to then-congressman

Newt Gingrich adopted the band's refrain "to create, you must destroy" from "Theme Song" on *Cereal Killers*. While they have never officially broken up, Too Much Joy called it quits after the *...Finally* album, releasing only the occasional odds and ends since then. Although they were poppy as all hell, Too Much Joy brought a refreshing sense of humor to punk and along with the **Dead Milkmen**, proved that the music could be just as funny as it was aggressive. In 2007, Too Much Joy got together for a one-off reunion to celebrate drummer Tommy Vinton's retirement from the police force. Vinton also later played with **pop-punk** visionaries Dirt Bike Annie.

Discography:
Green Eggs and Crack (Stonegarden, 1987); *Son of Sam I Am* (Alias, 1988); *Cereal Killers* (Alias/Giant/Warner Bros., 1991); *Nothing on My Mind* EP (Giant/Warner Bros., 1991); *Mutiny* (Giant, 1992); *...Finally* (Discovery, 1996)

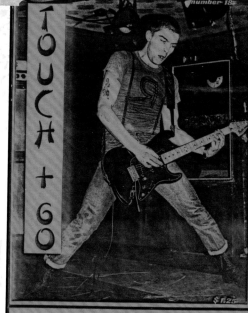

TRENCHMOUTH

1990-1996

LINEUP: Damon Locks (vocals/percussion); Chris DeZutter (guitar); Wayne Montana (bass); Fred Armisen (drums)

A severe gum infection that should be treated as soon as possible, Trenchmouth is also the name of the great and unclassifiable Chicago-based punk/**post-punk**/**hardcore**/**reggae**/funk hybrid band who helped make the 1990s scene a lot more interesting than it had any right to be. Debuting with the adventurous *Construction* album in 1991, Trenchmouth's quirky,

everything-but-the-kitchen-sink approach to music made them a thrilling band to listen to, but sadly almost unsellable in the U.S. market. Strangely enough, Trenchmouth's highly skilled drummer, Fred Armisen, later went on to great success as a cast member on *Saturday Night Live*.

Discography:
Construction of New Action: Volume 1: First There Was Movement (Skene!, 1991); *Inside the Future* (Skene!, 1993); *Trenchmouth Vs. the Light of the Sun* (Skene!/EastWest, 1994); *The Broadcasting System* (Skene!, 1996)

TRIBE 8

1991-2006

LINEUP: Lynn Breedlove (vocals); Leslie Mah (guitar); Lynn Payne (bass); Slade Bellum (drums, replaced by Jen Savage)

Through their raunchy stage shows, fiercely independent lesbian **queercore** band Tribe 8 worked furiously to smash dominant perceptions of gender. They released a number of early records on small labels before moving to the relatively larger **Alternative Tentacles** label. Lyrically, Tribe 8 eschewed political correctness by performing songs that openly proclaimed the joys of sexuality and demon-

strated the band's defiant refusal to be pinned down to any one political agenda (which often landed them in hot water). A Tribe 8 show was not so much a basic punk concert as it was an outrageous, provocative staged event with mock castrations or singer Lynn Breedlove strapping on a dildo to make her point graphically. Their important legacy as out punks was well recorded in Tracy Flannigan's *Rise Above: A Tribe 8 Documentary* (2003).

Discography:
Pig Bitch EP" (Harp, 1991); *By the Time We Get to Colorado* EP (Outpunk, 1995); *Fist City* (Alternative Tentacles, 1995); *Roadkill Cafe* EP (Alternative Tentacles, 1995); *Snarkism* (Alternative Tentacles, 1996); *Role Models for America* (Alternative Tentacles, 1998)

Tribe 8's Lynn Breedlove at the Michigan Woman's Music Festival.

T.S.O.L. at the
Whisky A Go Go, 1982.

T.S.O.L.

1978–2006

LINEUP: Jack Grisham (vocals); Ron Emory
(guitar); Mike Roche (bass); Todd Barnes
(drums)

Also known as True Sounds of Liberty,
T.S.O.L. was an early **hardcore** band from
California's Orange County, known for
their violent shows and an ever-changing
lineup (at one point a version of the band
was touring without any original members).
T.S.O.L. was started by vocalist Jack
Grisham and drummer Todd Barnes, who
had previously played together in Vicious
Circle, another band well known for rampant violence at its shows. (One story has
it that the guys simply changed their name
to T.S.O.L. because Vicious Circle had too
notorious a reputation to get gigs.) The
band started playing at affluent friends'
house parties, but their inherent love of
vandalism soon forced them out of the
houses and into the clubs. T.S.O.L. released
their self-titled debut EP in 1981 and followed it the same year with the hardcore
classic *Dance With Me*, an album that moved
the band into a less political and more
gothic/death rock direction (inspiring
fellow makeup-loving doom punks like
the **Misfits**). Although this shift confused
some in T.S.O.L.'s hardcore fan base, the
band continued in this direction for 1983's
Beneath the Shadows, which alienated even

THE NEW
T.S.O.L.
WITH
CRUCIF☆☆KS
AND
CONFLICT
SUNDAY JAN.15 STUMBLE INN
136 N. PARK AVE. 9.00 P.M.

Plane Crash
4 Killed

more fans. The band did, however, remain a central component of the Southern California scene, playing shows with **Bad Religion**, the **Dead Kennedys**, and **Social Distortion**—even making an appearance in **Penelope Spheeris'** punk tragedy, *Suburbia*.

After a Los Angeles show turned into a riot, Grisham quit T.S.O.L. to play similar music in Cathedral of Tears, and later toured and recorded in the 1990s as Joykiller and Tender Fury. Once Barnes dropped out as well, T.S.O.L. added guitarist and singer Joe Wood and drummer Mitch Dean to record several disturbing, metal-tinged T.S.O.L. records (at one point some of the members even hung around with Guns N' Roses). The original T.S.O.L. reunited at the end of the 1990s and continued to record and tour, although the band broke up for good (and probably for the best, considering the law of diminishing returns) in 2006.

Discography:

T.S.O.L. EP (Posh Boy, 1981); *Dance with Me* (Frontier, 1981; Epitaph, 1996); *Weathered Statues* EP" (Alternative Tentacles, 1982; Nitro 1997); *Beneath the Shadows* (Alternative Tentacles, 1982; Restless, 1989; Nitro, 1997); *Change Today?* (Enigma, 1984; Restless, 1997); *Revenge* (Enigma, 1986; Restless, 1997); *Hit and Run* (Enigma, 1987; Restless, 1997); *Thoughts of Yesterday 1981–1982* (Posh Boy, 1988; Rhino, 1992); *T.S.O.L. Live* (Restless, 1988); *Strange Love* (Enigma, 1990; Restless, 1997); *Live '91* (Triple X, 1991; Nitro, 1997); *Hell and Back Together 1984–1990* (Restless, 1992); *T.S.O.L./Weathered Statues* (Nitro, 1997); *Disappear* (Nitro, 2001); *Divided We Stand* (Nitro, 2003); *Who's Screwin' Who?: 18 T.S.O.L. Greatest Non-Hits* (Anarchy, 2005). **T.S.O.L./Slayer:** *Abolish Government* EP" (Sub Pop, 1996). **Cathedral of Tears:** *Cathedral of Tears* EP (Enigma, 1984). **Tender Fury:** *Tender Fury* (Posh Boy, 1988); *Garden of Evil* (Triple X, 1990); *If Anger Were Soul, I'd Be James Brown* (Triple X, 1991). **Jack Grisham/Mike Roche/Ron Emory/Todd Barnes:** *Live 1991* (Triple X, 1991). **Joykiller:** *The Joykiller* (Epitaph, 1995); *Static* (Epitaph, 1996); *Three* (Epitaph, 1997); *Ready Sexed Go!* (Epitaph, 2003)

2.13.61
LOCATION: LOS ANGELES

A publishing company run by renaissance punk **Henry Rollins** and named for his birthday, 2.13.61 specializes in books by cult authors and Rollins' own considerable body of work, releasing numerous volumes of Rollins' spoken word, poems, and musings that often resemble stand-up comedy. The company has gone beyond merely printing the boss' work—also releasing books and music by other artists Rollins admires, such as Nick Cave, Michael Gira (from the Swans), proto-beatnik Henry Miller, Exene Cervenka of **X**, Hubert Selby Jr., Glen E. Friedman

(who took many classic early punk and **skateboarding** photos), and spoken-word CDs by Rollins, Cervenka, and Selby Jr.

2 TONE
LOCATION: LONDON

Run by Jerry Dammers of the **Specials** as an imprint of the Chrysalis label, 2 Tone released records by the Specials, the Special AKA, Madness, the Selecter, Elvis Costello, the Beat (called the English Beat in the United States for contractual reasons), and many others—becoming known as the go-to label during the English-style **ska** revival. Dammers opened 2 Tone Records in 1979, inspired by the legacy of labels like Motown that had a recognizable style and musical direction—that inspiration also fit into his plan to release music by multiracial bands such as his own and the Selecter. 2 Tone was largely active during the late-1970s to early-1980s and was instrumental in exposing people around the world to the ska and rock-steady rhythms that regularly cracked the UK's top 10. After the original Specials dissolved—with members leaving to form Fun Boy Three—Dammers reconstituted the Specials under its original name of the Specials AKA, scoring its last major hit with the 1984 antiapartheid classic "Free Nelson Mandela."

Jerry Dammers of the Specials and 2 Tone Records performing in London, 1979.

U.K. SUBS

1976-present

CLASSIC LINEUP: Charlie Harper (vocals);
Nicky Garratt (guitar); Steve Slack (bass);
Pete Davis (drums)

Formed in the mid-1970s by leader and
vocalist Charlie Harper (a **Damned** aficionado
and professional hairdresser originally
named Manuel Vader, who had also been
in a **101'ers**-style pub-rock band called the
Marauders), the U.K. Subs were originally
named the Subversives. In 1977, the U.K.
Subs recorded sessions with disc jockey
John Peel as well as a live set at the **Roxy**.
Their first record, *Another Kind of Blues* (a
reference to a kind of pill particularly popular on the London scene at the time) was
released on Gem in 1979, and was the first
of many U.K. Subs titles beginning with
subsequent letters of the alphabet.

Based somewhat incongruously out
of Harper's South London salon, U.K. Subs
played many gigs with the like-minded
Crass and fostered a sense of working-class
pride absent from some of the artier permutations of punk and **post-punk** at the
time, specializing instead in revved-up
anthems such as "Stranglehold," "CID,"
and "Telephone Numbers." In 1979 the U.K.
Subs were featured in a rarely seen film by
Julien Temple called *Punk Can Take It*, and
that same year made it to the British TV
show Top of the Pops with "Stranglehold."
They weathered the punk drought of the
1980s, never disbanding, but instead
making numerous personnel changes,
consistently playing gigs, and recording—
even as punk's popularity in the U.K. steadily declined. One-time bassist Alvin Gibbs
later played with **Iggy Pop** in the late-1980s
and recounted his experiences in the book
Neighborhood Threat: On Tour with Iggy Pop.
The U.K. Subs continued making music

into the new millennium, with an ever-
evolving lineup that at one point included
Lars Frederickson of **Rancid**. Charlie Harper
is one of the true grand old men of punk,
playing on year after year for the sheer
fun of it; unlike the should-be-retired Mick
Jagger, Harper was your dad's age when he
started playing punk rock.

Discography:

Another Kind of Blues (RCA, 1979); *Brand New Age*
(Gem, 1980); *Crash Course* (Gem, 1980); *Live Kicks*
(Universe, 1980); *Diminished Responsibility* (Gem,
1981); *Endangered Species* (NEMS, 1982); *Flood of Lies*
(Scarlet-Fall Out, 1983); *Demonstration Tapes*
(Konexion, 1984); *Gross out USA* (Fall Out, 1985);
Left for Dead: Alive in Holland '86 (ROIR, 1986); *Raw
Material* (Killerwatt, 1986); *Japan Today* (Enigma,
1988); *Down on the Farm* (Castle, 1994); *Punk Is Back*
(Cannon, 1995); *Occupied* (Amsterdamned, 1997);
Riot (Cleopatra, 1997); *Sub Mission: The Best of the
UK Subs 1982–1998* (Fallout, 2000); *Mad Cow Fever*
(Fallout/Jungle, 2001); *Universal* (Captain Oi!, 2002);
Before You Were Punk (Anarchy Music, 2004)

The U.K. Subs in London, c.1980s

UK SUBS ☠
DC IRON CROSS
PHILLY's SADISTIC EXPLOITS
+ N.J.'s U.S. CHAOS

C.E. CENTER
35th + LANCASTER
PHILADELPHIA, PA.

LISTEN TO WKDU AND WXPN FOR DETAILS
91.7 FM 88.9 FM

FROM THE U.K.

ULTRAMAN

1986-1991, occasionally thereafter

LINEUP: Tim Jamison (vocals); Rob Wagoner (guitar); John Corcoran (bass); Mike Doskocil (drums, replaced by Mark Deniszuk)

In the 1980s, an article in *Maximum RocknRoll* described the scene in St. Louis (which long lived in the punk shadow of Chicago) as "apathetic." This ticked off the punks in local band White Suburban Youth, who responded by releasing a cassette called "So This is Apathy?" In 1986, the band's guitarist Rob Wagoner and singer Tim Jamison formed Ultraman, and by the late-1980s, they were known as the only consistently visible, gigging **hardcore** band in St. Louis, where the scene was defined more by funk-**ska**-punk outfits like The Urge and MU-330 (a fact that did indeed lend some credence to *MRR*'s original accusation). While playing ear-bleeding, loud hardcore (utilizing for a time the drumming of Mike Doskocil, raging provocateur of the town's *other* punk band, the **Stooges**-reminiscent Drunks With Guns), Ultraman also had a yen for melody on occasion. After having played countless shows at fondly remembered venues like the Bernard Pub (where they opened for **7 Seconds** and **MDC**), recording a few albums, and even managing to attain the punk holy grail of a European tour, Ultraman broke up in 1991—its members cross-pollinating the scene for years afterward. Ultraman reformed with various lineups into the 1990s and beyond, and as late as 2006, a version of the band with scene stalwarts Wagoner and Jamison performed with **Rancid** during one of their stops in St. Louis. Ultraman's longevity helped disprove the *MRR* charge, showing that smaller American cities did indeed produce a number of vital and enduring punk bands.

Discography:
Freezing Inside (New Red Archives, 1989); *Non-Existence* (New Red Archives, 1991); *The Constant Weight of Zero* (New Red Archives, 2004)

UNDERDOG

1985-1989, occasionally thereafter

LINEUP: Ritchie Birkenhead (vocals/guitar); Danny Derella (guitar, replaced by Chuck Treece); Russ "Wheeler" Iglay (bass); Dean Joseph (drums)

A **straight-edge** New York band, Underdog played their loud and intentionally aggressive straight-edge version of **hardcore** (occasionally dashed with some **reggae**) extensively in that city during the mid-1980s. Their 1989 Caroline release *Vanishing Point* was produced by Don Fury, who had done similar duty for nearly every other New York hardcore band worth mentioning. Underdog folded at the end of the decade following a nationwide tour. The band played with **Bad Brains** and the **Stimulators** at one of the final **CBGB** shows in 2006. While not the most famous or most popular band in the city's mid-1980s hardcore scene (nor the most consistent on keeping their straight edge), Underdog inspired countless new bands like **Youth of Today**, who helped keep the straight-edge scene constantly reinvigorated and vital.

Discography:
True Blue EP (New Beginning, 1986); *Vanishing Point* (Caroline, 1989; Go Kart, 1998); *The Demos* (Revelation, 1993, 1996)

THE UNDERTONES

1975-1983, 1999-present

LINEUP: Feargal Sharkey (vocals, replaced by Paul McLoone); John O'Neil (guitar); Damian O'Neil (guitar); Mickey Bradley (bass); Billy Doherty (drums)

Northern Ireland's answer to the **Ramones**, the Undertones are best known for their ode to young love, "Teenage Kicks," and for being the favorite band of the late great English DJ **John Peel**. First formed in Londonderry, Northern Ireland, in late 1975, the band didn't release their first record, *The Undertones*, until May 1979.

Seymour Stein of Sire records was apparently so enamored with the Undertones that when he heard "Teenage Kicks" (released on an EP by **Terri Hooley**'s

Good Vibrations label in 1978) on the radio, he pulled his car over and decided right then and there to sign the band. The resulting album was a gloriously innocent exploration of the joys of being a teen—surprising considering punk's limited subjective scope, and the crushing poverty and internecine warfare the Undertones had grown up in. The Undertones opened for the **Clash** on their 1979 tour of America and started to make inroads into the American and European marketplace. 1980's *Hypnotised* was a step forward, but still concentrated on short, poppy songs about (as one song went) "chocolate and girls." The record also included the sarcastic "My Perfect Cousin" and the beautiful "Wednesday Week," which showed that the Undertones had a musical sensibility all of their own.

On later albums, however, the Undertones became consumed by their lack of popularity and hamstrung by the need to advance the sound without losing old fans. A move in a more soulful direction (possibly influenced by singer Feargal Sharkey, whose later solo releases had a decidedly soulful flavor) was less successful, and the band called it quits after *The Sin of Pride* in 1983. Brother guitarists Damian and John O'Neil went on to form That Petrol Emotion, which saw moderate success during the 1980s and 1990s. In 1999 the Undertones reunited, replacing Sharkey with singer Paul McLoone (who was somehow able to channel Sharkey's voice). The resulting concerts and the 2003 album, *Get What You Need*, were received all too happily by a public with fond memories of the boys from Derry, and led to more tours, live performances, and recordings to please the public.

Discography:
Teenage Kicks EP" (Good Vibrations, 1978); *The Undertones* (Sire, 1979; Rykodisc, 1994; Castle/Sanctuary, 2003); *Hypnotised* (Sire, 1980; Rykodisc, 1994; Castle/Sanctuary, 2003); *Positive Touch* (Harvest, 1981; Rykodisc, 1994; Castle/Sanctuary, 2003); *The Love Parade* EP (Ardeck, 1982); *The Sin of Pride* (Ardeck, 1983; Rykodisc, 1994; Castle/Sanctuary, 2003); *All Wrapped Up* (Ardeck/Capitol, 1983); *Cher 'o Bowlies* (EMI, 1986); *The Peel Sessions* EP (Strange Fruit, 1986); *The Peel Sessions Album* (Strange Fruit, 1989); *The Very Best of the Undertones* (Rykodisc, 1994); *True Confessions (Singles = As + Bs)* (Castle/Sanctuary, 2003); *Get What You Need* (Sanctuary, 2003); *Dig Yourself Deep* (Phantom Sound & Vision, 2007). **Feargal Sharkey:** *Feargal Sharkey* (Virgin/A&M, 1985); *Wish* (Virgin, 1988); *Songs from the Mardi Gras* (Virgin, 1991)

The Undertones' Feargal Sharkey, 1980.

"Maybe once a fortnight, after a few days of listening to sizzling new releases and worrying that the music is merging into angst but otherwise characterless soup, I play 'Teenage Kicks' to remind myself exactly how a great record should sound."

—John Peel

UNIFORM CHOICE

1983–1989

LINEUP: Pat Dubar (vocals); Victor Maynez (guitar); Pat Longrie (drums)

A **straight-edge hardcore** band from Orange County, Californi,a well known for skirmishes between their fans during shows, Uniform Choice imitated **Minor Threat** both in look and musical style. Uniform Choice, circa 1986, were the most compelling and aggressive West Coast hardcore band, making pure and brutal music—anthems of unity and straight-edge power, and, um…unity, and um…straight-edge. Singer Pat Dubar and drummer Pat Longrie started the Wishing Well label, releasing albums and seven-inches by Uniform Choice, **76% Uncertain**, and Unity (who Dubar also performed with during the mid-1980s). After Uniform Choice broke up, Dubar later performed with the funk-metal group Mind Funk.

Discography:

Screaming (WIS, 1980); *Staring into the Sun* (Positive, 1980); *Region of Ice* (Giant, 1995); *Getting the Point Across (live)* (Lost & Found, 1996); *Screaming for Change* (Wishing Well, 1999)

UNNATURAL AXE

1977–1980, occasionally thereafter

LINEUP: Richie Parsons (vocals/guitar); Tommy White (guitar); Frank Dehler (bass, replaced by Joe Harvard, Jack Clark); Dom Deyoung (drums, replaced by others)

An early-period American punk band from Dorchester, Massachusetts, who played the Boston scene during the late-1970s, Unnatural Axe are remembered most for their songs "They Saved Hitler's Brain" and "Three Chord Rock." Their exciting live shows melded the best of 1960s rock with the fun and experimentation of the Boston scene, making them one of the only punk bands at the time who could just as easily play a frat party as a club. They played all of the usual Boston haunts like the **Rat**, Cantone's, and the Space, and famously opened for the Police before breaking up as the 1980s dawned. All of the band's record-

ings were later compiled on CD by Lawless records in the late-1990s. Unnatural Axe reformed sporadically after 2000.

Discography:

They Saved Hitler's Brain EP (Varulven, 1978); *The Man I Don't Want to Be* EP (Varulven, 1982); *Three Chord Rock* EP (Varulven, 1990); *Unnatural Axe Is Gonna Kick Your Ass* (Lawless, 1997)

UNWOUND

1991–2002

LINEUP: Justin Trosper (vocals/guitar); Vern Rumsey (bass); Brandt Sandeno (drums, replaced by Sara Lund)

Dealing in that peculiar breed of Northwest-style anti-conventional tonal music/noise-punk, Unwound released a steady stream of albums of particularly complex music on **Kill Rock Stars** nearly every year throughout the 1990s. Their sound was a compelling combination of introverted lyrics—somewhat reminiscent of the Washington, D.C., sound, occasionally bordering on **emo**—with high-pitched vocals and a noisy, feedback-laden guitar that garnered more than a few comparisons to **Sonic Youth** (or a noisier **Sleater-Kinney**). Unwound, for all their angst-driven lyrics, put on a surprisingly energetic show during years of relentless touring. Even though they were musically similar to other KRS bands (they originally formed in Tumwater, a small town near KRS's home base of Olympia, Washington), Unwound tended toward the abstract and obtuse, and were less politically active. The band's final record, 2001's *Leaves Turn Inside You*, was a double album, and a glorious, creative leap on a par with **Hüsker Dü** and the **Minutemen**'s best work during the golden age of **SST**. Singer/guitarist Justin Trosper and original drummer Brandt Sandeno also worked in an experimental side project, the Replikants. Unwound's second drummer, Sara Lund, came on board early on in 1992, after a stint in Witchypoo. On July 7, 2007, Lund took part in the **Boredoms**' 77-drummer concert event in Brooklyn, *77 Boadrum*.

Discography:

Fake Train (Kill Rock Stars, 1993); *New Plastic Ideas* (Kill Rock Stars, 1994); *The Future of What* (Kill Rock Stars, 1995); *Repetition* (Kill Rock Stars, 1996); *Challenge for a Civilized Society* (Kill Rock Stars, 1998); *Further Listening* (Matador, 1999); *Leaves Turn Inside You* (Kill Rock Stars, 2001)

URBAN WASTE

1981–1983

LINEUP: Billy Phillips (vocals, replaced by Kenny Ahrens); John Kelly, aka "Johnny Waste" (guitar); Andy Apathy (bass); Johnny "Feedback" Dancy (drums)

One of the best early-1980s New York **hardcore** bands, Queens' Urban Waste played their first show at the legendary and long-since-closed **A7** club in February 1982. The band members were tightly woven into the city's scene, hanging around with members of **Bad Brains** and **Kraut**, while bassist Andy Apathy was briefly a member of **Reagan Youth**. Singer Billy Phillips, guitarist Johnny Waste and drummer Johnny "Feedback" Dancy also formed Major Conflict. Urban Waste's only release was a self-titled seven-inch single; while not well known, this lone record is one of the most important early New York hardcore records, before the scene coalesced around the **straight-edge** movement.

Discography:

Urban Waste (Mob Style, 1982; Hungry Eye, 2004; Mad at the World, 2004)

URINALS/ 100 FLOWERS

1978–1983, 1996–present

LINEUP: John Talley-Jones (vocals/bass); Kjehl Johansen (guitar, replaced by David Nolte, Rod Barker); Kevin Barrett (drums)

This Los Angeles band of parodists, who started out as the Urinals and played around the UCLA campus in the late-1970s, had a striking, minimalist sound that influenced many punk bands at the time, particularly as the **Minutemen**. The original Urinals lineup included Delia Frankel on vocals and Steve Willard on guitars. They didn't stay long, after which the band stabilized as John Talley-Jones on vocals and bass, Kjehl Johansen on guitar, and Kevin Barrett on drums. The Urinals' first EP was produced by Vitus Matare, keyboardist for legendary L.A. **pop-punk** band the Last, and was released on the Urinals' own label, Happy Squid. Their second EP was recorded in a film-storing soundstage at UCLA.

In 1980, the Urinals changed their name to 100 Flowers (from a quote from

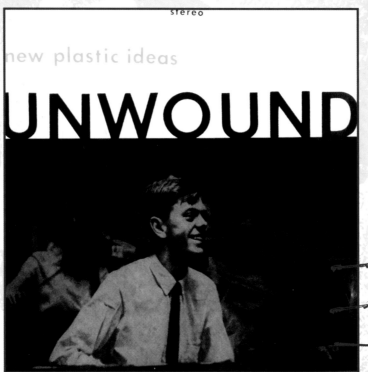

new plastic ideas

stereo

UNWOUND

Chairman Mao that stated, "Let 100 flowers bloom and 100 schools of thought contend") and continued to play sporadically. The band went on hiatus between 1983 and 1996. Much more influential on other bands and record collectors than on the general public, Urinals/100 Flowers material has been covered by Yo La Tengo and the **Gun Club** (among others). During their time, they opened for everyone from the Go-Go's (one of their first non-UCLA gigs) to **Black Flag** to **Sonic Youth**. Johansen left in 1998 and was replaced by David Nolte (from the Last) and then by Rod Barker. More recently, the band renamed themselves again, this time as the Chairs of Perception, the name they used when they played the 2007 South by Southwest festival in Austin, Texas.

Discography:
Urinal EP (Happy Squid, 1979); *Another* EP (Happy Squid, 1979). *Negative Capability? Check It Out!* (Amphetamine Reptile, 1997; Warning Label, 2004); *What Is Real and What Is Not* (Warning Label, 2003). **As 100 Flowers:** *100 Flowers* (1983, Happy Squid)

U.S. CHAOS
1982-1987, 1995-present
LINEUP: Skully (vocals); Gary Reitmeyer (guitar); Jack Gibson (bass); Spike (drums)

An early **hardcore** band from New Jersey (originally known as the Radicals) who have played around New York for years, U.S. Chaos became known for adopting the British **oi** style and fusing it with their unique brand of patriotic satire (which was somehow lost on most of the **skinheads** who came to their shows). They faced drastic lineup changed over the years, with bassists and drummers coming and going regularly. U.S. Chaos broke up in 1987, but managed to reunite for a few shows in 1992, eventually bringing on a full re-formation in 1995. The first U.S. Chaos single was pressed in 1984 and released in 1996, but early pressings are rare and worth quite a bit of money in punk collector circles. Sadly, guitarist Gary Reitmeyer died in 2007, but the band is currently soldiering on with Gary's sister Renee (from Blanks '77) on guitar.

Discography:
Blame It on Sam (Punkrockrecords, 1998); *Complete Chaos Anthology* (Punkrockrecords, 1998); *We Are Your Enemy* (split release with Statch & the Rapes; Punkrockrecords, 2001); *You Can't Hear a Picture* (Pure Impact/Razorwire, 2003; Punkrockrecords, 2003); *We've Got the Weapons* (Punkrockrecords, 2003)

Mensi is Back! the Amazing- ANGELIC UPSTARTS

Plus! The Infamous... U.S. CHAOS

2 Big Shows - Fri. March 8 Show Place Dover, Nj Sat. March 9 New York's Only Rock Hotel, NYC

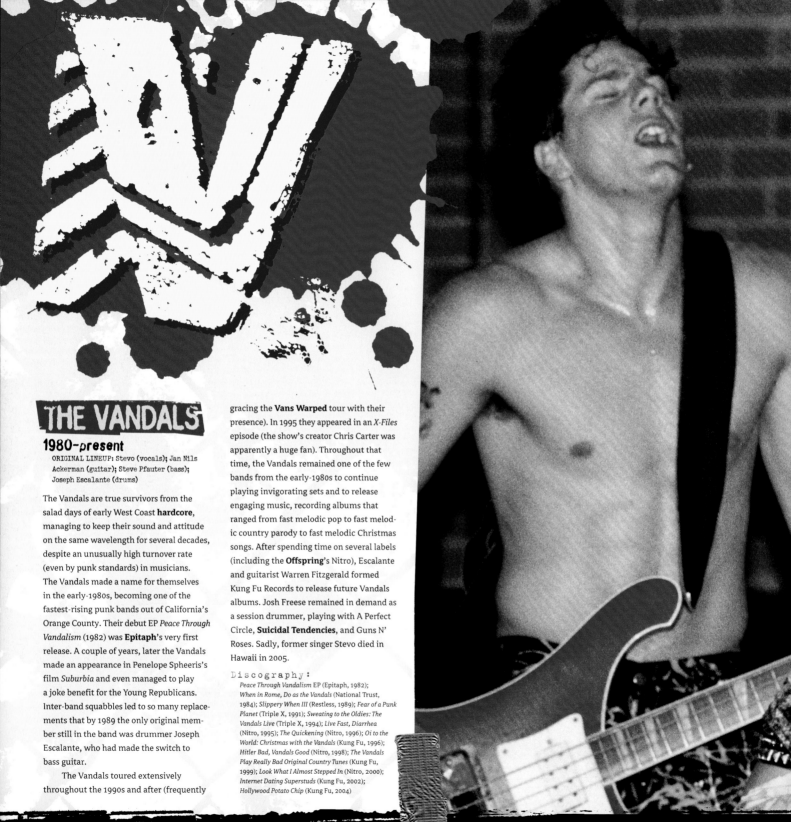

THE VANDALS

1980-present

ORIGINAL LINEUP: Stevo (vocals); Jan Nils Ackerman (guitar); Steve Pfauter (bass); Joseph Escalante (drums)

The Vandals are true survivors from the salad days of early West Coast **hardcore**, managing to keep their sound and attitude on the same wavelength for several decades, despite an unusually high turnover rate (even by punk standards) in musicians. The Vandals made a name for themselves in the early-1980s, becoming one of the fastest-rising punk bands out of California's Orange County. Their debut EP *Peace Through Vandalism* (1982) was **Epitaph**'s very first release. A couple of years, later the Vandals made an appearance in Penelope Spheeris's film *Suburbia* and even managed to play a joke benefit for the Young Republicans. Inter-band squabbles led to so many replacements that by 1989 the only original member still in the band was drummer Joseph Escalante, who had made the switch to bass guitar.

The Vandals toured extensively throughout the 1990s and after (frequently gracing the **Vans Warped** tour with their presence). In 1995 they appeared in an *X-Files* episode (the show's creator Chris Carter was apparently a huge fan). Throughout that time, the Vandals remained one of the few bands from the early-1980s to continue playing invigorating sets and to release engaging music, recording albums that ranged from fast melodic pop to fast melodic country parody to fast melodic Christmas songs. After spending time on several labels (including the **Offspring**'s Nitro), Escalante and guitarist Warren Fitzgerald formed Kung Fu Records to release future Vandals albums. Josh Freese remained in demand as a session drummer, playing with A Perfect Circle, **Suicidal Tendencies,** and Guns N' Roses. Sadly, former singer Stevo died in Hawaii in 2005.

Discography:

Peace Through Vandalism EP (Epitaph, 1982); *When in Rome, Do as the Vandals* (National Trust, 1984); *Slippery When III* (Restless, 1989); *Fear of a Punk Planet* (Triple X, 1991); *Sweating to the Oldies: The Vandals Live* (Triple X, 1994); *Live Fast, Diarrhea* (Nitro, 1995); *The Quickening* (Nitro, 1996); *Oi to the World: Christmas with the Vandals* (Kung Fu, 1996); *Hitler Bad, Vandals Good* (Nitro, 1998); *The Vandals Play Really Bad Original Country Tunes* (Kung Fu, 1999); *Look What I Almost Stepped In* (Nitro, 2000); *Internet Dating Superstuds* (Kung Fu, 2002); *Hollywood Potato Chip* (Kung Fu, 2004)

The Vandals take advantage of a Tucson church's open-door policy, 1984. (L to R) Chalmer Lumary, Stevo Jensen, fan.

VANS WARPED TOUR

The Vans Warped Tour is a huge traveling festival that promotes **skateboarding** culture, political activism, and (of course) the Vans product line. Initially featuring an eclectic and wide range of punk and **hardcore** bands, the Warped Tour has more recently skewed toward consumer-friendly **emo** (with the occasional hip-hop and **reggae** artist thrown in). The modest first tour happened in 1995, and included **Civ**, **Quicksand**, L7, and **No Use For a Name**. These days, the tour is an annual summer event, held at giant outdoor arenas with multiple stages, skate ramps, and ubiquitous corporate sponsorship. In terms of music, the Vans Warped Tour has traditionally featured older punk performers such as the **Damned** or **Joan Jett** during the day, and younger bands from the **Epitaph** label or **Fat Wreck Chords**, such as **Bad Religion** and **NOFX**, as the headliners. Providing valuable exposure and semi-steady gigging for a number of excellent punk groups of yesteryear, the Warped Tour has also helped launch the careers of numerous **pop-punk** bands such as **Good Charlotte** and Yellowcard, making it at best a necessary evil.

THE VARUKERS

1979-present

LINEUP: Rat (vocals); Biff (guitar); Sean (guitar); Marvin (bass); Ricardo (drums)

Hailing from the punk hotbed of Leamington Spa, England, the Varukers are one of the more important bands from the early British **hardcore** period and, at this point, one of the longest lasting (although only lead singer Rat remains from the original lineup). The story goes that Rat was so inspired after watching the **Sex Pistols** on *Top of the Pops*

A pleased customer at the Vans Warped Tour in Fullerton, California, 2004.

that he decided to fight the mind-numbing boredom of small-town English life by forming a punk band of his own. After a few years as a pedestrian punk band, the Varukers became creatively re-energized by the raw aggression of **Discharge**, and re-tooled their style to epitomize what many critics saw as the "Discore" sound. Ironically, in 2003, Rat started doing double duty as the lead vocalist for the newly reformed Discharge when their singer Cal refused to join up. While the Varukers are not well known in America, their first three records are a prime example of the furious Discore sound.

Discography:
Blood Suckers (Riot City, 1983); *Another Religion Another War* (Riot City, 1984); *One Struggle One Fight* (Liberate, 1985); *Still Bollox But Still Here* (We Bite, 1995); *Murder* (We Bite, 1998); *How Do You Sleep?* (Go Kart, 2000); *Retch Files* (Retch, 2001); *Massacred Millions* (Fallout/Jungle, 2001)

VATICAN COMMANDOS

1982-1985

LINEUP: Chuck Weaver (vocals); Richard Hall aka "Moby" (guitar, replaced by Mike Pollack); Jim Spadaccini (bass); Chip Moody (drums)

The Vatican Commandos were a Connecticut-based **hardcore** band who, for a time, featured a young Moby (aka Richard Hall, then billed as M.H.) on guitar—roughly a decade before he became the ubiquitous techno über-star. Originally called Disorder—before learning of a UK band with the same name—the Vatican Commandos recorded some fairly classic humorous hardcore. Songs like "Why Must I Follow" (apparently an answer song to U2's "I Will Follow") and "Hit Squad for God" are representative of the band's general focus. Although huge on the Connecticut scene during their time, the band rarely toured and eventually called it quits in 1985. Their first EP, *Hit Squad for God*, is particularly well worth tracking down.

Discography:
Hit Squad for God EP (Pregnant Nun, 1983), *Just a Frisbee* EP (Pregnant Nun 1983), *Point Me to the End* EP (Pregnant Nun, 1984)

THE VELVET UNDERGROUND

1965-1972

LINEUP: Nico (vocals); Lou Reed (vocals/
guitar); Sterling Morrison (guitar);
John Cale (vocals/bass/violin, replaced by
Doug Yule); Maureen "Mo" Tucker (drums)

Although essentially ignored during their
time, the Velvet Underground had an enormous effect on countless punk and indie
bands in the decades that followed, and also
served as the creative birthing place of punk
icons **Lou Reed** and John Cale. Even though
the famous saying about the band's massive
influence (most commonly attributed to
Brian Eno—it's loosely paraphrased as
"Although only a few thousand people
bought the Velvet Underground's records,
every one of them formed a band") may
be apocryphal, it reveals the astonishing
extent of their influence on punk and
underground music, with many considering
them nearly as important as the **Ramones**
or **Sex Pistols**.

With a name taken from an S&M
novel, the Velvet Underground was started
by literature student Reed and classically
trained John Cale as an experimental band,
playing repetitive drone music with dark,
drug-influenced lyrics. Their sound was
an amalgam of Reed's pop sensibility—
honed as a songwriter-for-hire for Pickwick
Records, where he wrote the novelty hit
"[Do] The Ostrich"—and Cale's work with
minimalist composer La Monte Young.
Original percussionist Angus MacLise, who
hated the thought of the rampant commer-
cialism involved in actually playing a gig *for
money*, was replaced early on by Maureen
Tucker on drums. (After spending several
years in India, MacLise died in 1979 in
Kathmandu.)

The collective of Reed, Cale, Tucker,
and guitarist Sterling Morrison had firmly
established the band's mixture of subversive pop and lengthy raga-like jams by 1965,
and clearly stood apart from the dominant
packaged pop scene (that Reed had helped
to nourish). After noticing them at a show
at the Café Bizarre, Andy Warhol took an
interest, packaging the band as a collective,
featuring **Nico** (an icy European model and
sometime singer who wasn't an immediate

good fit with the American quartet),
dancers, and a light show, calling it the
Exploding Plastic Inevitable. Whatever the
band's opinion of her, Nico brought a sense
of Weimar decadence to Reed's stark and
somber songs and her droning vocals on
masterpieces from their debut 1967 album
such as "All Tomorrow's Parties," "Femme
Fatale," and "I'll Be Your Mirror," helped
gain them a small but dedicated following.

Nico left the Velvet Underground
after the first record (considered a period-
defining classic now, it sold poorly at the
time) and began a career as a solo artist,
occasionally abetted by Reed and Cale. After
Nico's departure, Warhol lost creative interest and left the band to its own devices. The
band's second record was the more acerbic
and even less mainstream *White Light/White
Heat*, which contained the ultimate anti-
commercial epic "Sister Ray" (17 minutes
of pure giddy noise rock) and other classics
like the proto-punk title track. After *White
Light*, tensions between Cale and Reed came
to a boiling point, and Cale was forced out
of the band in September 1968, replaced by
bassist Doug Yule. For their third record,
simply titled *The Velvet Underground*, the
band abandoned some of their more
abstract and confrontational music and
ended up producing a work of quiet beauty.
Songs like "Pale Blue Eyes" revealed that,
despite the layers of feedback and cacophony,
Reed had an instinctive gift for telling
stories though song.

The Velvet Underground continued
to struggle to find a foothold in the United
States, where they were ignored by commercial radio and lambasted in the few
reviews that actually came out in mainstream media. The band tended to be more
comfortable playing in towns with vibrant
music scenes, such as San Francisco and
Boston, and in New York at bohemian
hangouts such as **Max's Kansas City**;
and failing that, Europe. After *The Velvet
Underground*'s abysmal sales, MGM let the
band go. Their last official album, *Loaded*,
was a conscious effort to get radio play
which, despite the band's best attempts,
would not pay off during the band's lifetime (shocking, considering that *Loaded*
included the first version of "Sweet Jane,"
which would later became a radio staple
and cover-version favorite). The Velvet

Underground returned to play an extended
residence at Max's Kansas City, minus
Tucker, who had left the band to have a
child, and by the end of the residence, Reed
had had his fill and departed as well. Yule
and his brother Billy (who had played on
Loaded) kept the band going for another
Velvets (in name only) album. The few
Velvet Underground fans that remained had
no appetite for the band after Reed's departure, and it died quietly not long after.

Reed went on to a successful career as
a solo artist, releasing landmark albums
such as *Transformer*, *Coney Island Baby*, and
Berlin. In 1990, Cale and Reed reunited to
record *Songs for Drella*, a concept album,
tribute, and apologia to the late Warhol.
Three years later, the original lineup of the
Velvet Underground reunited for a reunion
tour (including a few dates opening for U2),
but plans for future tours and recordings
ended when Morrison died of cancer in
1995. Reed, Cale, and Tucker continued
with solo careers of varying success. When
the band was inducted into the Rock and
Roll Hall of Fame in 1996, they were presented with the award by **Patti Smith**.

Discography:

The Velvet Underground & Nico (Verve, 1967, 1985);
White Light/White Heat (Verve, 1968, 1985); *The Velvet
Underground* (MGM, 1969; Verve, 1985); *Loaded*
(Cotillion, 1970); *The Velvet Underground Live at Max's
Kansas City* (Cotillion, 1972); *Lou Reed and the Velvet
Underground: That's the Story of My Life* (Pride, 1973);
Squeeze (Polydor, 1973); *1969 Velvet Underground Live
with Lou Reed* (Mercury, 1974); *VU* (Verve/Polygram,
1985); *Velvet Underground* (Polydor, 1986); *Another
View* (Verve, 1986); *The Best of the Velvet Underground*
(Verve, 1989); *Live MCMXCIII* (Sire/Warner Bros.,
1993); *The Best Of* (Global Television, 1995); *Peel
Slowly and See* (Polydor, 1995); *Loaded (Fully Loaded
Edition)* (Rhino, 1997); *Bootleg Series Volume 1: The
Quine Tapes* (Polydor, 2001)

The Velvet Underground in Paris,
January 1972: (L to R) Lou Reed,
John Cale, unknown cameraman, Nico.

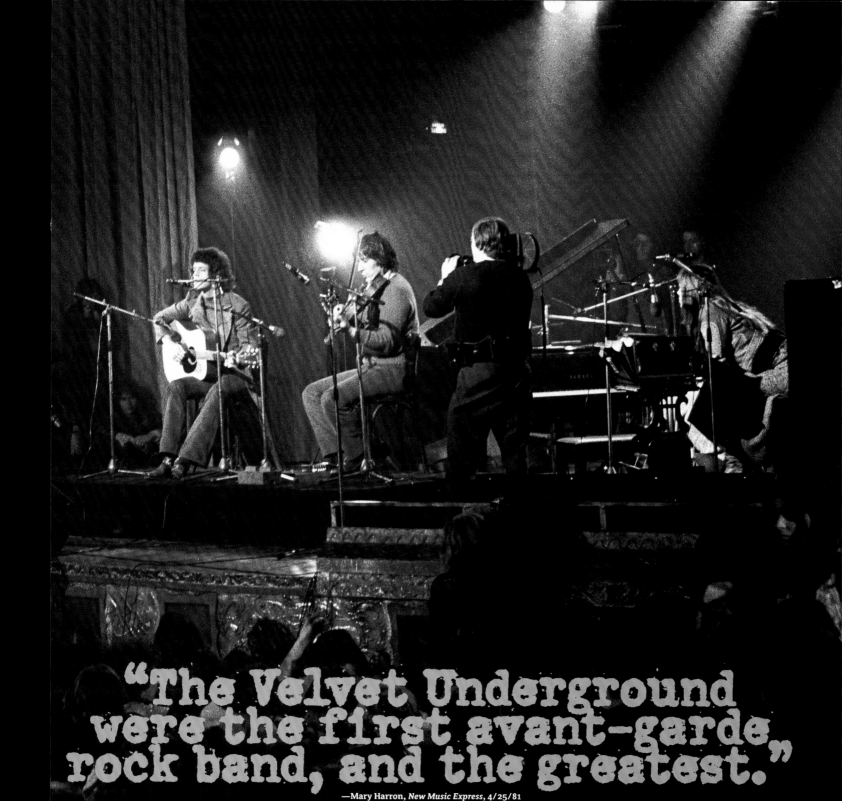

"The Velvet Underground were the first avant-garde rock band, and the greatest."

—Mary Harron, *New Music Express*, 4/25/81

VERBAL ASSAULT

1981–1991

LINEUP: Chris Jones (vocals/bass);
Pete Chramiec (guitar); Doug Ernest (drums)

A Newport, Rhode Island-based **hardcore** band (there weren't many), Verbal Assault played their first show in 1983 (in Providence with the **Circle Jerks**) and released their first EP through Kevin Second's **Positive Force** label. That EP, *Learn* (now considered by many a punk classic), was reminiscent of early **Minor Threat**, not least because it was produced by **Ian MacKaye**, who also contributed vocals to several tracks. A multitude of drummers and bass players came and went over the years, but Verbal Assault soldiered on with primary members Chris Jones on bass and Pete Chramiec on guitar. Chramiec later formed Rain Like the Sound of Trains and toured with Lois and Not from Space, while Jones became a cook. Despite their limited output, Verbal Assault were vital players in the early days of hardcore.

Discography:
The Masses (self-released demo, 1985); *Learn* EP (Positive Force, 1985); *Trial* (Positive, 1988); *On* (Groove, 1989); *Verbal Assault* (Groove, 1991); *Exit/On* (Groove, 1992); *On* EP (Razorwire, 2003); *Volume One: Masses and Learn* (Mendit, 2003)

Verbal Assault's Christopher Jones tries to find out how low the ceiling is at Berkeley's Gilman Street, 1987.

THE VIBRATORS

1976–present

LINEUP: Ian "Knox" Carnochan (vocals); John Ellis (guitar); Pat Collier (bass, replaced by Gary Tibbs); John "Eddie the Drummer" Edwards (drums)

Although bona fide punks of the classic British generation, the Vibrators were in actuality more of an English power-pop band who happened to be in the right place at the right time and were swept up into the punk scene. Prior to the Vibrators, singer Ian "Knox" Carnochan was a veteran of the rhythm-and-blues and pub-rock circuit, and brought a good deal of experience with him

to the band. For their parts, bassist Pat Collier and guitarist John Ellis had previously played in a local band called Bazooka Joe before meeting Knox and deciding to form an edgier band.

The Vibrators played their first gig in February 1976, getting on the bill a few months later at the famous **100 Club** punk festival (along with the **Sex Pistols**, **Subway Sect**, the **Buzzcocks**, the **Damned**, and the **Clash**). Even so, the band remained largely outsiders to the punk scene, possibly due to their generic look and propensity for power pop, as opposed to more raunchy punk. In 1977, the Vibrators released their first album, *Pure Mania*, which included their

best-known song, "Baby Baby." The band went through several breakups and re-formations (including the addition of Mark Duncan and, later, Nick Peckham on bass, Mickie Owen, Nigel Bennet and then Darell Bath on guitar), but continued to tour with everyone from **Iggy Pop** to the **Exploited** and **Die Toten Hosen**. With Knox's recent retirement, the band tours today with no original members.

Discography:

Pure Mania (Columbia, 1977; Sony, 1990); *V2* (Epic, 1978; Sony, 1999); *Batteries Included* (CBS, 1980); *Guilty* (Anagram, 1982); *Alaska 127* (Ram, 1984); *Fifth Amendment* (Ram, 1985; Anagram Punk, 2001); *Vibrators Live* (FM/Revolver, 1986); *Recharged* (FM/Revolver, 1988); *Meltdown* (FM/Revolver, 1988); *Disco in Moscow EP* (FM/Revolver, 1988); *Vicious Circle* (FM/Revolver, 1989); *Volume 10* (FM/Revolver, 1990); *The Power of Money: The Best of the Vibrators* (Continuum, 1992); *BBC Radio 1 Live in Concert* (Windsong, 1993); *Hunting for You* (Dojo, 1994); *Unpunked* (Vibes, 1996; Orchard, 1998); *We Vibrate: Best of the Vibrators* (Cleopatra, 1997); *French Lessons with Correction* (Anagram, 1997, 2003); *Rip up the City Live* (Receiver, 1999); *Best of the Vibrators* (Anagram Punk, 1999); *The BBC Punk Sessions (live)* (Captain Oi!, 2000); *Live at the Marquee 1977* (Orchard, 2000); *Public Enemy #1* (Harry May, 2000); *Demos and Rarities* (Orchard, 2000); *Noise Boys* (Receiver, 2000); *Guilty Alaska 127* (Anagram Punk, 2001); *Buzzin'* (Ripe and Ready, 2001); *Punk Rock Rarities* (Captain Oi!, 2001); *Live at CBGB (Gig) 2002* (Almafame, 2001); *Meltdown/Vicious Circle* (Anagram Punk, 2002); *The Independent Punk Singles* (Anagram Punk, 2002); *Energize* (Track, 2002); *Live at the Nashville and 100 Club* (Overground, 2003); *Live at the Cortex* (Overground, 2003); *Live: Near the Seedy Mill Golf Club* (Invisible Hands Music, 2004). **Knox:** *Plutonium Express* (Razor, 1983)

The Vibrators in London, 1977.

VICE SQUAD

1978–present

CLASSIC LINEUP: Rebecca Louise Bond aka "Beki Bondage" (vocals/guitar); Dave Bateman (guitar, replaced by Paul Rooney); Mark Hambly (bass, replaced by Michael Gianquinto); Shane Baldwin (drums, replaced by Tone Piper, then Kev Taylor)

Formed in Bristol, England, during the late-from the remains of local bands the Contingent and TV Brakes, Vice Squad helped to pioneer punk's second and more politicized wave in England. They were notable at the time for being fronted by a teenage female singer, Beki Bondage (Rebecca Louise Bond), who dressed the part of her provocative moniker and famously posed topless (though with arms strategically folded across chest) for *Sounds* magazine. Vice Squad released their first EP in 1980 on their own label, Riot City. The band was extremely popular for a number of years, but infighting tore them apart in 1985, when Bondage left over an argument about the issue of animal rights. After the departure of Bondage, who went on to form the band Ligotage, Vice Squad continued with new singer Lia. In 1998, Bondage decided to revive the Vice Squad name for a new generation and toured the punk festival circuit with a completely new backing line of musicians, going on to record new material.

Discography:

Last Rockers EP (Riot City, 1980); *Resurrection* EP (Riot City, 1981; Rhythm Vicar, 1999); *No Cause for Concern* (Zonophone/EMI, 1981; with bonus tracks, Captain Oi!, 2000); *Live in Sheffield* (cassette; UK Live, 1981); *Stand Strong, Stand Proud* (Zonophone/EMI, 1982); *Stand Strong* EP (Riot City, 1982; Captain Oi!, 2000); *State of the Nation* EP (Riot City, 1982); *Shot Away* (Anagram, 1985; Anagram Punk UK, 2002); *Live and Loud!!* (Link, 1988; Cleopatra, 1995); *Get a Life* (Rhythm Vicar, 1999; High Speed Recording, 2001); *Resurrection* (Rhythm Vicar, 1999); *The Complete Punk Singles Collection* (Anagram, 1999); *Lavender Hill Mob* (Combat Rock, 2000); *Lo-Fi Life* (Sudden Death, 2000); *The Very Best of Vice Squad* (Anagram Punk UK, 2000); *The Rarities* (Captain Oi!, 2000); *Bang to Rights: The Essential Vice Squad Collection* (EMI, 2001); *BBC Sessions* (live; Anagram Punk UK, 2002); *Rich and Famous* (EMI, 2003); *Riot City Years* (Phantom, 2005)

Vice Squad's Beki Bondage in disciplinary mode, 1980.

FLYERS

In the early days of punk, before the Internet provided bands with unlimited promotional tools, there was usually one way to publicize shows: flyers. Created with Sharpie scrawl and a few cut-and-pasted images, flyers were quickly mass-produced at local copy shops. (Punks with access to copiers at their office jobs became all-important links in the promotional chain.) The flyers were then pasted or taped up on strategically located telephone poles, traffic lights, walls, and wherever else possible before the cops showed up to remove them. In the book *Fucked Up and Photocopied*—Bryan Ray Turcotte and Christopher Miller's lucid and well-documented 1999 history of punk flyer art—the **Avengers** bassist Jimmy Wilsey recalled that making flyers "was fun because it was fast — you could draw something, get it copied, and have it pasted all over town in a matter of hours—it was an outlaw activity."

Many flyers were relatively crude in execution and concept, often giving only the names of the bands, their hometowns, the venue and time, and entry fee. However, some flyers came to be considered collectible artwork. (For example, the work of **Raymond Pettibon**, the house **SST** artist whose funny and explicit imagery graced

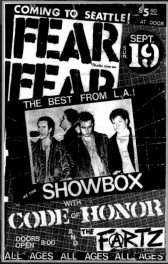

most **Black Flag** flyers, is now exhibited in galleries and museums.) Most punk flyers had a rough-and-ready collage aesthetic that, knowingly or not, drew straight from the political art repertoires of the **Situationists** and **Jamie Reid**—mostly by way of Reid's extremely influential graphic work for the **Sex Pistols**—and Jenny Holzer's satirical, cut-and-paste style.

The iconic look of the punk flyer was mostly solidified by the early-1980s and the rise of the **hardcore** touring circuit, though there were regional distinctions. Flyers from the Los Angeles area were particularly recognizable, often imitating Pettibon's jarring and surreal juxtapositions. Styles would also vary from one band to the next, with the more political bands emphasizing doctored **Ronald Reagan** clip art or horrific wartime imagery (most often from the Vietnam War). But even accounting for regional or creative variances, flyers almost always had the same basic needs: to be informative, quick, cheap, and striking.

Starting in the mid-1990s, widespread access to computers and graphic design programs brought a more diverse and sometimes even a (gasp) professional look to many punk flyers (though a helpful friend with copier access is still often a necessity). Even with the graphic art revolution, flyers remain *the* way for punks to get information out to the local community. Now in the days of Photoshop and InDesign, many punk flyers still look like cut-and-paste jobs, even though scissors and glue as design tools have since become obsolete.

> # "When asked why he left the deceased in the bathroom, wounded, and went out to get his methadone he said 'Oh! I am a dog' or similar words."
>
> —From police report on Sid Vicious from when Nancy Spungen was found murdered

SID VICIOUS

Born John Simon Ritchie (by some accounts, John Beverly) in London in 1957, Sid Vicious was to many (especially in the media) the "face" of punk rock, a James Dean-like icon of self-destructive tragedy. Vicious befriended **John Lydon** at school in 1975 and apparently was rechristened "Sid" after Rotten's hamster, (which for its part was supposedly named after the famously deranged Syd Barrett of Pink Floyd—a bit of unintentional foreshadowing). While Lydon joined the **Sex Pistols**, Vicious drummed with **Siouxsie & the Banshees** at their first show, and became a pseudo-**Bromley Contingent** fixture on the London scene, where he reportedly created the signature "pogo," the precursor to slam dancing.

In early 1977, Vicious replaced Sex Pistols' bassist Glen Matlock. His lack of actual playing ability was thought to be an acceptable tradeoff for his dynamic stage presence, based on his idol **Dee Dee Ramone**. While Vicious certainly did prove popular with audiences for his on-stage antics, an accelerating heroin habit (abetted by his American girlfriend, **Nancy Spungen**, a former **Heartbreakers** groupie and hardcore addict) was further destroying his already negligible bass-playing ability. (According to some accounts, Matlock was actually rehired as a substitute for Vicious when the

band recorded *Never Mind the Bollocks...*, although others claim that Steve Jones played on the tracks; what is certain is that Vicious, arguably the most infamous member of the Sex Pistols, did not even play on their most well-known recording.) Many accounts of Vicious's sharp decline during 1977 put most of the blame on Spungen and the toxic effect she had on him—some fans began calling her the Yoko Ono of the Sex Pistols. Spungen's influence aside, Vicious was self-destructive enough on his own, and the ill-fated American tour that started in early 1978 did nothing to alleviate his growing propensity for drugs and self-mutilation. One particularly telling story from the tour had Vicious one-upping a cowboy, who had put a cigarette out on his own arm, by cutting his own arm open, letting the blood spill onto his plate of eggs, and continuing to eat his breakfast, much to the cowboy's horror.

After the Sex Pistols broke up, Vicious spent much of the rest of 1978 trying to start a solo career, with the willing participation of some of punk's royalty. With Spungen as his purported manager, Vicious recorded a sublime cover of Sinatra's "My Way." In August 1978, the pair relocated to New York's fabled bohemian-celebrity hangout, the Hotel Chelsea (**Richard Hell**, William S. Burroughs, Dylan Thomas, and Dee Dee Ramone were also residents at various times). Vicious put together a backing

band with several members of the **New York Dolls**, as well as the **Clash**'s Mick Jones (who was in town recording *Give 'Em Enough Rope*) and they played in September at **Max's Kansas City**. The impromptu supergroup ended up performing five songs for about 20 minutes before Vicious's addled state ended the show prematurely. After a few more abortive gigs, Vicious decided to concentrate more on his addiction and spiraled even further downward.

On October 12, 1978, Vicious was arrested for the stabbing death of Spungen and was arraigned in a New York court that morning. **Malcolm McLaren** bailed him out a week later, but on October 22 Vicious attempted suicide by slashing his arms and overdosing on methadone. He survived this attempt but was arrested in November for fighting with **Patti Smith**'s brother Todd at Hurrahs. Sent back to prison on Rikers Island, he underwent forcible detox for seven weeks. Immediately after his release on bail in February 1979, Vicious returned to a friend's Greenwich Village apartment, overdosed on heroin, and was found dead the next morning. Ignominious end notwithstanding, Vicious lives on (somewhat strangely) as a punk icon, a romanticized version of the junkie as pin-up idol, his essence rather memorably captured later by Gary Oldman in the film *Sid and Nancy*.

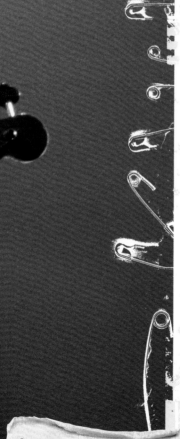

San Francisco, Jan. 14, 1978: Sid Vicious' last performance with the Sex Pistols.

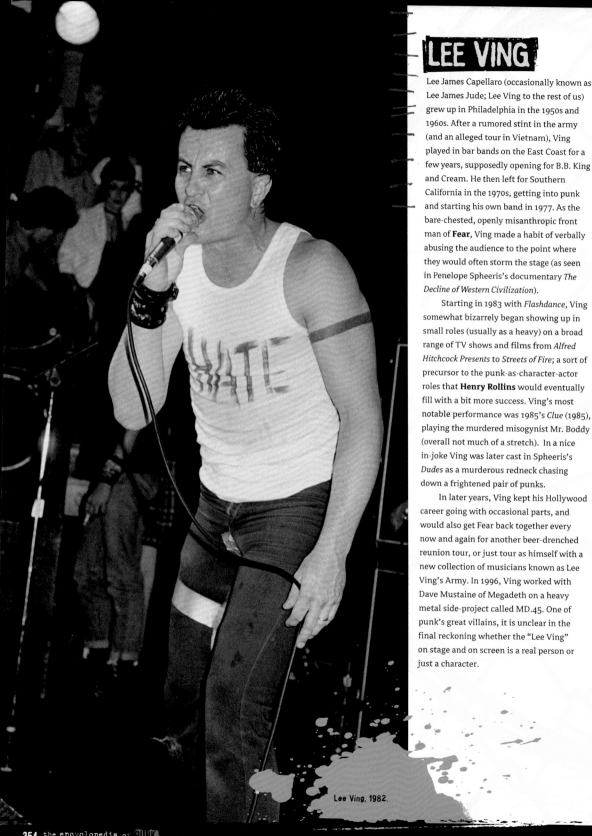

Lee Ving, 1982.

LEE VING

Lee James Capellaro (occasionally known as Lee James Jude; Lee Ving to the rest of us) grew up in Philadelphia in the 1950s and 1960s. After a rumored stint in the army (and an alleged tour in Vietnam), Ving played in bar bands on the East Coast for a few years, supposedly opening for B.B. King and Cream. He then left for Southern California in the 1970s, getting into punk and starting his own band in 1977. As the bare-chested, openly misanthropic front man of **Fear**, Ving made a habit of verbally abusing the audience to the point where they would often storm the stage (as seen in Penelope Spheeris's documentary *The Decline of Western Civilization*).

Starting in 1983 with *Flashdance*, Ving somewhat bizarrely began showing up in small roles (usually as a heavy) on a broad range of TV shows and films from *Alfred Hitchcock Presents* to *Streets of Fire*; a sort of precursor to the punk-as-character-actor roles that **Henry Rollins** would eventually fill with a bit more success. Ving's most notable performance was 1985's *Clue* (1985), playing the murdered misogynist Mr. Boddy (overall not much of a stretch). In a nice in-joke Ving was later cast in Spheeris's *Dudes* as a murderous redneck chasing down a frightened pair of punks.

In later years, Ving kept his Hollywood career going with occasional parts, and would also get Fear back together every now and again for another beer-drenched reunion tour, or just tour as himself with a new collection of musicians known as Lee Ving's Army. In 1996, Ving worked with Dave Mustaine of Megadeth on a heavy metal side-project called MD.45. One of punk's great villains, it is unclear in the final reckoning whether the "Lee Ving" on stage and on screen is a real person or just a character.

VIOLENT CHILDREN

1983-1985

LINEUP: Ray Cappo (vocals/drums); John "Porcell" Porcelly (guitar); Warren (bass)

Violent Children were a Connecticut-based **hardcore** band from the early-1980s who are most remembered as a breeding ground for future members of more influential hardcore bands. Guitarist John Porcell later went on to play in **Youth of Today**, **Shelter**, Young Republicans, Project X, and **Judge**, while singer/drummer Ray Cappo worked alongside Porcell in several of those bands. Violent Children were one of the early hard/fast bands who tried to preach **straight edge** as a way of proper living to the young punks. But apparently their dedication was not enough for Cappo and Porcell, who decided that straight edge was not something you merely sing about, it was worth dedicating a life to.

Discography:
Violent Children EP (United Nutmeg, 1984); *Rock Against Spindlers* (United Nutmeg, 1984, 1993); *Violent Children* (United Nutmeg, 1984); *Skate Straight* (Violent Records, 1991)

THE VOIDOIDS

1976-1982

LINEUP: Richard Hell (vocals/bass); Robert Quine (guitar); Ivan Julian (guitar); Marc Bell (drums

While **Richard Hell** was a brilliant songwriter, he needed musicians who were able to carry out his vision, and in his backing band the Voidoids—particularly the Coltrane-influenced guitarist Robert Quine and the inventive rock-oriented guitarist Ivan Julian—he found players who were more than up to the task. Drummer Marc Bell was no slouch, either; after the Voidoids broke up, Bell joined the **Ramones** (becoming Marky Ramone) and toured with them for the next 16 years, with a brief hiatus for rehab. Following his stint with the Voidoids, Quine recorded several jazzy solo records and played as a session man for many artists, such as Tom Waits, **Lou Reed**, and Matthew Sweet, before committing suicide by heroin overdose in 2004.

Discography:
Richard Hell & the Voidoids: *Richard Hell* EP (Ork, 1976); *Blank Generation* (Sire, 1977; Sire/Warner Bros., 1990); *Richard Hell/Neon Boys* EP (Shake, 1980); *Destiny Street* (Red Star, 1982; UK ID, 1988; Razor & Tie, 1995); *Funhunt: Live at the CBGB & Max's* (cassette; ROIR, 1990; ROIR/Important, 1990, 1995)

The Voidoids, 1976: (L to R) Richard Hell,
Marc Bell, Ivan Julien, Robert Quine.

WARZONE

1982-1997

LINEUP: Raymond James Barbieri,
aka Raybeez (vocals); Todd the Kid (guitar);
J-Sin (bass); Vinny Value (drums)

Among the most electrifying **hardcore**
bands on the New York scene in the 1980s
and '90s, Warzone went through numerous
personnel changes in their early years
before recording their seminal first album,
*Don't Forget the Struggle, Don't Forget the
Streets*. The album's title became the band's
defining slogan; Warzone and singer
Raybeez (Barbieri) are best known for
opposing the corporatization of hardcore
music (in which Raybeez admonished the
kids to "keep the faith," despite the many
temptations of corporate rock). Warzone
played a confrontational brand of hardcore

that became more militant as the band
(some of whom were not consistent in their
commitment) went **straight-edge** in the
mid-1980s. After a decade and a half of
leading the band, Raybeez died of pneu-
monia in 1997, ending a long and prolific
career as an elder statesman of the local
scene. Warzone disbanded after that, with
guitarist Todd the Kid going on to join
Murphy's Law, Chrome Locust, and punk-
metal band Danzig, while drummer Vinny
Value later played in Grey Value.

Discography:

Don't Forget the Struggle, Don't Forget the Streets
(Caroline, 1987; Another Planet, 1994); *Open Your Eyes*
(Caroline, 1989); *Warzone* (Caroline, 1992); *Old School to
the New School* (Victory, 1994); *Lower East Side* (Victory,
1996); *Sound of Revolution* (Victory, 1996); *Fight for
Justice* (Victory, 1997); *Victory Years* (Victory, 1998)

WASTED YOUTH

1981-1988

LINEUP: Danny Spira (vocals);
Chett Lehrer (guitar); Dave Kushner (guitar);
Jeff Long (bass); Allen Stiritz (drums)

A **hardcore** band who eventually (like so
many major West Coast hardcore bands)
went metal, Wasted Youth were, at times,
stylistically similar to early **Black Flag**.
Their ten-song *Reagan's In* EP (1981) included
an improbable 10 songs lasting all of 15
whole minutes, featuring the classic anti-
Reagan song, "Fuck Authority" (the album
cover depicts President **Ronald Reagan**
with a Manson-esque swastika carved into
his forehead). Guitarist Dave Kushner later
went on to play in Velvet Revolver with
Slash and Duff from Guns N' Roses, who
had long championed Wasted Youth.

Discography:

Reagan's In (Sanoblast, 1981; Restless, 1990, 1993);
Black Daze (Medusa, 1988; Restless, 1993);
Get out of My Yard (Medusa, 1990)

Wasted Youth's Dave Kushner with other, possibly wasted youths, 1983.

MIKE WATT

Onetime military brat and longtime resident of the working-class town of San Pedro, California, Mike Watt has played the bass (or as the elder statesman might put it, the "thud staff" or "boomstick") over the years with pivotal punk band the **Minutemen**—who introduced radical politics and free jazz to American punk—and later with everyone from **Iggy Pop** to the Beastie Boys. Watt's adeptness and organic way with the bass (as skilled and inventive as that in any prog-rock band) helped to dispel the notion that punks simply could not play. Watt also helped to propagate the **DIY** notion of touring "econo-style," unbound by common music industry trappings—booking one's own tours, driving cross-country in a van, crashing at local **squats** or on the floors of fans' homes, avoiding starvation on the road, and playing as many shows as possible. A typical scene from before a show in the 1990s might find Watt (by then a veritable sage in underground music) sitting behind a folding card table of band merchandise under a hand-lettered sign reading: "T-Shirts: $10." And yes, he would even sign that shirt for you, as long as you asked nicely.

Watt, the son of a navy engineer, first got into punk in the mid-1970s, forming the Reactionaries and later the Minutemen with his best friend D. Boon (Watt was quoted in the documentary *We Jam Econo: The Story of the Minutemen* as saying that they met when Boon "fell out of a tree on me.") The Minutemen's thrillingly complex jazz-punk, came to an abrupt end in 1985 with Boon's death in a car accident. After Minutemen fan Ed Crawford showed up on Watt's doorstep from Ohio (becoming "edfromohio" in the process), he, Watt, and the Minutemen's drummer George Hurley formed the indie-rock trio fIREHOSE, and played a folkier style of jazz-influenced

"If you're not playing, you're paying."

— Mike Watt

Watt works the boomstick while Iggy does his sexy dance on the 2007 Stooges tour.

music until their breakup in 1994. Since then, Watt has kept himself out of long-term band commitments, with the exception of Dos, a two-bass-player side project with his ex-wife (and former **Black Flag** member) Kira Roessler, that has been touring and recording off and on since 1985.

In 1995, Watt released the *Ball-Hog or Tugboat?* solo album, with cover art by **Raymond Pettibon** (who had done much of the Minutemen's cover art when they were on the **SST** label). As a testament to Watt's status in the punk community, nearly the entire indie-rock establishment turned up for the recording sessions, making the record a sort of celebrity-filled autobiography. The record featured **Henry Rollins**, Lee Ranaldo and Thurston Moore from **Sonic Youth**, the **Germs'** Pat Smear, J. Mascis of Dinosaur Jr., the Beastie Boys's Mike D, and so on. The witty anti-nostalgia screed "Against the '70s" (sung by Eddie Vedder of Pearl Jam, who also toured with Watt for the album) was a minor radio hit, the only one of Watt's career. The 1997 solo album *Contemplating the Engine Room* was a self-described "punk rock opera" that dispensed with the cameos and dealt heavily in Watt's relationship with his father (whose photo graces the cover). More recently, Watt has continued to play in a multitude of bands, including backing up Iggy Pop on a tour with the reconstituted **Stooges**, touring with a new group he calls the Missingmen, and even doing studio session work for *American Idol* Kelly Clarkson.

Beloved for his frank unpretentiousness and utter commitment to the independent production of music, Watt can best be compared in terms of reverence with that great punk saint, **Joe Strummer**. The name of a song from the one-off album *The Way Things Work*, recorded by Watt with a group named the Unknown Instructors (which featured former Minuteman Hurley and a couple ex-members of Saccharine Trust) in 2003 says it all: "Punk (Is Whatever We Made It To Be)." Long may Mike Watt's flannel fly.

Solo Discography:
Ball-Hog or Tugboat? (Columbia, 1994); *Contemplating the Engine Room* (Columbia, 1997); *The Secondman's Middle Stand* (Red Ink/Columbia, 2004)

THE WEIRDOS
1976–1980, occasionally thereafter
LINEUP: John Denney (vocals); Dix Denney (guitar); Cliff Roman (guitar); Dave Trout (bass)

The Weirdos were an influential band of 1970s West Coast Dadaist performance artists who recorded the classic Los Angeles punk anthem "We Got the Neutron Bomb," and also helped pioneer the ripped clothing and **DIY** look that dominated early punk fashion. The original lineup formed in 1976 with brothers John and Dix Denney on vocals and guitar, respectively, and no apparent desire for a drummer. Caving after their first few gigs, the Weirdos placed Nicky Beat behind the drums, which was about the closest they got to not being, well, Weirdos.

One of the things that distinguished the Weirdos as outsiders during the late-1970s was that they designed and created their own clothing, flyers, merchandise, and T-shirts in the pursuit of their philosophy of "weirdoism." Although initially reluctant to take on the label of *punk rock*, the Weirdos eventually became accustomed to the description after finding inspiration in the first **Ramones** album, and once they were featured alongside various other punk bands in a July 1977 *Time* magazine story (in which the author considers whether the "demon-eyed New Yorker" **Richard Hell** could become the "Mick Jagger of punk"). After the first blaze of punk weirdness, the Weirdos went on semi-hiatus during the 1980s, but reformed for 1990's *Condor* album, and toured sporadically afterward.

Although lumped in with a number of non-like-minded bands, the Weirdos were far smarter than the average punk band of the time, known particularly for their Dadaist tendencies, love of Marcel Duchamp and the music of Karlheinz Stockhausen, Captain Beefheart, and Miles Davis. Their timeliness and fashion sense epitomized the artistic ideal of the early L.A. punk scene and made the Weirdos one of the pivotal bands from that period, demonstrating punk's ability to be simultaneously adventurous and intelligent.

Discography:
Who? What? When? Where? Why? EP (Bomp!, 1979); *Action Design* EP (Rhino, 1980); *Condor* (Frontier, 1990); *Weird World: 1977–1981 Time Capsule Volume One* (Frontier, 1991)

The Weirdos'
Dix Denney, 1977.

PUNK AND FASHION

Punk fashion may sound like a contradiction in terms to many, but punk did spawn some of the most iconic "looks" and uniforms of the late-twentieth century. Loathe him or love him, the iconic image of Sid Vicious (resplendent in torn T-shirt, ripped jeans, and leather jacket) is as indelible a fashion statement as James Dean's look was in the 1950s. Punk revolutionized the way in which

clothing was worn by teens around the world. Suddenly, high fashion (although Malcolm McLaren certainly started the idea of expensive punk "fashion") was no longer the point, the point was to appear different, to be an individual, and, in the best DIY sense, to create a unique look. Sadly, this eventually led to not only the adoption of a more universal punk "uniform" but also to sickly thin models parading down the catwalk wearing ripped clothing and safety pins. And no one designer bothered to send a

royalty check to Richard Hell.

Punk fashion, for lack of a better term, has always varied hugely depending on the time period, scene, country, or city, ranging anywhere from the garish (safety pins, mohawks, leather, and bondage outfits) to the mundane (suspenders, Doc Martens, sweatshirts, shaved heads) and is no easier to define in the past than it is today. Here, however, is a brief primer.

When the American punk scene got started in New York, there was very

simply no fixed style. Richard Hell, a fixture on the local scene, had a particularly jagged look involving torn clothing with safety pins, which Malcolm McLaren was all too happy to appropriate for his store, which helped seed the look throughout the nascent London scene. Punks on both side of the Atlantic were similarly inspired by the Ramones' stylized uniform of ripped jeans, sneakers, leather jackets, and bowl haircuts.

In the late-1970s, many punks adopted the baroque look of spiked leather, bondage clothing, and brightly colored mohawks; variations of which became for years the stereotyped mass media image of "punk." At the same time, however, many punks at shows made no attempt to dress in any particularly rebellious fashion (attested to by the number of photos in this book from the 1970s and '80s where many, if not most, of the visible audience members looked in no way "punk"). A common denominator was, however, hair, which was nearly always worn short in reaction to the dreaded hippies and classic-rock fans of the 1970s. Hair was sometimes spiked up, unless it was in a mohawk, the latter of which was usually the only excuse to have long hair; unless one was a Ramone, in which case the wearer was grandfathered in.

After punk's first wave began to fizzle in the early-1980s, many in the burgeoning hardcore scene adopted a more stripped-down appearance. In scenes like Los Angeles and Boston, hardcore punks dressed to intimidate,

in reaction to the frequent beatings and assaults they had to endure. The shaved head (which very often did not indicate that one was a skinhead) was one way to affect a preventively tough appearance; militaristic or working-class clothing (combat boots, military surplus jackets, chains, torn jeans) did the rest. Long before grunge appropriated it, flannel shirts were, and are, often also part of the look, commonly tied around the waist as a concession to the frequent lack of air-conditioning in clubs where sweltering shows were held during the summer.

During the 1980s as well, skateboarding punks developed their own style of band T-shirts and baggy shorts (allowing more flexibility while skating; not doing much for those knees though).

Their style was later appropriated wholesale by merchandisers such as the much-loathed Hot Topic chain for resale to suburban youth who often didn't even know what a skateboard looked like.

In later years, **crust punks** and street punks took the classically extravagant 1977-era style and made it grubbier by several degrees of magnitude; as many crust punk lived in squats or on the streets, this was considerably easier than it sounds. Some crust punks also exaggerated the trend of wearing bracelets and jackets with metal studs and spikes (epitomized in early years by Brit-punks like Discharge and the Exploited), creating an even more intentionally aggressive appearance. (This leather-chain style had also spread in the mid-1980s to the heavy metal scene, some of whom, WASP for instance, took it to ridiculous extremes.)

Today, there is no single look within the punk scene. Many young punks tend to go for more of a low-profile, hardcore-era appearance, favoring Doc Martens or Converse footwear, black jeans, hooded sweatshirts (usually with a band logo sewed on), and sometimes a wool cap yanked low; anything much more elaborate than these garments is often the first signs of being a poseur. But, as much of the appeal of punk (particularly to teenagers) is the license it gives for reshaping one's appearance in strikingly original ways, many punks still make a point of crafting uniquely original modes of dress. In some countries, particularly Japan, vintage looks such as the rockabilly greaser or classic skinhead look still pop up in the punk scene from time to time, proving that punks can be just as nostalgic as any other subculture.

Vivienne Westwood (left) on stage with the Sex Pistols, 1976.

"The only reason I'm in fashion is to destroy the word 'conformity'."
—Vivienne Westwood

VIVIENNE WESTWOOD

Prolific fashion designer, and former partner and wife of **Malcolm McLaren**, Vivienne Westwood invented, adopted, and created many of the key punk clothing styles that are still considered totemic today. Starting in 1971, the former primary school teacher from a working-class Derbyshire family sold her abstract but fashionable designs at Let It Rock, Too Fast to Live, **Sex**, and Seditionaries, the succession of stores she ran McLaren at 430 Kings Road in London.

Westwood started out designing retro and Teddy Boy outfits (essentially British 1950s-style revivals) but soon moved on to zoot suits, and then the daring **Situationist**-slogan-inspired clothing that provided a uniform, for better or worse, for British punk fashion.

Following an exhibition in New York in 1973, Westwood and McLaren met the **New York Dolls**, and were generally inspired not just by the American glitter and glam scenes but also the clothing worn by New York punk icon **Richard Hell**. After returning to London, Westwood began designing cutting-edge clothing based on the torn outfits and bondage gear of the New York punks. When Sex opened in 1975, perverts, voyeurs, and curious budding punks who braved its graffiti-sprayed interior were treated to provocative clothing that had never been seen in a posh shop in England before, with a combination of shredded clothing displayed alongside leather and fetish outfits. After the shop was rechristened Seditionaries: Clothes For Heroes the following year, Westwood's designs gave the bondage look popular exposure, leading to a resurgence of the Carnaby Street scene, which had peaked in the 1960s.

After 1981, Westwood's designs left punk fashion behind to explore more gothic and **new wave** terrains. McLaren and Westwood broke up their marriage and business relationship acrimoniously in 1983, after which she continued to work as a designer. Westwood was awarded an Order of the British Empire in 1991, and in 2004, the Victoria & Albert Museum in London held a career retrospective of her work in 2004; both events giving an institutional nod to Westwood's anti-establishment fashions. In 2006 many of her fashions were exhibited at the Metropolitan Museum of Art in New York , making her fashion royalty on both sides of the Atlantic.

WHISKY A GO GO
LOCATION: LOS ANGELES

Centrally located on West Hollywood's Sunset Strip, the Whisky A Go Go first opened in 1963, and was billed as a discotheque (supposedly America's first). From the Whisky's opening it became a hipster hangout with bands and miniskirt-wearing women dancing in cages, making it (allegedly) the birthplace of go-go dancing. The Whisky was a focal point for the Sunset Strip riots of the 1960s, and important national acts played there throughout the '60s and '70s, including Jimi Hendrix, Otis Redding, the Who, Led Zeppelin, Roxy Music, and the Kinks. The Doors even performed as the house band for a time.

Although the Whisky primarily played host to mainstream rock groups, the management was astute enough to notice a new music movement, and started booking nationally known punk bands early on. A two-month stretch in late 1977 saw the **Ramones**, the **Talking Heads**, and the **Runaways** grace the stage. After initial resistance to local punk bands from L.A., the Whisky eventually relented and started having bands like the **Germs** and **X** in to perform. The Whisky closed in 1982, but reopened in 1986, becoming a focal point of the mid-1980s metal explosion, and continues to be an epicenter of the metal scene in L.A. to this day.

WHITE FLAG
1982–present
LINEUP: Al Bum (vocals); Jello B. Afro (bass); Pick Stix (drums)

A Sunnymead, California, band known for their quirky sense of humor and melodic **pop-punk** sound, White Flag started in 1982 with original members Al Bum on vocals (who left after the live *Feeding Frenzy* record), Jello B. Afro on bass, and Pick Stix on drums. Later members (the family tree is confusing as the band constantly revolved and members occasionally changed names) included Pat Fear (Bill Bartell), Trace Element, Doug Graves, and El Fee. White Flag went through numerous lineup changes, featuring a plethora of guest musicians who played in the band at one point or another, including the McDonald brothers from **Redd Kross**, Dale Crover from the **Melvins**, Greg Hetson from **Bad Religion** and the **Circle Jerks**, and Ken Stringfellow and Jon Auer of the Posies. White Flag is about as well-known for their music as they are for their T-shirts that parodied the **Raymond Pettibon** design of **Black Flag**'s "Police Story" logo. (White Flag's version featured a friendly cop who had just helped a young child rescue a kitten from a tree.)

Discography:
S Is for Space (Gasatanka, 1982); *Third Strike* (Gasatanka, 1984); *Desperate Teenage Lovedolls* (Gasatanka, 1984; SST, 1984); *(WFO)* (Starving Missile, 1985); *Peace* (split LP with "F"; Starving Missile, 1985); *Feeding Frenzy: Live in the City of Gold* (Bootleg Records, 1986); *Lead* (Bootleg Records, 1986); *Zero Hour* (Starving Missile, 1986); *Please Stand By* EP (Baratos Afins, 1986); *Wild Kingdom* (Positive Force/Gasatanka, 1986); *Sgt. Pepper* (Wet Spots, 1987); *Jail Jello* (split 12 with the Necros; Gastanka, 1987); *Thru the Trash, Darkly (Best of Compilation)* (Munster Records, 1993); *Step Back 10* (Just 4 Fun, 1994); *Sator vs. White Flag* (split CD; Warner Bros., 1994); *Skate Across America* (Mystic, 1995); *Empty Heaven* (Houston Party, 1999); *Eternally Undone* (Houston Party, 2002); *History Is Fiction* (Tutl, 2002; Phantom, 2003)

THE WIPERS

1976-1996

LINEUP: Greg Sage (vocals/guitar); Doug Koupal (bass, replaced by Brad Davidson); Sam Henry (drums, replaced by others)

A Portland, Oregon-based group led by the enigmatic Greg Sage, the Wipers were one of the earliest and most influential punk bands from the Pacific Northwest. From 1978, when their first single came out, through the dark years of the late-1980s and beyond, the Wipers kept to Sage's unique and honest vision of what rock 'n' roll should be, as opposed to what it was. The Wipers' uncompromising, independent approach helped lay the groundwork in the Pacific Northwest for much of what would follow, from the grunge explosion to the proliferation of successful independent labels such as **Kill Rock Stars** and Sub Pop.

The center of the Wipers has always been the famously antisocial Sage, with original members like bassist Doug Koupal and drummer Sam Henry both leaving in 1981 (later playing with the Jesus and Mary Chain and **Napalm Death**, respectively). While the Wipers did shows with many of Portland's other punk bands, they never really fit in as part of a scene. (Sage steadfastly refused to indulge in the marketing and promotional BS that the rock world required.) Despite numerous personnel changes, the Wipers continued to release music sporadically throughout the 1990s, with Sage also putting out solo material.

The Wipers were a longtime favorite of Kurt Cobain (some have charged that **Nirvana** and other grunge bands copied wholesale the Wipers' depressive lyrics and bursts of angry guitar noise) and he championed them in numerous interviews,

leading to a smattering of commercial success for the band in the mid-1990s. A Wipers tribute record with songs from popular bands such as Nirvana, Hole, and **Sonic Youth** was released in 1993. The fact that the Wipers became such a cornerstone band in American indie music, even with Sage's reluctance to publicize the band or to be involved in the machinery of stardom, is testament to both his commitment and vision.

Discography:

Is This Real? (Park Ave., 1980; Sub Pop, 1993); *Alien Boy* EP (Park Ave., 1980); *Youth of America* EP (Park Avenue, 1981; Restless, 1990); *Over the Edge* (Brain Eater, 1983; Restless, 1987); *The Wipers* (Enigma, 1985); *Land of the Lost* (Restless, 1986); *Follow Blind* (Restless, 1987; Dead Line, 1992; Gift of Life, 1995); *The Circle* (Restless, 1988); *The Best of Wipers and Greg Sage* (Restless, 1990); *Silver Sail* (Tim/Kerr, 1993); *The Herd* (Tim/Kerr, 1996); *Power in One* (Zeno, 1999); *3 CD Box Set: Is This Real?—Youth of America—Over the Edge* (Zeno, 2001). **Greg Sage:** *Straight Ahead* (Enigma, 1985); *Sacrifice (For Love)* (Restless, 1991). **Various Artists:** *Eight Songs for Greg Sage and the Wipers* EP (Tim/Kerr, 1992); *Fourteen Songs for Greg Sage and the Wipers* (Tim/Kerr, 1993)

WIRE

1976-1980, occasionally thereafter

LINEUP: Colin Newman (vocals/guitar); Bruce Gilbert (guitar); Graham Lewis (bass); Robert Grey, aka Robert Gotobed (drums)

One of the few original British punk bands to stretch the genre's parameters in unexpected directions, Wire paved the way for the infusion of synthesizers and dance rhythms into **post-punk** and **new wave**. Formed in late 1976, Wire recorded their amazing and lyrically abstract seminal first album just a year later. *Pink Flag* featured 21 songs that deconstructed punk rock nearly as completely and with as much excitement as groups like **Can** and visionaries like Brian Eno had deconstructed rock 'n' roll years earlier. *Pink Flag* did have its "traditional" punk moments, such as the proto-**hardcore** song "12XU," later covered by **Minor Threat**. (REM also covered the song "Strange" from *Pink Flag*.) But most Wire songs were haiku-like bursts of mysterious lyrics surrounded by buzzing guitars and the cryptic sound design of producer Mike Thorne.

If *Pink Flag* was a revelation, Wire had advanced stylistically even further by their next album, *Chairs Missing*, which followed the experimentation of *Pink Flag* by strip-

ping down songs to their skeletal structures and rebuilding them, creating an entirely unique musical style and language, a true Wire sound. The band's third album, 1979's *154*, was a further step in a direction that was years ahead of its time. Seemingly conflicted about where to go next after they had left both punk and traditional rock templates far behind, Wire took a multi-year hiatus during which the various members of the band busied themselves with solo projects. (An entire book could be written about the various permutations under which members of Wire performed and recorded since the 1980s.)

In 1987, the band regrouped, but instead of the old experimentation, Wire had moved in a dance rhythm direction, reminiscent of the decade's best British new wave bands, while also furthering their experiments in drones and bizarre soundscapes. Wire continued to record and tour, although, being slightly older than most punks, even during the 1970s, the band concentrated on short sets in which old favorites (such as "I Am the Fly") were completely reworked, wildly deviating from the original recordings. Wire continues to inspire bands such as Elastica, who actually had to pay Wire royalties for "borrowing" certain musical ideas.

Select Discography:

Pink Flag (Harvest, 1977); *Chairs Missing* (Harvest, 1978); *154* (Automatic/Warner Bros., 1979)

V0515
EVENT CODE
$20.00
IV0515
SECTION/AISLE
GA

CA   2X
GA6   84
RAW   SEAT
DEL409A
10MAY00

GA   GA6 84   ADULT
SECTION/AISLE   ROW/BOX SEAT   ADMISSION
GEN ADM STANDING   20.00
16 TO ENTER/21 TO DRINK
WIRE
NO REC/CAM/BOT/CAN/RESELL
IRVING PLAZA
17 IRVING PLACE/NYC
MON MAY 15.2000 8PM

Wire, c.1977.

X

1977–present

LINEUP: Exene Cervenka (vocals); Billy Zoom (guitar, replaced by others); John Doe (bass/vocals); D.J. Bonebrake (drums)

As members of the foremost and certainly most popular band to come out of the Los Angeles punk scene, the bohemian rockers of X blended roots rock, **rockabilly**, blues, and gospel in their potent and poetic punk songs. Led by charismatic poet Exene Cervenka and her ex-husband, bassist/singer **John Doe** (both out-of-towners, they met, fittingly, at a poetry workshop), X set the standard for combining roots rock and punk that would be followed by numerous other bands in the 1980s and '90s. In 1980, X became one of the first bands in the early L.A. scene to put out a major record. *Los Angeles* was produced by the Doors' Ray Manzarek, who not only knew a little something about the dark undercurrent of L.A. that was evident in the band's music but also saw in X some of the poetic resonance he had previously witnessed in Doors front man Jim Morrison. *Los Angeles* is a brilliant summary of the dangers and joys of living in the city during the chaotic days of the early punk scene. The record highlighted in particular the (strange and slightly-off)

vocal interplay between Cervenka and Doe, and Billy Zoom's raging mastery of the guitar (a decade older than the rest of the band, Zoom had honed his talents in various rockabilly combos).

Los Angeles and its two Manzarek-produced follow-ups, 1981's *Wild Gift* and 1982's *Under the Big Black Sun*, are priceless tales of love, loss, and debauchery; as a body of work, this trilogy established X as one of the most talented and thrilling American punk bands. By the time of the 1985 album, *Ain't Love Grand*, the production values had grown slicker, Cervenka and Doe's relationship had become unworkable, and Zoom was clearly growing tired of increasingly less-rocking material (he left soon after). The rest of the band reunited with guitarist David Alvin from the Blasters (later replaced by Tony Gilkyson), with whom they had worked on the Knitters side project. After an uninspired live album with Gilkyson, X went on hiatus for several years. In the interim, Doe starting taking an increasing number of acting jobs (particularly in music-oriented films like *Great Balls of Fire* and *Georgia*) and pursuing a solo music career that was more roots- and country-inflected than his rock-oriented

X at West L.A.'s Club 88, 1980: (L to R) Billy Zoom, Exene Cervenka, D.J. Bonebrake.

"We didn't have any radio or music industry interest, so here's a bunch of kids just screwing around with art and music, doing whatever comes into their mind, being totally left alone."
—Exene Cervenka

X's John Doe (left) and Exene Cervenka at L.A.'s Stardust Ballroom, 1979.

work with X. During the same time period, Cervenka worked on her poetry and writing, collaborating with **Lydia Lunch**, and taking part in the odd musical side project, like the Knitters.

In 1993, X (with Gilkyson) went back to work, releasing *Hey Zeus!*, a slower, more thoughtful work that found the band acknowledging their age while not succumbing to its responsibilities, as seen on the 1995 acoustic album *Unclogged*. While X has continued to make interesting music

since the early-1990s, and has occasionally reformed and toured (sometimes with Zoom back on guitar), their days as young and angry punks are long behind them, but their influence on the punk and roots scene is ongoing.

Discography:

Los Angeles (Slash, 1980; Slash/Rhino, 2001); *Wild Gift* (Slash, 1981; Slash/Rhino, 2001); *Under the Big Black Sun* (Elektra, 1982; Elektra/Rhino, 2001); *More Fun in the New World* (Elektra, 1983; Elektra/Rhino, 2002); *Ain't Love Grand* (Elektra, 1985; Elektra/Rhino, 2002); *See How We Are* (Elektra, 1987; Elektra/Rhino, 2002); *Live at the Whisky A Go-Go on the Fabulous Sunset Strip* (Elektra, 1988); *Los Angeles/Wild Gift* (Slash, 1988);

Hey Zeus! (Big Life/Mercury, 1993); *Unclogged* (Infidelity/Sunset Blvd., 1995); *Beyond & Back: The X Anthology* (Elektra, 1997). **Exene Cervenka and Wanda Coleman:** *Twin Sisters* (Freeway, 1985). **Exene Cervenka:** *Old Wives' Tales* (Rhino, 1989); *Running Scared* (Rhino, 1990); *Rage* EP (Kill Rock Stars, 1994); *Surface to Air Serpents* (Thirsty Ear, 1996). **Exene Cervenkova:** *Excerpts from the Unabomber Manifesto* (Year One, 1995). **Lydia Lunch/Exene Cervenka:** *Rude Hieroglyphics* (Rykodisc, 1995). **Auntie Christ:** *Life Could Be a Dream* (Lookout!, 1997). **Original Sinners:** *Original Sinners* (Nitro, 2002). **John Doe:** *Meet John Doe* (DGC, 1990); *Dim Stars, Bright Sky* (Imusic, 2002). **John Doe Thing:** *Kissingsohard* (Forward, 1995); *For the Rest of Us* EP (Kill Rock Stars, 1998); *Freedom Is...* (spinART, 2000). **Knitters:** *Poor Little Critter on the Road* (Slash, 1985)

X

CLUB 88
SAT.
JULY 28

X-RAY SPEX

1977-1979

LINEUP: Poly Styrene (vocals);
Jak Airport (guitar); Paul Dean (bass);
B.P. Hurding (drums); Lora Logic (saxophone,
replaced by Rudi Thompson)

Although they were later eclipsed by bands like the **Sex Pistols** and the **Clash**, X-Ray Spex were for a time one of the most exciting bands on the London punk scene. Their scarily charismatic leader, the dynamic Poly Styrene (Marian Elliott), was allegedly the one person whom **John Lydon** was frightened of. An anomaly on the mostly white and image-obsessed London scene, Styrene was a half-Somalian proto-**Riot Grrl** with braces and a girlie/neon wardrobe almost as loud as her mouth. Styrene decided to form X-Ray Spex after seeing the Sex Pistols. Her school mate Lora Logic added a saxophone to the band's already unique mix. (Logic later left, or was fired—depending on who's telling the story—and formed her own group, Essential Logic.) X-Ray Spex stunned the male-dominated punk world with their debut single, the anti-sexist rallying cry, "Oh Bondage, Up Yours!" It was a bona fide classic of the early punk years.

X-Ray Spex performed at the **RAR (Rock Against Racism)** concert at Victoria Park in April 1978, demonstrating to the other bands on the bill that there was a punk credibility penalty to be paid in following them onstage. That October, the band released their first album *Germfree Adolescents*, which included the classic single "The World Turned Day-Glo," though oddly not "Oh Bondage" (included later on the CD reissue). Much of the album was a concentrated attack on consumer culture, epitomized on songs such as "Art-I-Ficial" and "Warrior in Woolworths" (Styrene had worked behind the counter at the store), although Styrene later distanced herself from such narrow ideological perspectives. Due to mounting pressures and what some saw as Styrene's instability (she told an interviewer that she had been warned by a pink flying saucer to spread warnings about the "synthetic life"), the group disbanded in 1979.

Afterward, Styrene released sporadic solo work and converted to the **Hare Krishna** faith. A 1995 reunion album with Logic and bassist Paul Dean, *Conscious Consumer*, continued the band's culture critique and also highlighted Styrene's spiritual beliefs. In 2005, Styrene released an album called *Flower Aeroplane*, a collection of tracks she had recorded over the previous three decades, and started an organization called Fair Music to provide support for the various musicians who had played with her over time.

Discography:
Germfree Adolescents (EMI, 1978; Caroline Blue Plate, 1991); *Conscious Consumer* (Receiver, 1995). **Poly Styrene:** *God's & Goddesses* EP (Awesome, 1986); *Translucence* (UA, 1980; Receiver, 1990) *Flower Aeroplane* (Film Media & Entertainment Co., 2005)

X-Ray Spex's Paul Dean (left) and Polly Styrene in London, 1977.

Y.D.L.
1987–1989, 2005
LINEUP: English Nick (guitar/vocals);
Rishi (guitar); Dean (bass)

One of the sad truths about the inclusive nature of the NYHC scene of the mid-1980s is that unintended alliances occasionally formed, despite some bands' questionable politics and complete disregard for inclusionary thinking. A perfect example is Y.D.L., who were one of the more engaging **oi**-influenced **skinhead** bands of that time period. However, they were also self-identified as a "white pride" band and were close with **Skrewdriver**, an ugliness that severely limited their influence, and in the end, left them quite marginalized. Their entire output was recently re-released as the *Voice of Brooklyn* full-length LP.

Discography:
American Pride EP (Oi Core 1988), *Voice of Brooklyn* (Vulture Rock, 2005)

TIM YOHANNON

One of the most influential Americans involved in the **DIY** movement of the 1970s and 1980s, Tim Yohannon was an ex-hippie and longtime producer/publisher of both the original radio show *Maximum RocknRoll* (which started in 1977) and the definitive punk zine *Maximum RocknRoll*, which he organized in 1982 and kept going for more than twenty years. Yohannon was also instrumental in the founding of Berkeley's legendary **Gilman Street** collective and the Epicenter Zone record store collective. Through *MRR* Yohannon was partially responsible for creating and maintaining a punk scene outside of mainstream media and corporate consumer culture, but his uncompromising ideological stances on what actually constituted punk caused enormous controversy.

Although Yohannon's detractors thought him too obsessed with ideological purity, he was nonetheless one of the people most responsible for holding the larger American punk community together through the 1980s and '90s. Yohannon, who for many years ran the magazine while simultaneously holding down a day job in shipping and receiving at the University of California at Berkeley, died of lymphoma in 1998 at the age of 52.

> "Punk didn't die with Yohannon in the physical sense: It died in the sense that languages die. It now has no more native speakers left."
> —Gavin McNett, *Salon*, 4/17/98

YOUNG AND THE USELESS
1982–1984
LINEUP: David Scilken (vocals);
Adam Horovitz aka Adam O'Keefe (guitar),
Arthur Africano (bass); Adam Trese (drums)

A New York **hardcore** band who only lasted for about a year and a half in the early-1980s, the Young and the Useless included among their ranks future Beastie Boy Adam "Adrock" Horovitz (the two bands played some shows together). Less serious than most hardcore bands in the city at that time, the Young and the Useless specialized in hardcore renditions of AOR songs (Journey, Boston, the Eagles, etc.) and even tackled the soundtrack of *Grease*, adding a dash of humor and parodying the scene's self-importance. They only managed to release one record, the 1982 EP *Real Men Don't Floss*. This most promising of young New York bands gave their last performance at **CBGB** in October 1984.

Discography:
Real Men Don't Floss EP (Ratcage Records, 1982)

YOUTH BRIGADE (D.C.)
1981
LINEUP: Nathan Strejcek (vocals);
Tom Clinton (guitar); Bert Querioz (bass);
Danny Ingram (drums)

The Washington, D.C., **hardcore** band Youth Brigade was a decidedly shorter-lived phenomenon than the Los Angeles-based trio of the same name. Featuring former **Teen Idles** lead singer Nathan Strejcek and the Untouchables' bass player Bert Querioz, the band lasted from March to December of 1981. Youth Brigade released the *Possible E.P.* in 1981, and was featured on **Dischord**'s 1982 compilation *Flex Your Head*. Despite the short run, Youth Brigade were an influential D.C. band, where budding vocalist Strejcek began to come into his own.

Discography:
Possible E.P. (Dischord, 1981)

YOUTH BRIGADE (L.A.)
1980–1985, *occasionally thereafter*
LINEUP: Shawn Stern (vocals/guitar);
Adam Stern (bass); Mark Stern (drums)

The longer-lasting of two 1980s' **hardcore** bands with the same name was the Los Angeles-based Youth Brigade (the other was in Washington, D.C.). Featuring the trio of Toronto-born Stern brothers (Adam, Shawn, and Mark), Youth Brigade was originally formed by Mark and Shawn. They lived in the infamous Skinhead Manor, a **squat**/flophouse/rehearsal space used by the likes of the **Circle Jerks** and **Black Flag**, where the two of them had decided to start up the punk collective **Better Youth Organization** (BYO). Originally a **ska** band, Youth Brigade became a more coherent lineup when younger brother Adam joined the band on drums and helped with running BYO.

After Skinhead Manor was closed, the band held shows at the Godzilla club, before it, too, was closed. BYO began to release records, and in 1982 the Stern brothers used their bar mitzvah money to release the *Someone Got Their Head Kicked In* compilation (the title was taken from an incident at a show in which a **skinhead** attack left a fan in a coma), which featured the Brigade alongside **Bad Religion**, the **Adolescents**, and **Social Distortion**.

Following the success of the compilation, Youth Brigade went on the BYO tour with Social Distortion, which was documented in the movie *Another State of Mind*. In 1985, the original group disbanded for the first time as bassist Adam Stern left for art school. Shawn and Mark kept playing music as the more commercial-sounding Brigade for several years, continuing to produce **DIY** punk music, and playing and recording on occasion.

Discography:

Someone Got Their Head Kicked In (BYO, 1982); *Sound and Fury*, *What Price?* EP (BYO, 1984); *Sink with Kalifornija* (BYO, 1985, 1994); *Happy Hour* (BYO, 1994); *Come Again* (BYO, 1995); *To Sell the Truth* (BYO, 1996); *Out of Print* (BYO, 1998); *BYO Split Series, Vol. 2* (split with Swingin' Utters; BYO, 1999)

YOUTH OF TODAY

1985-1990

LINEUP: Ray Cappo (vocals); John Porcelly aka Porcell (guitar); Graham Philips (bass); Darren Pesce (drums)

Seminal New York **straight-edge** band Youth of Today (who are actually from Connecticut) are credited with the straight-edge movement's rise to prominence during the mid-1980s. Youth of Today were formed by ex-**Violent Children** members Ray Cappo and John Porcelly. Ardent straight-edge followers, Cappo and Porcelly were highly dedicated to the original **hardcore** scene as epitomized by bands like **7 Seconds** and **Negative Approach**; they would remain the core of the band through later personnel changes.

One of the earliest New York hardcore bands to tour cross-country and overseas, Youth of Today acted as a major force in spreading the gospel of straight edge and also Krishna Consciousness once Cappo became a follower. Cappo broke up Youth of Today several times as he struggled with internal personal conflicts between playing to the adulation of an audience and maintaining a spiritually pure life. Cappo, who later became known as "Ray of Today" (one of the least impressive names in punk history), settled the issue in 1990 by folding Youth of Today and creating the Krishna-core band, **Shelter**. There have been sporadic Youth of Today reunions, and no new recorded material, but the band is still revered as one of the most devoted and fiery of the 1980s straight-edge crew.

Discography:

Can't Close My Eyes EP (Positive Force, 1985); *Break down the Walls* (Wishing Well, 1987); *We're Not in This Alone* (Caroline, 1988); *Take a Stand Live* (Lost and Found, 1995)

Youth of Today's John Porcelly (left) and Ray Cappo, 1987

YOUTH OF TODAY

SUNDAY MAY 3rd
4:00-8:00 PM
all ages show

PAGAN BABIES

side by side

E.A.B.
EPILEPTIC ALBINO BULLFROGS

club pizazz

FRANKFORD & OXFORD AVES
PHILADELPHIA P.A.
[AT THE MARGARET-ORTHODOX STOP ON THE EL]

CLUB PIZAZZ IS LOCATED MINUTES FROM ROOSEVELT BLV I-95, AND THE TACONY-PALMYRA BRIDGE. ITS NOT HARD TO GET TO AT ALL UNLESS YOU ARE A DEADBEAT SLUG WHO IS TOO STUPID OR LAZY TO TRAVEL 15-20 MINUTES PAST CENTER CITY. SO DONT BE A TARD. CALL:

215-387-0789

CLUB PIZAZZ MAILING LIST. c/o A MEETING P.O.B 53557, PHILA. PA. 19105

Coming 5/8 - Henry Rollins Band + MORE

ADMISSION: ONLY 6$ CAN YOU DIG IT?

THE POLITICS OF PUNK

A common critique is that for all punk's talk of radicalism, anarchy, and social change, the political angle is really little more than a fashion statement as opposed to real advocacy. It's certainly true that the radical stances taken by bands such as the Clash (with their vocal support of the Sandinistas and other rebel groups) and the MC5 (who often played at being Maoists) have not always been that well-considered, or even followed up, and were often espoused more by the bands' handlers (Bernie Rhodes and John Sinclair,

respectively). But many bands and individuals—Crass and Fugazi being notable examples—have definitely taken punk's message of social change to heart, whether agitating for women's rights, combating the scourge of racism (both in the scene and within society at large), developing alternate and noncapitalist means of creating and distributing music, or just plain wanting to tear the whole fucking system down.

Inherent (and sometimes explicit) in the criticism of punk (sometimes from within) on these grounds was the idea that the movement was nothing more than a white boys' club, just as exclusionary as any other institution

or movement in mainstream society. This critique is of course hardly without merit, as for many years punk has drawn its ranks largely from the disaffected youth of suburbia, and a quick scan of the average audience at a show will usually reveal a majority of melanin-deficient males. While punk's call to revolution is in many ways supposed to be a direct refutation of the existing white male power structure, punks often seem to have a difficult time reaching beyond their socioeconomic comfort zone.

In short, punk has had a complex, ambiguous, and often contradictory relationship not just with its own

revolutionary impulses but also with issues of gender and race. Regarding the former, punk has from its very beginning marginalized many of the women in the movement. Exene Cervenka and others in the Los Angeles scene, for example, complained about the exclusion of women from the scene in general, and the pit in particular, as the popularity of hardcore grew, with all the genre's hyper-testosterone tendencies. This all happened despite the groundbreaking strides made by bands like the Slits and X-Ray Spex; when the Adverts featured a female bassist, she was almost immediately portrayed, much to her chagrin, as some kind of punk sex symbol rather than taken seriously as a musician.

In America, punk started out as even more male-dominated than in Britain, and continued that way for years. Well into the 1990s, there were few or any female members in most of the prominent punk bands. Women are still a distinct minority in the audience at shows, and were long made to feel unwelcome at many shows (particularly of the hardcore variety), where groping and outright sexual abuse were sometimes the norm. In *American Hardcore*, Steven Blush observed, "Hardcore boys saw girls as outsiders, even distractions." This male hegemony was rattled in the early-1990s by the rise of the Riot Grrrl movement, one of whose first innovations was the idea of the female-friendly pit (wherein women would form a ring around the outside so that others could slam without getting

SHAME
ON OUR
"REPRESENTATIVES"

bashed about by the guys). While there's no question that punk today is still a male-dominated domain, in America at least, there are now there are more female-centric bands as well as women in the audience, though whether that was because of Riot Grrrls kicking their way in, growing awareness on the part of men in the scene, or because the guys simply left for the boy-safe environs of heavy metal, is not known. What matters is that the scene has evolved into a more female-inclusive one over the last 30 years.

While there have definitely been positive developments in the punk scene over the past decade in terms of gender issues, race is another matter entirely. Although the punk ethos was always theoretically one of inclusion, most scenes were often hostile to any kind of outsiders; more often than not that hostility was extended to racial minorities. As with the exclusion of

women, in the early days of punk, this was less true in Britain than in America. In fact, one of the biggest bands on the early London scene, X-Ray Spex, was fronted by a half-Somalian female singer, something that would have been nearly impossible in the United States at the time. In the late-1970s, there was a close relationship between British punk rockers and fans of reggae, with ska being a particularly fertile genre for creative cross-pollination. This punk-reggae bridge was largely built and maintained by Brit-punks like DJ and filmmaker Don Letts, as well as reggae aficionado John Lydon, and world-music lovers like the Clash's Joe Strummer and Mick Jones.

On the other side of the Atlantic, however, punks had a more troubled relationship with race issues, with even more forward-thinking bands like Minor Threat and Black Flag performing songs ("Guilty of Being White" and "White Minority") that were sometimes, falsely or not, misconstrued as white-power anthems. Over the years there have been very few instances of minority punk bands, with a few exceptions like the mostly-Hispanic Los Crudos (who sometimes sang in Spanish). Even though for a time Bad Brains were one of the most popular bands in American hardcore, it was hardly a rare occasion for them to be the only African Americans at a show (James Spooner's documentary *Afro-Punk* is a well-informed look at the lack of minorities in the scene).

Perversely, although the American scene was much more white-oriented than that in Britain, white-supremacist skinheads, Nazi punks, and white-power bands like Skrewdriver were a substantially bigger issue in England than in America. While racial violence (motivated by skinheads or whoever) at shows in America was a relatively rare occurrence, in Britain, the rise of the racist and fascist National Front (who worked hard at recruiting punk skin-heads into its ranks) was a recurring problem. As a result, a wide umbrella of British punks and activists formed the Rock Against Racism movement, which helped fight intolerance in the scene and the nation throughout the late-1970s. Although the scene is in general slightly better integrated these days, and the Nazi element has for the most part been kicked to the side (any such bands who adhere to that ideology play exclusively to their own miniscule knot of fans, mostly at white-power rallies), punk in America and Britain remains a mostly Caucasian phenomenon.

It's impossible to say whether the continuation of punk's generally white and usually male membership is an indictment of its revolutionary promise, or if punk's ideological stance was simply another case of potential rebels biting off more than they could chew. Punk's DIY production and business ethos and anti-mainstream musical attitude may have helped revolutionize music and culture, but the older and more fraught issues of race and gender equality have proved much more stubborn.

NICK ZEDD

Although it may be difficult to define exactly what punk film is, Nick Zedd has been long regarded as one of the key innovators in that genre. With his first film, 1979's punk satire *They Eat Scum*—which director John Waters approvingly described as a "disgusting outlay of cheapness, decadence, nihilism and everyday cannibalism"—Zedd claims to have invented death rock, or at the very least the name. In films such as *Geek Maggot Bingo* (1983), which started the cream of the underground art and music scenes (including **Richard Hell**), Zedd sought to emulate transgressive schlock filmmakers like Herschell Gordon Lewis. In 1985, Zedd pioneered what he called the "cinema of transgression," creating bleak and violent films with Cassandra Stark, Richard Kern, and others. Zedd is also the author of two autobiographical books, *Bleed* (Hanuman Books, 1992) and *Totem of the Depraved* (2.13.61 Publications, 1997); and several noteworthy essays, such as the "Cinema of Transgression Manifesto" and the "Theory of Xenomorphosis" (on achieving transcendence through cognitive dissonance), both articles published in the *Underground Film Bulletin*.

Filmography:

They Eat Scum (1979); *The Bogus Man* (1980); *The Wild World of Lydia Lunch* (1983); *Totem of the Depraved* (1983); *Geek Maggot Bingo* (1983); *School of Shame* (1984); *Thrust in Me* (1985); *Kiss Me Goodbye* (1986); *Go to Hell* (1986); *Police State* (1987); *Whoregasm* (1988); *War Is Menstrual Envy* (1992); *Smiling Faces Tell Lies* (1995); *Screen Test 98* (1998); *Ecstasy in Entropy* (1998); *Tom Thumb in the Land of the Giants* (1999); *Elf Panties: The Movie* (2001); *Thus Spake Zarathustra* (2001); *Lord of the Cockrings* (2002); *I Was a Quality of Life Violation* (2002); *Electra Elf* (2004)

THE ZERO BOYS

1979-1982, occasionally thereafter

LINEUP: Paul Mahern (vocals/guitar); Terry Hollywood (guitar, replaced by Vess Ruhtenberg); John Mitchell (bass, replaced by David "Tufty" Clough); Mark Cutsinger (drums)

Just about the best thing musically ever to come out of Indianapolis, the Zero Boys played melodic **Ramones**-influenced **pop-punk** through the early part of the 1980s before speeding up slightly into a poppy **hardcore** band. The band debuted live only a few weeks after their first practice, and then recorded an EP in a friend's basement just a few months later. Their first album, 1982's *Vicious Circle*—an evocation of the faster style of hardcore then spreading throughout the scene—is still considered a 1980s hardcore landmark, with original copies selling for far too much on eBay. The band then toured relentlessly across the country and up to Canada, playing with the **Dead Kennedys**, **Minor Threat**, and **MDC**. After that tour, however, the Zero Boys took a permanent break, reuniting on occasion in later years. Singer/guitarist Paul Mahern went on to form the bands Datura Seeds and Dandelion Abortion, got into yoga, and also ran local indie label Affirmation Records. Mahern reformed the Zero Boys

in the late-1980s, with Vess Ruhtenberg replacing Terry Hollywood on guitar, but this lineup broke up in 1993. The Zero Boys have reunited several times, and threw a benefit show to save **CBGB** in 2005.

Discography:
Livin' in the 80's (Z-Disc, 1980; Lookout, 2000); *Vicious Circle* (Nimrod, 1982; Toxic Shock, 1988; Lookout/Panic Button, 2000); *History Of* (Affirmation, 1984); *Split 7"* (with Toxic Reasons; Selfless, 1991); *Make It Stop* (Bitzcore, 1991); *The Heimlich Maneuver* (Skyclad, 1993). **Datura Seeds**: *Who Do You Want It to Be?* (Toxic Shock, 1989)

ZERO CLUB
LOCATION: LOS ANGELES

During the late-1970s and early-1980s, the Los Angeles scene was still in its infancy and needed a respectable place where the punk crowd would not be the focus of taunts and abuse. As a result, the Zero Club was born, an L.A. after-hours performance space and bar that was partially financed by David Lee Roth of Van Halen.

("Diamond Dave" seems to have had a surprising tolerance for punk in those halcyon days, occasionally hanging at the Zero Club, which also saw the likes of **Henry Rollins**.) In Don Snowden's history of the L.A. scene, *Make the Music Go Bang!*, the Zero Club is described as "an uncensored after-hours speakeasy and straight sex club masquerading as an art gallery." Many L.A. scenesters were attendees at after-hours parties at the Zero Club, though with legendary barman Top Jimmy working the door, even members of the mighty Plimsouls would have to prove their punk credibility to gain entrance. A legend during its brief existence, the Zero Club was one the few places in L.A. where punks felt comfortable drinking and debauching with their own kind.

THE ZEROS
1976-1981

LINEUP: Javier Escovedo (vocals/guitar); Robert Lopez (guitar); Hector Peñalosa (bass, replaced by Guy Lopez); Baba Chenelle (drums)

Formed in 1976 by a quartet of high school friends in Chula Vista, California, the Zeros shared a keen appreciation for the **Stooges**, 1960s proto-punk, and garage rock. Singer/guitarist Javier Escovedo's brother Alejandro played with the **Nuns** and later with the Kinman brothers from the **Dils**. They gigged extensively in the late-1970s Los Angeles punk scene alongside bands such as **X**, the **Germs** (opening for them at their first-ever show in 1977), the Dils, the Plugz and the **Weirdos**. The Zeros were called the "Mexican **Ramones**," although it is unclear if this was always a compliment. After guitarist Robert Lopez quit the band, the Zeros, as a trio, relocated to San Francisco, where they had previously opened for the **Clash** in 1979, and played numerous times at the **Mabuhay Gardens**. Lopez later went on to a successful run in the 1980s and 1990s as El Vez, a sort of "Mexican Elvis" who reinterpreted classic songs by Presley and others.

Discography:
Don't Push Me Around (Bomp!, 1991); *Knockin' Me Dead* (Rockville, 1995); *Right Now!* (Bomp!, 1999)

The Zeros' Robert Lopez at the Masque.

ZOUNDS
1977-1983, occasionally thereafter

LINEUP: Steve Lake (vocals/bass); Nick Godwin (guitar, replaced by Lawrence Wood); Steve Burch (guitar); Jimmy Lacey (drums, replaced by Joseph Porter)

Considered by many fans of the genre to be one of the best **crust-punk** bands in history, Zounds was a dedicated band of anarcho-syndicalists in the classic British sense. Led by bassist/singer Steve Lake, a squatter and anarchist, Zounds was originally a collective who played freeform music somewhat inspired by the experimentation of the **Velvet Underground**, as well as bands that would prove influential on the **post-punk** scene such as **Can** and the Mothers of Invention. Like their comrades in **Crass**, Zounds was were inspired by the more politically active and true anarchistic elements of the punk scene in the late-1970s. They released their debut three-song EP, *You Can't Cheat Karma*, on **Crass Records** in 1980. The positive response to that EP, as well as their association with Crass, led to greater touring opportunities for the band. (Although playing in **squats** may not have been the most lucrative or comfortable of opportunities, it likely suited Zounds just fine.)

Despite their reputation for industriousness, the band was not prolific when it came to recording. Their one and only album, *The Curse of Zounds*, released on Rough Trade in 1982, was well-reviewed, but sold very poorly. Not long after, Zounds released the "Dancing" single, produced by **reggae** legend Mikey Dread. After several lineup changes, Zounds broke up the following year.

Still dedicated to smashing an unjust system, Zounds reunited in the 1990s for a one-off performance and cut the single "This Land" to benefit the McLibel Defense Fund in support of a pair of environmentalists who were sued for libel by McDonald's for distributing (but not writing) a pamphlet entitled *What's Wrong with McDonalds: Everything They Don't Want You to Know*. Today, Zounds stands out as one of several bands from the early-1980s whose dedication to their beliefs and anarchist politics are far better known and respected now than they were during their heyday.

Discography:
The Curse of Zounds (Rough Trade, 1982)

TIMELINE

MARCH 30, 1974—The "brudders" from Queens known as the Ramones play their debut show at The Performance Studio in New York and change the world of music forever, even if only a few people notice at the time.

1975—John Holmstrom and Legs McNeil found *Punk* magazine, both documenting and naming a movement. The first incarnation of *Punk* will last for 17 amazing issues.

NOVEMBER 6, 1975—The Sex Pistols play their first gig at St. Martin's Art College, kicking British punk to life.

1976—*The Ramones* is released to a confused public, who had forgotten that music didn't have to suck. A movement builds.

APRIL 16, 1977—The Weirdos smack the Los Angeles punk scene into high gear by hosting their first show, with support from the Zeroes and the Germs.

JANUARY 14, 1978—At San Francisco's Winterland Ballroom, a sneering Johnny Rotten stops the Sex Pistols' lethargic version of the Stooges' "No Fun" and walks offstage after asking the crowd "Ever get the feeling you've been cheated?" The Sex Pistols will not perform again for almost 20 years.

1979—Black Flag, created by electronics expert and Black Sabbath fan, Greg Ginn, inject hardcore with metal.

FEBRUARY 2, 1979—Sid Vicious fatally overdoses on heroin, cementing his position as the James Dean of punk.

DECEMBER 1979—The British release of the Clash's multifaceted masterpiece, *London Calling*, raises the creative bar for punk bands everywhere.

1980—Dischord Records is founded, allowing releases by the cream of the Washington, D.C., crop and setting the standard for long-lasting DIY punk labels.

DECEMBER 6, 1980—Darby Crash dies of a self-inflicted heroin overdose, further cementing the legacy of the Germs.

SUMMER 1985—"Revolution Summer" is declared in Washington, D.C. This does not lead to an overthrow of the government, but to lots of great music and art.

1988–1992—Bad Religion releases four seminal albums in a row (*Suffer*, *No Control*, *Against the Grain*, and *Generator*), demolishing the myth that hardcore died in 1986.

JANUARY 1989—Ronald Reagan leaves office. Reagan Youth debate changing their name.

1991—Riot Grrrl is unleashed upon the world. Media overreaction and distortion help kill it off in name not long after, but the increased visibility of women in punk music remains.

FEBRUARY 1, 1994—Green Day's major-label debut, *Dookie*, is released to huge success, paving the way for punk bands to enter the mainstream, for better and for worse.

1995—Keith Morris duets with teen idol Debbie Gibson on the Circle Jerks' cover of the Soft Boys' "I Wanna Destroy You." Despite this, the world does not end.

1996—The surviving members of the Sex Pistols reunite for the shameless money-grubbing "Filthy Lucre" tour, starting a trend of other first-wave punk reunion tours.

JANUARY 24, 2001—George W. Bush inaugurated as president of the United States. Punks detect new song material.

MARCH 18, 2002—The Ramones become the first punk band to be inducted into the Rock and Roll Hall of Fame.

DECEMBER 2002—Joe Strummer dies of undetected heart condition. A little bit of punk dies with him.

SEPTEMBER 2003—Black Flag does half-assed reunion show with only Dez, Robo, and C'el. Fans everywhere are forgiven for being less than overjoyed.

SEPTEMBER 15, 2004—Johnny Ramone joins Joey and Dee Dee in punk heaven.

OCTOBER 15, 2006—CBGB closes. At the final concert, Patti Smith's fitting eulogy suggests that although punk's birthplace is gone, the legacy has been dispersed throughout the universe on the wings of its ashes.

CURRENTLY—Thousands of great punk bands (possibly your own) are still touring, recording, and distributing their own music.

100 ESSENTIAL PUNK ALBUMS

Despite the relative brevity of this list of the greatest punk albums that are **not** Never Mind the Bollocks, Here's the Sex Pistols, this is a fairly good starting point for any student of punk.

The Adicts – *Songs of Praise*
The Adolescents – *The Adolescents* (Blue album)
The Adverts – *Parting the Red Sea with the Adverts*
Against Me – *New Wave*
Agnostic Front – *Victim in Pain*
Angry Samoans – *Back from Samoa*
AOD – *Wacky Hijinks of...*
Avail – *Over the James*
Bad Brains – *Bad Brains* (ROIR cassette)
Bad Religion – *No Control*
Big Black – *Songs About Fucking*
Bikini Kill – *The C.D. Version of the First Two Records*
Black Flag – *Damaged*
Bratmobile – *Potty Mouth*
Buzzcocks – *Singles: Going Steady*
Circle Jerks – *Group Sex*
Circle Jerks – *Golden Shower of Hits*
The Clash – *The Clash*
The Clash – *London Calling*
Conflict – *Standard Issue '82–'87*
The Cramps – *Gravest Hits*
Crass – *The Feeding of the Five Thousand*
Crime – *San Francisco's Still Doomed*
Cro-Mags – *The Age of Quarrel*
Dag Nasty – *Wig Out at Denko's*
The Damned – *Damned, Damned, Damned*
Dead Boys – *Young, Loud, and Snotty*
Dead Kennedys – *Fresh Fruit for Rotting Vegetables*

Descendents – *I Don't Want to Grow Up*
Descendents – *Milo Goes to College*
D.I. – *Team Goon*
The Dicks – *The Dicks 1980–1986*
The Dictators – *Go Girl Crazy*
Discharge – *Hear Nothing, See Nothing, Say Nothing*
D.O.A. – *Hardcore '81*
Dropkick Murphys – *Sing Loud, Sing Proud!*
Ex – *Singles Period*
The Exploited – *Horror Epics*
The Fall – *Live At The Witch Trials*
Fugazi – *13 Songs*
Generation X – *Generation X*

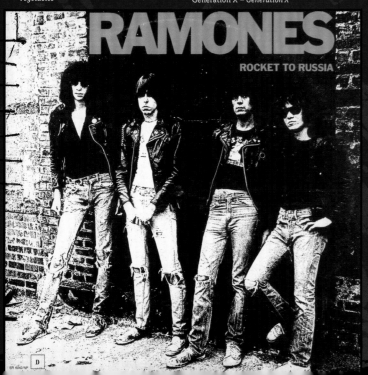

The Germs – *(MIA) The Complete Anthology*
Gorilla Biscuits – *Start Today*
Richard Hell and the Voidoids – *Blank Generation*
Hüsker Dü – *Zen Arcade*
The Jam – *In the City*
The Jam – *This Is the Modern World*
Jawbreaker – *Bivouac*
Kleenex – *Kleenex/LiliPUT*
Lurkers – *Fulham Fallout*
Meatmen – *Crippled Children Suck* EP
Metal Urbain – *Chef D'ouevre*
Millions of Dead Cops – *More Dead Cops*
Minor Threat – *Out of Step*
The Minutemen – *Double Nickels on the Dime*
Misfits – *Walk Among Us*
Naked Raygun – *All Rise*
Napalm Death – *Scum*
New York Dolls – *New York Dolls*
New York Dolls – *Too Much Too Soon*
999 – *999*
NOFX – *Punk In Drublic*
Operation Ivy – *Energy*
The Pogues – *Rum, Sodomy, and the Lash*
The Ramones – *Ramones*
The Ramones – *Leave Home*
The Ramones – *Rocket to Russia*
The Replacements – *Stink*
The Ruts – *The Crack*
The Saints – *Eternally Yours*
The Saints – *I'm Stranded*
7 Seconds – *Walk Together, Rock Together*
Sham 69 – *Herseysham Boys*
Patti Smith – *Horses*
Siouxsie and the Banshees – *Kaleidoscope*
Sleater-Kinney – *Call the Doctor*
The Slits – *Cut*
Sonic Youth – *Bad Moon Rising*

Stiff Little Fingers – *Inflammable Material*
Subhumans – *EP-LP*
Suicide – *Suicide*
Television – *Marquee Moon*
Tom Robinson Band – *Power in the Darkness*
Toy Dolls – *Dig That Groove, Baby*
U.K. Subs – *Another Kind of Blues*
The Undertones – *The Undertones*
Unnatural Axe – *Is Going to Kick Your Ass*
Vandals – *Peace Through Vandalism*
Various Artists – *The Blasting Concept*, Vol. 1
Various Artists – *Not So Quiet on the Western Front*
Various Artists – *Punk and Disorderly* – Vols. 1–3
The Vibrators – *Pure Mania*
Warzone – *Don't Forget the Struggle, Don't Forget the Street*
The Weirdos – *Weird World 1977–1981*
Wire – *Pink Flag*
X – *Los Angeles*
X-Ray Spex – *Germ-Free Adolescents*
Youth of Today – *Break Down the Walls*

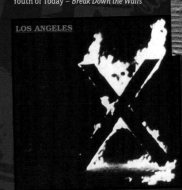

The Best, Shortest Punk Songs

Remember how those 16 beers seemed like a good idea at the time? Or that contest to finish the 72-ounce T-bone steak just to get it for free? Sometimes bigger isn't better. If Yes's *Tales from Topographic Oceans* (four LP sides, four songs!) has taught us anything, sometimes brevity is the soul of music. Below are 10 songs from bands who realized that sometimes getting things done quickly is not just more efficient, it's more fun as well.

The Descendents – "All!" (:01)
Napalm Death – "You Suffer" (:01.5)
The Descendents – "No, All!" (:02)
MDC – "Church and State" (0:27)
Circle Jerks – "Deny Everything" (0:28)
Black Flag – "Spray Paint the Walls" (0:32)
Circle Jerks – "In Your Eyes" (0:39)
Minor Threat – "Straight Edge" (0:45)
The Minutemen – "Please Don't Be Gentle with Me" (0:46)
Wire – "It's So Obvious" (0:52)

Ten beautiful songs, altogether constituting less than five minutes of musical joy.

TOP 10 PUNK DRUMMERS
(in no particular order)

BILL STEVENSON (Descendents/Black Flag/All)

MIKEY ERG (Ergs/Dirt Bike Annie)

RAT SCABIES (the Damned)

MARK LAFF (Subway Sect/Generation X)

T.J. QUATRONE (Serpico/Sleeper/Rule of Thumb)

EARL HUDSON (Bad Brains)

CHUCK BISCUITS (D.O.A./Circle Jerks/Danzig)

BRENDAN CANTY (Fugazi)

JEFF NELSON (Minor Threat/Egghunt)

IVOR HANSON (Faith/Embrace)

And yes, they could all put to shame those 20-minute-solo-playing heavy-metal guys.

10 BANDS WITH THE MOST VIOLENT SHOWS

Earth Crisis
The Exploited
Black Flag
Agnostic Front
SSD
T.S.O.L.
The Stranglers
Minor Threat
Cro-Mags
Skrewdriver

10 MOST POLITICALLY ACTIVE PUNK BANDS

1. Crass
2. Propaghandi
3. Anti-Flag
4. The Clash
5. Chumbawamba
6. The Minutemen
7. MDC
8. Minor Threat
9. Old Skull
10. Subhumans (Canada)

GREAT MOMENTS IN PUNK TELEVISION

The Young Ones meet the Damned – One of the highlights of British television comedy, *The Young Ones* (1982–84) was a surreal, anarchic sitcom about four hapless university students, including Vyvyan, who was so punk he had metal studs embedded in his forehead. The show had a fairly liberal booking policy with bands from Madness to Motörhead just happening to show up in the Young Ones' house each episode. In the second season's vampire-themed episode "Nasty," the Damned pop by to play their mid-period classic "Video Nasty," led by a particularly undead-looking Dave Vanian. The episode gets extra points for working in a reference to Leonard Cohen.

The Plasmatics on *The Tomorrow Show with Tom Snyder* – In the late-1970s and early-'80s, the chain-smoking and strangely cool Tom Snyder played host to a surprising number of new wave and punk bands on his show. Although the Jam, the Ramones, Iggy Pop, and Patti Smith are all well and good, though, few could beat the May 20, 1981, appearance of the barely punk trainwreck that was the Plasmatics. They played two songs and blew up a car.

Public Image Ltd. on *American Bandstand* – In May 1980, John Lydon ambled onto the set of Dick Clark's *American Bandstand* with Public Image Ltd., to lip-synch "Poptones" and "Careering." In truly sneering manner, Lydon took to the lip-synching with a vengeance, barely bothering to put the mic to his mouth while the recordings played, wandering about the studio while a baffled but amused crowd applauded.

Fear on *Saturday Night Live* – Halloween night, 1981: Thanks to John Belushi's guarantee of a cameo, Fear gets the coveted *SNL* musical guest slot. Fearing that the crowd would not appear punk enough, the producers bussed in a crew of Washington, D.C., punks to form a pit. The predictable result still managed to surprise the studio crew, who shut down the performance prematurely, showing that the band could, on occasion, live up to their name.

Sex Pistols on *Today* – Thanks to a cancellation by British pop-rockers Queen, on December 1, 1976, the Sex Pistols and their entourage (including a young Siouxsie Sioux) appeared on the *Today* show in the UK. There, the noticeably drunk host Bill Grundy antagonistically baited the band, while lecherously hitting on Sioux. Finally Grundy succeeded in coaxing an equally drunken Steve Jones into calling him a "fucking rotter," causing an instant sensation in the British press who decried "the filth and the fury" the next day.

The Top – On February 7, 1984, the premiere episode of a new kind of show was warming up in a Los Angeles studio. Executive produced by Harold Ramis and hosted by Chevy Chase, *The Top* was a revamp of scenester Peter Ivers' cult cable-access show *New Wave Theatre*, a kaleidoscopic variety-comedy-music program where bands like the Circle Jerks and Angry Samoans regularly showed up. The new show's combustible mix of mainstream and underground personalities detonated almost immediately after filming began, when a fight broke out between Chase and some punk hecklers in the audience (including Fear bassist Derf Scratch). Chase bolted after a few minutes and a cobbled-together episode (the show's one and only) aired months later, with Andy Kaufman filling in as host only four months before his death.

STRAIGHTEST STRAIGHT-EDGE LYRICS

MINOR THREAT, "Out of Step (With the World)" — "I don't smoke/Don't drink/Don't fuck/At least I can fucking think."

EARTH CRISIS, "Firestorm" — "No mercy, no exceptions/A declaration of total war/The innocents' defense, the reason its aged for."

DAG NASTY, "Under Your Influence" — "Twelve ounces of courage/Makes the world look better/You love the attention/You never had it before."

BOLD, "Nailed to the X" (Comparing straight edgers who marked their hands with the totemic "X" to being crucified):
— "Working together with straight clean souls/Nailed to the X."

UNIFORM CHOICE, "Straight and Alert" — "Straight and alert/Straight and alert/Being high doesn't mean that much to me."

SELECTED BIBLIOGRAPHY

It should be noted that this is not an exhaustive listing of books and articles on punk rock; it is simply a listing of publications that are the most reader-friendly to the general public, or at least the ones most easily accessible to a popular audience. This does not list every book on the subject, and many more websites and zines contain valuable information about punk rock and the subjects discussed in this volume.

Alexander, Allison, and Cheryl Harris, eds. *Theorizing Fandom: Fans, Subculture and Identity.* Cresskill, NJ: Hampton Press, 1998.

Alleyne, Mike. "White Reggae: Cultural Dilution in the Record Industry." *Popular Music and Society* 24, no. 1 (Spring 2000): 15–31.

Andersen, Mark. *All the Power: Revolution without Illusion.* New York: Akashic Books, 2004.

Andersen, Mark, and Mark Jenkins. *Dance of Days: Two Decades of Punk in the Nation's Capital.* New York: Soft Skull Press, 2001.

Antonia, Nina. "Johnny Thunders: A Reason to Believe." *Mojo Special Edition: Punk: The Whole Truth* (April 2005): 14–20.

Arnold, Gina. *Kiss the Girls: Punk in the Present Tense.* New York: St. Martin's Press, 1997.

Auslander, Philip. "Seeing Is Believing: Live Performance and the Discourse of Authenticity in Rock Culture." *Literature and Psychology* 44, no. 4 (1998): 1–26.

Azerrad, Michael. *Our Band Could Be Your Life: Scenes from the American Indie Underground.* Boston: Back Bay Books, 2002.

Bacelin, Jason. "Hard Day's Fight: Rancid Overcomes Death, Divorce and a Sore Back to Deliver Its Most Personal Album." *Scene Entertainment Weekly* 19, November 2003, 32.

Back, Les. "Voice of Hate, Sounds of Hybridity: Black Music and the Complexities of Racism." *Black Music Research Journal* 20, no. 2 (Autumn 2000): 127–49.

Bangs, Lester. "Innocents in Babylon." In *Mainlines, Blood Feasts, and Bad Taste: A Lester Bangs Reader*, edited by John Morthland, 259–299. New York: Anchor Books, 2003.

———. *Psychotic Reactions and Carburetor Dung.* Edited by Greil Marcus. New York: Vintage Books, 1988.

Banks, Abby. *Punk House: Interiors in Anarchy.* New York: Abrams Image, 2007.

Barrett, Leonard E., Sr. *The Rastafarians: Sounds of Cultural Dissonance.* Boston: Beacon Press, 1988.

Bayer, Jonah. "The State of Punk to Come." *Alternative Press* 18, no. 189, April 2004.

Beaujon, Andrew. "Out of Step with the World." *Spin* 19, no. 5, May 2003, 84–86.

Black, Johnny. "Oh Shit!" *Mojo Special Edition: Punk: The Whole Truth*, April 2005, 88–89.

Blush, Steven. *American Hardcore: A Tribal History.* Los Angeles: Feral House, 2001.

Bourdieu, Pierre. *Distinction: A Social Critique of Taste.* Cambridge, MA: Harvard University Press, 1984.

Brannigan, Paul. "A Riot of Our Own." *Mojo Special Edition: Punk: The Whole Truth*, April 2005, 124–28.

Bushell, Gary. "Ain't That a Kick in the Head." *Mojo Special Edition: Punk: The Whole Truth*, April 2005, 102–4.

Bushszpan, Daniel. *The Encyclopedia of Heavy Metal.* New York: Barnes and Noble Books, 2003.

Cameron, Keith. "Something's Gone Wrong Again." *Mojo Special Edition: Punk: The Whole Truth*, April 2005, 36–41.

Cartledge, Frank. "Distress to Impress?: Local Punk Fashion and Commodity Exchange." In *Punk Rock: So What*, edited by Roger Sabin, 143–54. London: Routledge, 1999.

Chanel, Kevin. "From Joey Cora to Joey Ramone: The Connection between Baseball and Punk Rock." *Zisk*, no. 2, Fall 1999.

———. Interview by Brian Cogan. January 5, 2003.

Colgreave, Stephen, and Chris Sullivan. *Punk.* New York: Thunder's Mouth Press, 2001.

Curtis, Deborah. *Touching from a Distance: Ian Curtis and Joy Division.* London: Faber and Faber, 1995.

D'Ambrosio, Antonino, ed. *Let Fury Have the Hour: The Punk Rock Politics of Joe Strummer.* New York: Norton Books, 2004.

Davies, Jude. "The Future of No Future: Punk Rock and Postmodern Theory." *Journal of Popular Culture* 29, no. 4 (Spring 1988): 3–26.

De Whalley, Chas. "Lift Off!" *Mojo Special Edition: Punk: The Whole Truth*, April 2005, 32–35.

Duncombe, Stephen. *Notes from Underground: Zines and the Politics of Alternative Culture.* London: Verso, 1997.

El Hefe. Interview by Brian Cogan via e-mail. May 6, 2004.

Ewen, Stewart. *All Consuming Images: The Politics of Style in Contemporary Culture.* New York: Basic Books, 1988.

Faloon, Michael. Interview by Brian Cogan. December 22, 2002.

Fish, Stanley. *Is There a Text in This Class?: The Authority of Interpretive Communities.* Cambridge, MA: Harvard University Press, 1980.

Foehr, Stephen. *Jamaican Warriors: Reggae, Roots and Culture.* London: MPG Books, 2000.

Ford, Simon. *Wreckers of Civilization: The Story of Coum Transmissions and Throbbing Gristle.* London: Black Dog, 1999.

Fox, Jeff. "How Publicly Admitting You Like the Dead Milkmen Can Destroy Your Professional Baseball Career! An Interview with Ex-Detroit Tigers Infielder Jim Walewander by Jeff Fox." *Chin Music*, no. 2, 1998.

Friedman, R. Seth. *The Fact Sheet Five Zine Reader.* New York: Three Rivers Press, 1997.

Frith, Simon. *Music for Pleasure: Essays in the Sociology of Pop.* New York: Routledge, 1988.

———. *Performing Rites: On the Value of Popular Music,* Cambridge, MA: Harvard University Press, 1996.

———. *Sound Effects: Youth, Leisure and the Politics of Rock and Roll.* New York: Random House, 1982.

Gencarelli, Thomas. "Reading Heavy Metal Music: An Interpretive Communities Approach to Popular Music as Education." Ph.D. diss., New York University, 1993.

Gimarc, George. *Punk Diary: 1970–1979.* New York: Backbeat Books, 2005.

Glasper, Ian. *Burning Britain: The Story of UK Punk 1980–1984,* Norfolk, UK: Cherry Red Books, 2004.

Goldman, Vivien. "Achtung Baby!: Siouxsie and the Banshees." *Mojo Special Edition: Punk: The Whole Truth*, April 2005, 62–65.

Gordon, Devin. "Car Tunes for New Grownups: Advertisers Tap the Music of a Previously Jilted Generation." *Spin* 16, no. 6, June 2000, 60.

Gorman, Paul. "Dressed to Kill." *Mojo Special Edition: Punk: The Whole Truth*, April 2005, 46–49.

Gray, Marcus. *Last Gang in Town: The Story and Myth of the Clash.* New York: Henry Holt, 1995.

Grossberg, Lawrence. "Reflections of a Disappointed Popular Music Scholar." In *Rock over the Edge*, edited by Roger Beebee, Denise Fulbrook, and Ben Saunders, 25–59. Durham, NC: Duke University Press, 2002.

Gunderloy, Mike, and Carri Goldberg Janic., eds. *The World of Zines: A Guide to the Independent Magazine Revolution.* New York: Penguin Books, 1992.

Harrison, Ian. "The Naked Truth." *Mojo Special Edition: Punk: The Whole Truth*, April 2005, 70–75.

Hasted, Nick. "Back to the Planet of Sound." *Uncut* Take 91, December 2004, 82–96.

Heathcott, Joseph. "Urban Spaces and Working Class Expressions across the Black Atlantic: Tracing the Routes of Ska." *Radical History Review* 87 (2003): 183–206.

Hebdige, Dick. *Cut 'n' Mix: Culture, Identity and Caribbean Music.* London: Comedia, 1987.

———. *Subculture: The Meaning of Style.* London: Routledge, 1979.

Hell, Richard. Interview by Brian Cogan via e-mail. July 6, 2005.

Heylin, Clinton, ed. *All Yesterday's Parties: The Velvet Underground in Print 1966–1971.* Cambridge, MA: Da Capo Press, 2005.

———. *From the Velvets to the Voidoids: A Pre-Punk History for a Post-Punk World.* London: Penguin Books, 1993.

Hillsbery, Kief. *What We Do Is Secret.* New York: Villard, 2005.

Holmstrom, John. Interview by Brian Cogan. August 11, 2005.

———, ed. *Punk: The Original.* New York: Trans-High, 1996.

Hurchalla, George. *Going Underground: American Punk 1979–1992.* Stuart, FL: Zuo Press, 2006.

Keithley, Joey. *I, Shithead: A Life in Punk.* Vancouver, BC: Arsenal Pulp Press, 2003.

Kellner, Douglas. "Advertising and Consumer Culture." In *Questioning the Media: A Critical Introduction*, edited by Roger Dowling and Ali Mohammadi, 329–344. Thousand Oaks, CA: Sage, 1995.

Kent, Nick. "The Lost Pistol." *Mojo Special Edition: Punk: The Whole Truth*, April 2005, 8–12.

King, Stephen A. "International Reggae, Democratic Socialism and the Secularization of the Rastafarian Movement, 1972–1980." *Popular Music and Society* 22, no. 3 (Fall 1998): 39–61.

King, Stephen, and Richard Jensen. "Bob Marley's 'Redemption Song': The Rhetoric of Reggae and Rastafari." *Journal of Popular Culture* 29. no. 3 (Winter 1995): 17–37.

Lahickey, Beth, ed. *All Ages: Reflections on Straight Edge.* Huntington Beach, CA: Revelation Books, 1997.

Leblanc, Lauraine. *Pretty in Punk: Girls' Gender Resistance in a Boys' Subculture.* New Brunswick, NJ: Rutgers University Press, 2002.

Levine, Noah. *Dharma Punx: A Memoir.* New York: Harper, 2003.

Levine, Robert. "A Nike Poster Upsets Fans of the Punk Rock Band Minor Threat in A Major Way." *New York Times,* July 4, 2005, C4.

Lisa, John. Interview by Brian Cogan via e-mail. August 31, 2005.

Lydon, John, Keith Zimmerman, and Kent Zimmerman. *Rotten: No Irish, No Blacks, No Dogs.* New York: St. Martin's Press, 1994.

Marcus, Greil. *In the Fascist Bathroom: Punk in Pop Music, 1977–1992.* Cambridge, MA: Harvard University Press, 1999.

———. *Lipstick Traces: A Secret History of the Twentieth Century.* Cambridge, MA: Harvard University Press, 1989.

McNeil, Legs. Telephone interview by Brian Cogan. June 9, 2005.

McNeil, Legs, and Gillian McCain. *Please Kill Me: The Uncensored Oral History of Punk.* New York: Grove Press, 1996.

McNeil, Legs, and Jennifer Osborne. *The Other Hollywood: The Uncensored Oral History of the Porn Film Industry.* New York: Regan Books, 2005.

McPeace, Shon. "Bad Brains Confound Categorization." *Arkansas Democrat-Gazette,* July 27, 2003, 54.

Medehurst, Andy. "What Did I Get: Punk, Memory and Autobiography." In *Punk Rock So What? The Cultural Legacy of Punk,* edited by Roger Sabin, 219–231. London: Routledge, 1999.

Middleton, Jasson. "D.C. Punk and the Production of Authenticity." In *Rock over the Edge,* edited by Roger Beebee, Denise Fulbrook, and Ben Saunders, 25–59. Durham, NC: Duke University Press, 2002.

Miles, Milo. "Rolling Stone Hall of Fame: The Clash." *Rolling Stone Magazine,* June 20, 2002, 87.

Miller, Steve. "Johnny Ramone: Rebel in a Rebel's World." *Washington Times,* March 12, 2004.

Mullen, Brendan. *Whores: An Oral Biography of Perry Farrell and Jane's Addiction.* New York: Da Capo, 2005.

Mullen, Brendan, and Don Bolles. *Lexicon Devil: The Fast Times and Short Life of Darby Crash and the Germs.* New York: Feral House, 2002.

Mulvaney, Becky Michelle. "Rhythms of Resistance: On Rhetoric and Reggae Music." Ph.D. diss., University of Iowa, 1985.

Murray, Noel. "Los Brothers Henandez." *The Onion* 41, no. 3, September 2005, 14–16.

Negus, Keith. "Popular Music: In Between Celebration and Despair." In *Questioning the Media: A Critical Introduction,* edited by Roger Dowling and Ali Mohammadi, 379–393. Thousand Oaks, CA: Sage, 1995.

NOFX. *Flipside,* July/August 1997.

NOFX. *Maximum RocknRoll,* June 1991.

O'Hara, Craig. *The Philosophy of Punk: More Than Noise.* San Francisco: AK Press, 1999.

Perry, Andrew. "The Nutters's Club." *Mojo Special Edition: Punk: The Whole Truth,* April 2005, 114–20.

Perry, Mark. *Sniffin' Glue: The Essential Punk Accessory.* London: Sanctuary, 2000.

Poulsen, Henrik Bech. *'77: The Year of Punk and New Wave.* London: Helter Skelter. 2005

Radaway, Janice. *Reading the Romance: Women, Patriarchy and Popular Literature,* Chapel Hill, NC: University of North Carolina Press, 1984.

Raha, Maria. *Cinderella's Big Score: Women of the Punk and Indie Underground.* Emeryville, CA: Seal Press, 2005.

Reynolds, Simon. *Rip it Up and Start Again: Postpunk 1978–1984.* London: Penguin Books, 2005

Rimbaud, Penny (JJ Ratter). *Shibboleth: My Revolting Life.* London: AK Press, 1998.

———. *The Diamond Signature.* London: AK Press, 1999.

Rivett, Miriam. "Misfit Lit: 'Punk Writing' and Representations of Punk through Writing and Publishing." In *Punk Rock: So What?,* edited by Roger Sabin, 31–48. London: Routledge, 1999.

Robbins, Ira. "Clubbed!" *Spin* 21, no. 6, August 2005, 78–82.

———. "How the West Was Lost." *Mojo Special Edition: Punk: The Whole Truth,* April 2005, 92–98.

———, ed. *The Trouser Press Guide to '90's Rock.* New York: Fireside/Simon & Schuster, 1997.

Rockwell, John "After Politics There's Rock, Disco or Pop Clubs to Visit."

New York Times, C22. August 8, 1980.

Rollins, Henry. *Get In the Van: On the Road With Black Flag.* Los Angeles: 2.13.61, 1994.

Rushkof, Douglas. *Media Virus: Hidden Agendas in Popular Culture.* New York: Ballantine, 1994.

Ruskin, Yvonne Sewell. *High on Rebellion: Inside the Underground at Max's Kansas City.* New York: Thunder's Mouth Press, 1998.

Ryan, Kyle. "Jon Langford." *The Onion* 41, no. 14, November 2005, 14–15.

Sabin, Roger. "Introduction." In *Punk Rock So What? The Cultural Legacy of Punk,* edited by Roger Sabin, 1–14. London: Routledge, 1999.

———. "I Won't Let That Dago By: Rethinking Punk and Racism." In *Punk Rock So What? The Cultural Legacy of Punk,* edited by Roger Sabin, 199–218. London: Routledge, 1999.

Sarig, Roni. *The Secret History of Rock: The Most Influential Bands You've Never Heard.* New York: Billboard Books, 1998.

Savage, Jon. *England's Dreaming: Anarchy, Sex Pistols, Punk Rock and Beyond.* New York: St. Martin's Press, 1992.

———. "In Search of Space." *Mojo,* January 2004, 85.

———. "Savage Jukebox." *Mojo Special Edition: Punk: The Whole Truth,* April 2005, 82–86.

Scabies, Rat, and Christopher Dawes. *Rat Scabies and the Holy Grail.* New York: Thunder's Mouth Press, 2005.

Shaw, Thomas Edward. *Black Monk Time: Coming of the Anti-Beatle.* Reno, NV: Carson Street Publishing, 1995.

Sinker, Daniel, ed. *We Owe You Nothing: Punk Planet: The Collected Interviews.* New York: Akashic Books, 2001.

Spicer, Al. *The Rough Guide to Punk.* London: Rough Guides, 2006.

Spitz, Marc, and Brendan Mullen, eds. *We Got the Neutron Bomb: The Untold Story of L.A. Punk.* New York: Three Rivers Press, 2001.

Sprague, David. "Rancid." In *Trouser Press Guide to '90s Rock,* edited by Ira Robbins, 595–596. New York: Fireside, 1997.

St. John, Warren. "A Bush Surprise: Fright-Wing Support." *New York Times,* March 21, 2004.

Straugsbaugh, John. *Rock till You Drop: The Decline from Rebellion to Nostalgia.* London: Verso, 2001.

Strauss, Neil. "Yep, the Clash was Musical, but Don't Tell Anyone." *New York Times,* January 5, 2003, sec. 2, 32.

Tabb, George. *Playing Right Field, A Jew Grows in Greenwich.* New York: Soft Skull Press, 2004.

———. *Surfing Armageddon: A Memoir.* New York: Soft Skull Press, 2006.

Taylor, Steven. *False Prophet: Field Notes from the Punk Underground.* Middletown, CT: Wesleyan University Press, 2003.

Taylor, Todd. *Born to Rock: Heavy Drinkers and Thinkers.* Los Angeles: Gorsky Press, 2004.

Thompson, Dave. *Alternative Rock.* San Francisco: Miller Freeman Books, 2000.

Thompson, Stacey. *Punk Productions: Unfinished Business.* Albany, NY: State University of New York Press, 2004.

Traber, Daniel. "L.A.'s 'White Minority': Punk and the Contradictions of Self-Marginalization." *Cultural Critique* 48, no. 1 (2001): 30–64.

True, Everett. *Hey Ho Let's Go: The Story of the Ramones.* London: Omnibus Press, 2002.

Turcotte, Bryan Ray, and Christopher Miller. *Fucked up and Photocopied: Instant Art of the Punk Rock Movement.* Corte Madera, CA: Ginko Press, 1999.

Tyler, Kieron. "Idiot Box!" *Mojo Special Edition: Punk: The Whole Truth,* April 2005, 106–9.

Unterberger, Richie. *Unknown Legends of Rock 'n' Roll: Psychedelic Unknowns, Mad Geniuses, Punk Pioneers, Lo-Fi Mavericks & More.* San Francisco: Miller Freeman, 1998.

Ward, Ed. "No Second Acts in Punk? Says Who?" *New York Times,* December 29, 2002, sec. 4, 7.

Warner, Charles. "Jah as Genre: The Interface of Reggae and American Popular Music." Ph.D. diss., Bowling Green State University, 1993.

Wilson, Lois. "Punk Smashers!" *Mojo Special Edition: Punk: The Whole Truth,* April 2005, 133–43.

Liner Notes

Fricke, David. Liner notes for the Velvet Underground, *Peel Slowly and See* (Polydor, 1995).

Hitchcock, Doug. Liner notes for the Embarrassment, *The Embarrassment* (Bar None, 1995).

Hudson, Mike. Liner notes for the Pagans, *Shit Street* (Crypt, 2001).

(Author not listed.) Wayne/Jayne County and the Electric Chairs, *Rock 'n' Roll Cleopatra* (Royalty Records, 1993).

Piccarella, John. Liner notes for Richard Hell and the Voidoids, *Blank Generation* (Sire/Warner Bros., 1990).

Smith, TV. Liner notes for the Adverts, *The Adverts Anthology* (The Devil's Own Jukebox, 2003).

ACKNOWLEDGMENTS

This book was a labor of love and also enormously difficult. I do not mean difficult in the sense of "doing the research," but difficult in the sense of "releasing" to the general public something of which I've always been very possessive. When I was young, punk gave me a sense of identity and belonging that I could not find elsewhere, and it was an epiphany when I discovered that there were other outcasts like me. When I first came to know punk in the early-1980s, it was not a phenomenon that was marketed—it was truly an underground experience, and we felt it should stay that way. We loved punk, obsessed about it, fought over it, and held it close to us, as if it was a sacred talisman that would lose its magic if revealed to the masses. Punk was something my friends and I regarded as ours solely. When we encountered other members of punk culture on the street, we would nod in silent recognition of a shared bond. So it seems strange to write about punk in a critical way for "outsiders," as I am doing here. As Maria Raha wrote in her book *Cinderella's Big Score*, "it feels a bit traitorous to criticize a community in which I have invested so much." In writing about punk and "revealing" it to the public, there is an inescapable feeling of betraying the other members of a private club. But then again, optimist that I am, I firmly believe that for the hundreds of thousands of outsiders who do not fit in with mainstream culture, discovering punk rock (even if through the pages of a book) might in some small way help them survive high school, college, or just the banality of everyday life.

This book was written by one person, aided and abetted by a huge cast of characters. I do not have the space to list everyone who contributed via conversation, information, guidance, or otherwise, but the following people were instrumental in the birth of this book, and it would be remiss of me not to mention the enormous debt I owe them.

For research help, which took several years and endless hours, I would like to thank especially Cynthia Conti, my chief researcher and frequent intellectual foil.

Her help in finding and organizing vast amounts of information and her company in coffee shops talking me through this for hours are much appreciated. Special thanks go also to my original research assistant, Lauren Jablonski, who helped get me started and also provided invaluable insight into modern punk fashion and music.

I'd also like to thank the many people who talked me through this project for free (or occasionally for beer), including: John Lisa (even more punk than me!); my old friend and bandmate John Pillarella; Maria Raha, the ever-generous author of the insightful *Cinderella's Big Score*, the best book on punk and gender; Marvin Taylor, who curates the downtown archives of New York University's Fales Library; John Holmstrom for his time and patience; Johnny Whoa-Oh; Mikey Erg; Legs McNeil; Richard Hell; El Hefe; Ivor Hanson; Thomas King for additional guidance and patience and his killer steaks and Tater Tots; Andrew Barber, always a huge help; Mike Faloon, a great writer and friend as well as the other members of the Blacksmiths for Literary Progress, Tim Hall and Ken Wohlrob; Bert Aldridge, who helped me in articulating my version of punk; Sal Cannestra for years of support and for naming his kid Milo, a very punk name; Robert Francos, photographer extraordinaire; Brendan Gilmartin, although he is now a sports yuppie; Sean Cogan for keeping me on the punk straight and narrow; Eloise Pillarella, who is the youngest and coolest punk I know; the old Staten Island punk crew from Neri's place; the Saint John's punk crew who got me through college; Jon Zimmerman of NYU for special encouragement; my colleagues M.J. Robinson, Marion Wrenn, Bill Phillips, Cheryl Casey, Sue Collins, Samuel Howard-Spink, Tony Kelso, Devon Powers, Mike Grabowski, and Laura Tropp, all of whom encouraged me in too many ways to count; the Molloy College Communications Department and its former chair, Alice Byrnes; the Molloy College Faculty Professional Center for their generous grant to continue this research; and Robert Conway, Vanessa Weiman, Kristi Ward, and Debra Adams, for their patience and guidance early on.

And in case you were wondering, these puppies do not just spring from the mind of the author. This book was immeasurably helped, guided, and midwifed by my editor, Chris Barsanti, who was not afraid to challenge me, all the while supporting and encouraging me; the book would certainly not have been possible without his help, nor anywhere as good. My deepest gratitude. And of course, I didn't design the book, that would be the wonderfully and insanely talented Phil Yarnall, who does work that makes Raymond Pettibon look like a first-year design student.

I would like to give special thanks to all past and present members of my band, In Crowd, for making me as punk as I am today. To my parents, Joseph and Ann Cogan, who never got the punk thing but who were glad I wasn't doing drugs and supported me anyway; my brothers, Joe and Sean, and their wonderful wives; my niece Cara and nephew Gavin; and my cousins/sisters Gina and Claudia, who have always been an inspiration. Also special thanks to my wonderful and loving wife, Lisa, who supported me throughout and helped me through this rewarding and difficult project.

Also, to all those who helped me and who are not mentioned here, my sincerest thanks, and I'll leave it at this: See you in the pit.

—Brian Cogan, New York
April 2008

RAMONES

IN CROWD

photo credits